The International Lesson Annual
1991–92
September–August

THE INTERNATIONAL LESSON ANNUAL 1991–92

September–August

A Comprehensive Commentary on
the International Sunday School Lessons
Uniform Series

Edited and with
Introductions by
HORACE R. WEAVER

Lesson Analysis by
WILLIAM H. WILLIMON
and
PAT McGEACHY

ABINGDON PRESS
Nashville

THE INTERNATIONAL LESSON ANNUAL—1991-92

Copyright © 1991 by Abingdon Press

All rights reserved.
No part of this work may be reproduced or transmitted in any form or by any means, electronic or mechanical, including photocopying and recording, or by any information storage or retrieval system, except as may be expressly permitted by the 1976 Copyright Act or in writing from the publisher. Requests for permission should be addressed in writing to Abingdon Press, 201 Eighth Avenue South, Nashville, TN 37202.

This book is printed on acid-free paper.

ISBN 0-687-19155-6

Library of Congress ISSN 0074-6770

Scripture quotations noted RSV are from the Revised Standard Version of the Bible, copyright 1946, 1952, 1971 by the Division of Christian Education of the National Council of Churches of Christ in the U.S.A. Used by permission.

Those noted King James Version are from the Authorized Version of the Bible.

Scripture quotations noted J. B. Phillips are from *The New Testament in Modern English*, by J. B. Phillips, copyright © J. B. Phillips, 1958, 1959, 1960, 1972.

Scripture quotations noted Goodspeed are from *The Complete Bible: An American Translation*, translated by J. M. P. Smith and Edgar Goodspeed.

MANUFACTURED IN THE UNITED STATES OF AMERICA

Editor's Preface

In closing my record of thirty-one years as editor of *The International Lesson Annual*, I want to express my appreciation for the inspiring support given me by Christian theologians, Christian educators, and various religious groups representing over a dozen religious backgrounds. During the years, I have been aware of writers whose mental and religious powers have included at least nine different languages. (In case you have wondered, I have studied nine languages also.) Those who have used foreign words in their sections of lessons have done so in order to clarify the meanings of difficult biblical passages, and I praise their abilities! The writers have been knowledgeable not only of languages but also of ancient history, geography, biblical poetry, comparative theologies, cosmologies, and other fields of study.

I challenge you readers of the *Annual* to keep an open mind to new ideas, many of which may be instilled in your heart and mind by God himself! I have sought such divine help for over fifty-five years, and suspect I will continue my searching for many years to come. In the thought-life of Paul, Christians face physical death, yet they also face a new, nonphysical (hence spiritual) existence (1 Corinthians 15:35-45). As a caterpillar metamorphoses into a beautiful butterfly, so our bodies will take on new and amazing forms in the life after death. Oh yes, we shall know and be known!

Horace R. Weaver, *Editor*

Contents

FIRST QUARTER
From the Damascus Road to Rome

UNIT I: CHOSEN BY GOD
(SEPT. 1–8)

LESSON		PAGE
	Introduction	11
1.	Chosen to Serve	12
	Sept. 1—*Acts 7:54–8:3; 9:1-22*	
2.	Working Together	20
	Sept. 8—*Acts 9:26-30; 11:19-30; 12:25*	

UNIT II: EMERGING LEADER
(SEPT. 15–29)

	Introduction	29
3.	Proclaiming the Good News	29
	Sept. 15—*Acts 13:1-3, 13-52*	
4.	Making People Whole	38
	Sept. 22—*Acts 14*	
5.	Working Out Differences	46
	Sept. 29—*Acts 15:1-35*	

UNIT III: TRAVELING PREACHER
(OCT. 6–27)

	Introduction	54
6.	Responding to Needs	54
	Oct. 6—*Acts 15:36–16:23*	
7.	Finding Courage to Choose	63
	Oct. 13—*Acts 16:16-40*	
8.	Finding the True God	71
	Oct. 20—*Acts 17*	
9.	Learning from One Another	80
	Oct. 27—*Acts 18:1–19:20*	

UNIT IV: DESTINATION: ROME
(NOV. 3–24)

	Introduction	88
10.	Serving the Church	88
	Nov. 3—*Acts 20*	
11.	Facing Crises	96
	Nov. 10—*Acts 21:17-40; 22:25–23:11*	
12.	Speaking Up for Your Faith	105
	Nov. 17—*Acts 25:13–26:32*	
13.	Proclaiming the Gospel	113
	Nov. 24—*Acts 27–28*	

SECOND QUARTER
Songs and Prayers of the Bible

UNIT I: SONGS FROM ANCIENT ISRAEL
(DEC. 1-22)

LESSON		PAGE
	Introduction..	122
1.	Song of Deliverance...	123
	Dec. 1—*Exodus 14:19-15:21*	
2.	Song of Triumph...	131
	Dec. 8—*Judges 4:4-5:31*	
3.	Song of Sorrow...	139
	Dec. 15—*2 Samuel 1*	
	Spiritual Enrichment Article:	
	Unto Us a Savior Is Born	
	Horace R. Weaver..	147
4.	Songs of Joy...	151
	Dec. 22—*1 Samuel 2:1-10; Luke 1:26-56*	

UNIT II: SONGS FROM FESTIVE OCCASIONS
(DEC. 29-JAN. 26)

	Introduction..	160
5.	Song of Praise...	160
	Dec. 29—*Psalm 8*	
6.	Song of Worship...	168
	Jan. 5—*Psalm 84*	
7.	Song of Gratitude...	176
	Jan. 12—*Psalm 103*	
8.	Song of Love...	184
	Jan. 19—*Song of Solomon 2:8-17*	
9.	A Song of Unreturned Love..	192
	Jan. 26—*Isaiah 5:1-7*	

UNIT III: SONGS AND PRAYERS OF THE CHURCH
(FEB. 2-23)

	Introduction..	201
10.	A Model for Prayer..	201
	Feb. 2—*1 Chronicles 29:10-13; Matthew 6:7-15*	
11.	Jesus' Prayer for Believers...	208
	Feb. 9—*John 17*	
12.	Being Servant of All...	216
	Feb. 16—*Philippians 2:1-11*	
13.	Song of God's Victory...	223
	Feb. 23—*Revelation 15:2-4; 19:1-8*	

THIRD QUARTER
Course 1: The Strong Son of God

UNIT I: MISSION AND MESSAGE
(MAR. 1–22)

LESSON		PAGE
	Introduction	231
	Spiritual Enrichment Article: The Gospel of Mark *Barbara Derrick*	232
1.	Entering God's Kingdom Mar. 1—*Mark 1:1-15*	233
2.	Affirming the Priority of People Mar. 8—*Mark 2:23–3:6*	241
3.	Ministering in Spite of Rejection Mar. 15—*Mark 6:1-13*	249
4.	Jesus Meets Needs Mar. 22—*Mark 7:24-37*	257

UNIT II: CONFESSION AND CRUCIFIXION
(MAR. 29–APR. 19)

	Introduction	265
5.	A Price to Pay Mar. 29—*Mark 8:27–9:13*	266
6.	Love Says It All Apr. 5—*Mark 12:28-37*	274
7.	Christ Died for You Apr. 12—*Mark 15:1-41*	282
8.	Death Is Not the End Apr. 19—*Mark 15:42–16:8*	290

Course 2: God's People in the World
(APR. 26–MAY 31)

	Introduction	298
9.	The Gift of Living Hope Apr. 26—*1 Peter 1:1-25*	299
10.	Called to Be God's People May 3—*1 Peter 2:1-25*	307
11.	Witnessing in Suffering May 10—*1 Peter 3:13–4:11*	315
12.	Excellent Exhortations May 17—*1 Peter 5:1-11*	323
13.	Growing in Grace May 24—*2 Peter 1:1-14*	331
14.	Living in the Light of the Future May 31—*2 Peter 3:3-14*	339

FOURTH QUARTER
Course 1: God's Judgment and Mercy

UNIT I: WARNINGS AND PROMISES FROM GOD
(JUNE 7–JULY 5)

LESSON		PAGE
	Introduction	347
1.	God's Justice Will Prevail	348
	June 7—*Obadiah*	
2.	Running Away from God	356
	June 14—*Jonah 1–2*	
3.	Disturbed by God's Grace	364
	June 21—*Jonah 3–4*	
4.	Good News for God's People	372
	June 28—*Nahum*	
5.	Faithfulness in Crisis	380
	July 5—*Habakkuk*	

UNIT II: A REMNANT IS SAVED
(JULY 12–19)

	Introduction	388
6.	Seek the Lord	388
	July 12—*Zephaniah 1–2*	
7.	Renewal of Life	396
	July 19—*Zephaniah 3*	

Course 2: Guidelines for Ministry

UNIT I: GUIDELINES FOR LEADING
(JULY 26–AUG. 9)

	Introduction	404
8.	Hold to Sound Doctrine	405
	July 26—*1 Timothy 1*	
9.	Train Yourself in Godliness	412
	Aug. 2—*1 Timothy 4*	
10.	Set Your Priorities	420
	Aug. 9—*1 Timothy 6:2c-21*	

UNIT II: GUIDELINES FOR SERVING
(AUG. 16–30)

	Introduction	428
11.	Respect God's Word	429
	Aug. 16—*2 Timothy 2:1-19*	
12.	Serve Faithfully	437
	Aug. 23—*2 Timothy 3:10–4:8*	
13.	Demonstrate Christian Living	445
	Aug. 30—*Titus*	

FIRST QUARTER
From the Damascus Road to Rome

UNIT I: CHOSEN BY GOD
Horace R. Weaver

TWO LESSONS   SEPTEMBER 1-8

This course of thirteen lessons concentrates on Luke's portrait of the Apostle Paul, as it is developed in the book of Acts. This study begins with the account of Saul's conversion in Acts 9 and concludes with his arrival in Rome.

The scripture passages are selected to demonstrate Luke's understanding of Paul—what and why he believed as he did, and how he translated those beliefs into a most meaningful life.

This study is divided into four units. Unit I, "Chosen by God," includes two lessons that concentrate on the uniqueness of Saul's conversion and the beginning of his witnessing. Unit II, "Emerging Leader," consists of three lessons that introduce Paul's early missionary evangelistic thrust. Paul's emerging Christian leadership is demonstrated by his skills in preaching and healing and his participation in the Jerusalem Conference.

Unit III, "Traveling Preacher," describes in four lessons Paul's missionary journeys: his call (probably in the presence of Luke) to Macedonia, his imprisonment in Philippi, his sermons at Athens, and his instruction of new disciples in Ephesus.

Unit IV, "Destination: Rome," consists of four lessons and follows Paul through his arrest, defense, appeal to Caesar, and arrival in Rome.

The individual lessons for unit I are as follows: "Chosen to Serve," September 1, shows Paul's dramatic encounter with the risen Lord. "Working Together," September 8, describes how Barnabas brought Saul to the apostles and supported his claim to conversion.

Contributors to the first quarter:

Pat McGeachy, Pastor, Downtown Presbyterian Church, Nashville, Tennessee.

Ronald E. Schlosser, Director, American Baptist Films, Valley Forge, Pennsylvania.

Michael Winters, Pastor, The Presbyterian Church of Berwyn, Chicago, Illinois.

LESSON 1   SEPTEMBER 1

Chosen to Serve

Background Scripture: Acts 7:54–8:3; 9:1-22

The Main Question—Pat McGeachy

Apart from the question, What must I do to be saved? (Acts 16:30), the main question in this week's lesson may very well be *the* question, What should I do with my life? It can be reworded in many different ways: What's the use? What's the point of life? How can I find meaning and purpose in it? And it may seem to be a question that young people starting out ask of parents, career counselors, ministers, and others. But I find an increasing number of older folks, not just those involved in the mid-life crisis but even those of us who are approaching retirement, asking this very question: What should I be doing?

For Saul of Tarsus the answer was burning and clear: Rid the world of those accursed Christians. And this he set out to do, with whip and cord. But he was colossally wrong! And knocked down in the road, blinded and broken, he was turned completely around, becoming the greatest protagonist for the very cause that he had originally attacked. My father (a clergyman) used to say, "If you want to know whether you are called into the ministry, try as hard as possible to get into something else; then, if you end up in the ministry you will know that you were called." There is a note of facetiousness in this saying, but Paul is living proof of its validity: You cannot escape from the call of God!

But not every voice that speaks to you in the night is the Holy Spirit. How shall we distinguish the false voices from the true? How shall we know what God has chosen us to do? A lady whom I know, aged 103, sits, as I write this, in a nursing home, blind and feeble but as alert as a sparrow. "Why does God keep me here?" she asks. "What am I supposed to be doing?" I can't answer her question, but I know what she means to me! And I suspect she means as much and more to hundreds of others. She has been chosen to serve in her way; in what way are you and I chosen?

Selected Scripture

King James Version

Acts 9:1-16

1 And Saul, yet breathing out threatenings and slaughter against the disciples of the Lord, went unto the high priest.

2 And desired of him letters to Damascus to the synagogues, that if he found any of this way, whether they were men or women, he might bring them bound unto Jerusalem.

3 And as he journeyed, he came

Revised Standard Version

Acts 9:1-16

1 But Saul, still breathing threats and murder against the disciples of the Lord, went to the high priest 2 and asked him for letters to the synagogues at Damascus, so that if he found any belonging to the Way, men or women, he might bring them bound to Jerusalem. 3 Now as he journeyed he approached Damascus, and suddenly a light from

SEPTEMBER 1   LESSON 1

near Damascus: and suddenly there shined round about him a light from heaven:

4 And he fell to the earth, and heard a voice saying unto him, Saul, Saul, why persecutest thou me?

5 And he said, Who art thou, Lord? And the Lord said, I am Jesus whom thou persecutest: *it is* hard for thee to kick against the pricks.

6 And he trembling and astonished said, Lord, what wilt thou have me to do? And the Lord *said* unto him, Arise, and go into the city, and it shall be told thee what thou must do.

7 And the men which journeyed with him stood speechless, hearing a voice, but seeing no man.

8 And Saul arose from the earth; and when his eyes were opened, he saw no man; but they led him by the hand, and brought *him* into Damascus.

9 And he was three days without sight, and neither did eat nor drink.

10 And there was a certain disciple at Damascus, named Ananias; and to him said the Lord in a vision, Ananias. And he said, Behold I *am here*, Lord.

11 And the Lord *said* unto him, Arise, and go into the street which is called Straight, and enquire in the house of Judas for *one* called Saul, of Tarsus: for, behold, he prayeth,

12 And hath seen in a vision a man named Ananias coming in, and putting *his* hand on him, that he might receive his sight.

13 Then Ananias answered, Lord, I have heard by many of this man, how much evil he hath done to thy saints at Jerusalem:

14 And here he hath authority from the chief priests to bind all that call on thy name.

15 But the Lord said unto him, Go thy way: for he is a chosen vessel unto me, to bear my name before the Gentiles, and kings, and the children of Israel:

heaven flashed about him. 4 And he fell to the ground and heard a voice saying to him, "Saul, Saul, why do you persecute me?" 5 And he said, "Who are you, Lord?" And he said, "I am Jesus, whom you are persecuting; 6 but rise and enter the city, and you will be told what you are to do." 7 The men who were traveling with him stood speechless, hearing the voice but seeing no one. 8 Saul arose from the ground; and when his eyes were opened, he could see nothing; so they led him by the hand and brought him into Damascus. 9 And for three days he was without sight, and neither ate nor drank.

10 Now there was a disciple at Damascus named Ananias. The Lord said to him in a vision, "Ananias." And he said, "Here I am, Lord." 11 And the Lord said to him, "Rise and go to the street called Straight, and inquire in the house of Judas for a man of Tarsus named Saul; for behold, he is praying, 12 and he has seen a man named Ananias come in and lay his hands on him so that he might regain his sight." 13 But Ananias answered, "Lord, I have heard from many about this man, how much evil he has done to thy saints at Jerusalem; 14 and here he has authority from the chief priests to bind all who call upon thy name." 15 But the Lord said to him, "Go, for he is a chosen instrument of mine to carry my name before the Gentiles and kings and the sons of Israel; 16 for I will show him how much he must suffer for the sake of my name."

FIRST QUARTER

16 For I will shew him how great things he must suffer for my name's sake.

Key Verse: He is a chosen vessel unto me, to bear my name before the Gentiles, and kings, and the children of Israel. (Acts 9:15)

Key Verse: He is a chosen instrument of mine to carry my name before the Gentiles and kings and the sons of Israel. (Acts 9:15)

As You Read the Scripture—Mike Winters

Acts 9:1-16. Saul of Tarsus (Acts 21:39) was a self-proclaimed persecutor of the church in the defense of Judaism (Galatians 1:13). He was first acknowledged as Judaism's defender at the stoning death of the deacon, Stephen (Acts 7:54–8:3). On a special mission against the disciples of the Lord, on the road to Damascus, Saul was suddenly confronted by the risen Lord. This confrontation resulted in Paul's conversion to Christianity. As a Christian, Saul proclaimed Jesus the Son of God, confounding the Damascus Jews (Acts 9:17-22).

Verse 1a. In 8:3, Saul is in a frenzy, wasting the church and imprisoning Jesus' disciples. Saul's persecution of the church continues in this verse.

Verses 1b-2. The high priest had apparent authority to extradite the followers of Jesus in order to punish them. Before the word "Christian" came into popular use (Acts 11:26), Jesus' disciples were called "followers of the Way."

Verses 3-15. The story of Saul's conversion also appears in Acts 22:6-16 and 26:12-18. In Galatians 1:13-17 Saul alludes to this conversion experience.

Verse 3. In 64 B.C. the ancient Damascus became a Roman province. Damascus was a city of the Decapolis under the Herods in the Province of Syria. During Saul's time, Damascus was not under Roman dominion (2 Corinthians 11:32). There were several synagogues in Damascus at this time.

At noon (Acts 22:6), the blinding light Saul experienced on the road to Damascus was the presence of the risen Jesus. It must have been somewhat like Jesus' transfiguration (see Matthew 17:2). In Exodus 40:35, the glory of the Lord is described as a cloud. In 2 Corinthians 4:6, however, the glory of the Lord is light.

Verses 4-5. Not until the moment of Jesus' epiphany did Saul realize that he was vicariously persecuting Jesus when he persecuted Jesus' followers (see Matthew 25:40).

Verse 6. Neither Saul's conversion nor the future direction of his life was clear at the moment of his encounter with Jesus on the road to Damascus. In Acts 22:10, Saul took the initiative to inquire of his future. Jesus said to him, "Go to Damascus, and there you will be told . . ." In Acts 26:16, while still on the Damascus road, Jesus readily explained to Saul his new role, bearing "witness to the things in which you have seen me [Jesus]."

Verse 7. The detachment of men who accompanied Saul on his Damascus mission saw the light (verse 22:9) but did not hear the voice. It is not clear whether Saul actually saw the risen Christ during this epiphany. The speechlessness of those who accompanied Saul is contrasted with Saul's immediate inquiry during the epiphany (contrast verse 5).

Verse 8. Saul was left helplessly blinded by the intensity of the light. But there is a sense here that Saul was reborn. Like a newborn baby whose very existence depends on the hands of those who care for it, Saul depended on the hands of those who accompanied him on the Damascus road.

Verse 9. This is an allusion to the darkness Jesus' disciples endured during the three days after Jesus crucifixion, until his resurrection. In this way, Saul could also say he endured the agony and grief and uncertainty the disciples endured.

Verses 10-16. At this point the focus of the story shifts. This is now Ananias's story. The pious Ananias was given the task to commission Saul to service in "the Way" he formerly persecuted, somewhat like the task given to Samuel to anoint the king of Israel (1 Samuel 9:16).

The Scripture and the Main Question—Pat McGeachy

Who Are You? (Acts 7:54–8:3)

The last thing we moderns ought to do is to psychoanalyze the people of the Bible. It is a hard temptation to avoid; the agonies of a Jeremiah (Jeremiah 20:7-12) or the madness of a Saul (1 Samuel 18:6-11) are wonderfully tempting to the amateur shrink. Indeed, Saul's final scene, in the spooky cave of the medium of Endor (1 Samuel 28) is so powerful that it almost demands the cast and chorus of an opera to bring it home with power.

But let us not attempt to diagnose (paranoia, schizophrenia?) these ancient heroes. We do not have them on the couch. We do not know what they would have told us about their inner hopes and fears, had we been intimate with them. Besides, what good does it do to call a condition by name, except to comfort those who like to file things away? The important thing is, what happened? What did they say? What did they do? And what can we learn from that?

But there is one other question: Why did Luke, the writer of Acts, guided by the Spirit, leave us with the tantalizing information that the young man Saul held the coats of those who stoned Stephen, and that he "was consenting to his death"? It must be that we, apart from any pretenses about our knowledge of abnormal psychology, are supposed to see what is obvious: that Saul was drawn into his fanaticism against the Christians by the zeal of his friends, and that, like most young radicals, he was swept up in the enthusiasm of the moment *to do a cruel deed in the name of righteousness.*

A pious Jew, even a Pharisee, would have known better than to join in a stoning. "Vengeance is mine," says the Lord (Deuteronomy 32:35). (See Paul's own rendition of this in Romans 12:19.) Why then are we told of this fanatical act of the young man Saul? Surely to make clear to all concerned that we have here a man driven by righteousness—as driven as Martin Luther in the sixteenth century, who tried to rid himself of guilt by flagellating himself in the icy fish pond at Wittenberg, or running daily to his priest to confess sin after sin, until, at last, the great doctrine of justification by grace, (Romans 3:23-24; 5:1; Ephesians 2:8-9) with its liberating power, came pouring in.

As amateur psychologists, we do not know whether the stoning of Stephen gnawed at the back of Paul's mind until it burst forth in hysterical blindness on the Damascus road. We dare not pretend to understand the

FIRST QUARTER

conversion experience in purely Freudian terms. But at the same time, we must understand that the Bible has revealed these facts to us for a purpose, namely, that Saul moved, in an instant, from fanaticism to fanaticism, from zeal for the house of Israel to zeal for the Herald of the new Israel, Jesus Christ.

Blindness (Acts 9:1-9)

Struck down in the road, blind, not from the darkness but from the Light of Lights, Paul was led helpless into Damascus (verse 8). In the valley of deep darkness ("the valley of the shadow of death," Psalm 23:4), there is a rod and staff to lead us. When it is dark, there is always the hope of a light to guide us (Isaiah 9:2; Psalm 119:105; John 1:5). But true blindness comes, not in the darkness of the pit, but in the blazing of the sun. (Do not, upon penalty of blindness, look fully into the face of the sun, even—perhaps especially—during an eclipse.) It is ultimately light, not darkness, that hides us from the truth.

> Great Father of glory,
>   pure Father of light,
> Thine angels adore thee,
>   All veiling their sight.
> All praise we would render:
>   O help us to see
> 'Tis only the splendor
>   of light hideth thee.
>   ("Immortal, Invisible, God Only Wise")

In that Damascus road darkness there shown a splendor too bright for human eyes, and Saul the Avenger was no more.

Humbly he was led, the blind by the blind (Matthew 15:14), to a room on a street called Straight (is their any significance in that name; compare Matthew 7:14 KJV?) in the house of a man named Judas (any significance there?). And there came to him there a man sent from God, named Ananias.

Brother Saul (Acts 9:10-19)

I am conducting a contest for the most important *one* word ever spoken. Perhaps it was, "Light," announced by God in Genesis 1:3. Maybe it was *YHWH* ("I Am," Exodus 3:14). Perhaps it was simply the word "word" itself (John 1:1). But for the present, my vote is for the simple word "brother," spoken by Ananias to Saul the persecutor on his bed of blindness.

Why are we told what Ananias said to Saul? Again we must steer clear of amateur psychology, but let me pose an imaginary conversation. It's years later, and Paul and Luke are walking on one of the long missionary treks that the two took together. (See the "we" passages in Acts, such as 28:11-14.) I can imagine the old friends talking, and Paul saying something like this: "Luke, old friend, we have known each other long enough for me to share this with you. When I was a young man, I did many wicked things in my attempt to prove my righteousness. But I think the worst thing I ever did was to stand there, an accessory to the fact, while they stoned Stephen to death. And he died just like Jesus, saying, 'Lord, forgive them' and 'receive my spirit.' Even in his death he was filled with a spirit of grace. And then, when I had come, blinded and helpless, to a dark bed in Damascus, one of the Christians came and called me 'Brother.' Brother! When I had been jailing his sisters and brothers! At that very moment, something like scales fell from my eyes, and I knew that all my attempts to keep the law were just so much dung. At that very moment I understood the meaning of God's grace. Before that moment I was blind, but now I see."

I don't know if that conversation ever happened, but I suspect it did. Otherwise, how did Luke know to tell it? And this I *do* know, that Saul was no longer the same person. He became Paul, and he devoted the rest of his life to taking that good news to every person and every town that he encountered.

What Shall I Do? (Acts 22:10)

In Paul's own account of this story, in his defense before the tribune in Jerusalem, he tells us that he asked Jesus, "What shall I do, Lord?" Up until this moment he had been highly self-motivated. He wasn't asking the question; he thought he knew the answer already. So do we. We keep saying things such as, "I know I ought to start going to church more regularly," "I know I ought to lose thirty pounds," "I know I ought to be a nicer person," "I know I ought . . ." But all those oughts, added together, amount to just so much self-righteous junk (Philippians 3:8). Even if we could do them all, we would be not a step closer to happiness and the kingdom. There is not a single thing we can do, or need to do. As the old song has it:

> Nothing in my hand I bring,
> Simply *to* thy cross I cling.
> ("Rock of Ages")

Of course, this doesn't answer the question of the young person wanting to know what career to follow, or the older person wanting to know where to retire to. But it does answer the question of my 103-year-old friend, and of everybody else: Why am I here? Answer: to receive the grace of God in Jesus Christ and to pass it on. And how can we do that? With a word, a smile, a hug, an affirmation, a kindness, a bag of groceries, a helping hand, a prayer, a verse of scripture—indeed, any act of love. For Paul, it meant becoming "all things to all people" (1 Corinthians 9:22)—in other words, identifying with others, and relating to them in such a way as to be able to communicate the grace of God to them. That is what Jesus did when he became a man. That is what we must do, every day. It is even possible for me to share the good news sitting here all alone at my typewriter. And it is possible for you, whatever your daily work, wherever you are at this moment. It is the calling of us all. We are chosen to serve.

Helping Adults Become Involved—Ronald E. Schlosser

Preparing to Teach

As you begin this new series of lessons on the life of the Apostle Paul, you may want to gather together additional resources to supplement the

FIRST QUARTER

background material provided by Dr. McGeachy and Dr. Winters. A good Bible commentary such as *The Interpreter's Bible* or *The Abingdon Bible Commentary* would be very helpful. Certainly a map showing the journeys of Paul, such as may be found in a Bible atlas or dictionary, or in the back of many Bibles, would prove a valuable learning aid. Try also to obtain a large map for use in the classroom.

You may wish to explore the use of videotapes on the Apostle Paul, either for personal enrichment or to show to your class at appropriate points during the study. A relevant series entitled *Discovering Paul* contains twelve twenty-minute episodes on three videocassettes, examining various aspects of Paul's life and work. Write or phone EcuFilm in Nashville for more information. (Address: 810 Twelfth Ave. South, Nashville, TN 37203. Phone: 1-800-251-4091.)

Another series on videotape, *The Life and Work of Paul*, contains six fifteen-minute episodes treating his early life, his conversion, and his missionary journeys. Produced by Family Films, it is available from Concordia Publishing House, 3558 S. Jefferson Ave., St. Louis, MO 63118-3963.

For today's lesson, you may wish to locate a copy of Robert Frost's poem "The Road Not Taken." It can be found in most poetry anthologies.

Carefully read the sections "As You Read the Scripture" and "The Scripture and the Main Question." These form the heart of the lesson. The ideas, insights, and suggestions in these sections should be employed throughout your lesson plan.

After introducing the main question, you might develop the lesson as follows:

    I. The character of Saul
   II. The conversion of Saul
      A. Locating Damascus
      B. Comparing accounts
      C. Seeing the light
      D. Encountering Ananias
      E. Choosing "the Way"
  III. The crossroads of life

Today's lesson will focus on three goals: (1) to examine the meaning of God's calling, especially in the lives of Saul and Ananias; (2) to consider the roads people take that lead them into or away from doing God's will; (3) to appreciate how Christian conversion can turn a person's life around.

Introducing the Main Question

The story of the conversion of Saul is probably well known by most persons in your class. The events are quite dramatic: the vision, the voice, the awareness of the risen Jesus, the instructions. But behind the events is the "Main Question" that Saul asks (Acts 22:10) and that Dr. McGeachy relates to our own lives: "Lord, what do you want me to do?"

Refer to Dr. McGeachy's statement in his opening commentary: "You cannot escape from the call of God!" How does the class react to this? Do the members agree or disagree? Why? Some may point to the story of Jonah, a well-known example of a person trying to avoid God's call. Moses had his

SEPTEMBER 1 — LESSON 1

excuses (see Exodus 3:10-11; 4:1, 10), as did Amos (Amos 7:14-15) and Jeremiah (Jeremiah 1:6). Ananias, as we shall see shortly, also protested.

Indicate that in today's lesson we will be coming to grips with what the call of God may mean for us personally.

Developing the Lesson

I. The character of Saul

Ask the class: "What do we know about Saul before his conversion?" Encourage the members to tell what they know about Saul's background and character traits and write them on the chalkboard or newsprint. The following Scripture references may help in making a list: Acts 7:58–8:3; 22:3-4, 26-29; Galatians 1:14; Philippians 3:4-6. (Saul was a Hebrew scholar, well educated, taught by the Pharisee Gamaliel, a Roman citizen by birth, a zealous persecutor of the early Christians.)

II. The conversion of Saul
  A. *Locating Damascus*

After mentioning Saul's zeal in persecuting the followers of Christ, read aloud Acts 9:1-2. Locate Damascus on a Bible map. In the city was a strict Jewish group, the "Covenanters of Damascus," intensely loyal to the Jewish law. These persons would be hostile to the Christians, and some Bible scholars think Saul may have had some relationship to this group in his campaign against early Christianity.

  B. *Comparing accounts*

There are three accounts of Saul's conversion in the Bible: one by Luke (Acts 9:3-16) and two by Paul himself (Acts 22:6-11 and 26:13-18). As you read aloud Luke's account, have half the class compare it with the account in Acts 22, and the other half with Acts 26. Discuss the similarities and differences. Although there are some differences in the details (did Saul's companions see the light and hear the voice?), there is no essential discrepancy. Saul had a profound encounter with the living Christ, which changed his life!

  C. *Seeing the light*

Both Dr. Winters and Dr. McGeachy comment on the blinding light that enveloped Saul. You may wish to explore light as a metaphor in the Scriptures. Jesus, of course, refers to himself as "the light of the world" (John 8:12; 9:5), and the Gospel writer sees this light as giving life to all persons (John 1:4-8). Also note Isaiah 9:2; Psalm 119:105; 2 Corinthians 4:6; and Matthew 17:2.

The hymn "Great Father of Glory" quoted by Dr. McGeachy, and the hymn by John Henry Newman, "Lead, Kindly Light," found in many hymnals, refer to two types of light: that which blinds and that which illumines. Saul encountered both kinds of light on the Damascus road, one leading to the other. The phrase "seeing the light" is particularly instructive in reference to Saul.

  D. *Encountering Ananias*

What a thrilling story is Saul's encounter with Ananias! How Ananias could bring himself to seek out Saul, that feared persecutor of the church, is difficult to comprehend. Other than the threat to his own life, what other excuses might Ananias have given when God asked him to visit Saul? What excuses might we give today under similar circumstances? (I'm too busy; it's

FIRST QUARTER

too much effort; let someone else do it; I wouldn't know what to say.) But Ananias trusted God and strode into the perilous meeting with quiet serenity. As Dr. McGeachy points out, his words of greeting to Saul must rank among the most beautiful expressions in all literature: "Brother Saul!" Imagine being called "brother" by one whose life you had come to take. Right there Saul had his Pentecost. Noble Ananias laid his hands upon him, healed him, and imparted the gift of the Holy Spirit to him.

E. Choosing "the Way"

Robert Frost's memorable poem "The Road Not Taken" has relevance here. If you can find a copy, you might want to read it now. It speaks of the decision the poet had to make when he came to a fork in a woodland road. He made his decision—to take the path less traveled—and it forever changed the direction of his life.

The Greek word translated "repentance" is *metanoia*, meaning "to turn around, to change direction." This is what happened to Saul when he met Christ on the road to Damascus and received his sight by the hand of Ananias on a street called Straight. It was an intersection in his life that forever set him on a new path.

Helping Class Members Act

III. The crossroads of life

Close the session by asking class members to share times when they encountered crossroads in their lives. Perhaps some may want to tell of their conversion experience. It may not have been as dramatic as Saul's, but it was as real and as life changing nevertheless. Others may be willing to tell of how they made a vocational decision, or sought direction for some other decision in their life. Let this be a time of sharing and mutual affirmation.

Planning for Next Sunday

Give some thought during the week to the persons who have had an influence on you or have been supportive of you. Read Acts 9:26-30; 11:19-30; and 12:25.

LESSON 2   SEPTEMBER 8

Working Together

Background Scripture: Acts 9:26-30; 11:19-30; 12:25

The Main Question—Pat McGeachy

If I asked you to define the word "gate-keeper," you would probably think first of somebody whose task it is to keep people out, like the sentry at

SEPTEMBER 8   LESSON 2

the gate of a palace or a military base, whose job is to challenge all comers and make sure that the wrong sorts of folk don't get in. But in fact the word can mean quite the opposite, and I propose to use it so in this lesson. Think rather of the doorman at a hotel, an important looking person with gold braid on his shoulders, looking something like an admiral, who graciously shepherds the guests into the lobby. A gate-keeper may not only be someone who keeps people out but also someone *who lets people in.*

If, in a group, there is a shy, quiet person who can't seem to catch the eye of the moderator and clearly is itching to say something, I, who have a very loud voice, like to run interference. I'll say something like, "Madam President, Charlie's trying to get the floor." And I call that gate-keeping.

Well, the best gate-keeper I know about is Barnabas. We first read about him in Acts 4:36, where we learn of his generosity. The apostles nicknamed him Barnabas, which, by their popular etymology, sounded like "son of encouragement." And that's a perfect description of him! For when next we meet him, he is gate-keeping for Saul, the former enemy of the church.

Our main question is thus a two-way question: How can I keep the gate for others, and who will keep the gate for me? Perhaps you have not asked it in just these terms, but it is a question worth asking and answering, for there is tremendous satisfaction to be found in serving as a Boswell to someone else's Johnson, or a Barnabas to someone else's Saul. And you can expect it to pay off for you in time, as we shall see. Sometimes, as in basketball, the one who shoots the goal is noticed more than the one who gives the assist, but he or she is equally important (see Psalm 84:10).

Selected Scripture

King James Version

Acts 9:26-30; 11:19-26, 29-30

26 And when Saul was come to Jerusalem, he assayed to join himself to the disciples; but they were all afraid of him, and believed not that he was a disciple.

27 But Barnabas took him, and brought *him* to the apostles, and declared unto them how he had seen the Lord in the way, and that he had spoken to him, and how he had preached boldly at Damascus in the name of Jesus.

28 And he was with them coming in and going out at Jerusalem.

29 And he spake boldly in the name of the Lord Jesus, and disputed against the Grecians; but they went about to slay him.

30 *Which* when the brethren knew, they brought him down to Caesarea, and sent him forth to Tarsus.

Revised Standard Version

Acts 9:26-30; 11:19-26, 29-30.

26 And when he had come to Jerusalem he attempted to join the disciples; and they were all afraid of him, for they did not believe that he was a disciple. 27 But Barnabas took him, and brought him to the apostles, and declared to them how on the road he had seen the Lord, who spoke to him, and how at Damascus he had preached boldly in the name of Jesus. 28 So he went in and out among them at Jerusalem, 29 preaching boldly in the name of the Lord. And he spoke and disputed against the Hellenists; but they were seeking to kill him. 30 And when the brethren knew it, they brought him down to Caesarea, and sent him off to Tarsus.

FIRST QUARTER

19 Now they which were scattered abroad upon the persecution that arose about Stephen travelled as far as Phenice, and Cyprus, and Antioch, preaching the word to none but unto the Jews only.
20 And some of them were men of Cyprus and Cyrene, which, when they were come to Antioch, spake unto the Grecians, preaching the Lord Jesus.
21 And the hand of the Lord was with them: and a great number believed, and turned unto the Lord.
22 Then tidings of these things came unto the ears of the church which was in Jerusalem: and they sent forth Barnabas, that he should go as far as Antioch.
23 Who, when he came, and had seen the grace of God, was glad, and exhorted them all, that with purpose of heart they would cleave unto the Lord.
24 For he was a good man, and full of the Holy Ghost and of faith: and much people was added unto the Lord.
25 Then departed Barnabas to Tarsus, for to seek Saul:
26 And when he had found him, he brought him unto Antioch. And it came to pass, that a whole year they assembled themselves with the church, and taught much people. And the disciples were called Christians first in Antioch.

19 Now those who were scattered because of the persecution that arose over Stephen traveled as far as Phoenicia and Cyprus and Antioch, speaking the word to none except Jews. 20 But there were some of them, men of Cyprus and Cyrene, who on coming to Antioch spoke to the Greeks also, preaching the Lord Jesus. 21 And the hand of the Lord was with them, and a great number that believed turned to the Lord. 22 News of this came to the ears of the church in Jerusalem, and they sent Barnabas to Antioch. 23 When he came and saw the grace of God, he was glad; and he exhorted them all to remain faithful to the Lord with steadfast purpose; 24 for he was a good man, full of the Holy Spirit and of faith. And a large company was added to the Lord. 25 So Barnabas went to Tarsus to look for Saul; 26 and when he had found him, he brought him to Antioch. For a whole year they met with the church, and taught a large company of people; and in Antioch the disciples were for the first time called Christians.

....

29 Then the disciples, every man according to his ability, determined to send relief unto the brethren which dwelt in Judaea:
30 Which also they did, and sent it to the elders by the hands of Barnabas and Saul.

29 And the disciples determined, every one according to his ability, to send relief to the brethren who lived in Judea; 30 and they did so, sending it to the elders by the hand of Barnabas and Saul.

Key Verse: **Then departed Barnabas to Tarsus to seek Saul, and when he had found him, he brought him unto Antioch. It came**

Key Verse: **Barnabas went to Tarsus to look for Saul; and when he had found him he brought him to Antioch. For a whole year they**

22

SEPTEMBER 8   LESSON 2

to pass, that a whole year they assembled themselves with the church, and taught much people. (Acts 11:25-26)

met with the church, and taught a large company of people. (Acts 11:25-26)

As You Read the Scripture—Michael Winters

Acts 9:26-30. Saul, a former persecutor of the church, is now preaching boldly in the name of Jesus. In verses 23-25, Saul escapes a Jewish plot to kill him in Damascus, fleeing to Jerusalem. There the disciples of Jesus are afraid of him. Barnabas, however, successfully dispels their anxiety. This enables Saul to preach boldly again, until the Hellenists seek to kill him. On learning of their desperate plot, the disciples escort Saul to the safety of Caesarea and then send him to Tarsus.

Verse 26. Here is Saul's first visit to Jerusalem as a Christian. In Galatians 1:18, Saul writes that his first visit to Jerusalem came three years after his conversion. The disciples' fear was based on their belief that Saul was still a persecutor of the church. They must have believed that Saul was feigning discipleship in order to entrap and persecute the true disciples.

Verses 27-29a. Barnabas is first introduced in verse 4:36. There his name is translated "son of encouragement." Barnabas, apparently, was influential among Jesus' disciples in Jerusalem.

We do not know how Barnabas became acquainted with Saul. He was clearly familiar with Saul's conversion story. Since Barnabas was Saul's advocate among the disciples in Jerusalem, Saul was able to preach freely. Saul and Barnabas were to become missionary colleagues to the Gentiles.

Verse 29b. The Hellenists were Greek-speaking Jews. The King James Version calls them Grecians. Verse 6:1 indicates that there was trouble between the Hellenists and the Hebrews the Semitic Jews who spoke Hebrew or Aramaic. Saul was a Hebrew, by his own testimony (see Philippians 3:5).

The Hellenists' provocation over Saul's comments was probably related to the stoning of Stephen, who was himself a Hellenist. All of the first deacons had Greek names (see Acts 6:5).

Verse 30. The "brethren" were Jesus' disciples. Where before they feared Saul, now they were Saul's protectors. They escorted him to the safety of Caesarea of Palestine, on the coast. From there he likely found a ship to take him to Tarsus, due north.

Verses 11:19-26. In Acts 10:11-16, Peter is in Joppa, on the coast, west of Jerusalem. While in a prayer trance, Peter has a vision in which he is invited to eat food that is not ritually permissible for a Jew to eat. In verses 10:23b-28, Peter goes to Caesarea, where he realizes that his vision in Joppa had prepared him to offer the gospel to a Gentile, Cornelius.

Until this time, the gospel had been preached only to the Jews. There were some in Cyprus and Cyrene, however, who had been preaching the gospel to the Greeks or Gentiles. When word of this reached Jerusalem, the church sent Barnabas to Antioch to verify that in fact Gentiles were believing in Jesus. Barnabas then took Saul from Tarsus, and the two of them taught in Antioch among the Gentiles for a year.

Verse 19. The persecution that followed Stephen's death served to spread the gospel into the Greek world. Phoenicia was the coastal region of the province of Syria. Cyprus is a Mediterranean island due west of Crete.

FIRST QUARTER

Antioch is on the south bank of the Orontes river, about fifteen miles from its mouth, beyond the western reach of Cyprus.

Verse 20. Cyrene is in North Africa south of Greece.

Verse 26. In Antioch, the name "Christian" is first applied to the believers in Jesus.

The Scripture and the Main Question—Pat McGeachy

Saul Needs Barnabas (Acts 9:26-30)

Before we get started on this lesson, we must at least notice that the New Testament is not clear about the times and people involved. According to Paul's own account (Galatians 1:11–2:10), which was written much earlier than Acts, he didn't go to Jerusalem immediately after his conversion but went to Arabia, presumably for a time of reflection and renewal before setting out on his missionary task (Galatians 1:17). Then, when he finally did get to Jerusalem, three years later (Galatians 1:18-20), he says nothing about Barnabas. In fact, he swears before God, as though it were a particularly important point, that Peter and James were the only apostles he saw. These early events in Paul's life took place before he and Luke became acquainted, so the good doctor may not have been aware of the exact details. In any event, we have to conclude that his arrival in Jerusalem did not happen immediately after his departure from Damascus.

But whenever it was, Luke tells us his first reception was not a happy one. This seems pretty easy to understand. How would you feel if, say, the village atheist suddenly announced that he had become a Christian and wanted to testify at prayer meeting in your church. I bet there would be a pretty long meeting of the official board over that one! And it would make a difference if there were somebody to speak up for him. There is weight to the old truism: It's not what you know, it's who you know. We can all use a "son of encouragement" at times.

The Bible tells about a good many people who, lesser lights themselves, are remembered primarily for the way in which they served as gate-keepers for others. Remember how Aaron served as mouthpiece for Moses in their attempt to get through to Pharaoh (Exodus 4:14-16)? Remember how Andrew sought out Peter and brought him to Jesus (John 1:40-41), and how Philip did the same for Nathanael (John 1:45-46), and how both Philip and Andrew did the same for some Greek-speaking Jews (John 12:20-22). Or think of the four fellows who went to all the trouble to let their friend down through a roof just to get him to Jesus (Mark 2:3-4). It is true there have been times when the disciples acted like guards, keeping people away from Jesus (Mark 10:13), but when they were doing their job, they were openers of doors.

Just as the church might have missed out on its greatest missionary if Ananias had not been there to welcome "Brother Saul" (Acts 9:17), we might have missed out on him if Barnabas had not been there to be gate-keeper before Peter and James. Can you think of similar opportunities in which you and I might serve as gate-keepers? Of course there are obvious ones, such as visiting newcomers to your community and inviting them to church, or greeting them at the door and introducing them to others, helping them to feel at home. But there can be many gates to keep, small and large. Imagine the full story built around these brief quotations:

SEPTEMBER 8   LESSON 2

"Pastor, I'm worried about Sally. She seems so discouraged and down; could you give her a call?"

"Chuck, this is none of my business, but I thought I smelled alcohol on your breath this morning. Have you got a problem or something?"

"What say we take some homemade soup over to those folks that just moved in down the street?"

"You know, Fred, you have such a gift with people, you'd make a great addition to our Barnabas club. What about coming to the meeting next Tuesday and meeting some of the members?"

I could go on, but perhaps you see what we are saying: You and I can be Barnabas to one another.

Barnabas Needs Saul (Acts 11:19-30)

Once again Barnabas seeks out Saul, this time with a specific job in mind. Antioch (now Antakya in southern Turkey) was a relatively large and important city north of Jerusalem. (Josephus says it was the third most important city in the Roman Empire.) It served as the center for the governor of the province of Syria. Apparently the church had begun to take root there partly because of bad news in Jerusalem. The persecution (11:19) that arose after Stephen's death caused many to flee, and wherever they went, they shared the gospel. We mustn't think that Paul and the Twelve were the only missionaries. The new church was filled with gate-keepers to the pagan world, and wherever they found themselves, they naturally offered the good news to those who would receive it.

Barnabas, by now apparently a very important person in the new church, was sent to Antioch to "see how things were going." And one of his first acts was to go looking for Saul. Ever the gate-keeper, he must have been thinking, "This is exactly the spot for Saul. He could be a powerful witness here, and it would probably do him a lot of good too." There are some people with a marvelous gift for seeing how person X will fit into situation Y. I can't do this very well myself, but those who can make excellent administrators, guidance counselors, and teachers. Gate-keeping is an art, and Barnabas had mastered it.

Apparently Saul had gone to his home town, which was a good distance further on around the curve of the Mediterranean from Antioch. Tarsus was "no mean city," famous for its schools, and Saul may very well have been there poring over the books and continuing to shape his understanding of the incredible new gospel he had received. Now comes Barnabas to say, "Up, up, my friend, and quit your books! It's time to put your faith to work. We need you at Antioch."

When the two went to work there, probably Barnabas was the leader, but his friend and pupil, Saul, quickly became the dominant figure. The world's greatest evangelist was beginning to discover his gifts. Thus the talents of Barnabas, a good man and spirit filled (11:24), and of Saul, rapidly developing his missionary skills, brought the church at Antioch to maturity. Two things must be noted: first, the term "Christian" first began to be used there (11:26), probably originally as an insult (compare the word "cretin," which comes from the same root word). Its ultimate root means, "follower of the Messiah (the anointed one)." Second, along with their theology, the Antioch church was inspired to be a generous people (11:29). Between them, Paul and Barnabas helped build a community whose word and deed were inseparable.

We Need Each Other

Gate-keeping doesn't seem like a very rewarding hobby. Other people seem to get the credit for our acts. But it doesn't, in fact, turn out that way. As Jesus promised, whoever loses life for the Lord's sake will find it. Barnabas, in gate-keeping for Saul, eventually reaped the rewards of a lifelong friendship (though it did have its ups and downs; see Acts 15:39). Moreover he had the satisfaction of seeing enormous good take place at the hands of his disciple.

I know a young actor who prefers directing to acting, because, he says, "I can accomplish so much more by working with others. As much as I love to act, I love even more seeing actors blossom into their full power under my direction." I know teachers whose greatest joy is the golden moment when their students experience understanding, parents who have rejoiced to help open the right doors for their children. At every turn in the road, from a police officer who helps a child find the way home to a pastor who leads a sinner to repentance, there is the deepest sort of satisfaction. Indeed, we are told, that is what makes the heavens rejoice (Luke 15:7).

The great Gate-keeper, is, of course, God (Revelation 21:25), and the gate God keeps is never shut. It is a gate built for invitation, not exclusion. And those of us who are privileged to be undershepherds (that means you and me both), the joy of helping others find the way to God's gate is reward enough.

> I would rather be a gate-keeper
> in the house of God,
> than a big shot
> in a wicked house.

Helping Adults Become Involved—Ronald E. Schlosser

Preparing to Teach

As people in the dramatic arts will acknowledge, it is not always easy to take a supporting role and play it well. All performers have a sense of pride, and those with talent and training naturally feel that they ought to be given the lead role. Yet in every play—indeed, in every endeavor in life—it is important to have good people in supporting roles.

In today's lesson we shall be focusing our attention on Barnabas, a man whose very name signified the kind of supportive person he was: "son of encouragement." In the process of looking at Barnabas and his relationship with Paul, we will be aiming at the following learning goals: (1) to recognize the need for Christian encouragement and support in the living out of one's life; (2) to identify the qualities that make for responsible Christian gate-keeping; (3) to explore ways one can provide a gate-keeping (supporting) role in working within the Christian community.

After introducing the main question, you might develop the lesson following this outline:

SEPTEMBER 8   LESSON 2

      I. Gate-keepers in the Bible
     II. A profile of Barnabas
    III. Barnabas the gate-keeper
    IV. Gate-keepers we know
     V. Responding to needs

Carefully read the sections "As You Read the Scripture" and "The Scripture and the Main Question." These form the heart of the lesson. The ideas, insights, and suggestions in these sections should be employed throughout your lesson plan.

Have available pencils or pens and a supply of three-by-five-inch index cards for use at the end of the session.

Introducing the Main Question

Basic and helpful ideas are presented in the section "The Main Question." These ideas are essential in identifying the central focus of the lesson.

Begin by writing the word "gate-keeper" on the chalkboard. Ask your class members to tell what the word means to them. Jot down their answers as they give them.

Note what Dr. McGeachy says about a gate-keeper. The image of a doorman rather than a sentry is the more positive one. Rather than keeping people out, a gate-keeper should let people in. The question this lesson will examine is twofold: Who have been gate-keepers for us, and how can we be gate-keepers for others?

Developing the Lesson

I. Gate-keepers in the Bible

The Bible is filled with stories of people being gate-keepers. Ask your class to think of some. Who opened doors of opportunity for others, or were supportive of someone when the going got tough? Dr. McGeachy names a few: Aaron, Andrew, Philip, the friends of the paralytic. Others might be mentioned: Miriam, Moses' sister, who arranged for her mother to nurse him as a baby (Exodus 2); the little Jewish maid who introduced Naaman to Elisha (2 Kings 5); Jonathan, who warned David of his father's wrath (1 Samuel 19); the boy with five loaves and two fishes who helped Jesus feed a multitude (John 6); Lydia, who opened her home to Paul and his companions (Acts 16).

II. A profile of Barnabas

Dr. McGeachy points to Barnabas as the best gate-keeper he knows. What does your class know about Barnabas? Write his name on the chalkboard and under it list the background information the class may give. Barnabas was the name given to Joseph, a Levite, by the apostles. He was a native of Cyprus and apparently was a man of some means. He sold a field and contributed the money to the work of the church (Acts 4:36-37). There is a tradition that Barnabas had gone to the University of Tarsus, where he first met Saul. Barnabas was the uncle of John Mark; both of them accompanied Paul on his first missionary journey.

FIRST QUARTER

III. Barnabas the gate-keeper

In the Scripture passages for study today, we discover some other things about Barnabas. Ask half the class to read silently Acts 9:26-30, and the other half to read Acts 11:19-30. Then discuss what additional insights into the character of Barnabas these two passages reveal.

1. Barnabas himself had real insight. He was the first to believe that Saul's conversion was genuine. He vouched for Saul before the other apostles. As Dr. Winters points out, Barnabas' influence among the apostles opened the door of opportunity for Saul to preach freely.

2. Barnabas also had foresight. He sensed the possibilities for Christian leadership in Saul. As the work grew in Antioch, Barnabas saw the need for another Christian worker. Remembering Saul, he went to Tarsus to invite him back to labor with him.

Locate Antioch on your Bible map. It is in the northern part of Syria, east of the seaport town of Seleucia. (It should not be confused with Antioch of Pisidia, in Asia Minor.) More will be said about Antioch next week, but point out that it was a large and important city in the Roman Empire. It was connected by trade routes with both East and West. As Dr. McGeachy notes, it was an ideal spot for Saul, with his culture and learning, to help the growing young church. And it was at Antioch that the followers of "the Way" were first called Christians.

IV. Gate-keepers we know

We have seen how Barnabas, the gate-keeper, opened doors for Saul. Now have the class members think of modern-day gate-keepers—specifically, persons who were influential and supportive in their lives. Everyone should be able to think of at least one person who made a difference in his or her life. Who was there to open a door at a crucial time or be an encourager when things looked gloomy? Spend some time allowing the members to share personal experiences of people who were gate-keepers for them.

Helping Class Members Act

V. Responding to needs

Dr. McGeachy suggests several brief scenarios where persons can be gate-keepers for others. It may be a phone call, a personal word of concern, a visit to new neighbors, or an invitation to a special meeting that would open a door to Christian love and concern.

Ask your class to think about needs that are evident in your church or community that could benefit from Christian gate-keeping. List these on the chalkboard as they are given. If the members are hesitant to mention things that may be too personal for public expression, suggest that they write them on index cards that you will pass out. Then, on the back of their cards, they might identify at least one situation from the list on the chalkboard or from their own personal list that they will attempt to address in the coming week. They should write down how they will try to be a gate-keeper in that situation—to be a door-opener, a supporter, an encourager, a friend willing to help.

Close with a time of quiet prayer when each can ask for God's blessing and support in the gate-keeping task they are to undertake.

SEPTEMBER 15   LESSON 3

Planning for Next Sunday

Ask the members to think through what they feel are the five most important tenets of the Christian faith. The background Scripture for next week is Acts 13:1-3, 13-52.

UNIT II: EMERGING LEADER
Horace R. Weaver

THREE LESSONS   **SEPTEMBER 15-29**

Unit II, "Emerging Leader," consists of three lessons that introduce Paul's early career as missionary, pastor, and advocate of Jesus Christ. This unit includes Paul's first apostolic conference in Jerusalem, and the marvelous contributions made by the Greek/Jewish convert Barnabas. Paul's emerging leadership is demonstrated by his preaching, healing, and apostolic authority. The focus of this unit is seen in the three titles of its lessons: "Proclaiming the Good News," September 15, asks, How shall we sum up our faith? "Making People Whole," September 22, asks, How can we become whole? "Working Out Differences," September 29, asks, What are some of the best ways to work out differences among us?

LESSON 3   SEPTEMBER 15

Proclaiming the Good News

Background Scripture: Acts 13:1-3, 13-52

The Main Question—Pat McGeachy

If you had to sum up the Christian message in a few words, what would those words be? You might, of course, use the simplest of all creeds: "Jesus is Lord" (1 Corinthians 12:3). But what would that mean to someone who knew nothing about Jesus? In the book of Acts there are five sermons (or at least the gist of them as remembered by the early church) that tell how the first missionaries summed up their faith. They are:

- Peter's sermon at Pentecost (Acts 2:14-40)
- Peter's sermon on Solomon's portico (Acts 3:12-26)
- Stephen's sermon (Acts 7:2-53)
- Paul's sermon at Antioch of Pisidia (our lesson this week)
- Paul's sermon in Athens (Acts 17:22-31)

FIRST QUARTER

And you may want to include Paul's defense before the tribune (Acts 22:3-21) and before Felix (Acts 24:10-21). A careful comparison of these indicates that they have much in common: They begin with Hebrew history, they tell of Jesus' fulfilment of prophecy and of his death and resurrection, and they conclude with a call to repentance.

In this lesson we have to do with one such sermon, that by Paul in Antioch. As we study it, you may want to think to yourself, "How would I tell this story to someone who had never heard it?" Thinking in this way will help us to sharpen our own faith, and to decide what is really fundamental or essential. If Jesus wants us to be his witnesses (Acts 1:8), we had better know how to give account of our faith. Good news is fun to share! Let's commit ourselves in this lesson to developing the skill necessary to share this, the best of all news, with understanding, conviction, and effectiveness. In other words, let's answer the question, How shall we sum up our faith?

Selected Scripture

King James Version

Acts 13:26-39

26 Men *and* brethren, children of the stock of Abraham, and whosoever among you feareth God, to you is the word of this salvation sent.

27 For they that dwell at Jerusalem, and their rulers, because they knew him not, nor yet the voices of the prophets which are read every sabbath day, they have fulfilled *them* in condemning *him.*

28 And though they found no cause of death *in him,* yet desired they Pilate that he should be slain.

29 And when they had fulfilled all that was written of him, they took *him* down from the tree, and laid *him* in a sepulchre.

30 But God raised him from the dead:

31 And he was seen many days of them which came up with him from Galilee to Jerusalem, who are his witnesses unto the people.

32 And we declare unto you glad tidings, how that the promise which was made unto the fathers,

33 God hath fulfilled the same unto us their children, in that he hath raised up Jesus again; as it is also written in the second psalm, Thou art my Son, this day have I begotten thee.

Revised Standard Version

Acts 13:26-39

26 "Brethren, sons of the family of Abraham, and those among you that fear God, to us has been sent the message of this salvation. 27 For those who live in Jerusalem and their rulers, because they did not recognize him nor understand the utterances of the prophets which are read every sabbath, fulfilled these by condemning him. 28 Though they could charge him with nothing deserving death, yet they asked Pilate to have him killed. 29 And when they had fulfilled all that was written of him, they took him down from the tree, and laid him in a tomb. 30 But God raised him from the dead; 31 and for many days he appeared to those who came up with him from Galilee to Jerusalem, who are now his witnesses to the people. 32 And we bring you the good news that what God promised to the fathers, 33 this he had fulfilled to us their children by raising Jesus; as also it is written in the second psalm,

'Thou art my Son,
today I have begotten thee.'

SEPTEMBER 15　　　　　　　　　　　　　　　　　LESSON 3

34 And as concerning that he raised him up from the dead, *now* no more to return to corruption, he said on this wise, I will give you the sure mercies of David.

35 Wherefore he saith also in another *psalm*, Thou shalt not suffer thine Holy One to see corruption.

36 For David, after he had served his own generation by the will of God, fell on sleep, and was laid unto his fathers, and saw corruption:
37 But he, whom God raised again, saw no corruption.
38 Be it known unto you therefore, men *and* brethren, that through this man is preached unto you the forgiveness of sins:
39 And by him all that believe are justified from all things, from which ye could not be justified by the law of Moses.

Key Verse: **Be it known unto you therefore, men and brethren, that through this man is preached unto you the forgiveness of sins. (Acts 13:38)**

34 And as for the fact that he raised him from the dead, no more to return to corruption, he spoke in this way,
　'I will give you the holy and sure blessings of David.'

35 Therefore he says also in another psalm,
　'Thou wilt not let thy Holy One see corruption.'

36 For David, after he had served the counsel of God in his own generation, fell asleep, and was laid with his fathers, and saw corruption; 37 but he whom God raised up saw no corruption. 38 Let it be known to you therefore, brethren, that through this man forgiveness of sins is proclaimed to you, 39 and by him every one that believes is freed from everything from which you could not be freed by the law of Moses."

Key Verse: **Let it be known to you therefore, brethren, that through this man forgiveness of sins is proclaimed to you. (Acts 13:38)**

As You Read the Scripture—Michael Winters

Acts 13:1-16a. On their first missionary journey, Saul and Barnabas passed through all of Cyprus, where, in Paphos, we learn that Saul was also known as Paul (verse 9). From Paphos, Paul sailed north to the coastal town of Perga in Pamphylia (verse 13), and then traveled north overland to Antioch in Pisidia (verse 14). In Antioch, on the sabbath day Paul was encouraged to preach.

Verses 16b-41. Paul's sermon outline follows the history of the Jewish people, beginning in Egypt and including the Exodus. He alludes to the conquest of Canaan. He glosses over the period of Judges to the time of King David. From David, being at the heart of Jesus' genealogy (Matthew 1:1), Paul leaps to the promised savior, Jesus (verse 23). After a brief allusion to John the baptist (verse 25), we see that the heart of Paul's gospel is the crucifixion and resurrection of Jesus.

Verse 26. Translating this verse literally from the Greek, it begins "Men, brothers, sons of Abraham." Likely, Paul was addressing only men. While both men and women attended the synagogue on Sabbath days, only men were allowed into the inner rooms of the building, where the worship service was conducted. "The family of Abraham" were the Jews. "Those . . . that fear[ed] God" were proselytes to Judaism.

FIRST QUARTER

Verse 27. Here is a dashing indictment against the Jews of Jerusalem. Paul says their failure to recognize Jesus only points to their failure to understand the prophets.

Verse 28. The Jews accused Jesus of perverting the nation, forbidding tribute to Caesar, and declaring himself a king (Luke 23:2). Pilate said, "Nothing deserving death has been done by him" (Luke 23:15*b*). But the Jews were urgent, demanding and shouting that Jesus should be crucified (Luke 23:23).

Verse 29. Paul echoes Peter's declaration, "What God foretold by the mouth of all the prophets . . . he thus fulfilled" (Acts 3:18). Peter also said that Jesus was put to death by hanging on a tree (Acts 10:39).

Joseph of Arimathea, a good and righteous man, a Jew, took Jesus' body from the cross and laid him in a new tomb (Luke 23:50-53).

Verse 30. This verse is contrasted with the previous verse. Whereas the Jews executed Jesus and buried him (though clearly, the Arimathean, Joseph, was looking for the kingdom of God), God raised Jesus from the dead.

Verse 31. For forty days after his passion Jesus presented himself alive to the apostles in Jerusalem (Acts 1:3-4*a*). On the day of Jesus' resurrection, Jesus said to the living eleven of his twelve disciples, "You are my witnesses" (Luke 24:48).

Verses 32-39. Paul's theology of justification by faith is quite immature at this point. See Romans 4 for his most mature statement of the concept.

Verse 32. Paul alludes to the Abrahamic covenant. God's covenant with Abraham and his descendants was the everlasting covenant. God said, "I will be their God" (Genesis 17:7-8). Paul has returned to common ground with the Jews, whom he addressed in verse 26 as "the family of Abraham."

Verse 33*a*. Paul's congregation are the children of the covenant, not because they are descendants of Abraham, but because one of Abraham's son's, Jesus, has brought them salvation. Paul quotes Psalm 2:7*b*. It is also quoted at Jesus' baptism (Luke 3:22*b*).

Verses 34-39. Paul quotes from the Old Testament: Isaiah 55:3 and Psalm 16:10*b*. David's blessing is Jesus, as stated in verse 23. Jesus and David are contrasted. David died and saw corruption. Jesus died and was raised from the dead. Through this incorruptible Jesus comes something the law of Moses could never give, forgiveness of sins.

The Scripture and the Main Question—Pat McGeachy

Having Been Sent (Acts 13:1-3)

If I remember my high school Latin correctly, the conjugation of the verb *mitto*, "to send," begins *mitto, mittere, missus est*. The past participle, from which we get our word *missionary*, means "having been sent." In plain English, a missionary is one who has been sent. Who sent Paul and Barnabas from one Antioch to the other? (I hope you have noticed that there are two different Antiochs in this story, one in Syria and one in Caria [called Pisidian Antioch]. They are not too far apart; look them up on your Bible map.)

Paul and Barnabas were sent in at least three ways: First, of course, the Holy Spirit called them (verse 2). Second, the leaders of the congregation confirmed the call by the laying on of hands (verses 1 and 3). By the way, we

SEPTEMBER 15   LESSON 3

know nothing of Simeon, Lucius, and Manaen. If, like Lucius, Simeon was from Cyrene, he could have been the Simon (Mark 15:21) who carried Jesus' cross. Tradition has it that this was a black man, and our Simeon is in fact nicknamed "Niger," which means "black." Third, of course, there was their own sense of having been sent. This is implied in their accepting the commission and setting out to fulfill it.

A Parenthesis on Cyprus (Acts 13:4-12)

This section is not assigned for our lesson this week, but we need to glance at it, if only to observe the change of name from Saul to Paul. In most other biblical accounts of a name change, we have a formula something like this: "No longer shall you be called [Abram, Jacob, Simon, etc.] but [Abraham, Israel, Peter, etc.]."

But here we have simply Luke's mention of the fact that Saul "is also called Paul." What could be the explanation?

1. It could simply be a reference to the fact that the proconsul, to whom they were speaking (verse 7), was also called Paul. But this is unlikely since Luke, who has been using the name Saul up till now, for the rest of the book calls him Paul.

2. It could just be Luke's poor attempt at a joke. Paul was "the least of the apostles" (1 Corinthians 15:9), and tradition has it that he was short in stature. Paulus means "small" in Greek.

3. More likely it had been one of Paul's names from birth. As a Roman citizen, he might well have been called by a Gentile name as well as by his Hebrew one. And now that he is beginning his full-time mission to the Roman world, he might have wished to be known not as "Saul" the Jew but as "Paul" the Roman. At any rate, from now on out, that is what we will call him.

The Setting for the Sermon (Acts 13:11-16)

The central place of worship for the Jews was the temple, but in every city where there were as many as "ten Jewish men," synagogues (the word means exactly the same thing as our word "congregation") were formed for prayer, reading of the Word, and teaching. Visiting teachers were welcome, especially in the outlying towns. With no telephones, newspapers, or radios, news traveled slowly, and those with the "latest" news were listened to with eagerness (see verse 44). (For another example of radical news spoken by a visiting teacher in a synagogue, read Luke 4:16-30.)

Please note (verse 16) that there were Gentiles ("you that fear God") as well as Jews in the congregation. We can suspect that most of them were pretty well versed by now in Jewish history, having attended the synagogue. But I suspect that this sermon, just as it is, would not speak to a modern audience. Would the average visitor in a pew in your church be able to identify Saul the son of Kish? If so, congratulations on the good job of Bible teaching going on in your synagogue.

The Sermon (Acts 13:17-41)

It would be interesting to deal with what is left *out* of this story. Why did Paul choose these particular Hebrew heroes? But let's see who he *does* include.

FIRST QUARTER

- *Verses 17-20:* God led the people during the simple early days of the judges until the time of Samuel, the last of the judges and the first of the prophets.
- *Verses 21-22:* They demanded a king, and God gave them Saul and David, and more, but promised a true king of David's lineage.
- *Verses 23-25:* Jesus is that true king, as heralded by John, the last of the prophets.
- *Verses 26-29:* Both the mistaken religious leaders and the ignorant pagan (Pilate) killed the true Messiah.
- *Verses 30-31:* But God raised him from the dead.
- *Verses 32-39:* This was all prophesied in your Scriptures.
- *Verses 40-41:* Therefore, repent and believe.

The Reaction (Acts 13:42-51)

As the saying goes, you win a few and lose a few. The sermon attracted unusual interest (verses 42-44), but it also attracted jealousy among the leaders. This is not very surprising. How would you feel if you had been proclaiming a particular doctrine with zeal and faithfulness all your life, and some stranger came along with a claim that your doctrine was wrong and his was right. It would take remarkable restraint for you to continue to believe in freedom of speech under those conditions.

"All right then," said Paul and Barnabas, in effect (verses 46-47), "I understand that you can't handle this, but in that case we are going to give it to those who *can* handle it, namely, the Gentiles."

The result was a great revival, but also a great schism (verses 48-51). Growth often involves pain, and sometimes it is necessary to "shake off the dust." This was the Jewish equivalent of treating someone as a heathen; the pious Jew would not bring into the Holy Land any dust from pagan territory. It is also a way of saying, "All right then, you have condemned yourselves; your blood be on your head." But the net feeling we are left with at the end of this sermon is one of gladness, gladness on the part of those who had thought themselves outside of the pale, without hope (see Ephesians 2:11-13). But now they have been given a new and living hope, and the last verse sums it up: "And the disciples were filled with joy and with the Holy Spirit."

Summing It Up

Suppose someone stopped you on the street and asked, "What does your faith mean?" How would you respond? Would you begin by saying, "Well, let me tell you a little Hebrew history? A long time ago a man called Abraham set out . . ." What would you include in that history, and what would you omit?

It seems clear to me that every evangelistic message will be different, depending upon what the listener already knows. If he is a Jew or a "God-fearer," that calls for one kind of approach; maybe we could use Paul's words just as we have them in Acts 13. But if he is a pagan, then a different tack will be called for. A good many years ago, a young man, clad in beads and jeans, stopped me in front of a church and asked, "Hey man! What's all this whoop-de-do about Jesus Christ?" I responded by saying, "Before I can answer that, you and I need to get to know each other a little better."

Just so. But I now think I would add one sentence. Before I can answer anybody I need to get to know myself a little better. What do *I* know about the faith of ancient Israel, and the meaning of prophecy? Just what scriptures do I trust that are fulfilled in Jesus Christ? You see, Jesus is not only the fulfilment of the ancient scrolls. He is also the answer to a deep longing in the human heart for Emmanuel, "God with us." And unless you and I have understood that longing, we will not have asked the question to which Christ is the answer.

Helping Adults Become Involved—Ronald E. Schlosser

Preparing to Teach

No city figures more largely in Paul's ministry than the Syrian city of Antioch. Here Barnabas brought him from Tarsus as his co-worker (Acts 11:26). Here he and Barnabas were commissioned as missionaries (Acts 13:2-3). From here Paul set out on his missionary journeys (Acts 13:4; 15:35-41; 18:22-23). Here he had his famous interview with Peter (Galatians 2:11). Antioch in Syria was the base of all of Paul's missionary activity.

But there is another Antioch, in Pisidia in Asia Minor. Paul stopped there on his first missionary journey and delivered a powerful sermon. Today's lesson might be considered a tale of two cities, a tale of two congregations, one sending, the other receiving. Plan to have a large Bible map in the classroom to enable the class to locate the two Antiochs.

Today's lesson has three learning goals: (1) to identify the truths that make up the heart of the Christian gospel; (2) to determine the place and importance of preaching in sharing one's faith; (3) to recognize the importance of the local church in carrying out the Christian mission.

After presenting the main question, you might develop the session around this outline:

I. The church reaches out.
II. The journey begins.
III. Sharing the good news.
IV. Lessons to be learned.

Carefully read the sections "As You Read the Scripture" and "The Scripture and the Main Question." These form the heart of the lesson. The ideas, insights, and suggestions in these sections should be employed throughout your lesson plan.

Introducing the Main Question

Central to the religion of Islam are its five pillars of faith: (1) bearing witness to the one true God (Allah) and acknowledging Muhammed as his messenger; (2) praying five times a day while facing Mecca; (3) giving alms to help the needy; (4) fasting from dawn to sunset during the holy month of Ramadan; (5) making a pilgrimage to Mecca at least once in your lifetime.

Pose this question to your class, as suggested by Dr. McGeachy: If you had to sum up the Christian faith in five fundamental principles, what would

FIRST QUARTER

they be? Suggest that the members take three or four minutes to think about this question and jot down the principles they would select. Then write all their suggestions on the chalkboard. From these have the class agree upon which five they feel are the most important. Indicate that in today's lesson we will be looking at what the Apostle Paul felt were the important truths to communicate in his sermons.

Developing the Lesson

I. The church reaches out.

Ask a class member to read aloud Acts 13:1-4. Locate Antioch (in Syria) on a Bible map. What does the class know about Antioch? Recall the lesson from last week, and refer to the comments in the opening paragraph under "Preparing to Teach," above.

Remembering that it was at Antioch that the followers of the Way were first called Christians, ask the class to list the characteristics of the local congregation there.

1. *A cosmopolitan church:* Antioch was a cosmopolitan city, and the church there had a cosmopolitan membership. Lucius, and perhaps Simeon also, was from Cyrene. Manaen was a member of Herod's court. Barnabas, as we saw last week, was a rather well-to-do landowner from Cyprus. Paul was a university-trained Pharisee from Tarsus.
2. *A generous church:* When the congregation at Antioch heard about the needs of their Christian brothers and sisters in Judea, they sent them relief (Acts 11:29-30).
3. *A praying church:* Acts 13:2-3 describes the members as "worshiping the Lord and fasting," and "fasting and praying." Great things happen when a church prays. Recall Jesus' words in Mark 9:29.
4. *A Spirit-filled church:* Verses 2 and 4 underscore the Spirit's moving in the lives of the members.
5. *A mission-minded church:* Refer to Dr. McGeachy's comments on the meaning of the words "mission" and "missionary."

II. The journey begins.

On your Bible map, follow the travels of Paul, Barnabas, and John Mark, as summarized by Dr. Winters in his comments on Acts 13:1-16a. Refer to Dr. McGeachy's explanation about Paul's name change in Cyprus. Note also that in this passage another change is indicated. Up to this point, whenever Barnabas and Saul had been mentioned, Barnabas' name came first (see Acts 11:30; 12:25; 13:2, 7). Barnabas had been the leader, the organizer. But now, for the first time, we read "Paul and his company." After this, Paul always seems to be the dynamic leader, the energetic spokesman.

III. Sharing the good news.

Ask the class to read silently Paul's sermon in Acts 13:16b-41. Suggest that they quickly scan verses 16-25 but focus more intently on verses 26-41. In this latter passage, have them underline words that seem to focus on the heart of his message.

Allow about five minutes for this quiet study, then discuss what the central points of Paul's sermon seem to be. Key words and phrases to focus

SEPTEMBER 15   LESSON 3

on are salvation, prophecy, fulfillment, resurrection, eyewitnesses, good news, promises, forgiveness, everyone that believes is freed.

Dr. McGeachy points out, in analyzing the sermons of Peter, Stephen, and Paul in the book of Acts, that all have these common elements: reference to the Hebrews' history, Jesus' fulfillment of prophecy of his death and resurrection, and a call to repentance and belief. The Greek word *kerygma* is used to describe the substance of the early apostolic preaching. This is the proclamation of the gospel that Paul refers to in 1 Corinthians 15:1-5.

Look back at your list of fundamental principles of the Christian faith, discussed at the beginning of the session. How does it compare with the *kerygma* of the early church? Should there be differences in emphases, given our twentieth-century culture?

If time allows, discuss the reaction to Paul's sermon as described in Acts 13:42-51. Refer to Dr. McGeachy's comments.

Helping Class Members Act

IV. *Lessons to be learned.*

Use the last part of your session to discuss these questions:

1. When we share our faith, how should we do it? Is every evangelistic message different, as Dr. McGeachy suggests?
2. What is the place and importance of preaching in proclaiming the gospel? Should preaching ability be the primary concern of a church looking for a new pastor?
3. What is the place of the local church in God's plan? Can Christian mission be carried out without the support of local churches?

Conclude by pointing out that from the first apostles to present-day missionaries, the primary goal, after preaching the gospel, has been to establish and support churches. The great achievements in missions through preaching, teaching, healing, and building have been possible because local churches first saw a need.

Planning for Next Sunday

Ask your members to read Acts 14 and consider what they would have done if they had been in Lystra and witnessed the healing of the crippled man.

LESSON 4   SEPTEMBER 22

Making People Whole

Background Scripture: Acts 14

The Main Question—Pat McGeachy

We have always known that the body and the spirit are closely related. It is common knowledge that when you feel better physically, you are sharper mentally, and that when you are in good spirits, your body works more effectively. Listen to the parallelism in Psalm 103:2-3:

> Bless the Lord, O my soul
> ....
> who forgives all your iniquity,
>   who heals all your diseases.

Or remember Psalm 32:3: "When I declared not my sin, my body wasted away."

Modern medicine is rediscovering this relationship. Investigation of the curious form of psychosis called multiple personality has revealed that sometimes a patient who has a severe rash when he is one of his various personalities can be completely free of it when he takes on another "self." If that is a little far out, it has been proven that many disorders are primarily psychological in origin. All of this has given rise to the practice of what some call holistic medicine, the treatment of a patient not simply as a machine called the body but as a whole person, body, mind, and spirit.

In the town of Lystra, Paul, filled with the good news, sensed in one of his hearers, a lame man, the coming of healing both to soul and body, and called him to stand up. As a result, the crowds tried to treat Paul as a god. But we do not have to be gods to experience this phenomenon. I have seen it in my own ministry, and in myself, and I suspect you have to. Let's examine Acts 14 with a view to answering the question, How can we become whole?

This is neither a medical nor a theological question; it is a faith question, and one that we can hope to answer in terms of our own lives. We will not find here a "quick fix" or a psychological trick to fool the gullible, but a genuine part of the Christian experience. True holiness is wholeness.

Selected Scripture

King James Version	Revised Standard Version
Acts 14:8-18	*Acts 14:8-18*
8 And there sat a certain man at Lystra, impotent in his feet, being a cripple from his mother's womb, who never had walked:	8 Now at Lystra there was a man sitting, who could not use his feet; he was a cripple from birth, who had never walked. 9 He listened to Paul speaking; and Paul, looking intently at him and seeing that he had faith to be made well, 10 said in a loud voice, "Stand upright on your feet."
9 The same heard Paul speak: who stedfastly beholding him, and perceiving that he had faith to be healed,	

10 Said with a loud voice, Stand upright on thy feet. And he leaped and walked.

11 And when the people saw what Paul had done, they lifted up their voices, saying in the speech of Lycaonia, The gods are come down to us in the likeness of men.

12 And they called Barnabas, Jupiter; and Paul, Mercurius, because he was the chief speaker.

13 Then the priest of Jupiter, which was before their city, brought oxen and garlands unto the gates, and would have done sacrifice with the people.

14 *Which* when the apostles, Barnabas and Paul, heard *of*, they rent their clothes, and ran in among the people, crying out,

15 And saying, Sirs, why do ye these things? We also are men of like passions with you, and preach unto you that ye should turn from these vanities unto the living God, which made heaven, and earth, and the sea, and all things that are therein:

16 Who in times past suffered all nations to walk in their own ways.

17 Nevertheless he left not himself without witness, in that he did good, and gave us rain from heaven, and fruitful seasons, filling our hearts with food and gladness.

18 And with these sayings scarce restrained they the people, that they had not done sacrifice unto them.

And he sprang up and walked. 11 And when the crowds saw what Paul had done, they lifted up their voices, saying in Lycaonian, "The gods have come down to us in the likeness of men!" 12 Barnabas they called Zeus, and Paul, because he was the chief speaker, they called Hermes. 13 And the priest of Zeus, whose temple was in front of the city, brought oxen and garlands to the gates and wanted to offer sacrifice with the people. 14 But when the apostles Barnabas and Paul heard of it, they tore their garments and rushed out among the multitude, crying, 15 "Men, why are you doing this? We also are men, of like nature with you, and bring you good news, that you should turn from these vain things to a living God who made the heaven and the earth and the sea and all that is in them. 16 In past generations he allowed all the nations to walk in their own ways; 17 yet he did not leave himself without witness, for he did good and gave you from heaven rains and fruitful seasons, satisfying your hearts with food and gladness." 18 With these words they scarcely restrained the people from offering sacrifice to them.

Key Verse: The same heard Paul speak: who stedfastly beholding him, and perceiving that he had faith to be healed, said with a loud voice, "Stand upright on thy feet." And he leaped and walked. (Acts 14:9-10)

Key Verse: Paul, looking intently at him and seeing that he had faith to be made well, said in a loud voice, "Stand upright on your feet." And he sprang up and walked. (Acts 14:9-10)

As You Read the Scripture—Michael Winters

Acts 14. On their first missionary journey, Paul and Barnabas began in Antioch of Syria, passed through Cyprus, sailed to Perga in Pamphylia, and traveled inland to Antioch of Pisidia. In Antioch, Paul preached. As a result, many Jews and devout Jewish proselytes followed Paul and Barnabas. Yet

FIRST QUARTER

controversy, stirred mainly by Jewish jealousy over the missioners' large crowds, provoked persecution against Paul and Barnabas (Acts 13:44-52).

From Antioch, Paul and Barnabas went to Iconium, where they preached. Again controversy flared, so that Paul and Barnabas had to flee to escape stoning (Acts 14:1-7).

They fled to Lystra of Lycaonia, where Paul healed a cripple. The overly enthusiastic citizens of Lystra attempted to deify Paul and Barnabas, who scarcely prevented the people from offering sacrifices to them (verses 8-18).

Vigilant Jews followed Paul and Barnabas to Lystra and stirred the people there against them. Paul was stoned and left for dead outside the city. But he survived, so that he and Barnabas were able to continue to Derbe, also of Lycaonia. There they preached and made many disciples and left, returning to Lystra, Iconium, and Antioch. Courageously, they returned to take time to develop the faith of the new disciples of Jesus (verses 19-24).

After a couple of brief layovers, Paul and Barnabas completed their journey, returning to Antioch of Syria. There they heralded their work abroad, declaring that they had "opened a door of faith to the Gentiles" (verses 24-28).

Verse 8. Lystra is eighteen miles south of Iconium, in the province of Lycaonia. The healing of the cripple is faintly reminiscent of Peter's healing story in Acts 3:2-8.

Verse 9. Paul looked intently at the cripple. In 3:4, Peter also gazed at his patient, seeking the cripple's attention. Paul, however, looked at the cripple, assessing the cripple's faith.

Verse 10. Paul shouted, "Stand upright on your feet." He did not touch the cripple. And the cripple sprang up and walked. In Acts 3:7-8, Peter took the cripple by the right hand; the cripple then leaped up and walked.

Verse 11. Although the people who witnessed Peter's healing of the cripple were filled with wonder and amazement (verse 3:10), their attitudes were reserved compared to the reaction of the people who witnessed Paul's healing. The people of Lystra deified Paul and Barnabas, shouting in their apparently unique dialect.

Verse 12. They called Barnabas, Zeus. Zeus was the chief of the Greek gods. Jupiter was the corresponding Roman deity. There had been a temple dedicated to Zeus at Athens. During the time of the Maccabeans (169 B.C.), the Seleucid king, Antiochus IV, compelled the Jews to call their temple in Jerusalem "Olympian Zeus" (See 2 Maccabees 6:2).

The Greek god Hermes was the equivalent of the Roman god Mercury. Hermes, Zeus' attendant, also spoke for Zeus. They called Paul Hermes because he was the chief speaker.

Verse 13. The priest of Zeus wanted to offer sacrifices to appease the god.

Verse 14. To Paul and Barnabas, their identification with Zeus and Hermes was scandalous. But to have allowed the priest to make sacrifice to them would have been a sacrilegious desecration. They were utterly horrified.

Verses 15-18. Paul and Barnabas urgently appealed to the natural theology of the priest and citizens of Lystra to turn from Zeus and Hermes to the living God of the rains and harvest. Thus they prevented the sacrifice.

SEPTEMBER 22   LESSON 4

The Scripture and the Main Question—Pat McGeachy

A Mixed Bag (Acts 14:1-7)

When you show up in the world with a gospel as radical as the Christian faith, you can expect some fur to fly. Initially, in Iconium, there was a popular response to Paul and Barnabas. A "great company" (verse 1) believed, both Jews and Gentiles. As usual, the apostles began their ministry with the people to whom their preaching should speak, those of the synagogue, who already had a background in the scriptures that foretold the coming of the Christ. And to a large extent it worked. But there were those (verse 2) who could not or would not believe. Even so (verse 3) they did their best, speaking boldly and doing signs and wonders (a foretaste of what would happen to the crippled man at Lystra). However, it doesn't take a highly motivated opposition long to put the squelch on a brand new movement, so the city became divided, evenly at first, but eventually the apostles were in the minority. (Notice that the word "apostle" in Acts has become a general term, not confined to the twelve original witnesses of the resurrection but including here Paul and Barnabas. The root meaning of the word "apostle" is "sent," and that very verb, *apostello*, is used at the beginning of this missionary journey (Acts 13:3), where it says that the church "sent them off.") But no amount of apostolic authority can succeed when the audience stops up its ears. Remember that there were times (Matthew 13:58) when not even Jesus could succeed. There is one thing that even God cannot do: give grace to one who will not receive it. So just before the rocks began to fly (verse 5), Paul and Barnabas skipped town and took the gospel to Lystra.

A Healing (Acts 14:8-10)

If you have ever been a public speaker, you will know that there are faces in every audience that stand out. Some of them are scowling, some of them are smiling and nodding, and some of them are just blank, like those of an adolescent trying to hide all feelings. I have learned that you can't always tell at a distance how someone is responding; I have had some of those scowling faces come up to me afterward and thank me for the message. But most of the time, you learn as a preacher to find those faces that are truly responsive, and I catch myself looking at them from time to time to make sure that I am getting through. You can tell a lot from their nonverbal signals, and sometimes they will even give you a verbal response like "Amen." It's comforting when you get that, but it is wise also to listen to the "Oh yeah?" corner as well.

Paul was a master reader of the human heart, perhaps second only to Jesus. In this case, we are told (verse 9) that he could, by looking intently, read the man's faith, and he found it sound. This made Paul bold to cry out, "Stand upright on your feet." And the fellow sprang up and walked (verse 10). This is by no means the only account of a healing by those who were so close to Jesus that they caught some of the Physician's gift. Perhaps the most dramatic example is the story of Peter and John and the lame man in Acts 3:1-10, which precedes Peter's sermon. Remember how he went "walking and leaping and praising God." Peter so possessed the gift that people felt better if only his shadow fell upon them (see Acts 5:12-16).

Allow me a brief etymological digression. Our word "health" comes from

FIRST QUARTER

an Anglo-Saxon root, *hal*, from which we derive a number of words, among them "whole" and, believe it or not, "holy." And it is worth mentioning that the word "salvation" is also related to healing; note the root word "salve," a healing ointment, hiding in it.

Jesus once dramatically pointed out the relationship between sin forgiven and the wholeness of the body when he healed the paralytic who had been let down through the roof (Mark 2:1-12). When the scribes called him a blasphemer because the told the man his sins were forgiven, Jesus demonstrated his authority by telling the man to walk, which he did. Jesus said to them, in effect (this is my way of wording it), "Anybody can say, your sins are forgiven, and who will know? But it's tougher to say, 'Take up your bed and walk,' because everybody will know." In so doing, Jesus relates the man's sin to his illness, and his healing to God's forgiveness.

Of course, we can't say that every specific sickness is due to a specific sin. Some of them obviously are—venereal diseases, for instance. But what about a baby who inherits such a sickness from its mother? In the case of the blind man related in John 9:1-3, Jesus plainly says that it was *not* this man's sin, or his parents', that caused his blindness. The question is a thorny one, baffling to theologians even before the time of Christ. The book of Job, which may be one of the earliest books of the Bible, was written to struggle with the origin of disease and leaves us in a state of humble wondering. But it is clear that sin and sickness are in *some* sense related, and that the healing of the body and the saving of the soul are in some sense related. Just as we are to love God with our whole being, body, mind, and heart, we can also become corrupt in our whole being, and it takes a whole gospel to make us both whole and holy.

Taken for Gods (Acts 14:11-18)

The people saw this healing as a miracle, and they called Barnabas, Zeus, and Paul, Hermes. Barnabas was probably taller and more imposing and Paul little and talkative. In Greek (and Roman) mythology Zeus (Jupiter) was the king of the gods, and Hermes (Mercury) their messenger. But the apostles would have none of it. They knew that they were ordinary mortals, like you and me. And by inversion, this means that you and I should be able to be healers too.

I remember our family physician, who would come to my bedside when I was sick. I have since learned that he was a troubled man and an alcoholic, but what I remember is his gentle smile, his tired eyes, and his comforting voice. From the very moment he entered the room, I would start to feel better. If that poor man could radiate such healing, how much more could be the gifts of a genuine Christian evangelist. I am not speaking here of an angry televangelist, shouting, and radiating judgment and anger, but a genuine witness for Christ, with the bearing of an apostle, eager to heal the whole person. I know such persons, and surely you do too. Let us pray for that gift in ourselves, and let us draw closer to Christ, that we may learn from him how to draw others into the healing circle.

The Wounded Healers (Acts 14:19-28)

And what did they do for the healers? They stoned them and left them for dead (verse 19), but they too were healed by the presence of the disciples gathered around them (verse 20), and went on to strengthen others (verse 22) until they came at last to the other Antioch, from which they had been sent. We do this to our healers. We kill off the gentle folk because they disturb our moral indignation. We don't *want* the prisoners to turn over a new leaf and the lepers to be clean and the lame to walk. We say we do, but we stone the healers, just as we crucified the Great Physician.

But "he was wounded for our transgressions . . . and with his stripes we are healed" (Isaiah 53:5). One of the ways in which Christ, and his apostles, comforts us in our pain is that he is able to say, "I know how it hurts." When you and I can learn, like Christ and like Paul, to enter the kingdom of God through many tribulations (Acts 14:22), then we too may have the power to see the faith and feel the hurt of those around us, and to lend them some of the strength that we have received from God. In that case, we will become "holistic" Christians, not yet fully whole, but whole enough to help other people find wholeness.

Helping Adults Become Involved—Ronald E. Schlosser

Preparing to Teach

Paul's missionary activities, described in the book of Acts, follow a predictable pattern: Enter a town. Find the Jewish synagogue. Preach to the Jews about Jesus and the resurrection. Get a mixed reaction. Face growing Jewish opposition. Turn to the Gentiles. Establish a church. Run for your life to the next town, and start all over. Add some bitter debate, some miracles of healing, and a little sheer violence, and you have the pattern pretty well in mind.

The lesson for this week continues the account of Paul's first missionary journey begun in last week's lesson. As you read Dr. Winters's summary of the journey in his comments on Acts 14, trace Paul's route on a Bible map and locate the various towns he visited. As in previous sessions, a large classroom map should be available to help your class follow the story as it unfolds.

Carefully read the sections "As You Read the Scripture" and "The Scripture and the Main Question." These form the heart of the lesson. The ideas, insights, and suggestions in these sections should be employed throughout your lesson plan.

The following outline may help you develop the lesson after you introduce the main question:

       I. Division at Iconium.
      II. Healing at Lystra.
         A. A cripple rises.
         B. A missionary rises.
     III. Homecoming at Antioch.
     IV. The work of a missionary.

The learning goals for the lesson will be (1) to become aware of the motivations of people who suffer illness or experience healing and (2) to discern the kinds of ministry persons can perform as Christian workers or missionaries.

FIRST QUARTER

Introducing the Main Question

In the section "The Main Question," Dr. McGeachy introduces the term "holistic medicine," referring to the treatment of the whole person—body, mind, and spirit. Begin the session by asking your class members what their attitude is toward holistic medicine. Is this a legitimate way of treating people? Do any of their doctors practice it? What has been their experience?

Push the discussion a little further by asking, "Should we as Christians seek out a doctor who is also a Christian, who appreciates the spiritual aspects of a person's life which may have an effect upon the healing process?"

Don't dwell long on this question or try to get a consensus. Indicate that you will be coming back to it later in the lesson.

Developing the Lesson

I. Division at Iconium.

Using your classroom Bible map, review briefly the journey of Paul and his companions thus far. We last left them in Antioch of Pisidia. Read aloud Acts 13:49-53. Point out that from Antioch Paul and Barnabas moved eastward along the Roman highway to Iconium, about a hundred miles on foot. Iconium was the capital of Lycaonia, a rugged inland district of Asia Minor.

Have someone read Acts 14:1-7. Ask: How did the response of the people of Iconium compare with that of the people of Antioch? (In both cases, there were some who believed and others who didn't, even to the point of physically threatening the apostles.) Refer to Dr. McGeachy's comments in the section "A Mixed Bag." Note Paul's practice of going to the Jews first with the gospel message, but also of reaching to the Gentiles when the Jews turned against him. When the opposition became intense and violence threatened, Paul would move on to the next town.

Ask the class: Are there times when one should give up trying to reach hardhearted people with the gospel? Note Dr. McGeachy's comment on this in his reference to the times when not even Jesus could succeed (Matthew 13:58). In fact, Paul and Barnabas did just what Jesus told his disciples to do in the presence of unbelief—they shook off the dust from their feet and traveled on (compare Acts 13:51 with Matthew 10:14).

II. Healing at Lystra.
A. A cripple rises.

Turn next to Acts 14:8-18. Instead of having the class follow along in their Bibles as the passage is read, ask the members to visualize the scene in their minds. (They may even wish to close their eyes.) They are to imagine they are there in Lystra as eyewitnesses. One group should try to experience what is happening from the point of view of the crippled man. Another group should picture themselves as spectators watching the events unfold.

After reading the passage aloud, explore with the first group how it must have felt to the cripple to be able to walk for the first time in his life. What did Paul see in his face, to interrupt his message and cause the man to be healed? See Dr. McGeachy's comments about nonverbal communication. Note also his and Dr. Winters's comparison of this healing with Peter's healing of the lame man in Acts 3:1-10.

SEPTEMBER 22   LESSON 4

Next explore with the second group their reaction as spectators to the healing. Would they have gone along with the crowd to worship Paul and Barnabas as gods, given the culture of the day? After hearing Paul's disclaimer, what might they have done? What questions would they have?

Discuss the motivations that compel people to action when they suffer illness or experience healing. People who are desperately ill may do desperate things to seek a cure. People who are cured—and perhaps their loved ones too—may show their gratitude in expansive ways to the one or ones they credit for the cure. Consider the dangers or benefits of such action. How can the Christian faith be a leavening influence?

B. A missionary rises.

Read aloud Acts 14:19-23. Discuss Paul's response to his misfortune. Instead of quitting after the stoning, he miraculously regained his strength and moved on. And then, courageously, he retraced his steps and revisited the same towns that had persecuted him. In fact, he visited Lystra a third time, where he took on Timothy as a traveling companion (Acts 16:1-3). Ever the missionary, Paul sought to strengthen the churches that had been established, encouraging the members and appointing leaders to guide the work.

III. Homecoming at Antioch.

Read aloud Acts 14:24-28. Follow Paul's journey back to Antioch on your map. Imagine the homecoming. What joy and thanksgiving must have been expressed! Can your class think of comparable events today that would cause such rejoicing?

Helping Class Members Act

IV. The work of a missionary.

Ask: In light of the accounts in Acts 14, what kinds of ministry can persons perform as Christian workers or missionaries? Here are some suggestions:

1. Witnessing: Everywhere Paul went, he preached the gospel.

2. Healing: Refer to Dr. McGeachy's comments that we all should be healers.

3. Encouraging and strengthening: This can be considered a part of healing, particularly when spirits are depressed, whether as individuals or congregations.

4. Identifying and training leaders: A church will thrive only if there is a strong group of committed lay people.

Close with a prayer for God's strength and counsel as we all endeavor to be Christian missionaries in the world.

Planning for Next Sunday

Read the background Scripture, Acts 15:1-35. Refer to next week's "Preparing to Teach" section to assign debaters or discussion stimulators.

LESSON 5　　　　　　　　　　　　　　SEPTEMBER 29

Working Out Differences

Background Scripture: Acts 15:1-35

The Main Question—Pat McGeachy

I suppose there has never been a church, or a family, or any other human institution, no matter how Christlike, that hasn't had its differences. Even Jesus and his parents were at cross-purposes on more than one occasion (Luke 2:48-49; John 2:4). Where there's life, there's strife. The question then is not what can we do to avoid having differences; we will always have them, and the more alive and energetic we are, the more we will have them. The question is what shall we do with them. We may not resolve them, but we may be able to do something to work them out.

In this lesson we will see the early church dealing with a controversy, and not a small one at that. In a way it is the same controversy we always seem to be having: that between the progressives and the conservatives. I wish we didn't have to use words like those because they quickly become labels, and we use them pejoratively. We call each other liberal or fundamentalist with a bit of a sneer in our voice, and the first thing you know we are into such misunderstandings that we don't seem to be able to communicate at all.

But we must! Conservatives need progressives to keep them from doing nothing, and progressives need conservatives to keep them from running off the end of the pier. We can't get along without one another. Therefore, let us look carefully at this first "General Conference" in Jerusalem, and see what we can learn in the way of skills that will enable us to conduct our affairs in such a way that our conflicts are turned into energy for good, and that the dignity of people is preserved in the process.

It was a knotty problem that confronted them, and feelings ran high, as they always do when deeply held convictions seem to be at stake. But they surmounted the difficulties. What can we learn from them to answer the question, How can we best work out our differences?

Selected Scripture

King James Version	Revised Standard Version
Acts 15:1-12	*Acts 15:1-12*
1 And certain men which came down from Judea taught the brethren, *and said*, Except ye be circumcised after the manner of Moses, ye cannot be saved.	1 But some men came down from Judea and were teaching the brethren, "Unless you are circumcised according to the custom of Moses, you cannot be saved." 2 And
2 When therefore Paul and Barnabas had no small dissension and disputation with them, they determined that Paul and Barnabas, and certain other of them, should go up	when Paul and Barnabas had no small dissension and debate with them, Paul and Barnabas and some of the others were appointed to go up to Jerusalem to the apostles and

SEPTEMBER 29   LESSON 5

to Jerusalem unto the apostles and elders about this question.

3 And being brought on their way by the church, they passed through Phenice and Samaria, declaring the conversion of the Gentiles: and they caused great joy unto all the brethren.

4 And when they were come to Jerusalem, they were received of the church, and *of* the apostles and elders, and they declared all things that God had done with them.

5 But there rose up certain of the sect of the Pharisees which believed, saying, That it was needful to circumcise them, and to command *them* to keep the law of Moses.

6 And the apostles and elders came together for to consider of this matter.

7 And when there had been much disputing, Peter rose up, and said unto them, Men *and* brethren, ye know how that a good while ago God made choice among us, that the Gentiles by my mouth should hear the word of the gospel, and believe.

8 And God, which knoweth the hearts, bare them witness, giving them the Holy Ghost, even as *he did* unto us;

9 And put no difference between us and them, purifying their hearts by faith.

10 Now therefore why tempt ye God, to put a yoke upon the neck of the disciples, which neither our fathers nor we were able to bear?

11 But we believe that through the grace of the Lord Jesus Christ we shall be saved, even as they.

12 Then all the multitude kept silence, and gave audience to Barnabas and Paul, declaring what miracles and wonders God had wrought among the Gentiles by them.

Key Verse: **But we believe that through the grace of the Lord Jesus Christ we shall be saved, even as they. (Acts 15:11)**

the elders about this question. 3 So, being sent on their way by the church, they passed through both Phoenicia and Samaria, reporting the conversion of the Gentiles, and they gave great joy to all the brethren. 4 When they came to Jerusalem, they were welcomed by the church and the apostles and the elders, and they declared all that God had done with them. 5 But some believers who belonged to the party of the Pharisees rose up, and said, "It is necessary to circumcise them, and to charge them to keep the law of Moses."

6 The apostles and the elders were gathered together to consider this matter. 7 And after there had been much debate, Peter rose and said to them, "Brethren, you know that in the early days God made choice among you, that by my mouth the Gentiles should hear the word of the gospel and believe. 8 And God who knows the heart bore witness to them, giving them the Holy Spirit just as he did to us; 9 and he made no distinction between us and them, but cleansed their hearts by faith. 10 Now therefore why do you make trial of God by putting a yoke upon the neck of the disciples which neither our fathers nor we have been able to bear? 11 But we believe that we shall be saved through the grace of the Lord Jesus, just as they will."

12 And all the assembly kept silence; and they listened to Barnabas and Paul as they related what signs and wonders God had done through them among the Gentiles.

Key Verse: **But we believe that we shall be saved through the grace of the Lord Jesus, just as they [the Gentiles] will. (Acts 15:11)**

FIRST QUARTER
As You Read the Scripture—Michael Winters

Acts 15:1-35. Christianity began as a Jewish sect. Its adherents were required to subscribe to the ancient rituals of Judaism. This meant obedience to the law of Moses and the entire deuteronomic code. There were many dietary restrictions. And there was circumcision: Male circumcision itself was the one ritual and visible sign that above all others signified initiation into Judaism.

The Gentile Christians found themselves not desiring to face the ritual of circumcision. They rather chose to embrace the simple message of Paul and Barnabas, that salvation came only through the grace of God by believing.

Circumcision was an issue that festered in the increasingly Gentile church. Finally, the apostles in Jerusalem were asked to resolve once and for all the issue of whether one had to first become a Jew before becoming a Christian.

During a special council the apostles decided that the gospel did not require Jewish circumcision. The council sent a letter to the emerging church among the Gentiles, requiring them only to abstain from that which had been offered to idols, from unchastity, and from what is strangled. This was a letter that was received with joy by the Gentiles in Antioch of Syria.

Verse 1. Circumcision is a Jewish ritual required as a sign of God's covenant with Abraham (Genesis 17:11). The men from Judea were Jewish Christians, possibly Pharisees (verse 5), who evidently came to Antioch with authority (authority of the Pharisees?) to declare circumcision a basic component of Christianity.

Verse 2. Paul and Barnabas became the principal spokespersons, dissenting against the circumcision directive. The church in Antioch commissioned Paul and Barnabas to go to Jerusalem to achieve clarity about the need to circumcise. It was not the first time the church in Antioch commissioned them (see 11:29-30).

Verse 3. As Paul and Barnabas made their way to Jerusalem, they likely lobbied their interest among the Gentiles in the churches in Phoenicia and Samaria, regions in North and Central Palestine, respectively.

Verses 4-5. Paul and Barnabas were typically upbeat about their experience among the Gentiles. The "party of the Pharisees," however, was not going to allow them to abrogate the issue of the need for circumcision before the church. The church in Jerusalem, decidedly Jewish, was the headquarters of the growing worldwide church.

Verses 6-7a. The issue was thoroughly debated among the apostles and the elders, the overseers of the church.

Verse 7b. Peter had problems with this issue. Here he recalls his experience, which opened the church to the Gentiles (Acts 10:44-48). But he is clearly identified in Paul's mind with the side of the circumcision (Galatians 2:8, 11-14).

Verses 8-9. Peter has in his mind the conversion of the Gentile, Cornelius, in Caesarea (see Acts 10:30-34).

Verses 10-11. Peter makes a sterling statement of the doctrine of justification by faith. Rhetorically, he asks the Jews, "Why burden the Gentiles with the law, which has been our own stumbling block? It is enough that the Gentiles be expected to come to salvation through the grace of God." (See Paul's own statement in Romans 3:24 and Ephesians 2:8.)

Verse 12. In time, thanks to Peter's remarks, the assembly respectfully

SEPTEMBER 29   LESSON 5

allowed Paul and Barnabas to continue where they had begun when they first arrived in Jerusalem (verses 3-4), reporting the conversions of the Gentiles and proclaiming all the good work God had done.

The Scripture and the Main Question—Pat McGeachy

A Question of Interpretation

Before we look closely at Acts 15, we have to face up to a problem in New Testament interpretation on which the scholars differ. The problem is that in the letter to the Galatians, which was written before Acts, Paul describes a conference in Jerusalem somewhat similar to this one. Was he talking about the same meeting? If so, there are some major differences. Look for a moment at Galatians 2:1-10. The event as Paul describes it was not a general meeting in which a vote was taken but a private conference with key leaders (Galatians 2:2), and the conclusion, in the Galatians account, does not mention the need to abstain from nonkosher food, but "only that they would have us remember the poor" (Galatians 2:10). So, if they were describing the same event, either Luke or Paul was mistaken.

Of course, as the four Gospels demonstrate, different people see the same things from different perspectives. But these discrepancies are marked. So some commentators conclude that there must have been two separate meetings. Perhaps in Galatians Paul is referring to the trip to Jerusalem by Barnabas and Paul, mentioned in Acts 11:30. You will have to decide for yourself.

An Appeal to Higher Authority (Acts 15:1-3)

Most problems can be worked out between the differing parties themselves, and this way is always best. If two individuals are willing to listen to each other, they don't need to involve the whole congregation, but sometimes it is necessary for the whole assembly to be called in. If *they* can't agree, then it is sometimes necessary to "go to Jerusalem" and seek the opinion of the wisest minds of the church. In some extreme conditions, sad to say, warring factions in the church go even further and take the matter to the secular courts (See 1 Corinthians 6:1-8).

In this case, the problem was apparently more than the local congregation in Antioch could manage. Some "Judaizers" were saying that the Gentile converts were not true believers because they did not keep the ancient customs of Moses, most particularly the sign of the covenant, circumcision. For Christians today, the sacrament of baptism has taken the place of circumcision, just as the Lord's Supper has replaced the Passover meal. But the early congregations, made up as they were of a mix of Jews and Gentiles, were still influenced strongly by the ancient traditions, and many of them must have been feeling pretty guilty with their newfound freedom in Christ. The appeal to works of righteousness always strikes a chord with the conscientious.

To put the question in more contemporary terms, it would be as though a group of very conservative Christians began to worry one of our congregations by saying something like this: "It isn't enough just to say you have been saved by grace. If you are a real Christian you will be a total abstainer, and you will refrain from dancing, card playing, going to the movies on Sunday, and wearing jewelry." There is a Puritan streak in all of us, and this appeal to holiness might worry some of us, especially those who had been raised in strict conservative homes.

In any event, the congregation at Antioch couldn't agree on whether the Judaizers were right, and they were sufficiently worried about it to send Paul and Barnabas (and others, verse 2) to go up to Jerusalem to ask the "higher authorities" for a ruling. It is doubtful that Peter and James (the brothers of Jesus) had at this early stage official titles, such as bishop. But there is no question that they were among the original founders of the church, having been intimate with Jesus from the beginning, and their opinions would be greatly respected. So one solution when there is a disagreement is: ask someone who knows more than you do to mediate.

Stating the Case (Acts 15:4-6)

The whole assembly welcomed them: the church, the apostles, and the elders. And the delegation from Antioch told the wonderful story about how God had been adding to their numbers, and how well things were going with the gospel to the Gentiles. But, as in Antioch, there were arguments from the other side. Those of the "party of the Pharisees" spoke out in favor of the necessity of circumcision and the ritual laws. We have come in our day to think of the word "Pharisee" as synonymous with "self-righteousness," but the Pharisees were respected people in the Jewish community. It is hard to argue with those whose principal fault is trying to do what is right!

Here we are given an example of another important thing to do with differences: Let people have their say. There is nothing much worse than coming home from a meeting and feeling that "nobody paid any attention to what I was trying to say." People who lose the argument without having had a chance to state their case are going to be very unhappy with the final decision.

Thorough Discussion (Acts 15:6-21)

This section can be divided into four convenient parts. First, there is much debate among the apostles and elders. It goes without saying that the problem has to be talked out.

Second, Peter gives a supportive speech. He reminds the assembly about his own experience with the dream of the "unclean" animals, which he had prior to the visit of Cornelius (see Acts 10), which concluded with the message, "What God has cleansed, you must not call common" (verse 15). From this, Peter had rightly discerned that "God shows no partiality" (verse 34), and the first Gentile converts were baptized (verses 47-48). On the strength of this experience, Peter is able to say that all of us, Jews and Gentiles, are saved by grace (Acts 15:11).

Third, Barnabas and Paul testify to the wonderful things that have happened under their ministry.

Fourth, a considered judgment is rendered by James, who seems to have been the chief leader of the Jerusalem church. (See Acts 12:17; 21:18; Galatians 1:19; etc.) He was a man respected as a devout Jewish Christian, who could be counted on to support the conservative cause, especially if tradition is correct and he is the author of the epistle that bears his name, in

SEPTEMBER 29 LESSON 5

which he takes the position that faith without works is dead (James 2:17). He argues from Holy Scripture, as a conservative should, but he points out that the Scriptures support Peter's argument. However, for the sake of the conscience of the Jewish members of the church, he thinks the Gentiles should abstain from nonkosher food (verse 20; compare Romans 14:1–15:6 and 1 Corinthians 8).

Conclusion (Acts 15:22-35)

After all this discussion and testimony, they took a vote (that is what "it seemed good" means in verses 22 and 28) on a compromise proposal, which was really a victory for the Gentile party but attempted (verse 29) to pacify the Judaizers at the same time. Moreover, they wrote this down in the form of an official pronouncement, which could be taken back to Antioch as a guide. There it was joyfully received (verse 31) and a kind of peace (verse 33) was achieved. (It should be noted that this issue was never finally put to rest in the early church and crops up often in the Epistles, most notably in the letter to the Galatians, in which Paul comes down firmly on the side of Christian freedom [Galatians 5:1-2]).

We have then some excellent guides for working out differences:

1. Talk it over.
2. Get help.
3. Go to the authorities.
4. Listen to both sides.
5. Consult the Scriptures.
6. Relate it to your own experiences.
7. Compromise (not give in, but respect each other's views).
8. Come to a prayerful, Spirit-led conclusion.
9. Write your conclusion down.
10. Get on with the business of the kingdom.

Such conferences as this one in Jerusalem have been going on since the beginning of religious history, and they will always be necessary as long as Christians are human beings. They are the stuff of which the life of the church is made. But we must follow the rules because it is better for us to spend our time fighting the Devil than one another.

Helping Adults Become Involved—Ronald E. Schlosser

Preparing to Teach

In raising today's main question, Dr. McGeachy refers to the terms "conservative" and "progressive" to describe the approaches people take when dealing with controversial issues. Where do you fit into the continuum between the two extremes? In your beliefs, are you firm and unbending in what you believe, or are you open to new interpretations? Can you accept compromise without being threatened? Would you be willing to give up personal preferences for the common good? Could you accept as binding the decisions of others, even if you disagreed with them?

These are the questions the early Christians had to face in dealing with the issues in today's lesson. To give your class a sense of what was involved,

FIRST QUARTER

identify one or two issues that you feel may elicit some differences of opinions among your members. For example, where do your members stand on the use of alcoholic beverages? Some churches have been terribly divided when one group or another has wanted to delete a statement about abstention from its church covenant. Other churches have almost come to a parting of the ways over money issues—whether to air-condition the sanctuary or to mortgage the building for an urban mission project or to allow the young people to hold a bake sale on the church property. Other differences may occur, as Dr. McGeachy suggests, over dancing, card playing, going to the movies, and wearing jewelry.

Select an issue and ask several of your class members to come prepared to debate (or discuss) the pros and cons of it. It might be well to meet with them beforehand to plan the presentation.

The learning goals for the lesson are (1) to examine the issues that divided the early Christians and (2) to explore ways of resolving them today.

Following the opening activity, the lesson might be developed in this way:

  I. Old customs die hard.
     A. A matter of salvation.
     B. A matter of fellowship.
 II. The struggle for a solution.
III. Guidelines for problem solving.
 IV. Putting principles into practice.

Carefully read the sections "As You Read the Scripture" and "The Scripture and the Main Question." These form the heart of the lesson. The ideas, insights, and suggestions in these sections should be employed throughout your lesson plan.

Introducing the Main Question

Begin by raising the issue you have selected for discussion or debate. Allow persons representing the differing opinions an equal opportunity to present their positions. Do not attempt to settle the issue. Cut off all discussion after ten minutes, indicating that the class members can take up the discussion if they like at the end of the session. Point out, as Dr. McGeachy does in "The Main Question," that the early church faced disagreements and controversy. In today's lesson we will try to learn from them to answer the question, How can we best work out our differences?

Developing the Lesson

I. Old customs die hard.

Ask someone to read aloud Acts 15:1-5. Use the comments by Dr. Winters and Dr. McGeachy to identify the issue that caused dissension in the church. In essence the question was, Should Gentiles be accepted as Christians without submitting to Jewish laws and customs first? The Antioch church said yes. Some Judaizers from Jerusalem said no.

A. A matter of salvation.

The principle at the root of this dissension was not the value of circumcision. It was whether any outside rite or ceremony should be a

SEPTEMBER 29   LESSON 5

prerequisite for salvation. If Christ is the sufficient Savior, a person is saved by his grace and not by any works of the law. Paul had no objection to circumcision as such. His objection was to the belief that it was essential to salvation.

Ask: Why did the Jewish Christians feel so strongly about their position? (Circumcision was the recognized symbol of their covenant relation with God. To deny circumcision, they felt, was the equivalent of denying God's covenant and kingdom.)

Ask: If you had been a Jewish Christian then, do you think you would have felt as strongly about the issue as they did? Why or why not? Would you be willing to compromise the point to bring about harmony in the church?

B. A matter of fellowship.

Beyond the issue of circumcision was another issue. Since Christians joined together in a love-meal, could Jewish Christians eat with Gentiles who did not observe Jewish dietary law?

Ask: In our churches today, can we fellowship comfortably with people who have different beliefs from ours—for example, those who are on different sides of the abortion issue, or the ordination of women, or prayer in public schools, or ministering to gays? How far should compromise go?

II. The struggle for a solution.

Ask: What was the solution to the problem arrived at by the early church? Read aloud Acts 15:6-21. Refer to Dr. McGeachy's comments on this passage. Then discuss these questions:

1. How do you feel about this compromise? Both faith and practice issues were involved. Are faith issues harder to compromise than practice issues? Why?
2. Should the principles enunciated in Acts 15:19-21 still apply to Christians today? Why or why not?
3. How do you feel about compromise today as a way of settling doctrinal disputes? Does this allow for the leading of the Holy Spirit, or is it just a practical means to reduce conflict?

III. Guidelines for problem solving.

Have the class list the steps the early Christians took to resolve their differences. Note Dr. McGeachy's summary in the section headed "Conclusion."

When mentioning point 3 ("Go to the authorities"), raise this question: How much influence do you think the opinions of Christian leaders should have on our own decision making?

Helping Class Members Act

IV. Putting principles into practice.

Return to the problem or issue discussed at the beginning of the session. In light of what has been said about compromise, can this issue be resolved through compromise? Work through a possible solution, if appropriate. Or discuss what steps may need to be taken before a resolution of the issue can be reached.

Conclude by identifying biblical principles one should follow in dealing with disagreements in the church. Consider these as starters:

FIRST QUARTER

1. The principle of our neighbor's good (1 Corinthians 8:9-13; 10:23-29).
2. The principle of the glory of God (1 Corinthians 10:31-32; Colossians 3:17, 23).
3. The principle of love (1 John 3:16-18; 5:1-5). As Christians, we may agree to disagree, but we should resolve always to love. Here there can be no compromise of principle. Faith and hope are integral parts of the Christian life, but love is fundamental to all.

Planning for Next Sunday

Read Acts 15:36–16:23 and identify the number of times Paul was called upon to make a decision.

UNIT III: TRAVELING PREACHER
Horace R. Weaver

FOUR LESSONS   **OCTOBER 6–27**

"Traveling Preacher" describes in four lessons incidents in Paul's missionary journeys: his call to Macedonia, his imprisonment in Philippi, his sermon at Athens, and his instruction of new disciples in Ephesus. The individual lessons are described as follows: "Responding to Needs," October 6, teaches us how to turn our reactions into (Christian) actions. "Finding Courage to Choose," October 13, asks if we would have the courage to make the kind of choices Paul and Silas made, and the wisdom to overcome evil with good. "Finding the True God," October 20, challenges us to inquire how we can recognize and worship the One True God. "Learning from One Another," October 27, asks, How do you know what you must believe, and the manner of your baptism?

LESSON 6   **OCTOBER 6**

Responding to Needs

Background Scripture: Acts 15:36–16:23

The Main Question—Pat McGeachy

There is a considerable difference between *acting* and *reacting*. Acting carries with it the idea of self-motivation, of taking the initiative, of deciding what to do and doing it deliberately. Reacting, on the other hand, seems to mean letting the world shape your agenda, responding to whatever wheel squeaks the loudest, having little or no control over what you do from one day to the next.

OCTOBER 6   LESSON 6

But when you stop to think about it, very few of our actions are just that. Occasionally you may decide something on your own: "I believe that I will go back to school and learn Spanish so I can visit Central America," or "Let's take our vacation in New England this year." But most of us do not have the luxury of shaping our lives beyond the most general plans. I may plan to do certain things today, but you can count on it, the phone will ring, somebody I care for will go to the hospital, the man won't deliver the furniture when he said he was going to, or suddenly I will have to go to Des Moines for some reason. That seems to be the way things are.

If that is indeed so, then what we need to do is to learn how to turn our reactions into actions, that is, to take whatever situations Providence thrusts us into and *act responsibly therein*. In this lesson, Paul, the traveling preacher, sets out with certain plans in mind: to visit his former congregations and see how they are doing. But at the outset he is thwarted by an unexpected argument with his best friend, Barnabas, then he gets a call from God to change his direction and go to Macedonia, and finally, he encounters a poor demonic slave girl, and his efforts to help her wind up landing him in jail. Was he acting or reacting? Let's see if we can discover from this lesson how to choose our reactions, so that when life hands us a lemon we can turn it into lemonade.

Selected Scripture

King James Version

Acts 16:9-12, 16-23

9 And a vision appeared to Paul in the night: There stood a man of Macedonia, and prayed him, saying, come over into Macedonia, and help us.

10 And after he had seen the vision, immediately we endeavored to go into Macedonia, assuredly gathering that the Lord had called us for to preach the gospel unto them.

11 Therefore losing from Troas, we came with a straight course to Samothracia, and the next *day* to Neapolis;

12 And from thence to Philippi, which is the chief city of that part of Macedonia, *and* a colony: and we were in that city abiding certain days.

....

16 And it came to pass, as we went to prayer, a certain damsel possessed with a spirit of divination

Revised Standard Version

Acts 16:9-12, 16-23

9 And a vision appeared to Paul in the night: a man of Macedonia was standing beseeching him and saying, "Come over to Macedonia and help us." 10 And when he had seen the vision, immediately we sought to go on into Macedonia, concluding that God had called us to preach the gospel to them.

11 Setting sail therefore from Troas, we made a direct voyage to Samothrace, and the following day to Neapolis, 12 and from there to Philippi, which is the leading city of the district of Macedonia, and a Roman colony. We remained in this city some days.

....

16 As we were going to the place of prayer, we were met by a slave girl who had a spirit of divination and

55

FIRST QUARTER

met us, which brought her masters much gain by soothsaying:

17 The same followed Paul and us, and cried, saying, These men are the servants of the most high God, which shew unto us the way of salvation.

18 And this did she many days. But Paul, being grieved, turned and said to the spirit, I command thee in the name of Jesus Christ to come out of her. And he came out the same hour.

19 And when her masters saw that the hope of their gains was gone, they caught Paul and Silas, and drew *them* into the marketplace unto the rulers.

20 And brought them to the magistrates, saying, These men, being Jews, do exceedingly trouble our city,

21 And teach customs, which are not lawful for us to receive, neither to observe, being Romans.

22 And the multitude rose up together against them: and the magistrates rent off their clothes, and commanded to beat *them*.

23 And when they had laid many stripes upon them, they cast *them* into prison, charging the jailer to keep them safely.

Key Verse: **A vision appeared to Paul in the night. . . . After he had seen the vision, immediately we endeavored to go into Macedonia, assuredly gathering that the Lord had called us for to preach the gospel unto them. (Acts 16:9-10)**

brought her owners much gain by soothsaying. 17 She followed Paul and us, crying. "These men are servants of the Most High God, who proclaim to you the way of salvation." 18 And this she did for many days. But Paul was annoyed, and turned and said to the spirit. "I charge you in the name of Jesus Christ to come out of her." And it came out that very hour.

19 But when her owners saw that their hope of gain was gone, they seized Paul and Silas and dragged them into the market place before the rulers; 20 and when they had brought them to the magistrates they said, "These men are Jews and they are disturbing our city. 21 They advocate customs which it is not lawful for us Romans to accept or practice." 22 The crowd joined in attacking them; and the magistrates tore the garments off them and gave orders to beat them with rods. 23 And when they had inflicted many blows upon them, they threw them into prison, charging the jailer to keep them safely.

Key Verse: **A vision appeared to Paul in the night. . . . And when he had seen the vision, immediately we sought to go on into Macedonia, concluding that God had called us to preach the gospel to them. (Acts 16:9-10)**

As You Read the Scripture—Michael Winters

Acts 15:36-41. On the eve of their second missionary journey, Paul and Barnabas separated. Barnabas planned to take John Mark (also called Mark), who had been with them on the first missionary journey. Apparently Mark abandoned that first journey in Pamphylia for, what seemed to Paul, unsatisfactory reasons (Acts 13:13). Thus Paul was unwilling to travel with him again. Barnabas and Mark sailed to Cyprus. Paul, choosing Silas, went through Syria and Cilicia.

Acts 16:1-5. In Lystra Paul met the disciple Timothy, whom he decided would accompany him on the journey with Silas.

Together they carried the decisions of the Jerusalem council, which declared that Gentiles did not have to receive circumcision to become a Christian (Acts 15:22-29).

Verses 6-8. It could be interesting to speculate the medium through which the Holy Spirit spoke to Paul, Silas, and Timothy, forbidding them to preach in Phrygia and Galatia. Perhaps they experienced some hostility.

Verses 9-10. The Holy spirit called Paul to travel with his missionary team to Macedonia, a Roman colony (verse 12). Within the province of Macedonia were Philippi and Thessalonica.

In verse 10 the grammatical person of the story changes from third person to first person. This may indicate that Luke, the author of Acts, also traveled with Paul's missionary team. If the mechanics of the grammar are the only clues to indicate that Luke joins the team, our clues become vague by verse 17. It is likely, however, that Luke was with them until they departed Philippi at the end of the chapter.

Verse 11. Sailing from Troas, the westernmost port of Asia Minor, the missionary team of Paul, Silas, Timothy, and Luke sailed for the isle of Samothrace (then famous for a mystery cult) and from there to the Philippian seaport of Neapolis, the gospel's port of entry into Europe.

Verses 12-15. In Philippi, on the sabbath day, Lydia heard Paul preaching by the riverside, the apparent customary place of prayer. She was already a worshiper of God. When Paul's message rang clear to her, she was baptized. Out of gratitude, she hosted the missionary team in her home.

When so much emphasis is put upon the need to make a faith decision, it is interesting to note here that in Lydia's case, it was God who made the decision and chose her. Notice that "the Lord opened her heart to give heed to what was said" (verse 14*b*). This is always the case. Without God's first act, the act of belief can never happen.

Verse 16. The place of prayer was at the riverside (verse 13). The slave had the power to communicate with the spirits (presumably evil spirits) and did so for the profit of her owners. This is not Paul's first encounter with sorcery (see Acts 13:6).

Verses 17-18. The slave acknowledged God in much the same way as the demons acknowledged Jesus: as their foe (Luke 8:28-29*a*). Compare Paul's words here with Luke's description of Jesus' exorcism in Luke 8:29*a*.

Verses 19-21. The exploiters of the slave cried "Unfair" when Paul took their source of profit from them. Dragging Paul and Silas to the most public of places, the agora, where, apparently, procedures of justice were conducted, they presumed to make a credible argument against Paul and Silas, appealing to inflammatory and racist rhetoric. Although, Christianity would have been an unlawful cult in the Roman Empire, it is more likely that Paul was seen as a Jewish evangelist. And though Judaism itself was acceptable in the empire, proselytizing was not.

Verses 22-23. Paul and Silas were brutally attacked by the gathering mob, and the magistrates had them jailed.

The Scripture and the Main Question—Pat McGeachy

A Shaky Beginning (Acts 15:36-41)

This missionary journey doesn't begin on a happy note; it begins with a quarrel between friends. The ostensible cause of the disagreement is the

FIRST QUARTER

question of John Mark's reliability. For some unexplained reason (Acts 13:13), he had left them in the middle of their last journey and gone to his home in Jerusalem (see also Acts 12:12). He was Barnabas's cousin (Colossians 4:10; the King James Version says he was his nephew), so Barnabas would want to stand up for him. But we know that Paul and Barnabas had already begun to drift apart to some extent. In Galatians 2:13 we learn that to some degree Barnabas leaned away from Paul's position and toward that of the Judaizers. Perhaps that difference came to a head over the business about Mark.

Whatever the reason, the two friends parted, never, as far as we know from the biblical record, to meet again. Barnabas is not mentioned again in Acts. However, Paul speaks of him in 1 Corinthians 9:6 and Colossians 4:10, and mentions Mark very positively in 2 Timothy 4:11. Barnabas took Mark with Timothy 4:11. Barnabas took Mark with him to Cyprus, his native land, where he would certainly have an interest. And Paul decided (an action, not a reaction) to go on with his plans, taking with him Silas. These two were destined to go through much together, and Silas would remain Paul's respected friend. (In some of the Epistles he is called Sylvanus; like Saul/Paul, he had both a Hebrew and a Greek name.)

Adding to the Team (Acts 16:1-5)

So the familiar list of countries and towns begins to unroll again; it's fun to trace them on the map and to think of the miles of walking that they did to Syria, Cilicia, Derbe, Lystra, Iconium. In Lystra he encountered another young man who was to become his "adopted" son (1 Corinthians 4:17), Timothy, whose name is attached to two of the letters. It seems that when God closes one door, another opens: In place of Barnabas comes the faithful Silas, in place of Mark, the disciple Timothy. It is important to note that Paul circumcised Timothy. Why do you suppose he did this when he had fought so hard to free the Gentile converts from this requirement? (In the case of another of his companions, Titus, this was not required; see Galatians 2:3.) Luke tells us that the reason was to pacify the many Jews they would be encountering; Timothy was a Jew according to the ancient measure: His mother was Jewish (his father was a Gentile). Perhaps Paul was being consistent with the argument of James (Acts 15:20) that the early church, though it should welcome its Gentile converts, should try not to offend its Jewish members.

A Night Vision (Acts 16:6-10)

The roll call of regions continues: Phrygia, Galatia, Mysia (which three they bypassed) and Troas. Again, things didn't go the way they had been planned. They were "forbidden by the Holy Spirit" to speak in Asia. This could mean either that they received a direct revelation or that they made a Spirit-filled judgment, based on the Jewish opposition that they discovered there. But it is interesting to note that in verse 7 it was "the Spirit of Jesus" who did not allow them to enter Bithynia. This is the only place in the New Testament where this phrase occurs (it is not in the King James Version, but the best ancient manuscripts have it). The Spirit of Jesus and the Holy Spirit are certainly used synonymously in these two verses. This is comforting to those of us who wonder when we pray if we are speaking to Father, Son, or Spirit. Apparently it is perfectly appropriate to confuse the three.

OCTOBER 6   LESSON 6

Then, in the night, in Troas, perhaps in a dream, a spirit appears. It is not described as the Holy Spirit but as a Macedonian native. Sometimes (if not most of the time) God comes to us in human form (see Genesis 18:1-2). Sometimes God speaks to us in dreams; more often in the understanding of our minds and the passions of our hearts. But there come times when the call is so clear and unmistakable that the only thing we can do is obey. Is Paul acting or reacting? At every turn he seems to be pushed aside, or shoved ahead, or called apart, not going where he had thought but ending up in unexpected places. This was going to have been a retracing of a previous route, but the trip had run into obstacle after obstacle, and now it was going to branch off in an entirely different direction. A cold Calvinist might say these changes were Paul's destiny; a warm Wesleyan might say he chose them in the Spirit. What difference does it make whether we say that God hardened Pharaoh's heart (Exodus 9:12) or that Pharaoh hardened his own heart (Exodus 98:32), as long as Pharaoh's heart was hardened (Exodus 8:19)? We are not free to choose or to shape our destiny, but we *are* free to respond to our destiny as we will.

I know of a famous physician, a medical missionary who was invited to preach in a great Manhattan pulpit. As he entered the church, an officer signaled him into the vestry and held up a large pulpit robe, something the good doctor had never worn. "Do I have to wear that thing?" the missionary asked. The vestryman shuffled with a little embarrassment, then said, "Well I guess you don't *have* to." "In that case," said the missionary, "I'll be glad to."

We can go willingly when God calls us, or we can go kicking and screaming. Or we can, like Jonah, flee by ship. Or, like Paul, we can turn our energy into the opposite direction. But sooner or later, our destiny will swallow us up, or we will be blinded by it on the road. How much better to go rejoicing wherever God leads us!

Rich Lady, Poor Lady (Acts 16:11-23)

So they came to Macedonia. And there, in Philippi, the leading city, almost immediately occurred two more unexpected encounters.

The first involved a wealthy businesswoman who became Paul's first convert in Europe, and who made her home available to the missionaries. Responding to that encounter brought the apostles much joy.

Not so with the second; it was a slavegirl, possessed of a demon and both used and misused by her owners. When Paul cast that demon out, the result was anger, false charges, and imprisonment.

In both cases Paul responded as he felt he ought: with the good news. In the one case the results were positive, in the other, though he brought peace to the young woman, he brought beatings upon himself. You convert one person and get invited to a fancy house, convert another and get thrown in jail. Christian compassion can lead you into all sorts of surprises; the more you try to love, the more you find yourself opened up to needy people who long for you to help them. In the end it may cost you your life.

Reacting

Sometimes I think this book ought to be called "The Reacts of the Apostles." Paul receives at least eight calls in this brief lesson:

59

FIRST QUARTER

- A call in his own heart to retrace his mission (15:36)
- A call from Barnabas, which he rejects (15:37)
- A call in the form of an encounter with a promising young man, whose gifts Paul recognizes (16:1)
- A negative call from the Holy Spirit, forbidding him to preach (16:6)
- A negative call from the Spirit of Jesus, not to enter Bithynia (16:7)
- A positive call from a man of Macedonia (16:9)
- A call of spiritual hunger from a wealthy woman (16:14)
- A cry for help from a poor slavegirl to whom his heart went out (16:16-18)

You never know where God is going to lead you. You set out in one direction and end up in another. The art of living the spiritual life is the art of learning to respond in joy and obedience. Sometimes we must answer no, sometimes yes. ("You gotta know when to fold 'em.") It may lead us into joys beyond our dreams, or troubles beyond our fears. But of one thing we can be absolutely certain: The God of grace will go with us. Or, better, perhaps, there is no place we can go where we cannot say, "Surely the Lord is in this place" (Genesis 28:16).

Helping Adults Become Involved—Ronald E. Schlosser

Preparing to Teach

As you read today's scripture, you will notice that Paul made some important decisions. The most significant one was the decision to turn westward and take the gospel to Europe. This relatively short trip across the Aegean Sea brought him into a new and different world. Macedonia had been the home base of Alexander the Great. The Roman Empire had been built on the remains of Alexander's great conquests. Philippi was a Roman colony, a proud city that viewed itself as the most important one in the district. The local residents tried to make their city as much like Rome as they possibly could. The local officials gave themselves elaborate titles and presumed that they were exactly like their counterparts in the imperial city. So Paul stepped into a new culture when he set foot on the continent of Europe.

In order to follow Paul's journey, have available again a map of the Mediterranean area in Bible times.

There are three learning goals for the lesson: (1) to consider the ways God speaks to us as we seek direction in life, (2) to recognize the qualities one needs to discern and do God's will and (3) to become aware of the possible consequences one faces in obeying God.

After introducing the main question, you might follow this outline in developing the lesson:

    I. The gospel reaches out.
       A. Guided by the Spirit.
       B. Called by the Spirit.
    II. The gospel changes lives.
       A. A businesswoman.
       B. A slave girl.
    III. The gospel calls for action.

OCTOBER 6   LESSON 6

Carefully read the sections "As You Read the Scripture" and "The Scripture and the Main Question." These form the heart of the lesson. The ideas, insights, and suggestions in these sections should be employed throughout your lesson plan.

Introducing the Main Question

Begin by referring to Dr. McGeachy's comments about acting and reacting. In the world of business management, persons are described as proactive or reactive. A manager who takes the initiative to make things happen is considered proactive. One who manages by responding to circumstances as they happen is called reactive. Ask you class members to consider which approach they usually follow as they live out their lives day by day. Which approach do they feel the Apostle Paul followed? They should keep this question in mind as they study today's scripture.

Developing the Lesson

I. The gospel reaches out.
   A. Guided by the Spirit.

Ask someone to read aloud Acts 15:26–16:8. Have the class members follow the course of Paul's travels on a map in their Bibles or on a large classroom map. Note that the journey begins in Syria (Acts 15:35).

Ask: What were some of the decisions Paul had to make as he began his second missionary journey? (Who to take with him, where he should go, the message he should deliver, whether or not to circumcise Timothy.) Were these proactive or reactive decision? (See Dr. McGeachy's comments.)

Comment on the two specific instances in which God gave directions to Paul about where and when not to preach. In verse 6 we read that Paul felt "forbidden by the Holy Spirit to speak the word in Asia." In verse 7 we see that Paul wanted to enter Bithynia but was not allowed to go there by "the Spirit of Jesus." Discuss with the members why they feel God sometimes closes one door and opens another. Both Dr. Winters and Dr. McGeachy speculate on the way the Holy Spirit may have guided Paul. How else does the Holy Spirit provide guidance or direction for action? (Inner revelation through prayer, circumstances, counsel of Christian friends, reading God's word, etc.)

   B. Called by the Spirit.

Have the class silently read Acts 16:9-10. What do they notice? Point out the change from third person to first-person plural, indicating that Luke joined the group. Also note Paul's decision to cross over into Europe (Macedonia) after seeing a vision.

What does your class think of visions as a means of communication? Ask: Does God still speak through visions today? Refer to Dr. McGeachy's comments on this.

II. The gospel changes lives.

Next have someone read Acts 16:11-12. Trace the route on the map. Give some background on Philippi (see "Preparing to Teach," above), noting that it was named for Philip of Macedon, the father of Alexander the Great.

Then divide the class into two groups. Assign one group Acts 16:13-15

FIRST QUARTER

to study, the other group Acts 16:16-18. After reading its respective passage, each group is to consider three questions:

1. What was the person in the story like before meeting Paul?
2. What change took place at conversion?
3. What does this say to us today?

Allow about five minutes for the groups to discuss the questions. Then bring the class together and share findings. The following ideas might be presented.

A. A businesswoman.

Lydia was a devout woman of some means, but without a knowledge of God's love in Christ. Lydia's need is everyone's need. A person may be a good, moral person and still need Christ. Without a knowledge of Christ, people are drastically limited in their knowledge of God. They lack the positive assurance that sins can be forgiven. When Lydia heard the good news, God "opened her heart," and she opened her home to the missionaries. It became their base in Philippi.

B. A slavegirl.

She was a person with some sort of mental illness, used by her unscrupulous owners for their own profit. Paul rebuked the evil force that seemed to control the girl, and she stopped her noisy outcries. She had been set free by Jesus Christ, and she was normal and sane. Christ can still touch troubled minds and bring wholeness.

Helping Class Members Act

III. The gospel calls for action.

Speculate on the "what ifs" in today's Scripture. What if Paul had gone with Barnabas to Cyprus? What if Paul had been allowed to go east, as he had planned? Suppose Christianity had moved eastward to India and China instead of westward to Europe; how might world history have been changed? What if Paul had played it safe and not responded to the cries of the slavegirl? What happened to him? (Read Acts 16:19-24.)

Encourage your class members to share personal experiences in which they made a difficult Christian decision that brought unexpected consequences. If they had know what was in store for them, would they still have made the decision? What possible consequences might we face today by being faithful to God? (Consider such things as speaking out against injustice, taking a stand on a moral issue, being involved in some community action project that is unpopular.) How deep is our commitment?

Close by reading the last paragraph of Dr. McGeachy's comments. Pray for God's Spirit to guide and strengthen us in all decisions we must make.

Planning for Next Sunday

Next Sunday's lesson continues the story of Paul at Philippi (Acts 16:16-40). Ask your class members to be thinking of their favorite hymns or gospel songs. Which of these have special meaning during difficult times?

LESSON 7   OCTOBER 13

Finding Courage to Choose

Background Scripture: Acts 16:16-40

The Main Question—Pat McGeachy

"Do not be overcome by evil," wrote Paul (Romans 12:21), "but overcome evil with good." We have, in today's episode, an incredible example of the power of goodness to resolve a very dreadful crisis. It has been said that there are three ways to deal with a bad situation: flee, fight, or face. All three of these are at times appropriate responses. Once, at the beginning of his ministry (Luke 4:29-30), Jesus had incurred the wrath of the people and was in danger for his life. On that occasion, perhaps simply because his hour had not yet come, Jesus quietly slipped away. He chose the method of flight as the best action at the time.

On another occasion (John 2:13-16), on encountering a situation where the poor were being victimized by the greedy keepers of the sacrificial customs, Jesus responded with a fight.

But most of the time, Jesus chose to face his accusers, knowing that it was for this purpose that he had come into the world. With steadfast purpose he went straight to the source of the trouble, and there confronted it with courage and wisdom. Note the resolution implied in Luke 9:51, or consider his willingness to argue toe to toe with his accusers in Matthew 22:15-46, which ends with the announcement that "from that day no one dared to ask him any more questions."

We find Paul and Silas, in our lesson this week, in an extreme situation: beaten, bound, and imprisoned. Let's look at their behavior under these circumstances, to determine if we can, how we would behave under similar conditions. At such times, would you and I have the courage to choose what Paul and Silas did, the wisdom to overcome evil with good? The result of their action was not only their own release but also the release of another, from a different sort of imprisonment. The jailer, by their witness, found the courage to change his whole life. Could you and I do the same?

Selected Scripture

King James Version

Acts 16:19b-34

19 And when her masters saw that the hope of their gains was gone, they caught Paul and Silas, and drew *them* into the marketplace unto the rulers,

20 And brought them to the magistrates, saying, These men, being Jews, do exceedingly trouble our city,

21 And teach customs, which are

Revised Standard Version

Acts 16:19b-34

19 But when her owners saw that their hope of gain was gone, they seized Paul and Silas and dragged them into the market place before the rulers; 20 and when they had brought them to the magistrates they said, "These men are Jews and they are disturbing our city. 21 They advocate customs which it is not lawful for us Romans to accept

not lawful for us to receive, neither to observe, being Romans.

22 And the multitude rose up together against them: and the magistrates rent off their clothes, and commanded to beat *them*.

23 And when they had laid many stripes upon them, they cast *them* into prison, charging the jailer to keep them safely:

24 Who, having received such a charge, thrust them into the inner prison, and made their feet fast in the stocks.

25 And at midnight Paul and Silas prayed, and sang praises unto God: and the prisoners heard them.

26 And suddenly there was a great earthquake, so that the foundations of the prison were shaken: and immediately all the doors were opened, and every one's bands were loosed.

27 And the keeper of the prison awaking out of his sleep, and seeing the prison doors open, he drew out his sword, and would have killed himself, supposing that the prisoners had been fled.

28 But Paul cried with a loud voice, saying, Do thyself no harm: for we are all here.

29 Then he called for a light, and sprang in, and came trembling, and fell down before Paul and Silas,

30 And brought them out, and said, Sirs, what must I do to be saved?

31 And they said, Believe on the Lord Jesus Christ, and thou shalt be saved, and thy house.

32 And they spake unto him the word of the Lord, and to all that were in his house.

33 And he took them the same hour of the night, and washed *their* stripes; and was baptized, he and all his, straightway.

34 And when he had brought them into his house, he set meat before them, and rejoiced, believing in God with all his house.

or practice." 22 The crowd joined in attacking them; and the magistrates tore the garments off them and gave orders to beat them with rods. 23 And when they had inflicted many blows upon them, they threw them into prison, charging the jailer to keep them safely. 24 Having received this charge, he put them into the inner prison and fastened their feet in the stocks.

25 But about midnight Paul and Silas were praying and singing hymns to God, and the prisoners were listening to them, 26 and suddenly there was a great earthquake, so that the foundations of the prison were shaken; and immediately all the doors were opened and every one's fetters were unfastened. 27 When the jailer woke and saw that the prison doors were open, he drew his sword and was about to kill himself, supposing that the prisoners had escaped. 28 But Paul cried with a loud voice, "Do not harm yourself, for we are all here." 29 And he called for lights and rushed in, and trembling with fear he fell down before Paul and Silas, 30 and brought them out and said, "Men, what must I do to be saved?" 31 And they said, "Believe in the Lord Jesus, and you will be saved, you and your household." 32 And they spoke the word of the Lord to him and to all that were in his house. 33 And he took them the same hour of the night, and washed their wounds, and he was baptized at once, with all his family. 34 Then he brought them up into his house, and set food before them; and he rejoiced with all his household that he had believed in God.

OCTOBER 13　　　　　　　　　　　　　　　　　　　　　LESSON 7

Key Verse: [The jailer] brought them out and said, Sirs, what must I do to be saved? And they said, Believe on the Lord Jesus Christ, and thou shalt be saved, and thy house. (Acts 16:30-31)

Key Verse: [The jailer] brought them out and said, "Men, what must I do to be saved?" And they said, "Believe in the Lord Jesus, and you will be saved, you and your household." (Acts 16:30-31)

As You Read the Scripture—Michael Winters

Acts 16:16-23. See the exegesis in lesson 6.

Verse 24. The warden put Paul and Silas in the dungeon, where their feet were shackled to the wall.

Verse 25. Paul and Silas were not the only prisoners there. Perhaps there were petty criminals, political prisoners, and felons as well. Paul and Silas witnessed the gospel even in their adversity. They prayed and sang hymns, which apparently was not offensive to tired and uncomfortable criminals. That the prisoners listened may have been a bit of a miracle in itself.

Verses 26-28. Compare Peter's escape from a Jerusalem prison in verses 12:6-11. Paul, unlike Peter, did not take advantage of the miraculous opening of the prison. One might wonder about the need for an escape story in light of the development in verse 35, where the magistrates decided to have Paul and Silas released the following morning.

Verse 26. The earthquake caused the dungeon walls to shift, allowing the shackles to fall out of their anchors in the wall. When the prison doors swung open, the prisoners would have been free to escape, dragging their shackles around their ankles.

Verse 27. Bearing the responsibility for the assumed escape of the prisoners, the warden prepared to commit suicide. To us it would seem to be an excessive action, given that the dungeon opened on account of a natural event. Perhaps the warden was anticipating drastic punishment, just as Peter's hapless sentries received when the angel aided him in his miraculous escape from prison (Acts 12:19).

Verse 28. The warden's presence, bathed in the lamplight that illuminated the way into the dungeon, would have been very clear to the prisoners. Yet the prisoners languishing in the darkness of the dungeon would have been invisible to the warden. The warden naturally would have expected the prisoners to take their freedom. Paul alleviated the warden's fears, declaring all prisoners present; thus he prevented the warden's suicide.

Verse 29. The warden rushed into the dungeon, among the prisoners, with the lamplight. "Appreciation" rather than "fear" would have been the appropriate emotion to send the warden prostrate before Paul and Silas. But if the warden had surmised that the gods kept the prisoners from escaping, and if the warden experienced Paul and Silas as the incarnation of those gods, then likely the warden would have trembled with fear.

Verse 30a. The warden brought only Paul and Silas out of the dungeon.

Verses 30b-31. Here is the formula for salvation. Paul declares that salvation comes only through faith in Jesus the Christ. What's more, from Paul's covenant theology, informed by God's covenant with Abraham, Paul declares that the warden's household will also be saved by that singular affirmation (see Genesis 17:7, where God establishes the covenant with Abraham and his descendants).

FIRST QUARTER

Verses 32, 34. Paul and Silas are invited into the warden's home, where they were given the nourishment of food, and where they imparted the nourishment of the gospel.

Verse 33. The warden washed the wounds Paul and Silas received during the mob violence and their public beating (verse 22).

Verses 35-40. The morning after the earthquake, the magistrates who ordered their beating and imprisonment gave an order releasing them. But Paul would not go. He was a Roman citizen, and it was illegal to beat citizens of Rome as public punishment. The magistrates, upon realizing this, came and offered their apology, after which Paul and Silas departed Philippi.

The Scripture and the Main Question—Pat McGeachy

When Right Meets Might (Acts 16:16-24)

When we last left our heroes, they had gotten off to a good start in Philippi, the principal city of Macedonia, making friends with the wealthy Lydia, whose heart was opened to the gospel. But suddenly, their affairs took an ominous turn, due to Paul's exorcism of a demon that possessed a slave girl. They had, as the folk saying goes, "quit preaching and gone to meddling."

When you fight a troublesome enemy with direct action, you had better be prepared to meet a counterattack. This is particularly true when you hit somebody where it hurts: in the pocketbook. "When her owners saw that their hope of gain was gone, they seized Paul and Silas" (verse 19). Better not tackle the establishment unless you can stand the reaction. When Martin Luther King and his friends decided to take direct action against the tragedy of discrimination in America in the fifties, they were careful to train their followers in the art of nonviolence, because they knew full well that the response of the establishment would be violent. King himself ended up a prisoner, not unlike Paul. If you can get a copy of it, read the letter he wrote from the Birmingham jail to see how the civil rights hero reacted to the punishment of his attackers.

One of the lessons of these verses is that you had better be prepared to take the consequences of your action, even if you are in the right. Although we can believe that right will conquer in the end (John 16:33), we must be realistic about the reaction that radical righteousness brings about in those whose position is attacked, especially if it is a position deeply entrenched in tradition, the undermining of which causes a loss, either of ego or, what is worse, money. Casting out demons is dangerous work.

A Midnight Sing (Acts 16:19-26)

What a prayer meeting! You will have heard of revivals where great and astonishing things happened, but when did you ever encounter one that resulted in an earthquake, the shattering of fetters, and the opening of doors? What sort of hymns would have done that? Of course, you can call it coincidence rather than cause and effect, but I have lived too long to believe very much in coincidence. Is it really possible to sing your way to liberation!

If you want to pursue this question in depth, I can direct you to some other prisoners with songs in their hearts. You ought to know Victor

OCTOBER 13   LESSON 7

Frankl's book, *Man's Search for Meaning*, the story of a brilliant Jewish psychiatrist's victory over the evils of a German deathcamp. And you might like to read Ernest Gordon's story, *Through the Valley of the Kwai*, in which life comes to a foolish playboy under the most horrible of circumstances. And you will certainly want to become familiar with the faith of Dietrich Bonhoeffer, which shines out of his *Letters and Papers from Prison*. All three of these stories (and there are others) are about a song in the night, the coming of a spiritual earthquake, the mighty victory of life over death.

In contrast, there are times when we cannot bring ourselves to sing. Read the mournful words of Palm 137, which contains some of the angriest verses in the Bible. It is a song about those who cannot, or will not, sing the Lord's song while they are captives in a foreign land. Their tormenters teased them, saying, "Sing us a Jew song." But they refused and hung up their lyres.

And yet . . . and yet, even in their bitterness and anger, there is a note of hope. For their anger is understandable, just as is the anger of blacks in segregated South Africa. And no honest passion, however inappropriate, is without its redeeming features. I have even heard of a prisoner being converted by the angry words of Psalm 137:9. He was sitting in a jail cell when he overheard a fellow prisoner down the block reading aloud from his Bible: "Happy shall he be who takes your little ones and dashes them against the rock!"

"What the [mischief] are you reading?" he snorted.

"I'm reading the Bible," answered the other.

In a somewhat subdued tone, the first prisoner said, "You mean there is stuff like that in the Bible? I always thought it was about love and stuff like that."

"It is," said the reader. "But it also deals with hurt and anger, and a lot of it is about prisoners like you and me. It's a pretty honest book."

"Pass it down to me," said the other, and the process of his salvation had begun.

We don't know what hymns Paul and Silas sang that night, but whatever the melody, it had both earthquake power and charms to soothe the savage beast.

A Conversion (Acts 16:27-34)

There is no more moving story in the Bible than the conversion of the jailer at Philippi. What led him to take that first step on the road toward wholeness (holiness)? Let's start by noting some things that evidently did *not* cause his change of heart.

He was not, as far as we know, a Bible student who had attended Sunday school all his life. More than likely, this was his very first encounter with the Christian faith.

He had not listened to a sermon by an evangelist, or a well-reasoned argument from a Christian theologian.

He had not attended a confirmation class, or a discussion group, or had any training in the faith.

He had probably never been to church, certainly not a Christian church, but may have visited a temple erected to one of the Greek or Roman gods.

He had certainly not grown up in the faith, like many of us.

From what we know of this man, we are only sure of one thing: he had

FIRST QUARTER

encountered the wonderful example of two men who reacted to their problems in a remarkable way: They sang and prayed when other people would have cursed, they remained in custody when other people would have run for their lives, and they kept him from killing himself when other people might have rejoiced in his death. In the face of this example, the jailer must have said something like this to himself: "I don't know what it is these people have, but I have been looking for it all my life!" He saw in them the strength, the inner peace, the courage, the love, the compassion, and the character that good people long for but few achieve. And so he asked the burning question of every heart, "What do I have to do to be like you? How can I too be whole, at peace with myself, saved?"

And Paul and Silas were not only the bearers of a sermon in their actions, but spoke the words as well: "Believe in the Lord Jesus." This word means more than "intellectual affirmation." It does not simply mean "accept the story of Jesus as true." It means a commitment of the whole person. It means "Lean your whole weight on Jesus Christ, and you will be saved." It means literally a con-version, a turning around of one's life, a start in a new direction.

One further word: He *and his whole family* were baptized (again, without a confirmation class). The conversion of this one man infected his whole family, running through them like a benevolent "disease," and there was much rejoicing in their household.

A Happy Ending (Acts 16:35-40)

Having won the day, Paul and Silas refused to take the easy way out of accepting a quiet release from prison but insisted on their full innocence, and were exonerated. They were not about to give in. Instead, they left town with their heads held high. When others might have been tempted to fight, to rage and curse the darkness, or to flee, to take the easy way out, they had faced their crisis and carried the day.

In answer then, to the main question of our lesson—how shall we deal with opposition—we shall behave just as our Lord did, with courage, confidence, and trust. We may be beaten and imprisoned. We may even die. But in the end the victory is ours. For Paul, and Silas, and Lydia, and the jailer and his family whose name we do not know, this is a day of rejoicing. No wonder that when Paul looked back on the congregation in this city, he loved them and was filled with gladness (read Philippians 1:3-11; 4:1, 4-7.) It was always his favorite church.

Helping Adults Become Involved—Ronald E. Schlosser

Preparing to Teach

So many of Paul's experiences are connected with prison that we often forget the harsh reality of the situation. In today's lesson we find Paul and Silas in prison, painfully held in stocks, backs bloody from a beating, alone in a strange city. Alone? No, not alone, for they had learned to live in the constant presence of the living Christ. This was the secret of their endurance.

How do we face difficult circumstances? In the main question, Dr. McGeachy suggests three alternatives: flee, fight, or face. As we see how

OCTOBER 13   LESSON 7

Paul and Silas reacted, we need to consider what we would do if we found ourselves in equally trying situations.

The learning goals for the lesson are threefold: (1) to consider ways persons cope with difficult circumstances, (2) to identify things that bind and imprison people today, and (3) to realize what salvation in Christ brings to a person.

After introducing the main question, you might develop the lesson following this outline:

> I. Imprisonment in Philippi
>   A. Shackles
>   B. Songs
>   C. Shaking
>   D. Salvation
>   E. Supper
> II. Imprisonment today

Carefully read the sections "As You Read the Scripture" and "The Scripture and the Main Question." These form the heart of the lesson. The ideas, insights, and suggestions in these sections should be employed throughout your lesson plan.

Have hymnals available for the session. You will be asking the class members to identify hymns that have special meaning for them. You might give some thought to this yourself before the session begins.

Introducing the Main Question

Begin by referring to Dr. McGeachy's comments in "The Main Question." Note what he says about the three ways people deal with a bad situation: flee, fight, face. Ask the members which of these options they usually take. Do some like direct confrontation? Why? Do others try to avoid conflicts? Are some harmonizers, attempting to reconcile disagreements or make the best of the trouble they encounter?

Ask: What kind of person was Paul? Review the events that led to his imprisonment, studied last week (Acts 16:16-22). Does the class think Paul expected his actions would lead to a beating and imprisonment? Would this have deterred him if he had known what was to befall him?

Developing the Lesson

I. Imprisonment in Philippi
   A. Shackles

Paul often referred to himself as a prisoner for Christ (see Ephesians 3:1; 4:1; 2 Timothy 1:8; Philemon 1:1, 9). The book of Acts tells about others who were imprisoned for their faith (see, for example, Acts 4:3; 8:3; 12:4-5). The hymn "Faith of Our Fathers" speaks of our Christian ancestors "chained in prisons dark." Can the class name some of them? Names like John Hus, William Tyndale, and John Bunyan immediately come to mind. The latter wrote his well-known book *Pilgrim's Progress* while behind bars. More recent "prisoners for Christ" include Dietrich Bonhoeffer, Martin Luther King, Jr., and countless others over the years, many of whom have been jailed for human rights demonstrations. Discuss with your class the pros and cons of being arrested for expressing one's beliefs. Is civil disobedience an appropriate form of Christian witnessing?

B. Songs

Paul and Silas were undoubtedly chanting portions of Psalms, with outbursts of praises to God. Dr. Winters notes in his comments on this verse that the other prisoners listened to this singing. The Greek word used here, *epakroanto*, is the imperfect middle tense of a rare verb meaning "to listen with pleasure." This hymn-sing experience was as much a benefit for the cellmates as it was for Paul and Silas. Ask your class members what hymns or gospel songs have special meaning for them. Is there a particular hymn they sing or hum when they face problems? "God Will Take Care of You" might be one. "Under His Wings" and "Jesus, Savior, Pilot Me" are also favorites of many.

C. Shaking

God's direct intervention through a natural phenomenon—an earthquake—might lead us to ask whether God intervenes in similar ways today. What does your class think? Can members point to occasions when a natural phenomenon seemed to be God's intervening hand in human affairs? One classic example is the miraculous rescue of the British army from Dunkirk in May 1940. While Christians in England prayed, over 335,000 Allied soldiers were transported across the English Channel aboard a motley fleet of a thousand vessels of all sizes and descriptions. The usually rough and treacherous channel remained calm and shrouded in a dense, protective fog during the tense days of the rescue. Many devoutly believe God had intervened to save the army.

D. Salvation

The jailer (warden) would have responded to his misfortune by fleeing, that is, by escaping through suicide. Stoicism (a philosophy to be discussed next week) had made suicide popular as an escape from troubles. The suicide of Cato furnished the Stoics a constant model for such teaching. When the jailer asked the question, "What must I do to be saved?" he may have meant how could he escape the punishment he would receive from his superiors (see Acts 12:19). Or the earthquake may have convinced him that Paul and Silas were able to call on supernatural powers, and he was afraid of such powers. Whatever he meant by his question, Paul related it to his need for eternal salvation. Compare Paul's "salvation statement" with the statement Peter made at the time of his imprisonment (Acts 4:12).

E. Supper

One of the marks of Christian fellowship is the breaking of bread (see Acts 2:42, 46). After Paul and Silas fully explained God's word to him, the jailer washed their wounds and took them to his own house. He and his family were baptized, and together they rejoiced in the Lord over a meal. What is there about a meal that provides a sense of real fellowship? Perhaps it is the sharing from a common pot, the experiencing of the same pleasurable aromas and tastes. Can the class give examples of times when meals have brought persons closer together in Christian fellowship?

Helping Class Members Act

II. Imprisonment today

Consider the things that bind or imprison people today. The most obvious, of course, are the addictive drugs that have ensnared people in a

OCTOBER 20   LESSON 8

costly and health-threatening habit. From hard drugs like heroin and cocaine to substances that are used at varying degrees of intensity, like alcohol, tranquilizers, and cigarettes, the effects are the same in making people captive to a habit. But addiction can take other forms. Sex, food, power, money can enslave a person. More will be said about these "false gods" next week. The point is that we all are subject to forces and desires that would make us captive.

The good news is that Jesus can save us from these things—in effect, from the sin that binds us, that separates us from God. Close the session by having the class discuss how Christ is the answer to the addict, whatever the addiction. How can Christ set us free from whatever enslaves us?

Planning for Next Sunday

The Scripture for next Sunday is Acts 17. Have the class give some thought to what or who may be contemporary idols or "gods" people worship today.

LESSON 8   OCTOBER 20

Finding the True God

Background Scripture: Acts 17

The Main Question—Pat McGeachy

"Seek first God's kingdom and righteousness," said Jesus (Matthew 6:33), "and all these things shall be yours as well." It is essential that we put first things first, or get our priorities straight. I don't know anybody who disagrees with this. But there are many spirits that speak to us in the night, many voices that call us to loyalty.

Perhaps the ancient Greeks were wiser than we know. They gave names to their gods: Eros, Ares, Aphrodite, and so on, and built temples to them. We moderns do not name our gods and fool ourselves into thinking that we do not worship them. It might be better if we identified them and their temples, as, for example:

Mammon	The Bank
Patria	The Capitol
Eros	The "Adult" Book Store
Leisure	The Country Club

(Thinking those up is a rather useful exercise, and kind of fun. We may add to our list before we get through with this lesson.)

But we need to put our main question, which is, With all these tempting idols around us, how shall we recognize and worship the One True God? Even those of us who do not profess to be religious have a nagging feeling

FIRST QUARTER

about God. Our hearts are restless. We construct in our minds temples to that unknown god. And we need a Paul to come and stand on our street corner and say, "As I pass among the test tubes of your sciences, the tanks of your armies, the platforms of your politicians, and the pulpits of your preachers, I perceive that you still long for One whom you seek but do not yet know. I am here to tell you about that One." Perhaps he might thus get our attention, and we would be willing to listen to the story of Jesus in a fresh and hopeful way. We are much like the Athenians (Acts 17:21), there's nothing we like better than news. Is it possible for us to hear the gospel as just that?

Selected Scripture

King James Version

Acts 17:22-34

22 Then Paul stood in the midst of Mars' hill, and said, *Ye* men of Athens, I perceive that in all things ye are too superstitious.

23 For as I passed by, and beheld your devotions, I found an altar with this inscription, TO THE UNKNOWN GOD. Whom therefore ye ignorantly worship, him declare I unto you.

24 God that made the world and all things therein, seeing that he is Lord of heaven and earth, dwelleth not in temples made with hands;

25 Neither is worshipped with men's hands, as though he needed any thing, seeing he giveth to all life, and breath, and all things;

26 And hath made of one blood all nations of men for to dwell on all the face of the earth, and hath determined the times before appointed, and the bounds of their habitation;

27 That they should seek the Lord, if haply they might feel after him, and find him, though he be not far from every one of us:

28 For in him we live, and move, and have our being; as certain also of your own poets have said, For we are also his offspring.

29 Forasmuch then as we are the offspring of God, we ought not to think that the Godhead is like unto

Revised Standard Version

Acts 17:22-34

22 So Paul, standing in the middle of the Areopagus, said: "Men of Athens, I perceive that in every way you are very religious. 23 For as I passed along, and observed the objects of your worship, I found also an altar with this inscription, 'To an unknown god.' What therefore you worship as unknown, this I proclaim to you. 24 The God who made the world and everything in it, being Lord of heaven and earth, does not live in shrines made by man, 25 nor is he served by human hands, as though he needed anything, since he himself gives to all men life and breath and everything. 26 And he made from one every nation of men to live on all the face of the earth, having determined allotted periods and the boundaries of their habitation, 27 that they should seek God, in the hope that they might feel after him and find him. Yet he is not far from each one of us, 28 for

'In him we live and move and have our being';

as even some of your poets have said,

'For we are indeed his offspring.'

29 Being then God's offspring, we ought not to think that the Deity is like gold, or silver, or stone, a representation by the art and imagination of man. 30 The times of

gold, or silver, or stone, graven by art and man's device.

30 And the times of this ignorance God winked at; but now commandeth all men every where to repent:

31 Because he hath appointed a day, in the which he will judge the world in righteousness by *that* man whom he hath ordained; *whereof* he hath given assurance unto all *men*, in that he hath raised him from the dead.

32 And when they heard of the resurrection of the dead, some mocked: and other said, We will hear thee again of this *matter*.

33 So Paul departed from among them.

34 Howbeit certain men clave unto him, and believed: among the which *was* Dionysius the Areopagite, and a woman named Damaris, and others with them.

Key Verse: **God that made the world and all things therein. . . . dwelleth not in temples made with hands, neither is worshipped with men's hands, as though he needed anything, seeing he giveth to all life, and breath, and all things. (Acts 17:24-25)**

ignorance God overlooked, but now he commands all men everywhere to repent, 31 because he has fixed a day on which he will judge the world in righteousness by a man whom he has appointed, and of this he has given assurance to all men by raising him from the dead."

32 Now when they heard of the resurrection of the dead, some mocked; but others said, "We will hear you again about this." 33 So Paul went out from among them. 34 But some men joined him and believed, among them Dionysius the Areopagite and a woman named Damaris and others with them.

Key Verse: **The God who made the world and everything in it. . . . does not live in shrines made by man, nor is he served by human hands, as though he needed anything, since he himself gives to all men life and breath and everything. (Acts 17:24-25)**

As You Read the Scripture—Michael Winters

Acts 17:1-9. Westward from Philippi, on the Via Egnatia, Paul, Silas, and Timothy passed through Amphipolis and Apollonia. Finally, they arrived at Thessalonica, where Paul debated the Scriptures with the Jews in their synagogue. Paul convinced some Jews, many Greeks, and many prominent women of the Christ. The Jews became jealous, successfully inciting some rabble to run the evangelists out of the city.

Verses 10-15. About fifty miles west of Thessalonica, in Beroea, the evangelists began their mission in the city's Jewish synagogue by examining the Scriptures for evidence of the Christ. The Jews were much more accommodating in Beroea than in Thessalonica and many believed, as did many prominent Greek men and women.

When the Jews of Thessalonica heard that Paul, Silas, and Timothy were in Beroea, they incited the crowds to violence there, too. Paul had to flee, but Silas and Timothy stayed until Paul sent for them from Athens.

Verses 16-21. Ancient Athens, the city of enlightenment, was situated

FIRST QUARTER

around the rocky hill called the Acropolis. Paul noticed that it was a religious city full of shrines and idols.

Athens was the seat of the Platonic and Peripatetic philosophies, as well as the Epicurean and Stoic. Paul debated in the city's Jewish synagogue and in the agora. But the philosophers were skeptical of his teaching. So they took him to the Areopagus, the supreme court of Athens, where Paul pled this new philosophy of Jesus risen from the dead among those who prided themselves the most intelligent in the world.

Verses 22-23. Alluding to the many idols and shrines Paul saw in Athens, he perceived that Athenians were very religious. Thus he found common ground with them, being religious himself.

He identified one of the gods of their pantheism as being the same God who he himself worshiped.

Verses 24-25. Paul declared this God supreme without acknowledging the existence of those gods, let alone an existing hierarchy of gods. He declared that this God did not dwell on the earth (see 2 Samuel 7:6), nor depend on any kind of interchange with the people of the earth, which is much different from the gods of the Greek and Roman mythologies.

Verse 26. Paul alludes to Adam and Eve as the first of creation. From their offspring has sprung every nation on the face of the earth. In other words, this God Paul proclaims is not the parochial god of the Jews but the God of the world. The Stoics also held that all humanity is interrelated.

This God also has predestined the rise and fall of nations. Certainly, this is an idea the Greeks in a Roman world could appreciate, since the Roman ways seemed to pollute the old way of the Greeks, although Paul probably had in mind the gospel opening to the Gentiles.

Verses 27-28. Appealing to the Stoic school of philosophy, Paul's first quote is possibly from a poem by a Cretan, Epimenides. The second is from the Cilician (the province from where Paul hailed) Aratus's *Phaenomena*.

The Stoics held that all events are the result of the will of the divine, and humanity is helpless to intervene.

Verse 29. Finally, Paul concluded with the pointlessness of idolatry.

Verses 30-31. If ignorance were ever an excuse for idolatry, the most intelligent people on earth can no longer worship those idols, nor appeal to ignorance of the Supreme God when they do. It is time for repentance to righteousness, where ignorance once reigned.

Paul, at last, appealed to the resurrection of Jesus, not by name or title of deity.

Verses 32-34. The resurrection was a stumbling block (verse 18). Some mocked Paul, but a few joined him.

The Scripture and the Main Question—Pat McGeachy

Surrounded by Gods (Acts 17)

Paul observed (17:16) that Athens was full of idols. In that day, and in that city, they were highly visible, and still are, for some of their temples are yet standing. (In the city where I live there is a full-sized replica of one of them). But the gods are sneakier than we think. Here is a list of a few of them that are hiding in the very words of the chapter that we are reading.

Apollonia (verse 1) was a city named after the most Greek of all the gods, Apollo, the god of healing, of light, and of truth.

Silas (verses 4, 10, etc.) is the short form of Silvanus (this is what Paul calls him in the Epistles; see, for example, 1 Thessalonians 1:1). Silvanus was worshiped as the helper of plowmen and woodcutters.

Athens (verses 15, 16, etc.) is, of course, named after Athena, a warlike battle goddess, defender of the city, tamer of horses, and, later, the embodiment of wisdom and purity. The Romans called her Minerva.

The Areopagus (verse 22) is a large outcropping of limestone, creating a smaller hill just under the Acropolis where the Parthenon sits. It is a sort of natural pulpit and was used as a public forum. It is also called Mars Hill, for Ares (Greek) and Mars (Roman) are the two names of the ancient god of war.

Dionysius (verse 34) is named after the god of wine and revelry, also called Bacchus.

Well, we could go on, but we'd never get to the question: How do we spot the true God in a world so full of lesser deities? So, let us proceed.

Overturning the World (Acts 17:1-9)

Before getting to Athens, we must pause briefly in Thessalonica, memorable because two of Paul's letters were written to the congregation there. We observe a repetition of the typical pattern Paul followed in each of the community: first, an attempt to reach the Jews of the synagogue, which met with limited success, and then a break with the synagogue because of the jealousy of those who could not, or would not, accept Paul's argument. According to Luke (verse 5), those of Thessalonica resorted to underhanded tactics, including lies and mob violence. Jason, in whose home Paul and Silas were apparently staying, may very well have been the relative of Paul mentioned in Romans 16:21. His name is a Greek substitute for the Hebrew name Joshua or Jesus.

It is noteworthy that once more, the insult of their enemies became a high compliment. They said of them, "They have turned the world upside down." Indeed they had, both the theological world of the Jews and the philosophical world of the Greeks, as we are about to see. And when Jesus becomes the Lord of your life or mine, our whole world is inverted, to the last detail. Just consider the phrase "Those who try to save their lives will lose them" (Luke 9:24), in comparison with the thinking of those in the marketplace around you. To one who spends every waking hour trying to get ahead, Jesus' words are upside-down. But they are truer than the truth of the world.

Briefly in Beroea (Acts 17:10-15)

Not content with expelling them from their own town, the enemies of Thessalonica followed Paul and Silas for fifty miles to the next and forced them to move on once more. But they did not leave before a start was made in building a Christian community in Beroea. Note that "they received the word with all eagerness," and that here, as in Thessalonica, significant Greeks and notable women were among the converts. It is characteristic of Luke that he pays attention to Gentiles and women, both in Acts and in the Gospel that bears his name. Here, as in many of his cities, Paul was not allowed to stay and enjoy the fruits of his labors. We do not have a letter to the Beroeans, and no further evidence of the life of that congregation, but from the good start that they seem to have made, we can assume they continued to grow and thrive, and to overturn their corner of the world.

Philosophizing (Acts 17:16-21)

In Athens, as in the other cities he visited, Paul began with the synagogue, where, as a rabbi trained in the Hebrew Scriptures, he was accustomed to arguing on familiar grounds. It was the logical starting place. But in Athens there was a difference. Though the "glory that was Greece" had long since faded (Socrates had been dead for 400 years), it was still a center of great intellectual activity. Let's say a word about the two schools of philosophy Luke mentions.

The Epicureans took their name from their leader, Epicurus, a famous Athenian thinker (b. 341 B.C.). The Epicureans did not believe in the gods at all but claimed that happiness was to be found in enjoying the physical world for all the pleasure that it could give. Popular thought has it that they were libertines, of a sort of "eat, drink, and be merry" school, but this is not the case. They believed in using wisdom to temper the pleasures of the world. Epicurus, for instance, disapproved of drunkenness, gluttony, and other sins of excess on the purely pragmatic grounds that in the long run they gave more pain than pleasure.

The Stoics, on the other hand (founded in Athens by Zeno of Cyprus, 336–264 B.C.; their name comes from the *stoa*, or porch, on which they met to argue), claimed that moral good came primarily from keeping the emotions and desires under strict control. Their iron discipline was much admired by the ancients, and they had many followers, including the emperor Marcus Aurelius.

You have to give the philosophers credit; they didn't agree with Paul's teaching, but they were sufficiently openminded to give him a chance to argue his case in public. One curious note: He was accused by some (verse 18) of preaching "foreign divinities—because he preached Jesus and the resurrection." In Greek this would be rendered "Jesus and anastasia." But whatever Paul meant, the bored philosophers were eager to hear something new (verse 21). So they give him a chance. Would you have?

The Sermon on Mars Hill (Acts 17:22-34)

This preachment is different from all the other sermons in Acts (see the discussion of apostolic preaching in "The Main Question," lesson 3) in that it starts not from Hebrew Scripture but from where the Athenians were. And its results were not, at first, terribly impressive (verses 32-34); only a few believed and followed him. Some have called it Paul's poorest sermon.

But it speaks to my condition as a modern American, trained to believe in the good life (like the Epicureans) and in rugged individualism (like the Stoics), and surrounded by dozens of false gods: Money, Pride, Pleasure, Ancestors, the Nation, Athletics, Movies, and on and on. None of these lesser gods is in itself evil. But though they pretend to offer ultimate happiness, they cannot. There is always a longing left for the true God (verse 27) that we long to feel after and find.

Though the false gods cannot save, they can destroy, as many a worshiper of Pleasure, or Sex, or Whatever has tragically discovered. Only when the true God comes do these take their proper places in our lives.

OCTOBER 20   LESSON 8

Why did the Athenians not believe? Because, Luke tells us (verse 32), they were upset "when they heard of the resurrection of the dead." To Greek philosophers this was foolishness (see 1 Corinthians 1:22-25). They wanted to believe that by their own righteousness, their own vaunted philosophies, they could achieve salvation.

We have in this chapter two sorts of people who find it all but impossible to kneel humbly before the truth that God in Jesus Christ has died, and risen, and saved us: the Jews of the synagogue, to whom this Jesus is weakness, and the Greeks of the Areopagus, to whom this philosophy is foolishness. But to those who believe, "Christ [is] the power of God and the wisdom of God" (1 Corinthians 1:24; see also Romans 1:16). There on that lonely outcropping of rock, Paul gave the answer to our great question: What shall we put first in our lives? Will we do it?

Helping Adults Become Involved—Ronald E. Schlosser

Preparing to Teach

One can't study the last half of Acts without a map. As was suggested in previous sessions, have a Bible map of the Mediterranean area available for reference purposes. On it locate Thessalonica, Beroea, and Athens, the three cities mentioned in today's scripture. Consult a Bible dictionary for background information on these cities.

Although attention will be given in the lesson to Paul's activities in each of these places, the major focus will be on Athens. The main question raised by Dr. McGeachy relates to Paul's encounter with the Greek philosophers in Athens.

In addition to "The Main Question," carefully read the sections "As You Read the Scripture" and "The Scripture and the Main Question." These form the heart of the lesson. The ideas, insights, and suggestions in these sections should be employed throughout your lesson plan.

After introducing the main question, you might develop the lesson using the following outline:

      I. Eyewitness news reporting
         A. Hostility in Thessalonica
         B. Friendly interest in Beroea
         C. Skepticism in Athens
            1. The city
            2. The marketplace
            3. The Areopagus
     II. Shaping one's personal witness

There are three learning goals: (1) to observe how Paul presented the gospel in several cities he visited; (2) to evaluate Paul's sermon in Athens; (3) to consider how we can witness today to people who worship "false gods."

Introducing the Main Question

Begin by referring to the first two paragraphs in "The Main Question," where Dr. McGeachy talks about modern gods people worship. He identifies some of these and their temples. You might continue the exercise, asking class members to add to the list. Here are additional suggestions:

FIRST QUARTER

Science	The Laboratory
Materialism	The Shopping Mall
Athletics	The Stadium
Militarism	The Pentagon
Pleasure/Fantasy	The Movie Theater

Raise the question Dr. McGeachy asks: How shall we recognize and worship the One True God? Mention that later in the session, when we look at Paul's experiences in Athens, this question will come into sharper focus.

Developing the Lesson

I. Eyewitness news reporting

Refer to a Bible map to point out the next three places Paul visited after he left Philippi: Thessalonica, Beroea, and Athens. Indicate that we will look briefly at the first two cities before concentrating more fully on Athens. To do this, divide the class into two groups, asking the first group to read Acts 17:1-9 and the second group Acts 17:10-15. Each group is to envision itself as a news reporting team observing the happenings recorded in the scripture. After reading their respective passages, the groups should discuss (1) what would be the major news story to report, (2) what might be the headline or the lead-in "hook" to introduce the story, (3) what was the outcome?

Allow about seven or eight minutes for the groups to work, then call the class together for reporting. Add the comments by Drs. Winters and McGeachy to flesh out the stories.

A. Hostility in Thessalonica.

Thessalonica was about ninety miles southwest of Philippi. It was one of the chief cities in Macedonia, an important commercial center and a military base. Both Jews and Greeks responded to Paul's preaching of the gospel, including some leading women. A small group of jealous Jews gathered together some rabble-rousers and, either for money or the promise of sport, urged them to attack Paul. When the apostle could not be found in the home of Jason, they seized Jason and some other Christians and dragged them before the authorities. Jason had to post bond that he would no longer give Paul lodging. "Local Man Accused of Conspiracy" might be the headline reporting the incident.

B. Friendly interest in Beroea.

Beroea was about fifty miles west of Thessalonica. As was his pattern, Paul found a synagogue and began to preach. The response of the Bereoans was encouraging. With eagerness they listened to Paul and with enthusiasm searched the scriptures to check on Paul's teaching. Again women of high standing were among the believers. But when troublemakers from Thessalonica began to stir up the town, Paul had to leave. A headline might read "New Religion Attracts Many Leading Citizens."

C. Skepticism in Athens.

Ask the class what they know about Athens.

1. The city.

Athens was the cultural and intellectual center of the ancient world. It was the university center for various philosophies. Refer to Dr. McGeachy's comments about the Epicureans and the Stoics. Dominating the city was a high hill called the Acropolis, on which stood the Parthenon, the temple of Athena. Part way up the slope was a mound called Mars Hill, where the court known as the Areopagus met. It was here that Paul delivered his famous sermon.

2. The marketplace.
Have the class read silently Acts 17:16-21. How might reporters headline these events? Not content with speaking about Christ in the Jewish synagogue, Paul soon was talking with crowds gathered in the *agora* (marketplace). At any time of day, one could find learned teachers and groups engaging in discussions of philosophic and religious things. Their first reaction to Paul was one of scorn, possibly because they recognized him as a Jew. But they gave him the opportunity to present his "new teachings" to the Areopagus.

3. The Areopagus.
Read Paul's sermon in Acts 17:22-34. In outline, Paul talked about (1) God's creation (verses 24-25), (2) God's purpose (verses 26-27), (3) God's power (verse 28), (4) God's personhood (verse 29), and (5) God's promise (verses 30-31). What was the response of the people? (Some mocked, some were indecisive, some believed.) What might the headlines of the *Athens Times* or lead news story on Athens' television have said? ("Preacher Fails to Win Wide Support"?) Was Paul's sermon a failure? Note Dr. McGeachy's comments on this.

Helping Class Members Act

II. Shaping one's personal witness
Return to the main question introduced at the beginning of the lesson: How shall we recognize and worship the One True God? Review the list of modern gods people worship, which the class drew up. Categorize them under three headings: (1) Idols of wood and stone (material possessions), (2) idols of flesh and blood (human idols, celebrities, people who compete for our allegiance and detract from our loyalty to God), and (3) idols of mind and heart (ideas, philosophies, life-styles that influence our priorities).

Ask the class: How would one witness to people who "worship" these false gods? What does the gospel of Christ say to materialism? To the thirst for power and prestige? To science or humanism? Discuss the kind of approach we might make to a friend who is absorbed in making money, wants to live life in the fast lane, or is an avowed agnostic. Should the proclamation of the gospel be shaped to meet people where they are, or is there a basic message that does not change no matter what the situation? What might Paul do if he were in our places today?

Close with a time of prayer, asking God for guidance as we consider how to witness to our friends.

Planning for Next Sunday

The background scripture for next week is Acts 18:1–19:20. Indicate that you will be giving a short quiz on this passage.

LESSON 9 OCTOBER 27

Learning from One Another

Background Scripture: Acts 18:1–19:20

The Main Question—Pat McGeachy

Voice, voices, voices. I grew up in a more or less homogeneous town in the southern United States. There was a token Jew there, and a Buddhist, a tiny Roman Catholic congregation, a small Episcopal church, a medium-sized Presbyterian community, three Methodist congregations, and sixteen Baptist churches. Most of us small boys knew what the rules were (though we didn't always keep them and got whipped when we got caught). I never met an agnostic till I was twelve, nor an atheist till I was in college. Pretty much everybody in town believed the same Anglo-Saxon Protestant theology, or kept quiet about it. (The Jew and the Buddhist, who operated a Chinese laundry, attended the Presbyterian church.)

And yet, I heard voices. By the time I was eleven years old I knew four theories of the atonement (Jesus saves us by taking our place at the judgment seat; Jesus saves us by licking the devil at Calvary; Jesus saves us by teaching us how to be good; and Jesus saves us by setting us a wonderful example of how to live) and two or three doctrines of baptism (immersion, sprinkling, and the baptism of the Holy Ghost). Whom was I to believe? Of course I knew what my mom and dad believed, but what did *I* believe? Even with no television evangelists, we struggled with that question.

The New Testament church was in the same boat. Whom do you believe? Paul (Acts 18:4, 11, 22)? The Jews of the synagogue (18:12)? Priscilla and Aquila (18:2, 26)? Gallio the proconsul (18:14)? Apollos (18:24)? John's disciples (19:3)? The high priest named Sceva and his sons (19:14)? Dozens of voices say, "This is what you must believe, and how you must be baptized." But who has the last word, either in my childhood town, or your childhood community, or the ancient cities of Corinth and Ephesus? It is a question we need to answer, for the sake of our very souls.

Selected Scripture

King James Version

Acts 18:24-28

24 And a certain Jew named Apollos, born at Alexandria, an eloquent man, *and* mighty in the scriptures, came to Ephesus.

25 This man was instructed in the way of the Lord; and being fervent in the spirit, he spake and taught diligently the things of the Lord, knowing only the baptism of John.

26 And he began to speak boldly in the synagogue: whom when Aqui-

Revised Standard Version

Acts 18:24-28

24 Now a Jew named Apollos, a native of Alexandria, came to Ephesus. He was an eloquent man, well versed in the scriptures. 25 He had been instructed in the way of the Lord; and being fervent in spirit, he spoke and taught accurately the things concerning Jesus, though he knew only the baptism of John. 26 He began to speak boldly in the synagogue; but when Priscilla

OCTOBER 27 — LESSON 9

la and Priscilla had heard, they took him unto *them*, and expounded unto him the way of God more perfectly.

27 And when he was disposed to pass into Achaia, the brethren wrote, exhorting the disciples to receive him; who, when he was come, helped them much which had believed through grace:

28 For he mightily convinced the Jews, *and that* publicly, shewing by the scriptures that Jesus was Christ.

Acts 19:1-6

1 And it came to pass, that, while Apollos was at Corinth, Paul having passed through the upper coasts came to Ephesus: and finding certain disciples,

2 He said unto them, Have ye received the Holy Ghost since ye believed? And they said unto him, We have not so much as heard whether there be any Holy Ghost.

3 And he said unto them, Unto what then were ye baptized? And they said, Unto John's baptism.

4 Then said Paul, John verily baptized with the baptism of repentance, saying unto the people, that they should believe on him which should come after him, that is, on Christ Jesus.

5 When they heard *this*, they were baptized in the name of the Lord Jesus.

6. And when Paul had laid *his* hands upon them, the Holy Ghost came on them; and they spake with tongues, and prophesied.

Key Verse: **When Paul had laid his hands upon them, the Holy Ghost came on them; and they spake with tongues, and prophesied. (Acts 19:6)**

and Aquila heard him, they took him and expounded to him the way of God more accurately. 27 And when he wished to cross to Achaia, the brethren encouraged him, and wrote to the disciples to receive him. When he arrived, he greatly helped those who through grace had believed, 28 for he powerfully confuted the Jews in public, showing by the scriptures that the Christ was Jesus.

Acts 19:1-6

1 While Apollos was at Corinth, Paul passed through the upper country and came to Ephesus. There he found some disciples. 2 And he said to them, "Did you receive the Holy Spirit when you believed?" And they said, "No, we have never even heard that there is a Holy Spirit." 3 And he said, "Into what then were you baptized?" They said, "Into John's baptism." 4 And Paul said, "John baptized with the baptism of repentance, telling the people to believe in the one who was to come after him, that is, Jesus." 5 On hearing this, they were baptized in the name of the Lord Jesus. 6 And when Paul had laid his hands upon them, the Holy Spirit came on them; and they spoke with tongues and prophesied.

Key Verse: **When Paul had laid his hands upon them [the disciples], the Holy Spirit came on them; and they spoke with tongues and prophesied. (Acts 19:6)**

As You Read the Scripture—Michael Winters

Acts 18:1-4. Corinth is on the isthmus between the Grecian mainland and the Peloponnese peninsula, west of Athens. In Corinth Paul befriended the exiled Italian Jews Aquila and Priscilla. They were tentmakers, or leatherworkers, by trade.

FIRST QUARTER

Verses 5-17. Silas and Timothy caught up with Paul in Corinth. The movements of Silas and Timothy are not clear from the point Paul had to leave Beroea (Acts 17:14-15). While Luke mentions in 17:16 that Paul waited for them in Athens, there is no indication that either one of them arrived, except that in 1 Thessalonians 3:1-2, it appears that Timothy, at least, made it to Athens with Paul.

In the year and a half Paul is in Corinth, he is able to baptize only Crispus, Gaius, and Stephanas, and presumably their families (see 1 Corinthians 1:14-15).

Verses 18-23. Priscilla and Aquila left Corinth with Paul, traveling as far as Ephesus. This marks the end of Paul's second missionary journey and the beginning of the third.

Verses 24-25. Apollos, a disciple of John the Baptist and a native of Alexandria in Egypt, visited Ephesus. Apparently he was a polished teacher, though his Christian teaching was deficient. He taught the teachings of John and thus probably a baptism of repentance only (Acts 19:2-4). It is not impossible that a "John the Baptist sect" existed in Ephesus, which may even have declared John the Christ.

Verse 26. Priscilla and Aquila are able to instruct Apollos in the gospel of Jesus (see Acts 19:2-5).

Verses 27-28. The term "brethren" is used to describe the collegial relationship those in the faith have. Here it is likely used to include both Aquila and Priscilla (a woman). The letter recommending Apollos to the Corinthians probably came from them. In Corinth, the capital of Achaia, Apollos' teaching was appreciated, and he was able to refute, or, literally translated from the Greek, "maintain the discussion," with the Jews. Paul was not as successful as Apollos in Corinth.

Acts 19:1. Meanwhile, Paul is traveling through Galatia, Phrygia (Acts 18:23), and Ephesus, where the Holy Spirit had once forbidden him to speak (Acts 16:6). Paul was in Ephesus for at least two years (19:10).

Verses 2-3. The Ephesian disciples had received instruction under Apollos and thus did not have the full gospel (18:25). It seems rather odd at this point for Paul to ask the Ephesians if they had received the Holy Spirit when they believed. If the Christians in Ephesus did not have any outward signs of faith, however, the question might not seem so odd. For the Holy Spirit works these outward signs in the followers of Jesus. In verse 6 they are glossolalia and prophecy (Paul later looked for other and probably more important signs of the Holy Spirit in believers, namely teaching, preaching, and love [1 Corinthians 12:28–13:1]).

Verse 4. Paul declares to the Ephesians the hallmark of John's message. John too declared the baptism of Jesus with the Holy Spirit (Luke 3:16).

Verses 5-7. Twelve Ephesians were convinced and received baptism in Jesus' name, and they gave evidence of this baptism through glossolalia and prophecy. Notice that the Holy Spirit is given when Paul "laid his hands upon them" (compare Acts 8:17).

The Scripture and the Main Question—Pat McGeachy

Beginnings at Corinth (Acts 18:1-4)

We know more about the Corinthian church than almost any other of Paul's congregations, because the two letters to the Corinthians constitute the longest Pauline material in the New Testament. It was a city about the size of Birmingham, Alabama, located at the intersection of two major trade routes: the north-south passage across the isthmus of Corinth from the mainland of Greece to the Peloponnesus (with Athens to the north and Sparta to the south; in classical Greece this was *the* busy thoroughfare), and the east-west passage over the same, which connected the Adriatic and Aegean seas (today there is a canal dug there, but in those days the ships had to be ported across the three-mile strip of land). It was a busy city, with active schools, sporting events, drama, commercial, and religious activities.

Paul began his work as usual, in the synagogue, and both Jews and Greeks believed. The most important thing that happened in this encounter was his meeting with Priscilla and Aquila, who became his good friends, fellow tentmakers, and loyal supporters of the gospel. We meet them not only here (and in verses 18 and 26) but also in Romans 16:3 and 2 Timothy 4:19. There are an excellent example of how important good lay people are to a preacher, even one of the statue of an apostle.

Talking Tough (Acts 18:5-11)

As usual, Paul ran into opposition. This time he reacted with a typical Jewish action: He shook out his garments (see Matthew 10:14; 27:25; Acts 13:51). You can't spend all your ministry barking up an empty tree; sooner or later you have to shake off the dust and go on to more fertile territory. In this case, Paul moved in with a Gentile, Titius Justus, and continued his revival. He even converted Crispus, the top person in the synagogue, and was given courage from God to keep up the good work. He remained a long time (verse 11) in Corinth.

Moving On (Acts 18:12-23)

Paul's opponents tried to get him in the secular courts, but, as usual, the courts sidestepped the issue (see the police and the magistrates in 16:38-39 and, for that matter, Pontius Pilate in Luke 23:13-16). One Sosthenes (verse 17) seems to have caught the brunt of things, though what he had to do with it, I don't know. Conceivably, he could have been the same Sosthenes mentioned in 1 Corinthians 1:1 as a co-worker with Paul. In this case he must have been beaten for his Christian convictions.

Then (verses 18-21) there comes a brief visit to Ephesus. On the way Paul stopped at a barber shop because of a vow. Usually a Nazirite vow (see Numbers 6:5, 18) was a pledge *not* to cut the hair, so either Paul had just completed a vow or was getting ready to make one and wanted his hair short to begin with. Why do you suppose he didn't stay very long in Ephesus (verse 20)? Whatever the reason, he couldn't have been in too much of a hurry because his second visit lasted for two years (Acts 19:10).

Something is causing Paul to keep moving. To Antioch he goes, then to Galatia and Phrygia, always encouraging the Christians along the way. How long should a pastoral call last? I know one minister who averaged as many as fifty a day. Some criticized him for not having many in-depth relationships, but, if Paul is a good example, this is not always necessary.

Apollos (Acts 18:24-28)

Of all the acquaintances of Paul whom we meet in this lesson, none is more interesting than Apollos. He was a well-educated man, skilled in

FIRST QUARTER

rhetoric (the art of public speaking) and trained in the Hebrew Scriptures. He was also "fervent in spirit" and a good teacher. When we are told (verse 25) that he knew only the baptism of John, this probably means that he baptized in the same way that John did, that is, not in the name of Jesus. On this matter he was helped by Priscilla and Aquila, who "expounded . . . the way of God more accurately."

This is one of the best examples in the New Testament of what I call "cross-pollinating Christianity." We can all learn from one another. It is a mistake to believe that it all depends on the articulate expositor; sometimes a quiet, steady steward has something to teach the more visible evangelist. The point is that Apollos, Aquila, and Priscilla make a terrific three-person team. They need each other, and together they accomplish much. To push the point to a practical matter: Methodists can learn from Baptists and Episcopalians from Presbyterians. We will do well to see the rich diversity of the Christian community rather than to spend all our energy straightening one another out. When we do the latter, as A and P did for Apollos, we must do it speaking the truth in love (Ephesians 4:15), so that together we can grow up into Christ.

Baptism in the Spirit (Acts 19:1-10)

When Paul came back to Ephesus, though he had only been there briefly on his first trip, he found a small community in business. But there was something wrong. The little group had gone through the formalities of induction into the faith; there had been a baptism of sorts, but there had been two things wrong with it: (1) It had not been in the name of Jesus, and (2) it had not included an experience of the Holy Spirit. The baptismal formula of Matthew 28:19 is "in the name of the Father and of the Son and of the Holy Spirit." From this paragraph in Acts 19 we see why the three names are necessary. To be baptized in the name of the *Father* is to enter into the faith of Israel as renewed by repentance, as John the Baptizer had taught. To be baptized in the name of the *Son* is to accept the grace of God in Jesus Christ and to know the forgiveness of sins. And to be baptized in the name of the *Holy Spirit* is to experience the charismatic power that the Christian experience should include. Anything short of this is less than the total commitment that makes for the well-rounded disciple.

We have, then, a case where Christian training, off to a shaky start, needs the fine tuning of the master, Paul, to bring it to full fruition. The result of this was a long stay in Ephesus. There was some criticism of the people of the Way (this is the first time we have heard that name for Christians since 9:2), which caused Paul to move his operation to the home of Tyrannus, where he continued for two more years.

The Seven Stripped Sons of Sceva (Acts 19:11-20)

This is one of the funniest stories in the Bible, if you like slapstick. But let's not let the vision of the naked exorcists running down the street cause us to miss the point. It is this: *You can't cast out demons in the name of somebody else's Jesus.* You can't build a Christian life in the name of the Jesus your mother believed in. You can't get to heaven in the name of the Jesus your pastor preached about. You can't do mighty works in the name of "the Jesus whom Paul preaches." You can only do it in the name of *your* Jesus.

OCTOBER 27   LESSON 9

It is not the opinions of Paul and Silas that matter, nor those of Priscilla, Aquila, Apollos, or any of the other characters we have met in this lesson. From each of these we learn something; their lessons cross-pollinate until we receive the whole gospel. But in the end it is our own understanding of the Word that makes the rich wholeness of the Christian life possible.

Who, then, possesses the truth? Jesus Christ alone is the way, the truth, and the life, and though we come to know Christ through the witness of everyone from Paul to Ananias of Damascus, it is Christ and Christ alone to whom we must give out utter allegiance. Sometimes it may be necessary for us to oppose Peter to his face (Galatians 2:11), or our preacher or our parents, and to put our trust in the one Jesus in whose name we can cast out demons: the Jesus who has come to live in our own hearts.

Helping Adults Become Involved—Ronald E. Schlosser

Preparing to Teach

Paul's life was a series of journeys. He traveled for Jesus. Paul went from Antioch, to Lystra, to Philippi, to Athens, to Corinth, to Ephesus, and finally to Rome. But he didn't travel alone. He had partners.

In today's lesson we will meet some of Paul's partners and supporters in ministry. The learning goals are (1) to recognize the importance of working together as partners in the community of faith, (2) to appreciate the continuing need for Bible study and instruction in the Christian faith, and (3) to be willing to receive new learnings about biblical truths.

After introducing the main question, you might develop the lesson using the following outline:

>   I. Partners and supporters
>   A. Aquila and Priscilla
>   B. Silas and Timothy
>   C. Titius Justus
>   D. Crispus
>   E. Gallio
>   F. Sosthenes
>   G. Apollos
>   H. Tyrannus
>   II. Truths from the lesson

Carefully read the sections "As You Read the Scripture" and "The Scripture and the Main Question." These form the heart of the lesson. The ideas, insights, and suggestions in these sections should be employed throughout your lesson plan.

Prior to the session, make copies of the following quiz:

Match the persons in the left column with the descriptions of them in the right column.

1. Aquila and   a. Eloquent but uninformed preacher from
   Priscilla   Alexandria.

FIRST QUARTER

2. Silas and Timothy   b. Supported Paul by refusing Paul's judgment before his court.
3. Titius Justus   c. Opened his home to Paul in time of trouble.
4. Crispus   d. Lay persons who shared their home and vocation with Paul.
5. Gallio   e. Traveled with Paul on his missionary journeys.
6. Sosthenes   f. Loaned Paul his lecture hall.
7. Apollos   g. Ruler of the synagogue in Corinth, who became a believer.
8. Tyrannus   h. Another ruler of the synagogue who became a scapegoat and was beaten.

Introducing the Main Question

Begin the session by passing out the quiz and asking the class to match the persons in the left column with the identifying statements in the right column. Indicate that these are people we will be studying in today's lesson.

Allow five minutes for the members to do the quiz. They can work together in twos and threes if they desire. Then refer to Dr. McGeachy's comments in "The Main Question" regarding conflicting voices. Mention that the persons in the quiz are some of the players in the dramatic events described in today's scripture.

Developing the Lesson

I. Partners and supporters

Perhaps the best way to cover the background scripture in today's lesson (Acts 18:1–19:20) is to have the class read it silently to check out the correct answers to the quiz. Allow eight minutes for the members to do this. Then deal with each of the persons mentioned, using the comments of Drs. Winters and McGeachy and the materials below to expand your discussion. The correct answers are 1-d, 2-e, 3-c, 4-g, 5-b, 6-h, 7-a, 8-f.

A. Aquila and Priscilla

Aquila is a Roman name meaning "eagle." He was born in Pontus, a province bordering on the Black Sea in what is now modern Turkey. Priscilla is the diminutive form of Prisca, the more formal name Paul calls her in 1 Corinthians 16:19. The couple came to Corinth about A.D. 49 when Claudius ordered all Jews to leave Rome. Later they returned to Rome, where they had a church in their home (Romans 16:3-5). In today's scripture we read how they opened their home to Paul, gave him employment as a tentmaker, and later traveled to Ephesus with him. They were also the ones who instructed Apollos in the faith. Discuss with your calls the qualities they had that made them good examples of Christian laypeople.

B. Silas and Timothy

Silas we met in Jerusalem (Acts 15:22), and Timothy joined Paul in Lystra (Acts 16:1). The two were traveling companions of Paul, who did follow-up work for the missionary in establishing churches and instructing new believers in the faith. Discuss with your class the need for follow-up work in any evangelistic campaign. How important is it to have trustworthy persons do this work?

C. Titius Justus

This godly Gentile in Corinth allowed Paul to use his house as a base for his preaching ministry in Corinth. He may have done this at considerable risk (remember what happened in Thessalonica when Jason opened his home to Paul; see Acts 17:5-9). Ask: Are we willing to open our homes as meeting places for Christian action groups whose causes may not be popular with the general public?

D. Crispus

The ruler of the synagogue and his family were won to Christ by Paul. Crispus is one of the few persons in Corinth whom Paul baptized (1 Corinthians 1:14). Paul felt his call was to preach, not baptize (1 Corinthians 1:17).

E. Gallio

Though this proconsul is not identified as a believer, he nevertheless supported Paul's right to preach. He established an important precedent by refusing to issue a verdict on religious matters. What does your class feel about the principle of the separation of church and state in our day?

F. Sosthenes

Identified as a ruler of the synagogue (Crispus's replacement or colleague?), he was attacked and beaten by hostile Jews who were frustrated that they could not punish Paul. He may have been, or become, a believer also (see 1 Corinthians 1:1). What would be our response today if we were punished for problems caused by someone else?

G. Apollos

Refer to Dr. McGeachy's comments about Apollos. This eloquent and learned man didn't object to receiving instruction from Aquila and Priscilla. He went to Corinth and became one of the leaders in the church there. Ask: What made the difference in Apollos's life? Are we open to receiving new learnings about the Christian faith that may help us to grow?

H. Tyrannus

This Ephesian may have been either a teacher of philosophy or a Jewish scribe who gave instruction in the law. Paul used his classroom to preach and teach after he was expelled from the synagogue.

Helping Class Members Act

II. Truths from the lesson

Picking up the last two points, that of Apollos's willingness to receive new teachings and Paul's daily debating (teaching) in the hall of Tyrannus, discuss with your class the place Christian education should have in the local church. How important is it for church members to study the Bible regularly and be instructed in their faith? Why don't more members take advantage of the Christian teaching being conducted in your church? What can be done about it?

Note also the supporting roles Christians can play in their church's ministry. Not everyone has the same talents. (See 1 Corinthians 12:27-31.) But we all need to work together in love.

Close by referring to Dr. McGeachy's remarks about cross-pollinating Christianity.

Planning for Next Sunday

Ask the class to read Acts 20 and consider how Christians should deal with partings (loss by moving, divorce, death, etc.).

UNIT IV: DESTINATION: ROME
Horace R. Weaver

FOUR LESSONS   NOVEMBER 3-24

"Destination: Rome" has four lessons and follows Paul through his arrest, defense, appeal to Caesar, and arrival in Rome. The lessons can be described as follows: "Serving the Church," November 3, challenges us: How should a Christian grieve? What is good grief? "Facing Crises," November 10, raises the query: How and when does one decide to take a stand against persons in leadership and authority? "Speaking Up for Your Faith," November 17, raises the supreme challenge: What do I truly believe, and why? "Proclaiming the Gospel", November 24, asks: Will the last years of our lives be filled with promise?

LESSON 10   NOVEMBER 3

Serving the Church

Background Scripture: Acts 20

The Main Question—Pat McGeachy

Paul's road ministry is drawing to a close. We are coming to the end of his missionary journeys. Of course there is much more to the story—Jerusalem, imprisonment at Caesarea Maritima, a shipwreck, Rome . . . But the principal seeds of his work have been sown, and now there will be many partings.

All human relationships involve risk. To love is to ensure that hurt will happen. Only a married couple that can contrive to die at the same instant can know a life without parting, and even they will have to deal with many broken relationships. They will move, their children will leave home, they will retire, they will change jobs. No life well lived is without grief. The question is then, will it be "good grief"?

In 1942, 491 people were killed in a tragic fire at the Cocoanut Grove Fire in Boston. In addition, many badly burned people were admitted to the hospitals of the area. Dozens of psychologists descended on Boston to interview grieving burn victims who had lost loved ones in the fire. It had long been known that burns heal more rapidly for mentally healthy people; therefore, it was assumed that those who were grieving would heal more slowly. Not so! Some grieving persons healed rapidly, indicating that they were grieving in a healthy way. They were able to talk about their deceased loved ones and to share their feelings with others.

In this lesson we shall learn from Paul how to deal with our partings, the inevitable result of the risks every meaningful life must have. As he brings

NOVEMBER 3   LESSON 10

his long journeys to an end, facing almost certain imprisonment and possible death, he is able to grieve over his losses as a Christian should. How should a Christian grieve? What is "good grief"? That is the main question for us this week.

Selected Scripture

King James Version

Acts 20:17-31
17 And from Miletus he sent to Ephesus, and called the elders of the church.
18 And when they were come to him, he said unto them, Ye know from the first day that I came into Asia, after what manner I have been with you at all seasons,
19 Serving the Lord with all humility of mind, and with many tears, and temptations, which befell me by the lying in wait of the Jews:
20 *And* how I kept back nothing that was profitable *unto you,* but have shewed you, and have taught you publickly, and from house to house.
21 Testifying both to the Jews, and also to the Greeks, repentance toward God, and faith toward our Lord Jesus Christ.
22 And now, behold, I go bound in the spirit unto Jerusalem, not knowing the things that shall befall me there:
23 Save that the Holy Ghost witnesseth in every city, saying that bonds and afflictions abide me.
24 But none of these things move me, neither count I my life dear unto myself, so that I might finish my course with joy, and the ministry, which I have received of the Lord Jesus, to testify the gospel of the grace of God.
25 And now, behold, I know that ye all, among whom I have gone preaching the kingdom of God, shall see my face no more.
26 Wherefore I take you to record this day, that I *am* pure from the blood of all *men.*
27 For I have not shunned to

Revised Standard Version

Acts 20:17-31
17 And from Miletus he sent to Ephesus and called to him the elders of the church. 18 And when they came to him, he said to them:
"You yourselves know how I lived among you all the time from the first day that I set foot in Asia, 19 serving the Lord with all humility and with tears and with trials which befell me through the plots of the Jews; 20 how I did not shrink from declaring to you anything that was profitable, and teaching you in public and from house to house, 21 testifying both to Jews and to Greeks of repentance to God and of faith in our Lord Jesus Christ. 22 And now, behold, I am going to Jerusalem, bound in the Spirit, not knowing what shall befall me there; 23 except that the Holy Spirit testifies to me in every city that imprisonment and afflictions await me. 24 But I do not account my life of any value nor as precious to myself, if only I may accomplish my course and the ministry which I received from the Lord Jesus, to testify to the gospel of the grace of God. 25 And now, behold, I know that all you among whom I have gone about preaching the kingdom will see my face no more. 26 Therefore I testify to you this day that I am innocent of the blood of all of you, 27 for I did not shrink from declaring to you the whole counsel of God. 28 Take heed to yourselves and to all the flock, in which the Holy Spirit has made you guardians, to feed the church of the Lord which he obtained with his own blood. 29 I know that after my

declare unto you all the counsel of God.

28 Take heed therefore unto yourselves, and to all the flock, over the which the Holy Ghost hath made you overseers, to feed the church of God, which he hath purchased with his own blood.

29 For I know this, that after my departing shall grievous wolves enter in among you, not sparing the flock.

30 Also of your own selves shall men arise, speaking perverse things, to draw away disciples after them.

31 Therefore watch, and remember, that by the space of three years I ceased not to warn every one night and day with tears.

departure fierce wolves will come in among you, not sparing the flock; 30 and from among your own selves will arise men speaking perverse things, to draw away the disciples after them. 31 Therefore be alert, remembering that for three years I did not cease night or day to admonish every one with tears."

Key Verse: They all wept sore, and fell on Paul's neck, and kissed him, sorrowing most of all for the words which he spake, that they should see his face no more. (Acts 20:37-38)

Key Verse: They all wept and embraced Paul and kissed him, sorrowing most of all because of the word he had spoken, that they should see his face no more. (Acts 20:37-38)

As You Read the Scripture—Michael Winters

Acts 20:1-6. After three months in Greece, Paul's entourage meets with the author, as the change to first-person plural indicates in verse 5.

Verses 7-12. On his last full day in Troas, after the sabbath (Sunday), Paul delivered a lengthy speech, apparently over the course of an evening meal. The Troasian, Eutychus, was present. Eutychus fell to his death from the third-story window, where he had drifted into sleep during the course of Paul's speech. By Paul's intercession, Eutychus was miraculously revived.

Verse 11. Paul departed Troas via the short overland distance to Assos, where his companions met him, having traveled by boat (verse 14).

Verses 13-16. The missionary tour intentionally bypasses Ephesus to prevent further delays. Paul's mind is set on Jerusalem. He may have carried a famine relief offering for the church there (Acts 24:17). He also had in mind a trip to Rome (Acts 19:21).

Verses 17-18a. Intending to bid farewell to the Asian church, Paul asked the Ephesian elders to make the thirty-six-mile trip south to Miletus.

Verse 18b. Paul avoided Asia in his first missionary journey (Acts 16:6). Although Ephesus was not Paul's first foot in Asia, it is true that Ephesus was the point where Paul made his first significant Asian impact.

Verse 19. Paul was in Ephesus for at least two years (Acts 19:10), and probably longer (19:31). In Ephesus the Jews were so stubborn and disbelieving and slanderous of the Way, Paul withdrew from them with his

NOVEMBER 3   LESSON 10

disciples (19:8-10). Paul's biggest trial in Ephesus, however, was over the Greek goddess of hunting, Artemis (19:23-40).

Verse 20. Paul was bold to declare the good of the gospel of Jesus Christ to the Ephesians. His use of the word translated from the Greek, "profitable," is intended to mean, "what is good for you." But the Greek word also conveys the sense of "advantageous." In the course of his ministry to the Ephesians, they struggled to weigh the advantage of Jesus the Christ over that of the goddess Artemis. Interestingly, the row over the goddess was, financially, a profit motive issue (19:24-25).

Verse 21. When Paul withdrew from the synagogue in Ephesus, he preached in the hall of the philosopher Tyrannus, where he proclaimed the gospel also to the Greeks (19:8-10).

Verses 22-23. Paul anticipated persecution at the hands of the Jerusalem Jews (Acts 21:27-36).

Verse 24. Paul's self-effacement is a theme he also declared to the Philippians (Philippians 3:7-8).

Verses 25-27. Paul could depart from the Ephesians with good conscience, because he had declared to all, forthrightly, the gospel.

Verses 28-29. The Greek word, translated "guardian" is also translated "bishop" in Titus 1:7 (compare 1 Peter 2:25). The word "episcopal" is derived from the same Greek word.

Paul used the shepherd analogy as a metaphor for the work the elders must do in Ephesus (Matthew 7:15 warned against wolves in sheep's clothing). The wolves are the encroachment of Judaism (from which they were free; see Ephesians 2:11-20) and pagan licentiousness (Ephesians 4:17-20).

Verse 30. Paul's greatest concern is the divisiveness that the leadership of the church may promote: different baptisms (Ephesians 4:5), different gifts (Ephesians 4:11), and different doctrines (Ephesians 4:14).

Verse 31. In all, Paul spent three years with the Ephesians.

Verses 32-38. Paul concludes his remarks and departs by ship with a tearful goodbye.

The Scripture and the Main Question—Pat McGeachy

Moving On (Acts 20:1-6)

There is a restlessness about Paul in this chapter. It had begun in 19:21, where we are told that "Paul resolved in the Spirit to pass through Macedonia and Achaia and go to Jerusalem, saying, 'After I have been there I must also see Rome.'" As one who has spent a lifetime answering the call of the Spirit to go here and there doing ministry, I can testify that there also come calls from the Spirit saying, "Go away."

Timing is important; Jesus would say things like, "My hour has not yet come" (John 2:4; compare John 13:1). Paul did not leave until "after the uproar ceased"; supposedly he didn't want to appear to be fleeing from the danger. But as soon as things had quieted down, he made a parting speech and left.

Luke takes us swiftly through Paul's final visit to Macedonia and Greece. We aren't even told what city it was in which he spent three months (verse 3), but almost certainly it was Corinth. During this stay Paul probably wrote the most thorough argument for his Gospel: the letter to the Romans. But in

FIRST QUARTER

spite of such stops (three months here, seven days at Troas), still Paul seems to be hurrying, anxious to get to Jerusalem (verse 16) in time for the Hebrew feast of Pentecost. When the Spirit is moving within us, we are soon on the move ourselves.

A Sleepy Fellow (Acts 20:7-12)

The story of Eutychus must have stuck in Luke's mind, because though he has been hurrying us through this last journey, he stops long enough to tell it. Notice that, beginning with verse 6, we are back in what some call the "we" passages, indicating that Luke was there and could give us a first-hand account of things.

Certainly there are a number of details that interest us: It was the first day of the week, the time for a Christian community to be gathering to break bread. Did the gathering begin at sundown "Saturday" night, which marked the end of the Hebrew sabbath? Or did it start on "Sunday" afternoon, as would seem to be indicated by Paul's intent to resume his journey the next day? And what of the act of "breaking bread," mentioned in both 7 and 11? It sounds very much as if Luke meant this as a liturgical act (see Acts 2:42, 46), either a fellowship meal or "agape," or perhaps even the Lord's Supper itself.

Another detail: "There were many lights" in the upper room where Paul was speaking. This gives me some sympathy for Eutychus, for the only time I ever passed out in church (not counting sleeping) was during a candle light service when the oxygen began to get very scant. Thus even if Eutychus were eager to hear Paul's message, he could have become drowsy if there were lots of candle fumes in the loft. Paul's sermon lasted for hours. Indeed, the whole service lasted until the following morning. Do you suppose we are missing something by cutting our worship with television precision to exactly 59 minutes on Sunday morning?

Anyway, this story ends happily, or, as Luke understates it, they "were not a little comforted" (verse 12). From what Paul said in verse 10, it is apparent that the first diagnosis, that he was dead, was mistaken. This is not an account of a healing by a prophet (compare 1 Kings 17:17-24 and 2 Kings 4:32-37) but a celebration of Paul's diagnostic skills. I will leave you to draw your own moral from the story. You can choose between "Beware of sleeping in church," "Don't sit in the window" (My mother used to call me Eutychus when I would perch on the porch railing), or "Keep your sermons short and to the point." My own belief is that the story is preserved simply to give us a taste of some of the details of what life was like in the first century of the church's existence.

A Stop in Miletus (Acts 20:13-17)

Paul planned not to stop in Ephesus; no doubt he had reason to believe it would not be safe. But he couldn't just sail on by with no contact. A case can be made that Ephesus was actually the center of Paul's ministry. Certainly he lived there for more than two years on his third journey (see Acts 19 and also 1 Corinthians 15:32; 16:8-9; and 2 Timothy 1:18). He had found there both opposition and opportunity, and he could not part from them for the last time without some healthy grief work. So he sent for the "elders" (verse 17; the Greek word is *presbuteros*). This may not have meant a specific office;

NOVEMBER 3   LESSON 10

later (verse 28) he calls them "guardians" (RSV) (KJV: "overseers"). But the more common translation of the term (*episcopos*) is "bishop." The point is that we'd better not make too much over fine distinctions in these formative years of the church's government. Let's just say it was the leaders of the church and let it go at that.

But let's add that it must have been specially important to Paul to talk to them, because given the distance between Miletus and Ephesus (about thirty miles), it would have taken at least three days to get the message to them that Paul needed them, and for them to make the journey.

A Healthy Goodbye (Acts 20:18-36)

Let's take a look at Paul's speech to the Ephesian leaders, verse by verse. It doesn't have much theology in it; it's mostly personal stuff, but that's what makes it so meaningful for us.

Verses 18-21: We've had a long time together, and I've tried to be a faithful preacher to you all.

Verses 22-23: I don't know what will happen next, but I feel in the Spirit that heavy things are ahead.

Verse 24: I'm not worried; indeed, I welcome a chance to minister in such circumstances.

Verse 25: The important thing is that we are probably saying goodbye for the last time.

Verses 26-27: Therefore I want to leave you with a clean slate on my record; I've never pulled my punches with you.

Verse 28: So you're in charge now; take the responsibility for leadership and feed the church (compare John 21:17).

Verse 29: There are going to be plenty of wolves about (compare Matthew 10:16).

Verse 30: Some of the troublemakers will be your own people.

Verse 31: Therefore, be alert; I never promised you a rose garden.

Verse 32: But I'm not worried about you; you are in God's hands.

Verses 33-34: I'm glad you can't accuse me of preaching for the money. (Compare Paul with some of today's handsomely rewarded religious leaders.) I've been willing to handle my own needs.

Verse 35: The whole thing boils down to grace; it's better to give than to receive. Being a Christian means losing your life for others; you've seen my example, now live it yourselves.

Verses 36-38: Paul's speech ends with verse 35, but all the nonverbal stuff that happens after the talk is just as much if not more important. Listen to the physical acts: kneeling, weeping, embracing, kissing, looking at faces they may never see again. It is a beautiful picture. I, who was raised by dour Scots, am jealous of Paul's Mediterranean background, where it was not unseemly for people to let their feelings be freely expressed.

In the Cocoanut Grove fire studies, mentioned in "The Main Question," it was apparent that healthy grief work means being able to talk about the person you are losing, or have lost. We live in a society that denies death, pretends it is "only sleep," invents euphemisms for it ("passed away," "kicked the bucket"). But there is no way to avoid the harsh reality that as long as we live in this world, we will have tribulation (John 16:33).

Therefore, since we have many partings to face, we can learn from Paul to do it with passion and compassion. As Jesus wept in the garden in

FIRST QUARTER

anticipation of his death, and as Paul wept with the leaders of the Ephesian church, so must you and I weep together. For we too do not know if we will ever see each other again in this world. Let's have some flowers for the living. Let's speak loving truths to one another. A friend of mine once said to me, on the occasion of his wife's death, "We never thought this would happen to us." What incredible blindness! It will happen to us all. Let's then begin to do good grief work with one another, starting now.

Helping Adults Become Involved—Ronald E. Schlosser

Preparing to Teach

The time of holy fellowship Paul shared with the elders from Ephesus was a high point in his life. Christian workers count it a priceless reward when they are privileged to be in the presence of colleagues with whom their lives are eternally bound by a common devotion to Christ. These elders would not have given such devotion to a stranger, however eminent. Some of them had been won to Christ by Paul's ministry. They had accepted official responsibility in the church at his invitation. He had spent over two years teaching them. They had watched him at close range. He had won their respect. When he asked them to meet him in Miletus, there was no hesitation. They walked the thirty-plus miles each way to greet him—and to say a final goodbye.

In today's lesson we will be looking at this farewell meeting between Paul and his Ephesian friends. But before doing this, you may want to review the events that transpired following the conclusion of last week's scripture. Read the account of Paul's encounter with the silversmiths, recorded in Acts 19:21-41. Then, with a map in hand, trace Paul's travels mentioned in Acts 20:1-17.

Prior to the session, copy the following questions on the chalkboard:

1. No life well lived is without grief—agree or disagree?
2. Is there such a thing as "good grief"?
3. How should Christians handle grief?

These questions will be used in the opening activity when you introduce the main question. Also have pencils and paper on hand, for use later in the session.

There are two main learning goals for today: (1) to explore the meaning of grief and how best to deal with it as Christians and (2) to be encouraged to continue one's Christian service no matter what the cost.

After introducing the main question, you may want to develop the lesson using the following outline:

    I. Setting the scene
   II. Examining Paul's message
      A. Confession: Paul's account of his discipleship
      B. Concern: Paul's recognition of dangers he will face
      C. Caution: Paul's warning of adversity ahead
      D. Commendation: Paul's blessing and promise
  III. Coming to conclusions

NOVEMBER 3   LESSON 10

Carefully read the sections "As You Read the Scripture" and "The Scripture and the Main Question." These form the heart of the lesson. The ideas, insights, and suggestions in these sections should be employed throughout your lesson plan.

Introducing the Main Question

Begin the session by referring to the comments by Dr. McGeachy in the section "The Main Question." Point out the three questions you have written on the chalkboard, which are taken from Dr. McGeachy's comments. Ask the class to divide into groups of two or three to discuss these questions for about five minutes. Then call everyone together for feedback. It doesn't matter if the groups have not addressed every question or have not come to any consensus in their answers. Indicate there will be an opportunity at the end of the session to look at the questions again, after there has been input from the Bible study.

Developing the Lesson

I. Setting the scene

Remind the class of where the lesson ended last week, and briefly summarize the events recorded in Acts 19:21-41. Then, to set the scene for Paul's meeting with the Ephesian elders, read aloud Acts 20:1-17, sharing the comments of Drs. Winters and McGeachy on these verses. Trace Paul's travels on your classroom Bible map, noting such places as Corinth, Philippi, Troas (where Eutychus fell asleep), Assos, Mitylene, Chios, Samos, and finally Miletus. Underscore Paul's desire to meet with the church leaders of Ephesus, noting why he had so much affection for them.

II. Examining Paul's message

Ask the members to gather again into the groups of two or three they were in earlier. Indicate that they should read Acts 20:18-35, either aloud or silently, and then pick out four or five important points that Paul makes in his message to the elders. They should state these points in their own words, jotting them down on paper, which you will provide.

Allow about ten minutes for this small group study, then call the class together for a time of sharing. If responses are slow in coming, use the following as one way to highlight Paul's thoughts:

A. Confession: Paul's account of his discipleship

Paul reminds his Ephesian friends that his life among them was known to all and that it was characterized by humility, tearful concern, trials, and the faithful proclamation of the Word of life.

B. Concern: Paul's recognition of dangers he will face

Paul knew that unforeseen troubles were in store for him, but he assured his friends that the troubles meant nothing to him. His whole life had been devoted to the cause of Christ, and that would continue to be his goal no matter what came his way.

C. Caution: Paul's warning of adversity ahead

Paul also saw difficult days coming for the church. It is the responsibility of shepherds to care for their flock, to protect them from evil marauders that would seek to divide and conquer.

FIRST QUARTER

D. Commendation: Paul's blessing and promise
Even as Paul stated it, his Ephesian friends knew from their own experience that a life of service is a life of riches and happiness, both in this life and the next.

After the members have shared their own ideas, read Dr. McGeachy's summation of this passage. Then read aloud Acts 20:36-38, noting the emotionally charged scene described. Discuss the benefits and dangers of getting involved in highly emotional situations.

Helping Class Members Act

III. Coming to conclusions
Return to the questions the class discussed at the beginning of the session. In light of the Bible study just completed, what conclusions can we make about handling grief? Is grief a part of a well-lived life? What is the difference between "good grief" and "bad grief"?

Perhaps there are class members who would be willing to share their own experiences with grief, either their own or that of people they know. Or you might deal with public expression of grief. For example, at a funeral, is it helpful for a grieving family to be surrounded by openly grieving friends? Should Christians attempt to fight back tears in order to bring comfort and encouragement to the grievers?

Conclude the session by reading the final paragraph of Dr. McGeachy's comments. Perhaps the class might suggest ways we can "begin to do good grief work with each other."

Planning for Next Sunday

The background scripture for next week is rather long: Acts 21:17-40; 22:25–23:11. Ask your members to read it carefully and consider whether Paul made the right decision to go to Jerusalem.

LESSON 11   NOVEMBER 10

Facing Crises

Background Scripture: Acts 21:17-40; 22:25–23:11

The Main Question—Pat McGeachy

Paul never intended to start a new religion. He was a reformer, not a revolutionary. The same can be said for many of our heroes:

Jesus did not set out to found the Christian Church; he set out to call Israel to its true heritage.

Martin Luther did not set out to found the Lutheran Church; he set out to call the medieval Catholic church to its true heritage.

NOVEMBER 10   LESSON 11

John Wesley did not set out to found the Methodist Church; he set out to call the Church of England to its true heritage.

We could name others; all the great reformers wanted to preserve that which was right and good in their traditions.

As proof of his own thoughts along these lines, Paul attempted (Acts 21:17-26) to purify himself according to the ancient traditions of Israel. He was not doing this merely for political reasons, although he clearly had a political purpose, but because he was identifying in truth with the religion of his ancestors.

But they would not have it; he came to his own, and his own people received him not (John 1:11). So Paul, a Hebrew of the Hebrews and a Pharisee of the Pharisees (Philippians 3:4-6), attempted to be true to his heritage. He wanted to say loud and clear that he was not attempting to "start a new religion." He did his best to follow their suggestion that he "purify himself."

So when those who would push him back to classical Judaism appeared to be winning the day, Paul spoke in Greek (21:37) and gained the attention of the tribune. From then on, he was in the hands of the secular authorities and was eventually to arrive in Rome. We have to ask with Paul our main question, namely: When do you decide that you have to make the break? He had tried to be both Jew and Christian, but since that wasn't going to work, he must side with Christ alone. When do you and I draw the line?

Selected Scripture

King James Version

Acts 21:26-33; 37-39

26 Then Paul took the men, and the next day purifying himself with them entered into the temple, to signify the accomplishment of the days of purification, until that an offering should be offered for every one of them.

27 And when the seven days were almost ended, the Jews which were of Asia, when they saw him in the temple, stirred up all the people, and laid hands on him,

28 Crying out, Men of Israel, help: This is the man, that teacheth all *men* every where against the people, and the law, and this place: and further brought Greeks also into the temple, and hath polluted this holy place.

29 (For they had seen before with him in the city Trophimus an Ephesian, whom they supposed that Paul had brought into the temple.)

30 And all the city was moved,

Revised Standard Version

Acts 21:26-33; 37-39

26 Then Paul took the men, and the next day he purified himself with them and went into the temple, to give notice when the days of purification would be fulfilled and the offering presented for every one of them.

27 When the seven days were almost completed, the Jews from Asia, who had seen him in the temple, stirred up all the crowd, and laid hands on him, 28 crying out, "Men of Israel, help! This is the man who is teaching men everywhere against the people and the law and this place; moreover he also brought Greeks into the temple, and he has defiled this holy place." 29 For they had previously seen Trophimus the Ephesian with him in the city, and they supposed that Paul had brought him into the temple. 30 Then all the city was aroused, and the people ran togeth-

FIRST QUARTER

and the people ran together: and they took Paul, and drew him out of the temple: and forthwith the doors were shut.

31 And as they went about to kill him, tidings came unto the chief captain of the band, that all Jerusalem was in an uproar.

32 Who immediately took soldiers and centurions, and ran down unto them: and when they saw the chief captain and the soldiers, they left beating of Paul.

33 Then the chief captain came near, and took him, and commanded *him* to be bound with two chains; and demanded who he was, and what he had done.

er; they seized Paul and dragged him out of the temple, and at once the gates were shut. 31 And as they were trying to kill him, word came to the tribune of the cohort that all Jerusalem was in confusion. 32 He at once took soldiers and centurions, and ran down to them; and when they saw the tribune and the soldiers, they stopped beating Paul. 33 Then the tribune came up and arrested him, and ordered him to be bound with two chains. He inquired who he was and what he had done.

37 And as Paul was to be led into the castle, he said unto the chief captain, May I speak unto thee? Who said, Canst thou speak Greek?

38 Art not thou that Egyptian, which before these days madest an uproar, and leddest out into the wilderness four thousand men that were murderers?

39 But Paul said, I am a man *which am* a Jew of Tarsus, *a city* in Cilicia, a citizen of no mean city: and, I beseech thee, suffer me to speak unto the people.

37 As Paul was about to be brought into the barracks, he said to the tribune, "May I say something to you?" And he said, "Do you know Greek? 38 Are you not the Egyptian, then, who recently stirred up a revolt and led the four thousand men of the Assassins out into the wilderness?" 39 Paul replied, "I am a Jew, from Tarsus in Cilicia, a citizen of no mean city; I beg you, let me speak to the people."

Key Verse: **The night following the Lord stood by him and said, Be of good cheer, Paul: for as thou hast testified of me in Jerusalem, so must thou bear witness also at Rome. (Acts 23:11)**

Key Verse: **The following night the Lord stood by him and said, "Take courage, for as you have testified about me at Jerusalem, so you must bear witness also at Rome." (Acts 23:11)**

As You Read the Scripture—Michael Winters

Acts 21:17-26. The first stop in Jerusalem was at James's. The elders gathered there to hear Paul recount his evangelistic activities among the Gentiles.

Because it was believed that Paul taught the Jews among the Gentiles not to circumcise their sons, Jerusalem was a very dangerous place for Paul, as he had been warned (21:4, 10-12).

Paul took the Nazirite vow in hopes of demonstrating his earnest commitment to his Judaic roots.

NOVEMBER 10　　　　　　　　　　　　　　　　　LESSON 11

Verse 26. In fulfilling the vow of separation to the Lord, the law required of the Nazarite the following offerings: unblemished yearlings, both a male lamb for a burnt offering and an ewe as a sin offering; an unblemished ram as a peace offering; a basket of unleavened bread; cakes of fine flour mixed with oil; unleavened wafers spread with oil; cereal and drink offerings (Numbers 6:13-15). This would have been rather costly. Paul was advised to pay the expenses of the four men who were to join him in the Nazirite vow (verse 24).

Verses 27-28. As he had been warned by the prophet Agabus, the Jews at Jerusalem arose to persecute Paul (verses 10-11). Actually, it was the Jews of Asia visiting Jerusalem who fanned the flames of violence against Paul. These Asian Jews were those who before had hampered Paul, perhaps in Ephesus. Their charges against Paul were untrue, as Paul never took any liberties against Judaism, except those allowed in the letter from the Jerusalem council, which permitted Gentiles to become Christians without first submitting to the Jewish rite of circumcision (Acts 15:23b-29). It is very possible that Paul brought the Gentile Trophimus (verse 29) into the temple as far as the Court of the Gentiles. This would have been allowed. Much more serious would have been taking the Gentile into the temple proper. This, apparently, was the Asians' accusation.

Verse 29. Trophimus was one of the Asians who accompanied Paul on the last leg of this third missionary journey (Acts 20:4).

Verse 30. It is not likely that all the city turned against Paul. There are those who by conscience could not have participated in this kind of violence, especially the brothers and sisters of the church who welcomed Paul into Jerusalem (verse 17). Still, there were enough who became enraged over the slander of the Asians that Paul's life was in jeopardy.

Verses 31-33. The tribune, in charge of a Roman division of as many as six hundred soldiers, was alerted to the disruption. In order to regain order, the tribune arrested Paul.

Verses 33, 38. Paul was bound in double chains because the tribune believed Paul to be one of the Assassins, a terroristic network seeking Judean independence from Rome.

Verses 37, 38a. In the Greek language, Paul declared that he was not one of the Assassins, but a Jew from Cilicia.

Verses 39b-40. Paul was granted an opportunity to speak to his persecutors, and he did so in Hebrew so there would be no mistake that he was serious about his own Judaic roots.

Acts 22: 25-29. Paul was detained for flogging until he declared his Roman citizenship. It was illegal for a Roman citizen to be beaten.

Acts 21:30–23:11. The tribune arranged for a hearing before the chief priests, during which Paul was insubordinate to the high priest. But when he seized the opportunity to pit the two major sects, Sadducees and Pharisees, against each other, Paul was detained again, this time for his protection. It was while he was in custody that Paul experienced the call to go to Rome.

The Scripture and the Main Question—Pat McGeachy

An Act of Purification (Acts 21:17-26)

There are difficulties with this passage. It is not clear exactly what sacrifice Paul was asked to participate in, but we will assume that it was a rite of cleansing related to the vows of a Nazirite (Numbers 6:13-20). He may have gone through the whole process himself, because we know that he had recently taken such a vow (Acts 18:18), or he may simply have been underwriting the expenses of the four men; to do so was considered a sign of piety. But the more important question is, *Why* did he do it? Obviously James wanted him to help put to rest the rumors among the Jews of Jerusalem that Paul was encouraging good Jews not to undergo circumcision. (It was to prevent just such talk that Paul had had Timothy circumcised; see Acts 16:3.)

We can only conclude that this is all a part of Paul's continued willingness to be "all things to all" (1 Corinthians 9:22). He had made his position clear to the Corinthians (9:19-20): "For though I am free from all men, I have made myself a slave to all, that I might win the more. To the Jews I became as a Jew, in order to win Jews; to those under the law I became as one under the law—though not being myself under the law—that I might win those under the law." We are well aware that Paul would have been very angry at his Gentile converts if he found them drifting into legalism. Look at how upset he sounds in the letter to the Galatians (3:1, 5:1)! He is thus not condoning a legalistic life-style, but he is showing respect for those who have respect for the law. Though he is a Christian, Paul is still a Pharisee (Acts 23:6) and is certainly no libertine.

In a way, Paul's action here makes us think of what Jesus said in the Sermon on the Mount (Matthew 5:17-18): "Think not that I have come to abolish the law and the prophets; I have come not to abolish them but to fulfil them. For truly, I say to you, till heaven and earth pass away, not an iota, not a dot, will pass from the law until all is accomplished." The law is still our good "schoolmaster" (Galatians 3:24—RSV: "custodian") and to be respected. The point is, we do not have to fulfill it; it has already been fulfilled in Jesus Christ.

At any rate, Paul was trying to be a good Jew and to dispel any notion that he was subversive to his ancestral traditions. In this respect he was using the same logic that he employed in writing to the Romans and the Corinthians about the eating of meat that had been offered to idols (1 Corinthians 8; Romans 14:1–15:5; see especially Romans 15:1). It is one thing to make legalistic demands on oneself or others; it is quite another to keep oneself legally pure for the sake of others.

The Fight at the Temple (Acts 21:27-40)

If James and Paul had thought Paul's purification would keep him out of trouble, they were certainly disappointed. At any rate, Paul's enemies were not impressed with his attempt to act like a good Jew. Aided by other Jews from Asia and encouraged by rumors (such as the fact that he had been seen with an Egyptian), they seized Paul and were about to kill him. The tribune, whose job it was to keep the peace, bound Paul and "rescued" him at the last minute. (Have you ever noticed how it is usually the person who didn't start the fight who gets penalized by the referee?) The scene was one of such confusion that the authorities could make no sense of it, but suddenly, in the midst of the shouting, the tribune was astonished to hear some Greek words.

Greek was the language of commerce and trade and for all communication among foreigners in those days, just as French was during the

NOVEMBER 10   LESSON 11

Renaissance and as English is rapidly becoming in the world today. On hearing Greek, the tribune first sought to identify Paul with someone on his "most wanted" list, an Egyptian who had been stirring up trouble. But Paul identified himself both as a Jew and a citizen of Tarsus and was allowed to speak to the people.

The Defense Before the Barracks (Acts 22:1-24)

This section is not included in our background scripture for this week, but it should be read, for it gives us yet one more account of Paul's conversion, and reminds us how intensely personal his faith is. He is not using logic or philosophy in his explanation; he doesn't even argue from Scripture; he is simply talking about his own personal religious experience.

But they wouldn't let him finish. As soon as he began to talk about how Jesus had sent him to the Gentiles (22:21-22), they went into a righteous frenzy, which led the tribune to resort to police brutality (verse 24) to try to beat the truth out of them.

A Citizen of Rome (Acts 22:25-30)

This time Paul is saved by appealing to his Roman citizenship. Unlike the tribune, who had bought his papers, Paul had been born of parents who were citizens. (Some say they had perhaps received their citizenship from Mark Anthony, as a reward for their help during his campaign in Palestine.) At any rate, it makes the tribune think twice about beating him; instead, he decided to get at the truth by another way, one not strictly legal but less embarrassing than charges of brutality to a citizen. He orders the leaders of the Sanhedrin to come and make clear what charges they have against them. It was not strictly a trial, because it is doubtful that Lysias (we know his name from 23:26) would have referred the matter to the Jews rather than the Roman governor, and besides, Paul has the opening words.

Before the High Priest (Acts 23:1-11)

Before Paul could get out more than a sentence, he was struck on the mouth, to which he replied in fury. When he found out that it was the high priest he has called a "double-dyed hypocrite" (that's what "whitewashed wall" means), Paul apologized and then turned the whole thing into a free-for-all by getting the Pharisees and Sadducees to arguing among themselves over the doctrine of the resurrection, a matter they had been disagreeing over for years. The end result was another violent confrontation from which Paul was once more rescued by arrest and carried into the military barracks.

That night, Luke tells us, "the Lord stood by him" and called him to take courage.

You'll Have to Throw Me Out

All of his life Paul remained a Jew, though he was in the end vilified, beaten, and rejected by his own people. Today, some Jews who have become Christians like to speak of themselves as "completed Jews," for they feel that Jesus, being the fulfillment of messianic prophecy, is what their Judaism was leading them toward all their lives. So Paul believed and taught, attempting in every one of his missionary journeys to go first to the synagogues. He liked to say that the good news of Jesus came "to the Jew first, and also to the Greek" (Romans 1:16). His last days in Jerusalem followed closely those of his Lord: dragged from one hearing to another, to the Romans and to the Jews. But unlike Jesus, Paul didn't keep his mouth shut (Isaiah 53:7). He went out kicking and screaming, so to speak, until the very end, hoping and believing that all Israel would believe the gospel (see Romans 11:25-26).

Until the end of his life, John Wesley remained a priest of the Church of England. Martin Luther and John Knox would have still been priests of Rome if they had not been excommunicated. The main question for me is easy to answer this week: They'll have to throw me out! I mean by that that the church to which I belong is a part of the one holy catholic church, and as long as I am around, I am going to do my best to see to it that my church is true to the truth. I don't intend to start a revolution, but to brighten the corner where I am.

I remember once seeing two churches on a rural highway. One bore the sign

THE TRUE CHURCH
OF JESUS CHRIST

while on the other were the words

THE *ONLY* TRUE CHURCH
OF JESUS CHRIST, INC.

I don't know what started that fight, but if they had been more like Paul, they might have stayed together until the coming of the day when every knee should bow before the one true Lord (Philippians 2:10).

Helping Adults Become Involved—Ronald E. Schlosser

Preparing to Teach

When Paul was making his farewell to the Ephesian elders, he mentioned that he had been warned by the Holy Spirit in every city "that imprisonment and afflictions" were ahead of him (Acts 20:23). Once again, while in Tyre waiting for the ship's cargo to be unloaded, Paul was warned about going to Jerusalem. Moving on to Caesarea, Paul spent a few days with Philip, the evangelist, where the warning was dramatically underscored again by a prophet named Agabus (Acts 21:11). All at once Paul was deluged by the tearful pleas of his friends to give up the idea of his trip to Jerusalem. His response in Acts 21:13 is one of the greatest declarations of courage and commitment to be found anywhere. This moment of tearful struggle ends with the words, "The will of the Lord be done." It cannot help but remind us of Jesus' Gethsemane prayer, and his similar cry for the Father's will. Paul could face his Jerusalem because Jesus had so clearly shown the way.

In today's lesson we will go with Paul into that threatening city and see how he handled the trouble that befell him. In doing so, we will be focusing on two learning goals: (1) to consider at what point we must take a stand concerning our faith, regardless of the risk, and (2) to determine to what

NOVEMBER 10   LESSON 11

extent we should "become all things to all persons" in order to relate to people to whom we are to be witnesses.

After introducing the main question, you might develop the lesson following this outline:

      I. The place of ritual and tradition
     II. Acting on one's convictions
    III. Insights for today

Carefully read the sections "As You Read the Scripture" and "The Scripture and the Main Question." These form the heart of the lesson. The ideas, insights, and suggestions in these sections should be employed throughout your lesson plan.

Introducing the Main Question

In the section "The Main Question," Dr. McGeachy points to times in the Bible and in church history when people had to take a stand concerning their beliefs. It may have involved breaking with tradition or doing something never done before. It usually involved risk and often resulted in persecution.

To get your class thinking about contemporary implications, raise some current issue that seems to divide "traditionalists" and "progressives." For example, there exists today a debate over the value of Christian rock music, particularly heavy metal rock. Youth workers who argue in favor of Christian rock say that this kind of music speaks to today's youth. By putting the gospel in the music idiom that appeals to the young, you are going to attract them and win them for Christ. Those opposed to such music say that this is an example of the world taking over and altering Christian values. This kind of music, they argue, is associated with the drug culture, loose sex, and even Satanism, and should not be a part of the Christian life-style.

What does your class think? Are traditional Christian values being threatened by so-called "Christian" rock music? In an effort to relate to youth, is it legitimate to try to put the gospel into new forms that youth can understand? At what point does one draw the line?

Don't allow the discussion to go beyond ten minutes. Your purpose is not to resolve this issue but to illustrate how persons with traditional values often disagree with people they feel are doing unorthodox and harmful things.

Developing the Lesson

I. The place of ritual and tradition

Tying in with the preceding discussion, refer to Paul's statement in 1 Corinthians 9:19-23, where he says he has "become all things to all men, that I might by all means save some." This may be the reason why he decided to go through the act of ritual purification described in today's scripture (Acts 21:17-26). What does your class think? See Dr. McGeachy's comments on this.

Ask: How important is it to keep traditions in religion? What values do traditions have? What dangers might rigid traditionalism bring? How do

FIRST QUARTER

you respond to such statements as "We always do it this way," or "Pastor So-and-So never did this"?

II. Acting on one's convictions

Read Acts 21:27-36 aloud. Did Paul anticipate such a thing would happen to him? Refer to the numerous warnings he had (see the opening paragraph above in "Preparing to Teach").

Ask: In light of all the warnings, why did Paul want to go to Jerusalem? (First, he wanted to attend the feast of Pentecost, as mentioned in Acts 20:16. This feast had a double significance for Paul. As a Jew, he would revere the feast as a time of great rejoicing and sacred obligation. As a Christian, he recognized Pentecost as the day God's Holy Spirit had come upon Christ's followers in a mighty way. Paul's own life in Christ had been kindled as a result of that Pentecost flame. Second, he wanted to share the good news of the spread of the Christian faith with the Jerusalem church—see Acts 21:19-20. What an uplifting experience that would be. Third, we know from Paul's letters—for example, 2 Corinthians 9—that he was carrying a considerable sum of money from the churches of the Gentile world as a gift to the Jerusalem church. It was important to him that the gift be presented and understood as an expression of love and concern Gentile Christians had for their fellow believers in Jerusalem.)

Read Acts 21:37-40, then remind the class that Paul's account of his conversion was referred to in the lesson for September 1. Continue readings Acts 22:22-23:11. Note Dr. McGeachy's comments on this passage.

Ask: In light of what happened to Paul and what was yet to come, do you think Paul should have gone to Jerusalem? Were there any alternatives? Underscore Paul's declaration in Acts 21:13-14.

Helping Class Members Act

III. Insights for today

What lessons can we learn from today's study? First, we need to determine to what extent we should adapt our Christian witness and the way we approach people to the cultural and social settings in which we find ourselves. Paul spoke Hebrew on one occasion and Greek on another, in each case to identify with the persons to whom he was speaking. He performed certain ritualistic acts in order to relate to Jewish Christians. He used his Roman citizenship to accomplish another purpose. How far should we follow the policy of becoming all things to all people in order to win some?

Second, at what point do we take a stand, lest we compromise our faith? There is just so much adaptation one can do. To determine that point is not easy. But whenever we reach that point, we should be ready like Paul to stand there, regardless of the consequences. Does your class agree? Why or why not?

Close with a prayer for God to grant us wisdom to know how best to share our Christian faith with others.

Planning for Next Sunday

The background Scripture for next week is Acts 25:13-26:32. Ask your class members to read it and then list the key events in their life that influenced their faith.

LESSON 12   NOVEMBER 17

Speaking Up for Your Faith

Background Scripture: Acts 25:13–26:32

The Main Question—Pat McGeachy

Most of us, when we hear the word "apology," think of somebody making excuses for something that he or she is ashamed of. But that is not the root meaning of the word. It does not mean "alibi" but, more properly, "explanation." In fact, one of the disciplines still taught in some theological seminaries is *apologetics,* meaning the art of explaining to others why you believe as you do.

Paul's speech before Agrippa is an apology of the sort we mean, and it is a dandy one. Some say he "almost persuaded" Agrippa to believe. Certainly Paul got the attention of the king, and though he didn't manage to convert him, he did convince him that he should be allowed to go to Rome, which is what he had asked for (25:12). Agrippa, as he was called here, held the full title of Herod Agrippa II and ruled after the death of his father, though not immediately, for he was only seventeen at the time, so the petty kingdom remained under a proconsul until Agrippa could be appointed in 50 A.D. Agrippa, like most of the Herods, was a friend of the Caesars and, by reputation, a wicked man. His sisters, Bernice and Drusilla, had an even worse reputation. Paul had nothing to lose, so he gave it his best shot and came away with his heart's desire; At last he was going to Rome.

In this week's lesson we will want to look at Paul's "apology" and see what we can learn that will make us more skilled in speaking up for our own beliefs. I sometimes hear today's young Christians say things like "I'm not sure what I believe." If you mean by that "There's a lot I'm uncertain about," then we can all agree with that. None of us knows it all. But if you mean "I have never really decided for myself what truly matters," then there is work for you to do.

We can sum up the main question for this week's lesson in a very few words: What do I truly believe, and why? From Paul's example we can begin to answer that for ourselves.

Selected Scripture

King James Version

Acts 26:1-8, 22-23, 27-29

1 Then Agrippa said unto Paul, Thou art permitted to speak for thyself. Then Paul stretched forth the hand, and answered for himself:

2 I think myself happy, king Agrippa, because I shall answer for myself this day before thee touching all the things whereof I am accused of the Jews:

Revised Standard Version

Acts 26:1-8, 22-23, 27-29

1 Agrippa said to Paul, "You have permission to speak for yourself." Then Paul stretched out his hand and made his defense:

2 "I think myself fortunate that it is before you, King Agrippa, I am to make my defense today against all the accusations of the Jews, 3 because you are especially familiar

FIRST QUARTER

3 Especially *because I know* thee to be expert in all customs and questions which are among the Jews: wherefore I beseech thee to hear me patiently.

4 My manner of life from my youth, which was at the first among mine own nation at Jerusalem, know all the Jews;

5 Which knew me from the beginning, if they would testify, that after the most straitest sect of our religion I lived a Pharisee.

6 And now I stand and am judged for the hope of the promise made of God unto our fathers:

7 Unto which *promise* our twelve tribes, instantly serving *God* day and night, hope to come. For which hope's sake, king Agrippa, I am accused of the Jews.

8 Why should it be thought a thing incredible with you, that God should raise the dead?

....

22 Having therefore obtained help of God, I continue unto this day, witnessing both to small and great, saying none other things than those which the prophets and Moses did say should come:

23 That Christ should suffer, *and* that he should be the first that should rise from the dead, and should shew light unto the people, and to the Gentiles.

....

27 King Agrippa, believest thou the prophets? I know that thou believest.

28 Then Agrippa said unto Paul, Almost thou persuadest me to be a Christian.

29 And Paul said, I would to God, that not only thou, but also all that hear me this day, were both almost, and altogether such as I am, except these bonds.

4 "My manner of life from my youth, spent from the beginning among my own nation and at Jerusalem, is known by all the Jews. 5 They have known for a long time, if they are willing to testify, that according to the strictest party of our religion I have lived as a Pharisee. 6 And now I stand here on trial for hope in the promise made by God to our fathers, 7 to which our twelve tribes hope to attain, as they earnestly worship night and day. And for this hope I am accused by Jews, O king! 8 Why is it thought incredible by any of you that God raises the dead?"

....

22 "To this day I have had the help that comes from God, and so I stand here testifying both to small and great, saying nothing but what the prophets and Moses said would come to pass: 23 that the Christ must suffer, and that, by being the first to rise from the dead, he would proclaim light both to the people and to the Gentiles."

....

27 "King Agrippa, do you believe the prophets? I know that you believe." 28 And Agrippa said to Paul, "In a short time you think to make me a Christian!" 29 And Paul said, "Whether short or long, I would to God that not only you but also all who hear me this day might become such as I am—except for these chains."

NOVEMBER 17 LESSON 12

Key Verse: I continue unto this day, witnessing both to small and great, saying none other things than those which the prophets and Moses did say should come. (Acts 26:22)

Key Verse: To this day I have had the help that comes from God, and so I stand here testifying both to small and great, saying nothing but what the prophets and Moses said would come to pass. (Acts 26:22)

As You Read the Scripture—Michael Winters

There was no specified crime against the state to maintain Paul's detention (Acts 26:31*b*) in Caesarea (23:33). As the Jews became more desperate, their indictments against Paul increased. They had charged him falsely with "teaching . . . everywhere against the people and the law" and defiling the temple (21:28), and with being "a pestilent fellow, an agitator" and a Nazarene (verse 24:5). Paul was detained for more than two years under the administration of Governor Felix (24:27*a*). Governor Festus continued Felix's policy "to do the Jews a favor" (24:27*b*; 25:9*a*), keeping Paul's case before the Jews.

Acts 26:1. Agrippa was the great-grandson of Herod the Great, the king of Judea at the time of Jesus' birth. Agrippa became king by the appointment of the emperor, Claudius. His relationship with his sister, Bernice (25:13), was incestuous and considered scandalous.

Agrippa asked Festus to present Paul's case before him and his sister (25:22-23).

Verses 2-3. Perhaps Paul felt fortunate to appeal his case to Agrippa because he was able to speak to such a powerful person in the region. Agrippa's reign increased under two emperors, Claudius and Nero. Or perhaps Paul assumed that Agrippa was acquainted with Judaism because of his family's long service in the region, especially since Agrippa once was an advocate in Rome for the Jewish office of the high priest (although, it must be stated clearly, Agrippa was not a Jew).

Verses 4-5. Though Paul was born in Cilicia, he was thoroughly Jewish. He had been circumcised when he was eight days old, having been born of Jewish parents of the tribe of Benjamin. He was a Pharisee who was meticulously cautious to obey the entire Mosaic and Deuteronomic code (Acts 22:3; Philippians 3:5-6).

Verses 6-8. By the words "And now" in verse 6, he admitted that his zeal as a Jew was misdirected. He had now come face to face with the hope of the resurrection (verse 8). Paul had confused the hope of the Holy Spirit (Acts 2:38-39) and the messianic hope all of Israel expected with the hope of the resurrection, which was a partisan doctrine among the Jews, held mostly by the Pharisees (23:8). But not even the Pharisees were able to acknowledge Jesus' resurrection.

Verses 9-21. From his days as the chief persecutor of the church, Paul recounted his conversion on the Damascus road and divine commission to preach to the Gentiles. He clarified the real charge against him: declaring the God of the Jews to the Gentiles.

Verses 22-23. Paul affirmed the prophetic declarations: The Christ was to be the suffering servant, "despised and rejected . . . a man of sorrows . . . like a lamb that is led to the slaughter" (Isaiah 53:3-7), and, keeping in mind Paul's mission to the Gentiles, God had given Israel as "a covenant to the people, a light to the nations" (Isaiah 42:6*b*).

FIRST QUARTER

Verses 24-27. Paul is perceived as fanatical by both Festus and Agrippa, the first thinking him mad, the second being perhaps amused that Paul presumed to make him a Christian.

Verses 28-29. Paul's response to the smug Agrippa was that he desired to make him, Festus, Bernice, the military tribunes, and those prominent in the city, all present for Paul's defense, Christians (25:23).

Verses 30-32. Paul's defense is successful. He is deserving to be free. Yet by virtue of his appeal to Caesar (25:12), he is to be bound over to the Caesar's custody.

The Scripture and the Main Question—Pat McGeachy

The King Comes to Caesarea (Acts 25:13-23)

For more than two years Paul languished in the prison at Caesarea (24:27); finally he had been given a hearing before Festus, the new governor, and had appealed to Caesar (25:11-12). So he was about to go to Rome at last. But there remained one more hurdle: King Herod Agrippa.

Before pushing on with the story, let's get our names straight because they are confusing. For one thing, there are a number of places named Caesarea (just as there are a number of places in the United States named Washington, Lincoln, Monroe, Jefferson, etc.). The most prominent Caesarea in the Gospels was Caesarea Philippi, a lovely spot where the Jordan rises from the snows of Mount Hermon. It was there that Jesus heard Simon Peter's great confession (Matthew 16:13-20).

But this Caesarea is on the coast (and is therefore sometimes called Caesarea Maritima). It was an important port, with an artificial harbor built by Herod the Great that rivaled that of Athens. To this day it is an interesting place to visit, with the remains of an impressive aqueduct, a great amphitheater, and other buildings. It was a kind of second capital for Israel in Roman times (much as Tel Aviv became in the modern era). Paul was imprisoned there, probably for two reasons: One, he would be much safer from the angry forces in Jerusalem, and, two, it was the port from which he would eventually set sail to Rome.

As for King Agrippa, there were several of those too. The Agrippa of this lesson was the great-grandson of Herod the Great, the founder of Caesarea and the murderer of the children of Bethlehem (Matthew 2:16). Agrippa's father, Herod Agrippa I, had been a favorite of the Roman emperor Claudius, and young Agrippa was being educated in Rome with the emperor's children at the time of his father's death. Eventually he succeeded to the title of king.

Like all the Herods, Agrippa was a strange and wicked man. He had many strengths but was morally weak. The woman Bernice, who appears in the story as though she were his wife and queen, was actually his sister; this incestuous relationship was an abomination to the Jews, but they had to tolerate him as their ruler; he *was* fully familiar with Jewish customs, as had been his father before him.

Now he has come in great pomp to Caesarea, and Festus, struggling with keeping on good terms with the Jews (you know, he and Felix and all the other Roman authorities were a lot like Pontius Pilate; they had a hard time making up their minds) makes one more attempt to settle Paul's case properly by bringing him before the king. What will happen this time? Jesus had predicted (Matthew 10:18) that his followers would be dragged before governors and kings for his sake, and had promised that God would tell them what to say in such a time. And Paul needed little help, for he was a master speaker.

A friend of mine once told me that he had to preach before the Queen of England, who visited his parish in Scotland. He agonized over it for weeks, and then one day it came clear to him: "You idiot; every Sunday you preach before the King of Kings and you don't worry like this. Take it easy." So he did, and I'm sure the queen got more out of the sermon than she otherwise would have.

A Sermon Preached to a King (Acts 26:1-29)

Paul makes no apologies for his apology. He begins (verses 2-3) with some polite flattery to the king, reminding him that he has some familiarity with the traditions of his subjects. He then tells briefly (verses 4-5) of his upbringing as a pious young Jew and a strict Pharisee. Then (verses 6-8) he states his case in the firmest way, saying, in effect, "I am being tried for the very thing the Jews say that they have longed for all of their lives!"

He admits (verses 9-12) that he himself had refused to believe this glad good news when first he encountered it, and like his own enemies now, he had persecuted the church, believing it to be God's will that he should destroy it.

But then came the event (verses 13-15) by now thoroughly familiar to one who has been studying the book of the Acts: the Damascus road experience. In the last analysis, all his Pharisaical upbringing is cast aside as refuse (Philippians 3:8), and he puts the whole weight of his testimony on his personal relationship with Jesus Christ.

Then (verses 19-23) Paul tells how effective his witness has been to the people of the Gentile world, reaffirming the two main points with which he began, namely, that Christ has risen and that this is the very thing that the Hebrew Scriptures themselves had predicted.

Suddenly (verse 24), Festus interrupts with a guffaw: "You're crazy, Paul!" But Paul will not be dissuaded. He turns the argument again to Agrippa, reminding him that he is well trained in the prophets (verse 26). "I know you believe them," he says, asking, in effect, "Why not believe in the Christ to whom the prophets point?"

Agrippa's reply is difficult to translate. More than likely it should be read as sarcastic, as it appears in the Revised Standard Version, rather than as the "almost persuaded" found in the King James Version. But it was clear that Paul would have liked to convert the king. What do you suppose might have been the history of the rest of the world if he had?

And the Result (Acts 26:30-32)

After all the hearings and proceedings of the trial of Jesus, Pilate ended up saying, "I find no fault with this man" (Luke 23:4) and turned him over to others. Agrippa now does the same with Paul. "He is doing nothing to deserve death or imprisonment." So in a way, the speech was a success. Agrippa may not have been converted, but Paul was declared innocent of the charges of the Jews. No doubt Festus will report to Caesar that Paul is innocent, and this may mean that he will be acquitted by Caesar.

FIRST QUARTER

Unfortunately, the book of Acts ends before we find the answer to that question.

Apologizing

You and I might now to some good purpose ask ourselves, "What if I had to defend my faith before the king? (Or the Supreme Court, or the president?) Or if that is too frightening, try something closer to home: "What shall I say when my neighbor asks me what I believe?" I think there is some genuine guidance for us in Paul's apology to Agrippa and would like to conclude with a list of rules entitled "How to Defend Your Faith."

1. Don't be afraid to speak up. (Paul treated Agrippa with respect, as we should all to whom we witness, but he spoke plainly and with conviction.)
2. Start where the person is. (Paul began and ended by reminding Agrippa of his good understanding of the Scriptures.)
3. Know your Bible. (The central truth of Paul's argument is that Jesus is the fulfilment of the Scriptures.)
4. Tell about your own personal relationship to Jesus. (Paul spends a good bit of time talking about his own conversion. You don't want to clobber other people with your own spirituality, or bleed all over them with your past guilt, but the Christian faith can't be passed on as though it were a telegram or a mimeograph sheet. It is a highly personal experience and must be treated as such.
4. Give some examples (as Paul did) of the way the gospel has worked in other people's lives.
5. Above all, be yourself, prayerfully desiring the good of the one to whom you speak and relying on God to put the right words in your mouth.

In short, evangelism, the telling of the good news, is more than just talk. It is words, of course, as Paul used them here. But it is also deeds. And it is a matter of our life-style. What really almost persuaded Agrippa here was not the rhetoric but the courage, not the message but the man himself. Paul carried Christ with him (Philippians 1:21), and in every encounter those who met the apostle could see Jesus.

Finally, don't worry if you don't win. Even the greatest evangelist had a few rained out.

Helping Adults Become Involved—Ronald E. Schlosser

Preparing to Teach

As a result of his being taken into custody, the Apostle Paul had a chance to speak to several of the leading rulers of his day. And in almost every case, he made it an opportunity to tell about his faith. The question was raised in last week's lesson: Should Paul have insisted on going to Jerusalem at the risk of his life? One answer is that by doing so, he got the chance to witness to governors, kings, and presumably, even to Caesar himself.

Dr. McGeachy tells about a friend of his who agonized over preaching before the Queen of England. Suppose you had an opportunity to share

NOVEMBER 17 — LESSON 12

your faith with the president of the United States. How would you do it? What would you say? Would your testimony be different if you had to give it instead to the head of the Communist Party, or if you had to defend your faith before a Communist tribunal?

In today's lesson we will discover how Paul adapted his testimony to the situations in which he found himself. There are two primary learning goals: (1) to consider what Festus the governor might have written about Paul after hearing his defense before Agrippa and (2) to develop a set of guidelines for engaging in personal witnessing.

After introducing the "Main Question," you might follow this outline to develop the lesson:

  I. Setting the scene
 II. Paul's defense before Agrippa
     A. Personal credentials
     B. Vendetta against Christians
     C. Conversion and calling
     D. Declaration of faith
III. Reactions to Paul's testimony
 IV. Guidelines for witnessing

Carefully read the sections "As You Read the Scripture" and "The Scripture and the Main Question." These form the heart of the lesson. The ideas, insights, and suggestions in these sections should be employed throughout your lesson plan.

You will need pencils and paper to distribute to your class for the opening activity. Prior to the session, work on that activity yourself, in order to help your class do the same thing.

Introducing the Main Question

Begin by asking the class this question: If you had to list key events in your life that influenced your faith, what would they be? Refer to "The Main Question" presented by Dr. McGeachy, noting that in Paul's "apology" before Agrippa, he talked about his own faith journey.

Draw a line on the chalkboard to represent a time line of your life. Locate points along the line that signify incidents that affected your faith, either positively or negatively. You may wish to indicate high points with marks above the line, and low points with marks below the line, thus:

Briefly share your faith journey. Then distribute pencils and paper and ask the members to plot out their own "faith lines." Again, these are incidents or events that affected their faith one way or the other, such as their conversion experience, a vocational commitment, marriage, illness, death of a loved one, and the like.

FIRST QUARTER

Allow about five minutes for this individual reflecting and drawing, then move on to the next activity, indicating that you will be getting back to these faith lines later in the session.

Developing the Lesson

I. Setting the scene

Do a quick summation of Acts 23:16–25:27, noting the plot on Paul's life, his trip to Caesarea, his appearances before Felix and Festus, and Festus's desire to have King Agrippa hear his case. See the comments by Drs. Winters and McGeachy for background. Both commentators give helpful information about King Agrippa.

II. Paul's defense before Agrippa

Ask the class to read silently Acts 26:1-23 and suggest an outline of Paul's defense. The following outline, derived from Dr. McGeachy's comments, can form the basis of your study.

  A. Personal credentials

Compare Paul's description of himself with his statement in Philippians 3:4-7. Why do you suppose Paul emphasized his being a Pharisee and his belief in the resurrection of the dead? (Remember that Agrippa was familiar with the customs of the Jews and that a similar reference to the resurrection before the Sanhedrin had prompted the Pharisees to acquit him—see Acts 23:6-9.)

  B. Vendetta against Christians

Why did Paul bring up his earlier persecution of the followers of Jesus? Was he proud of this episode in his life? (He wanted to underscore his piety, his zealous desire to do God's will, and his high regard for Jewish traditions. After all, he was being accused by the Jews of violating their laws—see Acts 24:5-6; 25:8, 18-19.)

  C. Conversion and calling

This account of Paul's conversion was referred to in lesson 1. When comparing it with his defense before the crowd at the time of his arrest (Acts 22:3-22), we note that in this case he was not cut off after saying he was called to bring the good news of Jesus to the Gentiles. His message was one of forgiveness and reconciliation.

  D. Declaration of faith

Paul amplifies his message and ties it to the reason he was arrested. What does your class think of Paul's testimony?

III. Reactions to Paul's testimony

Read aloud Acts 26:24-32. What were the reactions of Festus and Agrippa? Speculate what Festus might have written about Paul in his letter to Caesar (see Acts 25:26-27). Consider what can be gleaned from the scripture about Festus's character—his ability (or inability) to make a decision and take action, his fairness, his open-mindedness, his political acumen, his religious concepts. Note the conclusion of Agrippa, Festus, and the others who had heard Paul (Acts 26:31).

Discuss Agrippa's comment in verse 28 about trying to make him a Christian. Was Agrippa being sarcastic, or was he impressed by Paul's zeal and sincerity? Certainly Paul's statement in verse 22 about receiving God's help to carry out his ministry must have made some impression on the king.

NOVEMBER 24　　　　　　　　　　　　　　　　　　LESSON 13

Helping Class Members Act

IV. Guidelines for witnessing

Ask the class members to look again at their faith lines done at the beginning of the session. Which of the events marked on them would they use when sharing their faith with another person? In an earlier lesson you encouraged class members to share their testimonies. Are there others who would like to share their faith with the rest of the class now?

Conclude by asking the class to list guidelines to follow when witnessing. Refer to the list Dr. McGeachy has compiled under the heading "How to Defend Your Faith."

Planning for Next Sunday

Ask the class to read Acts 27 and 28 and to speculate on what they would like to do when they retire.

LESSON 13　　　　　　　　　　　　　　　　　　NOVEMBER 24

Proclaiming the Gospel

Background Scripture: Acts 27–28

The Main Question—Pat McGeachy

"And so we came to Rome" (Acts 28:14). It was not exactly a triumphant entry. Paul was arriving a prisoner and under house arrest, having barely survived a severe storm and a shipwreck. And yet it was a mighty moment in its own way. Members of the congregation in Rome (28:15) came for miles down the road to greet him, so that Paul "thanked God and took courage." At long last, after many miles, many difficulties, many congregations, many friends, many enemies, he is arriving in the center of the known universe, the capital of Caesar's empire. The great missionary and the great city have finally met.

We do not know what became of Paul after this. The book of Acts ends here, with Paul preaching and teaching, and awaiting whatever fate God has in store for him. According to most traditions he eventually met his death there, a martyr for the Christ he had so faithfully served. Did this happen at the end of the two years mentioned in 28:30? Or was he released this time to minister further until a second arrest? There is even a tradition that he went on to Spain with the gospel before his life ended.

We know nothing of this for sure. But there is one thing we *do* know for sure: He never stopped proclaiming the gospel. There is a temptation for all of us, especially as our lives near their close (I'm guessing Paul to be in his early sixties at this time) to want to retire, to give up, to "take a well-deserved and much-needed rest." And certainly one ought not to keep on at sixty

FIRST QUARTER

behaving like a thirty-year-old. But we should never "retire" in the sense of giving up. These years have the opportunity to be the best and most creative of all our years. They may (certainly, will) involve physical decline and eventual death. But though our life-style will change, we must not retire *from* life but *to* new beginnings. Our main question: Will our last years be filled with promise?

Selected Scripture

King James Version

Acts 28:21-31

21 And they said unto him, We neither received letters out of Judaea concerning thee, neither any of the brethren that came shewed or spake any harm of thee.

22 But we desire to hear of thee what thou thinkest: for as concerning this sect, we know that every where it is spoken against.

23 And when they had appointed him a day, there came many to him into *his* lodging; to whom he expounded and testified the kingdom of God, persuading them concerning Jesus, both out of the law of Moses, and *out of* the prophets, from morning till evening.

24 And some believed the things which were spoken, and some believed not.

25 And when they agreed not among themselves, they departed, after that Paul had spoken one word, Well spake the Holy Ghost by Esaias the prophet unto our fathers,

26 Saying, Go unto this people, and say, Hearing ye shall hear, and shall not understand; and seeing ye shall see, and not perceive:

27 For the heart of this people is waxed gross, and their ears are dull of hearing, and their eyes have they closed; lest they should see with *their* eyes, and hear with *their* ears, and understand with *their* heart, and should be converted, and I should heal them.

Revised Standard Version

Acts 28:21-31

21 And they said to him, "We have received no letters from Judea about you, and none of the brethren coming here has reported or spoken any evil about you. 22 But we desire to hear from you what your views are; for with regard to this sect we know that everywhere it is spoken against."

23 When they had appointed a day for him, they came to him at his lodging in great numbers. And he expounded the matter to them from morning till evening, testifying to the kingdom of God and trying to convince them about Jesus both from the law of Moses and from the prophets. 24 And some were convinced by what he said, while others disbelieved. 25 So, as they disagreed among themselves, they departed, after Paul had made one statement: "The Holy Spirit was right in saying to your fathers through Isaiah the prophet:

26 'Go to this people, and say,
You shall indeed hear but never understand,
and you shall indeed see but never perceive.

27 For this people's heart has grown dull,
and their ears are heavy of hearing,
and their eyes they have closed;
lest they should perceive with their eyes,
and hear with their ears,
and understand with their heart,
and turn for me to heal them.'

NOVEMBER 24　　　　　　　　　　　　　LESSON 13

28 Be it known therefore unto you, that the salvation of God is sent unto the Gentiles, and *that* they will hear it.

29 And when he had said these words, the Jews departed, and had great reasoning among themselves.

30 And Paul dwelt two whole years in his own hired house, and received all that came in unto him,

31 Preaching the kingdom of God, and teaching those things which concern the Lord Jesus Christ, with all confidence, no man forbidding him.

28 Let it be known to you then that this salvation of God has been sent to the Gentiles; they will listen."

30 And he lived there two whole years at his own expense, and welcomed all who came to him, 31 preaching the kingdom of God and teaching about the Lord Jesus Christ quite openly and unhindered.

Key Verse: Paul dwelt two whole years... preaching the kingdom of God, and teaching those things which concern the Lord Jesus Christ, with all confidence, no man forbidding him. (Acts 28:30-31)

Key Verse: He lived there two whole years ... preaching the kingdom of God and teaching about the Lord Jesus Christ quite openly and unhindered. (Acts 28:30-31)

As You Read the Scripture—Michael Winters

After an adventuresome journey (Acts 27:1–28:14*a*) under Roman custody in order to stand before Caesar to defend himself against insubstantial Jewish charges, Paul arrived in Rome (28:14*b*), where he was held under house arrest (28:16).

Acts 28:21. By Paul's invitation, the Jews of Rome came to Paul (verses 17 and 23). Apparently, those assigned to prosecute Paul's case failed to file the charges. Or perhaps they defaulted because there was no case in the first place (26:31).

Verses 22, 31. In Acts 17:21, the Athenians were opened-minded but their commitment was academic. On the other hand, the Roman Jews expressed an open-minded desire to hear Paul, though they were doubtful about Christianity.

Christianity was first considered a sect of Judaism. The Pharisees and Sadducees were also Jewish sects. The Roman Jews had heard only evil things about Christianity and thus believed it was a heretical sect.

Verse 23. Rather than appealing to his personal experience, especially his conversion on the Damascus road (Acts 9:1-22), Paul meets them on common ground: the law of Moses and the prophets. From this very Jewish foundation, Paul introduced Jesus Christ to the Roman Jews.

Verse 24. Some of Paul's audience heard and understood and believed. Others heard, but the message was jumbled and incoherent.

Verses 25*a* and 29. It is interesting that the Roman Jews, rather than taking issue with Paul, as they did in so many other places when he won converts to Jesus (Acts 13:45; 17:4-5*a*), took issue among themselves. Some ancient texts add verse 29, "And when he had said these words, the Jews departed, holding much dispute among themselves," a reprise of verse 25*a*.

FIRST QUARTER

Verses 25b and 27. Paul understood Isaiah 6:9-10 (Isaiah's commission to prophecy) as the reason the Jews rejected the gospel of Christ. It is a difficult passage, in that it seems to make God the cause of the Jewish failure to hear and to see and to understand. In Isaiah 6:10 God says to the prophet, "Go . . . make the heart of this people fat." But when Paul quotes it, the "dull" heart is not of God's doing but rather reflects his view of a basic immaturity of Jewish faith (see also 2 Corinthians 3:12-17, where Paul alludes to the story of Moses' veil, oddly turning it into a metaphor of Jewish inability to see the gospel freedom of Christ).

Verse 28. Ultimately, because the Jews will not hear and will not see and will not understand, the gospel is proclaimed to the Gentiles. And at that point, especially, since Gentiles were able to become Christians without submitting to Jewish ritual (Acts 15:23-29), Christianity ceased to be a Jewish sect.

Verse 30. This is not the only occasion that Paul chose to pay his own way (see Acts 18:3).

Apparently, it was unimportant to the conclusion of Luke's account of the acts of the apostles to give the outcome of Paul's case before Caesar. The ultimate point was to show how Christianity came to the capital of the empire.

This is some debate about the disposition of Paul's case. Was he acquitted? Perhaps, but it is more likely that Paul was convicted and executed, but not on the Jewish charges. The Jewish case against Paul had failed (26:31). It is more likely that Paul was found guilty on new charges. For the church failed to remain a Jewish sect and thus by Roman law would have been banned.

The Scripture and the Main Question—Pat McGeachy

A Fantastic Voyage (Acts 27:1–28:14)

I wish we could spend more time on chapter 27 because it is the most dramatic passage in the book; indeed, it is one of the most exciting episodes in all of Holy Scripture. Luke was surely on board; this is the climax of the last of the "we" passages. He was no seafarer but a good observer, and we are given a number of interesting hints about early navigation.

Throughout the passage we are struck by the dominant figure of Paul, who, though he was a prisoner, was clearly looked to by all, including his captors, for advice and inspiration. In addition to his courage and faith, Paul also had considerable wit and common sense, and seems to have won the respect of all who journeyed with him. From the beginning (see Acts 27:3), Julius, the centurion in charge, took a liking to Paul and gave him many privileges.

The ship from Alexandria that they took at Myra (verse 6) was certainly a grain freighter, many of which attempted to make Rome each year. The Roman demand for Egyptian grain was enormous, and disruption of the trade caused more than one emperor considerable political difficulty. For a time the voyage was without incident, though there was much argument as to how to proceed, and apparently (verse 12) the majority prevailed! Odd that they would take a vote among prisoners and crew over a decision that we would think the captain or the owner ought to make.

Then the great storm came. It is called Euroclydon in the King James Version, which is a transliteration, and "the northeaster" in the Revised

Standard Version. The name "northeaster" (properly pronounced "nor-easter") has its origins among English seafarers and refers to what we would today call a hurricane or a tropical storm. Such winds invariably begin to blow from the northeast because of the counterclockwise motion of the cyclone as it emerges from the tropics. If this was an Atlantic hurricane that moved into the Mediterranean, that would have been a bit unusual, but it was certainly, as they said where I was a lad, a "stemwinder."

One interesting note: After fourteen days of seasickness, Paul apparently not only encouraged them to eat (verse 33) but broke bread in their presence in what sounds very much like a Eucharist (27:35). We should not be surprised that someone with a tradition of singing hymns in prison (16:25) would offer the Lord's Supper in a hurricane.

I do not enjoy heavy seas, but I wish I could have been a fly on a bulkhead during that trip, observing Paul at his best in a crisis. If he was not very much like his Master in his appearance before the tribunals in Jerusalem, he was certainly like him in his tranquility during the storm on the Sea of Galilee (Mark 4:35-41).

By the way, if I were translating Acts, I would render the phrase in 28:13 "we made a circuit" (which is translated as "we fetched a compass" in the King James Version), as "we did a three-sixty."

Rome at Last (Acts 28:14-16)

Luke's chronicle is now complete. He has told the story of the spread of Christianity, beginning in Jerusalem (Luke 24:47) and spreading throughout the Roman empire, which constituted most of the known world. He does not finish the story to our satisfaction. What *happened* to Paul and his friends? Did Luke meet his end there in Rome too? If not (and most scholars think not), then why did he leave us in the dark? Was he planning a trilogy: I Luke, Acts, and II Luke, which never got finished? We won't know in this life.

But what we do know fills us with hope. To begin with, the church at Rome was already very vital (was it founded by Peter?). Members came down the Appian way to the Forum, a distance of forty miles, to welcome the newcomers. (Three Taverns was a few miles closer toward Rome.) Their welcome lifted Paul's spirits, filling him with courage.

When they arrived in Rome, he was able to live on "his own recognizance," under "house arrest." I have never been arrested (unless you count being stopped by the highway patrol), but I have spent more than a decade working with prisoners, and I can tell you that even in minimum security prisons there is a strong desire to want to be somewhere else. Yet Paul seems to have functioned there very well. When he could not go to the synagogue to visit the Jewish leaders (verse 17), he asked them to come to see him, so that he could, as had been his tradition from the beginning, inform them of the gospel.

The Same Old Gospel (Acts 28:17-28)

Paul begins his case with the Roman Jewish community by making it clear that he was innocent of any crime against Israel. And apparently (verse 21) this was well received; there had been no negative report about Paul. (Of

FIRST QUARTER

course, considering the weather, mail service between Jerusalem and Rome must have left something to be desired.)

Like some of the Athenians (Acts 17:32), they wished to hear more about Paul's views, for Christianity had apparently already been troubling them. And though some (verse 24) were apparently convinced by his arguments on the appointed day, they all went away, arguing among themselves (verse 25). This prompted Paul to turn to the well-worn quotation from Isaiah 6:9-10 about stiff-necked people who can hear and see but don't really listen and perceive. It is quoted in *all four* of the Gospels (Matthew 13:14-15; Mark 4:12; Luke 8:9-10; John 12:39-40), making it one of the most oft-repeated passages in the Bible.

So in effect (verse 28) Paul finally shakes the dust of his feet off against his own people (compare Matthew 10:14) and turns his full attention to the Gentile world, which is hungry for the gospel.

Paul at the End (Acts 28:30-31)

So we find our hero, comfortably lodged (albeit at his own expense; apparently his many friends were supporting him with house rent and groceries), "preaching the kingdom of God and teaching about the Lord Jesus Christ quite openly and unhindered." This doesn't sound like Roman persecution as we have heard about it, with Christians forced to flee into the catacombs. Apparently Paul arrived at a time when the air was fairly free for diverse ideas and opinions.

Soon this would change. If Paul was not to die because of his crimes against Jerusalem (he had been given a clean bill of health on that by Festus and Agrippa, and no letter had come to Rome from the Jewish authorities), there was one thing left that would get him: *Here in Rome, Caesar's own city, he was teaching about a God who stood above all gods.* No self-deified Roman emperor could possibly tolerate such arrogance. He no doubt met his end for refusing to fall down and worship Caesar, preferring to serve the Christ who had kept him safe for these many years.

Your Own Last Days

As I write this I am looking forward to my sixtieth birthday. Perhaps you too have one of those milestone years coming up. If so, I commend both to you and myself the closing sentence of the book of the Acts: "And he lived there . . . at his own expense, and welcomed all who came to him, preaching the kingdom of God and teaching about the Lord Jesus Christ quite openly and unhindered."

Don't retire from the world—retire *to* the world. Get yourself another job. A friend of mine presided in Florida as a pastor over thousands of funerals of eastern executives who came down looking forward to spending years on tranquil tropical golf courses. Many of them proceeded immediately to have strokes and die, for they had nothing to live for. (My pastor friend did the same thing when he no longer had his church to give meaning to his life.) Don't let that happen to you. If you are very young, it is all the more important that you get this message: Devote the closing days of your life to something that really matters.

If you are at a loss to decide what that might be, then take a letter from Paul's notebook. He spent his whole life telling the world about the grace

NOVEMBER 24   LESSON 13

made known in Jesus, and he was not about to quit now. Let's you and I make a covenant that we will continue to search for Rome, wherever it may be for us, and if and when we find it, or if we don't, wherever God plants us, let us bloom there, with the gospel.

Helping Adults Become Involved—Ronald E. Schlosser

Preparing to Teach

We cannot read the closing chapters of Acts without recognizing the profound contribution the Apostle Paul made to the Christian faith. Paul's conversion occurred when the church was about four years old. By the time Paul arrived in Rome, some twenty-five years later, the church had grown and expanded to the far reaches of the Roman empire. Much of this growth can be attributed to the evangelistic and missionary efforts of Paul. In addition, he put his organizing genius into his evangelistic program. He started local churches and saw to it that they had proper leadership. He also did much to articulate and interpret the basic tenets of the Christian faith. What a debt we owe Paul for being a true pioneer of the faith!

As you read Acts 27 and 28, follow Paul's journey to Rome on a Bible map. Be prepared to tell in your own words the highlights of this journey up to the beginning of the passage we will be looking at more closely in the session (Acts 28:17-31).

There are two learning goals: (1) to appreciate what Paul was able to do despite his imprisonment and (2) to determine what we can do so that the gospel message is not hindered.

After introducing the main question, you might develop the lesson around the following outline:

                I. Journey to Rome
              II. Making contacts
            III. Home Bible study
            IV. Faithful to the end
                A. Facing retirement
                B. The unhindered gospel

Carefully read the sections "As You Read the Scripture" and "The Scripture and the Main Question." These form the heart of the lesson. The ideas, insights, and suggestions in these sections should be employed throughout your lesson plan.

Introducing the Main Question

Begin by asking your class members to speculate on what they would like to do when they retire. Where would they like to live? Would they want to take a part-time job? Do they have an avocation? Would they get involved in volunteer work? Would they like to travel?

If class members are already retired, ask them to tell what they do to keep themselves busy. What are the joys of retirement? The disappointments? The things future retirees should plan for?

After a time of sharing, refer to the main question introduced by Dr. McGeachy. How great is the temptation to "give up," to take it easy, to sit

FIRST QUARTER

back and relax? In today's scripture study we shall see that Paul kept active despite being held in custody, perhaps facing the end of his life. He continually found opportunities to witness for Christ.

Developing the Lesson

I. Journey to Rome

Tell the story of Paul's journey to Rome (Acts 27:1–28:16) in your own words. Or refer to the comments by Dr. McGeachy on this passage. Trace Paul's route on a map of the Mediterranean world. You might raise these questions with the class:
1. Early in the voyage, Paul sensed a crisis in the making and boldly gave advice, which was ignored (Acts 27:9-11). How do you feel when advice you give is not taken seriously? Do you take advice as easily as you give it?
2. There were times during the voyage when Paul seemed to be in charge. How do you explain this?
3. What does the term "providence" mean? Were there "providential" happenings in this story?

II. Making contacts

Read aloud Acts 28:17-22. Since Luke and Aristarchus (Acts 27:2) were with Paul and not prisoners, what might they have been doing during the first few days in Rome? Who, for instance, found the lodging for Paul? Who made contacts with the Jewish leaders? What else might they have done?

Ask: Why did Paul want to speak to the Jewish leaders first? What was Paul's pattern of witnessing wherever he went? Why might the Jews be fearful of Paul? (Paul always sought out the Jews first to tell them about Jesus the Messiah. The Jews in Rome were probably a frightened and cautious group. Only a few years before most of the Jews seemed to have been purged from Rome. Those remaining certainly did not want to become involved in anything that would cause them trouble. So Paul was careful to assure them that he had not come to make any charges against them. Indeed, he wished them well and wanted to share with them the gospel of Christ, the "hope of Israel.")

Ask: Why were the Jews in Rome more open to hearing Paul's message than the Jews in the other cities he visited? (See Dr. Winters's comments on Christianity's being considered a Jewish sect. In this regard, note also the reason why Paul was ultimately convicted when the Jewish case against him failed. As a new religion, Christianity would have been banned by Roman law. Paul was found guilty on new charges, as Dr. Winters points out.)

III. Home Bible study

Next read Acts 28:23-28. The scene resembles what we might describe today as a "home Bible study." Paul gathered a number of interested people in his home and discussed Scripture with them, and they engaged in dialogue and discussion. Of course, the meeting lasted much longer than most home Bible studies ("from morning till evening," verse 23), and probably there was more preaching than discussion, but the pattern was set. The concluding verses of Acts indicate that many people visited Paul in his home during the two years he lived in Rome, where "preaching" and "teaching" were carried on.

NOVEMBER 24   LESSON 13

Ask: What are the benefits of holding Bible studies in one's home today? Might there be any problems?

Refer to the comments of Drs. Winters and McGeachy about the content and outcome of the meeting with the Jews.

Helping Class Members Act

IV. Faithful to the end
  A. Facing retirement

Dr. McGeachy raises the question: Will our last years be filled with promise? Paul certainly didn't retire or give up when he was placed under house arrest in Rome. Neither should we when we face the last years of our life. Discuss with the class what can be done for Christ and his kingdom's work after one "retires" from active employment. Try to be specific, mentioning tasks one can do in one's own church and community.

  B. The unhindered gospel

If retirement is still a long way off for most of your class members, you may want to discuss what one can do today to share the gospel "openly and unhindered," as it is put in the final words of Acts (verse 31).

Ask: What hinders the church today from being as God would have it be? Have your class suggest hindrances to church growth. How can these be overcome? Where do your members find it most difficult to be Christlike themselves? What can they do to deal with these things?

Conclude with at time of sentence prayers, encouraging your members to pray for God's guidance and strength to be faithful witnesses in the world.

Planning for Next Sunday

A new quarter's study begins next week. The lessons will deal with "Songs and Prayers of the Bible." To prepare for the new study, ask the class to read Exodus 14:19–15:21.

SECOND QUARTER
Songs and Prayers of the Bible

UNIT I: SONGS FROM ANCIENT ISRAEL
Horace R. Weaver

FOUR LESSONS   DECEMBER 1-22

This quarter's study invites students to be aware of the richness of the songs and prayers of the Bible. With a wide variety of texts chosen from different parts of Scripture (both Old and New Testaments), the lessons remind us that much of our biblical faith comes from songs to be sung.

The titles for each of the three units of this quarter are as follows: unit I, "Songs from Ancient Israel"; unit II, "Songs from Festive Occasions"; unit III, "Songs and Prayers of the Church."

Unit I, "Songs from Ancient Israel," present four poems or songs from Israel's earliest days. The mood of these selections ranges from one of triumphant joy over God's acts of salvation to one of deep lament over the loss of national leaders. The fourth lesson, which falls on Christmas Sunday, tells how Luke took up one of these ancient songs as the basis for Mary's jubilation in her hymn, the Magnificat.

The individual lessons for unit I are as follows: "Song of Deliverance," December 1, asserts that our God is a God of deliverance and that when we experience deliverance, what else can we do but sing? "Song of Triumph," December 8, asks: In what ways can we see leadership as one of God's good gifts? "Song of Sorrow," December 15, deals with David's lament for Saul and Jonathan and raises the question, What is Christian grief? "Songs of Joy," December 22, asks: Are there circumstances so depressing that only an act of the loving God can turn them to joy?

Contributors to the second quarter:

Robert G. Rogers, Professor of Religion, Hampden-Sydney College, Hampden-Sydney, Virginia.

Horace R. Weaver, Executive Editor of Adult Curriculum Resources, The United Methodist Church, retired; Editor of *The International Lesson Annual.*

William H. Willimon, Minister to the University, Professor of the Practice of Christian Ministry, Duke University, Durham, North Carolina.

LESSON 1   DECEMBER 1

Song of Deliverance

Background Scripture: Exodus 14:19–15:21

The Main Question—William H. Willimon

The serious, white, Western reporter commented, "Here in South Africa, funerals of slain black South Africans begin as religious services but are quickly transformed into something like political demonstrations."

Behind him jumped, danced, shouted, and sang scores of black women. They had come to a funeral. A funeral that had begun with weeping and lamentation had erupted into people dancing and singing of liberation. Somehow, religion and politics, grief and joy, had gotten all mixed up in the swirling rhythms of these dancing women, in a way in that an NBC reporter could not understand.

What is an appropriate response to life when we are defeated, cast down, disappointed? We can weep. And crying is OK, as far as it goes. But sometimes we sing. We sing to take away the pain. We sing because music gives voice to our deepest feelings. We sing because music lifts us above the present, the status quo, things as they are, and shows us what, by God's grace, can be.

It is no accident that God's people tend to be singing people. It is no accident that the Christian season of Advent, which we enter this Sunday, is a season of singing. "Come, Thou Long Expected Jesus" and "O Come, O Come, Immanuel," are typical of the hymns of Advent. God's people are those who look for, expect, and sing about God's advent into our lives in Christ.

An appropriate Advent question: What are you waiting for? What is there in your life that can only be set right, healed, made good by the presence and acts of God?

Today's lesson deals with those questions by asserting that our God is a God of deliverance, and that when we experience deliverance, what else can we do but to sing?

Selected Scripture

King James Version	Revised Standard Version
Exodus 15:1-10, 13	*Exodus 15:1-10, 13*
1 Then sang Moses and the children of Israel this song unto the Lord, and spake, saying, I will sing unto the Lord, for he hath triumphed gloriously: the horse and his rider hath he thrown into the sea.	1 Then Moses and the people of Israel sang this song to the Lord, saying, "I will sing to the Lord, for he has triumphed gloriously; the horse and his rider he has thrown into the sea.
2 The Lord *is* my strength and song, and he is become my salva-	2 The Lord is my strength and my song,

SECOND QUARTER

tion: he *is* my God, and I will prepare him an habitation; my father's God, and I will exalt him.

3 The Lord *is* a man of war: the Lord *is* his name.

4 Pharaoh's chariots and his host hath he cast into the sea: his chosen captains also are drowned in the Red sea.

5 The depths have covered them: they sank into the bottom as a stone.

6 Thy right hand, O Lord, is become glorious in power: thy right hand, O Lord, hath dashed in pieces the enemy.

7 And in the greatness of thine excellency thou hast overthrown them that rose up against thee: thou sentest forth thy wrath, *which* consumed them as stubble.

8 And with the blast of thy nostrils the waters were gathered together, the floods stood upright as an heap, *and* the depths were congealed in the heart of the sea.

9 The enemy said, I will pursue, I will overtake, I will divide the spoil; my lust shall be satisfied upon them; I will draw my sword, my hand shall destroy them.

10 Thou didst blow with thy wind, the sea covered them: they sank as lead in the mighty waters.

....

13 Thou in thy mercy hast led forth the people *which* thou hast redeemed: thou hast guided *them* in thy strength unto thy holy habitation.

Key Verse: **The Lord is my strength and song, and he is become my salvation: he is my God, and I will prepare him an habita-**

and he has become my salvation; this is my God, and I will praise him,
my father's God, and I will exalt him.

3 The Lord is a man of war;
the Lord is his name.

4 "Pharaoh's chariots and his host he cast into the sea;
and his picked officers are sunk in the Red Sea.

5 The floods cover them;
they went down into the depths like a stone.

6 Thy right hand, O Lord, glorious in power,
thy right hand, O Lord, shatters the enemy.

7 In the greatness of thy majesty thou overthrowest thy adversaries;
thou sendest forth thy fury, it consumes them like stubble.

8 At the blast of thy nostrils the waters piled up,
the floods stood up in a heap;
the deeps congealed in the heart of the sea.

9 The enemy said, 'I will pursue, I will overtake,
I will divide the spoil, my desire shall have its fill of them.
I will draw my sword, my hand shall destroy them.'

10 Thou didst blow with thy wind, the sea covered them;
they sank as lead in the mighty waters."

....

13 "Thou hast led in thy steadfast love the people whom thou hast redeemed,
thou hast guided them by thy strength to the holy abode."

Key Verse: **The Lord is my strength and my song, and he has become my salvation; this is my God, and I will praise him, my**

DECEMBER 1   LESSON 1

tion; my father's God, and I will father's God, and I will exalt him.
exalt him. (Exodus 15:2)   (Exodus 15:2)

As You Read the Scripture—Horace R. Weaver

Moses led the "children of Israel" in search of freedom from Egyptian slavery. Moses' people were a motley group, undisciplined in both their faith in Yahweh (the Lord God) and the leadership of Moses. Moses' leadership was under considerable duress, for he and his people were without military arms of any kind. Exodus 14:6-9 helps us understand their fear and conviction that they would all be destroyed: The Pharaoh had "six hundred picked chariots and all the other chariots of Egypt with officers over all of them." The Pharaoh's "horses and chariots" and his horsemen and his army pursued Moses and his people.

Moses, observing and understanding the fear of his people, said, "Fear not, stand firm, and see the salvation of the Lord. . . . The Lord will fight for you, and you have only to be still" (14:13-14). Several centuries later the psalmist will say, "Be still and know that I am God."

Exodus 14:19. Bible scholars are convinced that the phrases "angel of God" and "pillar of cloud" are synonyms and symbolize the protecting presence of Yahweh. There is nothing more helpful than to be aware of God's presence.

Verse 20. The cloud (symbolizing the divine presence) and the darkness of night separated the two forces, so that each was hidden from the other. Modern warfare includes such miracles of invisibility (smoke screens, camouflage, etc.). In Hebrew the sea is called the Sea of Reeds, not the Red Sea. This sea of reeds was a shallow body of water, probably in the area of Lake Timnah. During a storm the shallow waters were driven back, causing the Egyptian chariots to get stuck in the mud and be unable to operate; when the waters returned, the Egyptians were drowned. The people of Israel walked on dry land (14:22-25).

Exodus 15:1. Moses and the people of Israel sang a song to the Lord, the first verse of which was taken up by Miriam later (verse 21):

> I will sing to the Lord, for he has triumphed gloriously;
> the horse and his rider he has thrown into the sea.

Miriam must have been in a religious ecstasy as she realized the significance of what God had done through her brother, Moses. She not only sang but also danced, in the traditional ways of her people as they expressed their gratitude to God. Miriam's religious experience encouraged her to take a timbrel in her hand ("And all the women went out after her with timbrels and dancing," verse 20) to praise God.

The form of this song in Hebrew is that of a victory dance/song. We read in the Bible of several occasions when women celebrated victories by singing and dancing (Judges 5:1-31; 11:34; 1 Samuel 18:6). Perhaps it is puritanical attitudes that prevent us from joyfully dancing in our times of religious festivities.

Verses 2-18. If we assume Moses wrote these verses, then he was familiar with the themes and vocabulary of the Judaism of 600 B.C. and knew of

SECOND QUARTER

David's warfare with Philistines. It seems likely that a very pious and God-loving man wrote verses 2-18 in honor of Moses' achievements.

Verse 2.

> The Lord is my strength and my song,
> and he has become my salvation.

This verse is taken from Isaiah 12:2 (also Psalm 118:14). The phrase "my father's God" means "this is my God."

Verse 3. God as "man of war" refers to the notion of a holy war, an idea frequently expressed in Judges.

Verses 4-5. The Egyptian chariots and officers were destroyed as the sea engulfed them.

Verse 6. The Lord always had power to achieve his purposes.

Verses 9-10. What the enemy (Egypt) said they would do to Israel is contrasted to what God's "breath" (as in creation) can do at any time.

The Scripture and the Main Question—William H. Willimon

Grief as Adjustment to Defeat

We need not be taught how to grieve. Grief comes quite naturally. Say farewell to someone you love, lose hope, face death (and don't we all?)—you'll grieve. A popular book was called *Good Grief.* It's good for us to grieve, to let it out, to cry, to wail, to shake our fists in rage. Go ahead and cry. Grief is natural, expected, normal. Go ahead and grieve. It is therapeutic. You'll feel better afterward.

But not much better. Because grief, once vented, only awaits more grief, life being what it is, death being what it is, namely, omnipresent. Our grieving, at its therapeutic best, is unlike that of the dancing South African women. Our grief is the last, anguished outcry, the brief, protesting whimper of people who are learning to resign themselves to the facts of life and death. Our grief is rage on our way to accepting things as they are. This is the way the world works.

After Good Friday, the disciples showed what sensible, mature people they were. They grieved, but they didn't go on and on. By Sunday, they were beginning to feel much better, which means that they had begun to relent to things as they are. It was a good campaign while it lasted, though we failed to get him elected Messiah. What can anybody do about Caesar?

"I'm going fishing," one of them said. Keep busy, then it won't hurt so much. Back to business as usual. Thank goodness for the anesthetizing effect of the routine.

Grief is the natural, predictable, psychic mechanism by which we humans adopt to the status quo, to the facts as they are. Therefore our world values people who learn to march about, those who dance or sing.

Sorrow Turned to Song

Today's text comes from Exodus. We have followed the Hebrew slaves, through the ten plagues and Pharaoh's stubborn refusal to let God's people go, through the terrible awe-filled night when there was weeping in the homes of the Egyptians and the excited, hasty exodus from the homes of the Hebrews.

Pharaoh, in his unbalanced, crazed grief over the death of his own son (Pharaoh showed no grief at killing the children of the Hebrews) told Moses and his people, "Get out of here and don't stop until you are someplace other than Egypt."

Eventually, Pharaoh got hold of himself. "I must have been crazy," he said, "to let those Hebrews go. It will wreck the economy. These things ought to be done gradually."

"You were upset," said Pharaoh's cabinet member. "Your grief almost got the best of you. Put yourself together and act like a real leader."

So Pharaoh sent his chariots, horses, and soldiers to bring the Hebrews back. What did those Hebrews think when they looked over their shoulders and saw the cloud kicked up by the hosts of Egypt, mightiest army in the world, on their heels in hot pursuit?

So this is how it shall end, for us, they thought. Standing out here on the very edge of freedom, almost there but not quite, slaughtered by a power greater than our own. If you wanted to weep, weep now, Israel.

God as it turned out, had other things in mind. When the roaring of the Red Sea had ceased, the devouring and liberating waters were again calm, and the slaves stood for the first time on dry, free ground, then you could hear music. Music? It is odd, old, primitive music, possibly one of the oldest fragments in the Bible, in this song of Moses. It's a song growing louder and more compelling, a strange rhythm of liberated people. There, out on the edge of the mighty empire, at the edge, where we would not have gone had we not been pushed, and called, we find Moses singing. "When I think about how I almost didn't get over," sings the spiritual.

How they sing and dance, these former slaves whose bodies ought to be exhausted and bent from too much work and too much bowing before the tyrant. The tambourines have brought them to their feet, and tired as they are, they cannot be still. They do not tire because they have within them the most energizing force in the world—hope. They have given death the slip. Listen to Moses' song and you will hear praised the name of a God stronger than Pharaoh.

> The Lord is my strength and my song,
> and he has become my salvation
> this is my God, and I will praise him.
> (Exodus 15:2)

How Can We Sing?

If we had tambourines, would we use them? We are modern and therefore cynical about such primitive outbursts. Tambourines are simple, primitive instruments to our sophisticated, well-trained ears. We don't believe in miracles, because we believe not in God but in Pharaoh. How much of your dollar goes to pay for his horses and riders? The empire, its corporations, and its bureaucrats may treat us as slaves, but at least we know its boundaries and, with a little grief, a tranquilizer or two, we can adjust. We are not undereducated, primitive, uncontrolled people. We can adjust.

Yet in our modern, Western cynicism, there is something, something deep within us, that responds to the haunting rhythms of Moses' song. We

SECOND QUARTER

listen to these people who have had so little to sing and dance about, and even our cynical toes began to tap to the beat of Moses.

Be careful about tapping your toes to such a beat; you might join Moses in this song of freedom. Songs of deliverance like this one disrupt, make people dance, turn funerals into victory rallies, create a critical space between us and the deadly status quo. When there is no one like Moses to sing, we don't dance, we fall into line, march in step, attend meetings.

Death, defeat, disappointment, disillusionment—how are they transformed into song? *By the surprises of a living God* who won't let Pharaoh have the last word, who recognizes the boundaries of no empire, even that one ruled by death. This God parted the Red Sea waters and rolled away the stone from the tomb, and those who gather to tell of his works do so best through song. Women, who never had anything to sing about, went wild with tambourines at the Exodus. A young woman named Mary sang at the good news of a Son, "My soul magnifies the Lord, and my spirit rejoices in God my salvation." And it was to women, come out to his tomb with spices to dress his decaying body, that the angel said, "Fear not, He is not here. He is risen. Go, tell." And they danced all the way back to the despairing disciples. As Paul says, "We do not grieve as those who have no hope." Why? Because *we believe in a God who delivers*.

One reason why it is important for us to gather and to sing songs of deliverance like the Song of Moses is that we thereby remind ourselves, in times of deep need, that our God comes to help us. A God who sits back passively without responding is hardly worth having.

Of course, to some, it may seem as if we believers sit back and wait for God to do for us what we ought to do for ourselves. Karl Marx charged Christianity with being a form of drug to keep people in bondage. Yet as we see in today's lesson, our faith in God the Deliverer is also a path to liberation. We don't have to settle in and accept things as they are. Here is a God who makes a way, even when it seems that there is no way. Even as God made a way out of Egypt, God makes the means for us to overcome whatever bondage we may be suffering.

In the depth of the Depression in the 1920s, the brilliant and cynical H. L. Mencken was visiting in a black church on the southside of Chicago. He was, like many who enter the worship of such a church for the first time, deeply moved by their singing.

Mencken was invited by the preacher to say a few words. "I'd like to know," he said, "how on earth, with all the troubles you have, you've got anything about which to sing."

Back toward the rear of the church, a woman shouted, "Mister, we've still got Jesus." And to Mencken's befuddlement, the place erupted in singing and praise.

Helping Adults Become Involved—Robert G. Rogers

Preparing to Teach

For the next four lessons you and your class will be studying songs from ancient Israel. Although set in different time periods, the four biblical stories all share a common theme: song as a human response to God's activity in the world.

Spend some time skimming over the biblical readings for this and the

DECEMBER 1   LESSON 1

next three lessons: Exodus 15:1-10, 13; Judges 5:1-11; 2 Samuel 1:17-27; 1 Samuel 2:1-5; Luke 1:46-55. As you read, try to look at the four lessons as a whole. Notice especially how song responds to a variety of human emotions. Think for a few moments about the importance of song in your own life. What particular hymns or even popular songs "capture" the various moods that you experience in your own life?

Your specific aim in this first lesson is to focus on the mood of joy. In particular, you want your class to focus on the joy felt by the Israelites as they experienced God's deliverance from slavery.

Introducing the Main Question

Commence the lesson by reminding the class of Dr. Willimon's observation that "God's people tend to be a singing people." In the Advent season, it is especially appropriate to remind ourselves of the importance of song in the life of the church. Ask class members to think about the various types of songs in each worship service. Suggest that different songs (or hymns) are used to reflect different moods, such as praise or thanksgiving or sorrow. Jot down on the blackboard hymns suggested by class members. Also note the occasions when these hymns are most effectively used.

Spend a few moments exploring the significance of song for individual lives. On what occasions did individual class members feel like "breaking out in song?" Perhaps it was an experience in nature, such as a beautiful sunset. Or, a medical doctor may have said that a seriously ill family member would recover. Point out that song usually gives voice to personal feelings.

Developing the Lesson

For this portion of the lesson, build on Dr. Willimon's work. In particular, note how he discusses the combination of grief and joy in describing the Song of Moses. Your task is to present both human emotions as you develop the lesson in three sections:

        I. Free at last
       II. Deliverance as challenge
     III. Sing a joyful song

I. Free at last

You want your class to experience what it must have felt like to be an Israelite standing on the safe side of the Red Sea. (The scriptural exegesis by Dr. Weaver can help you describe the scene.) Retell briefly the story of Hebrew slavery under the Pharaoh. Remind the class of the bitterness of slavery and the attempts by Moses to persuade Pharaoh to let the Israelites leave. Portray Moses as God's agent in this confrontation with Pharaoh. Note also that the Israelites were not immediately willing to follow Moses. He demanded risk taking. Point out the hopelessness of the Israelites' situation when they were pursued by the Egyptian army. Describe how feelings of despair gave way to joy after the miraculous crossing through the water.

Ask class members to imagine what their feelings would have been in that situation. Undoubtedly, each member has had times when he or she felt enslaved by a particularly bad set of circumstances. Ask them to describe

SECOND QUARTER

their feelings of elation when the burden was lifted from them. Now you can refer specifically to Exodus 15:2, where Moses expresses joy at release from captivity. Point out that his song expresses joy and praises God at the same time.

II. Deliverance as challenge

In this section you want to challenge the class to think of deliverance as the start of a process, not the end. Build on Dr. Willimon's notion that songs of deliverance, such as that of Moses, challenge us (and the Israelites) to continue to grow spiritually. How understandable it would have been for the Israelites to celebrate their freedom by disappearing into the desert to live their lives free from the Egyptian yoke of oppression. Yet remind the class that the biblical story has Moses leading the Israelites to Mount Sinai, where they accept the responsibility of living in covenant with God. Deliverance from slavery was just the beginning of a spiritual journey.

Now consider with the class your own congregation's life. Think of a problem in the church that has burdened the entire congregation. Identify some of the ways that God works through church members to "deliver" the congregation. Did the divine-human partnership offer new possibilities for Christian growth?

Conclude this section by recalling the purpose of the Advent season in the Christian calendar. As we await the deliverance offered by the Christ-Child, we are challenged to find new ways of loving and serving the human community.

III. Sing a joyful song

Consider again the entire Song of Moses. Point out the way it describes God's work in the world. What characteristics of God gave Moses a joyful confidence? Suggest that two facets of God are described. First, there is the initial act of salvation itself (deliverance from slavery in Egypt). A second characteristic is equally important: God continues in a relationship with the human community. Exodus 15:13 speaks of the "steadfast love" of God for his people.

Explore ways in which the Song of Moses describes God's activity in the world today. Acts of deliverance and the promise of continued relationship are as available for believers today as they were for the people of Israel. Remind the class that acts of deliverance need not be as spectacular as those recorded in the Bible. God works in ways suitable to the situation. At this point ask class members to share briefly an example or two of God's "quiet work" in your congregation.

Songs of joy enable us to respond to God's work in the world, whether the occasion is grand and spectacular or more simple and less public. The joyful songs of Advent reflect both the grandeur and the simplicity of the birth of a child at Bethlehem.

Helping Class Members Act

Ask class members to think in the coming week about one incident in their lives wherefrom they felt delivered by God. What was their response at that moment? Remind them again that God often works in small ways, not just through mighty acts.

DECEMBER 8 LESSON 2

Planning for Next Sunday

The assignment for next Sunday is the story of Deborah and Barak, and it takes place after the Israelites have settled in the land of Canaan. It is a time of turmoil and difficulty for the people. The class should read Judges 5:1-11 carefully.

LESSON 2 DECEMBER 8

Song of Triumph

Background Scripture: Judges 4:4–5:31

The Main Question—William H. Willimon

History is a long story of how, in times of crisis, someone has stepped to the front and become a leader. It is difficult to imagine how, during World War II, the forces of fascism would have been defeated without leaders like Roosevelt and Churchill. In today's scripture, Deborah and Barak step to the front of the state of Israel's history and take charge.

The Bible rightly speaks of good leaders as gifts of God. At all times and places, God has graciously sent us the leaders we need. Of course, leadership is a two-way street. Some lead, but their leadership means little if there are not others to follow. So in Deborah's song of triumph, she rightly notes,

> That the leaders took the lead in Israel,
> that the people offered themselves willingly,
> bless the Lord!
> (Judges 5:20)

Challenging, difficult times demand capable, bold leaders. Without leaders, we are subject to despair and hopelessness. Fortunately, God gives us people like Deborah and Barak. In what ways can we see leadership as one of God's good gifts? That is the main question behind today's scriptural song.

Selected Scripture

King James Version

Judges 5:1-11

1 Then sang Deborah and Barak the son of Abinoam on that day, saying,

2 Praise ye the Lord for the avenging of Israel, when the people

Revised Standard Version

Judges 5:1-11

1 Then sang Deborah and Barak the son of Abinoam on that day:

2 "That the leaders took the lead in Israel,

SECOND QUARTER

willingly offered themselves.

3 Hear, O ye kings; give ear, O ye princes; I, *even* I, will sing unto the Lord; I will sing *praise* to the Lord God of Israel.

4 Lord, when thou wentest out of Seir, when thou marchedst out of the field of Edom, the earth trembled, and the heavens dropped, the clouds also dropped water.

5 The mountains melted from before the Lord, *even* that Sinai from before the Lord God of Israel.

6 In the days of Shamgar the son of Anath, in the days of Jael, the highways were unoccupied, and the travellers walked through byways.

7 *The inhabitants of* the villages ceased, they ceased in Israel, until that I Deborah arose, that I arose a mother in Israel.

8 They chose new gods; then *was* war in the gates: was there a shield or spear seen among forty thousand in Israel?

9 My heart *is* toward the governors of Israel, that offered themselves willingly among the people. Bless ye the Lord.

10 Speak, ye that ride on white asses, ye that sit in judgment, and walk by the way.

11 *They that are delivered* from the noise of archers in the places of drawing water, there shall they rehearse the righteous acts of the Lord, *even* the righteous acts *toward the inhabitants* of his villages in Israel:

that the people offered themselves willingly,
bless the Lord!

3 "Hear, O kings; give ear, O princes;
to the Lord I will sing,
I will make melody to the Lord, the God of Israel

4 "Lord, when thou didst go forth from Seir,
when thou didst march from the region of Edom,
the earth trembled,
and the heavens dropped,
yea, the clouds dropped water.

5 The mountains quaked before the Lord,
yon Sinai before the Lord, the God of Israel.

6 "In the days of Shamgar, son of Anath,
in the days of Jael, caravans ceased
and travelers kept to the byways.

7 The peasantry ceased in Israel, they ceased
until you arose, Deborah,
arose as a mother in Israel.

8 When new gods were chosen, then war was in the gates.
Was shield or spear to be seen among forty thousand in Israel?

9 My heart goes out to the commanders of Israel
who offered themselves willingly among the people.
Bless the Lord.

10 "Tell of it, you who ride on tawny asses,
you who sit on rich carpets
and you who walk by the way.

11 To the sound of musicians at the watering places,
there they repeat the triumphs of the Lord,
the triumphs of his peasantry in Israel.

DECEMBER 8　　　　　　　　　　　　　　　　　　　　　　LESSON 2

then shall the people of the Lord go down to the gates.

"Then down to the gates marched the people of the Lord."

Key Verse: I will sing unto the Lord; I will sing praise to the Lord God of Israel. (Judges 5:3)

Key Verse: To the Lord I will sing, I will make melody to the Lord, the God of Israel. (Judges 5:3)

As You Read the Scripture—Horace R. Weaver

The judges were officials (both male and female) with authority to administer justice by trying cases in law, or, in a special sense, military leaders who had authority to deliver and govern their people in times of oppression. Their authority might be confined to one tribe (as with Samson, Judges 15). Some of the judges were contemporaries of one another, which suggests that judges did not succeed one another as did kings. This kind of government held sway during the period between the times of Joshua and of David.

There were thirteen judges, six who were classified as major judges (Othniel, Ehud, Deborah, Gideon, Jephthah, and Samson, whose roles were classified as deliverers) and seven as minor judges.

The story of Deborah appears in two forms. Judges 4 is a prose account; Judges 5 is poetic and is called the song of Deborah. This is an ancient ode of victory celebrating the last native Canaanite uprising against the Israelites, and the winning of the fertile Plain of Esdraelon Israel.

Judges 5:1. "Then sang Deborah and Barak . . . on that day." Deborah (in the prose section of chapter 4) had challenged Barak to lead a sizeable Israeli army against the Canaanites, who were living in the plush area called the Plain of Esdraelon. Barak agreed to participate if Deborah would go with him into the battle. "On that day" refers to the day of triumph over the Canaanite forces of Sisera (with their hundreds of iron chariots).

Verse 2. Deborah and Barak look back with pride

> that the leaders took the lead in Israel,
> 　that the people offered themselves willingly,
> 　bless the Lord!

Verse 3.

> Hear, O kings; give ear, O princes;
> 　to the Lord I will sing,
> 　I will make melody to the Lord, the God of Israel.

Deborah engages in mockery, for she knows the kings (such as Sisera) are dead. Yet her spirit produces songs within her heart.

Verse 4. "Lord, when thou didst go forth from Seir . . . the earth trembled" expresses Deborah's and Barak's faith in God's support of Israel against Sisera.

Verse 5. "The mountains quaked before the Lord" is a poetic way of expressing faith that God was active in their behalf, not only in times of need at Mount Sinai but also as they faced the strong Canaanite military forces.

Verses 6-7. "In the days of Shamgar" refers to the militant judge whose

SECOND QUARTER

home was located in the Canaanite city of Beth-anat in Galilee. Shamgar successfully led a local group in war against some Philistines, whose military weapons (such as iron chariots and iron spears and helmets) frightened the Israelites, so that "caravans ceased and travelers kept to the byways." Shamgar's activities preceded those of Deborah, who was judge in 1125 B.C.

Verse 7. Perhaps Barak or some of the women honored Deborah with

> The peasantry ceased in Israel, they ceased
> until you arose, Deborah,
> arose as a mother in Israel.

Verse 9. Deborah's compassion:

> My heart goes out to the commanders of Israel
> who offered themselves willingly among the people.
> Bless the Lord.

Deborah's compassion reflects the Philistine and Canaanite use of metal weapons. Hebrew slingshots had to match iron swords and iron-tipped arrows.

Verses 16-18. Actually, only six of the twelve tribes participated in the war. Why? Deborah and Barak could only ask questions, such as "Reuben, why did you tarry among the shepherds? Why was there great searching of heart?" (i.e., why didn't you immediately join your brethren?) "Dan, why did you abide with the ships" (i.e., why didn't you immediately join your brethren?) So with Asher, who was content to sit still at the coast of the sea.

The Scripture and the Main Question—William H. Willimon

The Leaders Took the Lead

It was a rather familiar story in history. Israel was at the point of great crisis. Faced with the superior forces of the Canaanites with their "nine hundred chariots of iron" (Judges 4:3), the people were terrified. For a while, it seemed as if God's great plans for his Chosen People, to bring them to their own land, would be ended by the violence of the Canaanites. The liberating Exodus out of Egyptian slavery would be as nothing. What was going to happen?

Then, Deborah and Barak stepped to the front, and the story took an amazing, rather miraculous turn. This rather disordered, weak collection of tribes defeated the enemy. "The leaders took the lead in Israel, . . . the people offered themselves willingly" (5:2).

Sometimes we Americans seem to have a bit of prejudice against strong leaders. Our constitutional system of checks and balances is meant to ensure that our leaders remain democratic leaders and not dictators, ruling with the consent of the governed. Presidential power is carefully balanced with congressional power because our country was born out of a struggle against monarchy and dictatorial leadership styles.

But we Americans should not forget that while leadership ought to be constitutionally limited, it also ought to be strong enough to protect and govern the people. Leadership strength can be abused, and when strong leadership uses its strength for unjust ends, that is tragic. But strong leadership can use its strength for good ends, and when it does, then that is nothing short of a blessing of God.

Great human misery is created when a government is too weak to govern, when leaders are ineffective. When things are going fairly well in a society, the people can be rather nonchalant about good leaders. It doesn't take much of a leader to govern when things are going well. But when things are going poorly, when the nation is threatened by outside enemies or the economy slumps or there is some internal crisis, we need to know that someone is in charge, that our leaders understand the problem and have adequate solutions.

Was Deborah, in her song of triumph, overstating the case when she blessed the Lord because Israel had been well led to victory? No. Good, wise, and just leaders are nothing less than a gift of God.

I remember, in a college history class, a young professor lecturing on the inadequacies of Franklin Roosevelt as a president. He noted that Roosevelt came dangerously close to abusing presidential power, that some of his ideas did not work and that some of his programs were ineffective.

There was one student in the class who was much older than the rest of us. He had come to college after a lifetime of working in a nearby textile mill. His experiences there gave him a perspective on things that we younger students did not have.

He challenged the young professor and questioned some of his judgments about Roosevelt. When the professor asked him to back up his assertions with facts, the man replied, "During the thirties, we were so poor that we only had one meal a day, and that was only some corn grits with a little fatback. My daddy was out of work. My mother was ill. We were desperate. When we got word that Franklin Roosevelt was elected, my mother had all of us get down on our knees and thank God for Mr. Roosevelt and to ask God to help him be a good president."

Of course, when one is doing well, when one is on the top of society rather than the bottom, when one has enough to eat and one's children are well taken care of, then it matters little who is in charge. However, when one is desperate, on the bottom, without hope, good leadership is nothing less than a gift of God, a triumph of God's grace within our world.

The Triumphs of the Lord

We rightly remember Deborah and Barak because, when the people needed bold leadership, they stepped to the front and led. However, if many in your class read the whole of today's scripture, beginning early in chapter 4 of Judges, they may be wondering why we are praising such violent, warlike actions as part of God's work. You may want to confront that troublesome issue in today's class.

Of course, Deborah and Barak lived in violent, chaotic times. The Canaanites and their leaders had one goal in mind, to wipe these invading Israelites off the face of the earth. Desperate circumstances often call for desperate actions by the nation's leaders. When asked if he agonized over the decision to drop the atom bomb on Hiroshima, president Harry Truman replied, "No. It saved American lives."

However, more than that is being said in today's scripture. Note that in the song of Deborah, the claim is made that it was *the Lord* who triumphed. The war against the Canaanites was a holy war; that is, it was a war in which

SECOND QUARTER

God took the side of those who had nothing on their side except their faith in God and no one to fight with them except a faithful God.

So the song claims that it wasn't just the Israelites who fought, but God who marched with them (5:4). These were not just the triumphs of brave people in the nation, they were the triumphs of the Lord (5:11) who led the poor people of Israel.

We are rightly suspicious about the concept of a "holy" war in which God fights on our side. It sounds like a terribly perverted rationale for bloodshed. However, within the biblical faith of Israel, holy war is actually a means of checking some of our violence.

Here, God is taking the side of those who are weak, vulnerable, and impoverished against the rich, strong, and powerful. Without God, they have no hope. It is difficult to believe that God is on the side of justice unless we also believe that God is willing to become involved in struggles for justice, to take sides against injustice. Here is a God who does not just sit back, contentedly detached in the heavens, but enters into our world and our history to set things right.

Also, if God is fighting for us, then we should not be so quick to fight for ourselves. We need not crusade and kill others to get our way. God is busy working to bring about righteousness. The moment that we begin believing that God is not active, that it is all left up to us, we are on the way to taking matters in our own hands, and then we are on the way to violence.

To the Lord I Will Sing

As the Song of Deborah makes clear, this is *God's* triumph, not ours, so we need not be smug, claiming the victory as our own, but should rather be grateful and obedient to God. We must be slow to claim our triumphs as God's triumphs, as if there were a direct relationship between what we want in life and what God wants for us. However, if we triumph over adversity, in our personal or national lives, if we see justice get the best of oppression, then it is because of the loving actions of God rather than our own efforts.

Sadly, in today's world you and I are more apt to ascribe our triumphs to ourselves, our adept leaders, our superior technology, or our innate goodness than to the work of God. We don't do all that much singing to God when things go well for us because, in our eyes, God really had nothing to do with it. We believe that good fortune is our right, not God's gift. We believe that we deserve for things to go well, so we don't really need God to deliver us. We are so busy delivering ourselves.

Then comes the season of Advent, as we prepare ourselves for a God who comes to us as a baby, a gift for people who cannot save themselves by themselves. The child in the manger reminds us: The things that need doing most in our lives come as gifts from a loving God.

And remembering, we sing.

Helping Adults Become Involved—Robert G. Rogers

Preparing to Teach

This lesson features another song of celebration: the triumph of the Israelites over the Canaanites. It is somewhat similar to the last lesson, but here the focus is on leadership in a time of crisis.

DECEMBER 8　　　　　　　　　　　　　　　　　LESSON 2

Read Judges 5:1-11 carefully. (Also skim through Judges 4:4-24 for background to the story.) Notice that in describing the triumph it celebrates the roles of both leaders and followers and places them under the direction of God. What traits of Deborah and Barak do you most admire?

In presenting this lesson, you will want to help the class discover God's role in calling leaders in a time of crisis. It is equally important to emphasize that good followers are needed and that God can direct both leaders and followers toward good ends.

Introducing the Main Question

Begin by emphasizing that the song is a celebration of Deborah and Barak's leadership, but it is also a celebration of God's work in redeeming the "peasantry of Israel." Refer to Dr. Willimon's approach, where the song is not just celebrating military victory but also celebrating God's act in sending leaders and empowering followers. In setting the scene, it is important to emphasize God's role in providing whoever is needed to guide his people.

After setting the scene, spend some time with the class, listing characteristics of both good leaders and good followers. You might put these on the blackboard or flipchart for later reference. Some members of the class may view themselves only as followers. Make sure that their thoughts are included as part of the class list.

Developing the Lesson

When introducing the lesson, you asked for the characteristics of good leaders and good followers. Now you want to build on the work of these lists to suggest the relationship between leaders and followers. In particular, you want to demonstrate the role of God within this interaction. To accomplish this, develop three sections:

　　　　　　　　I. Leadership as opportunity
　　　　　　　II. The necessity of followers
　　　　　　　III. God's triumph

I. Leadership as opportunity

Retell the story of Deborah and Barak, which led up to their Song of Triumph. The Israelites had entered the land of Canaan, but they were hard pressed by the Canaanite inhabitants. There was a need for someone to save Israel. God worked through Deborah and Barak; Deborah, in particular, was a key figure. As a judge, she already had a position of leadership among the people. In advising Barak, she had to adapt her concern to all of the people rather than considering just an individual legal dispute.

List leadership characteristics that Deborah exhibited. Put these on the board beside the traits already listed by the class. Examine the list together. What makes Deborah's contribution unique? Point out that one of her strengths was the ability to work cooperatively with Barak, the commander of the Israelite troops.

Now turn inward, toward your own church. Who are some of the leaders within the congregation? What distinguishes their styles of leadership? You

SECOND QUARTER

might note that different people can be leaders in different circumstances. We all have gifts to offer at the appropriate time.

Conclude this section by reminding the class that opportunities for leadership come in all of our lives; often, it is an unexpected opportunity. Yet as Christians, we should be open to those opportunities that God provides to work in behalf of his people and the world.

II. The necessity of followers

Commence this section by stating the obvious: Leaders need followers in order to accomplish a task. In ancient Israel, as in the contemporary church, there must be those who are willing to listen and follow the direction laid by others. The biblical story does not record for us the thoughts of the "peasantry of Israel." However, you and the class might try to list some of the characteristics that you think would have been necessary for followers in that time. What amount of personal discipline was necessary to ensure the triumph of the Israelites? Compare some of these traits with those on the board already listed by the class.

Acknowledge that it is often difficult to take orders from others. Most humans would rather be the one giving the directions and expecting others to follow. Yet to be a good follower, it is necessary to curtail one's personal need to be in charge. Shift attention to the modern day. Note that the church, like ancient Israel, needs a good, sturdy "peasantry" to do its work.

Remind your people of the personal satisfaction that comes to those who do a task well, even if the task seems small and relatively unimportant. Cite Paul's instruction to the Corinthians (I Corinthians 12), that the body of the church is comprised of many different members. Each has something to contribute to the entire body. The lesson is obvious, therefore. Each follower is needed to help the church function as a whole.

III. God's triumph

Let Judges 5:11 set the tone for this section. Clearly, the defeat of the Canaanites by the Israelites was a human enterprise, but it was under God's guidance. The peasants triumphed; Deborah and Barak triumphed; so, too, did God. By working in and through both leaders and followers, God led his people to triumph.

Refer to Dr. Willimon's observation that too often in the modern age, humans ascribe triumphs to themselves; they forget God's involvement in the world. Indeed, boasting is a game well played in the human community. Pose this question: Can the knowledge that we are loved by God help reduce our need to promote ourselves in public?

After discussing the question for a few moments, conclude this section by reminding everyone of the Advent message. God revealed himself to the human community through the simplicity of a child. Whether called to be leaders or followers, we should be grateful for the opportunity, and therefore minimize the claims of self-pride.

Helping Class Members Act

Suggest that in the coming week each class member envision a situation in the church where his or her personal traits would be best suited to being a follower. Then members should imagine a situation where God might call them to be leaders. Reiterate the significance of both roles; neither is more important than the other.

Planning for Next Sunday

Next Sunday the class will be discussing a song of lament. They should read 2 Samuel 1:17-27 carefully. It is a moving passage in which David mourns the death of King Saul and Jonathan, his son. What virtues of friendship does David describe?

LESSON 3   DECEMBER 15

Song of Sorrow

Background Scripture: 2 Samuel 1

The Main Question—William H. Willimon

"It seems as if I am always having funerals in my life," she said. She was speaking of the way that grief is a persistent, ever-present part of life. We grieve at the deaths of our close friends and family, but we also have other losses that cause us pain. Your marriage ends, your children leave home for college, you retire, you graduate—grief is a part of life.

William Sloane Coffin, former pastor of Riverside Church in New York, noted the reactions he encountered from some fellow pastors during the first months after the death of his teenage son. Some offered "comforting words of Scripture" to suggest that he look for God's will or some blessing in the middle of his tragedy. Others offered simple, easy answers in well-meaning but misguided attempts to take away some of his pain. But "the reality of grief is the absence of God," Coffin noted, and we must all guard against easy words offered "for self-protection, to pretty up a situation whose bleakness [we] simply [cannot] face" ("My Son Beat Me to the Grave," *A.D.*, June 1983, p. 26).

Perhaps you have gone through some experience of grief recently. Surely, all of us have been in situations where we attempted to comfort some grieving person. The predominant response to death or the presence of tragedy and the resultant pain is "I didn't know what to say." What do we say? Does our biblical faith offer us insights that make a difference in the way we respond to grief? Today's lesson concerns our everyday, persistent experiences of grief. Our study of David's Lament for Saul and Jonathan raises the question, What is Christian grief?

SECOND QUARTER
Selected Scripture

| King James Version | Revised Standard Version |

2 Samuel 1:17-27

17 And David lamented with this lamentation over Saul and over Jonathan his son:

18 (Also he bade them teach the children of Judah *the use of* the bow: behold, *it is* written in the book *of* Jasher.)

19 The beauty of Israel is slain upon thy high places; how are the mighty fallen!

20 Tell *it* not in Gath, publish *it* not in the streets of Askelon; lest the daughters of the Philistines rejoice, lest the daughters of the uncircumcised triumph.

21 Ye mountains of Gilboa, *let there be* no dew, neither *let there be* rain, upon you, nor fields of offerings: for there the shield of the mighty is vilely cast away, the shield of Saul *as though he had* not *been* anointed with oil.

22 From the blood of the slain, from the fat of the mighty, the bow of Jonathan turned not back, and the sword of Saul returned not empty.

23 Saul and Jonathan *were* lovely and pleasant in their lives, and in their death they were not divided: they were swifter than eagles, they were stronger than lions.

24 Ye daughters of Israel, weep over Saul, who clothed you in scarlet, with *other* delights, who put on ornaments of gold upon your apparel.

2 Samuel 1:17-27

17 And David lamented with this lamentation over Saul and Jonathan his son, 18 and he said it should be taught to the people of Judah; behold, it is written in the Book of Jashar. He said:

19 "Thy glory, O Israel, is slain upon thy high places!
How are the mighty fallen!

20 Tell it not in Gath,
publish it not in the streets of Ashkelon;
lest the daughters of the Philistines rejoice,
lest the daughters of the uncircumcised exult.

21 "Ye mountains of Gilboa,
let there be no dew or rain upon you,
nor upsurging of the deep!
For there the shield of the mighty was defiled,
the shield of Saul, not anointed with oil.

22 "From the blood of the slain,
from the fat of the mighty,
the bow of Jonathan turned not back,
and the sword of Saul returned not empty.

23 "Saul and Jonathan, beloved and lovely!
In life and in death they were not divided;
they were swifter than eagles,
they were stronger than lions.

24 "Ye daughters of Israel, weep over Saul,
who clothed you daintily in scarlet,
who put ornaments of gold upon your apparel.

DECEMBER 15   LESSON 3

25 How are the mighty fallen in the midst of the battle! O Jonathan, *thou wast* slain in thine high places.

26 I am distressed for thee, my brother Jonathan: very pleasant hast thou been unto me thy love to me was wonderful, passing the love of women.

27 How are the mighty fallen, and the weapons of war perished!

Key Verse: **Saul and Jonathan were lovely and pleasant in their lives, and in their death they were not divided: they were swifter than eagles, they were stronger than lions. (2 Samuel 1:23)**

25 "How are the mighty fallen in the midst of the battle!

"Jonathan lies slain upon thy high places.

26 I am distressed for you, my brother Jonathan;
very pleasant have you been to me;
your love to me was wonderful,
passing the love of women.

27 "How are the mighty fallen, and the weapons of war perished!"

Key Verse: **Saul and Jonathan, beloved and lovely! In life and in death they were not divided; they were swifter than eagles, they were stronger than lions. (2 Samuel 1:23)**

As You Read the Scripture—Horace R. Weaver

Do you remember, from your childhood days, being asked, "Who killed Cock Robin?" We face a similar question in this session: Who took the life of King Saul?

First, 1 Samuel 31:

> The Philistines fought against Israel; and the men of Israel fled before the Philistines and fell slain on Mount Gilboa. . . . The battle pressed hard upon Saul, and the archers found him; and he was badly wounded by the archers. Then Saul said to his armor-bearer, 'Draw your sword, and thrust me through with it, lest these uncircumcised come and thrust me through, and make sport of me.' But his armor-bearer would not; for he feared greatly. Therefore Saul took his own sword, and fell upon it. And when his armor-bearer saw that Saul was dead, he also fell upon his sword, and died with him. Thus Saul died, and his three sons.

Clearly, Saul killed himself!

Second, 2 Samuel 1:1–16: In this view an Amalekite claims he killed King Saul. The Amalekite appeared before David with "clothes rent and earth upon his head" (1 Samuel 1:2). He told David he had escaped from the camp of Israel, that "the people also have fallen and are dead; and Saul and his son Jonathan are also dead" (1 Samuel 1:4*b*). He told David he was on Mount Gilboa and witnessed "Saul leaning upon his spear," and that Saul begged him to "stand beside me and slay me. . . . So I stood beside him, and slew him, because I was sure that he could not live after he had fallen" (1 Samuel 1:6, 9-10).

Did the Amalekite purposely lie, hoping David would approve his killing King Saul and give him a reward? Did he really take "the crown which was

SECOND QUARTER

on his head and the armlet which was on his arm" and bring them "here to my lord"?

If Saul killed himself, did David know it, yet order the Amalekite's death? (1 Samuel 1:15).

1 Samuel 1:17. On learning of the death of King Saul and his son Jonathan, David composed one of the finest odes on friendship that has ever been written. David praised the virtues of Saul and the prowess of both Saul and Jonathan. David was known as a gifted musician and composer of songs.

Verse 19. David sang:

> Thy glory, O Israel, is slain upon thy high places!
> How are the mighty fallen!

David honored and loved Israel's first king, and his son Jonathan.

Perhaps this is the time to refer to Hebrew poetry. There are three major types of poetry. In the first sort, termed *synonymous*, the second line (called a stich) repeats the thought of the first:

> For there the shield of the mighty was defiled;
> the shield of Saul, not anointed with oil.
> (2 Samuel 1:21b)

In the second sort, termed *synthetic*, the second stich supplements or completes the first; for an example, see verse 19, quoted above.

In the third sort, termed *antithetic*, the second stich presents some antithesis to the first line:

> He will guard the feet of his faithful ones;
> but the wicked shall be cut off in darkness.
> (1 Samuel 2:9)

Verse 20. "Tell it not in Gath" nor in Ashkelon, two of the major Philistine cities in Judah,

> Lest the daughters of the Philistines rejoice,
> lest the daughters of the uncircumcised exult.

Verse 21. David speaks in anger:

> Ye mountains of Gilboa,
>   let there be no dew or rain upon you,
>   nor upsurging of the deep!
> For there the shield of the mighty was defiled,
>   the shield of Saul, not anointed with oil [as for a king].

Verse 22. In poetic language the arrow and the sword were considered devouring monsters that drink the blood and eat the fat of their victims.

Verse 23. David, lonely and unloved in his own family relationships, felt the pain of divisiveness.

> Saul and Jonathan, beloved and lovely!
> In life and in death they were not divided;

DECEMBER 15   LESSON 3

Verses 25b-26. David's memories:

> Jonathan lies slain upon thy high places.
> I am distressed for you, my brother Jonathan;
> very pleasant have you been to me;
> your love to me was wonderful,
> passing the love of women.

Verse 27.

> How are the mighty fallen,
> and the weapons of war perished!

David senses the folly and futility of war!

The Scripture and the Main Question—William H. Willimon

Accepting the Reality of Grief

I suppose that the first thing we ought to note, as we begin our study of 2 Samuel 1:17-27, is that David grieved. He gave public, open, poetic expression to his great grief for Saul and Jonathan. David's own deep and abiding faith in God in no way insulated or protected him from the experience of grief; in fact, his faith in God helped him to be open about his grief.

Perhaps that seems a trite, self-evident observation. Of course David grieved. Two people whom he loved deeply are dead. His grief is natural and expected. Yet there are some people who seem to feel that if we *really* had firm faith in God, somehow our faith would enable us to sidestep grief. We would be able to console ourselves with some sort of religious reassurance that would take away our pain and enable us to face bereavement and loss with smiling confidence.

So, let us begin by noting that David grieved.

In his book *Don't Take My Grief Away* (Harper & Row, 1979), Douglas Manning notes the intolerance of our society to people in grief. Parents, friends, even clergy offer support to the bereaved "by finding subtle but effective ways to take grief away" (pp. 64-65). A mother asks her grieving daughter if her crying "really helps." Friends say that it is "time to move on." Neighbors take the new widow aside and tell her that she should try to "be strong" as if her grief were a sign of weakness.

While these acts are often well intended, Manning says that they are not always the loving thing to offer grieving people. They fail to respect the reality of another's grief; we are acting as if we know better than the bereaved the real significance of their grief. They imply that the grieving person is pathetic, that tears are a sign of weakness or uncertain faith. Such actions may, in Manning's words, leave the griever "wondering if she is weak or even crazy."

The pain we feel, on occasions of bereavement and loss, is our spirit's way of telling us that our situation is serious. We must not ignore the reality of our grief or attempt to flee the pain. This means that grief, far from being a sign of weakness, is often a sign of strength, a sign that we are courageous enough to face the reality of loss. Weakness would be to deny or to medicate (through drugs or alcohol) the pain, and not to face the grief.

SECOND QUARTER

Psychologists often speak of "grief work," and that is how it often feels—like work. Grief takes time and effort. As May Sarton puts it, "The only way through pain... is through it, to absorb, probe, understand exactly what it is and what it means. To close the door on pain is to miss the chance for growth, isn't it?... Even the most terrible shock has somehow to be built into the fabric of the personality" (*Recovering: A Journal*, W. W. Norton, 1980, p. 13).

And of course, this is exactly what David did in his eloquent lament in 2 Samuel 1:17-27. He used his poetic skills to give vent to his anger, his hurt, his deep sense of regret. He did not deny the pain or prattle on about how their deaths were "God's will," or indulge in cheap consolation. He grieved.

Grief Work

Sometimes in the seminary class I teach on worship, when we are studying funerals, a student will ask, "Who is the funeral for, anyway?" It is a good question. Until we can answer that question, we really do not know how to plan or lead Christian funerals.

The most obvious answer is that funerals are for the family and close friends of the deceased, who are going through the acute crisis of grief at the loss of a close relative or friend. Yet we must remember that they are not the only ones going through grief. Life being what it is, all of us are either preparing to grieve or still dealing with past grief. So in this sense, a funeral is for all of us. We are all continuously engaged in "grief work." This fact makes funerals significant as educational experiences. Here is where the Christian community gives people help in preparing to grieve.

I wonder, as we read David's eloquent lament for these two dead men, if perhaps people in earlier generations were more adept than we in dealing with their grief. Fewer people attend funerals these days. Many people must bear their loss alone, without the presence of close family and friends. Do we really confront our loss, or do we hide from it? Do you believe that your own church does a good or a poor job of helping people through their grief and enabling them to do necessary grief work?

Ira Nerken, director of Widowed Persons Grieving Support Groups, based in Washington, D.C., says of our loss and bereavement, "Unless processed through grief, pain will eventually find a way out in illness or depression, or will lead the griever to avoid all the deep feelings with which it is associated, preventing her from ever again feeling love or enjoying herself as deeply as before" ("Making It Safe to Grieve," *The Christian Century*, Nov. 30, 1988, pp. 1091-95).

In other words, grief turned inward, pain kept silent and unexpressed, can be most destructive. Studies show that husbands whose wives died by accident or violence are sixty-six times more likely to kill themselves. Women who die of heart disease are six times more likely than other women to have been bereaved in the past six months. Heart disease among widowers under forty-five has been found to be ten times the rate among married men of the same age. "In a sense," notes the *Harvard Mental Health Letter* (March 1987), "people do die of a broken heart." Spouse loss is classified as the most stressful of all bad events in life.

Music is the means by which we express our deepest emotions, both positive and negative. David, in his great grief, turned to music and gave

DECEMBER 15   LESSON 3

voice to his feelings of lamentation. At funerals, isn't it interesting that music often plays such an important role in the service?

Good Grief

We are now in the Christian season of Advent, the time of preparation for Christmas. This Christmas, as every Christmas, people who have experienced recent bereavement or loss will feel that loss more acutely during the holiday season. There will be one less present under the tree, one less place at the holiday dinner table. Therefore, this provides an excellent occasion for your adult class to ponder the significance of David's song of lament and to think together about grief.

As Paul once said, "We do not grieve as those who have no hope." Yet we still grieve. Nothing about the faith of Christians removes the pain of loss and bereavement. In fact, knowing how dear each human life is to our loving God, knowing how God agonizes over each person's life, convinces us that God understands our grief and stands beside us in our times of pain and anguish.

Knowing the presence of a loving God may not take away the pain, but it certainly makes the pain more bearable.

Helping Adults Become Involved—Robert G. Rogers

Preparing to Teach

You will be teaching about a different type of song in this lesson. Whereas the previous two lessons dealt with celebration, this one deals with lamentation. As you prepare for this lesson, it might be useful to think about those emotions caused by the death of a friend or family member.

Read 2 Samuel 1:17-27 and also 2 Samuel 1:1-16 for background to David's song of lamentation. Notice particularly how David grieves for his close friend, Jonathan.

Your aim in this lesson is to demonstrate that pain due to the loss of another human being is real; it is not to be trivialized. Pain, like joy, is part of the range of human experiences. It is appropriate that we study a song of lament, which fits the occasion so readily.

Introducing the Main Question

In his exposition, Dr. Willimon points out the reality of pain for those who grieve for a loved one. In opening up the topic, be aware of those in your class who are recently bereaved. This lesson may be rather difficult for them to study. You might indicate some of your own personal experience with grief as a means of reassuring everyone that it is acceptable to discuss death and grief.

To understand David's pain, we must look at our own. Ask those who are willing to do so to share their own reactions to the death of someone with whom they were close. What words describe their feelings? Can they recall any song or hymn that was comforting during the time of acute loss?

You should also spend a few minutes contrasting the themes of a song of lament with those of a song of celebration. This would provide a good

SECOND QUARTER

review of lessons 1 and 2. Point out how God is praised in each. Is there any significant difference between the two types?

Developing the Lesson

After a brief period of discussion, you will want to explore, with sensitivity, what the death of a loved one means to those who remain behind. By doing this, your class will explore some of the reasons for grief while affirming the process that can heal the bereaved. Proceed with the lesson under three headings:

> I. The cost of friendship
> II. Lamentation and grief work
> III. Divine love and healing

I. The cost of friendship

Clearly, David had a deep, abiding affection for his friend Jonathan. David also greatly respected Saul, the king. David and Jonathan's friendship was based on common experiences they had shared. Such friendship has great rewards. It also carries a risk. The more one is involved intimately with another person's life, the greater the loss when that relationship is ruptured by death.

Have class members speak about friends they have had or currently have. What benefits have come to both parties through these friendships? Likely they have shared personal triumphs and defeats. Probably they have expanded each other's horizons. Perhaps they have even challenged each other's views on moral issues. The point is that true friendship takes a commitment of time, personal concern, and, on occasion, even material resources. Conclude this section by noting that true friendship demands a great deal of both parties. However, the possibilities of personal growth only occur when we are willing to risk a sharing of ourselves with others in a trusting relationship.

II. Lamentation and grief work

Begin by asserting that death brings conflicting emotions to the living. We feel a sense of loss or sadness; we also may feel abandoned and even angry that we have been left behind. If we have invested in someone, we quite naturally tend to resent his or her leaving us. Affirm these responses as being legitimate. The bereaved should not feel guilty about these feelings. (Of course, one should eventually move beyond resentment to a sense of thanksgiving for the life well lived.)

Note the value to David of the song that he composed. It allowed him to let his innermost feelings "get out." As a rule, it is not healthy to keep our feelings about death tightly bound up within us. Good "grief work" demands that we face our feelings honestly and accept them as a necessary response to death. This helps us to get on with the business of living.

Having spoken about the legitimacy of grief work, turn to the question of how to help one who is grieving. You might begin by commenting on Dr. Willimon's rejection of "easy answers" as a means of explaining the meaning of death. Why are these answers not helpful? What necessary "grief work" do such answers often cut off? Members of the class should be encouraged

DECEMBER 15   LESSON 3

to share those acts or words from others that have helped in their own time of grief.

III. Divine love and healing

Having looked at the cost of friendship and the necessity of grief work, it is time to look at what role God and the church family can play in the healing process. It would be useful at the outset to acknowledge that a loving God does not take away the pain of loss; his presence, however, does help us to bear the pain.

Focus especially on the role of the church family as agents of a loving God. Name some specific ways in which church members can help the recently bereaved. For example, those who mourn can be included in social functions. (It is important, of course, to move at the pace set by the grieving member.) Turn to the class for other suggestions on how to demonstrate God's love and concern through human words and deeds. During the discussion, you might mention that we need to be sensitive when ministering to those who are grief-stricken. What is helpful to one may be a hindrance to another. Your pastor might be helpful in offering guidance to those who would minister.

Helping Class Members Act

For the coming week, class members might meditate on two facets of the lesson: (1) the value of a specific friendship and (2) useful ways to reach out to a bereaved person in the community. Perhaps reflecting on the value of friendship will aid in ministering to those who mourn.

Planning for Next Sunday

Next Sunday is the last lesson in the series on songs from ancient Israel. It describes the joy of two Jewish women: Hannah and Mary.

Encourage class members to read 1 Samuel 2:1-5 and Luke 1:46-55 carefully. Both passages express great joy at the birth of a child. What better way to celebrate the last Sunday in Advent.

Unto Us a Savior Is Born
HORACE R. WEAVER

After the ministries of Nehemiah and Ezra in the fifth century B.C., a new attitude toward God emerged. Ezra brought the law (the Torah) to Judah and read it to Israel at the Water Gate. The people needed the law and Ezra's emphasis on obedience to the Torah brought unexpected results.

Ezra encouraged the reading of the law as the major religious event of the day. If a Jew wanted an interpretation of God's purposes on any matter, he or she sought a learned person (a rabbi) who could interpret the Word. No longer did a person go to a prophet, and sometimes not even to a priest. Psalm 74:9 states:

SECOND QUARTER

> There is no longer any prophet,
> and there is none among us who knows how long.
> How long, O God . . . ?

In the days of Zechariah, Elizabeth, Joseph, and Mary, the main source for religious and legal information came from the written Word, the Torah. God was present, all right. But the Deity's responses were available only in "the Book." God no longer communicated directly. No prophetic voice succeeded Haggai and Zechariah. As the Syrian Apocalypse of Baruch stated, "The prophets have lain down to sleep" (85:3).

People longed for the coming of the Messiah, who would pour out the prophetic and quickened Spirit. Luke's Gospel describes the fresh breath of the new Spirit.

The Coming of John

Luke begins by referring to two types of authoritative persons: King Herod, king of Judah, and a priest named Zechariah. Herod represents the evil, sensuous immorality of the time. He died in 4 B.C. Just prior to that time, the cousins John and Jesus were born. (Yes, our calendars are off by probably six years.)

John's father, Zechariah, was opposite in nature to Herod. He and his wife Elizabeth belonged to the priestly class and apparently were quiet and faithful to their faith in God. Zechariah and his son would prove to be many times more significant to mankind than was Herod. But they were childless. They had no son to continue their priestly duties. "Now while he was serving as priest before God when his division [the eighth of 24] was on duty, according to the custom of the priesthood, it fell to him by lot to enter the temple of the Lord and burn incense. . . . And there appeared to him an angel of the Lord. . . . And Zechariah was troubled when he saw him, and fear fell upon him" (Luke 8-12). He was told that his wife Elizabeth would bear him a son, and his name would be John. Zechariah's ministry included morning and evening prayers. One prayer that he would have offered was "The Lord bless you and keep you; the Lord make his face to shine upon you, and be gracious unto you: the Lord lift up his countenance upon you and grant you peace" (Numbers 6:24-26).

Zechariah, having fulfilled his tasks by burning the incense and placing new bread on the table, was ready to offer the benedictions. But he could not give the benedictions. He was speechless [aphasia] and had to pantomime his prayers. His inability to speak may well have caused the worshipers to assume the Deity had spoken directly to him.

The messenger ("angel") told Zechariah that John would be a Nazirite (he would drink no wine nor strong drink) and would be filled with the Holy Spirit. Not for four hundred years had such a promise been spoken! John would go before God "in the spirit and power of Elijah . . . to make ready for the Lord a people prepared" (1:17).

Elizabeth Conceives

The angel Gabriel, who had been with Zechariah in the temple, appeared to Mary. She was told, "Behold you will conceive in your womb and bear a son, and you shall call his name Jesus" (1:31). Jesus is the Greek form of the

UNTO US A SAVIOR IS BORN

Old Testament name Joshua, or Jeshua. We have been told that almost fifty boys carried that name when Jesus received it too.

Gabriel Told Mary:

> The Holy Spirit will come upon you
> and the power of the Most High will overshadow you;
> therefore the child to be born will be called holy,
> the son of God.
> (1:35)

There are seventy titles synonymous with the word "Messiah," some of which are the Holy One, the Begotten, the Logos, the only Begotten, and the Christ. Surely Mary was aware of the meaning of this title, son of God—her son, Jeshua, was/is the Messiah!

Mary Goes to Judah

Mary, on learning of her pregnancy, goes (with Joseph) to the hill country of Judah, about three miles west of Jerusalem to Ain Kerem, where Elizabeth and Zechariah lived. Elizabeth gives birth to John, at which time Zechariah's aphasia disappears. He ordered that his son be named John. Later on John would declare his cousin Jesus to be the Messiah. Joseph and Mary went to the city of David (Bethlehem, "house of bread") to be enrolled, as was required by Caesar Augustus. The dates implied by the scripture are difficult to adjust. P. Sulpicius Quirinius was viceroy of Syria in 10-7 B.C. and governor of Syria in A.D. 6. Luke was probably thinking, not the governor of Syria, but of the viceroy of Syria. These dates (10-7 B.C.) fit in well with our awareness that our calendar is off by several (5-6) years.

Luke: Emperor Caesar Augustus

Luke carefully shares significant information that is easily lost by the magnificent way in which he presented his knowledge of the relationship between Augustus Caesar and Jesus. The basic questions were/are: Who is *soter* (savior) and *divi filius* (son of God)? Who brought the *euangelion* (good news) to all mankind? Who brought peace (*shalom*) to mankind? What male choir outshone all other male choirs? Who was King of Kings, and Lord of Lords?

Luke, in introducing Caesar Augustus (the supreme ruler of the Roman Empire) portrays him as an agent of God. It was due to Caesar Augustus's edict of registration that Jesus was born in the city of David. Augustus Caesar ruled for 42 years (27 B.C.–A.D. 14). We know Herod the Great ruled under the authority of Augustus Caesar. Herod died in 4 B.C. In 6 B.C. he ordered the death of all male Jewish babies (born in Bethlehem) who were two years of age or younger (so Matthew). Herod feared the coming of the Messiah.

Augustus Caesar's reign was noted for his concern for international peace. Caesar ordered all piracy throughout the empire to cease. His naval forces established law and order on the seas. All persons could now travel safely by sea. Caesar also ordered military forces to clear the land of brigands and he ordered the construction of military stations to be located

SECOND QUARTER

every mile (*stadia*) throughout the Roman Empire. The Apostle Paul and his many friends would have used these highways with gratitude.

Caesar ushered in a new age, the age of peace—the famous *Pax Romana*. On January 1, 42 B.C., Caesar was recognized as a god by the power of the Roman senate. At the same time he was named Octavian and was given the title *divi filius* (son of god). It was in 27 B.C. that the senate bestowed on him the title of Augustus ("divine") Caesar, which gave him the supreme position in the restored republic. From this time on he was Emperor (*imperator*) Caesar Augustus. (Note that his family name was Caesar; during the decades various members of that family assumed the title of Augustus (meaning "divine"), such as Nero Caesar and Domitian Caesar; the latter ruled at the time of the writing of Revelation.)

The Roman senate ordered the erection and consecration of an altar honoring Augustus Caesar. The altar was placed in the Campus Martius, which is still on display in Rome. All peoples east of the Mediterranean world hailed Augustus as "savior" and "god" and/or the "son of God." These are the same words used in referring to Jesus as savior and son of god (*divi filius*). Such persons as Paul, Luke, Titus, Sylvanus, Priscilla, and Aquila would have been ordered to bow before the various Caesar images (deities) of those days, as Revelation 13 illustrates. We know many refused to worship man-declared, human-made deities! Phrases such as "sotera tou sympantos, Augustus" ("savior of the whole world, Augustus") were a cause of anguish for followers of Jesus Christ. Caesar's birthday (Sept. 23) was celebrated by use of the statement, "[The birthday] of the god [Augustus Caesar] has marked the beginning of the good news [*euangelion*] through him for the world."

Luke recognized the vanity, idolatry, and basic dishonesty of such a senatorial claim. Luke skillfully declared that the euangelion (good news) comes not through or by the imperator (emperor), but through a child who was born in a manger in Bethlehem, the city of David (not Rome). The good news comes, as Luke states it, through a poor family with Jewish names: Mary and Joseph and, of course, Jesus. It was a group of lowly shepherds, not the nobility of the Roman senate, who heard the magnificent male choir of the heavenly host singing: "I bring you good news [*euangelion*] of a great joy which will come to all the people; for to you is born this day in the city of David [Bethlehem] a Savior, who is Christ the Lord" (Luke 2:10-11). Note: Luke avoids the use of *euangelion* in his Gospel and uses it only twice in Acts (15:7; 20:24). However, Luke uses the word *euangelizesthai* ten times. Luke is purposely careful not to contradict the family of Caesars, who assume they are the ones who have brought in the good news for all the world.

Luke writes carefully, for he seeks not to irritate the political and military structures of Rome but to affirm that "good news" arises, not from the senate's action in Rome, but from God's (not the emperor's) actions, not from phrases such as *Ave Caesar* (hail, Caesar), but from the angelic phrase, *Ave Maria* (Hail, Mary). We are impressed with how carefully Luke chooses his words and phrases, which could well have caused his death if they had been understood by the senate. Luke is writing about 85 B.C. The Caesar of Luke's days lived 81-96 A.D., led by the "beast" of Domitian.

Luke is excitedly and amazingly aware that a new era of human history has begun in the birth and eventually the ministry, death, and resurrection of Jesus, the Messiah (which title in Greek is *Christ*). Luke portrays the child Jesus, born under *Pax Romana*, as one who will be hailed as the King, the

DECEMBER 22   LESSON 4

One who is to come in the name of the Lord, and one through whom, sometime, there will be peace in heaven and glory in the highest heaven (Luke 19:38).

LESSON 4   DECEMBER 22

Songs of Joy

Background Scripture: 1 Samuel 2:1-10; Luke 1:26-56

The Main Question—William H. Willimon

If your church has been celebrating the Christian season of Advent, and I hope that it has, then you have restrained yourself throughout the Sundays of Advent, confined your singing to slow-moving, somewhat somber hymns of hope, anticipation, expectancy. "O Come, O Come, Emmanuel, and ransom captive Israel." This Sunday, anticipation has become fulfillment. Now we are at last ready to sing of Christmas. Christmas is the season of singing.

No gospel does this better than Luke. Luke tells of the birth of Jesus with song and poetry rather than prose. Mary hears that she is going to be a Mama—she sings. The angels sing, Elizabeth sings, Simeon sings, everybody sings. (Everybody, that is, but poor Zechariah!)

In your own life, you know what this is like. You are moving through your ordinary, prosaic day, washing to be done, letters to be written, dusting to be done. Then there is a telephone call, a knock at the door. Some good news meets you, and what is your immediate, unconscious, innate response to you? You *sing*. Suddenly, quite without conscious effort, you go about the rest of your day with a song. Mary's good news, as did the good news to Hannah before her, evoked exactly the same response.

> My soul magnifies the Lord,
> and my spirit rejoices in God my Savior.
>
> ....
>
> He has put down the mighty from their thrones,
> and exalted those of low degree.
> (Luke 1:46-47, 52)

Is there something in your life that could only be set right by the intervention of a loving God? Are there circumstances that are so depressing that only an act of God can turn them to joy? These are the questions for which the songs of Mary and Hannah are a biblical response.

SECOND QUARTER

Selected Scripture

| **King James Version** | **Revised Standard Version** |

1 Samuel 2:1-5

1 And Hannah prayed, and said, My heart rejoiceth in the Lord, mine horn is exalted in the Lord: my mouth is enlarged over mine enemies; because I rejoice in thy salvation.

2 *There is* none holy as the Lord: for *there is* none besides thee: neither *is there* any rock like our God.
3 Talk no more so exceeding proudly; let *not* arrogancy come out of your mouth: for the Lord *is* a God of knowledge, and by him actions are weighed.
4 The bows of the mighty men *are* broken, and they that stumbled are girded with strength.
5 *They that were* full have hired out themselves for bread; and *they that were* hungry ceased: so that the barren hath born seven; and she that hath many children is waxed feeble.

Luke 1:46-55

46 And Mary said, My soul doth magnify the Lord,
47 And my spirit hath rejoiced in God my Saviour.
48 For he hath regarded the low estate of his handmaiden: for, behold, from henceforth all generations shall call me blessed.
49 For he that is mighty hath done to me great things; and holy *is* his name.
50 And his mercy *is* on them that fear him from generation to generation.
51 He hath shewed strength with his arm; he hath scattered the proud in the imagination of their hearts.

1 Samuel 2:1-5

1 Hannah also prayed and said,
  "My heart exults in the Lord;
    my strength is exalted in the Lord.
  My mouth derides my enemies,
    because I rejoice in thy salvation.

2 "There is none holy like the Lord,
    there is none besides thee;
    there is no rock like our God.
3 Talk no more so very proudly,
    let not arrogance come from your mouth;
  for the Lord is a God of knowledge,
    and by him actions are weighed.
4 The bows of the mighty are broken,
    but the feeble gird on strength.
5 Those who were full have hired themselves out for bread,
    but those who were hungry have ceased to hunger.
  The barren has borne seven,
    but she who has many children is forlorn."

Luke 1:46-55

46 And Mary said,
  "My soul magnifies the Lord,
47 and my spirit rejoices in God my Savior,
48 for he has regarded the low estate of his handmaiden.
  For behold, henceforth all generations will call me blessed;
49 for he who is mighty has done great things for me,
    and holy is his name.
50 And his mercy is on those who fear him
    from generation to generation.
51 He has shown strength with his arm,
    he has scattered the proud in the imagination of their hearts,

DECEMBER 22   LESSON 4

52 He hath put down the mighty from *their* seats, and exalted them of low degree.
53 He hath filled the hungry with good things; and the rich he hath sent empty away.

54 He hath holpen his servant Israel, in remembrance of *his* mercy;
55 As he spake to our fathers, to Abraham, and to his seed for ever.

Key Verse: **My soul doth magnify the Lord, and my spirit hath rejoiced in God my Saviour. (Luke 1:46-47)**

52 he has put down the mighty from their thrones,
and exalted those of low degree;
53 he has filled the hungry with good things,
and the rich he has sent empty away.
54 He has helped his servant Israel, in remembrance of his mercy,
55 as he spoke to our fathers, to Abraham and to his posterity for ever."

Key Verse: **My soul magnifies the Lord, and my spirit rejoices in God my Savior. (Luke 1:46-47)**

As You Read the Scripture—Horace R. Weaver

The Scripture background for today's study is from 1 Samuel 2:1-10 and Luke 1:26-55. We will observe how readily Mary borrowed from the song of Hannah. The Magnificat includes much from Hannah's song of joy and thanksgiving to God. Mary, of course, added new verses of praise.

Elkanah had two wives: Peninnah, who had several sons and daughters, and Hannah, who had none, though she prayed for years for a son (1 Samuel 1:11). As Hannah prayed, Eli, the head priest at Shiloh, thought she was a drunken woman, for only her lips moved. But she was speaking to God from the heart. When Eli realized the earnestness of her prayer, he said, "Go in peace, and the God of Israel grant your petition" (1:17). In due time she conceived and bore a son—Samuel.

In keeping with the vow she had made to the Lord, Hannah, after she had weaned Samuel, took him to Eli the priest at Shiloh and said to him: This is my son, Samuel—I have lent him to the Lord, as long as he lives!

1 Samuel 2:1. Note the fine use of parallelism in this selection of Hebrew poetry, throughout the ten verses. Each line (stich) generally receives two or three accents per line. The pattern of these accents makes up the poem's meter.

Hannah sings, using synthetic parallelism (see lesson 3),

> My heart exults in the Lord,
>   my strength is exalted in the Lord.

The King James Version correctly uses the word "horn" in this verse, a lovely metaphor for a wild animal (a deer or a ram) carrying its head high in triumph and awareness of its strength.

> My mouth derides my enemies,
>   because I rejoice in thy salvation.

The King James Version translation reflects the meaning of the Hebrew verb used here, translated as "gaping," which refers in turn to the ancient Hebrew gesture of contempt (see Psalm 35:21 for another example).

SECOND QUARTER

Verse 2.

> There is none holy like the Lord,
> there is none besides thee;
> there is no rock like our God.

Because God is holy, there is "no rock" to be compared with him as a source of stability and strength in time of need.

Verse 3. Addressing the enemies of Israel, Hannah says:

> Talk no more so very proudly,
> let not arrogance come from your mouth.

Verses 6, 8.

> The Lord kills [brings death] and brings to life [birth];
> ....
> He raises up the poor from the dust.

The Lord is concerned about those sleeping in garbage heaps at night and seeking alms for bread.

> he lifts the needy from the ash heap,
> to make them sit with princes and inherit a seat of honor.

Verse 9. "He will guard the feet of his faithful ones."

Luke 1:46-55. My soul magnifies the Lord! Verses 46*b* to 50 offer personal thanksgiving to God for his mighty acts.

Verse 47. "And my spirit rejoices in God my Savior."

Verse 48*a*. This verse seems to apply to Elizabeth, for God has regarded her "low estate" (i.e., childlessness), while 48*b* applies to Mary, "for behold, henceforth all generations will call me blessed."

Verse 49. This verse can well apply to both Elizabeth and Mary:

> For he who is mighty has done great things for me,
> and holy is his name.

Verses 51-55. In these lines the song moves from personal thankfulness to praising God for his mighty acts.

Verses 51-52.

> He has shown strength with his arm,
> he has scattered the proud in the imagination of their hearts,
> he has put down the mighty from their thrones,
> and exalted those of low degree.

Verses 53-54. God's biases are described:

> he has filled the hungry with good things,
> and the rich he has sent empty away.
> He has helped his servant Israel,
> in remembrance of his mercy.

Verse 55. The canticle concludes with references to God's ancient promise:

DECEMBER 22　　　　　　　　　　　　　　　　　　LESSON 4

> As he spoke to our fathers,
> to Abraham and to his posterity for ever.

The Scripture and the Main Question—William H. Willimon

Music and Liberation

Would you sing if you were Mary? After all, Mary's being "great with child" is not something she could explain or understand, not something she had chosen or planned. It put her in a bad way with her fiance. The angel told Mary to "fear not," but old Simeon told Mary the truth of what it meant for her to be "blessed among women" when he predicted that "a sword will also pierce your side." Motherhood would not be easy for Mary. Yet Mary sang:

> My soul magnifies the Lord,
> and my spirit rejoices in God my Savior.

This is no lullaby Mary sings. The words thunder forth like a battle chant:

> He has shown strength with is arm
> he has scattered the proud in the imagination of their hearts,
> he has put down the mighty from their thrones,
> ....
> and the rich he has sent empty away.

Not too sweet a Christmas carol, I think. It's a song about someone low going up, someone up high being brought low. You won't hear women singing like this except in Soweto, Warsaw, Harlem, or South Chicago.

A couple of years ago the government in Pretoria banned the lighting of candles or the singing of Christmas carols in Soweto. When asked why by the press, the South African Scrooge replied, "You know how emotional black women are. Christmas carols have an emotional effect upon them." (*St. Louis Post-Dispatch*, Dec. 27, 1985). You let a poor Jewish woman like Mary sing, a black mother in Soweto sing, you don't know where it might lead.

I'm a child of the sixties. When the German magazine *Der Spiegel* did a special issue this summer on my student years, "Der Wilden Sechstige" ("The Wild Sixties"), most of the article was about *the music* of the sixties. You can't understand what drove rebelling, protesting, out-of-control students into the streets of Detroit, Berlin, Paris, Chicago, or Duke if you never heard Janis Joplin, if you never heard Dylan whine "The Times They Are A'Changin'," if you never sat at a Jimi Hendrix concert and felt a solid wave of piercing sound rush past you with such force that it would part your hair. The sixties, a time of violence, peace, protest, civil rights, and a changing world order, began as a nearly spontaneous street outburst of boogie. It was a world torn loose with a solid wall of hard rock sound, or a group of Christians, hands joined, singing "We Shall Overcome."

"Music hath charms to soothe a savage breast." True, but it also hath power to release, cut loose, pull down, raise up. Imagine Mary's Magnificat sung, not by Anita Bryant accompanied by the Oral Roberts Singers, but by Janis Joplin backed up by the Rolling Stones, and you'll get my point.

SECOND QUARTER

A while back my choir director was lamenting that the teaching of choral music has declined in schools in the past few years. This affects recruitment of students for our chapel choir. In a time of a grim, "back-to-basics" educational mentality, we don't bother much with "frills" like music.

I find that tragic. The other night, I found a medical student here, late, playing the organ for all that he was worth. He's going to be a doctor, but when he wants to soar, he can be an organist.

"There will be days," I prophesied, "when your only protection from insanity as a physician will be that keyboard."

Liberating Joy

Think, this December, of all those brothers and sisters, near and far, who've lost the ability to sing. Voiceless, rendered speechless. Mary was young, unmarried, poor. Hannah before her was old, childless, poor. In that society, in that day, what had women like this to sing about?

A missionary once told me that when a child is utterly emaciated and near death, that child no longer cries. Tears dry up, and the child is silent. The hunger is so deep it has moved beyond pain, beyond feeling, to utter, empty silence. If you are hurt often enough, deep enough, disappointed, defeated, pushed down enough, before long you become withdrawn, quiet, silent.

The government is proud to report that Soweto is silent this Christmas. Santiago has accepted its dictator and is at peace this Noel. Harlem has stopped hoping for the holidays. The world has its brand of "Silent Night," but there is nothing holy or bright about it. I can't remember a Christmas when there were not enough starving children, enough grieving mothers, enough newly opened graves or raging King Herods to mock our happy yuletide music and silence our singing.

First-Century Judea, in the December darkness, without a star in the sky, people shut up in the darkened houses for fear of Roman soldiers, streets deserted and fearfully quiet . . . (One way to handle an oppressive situation in a place like Nazareth is to keep your head down, your mouth buttoned shut.) There, in the dark silence, a pure, clear, feminine voice cut through the night:

> My soul magnifies the Lord
> ....
> has put down the mighty from their thrones,
> and exalted those of low degree.

Before Herod knows what's happening, the streets are full of chanting, restless people on the move, and Herod regrets that he gave his troops time off for Christmas.

What happens to people when death walks in their front door? Numbed, speechless, silent.

"I didn't know what to say," friends will say. What is there to say in front of such a terrible presence? He's better off, now. I want you to know that we're thinking about you. It's God's will. Eventually, you'll get over this.

See? So trite. Such inadequate words. Might as well keep quiet. And that's just what most of us do. Keep quiet. Accept. Resign ourselves. Adjust. Quietly adapt.

Then a grieving family gathers at the church to confront its loss. And what does the church make them do? The church makes them sing. See them singing through their tears "A Mighty Fortress Is Our God." The church coaxes them to sing even when they don't feel like it. I tell you, such singing is pure defiance, stunning faith, clench-fisted revolution, impudent in the face of death's omnivorous presence. Death hates music, as do all tyrants.

In her singing, Mary becomes the premier disciple, a model for us all. She is the very first to hear the announcement that God is with us and the very first to believe. As Martin Luther once said in a Christmas sermon, three miracles occurred at Christ's nativity: God became human, a virgin conceived, Mary believed. For Luther, the greatest miracle that first Christmas was the last. Mary believed. Despite all the oppression, closed doors, brick walls, blind alleys, and dark, silent death, she believed. She sang.

Later, in chapter 11 of Luke's Gospel, when a well-meaning woman pronounces blessings on Jesus' mother, Jesus responds that the blessed are not those who claim biological kinship with him. ("My family have been members of this church since 1932.") The blessed are those *who hear and do God's word*. Mary is called "blessed among women" because she hears and responds. She sings. Thus she is a model for us, though she is rightly called the very first disciple.

Joy Mixed with Pain

Sure, there will be dark days ahead for Mary. Her joy as a mother will be mixed with much pain, as it is for any mother. Just down the road, in Ramah, mother Rachel weeps for her slaughtered babies, as others will weep for Mary's son. But for now, her faith enables Mary to sing.

And your life too, is not all Christmas carols and joy. Dark, cold January days lie just beyond our yuletide gladness. The days grow short, the nights are long. But for now, our faith enables us to sing. We sing because we believe; we believe as we sing.

> My soul magnifies the Lord
> and my spirit rejoices in God my Savior.

Helping Adults Become Involved—Robert G. Rogers

Preparing to Teach

This is the last lesson in the unit on songs from ancient Israel. Review the past three lessons and class sessions. Are there any remaining issues or questions that should be brought up in class this Sunday?

This is also the last Sunday in Advent. It is especially helpful to have Hannah and Mary "sing their songs." Read carefully 1 Samuel 2:1-5 and Luke 1:46-55. You might notice similarities between the stories of the two women. Can you personally identify with their joy?

Your central aim in this lesson is to demonstrate God's loving presence in the midst of human joy. Birth, like death, is part of the human drama. Humans need to affirm God's creative power.

SECOND QUARTER

Introducing the Main Question

Everyone loves a new baby. In the freshness and innocence of new life, we sense a rebirth of ourselves. Suggest that the Advent season precisely reflects this mood. Dr. Willimon particularly sets forth Mary's response of expectation. Call attention also to the joy of Hannah, who lived so many centuries prior to Mary. Point out the similarity between the songs of the two women. Both were of humble origin, and both expressed great joy at the birth of a child. Each woman's song praises God for this "miracle." Mary's Magnificat is modeled on the song of Hannah. Undoubtedly, as a young Jewish woman, she had heard Hannah's story.

Ask the class if we, today, can reach across the centuries and share with Hannah and Mary the thrill of expectation. Point out how important it is for men as well as women to hear a woman's perspective on the birthing process.

Developing the Lesson

You want to maintain a class mood of expectation. You will also want to help your people realize that loving a child carries a cost. Children are not born for the convenience of adults.

Develop the lesson in three sections:

        I. The mood of expectation
       II. The joy of new life
     III. The need to let go

I. The mood of expectation

In developing this section, point out that both Hannah and Mary viewed the birth of a child as a gift from God. In the case of Hannah particularly, she and her husband had waited many years for this "miracle" to occur. You need to be sensitive to the possibility that there are class members who are unable to bear children, despite their desire to do so. Do not give the impression that the inability to conceive is somehow a result of God's disfavor. Infertility is painful enough for a couple without having the added burden of guilt over some imagined sin.

It would be useful to emphasize the role of the entire church family in awaiting the birth of a long-expected child. Perhaps there is an expectant couple in the church whom you can cite as model. As the weeks progress toward the time of birth, everyone connected with the family begins to feel a sense of anticipation. We wait with the parents-to-be even as Hannah, Mary, and their husbands waited so many centuries ago.

II. The joy of new life

At the time of birth, there is an initial burst of joy. Turn the class's attention to both scriptural passages. Dr. Willimon points out that each woman's song has an element of "strong defiance" in its joy. We sense that each woman, humble and poor though she was, realized that she alone, with God's help, was bringing something special to the world. Mention that each child born has the capacity to be a special blessing in the world.

Help class members realize that each generation is part of the "chain of life." Spend a few moments pondering the question, How is bearing and raising a child a statement of our faith in the future?

New life brings great responsibility. We need to care for and nurture each new baby in our midst. This is a good way to help couples who are childless know that they are needed. Develop with the class ideas about the role of the entire church family in nurturing infants. Point out that the natural parents need the support and encouragement of the rest of the congregation. All of us have mutual responsibilities for helping the next generation face the future.

III. The need to let go

Begin this section by referring back to the two biblical mothers. Both soon faced a time when their sons became young men and had to follow their own calling. Hannah gave up her son, Samuel, to be trained by Eli as a priestly leader. Mary gave up her son, Jesus, to be messiah and savior for all people.

Reflect with the class how difficult it must have been for each woman to be separated from the one to whom she had given birth. How difficult it is for parents in every generation to face this inevitable time of separation. Indeed, all church members know the joy of seeing youngsters grow up in the church fellowship, but all have experienced the time when the young man or woman moves away to make a new life for himself or herself in the adult world. Suggest that our feelings are frequently mixed. One side of us wants to keep them forever young and innocent. (We may be trying to preserve our own youthfulness in the process.) The other side wants the young people to grow up and take their rightful place as responsible adults. Ah, how difficult it is to let them go!

Conclude this section by making reference to the Christmas message: the willingness of God to "let go" in giving his son to the human community. Knowing what lay ahead for Jesus, God still sent the Son to become "enfleshed" with the human family. The greater the love, the more that must be given up.

Helping Class Members Act

As your people look toward the promises of Christmas as fulfilled in the nativity of Jesus, they might ponder the joy and the responsibility that the birth of Jesus brings to Christians. To adore the infant is to accept the claims of the adult man on our lives.

Your class might also reflect on what role each can play in welcoming new babies into the church family.

Planning for Next Sunday

Next week begins a new unit entitled "Songs from Festive Occasions." All are drawn from the Old Testament.

They should read Psalm 8. This is a magnificent hymn celebrating God's lordship over the earth and the place of humanity within that wondrous creation. Suggest that the class pay special attention to the divine-human relationship as expressed therein.

UNIT II: SONGS FROM FESTIVE OCCASIONS
Horace R. Weaver

FIVE LESSONS   DECEMBER 29–JANUARY 26

Unit II examines a sampling of texts used at gatherings in the life of the people of Israel. Three of the five lessons in this unit deal with texts from Israel's hymnbook, the book of Psalms. The fourth lesson describes the love songs of the Song of Solomon. The last lesson features a different kind of love song, dealing with Israel's failure to return God's love.

The individual lessons are as follows: "Song of Praise," December 29 asks, What is the significance of human life? "Song of Worship," January 5 asks, Is there something in your life that could only be set right by the intervention of a loving God? "Song of Gratitude," January 12, asks, From whence springs a sense of gratitude? "Song of Love," January 19, asks, Just what is a Christian view of sex—dare we read the Song of Solomon (or do we dare not to read this biblical book)? "A Song of Unreturned Love," January 26, asks, What does God do when we fail to be faithful and loving to the Deity?

LESSON 5   DECEMBER 29

Song of Praise

Background Scripture: Psalm 8

The Main Question—William H. Willimon

What is the significance of human life? That is the question we will ponder today as we study one of the great psalms of the Bible.

Modern life has a way of making us feel rather small and insignificant. To my government, I am not a citizen, a name. I am a number. I am Social Security number 249-72-0710. To my bank, my insurance company, my employer, I am a number within a computer. Try corresponding with your credit card company or insurance company about a mistake on your billing. You are not having a conversation with a person. You are trying to make sense to a machine. That will make you feel small and insignificant!

Some of this is rather harmless, part of the aggravation of living in a technological computer age. But does all of this lead to more sinister complications as we are made to feel like mere cogs in a great, clanking machine?

Last year, nearly 1,800 New Yorkers were murdered by their fellow citizens. Our country has one of the highest infant mortality rates of any industrialized country in the world. All of this in a society that is founded on the belief in the integrity, the rights, and the freedoms of the individual. It is ironic that in actual practice, such a society has a way of making many of its citizens feel small and insignificant.

DECEMBER 29   LESSON 5

The poet who wrote Psalm 8 lived in a pretechnological age. Although he knew nothing about computers or social security numbers, he did know what it was like for a human being to feel very small and insignificant in so great a universe. This ancient psalmist raised some of the same questions about the place of human life in God's great scheme of things and came to some startling, and most helpful, answers.

"What is man, that thou art mindful of him?" That ancient question from the pages of the Psalms sounds as new and fresh as the headlines in this morning's newspaper.

What is the significance of human life?

Selected Scripture

King James Version

Psalm 8

1 O Lord our Lord, how excellent *is* thy name in all the earth! who hast set thy glory above the heavens.

2 Out of the mouth of babes and sucklings hast thou ordained strength because of thine enemies, that thou mightest still the enemy and the avenger.

3 When I consider thy heavens, the work of thy fingers, the moon and the stars, which thou hast ordained;

4 What is man, that thou art mindful of him? and the son of man, that thou visitest him?

5 For thou hast made him a little lower than the angels, and hast crowned him with glory and honour.

6 Thou madest him to have dominion over the works of thy hands; thou hast put all *things* under his feet:

7 All sheep and oxen, yea, and the beasts of the field;

8 The fowl of the air, and the fish of the sea, *and whatsoever* passeth through the paths of the seas.

Revised Standard Version

Psalm 8

1 O Lord, our Lord,
   how majestic is thy name in all the earth!

   Thou whose glory above the heavens is chanted
2 by the mouth of babes and infants,
   thou hast founded a bulwark because of thy foes,
   to still the enemy and the avenger.

3 When I look at thy heavens, the work of thy fingers,
   the moon and the stars which thou hast established;

4 what is man that thou art mindful of him,
   and the son of man that thou dost care for him?

5 Yet thou hast made him little less than God,
   and dost crown him with glory and honor.

6 Thou hast given him dominion over the works of thy hands;
   thou hast put all things under his feet,

7 all sheep and oxen,
   and also the beasts of the field,

8 the birds of the air, and the fish of the sea,
   whatever passes along the paths of the sea.

SECOND QUARTER

9 O Lord our Lord, how excellent *is* thy name in all the earth!

Key Verse: O Lord, our Lord, how excellent is thy name in all the earth. (Psalm 8:9)

9 O Lord, our Lord,
 how majestic is thy name in all the earth!

Key Verse: O Lord, our Lord, how majestic is thy name in all the earth. (Psalm 8:9)

As You Read the Scripture—Horace R. Weaver

In high school days our family obtained water from a pump in the back yard. Many times we had to "prime the pump"—we poured a quart of water in the top of the pump, and soon water rose to the top. For me, reading from the Psalms primes the pump of faith. I am challenged to think the psalmists' thoughts and catch some of their faith and vision.

The Jews did not systematically use the Psalms in the literature of the synagogue. They were not used as Scripture lessons, since the lessons were always taken from the Law and the Prophets. Psalms were used by early Christians because the Jews began reciting and singing psalms in their synagogues in the first century. It is said ninety-three passages from the Psalms are quoted in the New Testament.

I wonder whether Psalm 8 is the favorite hymn of many scientists? The author primed the pump as he meditated about the wonder of the heavens and the place of persons in God's scheme of creation. Psalm eight opens and closes with the same refrain.

Psalm 8:1, 9.

> O Lord, our Lord,
> how majestic is thy name in all the earth!

The words "O" and "Our" suggest a group of persons, perhaps a congregation (which would include at least ten or more men). "How majestic" points to the mind-boggling view many persons have of God and his creation, and the amazing nature of man.

Verses 1*b*, 2. The first stanza (strophe) of adoration is introduced:

> Thou whose glory above the heavens is chanted
> by the mouth of babes and infants.

That is, the most learned persons in astronomy, nuclear physics, chemistry, biology, and other sciences often find themselves inarticulate in the presence and fullness of the mind of God. "The heavens declare the glory of God, and the earth displays his handiwork." The noblest hymns persons can create to praise God's glory in creation are like the babblings of babes.

> Thou hast founded [a mighty fortress] because of thy foes,
> to still the enemy and the avenger.

The mighty fortress of God's designing is impregnable against any attempt to challenge God's power.

Verses 3-4. The second stanza, also of two verses, contemplates the magnificence of the heavens, the moon and the stars. Today astronomers look through radiotelescopes and marvel at God's creativity. One such astronomer at Greenbanks Observatory recently showed me a view on the screen of the universe as it existed two billion years ago, before earth knew of any flora and fauna! Yet, I was told, we could see the elements that would make the DNA of all living things. God is creatively at work!

> What is man that thou art mindful of him,
>   and the son of man [a synonym for man] that thou dost care for him?

God loves each and all enough to care what happens. Yes, the psalmist says, God cares for the hungry and dying.

Verses 5-6.

> Thou hast made him little less than God (with the potential of being truly human—loving, aesthetic, kind, honest, openly related to God)
>   and dost crown him with glory and honor.
> Thou hast given him dominion over the works of thy hands;
>   thou hast put all things under his feet.

As Genesis 1:26 states, Man, being capable of the highest ideas and noblest morality, is responsible for care of all living beings.

> all sheep and oxen;
>   and also the beasts of the field.
>   the birds of the air, and the fish of the sea.

Having such dominance, human beings are responsible for what happens to the rain forests, to the atmosphere, to acid rain, to filthy shores, to . . . ad infinitum.

The Scripture and the Main Question—William H. Willimon

How Majestic in All the Earth

We wonder about the original setting for Psalm 8. Did the psalmist think these beautiful thoughts while gazing up into a vast, Near Eastern starlit sky? Perhaps the psalmist was a shepherd, someone accustomed to working out in the fields, lying on his back, looking up into the heavens. Such a person would have written, "When I look at thy heavens, the work of thy fingers, the moon and the stars which thou hast established" (verse 3).

Or perhaps the psalmist came to these lines while standing on a high cliff overlooking the vast, roaring waves of the ocean, and therefore meditated upon all the teeming, unseen life that "passes along the paths of the sea" (verse 8).

Whatever the originating context, we feel as if we are in the presence of a human being who is overwhelmed by the majesty and the greatness of nature. Have you had similar experiences? I remember, as a teenager, four of us went on a camping trip across the United States. We were typical, raucous, carefree male teenagers. One afternoon we reached the national park at the Grand Canyon. We followed a line of talkative tourists who were making their way to the canyon rim to watch the sunset over the canyon. We really had no idea of what we would see; we were simply having a good time, following everyone else.

SECOND QUARTER

When we reached the rim of the Grand Canyon, the sun was setting, and the whole scene was a vast canvas of red, green, blue, and brilliant orange. Hundreds of people stood there in stunned awe and respectful silence. We too were transformed from rather casual, lighthearted teenagers to awestruck, wondering admirers of the beauty of God's creation.

If someone that afternoon had read Psalm 8 aloud to the rest of us, it would have been a perfect statement for how all of us felt: "O Lord, our Lord, how majestic is thy name in all the earth!"

Ponder, just for a moment, the vastness of the universe, with its galaxies upon galaxies, its innumerable stars and suns and planets, and one is overwhelmed by the greatness of nature.

That insight can have twofold significance for us humans. In one sense, to confront the greatness of the universe, the wonders of nature, can fill one with a sense of wonder and awe. On the other hand, it can make one human being seem so small and insignificant when set next to the vastness of it all.

I remember a graduate student in biology telling me that when she had studied nature through her microscope, had pondered the complexity of nature, the sheer size of it all compared to the smallness of humanity, it caused her faith to waver. Human life seemed so accidental, so small and insignificant.

So the psalmist looks upon the wonders of nature and feels not only gratitude and respect for the creativity of God but also a sense of insignificance. The psalmist asks, "What is man that thou art mindful of him, and the son of man that thou dost care for him?" (verse 4).

Human existence, for all its greatness, is just one tiny, little speck within so vast a universe. Why should the great creator of all this care for something so small and insignificant as the human animal?

Dominion over the Works of Thy Hands

When the Bible speaks of nature and its wonders, it not only says that nature is beautiful and awe-inspiring. The Bible, including Psalm 8, makes a rather stunning assertion: God set all this teeming creation in motion for one reason above all others—to make human life possible. Did you hear that in the Psalm? Over time, over what may have been billions of years, little by little, God coaxed from this buzzing mass of creatures a creature so like God's own self that it was said to be in the very image of God (Genesis 1-2). This creature, male and female, is the crowning glory of God's creativity.

I'm talking about you. You, me, all of us are in the image of God. And Scripture claims that the whole creation, the crickets, sheep, oxen, "beasts of the field, the birds of the air, and the fish of the sea" live for our sakes. We alone enjoy such a direct relationship with God.

I suppose that sounds incredibly presumptuous or arrogant. Not so, says the ancient Hebrew who, on one starlit night in July, stood on a Near Eastern hillside, gazed into the heavens, and exclaimed (verses 5-6):

> Yet thou hast made [us] little less than God,
>   and dost crown [us] with glory and honor.
> Thou hast given [us] dominion over the works of thy hands;
>   thou has put all things under [our] feet.

Little less than God. Sure, compared to the vastness of the starry heavens we are but small specks of matter in a great universe. But the Bible says we have no equal in all creation. Of all the creatures, we are the only ones invited to talk to, to work with God. God has given us dominion, given us the earth and told us to subdue it. Listen to Genesis: "So God created man in his own image . . . Male and female he created them. And God blessed them, and God said to them, 'Be fruitful and multiply, and fill the earth and subdue it; and have dominion over the fish of the sea and over the birds of the air and over every living thing that moves upon the earth' " (Genesis 1:26-29).

No other creature is so like God. While we don't really know precisely what "in the image of God" means, we can infer that it has something to do with dominion, with being partners with God in caring for the garden God has planted. Genesis says that God chose not to rule the world directly. God chose not to oversee every little, tiny detail, like some insecure boss who can never let go but insists on having his hands on everything that happens in the office. God puts us in charge—us!

And we need to be faithful stewards, not wasting any of God's creation, caring for all of God's creatures since God spent so much time and effort creating every one. Far from destroying the garden with waste and pollution, the good steward is always looking for ways to increase and enhance life in God's garden. Realizing that God has made it all for us, with loving care, believing that God has entrusted to us the maintenance of a beautiful, varied, and wonderfully rich creation, it makes a difference to us what happens to the whooping crane, the snail darter, another human being.

Little Less than God

Isn't it interesting, whenever someone is caught in some act of violence, some moral failure, some sexual indiscretion, people inevitably say, "Well, he is only human." It's meant to describe us at our immoral, bumbling worst. Only human!

And it's just that attitude that today's scripture is meant to combat. We are human! God has put *us* in charge! We are co-creators, co-workers with God. God's garden is all ours. The whole, wonderful creation exists for our livelihood, cultivation, protection, and delight. We are human! We are little less than God!

Here is a great antidote to the widespread despair, self-doubt, and self-hatred many humans feel today—the biblical proclamation that God has created us, little less than God, the very pinnacle of all creation, and given us dominion.

We are human!

Helping Adults Become Involved—Robert G. Rogers

Preparing to Teach

This lesson commences a series of five on songs from festive occasions. All are taken from the Old Testament and were generally used in a congregational worship setting. Read briefly the following biblical passages to get a feel for the entire series: Psalms 8, 84, 103; Song of Solomon 2:8-17; Isaiah 5:1-7. Notice that all five speak of love or beauty. Also, in each nature language is used to convey religious truth.

SECOND QUARTER

Now read Psalm 8 again carefully. You will notice that it glorifies both God and humanity. It would be useful to glance at Genesis 1, the story of creation, upon which much of Psalm 8 is based. As you read the psalm, think of the universe itself. Try to imagine both religious and scientific perspectives on the wonder of creation. (Both views can complement and enhance our appreciation of God's handiwork.)

Your aim in this lesson is to guide the class in exploring a hymn of praise. They will learn not only what it says about God but also what it tells about man and woman and our collective responsibility on earth.

Introducing the Main Question

It is easy to take the good things of the earth for granted. We expect the sun to warm us; we suppose that the rains will come and that the earth will bring forth produce. How easy it is for us humans to abuse and misuse those natural resources that have been given to us. It is equally true that we often treat our fellow humans as dispensable objects. We take others for granted, forgetting that they are "in the image of God."

Set the scene for the lesson by suggesting that there is a clear link between God and the human family and between both of them and the created order. God has created, and we are obligated to help sustain that creation. Suggest that all of life is a gift: human life and other forms in the universe. Particularly emphasize that as we give thanks for God's creation of humanity, we are reminded of our role as stewards of all creation.

Developing the Lesson

In working with Psalm 8, it is natural to maintain a sense of awe. This brief and beautiful biblical passage invites us to enter into a worship experience. Develop the lesson in three portions:

> I. The wonder of creation
> II. In the image of God
> III. Dominion and responsibility

I. The wonder of creation

Commence by referring back to the exposition by Dr. Willimon. Everyone has been awestruck on occasion by the magnitude of the universe. Invite the class to speak about their "awe experiences." Perhaps they have been moved by beautiful sunsets or a majestic range of mountains or beautiful wildflowers by the road. Many are moved when looking for the first time into the face of a newborn infant. Remind people as they share these experiences that they were in the presence of God, the author of beauty in the world.

Next, turn to the biblical record. Call attention to the parallels between Genesis 1 and Psalm 8. The latter assumes the goodness of creation as found at the beginning of the biblical record. Point out the link that biblical writers make between the person of God and various aspects of his creation. Invite others to suggest favorite biblical passages or stories that describe the created order.

DECEMBER 29   LESSON 5

II. In the image of God

Begin this section of your lesson by pointing to Psalm 8:4-5. Be sure that women feel included in the category even though only "man" is mentioned. You might read aloud Genesis 1:26-28, noting that "male and female" are both mentioned in the creation story. You could describe man and woman as being in a partnership or covenant relationship with God from the very beginning of recorded time. We are described as being crowned with "glory and honor."

With the biblical background in mind, refer back to previous lessons this quarter. Each lesson affirmed the value of every human being, from the humblest to the most powerful, from a Hannah or Mary to a Moses or David. Build on this sense of the value of humans. Think with class members about the implications of this belief. For example, what should we think of people from different cultural backgrounds or races or religious beliefs if we truly affirm all persons to be created in God's image? Unless we struggle against the temptation of being self-centered, how simple it is to assume that we are made closer to God's image than someone else.

It would be good to spend some time examining our own culture. In what ways do we minimize the value of other humans? What powers operate in our society to make people feel worthless, no longer in God's image? These are the practical implications of taking Psalm 8 seriously.

III. Dominion and responsibility

This third section ties together the first two admirably. If we are heirs to a magnificent creation, and we have an exalted place within it, what is our responsibility? Ask your people to begin by citing what they believe distinguishes man and woman from the rest of the creatures. Is it our intelligence? Our ability to have a covenant relationship with God? Is it the power of humans to greatly manipulate or change their environment that is unique? You want them to see that we have power that is not to be taken lightly. "Dominion" over God's handiwork carries a tremendous burden to use such trust wisely. Perhaps some class members are active in conservation groups. They might tell briefly about the concerns of some of the well-known organizations.

Turn to your local community or region of the state. How can church people usefully join hands with other neighbors to care for the earth and its creatures? Mention that ecological problems involve solutions that demand a balancing of legitimate human needs such as food and shelter with human wants, which are often selfish or exploitative.

Conclude by stating that if we take Psalm 8 seriously, responsibility for the earth is not optional; rather, it is a deeply moral issue.

Helping Class Members Act

In the coming week members of the class might give attention to two issues: First, what is the human potential that each of us has if we truly affirm our creation as being in God's image? Second, what is one local problem in the natural or human environment that needs attention? Could they suggest church involvement with others to address this problem?

SECOND QUARTER

Planning for Next Sunday

The next lesson in the series emphasizes the beauty of the temple as a "dwelling place" for God. Class members should read Psalm 84 carefully. Notice that the psalmist links the beauty of creation with beauty in the worship setting. It is particularly useful to look at nature language as it describes the worship center.

LESSON 6　　　　　　　　　　　　　　　　　　　JANUARY 5

Song of Worship

Background Scripture: Psalm 84

The Main Question—William H. Willimon

I was visiting her, trying to encourage her to be more active in the church. Her name had been on our church rolls for many years, but to my knowledge, she had only attended rarely. I told her about some of our new programs, our new Choir Director, some of the things we were doing on Sunday morning. Then, she looked directly at me and asked me, "Pastor, why come to church on Sunday morning? I try to live a good life. But I just can't see why it's important for me to come to church, sit there on Sunday morning, pray and sing."

I am somewhat embarrassed to say that hers was a question for which I had no ready answer. Why worship? It's a fundamental, basic question. How would you answer?

We live in a no nonsense, practical, utilitarian society. We Americans tend to value all experiences for their utility, their usefulness. "What good will this do me?" We want to know.

Therefore, when asked, Why worship? we are likely to point up all of the valuable, therapeutic reasons for worshiping God. Worship will "help you make it through the week," or "You will feel a real sense of peace," or "You will have the opportunity to think and to learn more about your faith." While all of these statements may be true to our experiences of Sunday worship, do they really get to the heart of the matter? What makes our experiences of worship different from any other public experience of therapy, education, or group fellowship? What is the most basic reason for why we are here?

Why worship? That's the question behind today's study of Psalm 84.

JANUARY 5 LESSON 6

Selected Scripture

| **King James Version** | **Revised Standard Version** |

Psalm 84

1 How amiable *are* thy tabernacles, O Lord of hosts!

2 My soul longeth, yea, even fainteth for the courts of the Lord: my heart and my flesh crieth out for the living God.

3 Yea, the sparrow hath found an house, and the swallow a nest for herself, where she may lay her young, *even* thine altars, O Lord of hosts, my King, and my God.

4 Blessed *are* they that dwell in thy house: they will be still praising thee. Selah.

5 Blessed *is* the man whose strength *is* in thee; in whose heart *are* the ways *of them.*

6 *Who* passing through the valley of Baca make it a well; the rain also filleth the pools.

7 They go from strength to strength, *every one of them* in Zion appeareth before God.

8 O Lord God of hosts, hear my prayer: give ear, O God of Jacob. Selah.

9 Behold, O God our shield, and look upon the face of thine anointed.

10 For a day in thy courts *is* better than a thousand. I had rather be a doorkeeper in the house of my God, than to dwell in the tents of wickedness.

11 For the Lord God *is* a sun and shield: the Lord will give grace and

Psalm 84

1 How lovely is thy dwelling place,
    O Lord of hosts!
2 My soul longs, yea, faints
    for the courts of the Lord;
my heart and flesh sing for joy
    to the living God.

3 Even the sparrow finds a home,
    and the swallow a nest for
        herself,
where she may lay her young,
    at the altars, O Lord of hosts,
        my king and my God.
4 Blessed are those who dwell in thy
        house,
    ever singing thy praise! *Selah*

5 Blessed are the men whose
        strength is in thee,
    in whose heart are the highways
        to Zion.
6 As they go through the valley of
        Baca
    they make it a place of springs;
    the early rain also covers it with
        pools.
7 They go from strength to
        strength;
    the God of gods will be seen in
        Zion.

8 O Lord God of hosts, hear my
        prayer;
    give ear, O God of Jacob! *Selah*

9 Behold our shield, O God;
    look upon the face of thine
        anointed!

10 For a day in thy courts is better
        than a thousand elsewhere.
    I would rather be a doorkeeper
        in the house of my God
    than dwell in the tents of
        wickedness.

11 For the Lord God is a sun and
        shield;

SECOND QUARTER

glory: no good *thing* will he withhold from them that walk uprightly.

12 O Lord of hosts, blessed *is* the man that trusteth in thee.

Key Verse: **My soul longeth, yea, even fainteth for the courts of the Lord: my heart and my flesh crieth out for the living God. (Psalm 84:2)**

he bestows favor and honor.
No good thing does the Lord withhold
  from those who walk uprightly.

12 O Lord of hosts,
  blessed is the man who trusts in thee!

Key Verse: **My soul longs, yea, faints for the courts of the Lord; my heart and flesh sing for joy to the living God. (Psalm 84:2)**

As You Read the Scripture—Horace R. Weaver

The author of Psalm 84 may well have been a pilgrim to Solomon's temple. He personally loved and valued the peace of God that surrounded the temple area. It is significant that the poet does not refer to specific priestly activities. He does not refer to the various feasts, nor to cultic activities (such as the burning of incense, slaughter of animals for sacrifice, the singing of psalms by Levites, etc.). The psalmist highly valued his experiences in the temple, for in and through the ritual he felt touched by the presence of God.

Psalm 84:1-2. The psalmist longs for the temple because there he experiences best the presence of God:

> How lovely is thy dwelling place,
>   O Lord of Hosts!

The Lord of Hosts and the Lord God of Hosts are titles for God that express the Deity's universal sovereignty.

The psalmist sings that his whole life is affected by knowing and experiencing the presence of God; his soul, heart, and flesh sing for joy!

> My soul longs, yea, faints
>   for the courts of the Lord;
> my heart and flesh sing for joy
>   to the living God.

The phrase "the living God" is emphasized in contradistinction to the lifeless idols and vain objects being worshiped by pagans and apostate Jews.

Verses 3-4. The happiness of living in the temple is set forth:

> Even the sparrow finds a home,
>   and the swallow a nest for herself,
> where she may lay her young,
>   at thy altars, O Lord of Hosts.

The contemplation of God's care for the sparrow and swallow is a deeply religious experience.

Verses 5-7. These verses speak of the pilgrims' quest.

Note the difference in verse 5 between the King James and the Revised Standard versions. The King James Version reads: "Blessed is the man," while the Revised Standard Version speaks of men in the plural:

> Blessed are the men whose strength is in thee,
> in whose heart are the highways to Zion.

In Hebrew the word "heart" refers to a person's attitudes, hopes, dreams, and intentions; these are the highways to Zion, to the supreme place of worship. Those with good intentions may "go through the valley of Baca," which is dry and arid area, yet "make it a place of springs." Such persons "go from strength to strength" as their excitement for worship increases; they are not fatigued by their journey.

Verses 8-9. These verses are a petition:

> O Lord God of hosts, hear my prayer;
> give ear, O God of Jacob!
> Behold our shield [i.e., we implore], O God;
> look upon the face of thine anointed [i.e., the king].

Verses 10-12. These verses tell us to trust in the Lord. The speaker—a pilgrim, Levite, priest, or possibly soldier at the temple—is thrilled by the privilege of being able to worship the Lord there. He "would rather be a doorkeeper in the house of . . . God," with all its privileges—welcoming pilgrims to approach the temple area, seeing that the sanctuary is not defiled by unclean persons or animals—"than dwell in the tents of wickedness" (i.e., yearning for sensuality, wealth, and power).

"For the Lord God is a sun and shield"—that is, a source of protection for both pilgrims and priests/Levites when needed.

> No good thing does the Lord withhold
> from those who walk uprightly.
> O Lord of Hosts
> blessed is the [person] who trusts in thee!

The Scripture and the Main Question—William H. Willimon

How Lovely Is Thy Dwelling Place

"How lovely is thy dwelling place, O Lord of hosts!" (Psalm 84:1). Thus begins the beautiful psalm that was undoubtedly sung by the congregation on their way into the great temple. To enter the vast temple was to enter the very house of God.

Of course, we know that our great God is much bigger than our places of worship. We do not confine God within our sanctuaries. Sometimes people say that they feel closer to God when they are walking alone in the woods—or playing on the golf course. Theoretically, God is present there as well as in our churches.

However, whereas God is not limited, we are. Undoubtedly, people can worship on a golf course, but how often do they? We human beings find it most helpful to have some place set apart, some designated time to gather to worship. So we build churches, adorn our sanctuaries. These holy places help us distracted humans to focus, to gather our thoughts and feelings.

A friend of mine has begun a church in a new suburban area. When the first members gathered to form the new congregation, their new pastor hoped that they could simply form a congregation, get on with their business, and avoid getting entangled in expensive and time-consuming building programs. They met in a local elementary school cafeteria. He hoped that would be enough for the people. But it wasn't. They quickly tired of the drab cafeteria and began planning a church building of their own.

"I found," said my friend, "that my people really needed a place, some building set apart. They live in a very mobile, unstable community. People are always moving in and moving out. They needed someplace that was permanently set apart for worship and service to God and nothing else. They needed a church."

Most of us are like that. Although we know that God is not confined to our places of worship, we find it helpful to have some place where we regularly focus upon God.

Another pastoral friend of mine was assigned to an urban church in a rapidly deteriorating neighborhood. Like many aging urban churches, this church was once a great downtown congregation. Now they had dwindled to a very small congregation that struggled to keep their large, but now mostly unused, building in repair.

"At first I really resented all of the time and effort that we were having to put into that old building," said my friend. "I looked upon it as a decaying tomb, a waste of money. But gradually, I came to understand why my people loved that old building. In that neighborhood, it was the one place of beauty and quiet. Everything else was in decay. It was a landmark, but more than that, it was a sign that God had not abandoned them, that the church was there. That old building was like a sacrament—an outward and visible sign—that God was there, even there."

A rock in the middle of a transient, unstable world; a sign and sacrament of God's presence among us; our churches are beloved because they serve as visible reminders of Emmanuel, God with us. So the psalmist can sing of his fellow worshipers, "Blessed are those who dwell in thy house, ever singing thy praise!" (84:4).

The Courts of the Lord

When asked by a utilitarian, pragmatic society, "Why worship?" the church has been all too quick to point out all of the useful aspects of our Sunday worship. Someone has called us the "therapeutic society." That is, we value other people, all experiences, only for what they can do for us as individuals. Will this make me feel better? Will it help me make it through the week? Will it help me to have a happier family life?

The trouble with thinking this way about worship is that worship is so shockingly nonutilitarian. At its best, worship has no "point" other than to bring us close to God. Whenever worship is used for something else, becoming a means to some other end, worship is being used and therefore abused.

The writer of Psalm 84 tells us that he comes to the temple because he longs to be close to God. When it comes down to it, there is really no other or better reason for us to be here on Sunday morning than that.

As a child, I remember services of worship in which all of the singing, music, prayers, and Scripture before the sermon were seen as "preliminaries" for the main event of sitting and listening to the sermon. When you came home from worship, people would sometimes ask, "Well, what did the preacher say?"

In other words, the main function of Sunday was to come listen to the preacher. I even remember a preacher standing up before the sparse congregation on a cold winter Sunday and thanking us all for coming to hear him! It seemed not to occur to him that we were all there to be with God, not just to hear him!

In other situations, the congregation, rather than the pastor, becomes the central focus of worship. The service seems to be concocted to make the congregation feel something, or believe something, to instruct them in correct social attitudes or right behavior. Church comes perilously close to school. "I can't figure out the difference between what we do here on Sunday morning and what we do at the Wednesday lunchtime meeting of my civic club," I overheard one layperson say. That is a devastating indictment upon human-centered worship.

Let the psalmist say it for us. There really is no greater point to worship, no better reason to be here, than simply to come into the presence of God.

Blessed Are Those in Thy House

If I were to ask you, "What good does being a friend of Jane Smith do you?" you might be somewhat offended by the question. After all, being a friend to someone is not a matter of getting some "good" out of that person. That would be using the person to get something that you wanted and that would be much less than real friendship. No, you are a friend to Jane Smith because you enjoy being with her, you like to be in her presence—that and nothing more.

However, upon further reflection, you have gotten some "good" out of your friendship with Jane. She has helped you to appreciate good music, or she has taught you how to sew. But you didn't spend time with Jane in order to get instruction in tailoring or music appreciation. Friendship is enjoyed for its own sake, even though good friendship has some wonderful byproducts.

Worship is much like that. We come to worship for no other better reason than that we love to be with God. We love to focus our lives upon God, to attune our ears to whatever God may be trying to say to us. That's why we are there on Sunday morning.

However, while we worship God, we sometimes do feel a new sense of peace and well-being. We do receive new strength to make it through the week. Sometimes we are motivated for greater service of God in the world. Sometimes we are made honestly to examine our lives in the light of God's will.

But the main reason we are there is the same as that of the psalmist: "My soul longs, yea, faints for the courts of the Lord; my heart and flesh sing for joy to the living God" (84:2).

This is the exuberant, unrestrained joy at being close to the God who loves and is therefore loved. So when asked, "Why worship?" we really have

SECOND QUARTER

no better response than, "We love because he first loved us." Why worship? An answer to such a question only makes sense to one who is in love. It's like asking someone who is in love, "Why kiss someone?" Behavior like kissing only makes sense to those who are in love. Worship is somewhat like that.

The psalmist concludes by exclaiming, perhaps at the end of the service, "A day in thy courts is better than a thousand" anywhere else.

Helping Adults Become Involved—Robert G. Rogers

Preparing to Teach

The central theme for this lesson is that of beauty. In the previous lesson, the beauty of God's universe was proclaimed. Now you will be paying attention to a particular portion of that universe: the worship center.

Read Psalm 84 and study it carefully. Notice how God's "dwelling place" is linked with the call for upright, righteous behavior on the part of the worshipers. Verse 10 addresses this specifically. How do you think worship can reinforce a moral way of life?

You might reflect on your own church building. What features make it beautiful? Is it the stained-glass window? A lovely, well-used parlor? Perhaps there is an old church bell or steeple that adds a distinctive mark to your building.

Your aim is to help the class consider the purpose of worship and the role of a worship center within that purpose. In the process, you and they will be examining how your church building is currently being used.

Introducing the Main Question

It is easy to take worship and even the worship center (the sanctuary and the rest of the building) for granted. Most people attend church weekly, but the event can become humdrum. Sometimes families rush to get there. They arrive harried and ill-prepared to absorb the joy and tranquility that a worship experience can provide. Too frequently, the mundane cares of the world bar us from seeing beauty in the service, in the sanctuary, in the parishioners assembled there. We may unintentionally shut out the central focal point of the worship experience—God himself!

Spend several minutes discussing worship. What do class members appreciate within a worship service? What factors can we individually control to make worship most meaningful personally?

Developing the Lesson

Psalm 84:2 describes the pure joy of worship for its own sake. Read it aloud as an introduction to the three sections of the lesson you will be developing:

> I. The dwelling place of God
> II. Authentic worship
> III. Worship and stewardship

I. The dwelling place of God

Too often we have a tendency to "humanize God." We use language of the Lord that is limiting; we ascribe to the Creator human features. This is understandable, but it needs to be placed in perspective. If we believe that God is all-powerful and ever-present throughout the universe, then he does not "dwell" in a particular place or building. To locate God in one building is to limit his activity in the world. The Israelites were well aware of this potential problem. They forbade any attempts to make a statue of God, lest the worshipers confuse an object made by humans with the reality of God.

It is worth spending a few moments discussing the issue just described. Remind your people that God is not limited to or contained by any particular building. He is in the home, at the school, in the marketplace, and in the church. The Lord is present at the occasion of worship by those who love him; he is also present with those who do not yet know him.

You might also explore the problem that some Israelite kings created. They claimed that they were in charge of "God's house," since they were the leading political power in the land. There is an obvious heresy in this line of reasoning. If God "dwells" in the temple, and if the temple is controlled by the ruler, then God is potentially subordinate to the king. Reflect for a few moments the modern day. Do some religious leaders seek to control the contemporary "dwelling place"—the church building? How often do we hear the phrase "That is Reverend X's church"?

As you conclude this portion of the lesson, however, do remind yourselves of the point that Dr. Willimon makes. A church building does provide a central place in which the community of faith can gather. In that sense it is the "dwelling place" of God and his people.

II. Authentic worship

What is essential to worship? We know that a worship service should not be a professional performance by minister and choir. Rather, the parishioners should be led to a group experience that satisfies the spiritual hunger of each individual.

In developing the lesson at this point, concentrate on the essential characteristics of worship. You might jot down on the blackboard the basic ingredients for worship as suggested by class members. Perhaps a key factor is that worship be inclusive. Everyone in the sanctuary should feel that he or she has something to contribute to the gathered community. Do people of all ages and backgrounds feel comfortable in the worship setting of your church? What might be changed (if change is needed) to ensure that everyone feels personal involvement on Sunday morning?

III. Worship and stewardship

Worship should be the culminating experience of any congregation's collective faith. However, it should not suffice for Christians to attend worship, return home, and not be concerned about the church and its building until the following Sunday. As you develop this section of the lesson, you want to examine how your church building is used throughout the week. In brief, is the building serving needs beyond those of Sunday worshipers? You have a marvelous resource in your class members. Ask various ones to share their understanding of how the church building is used. All of you will undoubtedly discover that the building serves a variety of church and community organizations. There may be some dissension, however, when the full range of activities is made known. Some church people prefer that the "beautiful parlor" only be used by certain groups in the church. How should the church balance the competing claims of those

SECOND QUARTER

who need to keep some rooms "beautiful" and those who need to have a church building that is used by a variety of ages and groups?

Turn to the more difficult topic of the yearly budget. How is money spent within the building? What priorities are evident in the way that funds are dispersed for various rooms in the building? As you and your group have a dialogue on these concerns, you are engaging in the act of being good stewards.

Helping Class Members Act

Suggest that concerned class members spend some time in the coming week thinking about the issue of worship and stewardship. Perhaps they could make some helpful suggestions to the appropriate church committees.

Planning for Next Sunday

Next Sunday's reading is Psalm 103. It is very familiar to most people. As class members read and study, they should try to envision various human circumstances when this psalm would be comforting.

LESSON 7   JANUARY 12

Song of Gratitude

Background Scripture: Psalm 103

The Main Question—William H. Willimon

As a parent, some things amaze me about children. For example, I am amazed by how many human virtues, which we consider to be worthwhile, come to use through training, education, or example, but not through birth. Many things that make us human do not come naturally.

Take gratitude, for instance. I have discovered that gratitude, a sense of thankfulness for the gifts of life, is not an innate human characteristic. We must be taught to be grateful.

I see this in my own children. Children are not born with an overwhelming sense of gratitude. Parents must continually say to them, "Say 'thank you' to the nice lady for the candy." If they were not made to say thanks, they wouldn't say thanks.

As a pastor I have sometimes observed that some people seem to be "givers" and others seem to be "takers." That is, whenever an appeal is made for gifts, say, to missions or overseas relief, some people can always be counted upon to do their part. Others can always be counted upon to do nothing. Some people seem to have an overflowing sense of gratitude for what they have been given in life and desire to share their goods with others.

JANUARY 12   LESSON 7

Other people feel that what they have is what they earned, their own achievement, the result of their labors, not of God's or others' gifts.

What makes the difference? From whence springs a sense of gratitude? These are some of the questions behind today's lesson from Psalm 103, one of the great thanksgiving hymns of the Bible.

Selected Scripture

King James Version

Psalm 103:1-17

1 Bless the Lord, O my soul: and all that is within me, *bless* his holy name.

2 Bless the Lord, O my soul, and forget not all his benefits:

3 Who forgiveth all thine iniquities; who healeth all thy diseases;

4 Who redeemeth thy life from destruction; who crowneth thee with lovingkindness and tender mercies;

5 Who satisfieth thy mouth with good *things; so that* thy youth is renewed like the eagle's.

6 The Lord executeth righteousness and judgment for all that are oppressed.

7 He made known his ways unto Moses, his acts unto the children of Israel.

8 The Lord *is* merciful and gracious, slow to anger, and plenteous in mercy.

9 He will not always chide: neither will he keep *his anger* for ever.

10 He hath not dealt with us after our sins; nor rewarded us according to our iniquities.

11 For as the heaven is high above the earth, *so* great is his mercy toward them that fear him.

12 As far as the east is from the west, *so* far hath he removed our transgressions from us.

13 Like as a father pitieth *his*

Revised Standard Version

Psalm 103:1-17

1 Bless the Lord, O my soul;
   and all that is within me, bless
     his holy name!

2 Bless the Lord, O my soul,
   and forget not all his benefits,

3 who forgives all your iniquity,
   who heals all your diseases,

4 who redeems your life from the
     Pit,
   who crowns you with steadfast
     love and mercy,

5 who satisfies you with good as
     long as you live
   so that your youth is renewed
     like the eagle's.

6 The Lord works vindication
   and justice for all who are
     oppressed.

7 He made known his ways to
     Moses,
   his acts to the people of Israel.

8 The Lord is merciful and gracious,
   slow to anger and abounding in
     steadfast love.

9 He will not always chide,
   nor will he keep his anger for
     ever.

10 He does not deal with us according to our sins,
   nor requite us according to
     our iniquities.

11 For as the heavens are high
     above the earth,
   so great is his steadfast love
     toward those who fear him;

12 as far as the east is from the west,
   so far does he remove our
     transgressions from us.

13 As a father pities his children,

SECOND QUARTER

children, *so* the Lord pitieth them that fear him.

14 For he knoweth our frame; he remembereth that we *are* dust.

15 *As for* man, his days *are* as grass: as a flower of the field, so he flourisheth.

16 For the wind passeth over it, and it is gone; and the place thereof shall know it no more.

17 But the mercy of the Lord *is* from everlasting to everlasting upon them that fear him, and his righteousness unto children's children.

Key Verse: **The Lord is merciful and gracious, slow to anger, and plenteous in mercy. (Psalm 103:8)**

so the Lord pities those who fear him.

14 For he knows our frame;
he remembers that we are dust.

15 As for man, his days are like grass;
he flourishes like a flower of the field;

16 for the wind passes over it, and it is gone,
and its place knows it no more.

17 But the steadfast love of the Lord is from everlasting to everlasting
upon those who fear him,
and his righteousness to children's children.

Key Verse: **The Lord is merciful and gracious, slow to anger and abounding in steadfast love. (Psalm 103:8)**

As You Read the Scripture—Horace R. Weaver

Psalm 103 expresses God's love for persons in superlative ways. This divine love is unique, for the Deity is always "in love" with his human creatures. The psalmist's deep sense of gratitude is twofold: God has forgiven the writer's sins and has brought healing from a desperate illness (verses 3-4). God's deep concern for the healing of broken covenants (sins) and for destructive illness calls for the soul to bless the Lord for all his benefits.

The psalmist has experienced God's love and care in sins forgiven and for recovery from desperate illness. It is because of his certainty of God's concern that the poet cries out

> Bless the Lord, O my soul;
> and all that is within me, bless his holy name!

The grateful poet uses an interesting literary device for Psalm 103: There are twenty-two letters in the Hebrew alphabet; just so, there are twenty-two verses in his psalm.

Psalm 103:2-5. The psalmist exhorts himself to "forget not all his benefits." He then proceeds to name these benefits God has given him, and for which he in turn will bless God

> who *forgives* all your iniquity,
> who *heals* all your diseases,
> Who *redeems* your life from the Pit,
> who *crowns* you with steadfast love and mercy,
> Who *satisfies* you with good as long as you live
> so that your youth is *renewed* like the eagle's.

To renew your youth "like the eagle's" refers to the majestic nature of the eagle, its superior size, strength, and longevity. The list of benefits is cause for rejoicing and blessing the Lord.

Verses 6-8. A brief survey of God's gracious acts to Israel is given.

These verses move from personal benefits from God to God's concern for all who are oppressed. The Deity wants all peoples to know that

> The Lord works vindication
> and justice for all who are oppressed.

This is extended not just to Jews but people from around the world.

> He made known his ways to Moses,
> his acts to the people of Israel.

Exodus 33:13-16 describes how Moses asked Yahweh: "Show me now thy ways, that I may know thee and find favor in thy sight." The response of the Lord did not include specific physical directions; rather, he said, "My presence will go with you." Moses responds: "Is it not in thy going with us, so that we are distinct, I and thy people, from all other people that are on the face of the earth?"

Verse 8 sounds like the voice of Hosea, whose life experiences with Gomer illustrated the "steadfast love" of God toward all kinds of people—even the prostitute Gomer.

Verses 9-11. Does God always have good attitudes toward those who continually sin?

> He will not always chide,
> nor will he keep his anger for ever.

Yet . . .

> For as the heavens are high above the earth,
> so great is his steadfast love toward those who fear him.

But . . . Is God's steadfast love dependent on whether persons *fear* him? How do you theologize on reading Psalm 97:10-11?

> The Lord loves those who hate evil;
> he preserves the lives of his saints;
> he delivers them from the hand of the wicked.

Verse 17.

> But the steadfast love of the Lord is from everlasting to everlasting
> upon those who fear him,
> and his righteousness to children's children.

The Scripture and the Main Question—William H. Willimon

The Lord Is Merciful and Gracious

Psalm 103 is typical of many of the thanksgiving psalms in the Bible in that it is formed on a typical "think-thank" motif. That is, the psalmist thinks about God's acts of mercy and goodness in the past and is moved to thanksgiving. In the opening verses of the psalm, the psalmist remembers such divine gifts as healing, forgiveness, redemption, and vindication. Remembrance of these divine acts leads to gratitude and thanks.

In a way, Psalm 103 typifies Christians at worship. Sometimes people criticize the church for being traditionalist, spending too much time with old words, recalling old events, pondering ancient history. On Sunday morning, listening to us reading, studying, and preaching from Scripture, someone might get the idea that we Christians care about nothing but the past.

Yet this remembrance is a holy, essential activity. We recall God's acts of love in the past so that we might be better able to see God's love among us today. The psalmist remembers God's love toward Moses in the Exodus (Psalm 103:7) and that leads the psalmist to assert for today, "The Lord is merciful and gracious, slow to anger and abounding in steadfast love" (verse 8).

On the basis of what we know about God's actions in the past, we are able to assert something of the nature of God in the present.

What would we be like without this holy recollection? As the old song says, we gather to "count our many blessings." We gather to claim our lives as gifts. Without such remembrance, we would be in danger of becoming self-centered, smug, arrogant, because we had forgotten the grace (i.e., gift) on which our lives are based.

Perhaps this accounts for the selfishness among many in our society. We have built a society that deludes many into thinking that they are self-made men and women. What I have is what I earned. I have a right to my life and my possessions. There's not much room for grace in that sort of world.

Do you know who are the highest percentage givers in the United States? Those who give the highest percentage of their income to churches and charity are those with incomes of under $10,000 per year. Generosity, it would seem, has little to do with the magnitude of one's income. It has to do with the nature of one's outlook upon life. Is my life of my own devising, or is my life a gift?

As a pastor, I do not know exactly how people come to a sense of gratitude. I wish that I did. However, it doesn't take long to recognize a person with a well-developed sense of the graciousness of God. Such people are appropriately humble. They do not speak of their children as their personal achievements. They do not boast and brag about their attainments. Rather, they have a sense of amazement that life should be so good and rewarding, as if what they have is unexpected and undeserved.

I remember an older preacher telling me, "Anytime religion is presented mainly as something *we* are supposed to do, then it really isn't the Christian religion. The Christian religion is a story of something that *God* has done before it is anything about what we are to do."

That's not a bad test for biblical faith.

The Steadfast Love of the Lord

Note that Psalm 103 expends most of its verses talking about God, not us. There are some Psalms, particularly the psalms of lament, that expend most of their verses in talking about the status of the psalmist—his illness, his distress, and so on. But this psalm centers itself upon God. Most of biblical faith, including this psalm, is *theocentric*; that is, it is centered on God.

Perhaps this can be said to be the whole point of worship, the whole meaning of church—to center ourselves a little more on God and a little less on ourselves. So the psalm is a long enumeration of all the works and gifts of God.

How well do you think that we accomplish this God-centeredness on Sunday morning? My image of many of us on Sunday is that we come with our little notepads; then, in the sermon, we receive our assignments for the week. This week, work on your marriage, or your bad habits, or your attitudes toward others. Come back next Sunday, and we'll give you another list of assignments. Worship of God thus degenerates into moralistic, carping triviality, and church becomes not too different from a meeting of any other civic club.

Not much room for God in that scheme of things, is there, as we go about working out our own salvation? We don't come reaching out for grace, because we don't need any as we go about becoming always bigger and better in our goodness. We don't pray for forgiveness because we have no strong, clear vision of a God who forgives. Our God becomes transformed into a mildly helpful moral critic who does little more than encourage us to be good.

The psalmist knows better. The thing that keeps us going in life, in the good times and in the bad, is the grace of God, not our own efforts. Fortunately, our God doesn't just stand beside us on Sunday morning, but throughout our lives, in the sunshine and the rain. Our God's love is *steadfast*.

Bless the Lord

What is the purpose of our study of Scripture, our attendance at Sunday worship? Someone answers, "The point is to realize where you have gone wrong and then work to set your life right." This is partly right but mostly wrong.

Certainly, in church, we examine our lives and try to correct ourselves. But our lives, values, habits, and ethics must be examined by a yardstick more significant than our own opinions. God's works are an indication of what God wants for us.

Therefore, Christians are called to be forgiving and merciful people, not simply because those are nice attributes that other people admire, but because God has so often forgiven and shown mercy to us. As the psalmist says, "He does not deal with us according to our sins" (thank God!) but rather "As a father pities his children, so the Lord pities those who fear him" (verses 10, 13).

Our ethics, our standards for Christian behavior, arise out of our vision of God. So sometimes the most ethical thing we can do on Sunday morning, the activity that does the most to form us into better people, is to keep looking at God, to keep at the never-ending task of taking God more seriously and ourselves a little less so.

Therefore, our creeds, our hymns, our reading of Scripture, in which we recall the works of God and remember the history of God's steadfast love toward us, is constantly forming and reforming us into new people. Hymns of praise usually occupy the first pages of any hymnal, thus indicating praise

SECOND QUARTER

of God as the primary task of worship, the first and foremost Sunday activity. In our songs of praise, we think-thank. We bless the Lord, and in so doing we are blessed. Remembering how much we owe to the love and graciousness of God, we become more loving and gracious ourselves. Our theocentric gratitude leads to great moral rectitude, not as the main point of our being in church but as a gracious byproduct of our worship and praise of God. As 1 John says, we love because we know that God first loved us.

Helping Adults Become Involved—Robert G. Rogers

Preparing to Teach

This week you will be leading the class in the study of a psalm of thanksgiving. Begin your preparation by reading Psalm 103. Notice the wide range of topics covered, examples of God's graciousness for which the psalmist is thankful. He expresses thanksgiving for recovery from illness, for acts of salvation for the entire people, for forgiveness of sins, and even for the creation in its entirety. Try to imagine the occasions in the Jerusalem temple on which this psalm was recited.

You might spend time reflecting on blessings in your own life for which you are personally thankful. What prayers or meditations help you in your response of gratitude to God? You might also consider deeds, as well as words, that offer appropriate responses of thanksgiving to God.

Your aim is to help the class see the relationship between God's blessings and our gratitude. You will especially emphasize God's graciousness to the human community.

Introducing the Main Question

What are the ways in which God blesses the human community? Psalm 103 suggests that all of life is a blessing from God. The Israelites began many worship services with the phrase "This is the day the Lord has made. Let us rejoice and be glad in it." What a marvelous place to begin a discussion of thanksgiving to God.

For what specific blessings of life do class members have reason to give thanks? These may range from good health to love of family to appreciation of nature. Jot down some of the general categories cited. Read aloud Psalm 103:1-5 and note how many of the members' blessings are identified as acts of God in these five verses.

In the face of the multitude of blessings, how should we respond in gratitude? Suggest that both words and deeds are signs of thanks to the Lord. Spend a few moments discussing specific examples of word or deed that illustrate our gratitude.

Developing the Lesson

The class has been thinking about the types of blessings that God gives and some of the ways we might respond. Now you want to expand this thinking and develop the lesson in the following three ways:

        I. The act of remembrance
       II. A variety of gifts
     III. The faithfulness of God

JANUARY 12   LESSON 7

I. The act of remembrance

As Dr. Willimon suggests, the Christian church is a community of faith that remembers. Indeed, the biblical record, in which our faith is historically rooted, is a record of remembrance. There are at least three levels of remembrance that you might explore: the history of the entire people of faith through the generations, the special history of your own congregation, and individual lives that have been graced by God's blessing. Develop with the class a biblical perspective on salvation history. What are the major biblical events (in both testaments) that provide "chapters of remembrance"? You could start with the creation of the world, then follow with the Exodus from slavery in Egypt, then move to the giving of the Ten Commandments at Mount Sinai. Work briefly through to the New Testament and highlights in the life of Jesus.

Now consider the central blessings given in the history of your own church. What are some of the major chapters in that history? Thinking about this will provide a distinctive way for older members to share with the younger ones some of the earlier history of your church.

The third category, that of individual blessings, has already been discussed in part earlier in your lesson. You may want to allow for any further reflections by individuals. What you need to do now, though, is look at particular ways that your church remembers. Do you use specific creeds of faith in the worship service? Perhaps there are hymns that are especially loved by the church. What are some of the other ways that you remember and celebrate God's past graciousness?

II. A variety of gifts

Start by referring to the Hebrew concept of life itself as a divine gift. Remind the class of what we all know: Each human is unique and has his or her own combination of strengths and weaknesses. God places in each of us some innate abilities. In life, we can build on these abilities and become proficient in certain ways. Discuss for a few moments the idea of our abilities being a divine gift. What are some of the obvious talents that various class members are aware of in their own lives?

In the course of the sharing, raise the issue of human responsibility for developing abilities, both ours and those of others with whom we have relationships. You might also allude to the human tendency to squander abilities on occasion. There is the need to use a divine gift wisely.

There is also another way in which God bestows his gifts on us. When we despair or are in trouble, we can receive divine solace, support, and encouragement. This type of gift has nothing to do with our innate abilities. Rather, it reflects the human condition and our need to accept divine grace. In thinking on this aspect of God's gifts, ask if there are other ways in which your class members have experienced God's self-giving. The obvious one, of course, is in the gift of his Son to the world.

III. The faithfulness of God

Move into this section of the lesson by reading aloud Psalm 103:17-18. "Steadfast love" is not fickle. It can be counted on; God's love, as the psalmist describes it, far exceeds the limitations of human love. Unlike us mortals, God does not "fall in love or out of love." The creeds, the hymns, and the prayers of the church all celebrate the steadfastness of this divine love.

SECOND QUARTER

Point out that God's love is freely given. However, the psalmist rightly reminds us that we have an obligation to keep God's commandments. This relates directly to the covenant relationship that God has with the human community. Whereas our faithfulness is sometimes limited by human frailty, we are nevertheless commanded to do our best to respond to God's love.

What are some of the favorite hymns of class members that celebrate God's faithfulness? You might begin by listing your own favorite hymn. How does it express God's love? There may also be other psalms that are class favorites. Psalm 100 is a favorite of many faithful folks. It too speaks of God's "steadfast love to all generations."

Helping Class Members Act

For the coming week, suggest that your people make a personal list of specific acts of divine grace for which they are thankful.

They might also think about ways to remember God's graciousness, useful not only for them but also for training the youth of the church.

Planning for Next Sunday

Next Sunday's lesson is a celebration of love. The reading is taken from the Song of Solomon (2:8-17), and it is perhaps the most beautiful picture of human love to be found in the Bible. Encourage class members to think of love between humans as one of the greatest of God's gifts.

LESSON 8   JANUARY 19

Song of Love

Background Scripture: Song of Solomon 2:8-17

The Main Question—William H. Willimon

How our views of love and sex have changed in the past few years! Before we all got "liberated," sex was one of those unmentionable subjects, human behavior that it was reasonable to suppose that nearly everyone did but that almost no one ever dared to talk about. The labels "Victorian" and "Puritan," whether they actually relate to the true nature of historical Victorians or Puritans, signified our former carefully suppressed dealings with sex.

The comedian Bill Cosby said that when he was young, his father always encouraged him to talk over any questions or problems. Attempting to obey his father, one evening at the dinner table young Cosby asked, "Dad, where do babies come from?" Cosby's father got up from the table, quietly asked his son to accompany him into another room, sat him down, and said, "If I ever hear you talk like that again, I'll give you a spanking you won't forget."

JANUARY 19   LESSON 8

Particularly in the context of religion, the very mention of sex was taboo. A pastor friend of mine recalls the time when, as he was greeting his parishioners after church one Sunday, a little girl ran up and said, "Pastor, we are so excited. Our cat just had five babies." The little girl's horrified mother grabbed her daughter, pushed her away, and said, "Oh, Pastor, I can't imagine where she learned to talk like that. We certainly don't talk about that kind of thing at home!"

It's enough to make one ask, "Just what is a Christian view of sex?" Is this some unmentionable subject that should not be examined in the context of an adult Sunday school class? Or is sex a biblical concern? For guidance, let us turn to a little known biblical book, the Song of Solomon.

Selected Scripture

King James Version

Song of Solomon 2:8-17
8 The voice of my beloved! behold, he cometh leaping upon the mountains, skipping upon the hills.

9 My beloved is like a roe or a young hart: behold, he standeth behind our wall, he looketh forth at the windows, shewing himself through the lattice.

10 My beloved spake, and said unto me, Rise up, my love, my fair one, and come away.

11 For, lo, the winter is past, the rain is over *and* gone;
12 The flowers appear on the earth; the time of the singing *of birds* is come, and the voice of the turtle is heard in our land;

13 The fig tree putteth forth her green figs, and the vines *with* the tender grape give a *good* smell. Arise, my love, my fair one, and come away.
14 O my dove, *that art* in the clefts of the rock, in the secret *places* of the stairs, let me see thy countenance, let me hear thy voice; for sweet *is* thy voice, and thy countenance *is* comely.

15 Take us the foxes, the little

Revised Standard Version

Song of Solomon 2:8-17
8 The voice of my beloved!
   Behold, he comes,
leaping upon the mountains,
   bounding over the hills.
9 My beloved is like a gazelle,
   or a young stag.
Behold, there he stands
   behind our wall,
gazing in at the windows,
   looking through the lattice.
10 My beloved speaks and says to me:
"Arise, my love, my fair one,
   and come away;
11 for lo, the winter is past,
   the rain is over and gone.
12 The flowers appear on the earth,
   the time of singing has come,
and the voice of the turtledove
   is heard in our land.
13 The fig tree puts forth its figs,
   and the vines are in blossom;
   they give forth fragrance.
Arise, my love, my fair one,
   and come away.
14 O my dove, in the clefts of the rock,
   in the covert of the cliff,
let me see your face,
   let me hear your voice,
for your voice is sweet,
   and your face is comely.

15 Catch us the foxes,

foxes, that spoil the vines: for our vines *have* tender grapes.

the little foxes,
that spoil the vineyards,
for our vineyards are in blossom."

16 My beloved *is* mine, and I *am* his: he feedeth among the lilies.

16 My beloved is mine and I am his, he pastures his flock among the lilies.

17 Until the day break, and the shadows flee away, turn, my beloved, and be thou like a roe or a young hart upon the mountains of Bether.

17 Until the day breathes
and the shadows flee,
turn, my beloved, be like a gazelle,
or a young stag upon rugged mountains.

Key Verse: **Many waters cannot quench love, neither can the floods drown it. (Song of Solomon 8:7)**

Key Verse: **Many waters cannot quench love, neither can floods drown it. (Song of Solomon 8:7)**

As You Read the Scripture—Horace R. Weaver

The Song of Songs is a series of some twenty love songs, none of which speak directly to a person's love for God. Rather, they speak of human love at its sensuous and loving best. True, as with Adam and Eve, love comes from the Creator, Yahweh Elohim (the Lord God). Apparently these songs were collected by an unknown editor at different periods of time (perhaps during five centuries, beginning with Solomon), as is noted by the use of the Hebrew preposition *lamed* (in 1:1), which has a variety of meanings: by Solomon, belonging to Solomon, to Solomon, for Solomon, and concerning Solomon. There is no adequate evidence in the context to know which meaning of the preposition was intended. Were they songs written by Solomon or for Solomon, or a group of songs "belonging to" Solomon?

The Song of Songs is the only book in the Bible that presents its message in the form of monologue, with practically no dialogue. It is the only book in the Bible that is intentionally secular, with no apparent theological, religious, or moral attributes. Nowhere is the presence of God referred to. To be sure, there have been several attempts to make these songs appear to be religious. This is done by accepting an allegorical interpretation of the Songs. Both Jews and Christians tortured and twisted the meanings of various of these songs. As early as A.D. 150 the Jewish Talmud offered impossible interpretations, and by A.D. 500 the Targum interpreted the bridegroom as Yahweh and the bride as the Jewish nation. Origen, an early bishop, claimed there were two interpretations of the Song of Solomon. The first emphasized Solomon's marriage to the pharaoh's daughter. In the second, and most important, the bridegroom was not Solomon but Christ, and the bride was the church. The Roman Catholic church identified the bride with the Virgin Mary. It seems best not to accept the early church's allegorical interpretations of Scripture. We must not let eisegesis replace exegesis!

Song of Songs 2:8. "The voice of my beloved" means "Hark!" The maiden hears the voice of her beloved, as sweet as the morning cooing of the turtledove. She loves to be awakened by the music of his love. "He comes ... leaping," gracefully and magnificently, hyperbolically "leaping upon the mountains, bounding over the hills."

Verse 9.

> My beloved is like a gazelle,
>   or a young stag.

His strength and fitness calls for appreciation.

> Behold, there he stands
>   behind our wall,
> gazing in at the windows,
>   looking through the lattice.

Her lover hopes to see his beloved as he peeks through the windows. He too can hardly wait until he sees her.

Verse 10. But love is more than seeing or awareness of another's presence: "My beloved speaks and says to me." The speech of true love always includes these questions: How can I say that I love you? How many ways can I express it? And why do you love me?

Verse 11. "The winter is past, the rain is over and gone," refers to the rainy season, at the end of which the growing season starts in earnest—then, of course the harvest.

Verse 12. After the harvest,

> The flowers appear on the earth,
>   the time of singing has come,
> and the voice of the turtledove
>   is heard in our land.

That is, a year has passed, and new life has come to the two lovers.

The turtledove was a migratory bird in Palestine, whose appearance signaled that spring—new life—was ahead.

Verse 14. "Oh, my dove" is a word of endearment. In the Middle East doves nest in the face of cliffs—"in the clefts of the rock." The maiden still speaks to her lover:

> let me see your face,
>   let me hear your voice,
> for your voice is sweet,
>   and your face is comely.

Verse 16. This is true love:

> My beloved is mine and I am his,
>   he pastures his flock among the lilies.

Verse 17. The heat of the day becomes the cool of the evening:

> Until the day breathes
>   and the shadows flee,
> turn, my beloved, be like a gazelle,
>   or a young stag upon rugged mountains.

SECOND QUARTER

The Scripture and the Main Question—William H. Willimon

The Voice of My Beloved

We ought to begin by noting that the Christian church has had a poor record in its historical dealings with sex. For centuries, the witness of biblical books like the Song of Solomon notwithstanding, the church acted as if sex were merely a necessary evil. In the Middle Ages, marriage was suspect, and celibacy (remaining unmarried) was considered the highest state of Christian existence. We Christians always tended to value spiritual things over physical things. Despite the fact that our Christian faith began when "the Word became flesh," despite Jesus' teachings about the proper use of all God's gifts, material and spiritual, we later Christians rarely mention money, politics, jobs, or sex as having great consequence for living the Christian life.

Of course, neatly separating our world into physical and spiritual spheres makes it easier to be faithful. We can keep our religion "pure" by focusing only on the spiritual, and then run our business, spend our money, cast our ballots, and have sex as we want to! Such separation makes life less complicated. Whether it makes life more Christian is quite another matter.

The perverted notion that sex is evil has many sources. Platonic dualism, which influenced Christian theology in the Middle Ages, was one source. Some medieval biblical interpreters, in order biblically to show that marriage was evil, cited Luke 14 where a man missed the great banquet because he had married a wife!

St. Ambrose called marriage a "galling burden," and Jerome taught that the main value of marriage was that it was helpful in producing future virgins!

The church as a whole weathered these extremist viewpoints. But until the Protestant Reformation, marriage held a distinctly second-class status, and sex itself, under any conditions, was held suspect. In recent years we have come to realize how unbiblical these negative views of sex are. The Protestant Reformers, in their Service of Marriage, argued that "Marriage is an honorable estate, instituted of God." Genesis teaches that sex was God's good idea. God created us, says Genesis, male and female, in God's own image (Genesis 1:27). God's first commandment to us was to "be fruitful and multiply," which is a difficult command to obey without engaging in sex! Any sinfulness in our sexuality is not due to the way we were created but to the fallen way that we abuse creation.

Anyone in the church who would teach that sexuality is inherently bad must come to terms not only with the first chapter of Genesis but also with one of the most unusual books in the Bible, the Song of Solomon. There, in an unabashed poem to the love between a man and a woman, we see displayed a biblical view of human love and sexuality.

My Beloved Is Mine

Today's scripture demonstrates to us that the Bible itself is not squeamish on the subject of sex. The Song of Solomon is an exuberant celebration of the joys of love, including erotic, sexual love, between a man and a woman.

I remember the first time I heard the words of the Song of Solomon. I was in a college religion course at the time (why did I have to wait until I got to college before I heard this book of the Bible even mentioned?). We were discussing, as you have undoubtedly discussed in your adult class, whether or not the Bible is really relevant to the concerns of modern people.

The wise professor flipped open his Bible to the Song of Solomon and began reading. The classful of nineteen-year-olds was transfixed. It was some of the most beautiful love poetry they had ever heard. In the words of these two young Hebrew lovers, they heard their own romantic yearnings.

> My beloved speaks and says to me:
> "Arise my love, my fair one,
>   and come away;
> for lo, the winter is past,
>   the rain is over and gone."
> (2:10-11)

Suddenly the ancient Bible took on fresh and exciting new relevance. We heard in the words of Scripture the voice of our own yearnings and concerns. Ever since that day, as a Christian I have been glad that the Song of Solomon was in our Bible. At times, this Hebrew love poem has been somewhat of an embarrassment to the church. (We are always embarrassed when the Bible doesn't say what we think it ought to say!) Medieval biblical interpreters, because this book did not fit their own preconceptions about the sinfulness of all sex, tried to allegorize away the Song of Solomon. They tried to say that this wasn't really a love poem rather a poem about the church as the Bride of Christ. The young man in the poem is Jesus; the young woman is the church.

But their explanations did not work. The Song of Solomon is the only book of the Bible that never mentions God. So why would they leave it in the Bible? Why, with all the noble religious sentiments that ought to be expressed, with all the more "appropriate" subjects to discuss, is the Song of Solomon in our Bibles?

I think it stands there, in the heart of our Bibles, as a joyful, exuberant celebration of the gifts of love and sex. Anyone who thinks that our faith, the faith of Israel and the church, is just for stuff-shirts and prudes ought to read the Bible—the *whole* Bible.

The Song of Solomon reminds us that sexuality, and the romantic love it elicits, is a gift of God. There is no denying that sex is seen in the Bible as a potentially troublesome and frequently abused gift of God, as are any of God's good gifts. But sex is a gift of God. And God does not give evil gifts.

Perhaps that message has gotten across to people today. We have learned that Christians are free to exercise and to enjoy our sexuality in responsible, covenanted ways. But sometimes, in recent years, it seems as if we have exchanged our perversion of acting as if sex does not exist for an equally perverted obsession with sex. We have ceased acting as if sex were the one unmentionable subject and started acting as if we have no other subject worth speaking about! What is the great obsession of our movies, plays, and television programs? Sex.

The Song of Solomon is not in our Bibles to reinforce our preoccupation with sex as *the* most significant aspect of the human being. It is only one among many books of the Bible. As I said earlier, I think it is wonderful that the Song of Solomon is in our Bibles. But it cannot be read or interpreted alone. Sex is *one* of God's gifts to us, along with the gifts of responsibility,

SECOND QUARTER

selfless love, commitment, children, and sacrifice. We believe that sex is most joyful and enjoyable when exercised within the context of a committed, self-giving, exclusive, and life-long relationship, rather than enjoyed for its own sake.

In other words, just as the Song of Solomon must be set in the context of all the other claims of the Bible upon our lives, so sex must be set in the context of all the other commitments and virtues that make us full, functioning, and faithful disciples. Then, and only then, can we speak of our sex and love as good, as in the image of God.

Helping Adults Become Involved—Robert G. Rogers

Preparing to Teach

This is the fourth in your series on "Songs from Festive Occasions." The focus this Sunday is on human sexual love. Read carefully the Song of Solomon 2:8-17. You might also wish to review Genesis 1:27-28, where God affirms male and female sexuality.

Sex and human sexuality are difficult subjects to discuss for many people. You will want to read Dr. Willimon's exposition and Horace Weaver's exegesis carefully. Dr. Willimon offers a brief view of Christian history and sexuality. Notice how Christians have often denied the value of the physical and sexual. What are your own feelings on the subject? Dr. Willimon also notes our contemporary culture's misuse of human sexuality. You might clip out several advertisements from magazines as illustrations of the misuse of sex to sell a product.

Your main aim is to affirm our sexuality as good, a gift from God. You will be noting its misuse in contemporary culture and suggesting the value of a committed, faithful love relationship.

Introducing the Main Question

We live in a culture that is permeated with heavily charged sexual themes. We use sex to sell cars as well as clothing. Yet it has not always been so. In recent history, sex and even any mention of it were repressed. We seem to have gone from one extreme to another.

Spend a few moments discussing with the class their views on sexuality in our culture. Why is sex so prominent in our day? Why are we so preoccupied with that one dimension of human existence? Conclude by reminding the class that the flaunting of sexuality is really a form of exploitation, a misuse of God's gift to man and woman.

Developing the Lesson

Read aloud the first portion of the Song of Solomon 2:16. This gives biblical validity to sexual love between man and woman. You will be developing three main themes:

> I. Affirming human sexuality
> II. Sex and contemporary culture
> III. Sexuality and commitment

JANUARY 19   LESSON 8

I. Affirming human sexuality

Spend time reviewing in general terms historic Christian views of sexuality. Refer to Dr. Willimon's brief summary. Remind the class of the tendency to divide each human into two parts: body and soul. In the process, it is easy to assume that the physical body is less valuable than the soul or spiritual side of a human being. Perhaps some of your people grew up with this idea of dividing each human into two parts.

Suggest that those who wish might share what they were told about the body and sex when they were children. How were they introduced to their awareness of human sexuality? (Not all people will feel comfortable sharing this part of their past.) Class members will have a wide range of views on sex. Avoid letting judgments be made about individual views.

Now turn to the biblical reading for this lesson. Point out the "language of love," particularly the word "beloved." What feelings does this word convey? Mention also the use of nature imagery in this love poem. Perhaps the biblical author is telling us that God, as Creator, affirms a sexual relationship in every order of creation: from flowers and trees to animals and humans.

End this section by spending a few moments on the "language of love." Pose the following question to the class: How do we tell a member of the opposite sex that we love him or her? During this brief exercise, affirm that each couple has its own meaningful love language. As one speaks with one's "beloved," one is participating in God's gift as expressed in Genesis 1:27-28, "male and female he created them. And God blessed them, and God said to them, 'Be fruitful and multiply'." We are spiritual beings, and we are sexual beings as well.

II. Sex and contemporary culture

In this section you will be seeking a balance: affirming sexuality but denying those things that abuse or misuse it. You and the class have established the claim that human sexuality is a gift from God. Yet it needs to be used wisely.

Show the ads that you have clipped from magazines and tell how, in your opinion, they exploit sex to sell a product. Now ask class members to contribute their own views on misused sexuality in contemporary culture. We need to analyze how God's gift of "healthy sexuality" is being turned to a pursuit of the wrong ends.

Suggest that an "obsession with sex" lets us view members of the opposite sex as objects rather than as individual humans. What happens when we are viewed by others in this nonpersonal way as an object? Suggest that women especially have been treated this way. Sexual harassment and even abuse or rape become acceptable if another human being is merely a sex object.

Some of your class may believe that there is too much talk about sexual matters in our culture. Help them distinguish between discussing human issues of sexuality and using sex for commercial purposes. It is good to discuss who we are as sexual beings—even in the church! Sex does not disappear simply because we refuse to talk about it.

III. Sexuality and commitment

Open up this section by referring to the assigned biblical passage again. Note that there is a mutual love between the man and the woman described in the Song of Solomon. They have eyes only for each other. The biblical

SECOND QUARTER

author tells us of a mutual attraction and fidelity. The beauty of each to the other is celebrated. Invite the class to consider the possibilities for personal growth in such a love relationship. You might begin the conversation by suggesting that "openness" is a significant benefit. There is no need to hide one's feelings from the other. Neither is there any desire to hide the relationship from the larger community. What other benefits come to those who know that they are loved by another? As people respond, jot down the major points on the blackboard, so that all can see and reflect together.

After a few moments of discussion, mention that the highest value of such commitment is that it is sanctified by God. In turn, the human community of faith blesses and affirms the union through the sacrament of marriage. Sexuality thus becomes a major aspect of a relationship of trust.

Helping Class Members Act

In the coming week, ask class members to think on several issues. First, they might look at ads more closely and analyze how sexuality is being used. Second, they should reflect on what Christian adults might teach youth about sexuality.

Planning for Next Sunday

Next Sunday's lesson is the last in the series on "Songs from Festive Occasions." It speaks of love that is "unreturned."

The class should read Isaiah 5:1-7 carefully and notice how the prophet uses nature imagery to describe the relationship between God and his people.

LESSON 9   JANUARY 26

A Song of Unreturned Love

Background Scripture: Isaiah 5:1-7

The Main Question—William H. Willimon

About the saddest thing I know is love that is offered and given but unreturned.

Here is a teacher who has expended her whole life offering education to her students. She spent many years and most of her resources to get the education she needed to be a good teacher. She forsook other, more lucrative employment because she felt called into the field of education.

JANUARY 26   LESSON 9

But after her years of teaching, she is becoming disillusioned and embittered. Her students are unattentive and undisciplined. She sees few concrete results of her labors. "What good have I done?" she asks herself. Unreturned love.

As a pastor, I have seen it. When someone offers love to another person and is rejected, that is one of the most painful blows one can receive in life. The person whose spouse is unfaithful must work hard not to be an embittered, resentful, hateful person. Infidelity is a cruel situation in which the person who has suffered the infidelity feels betrayed. Love was promised but not returned.

When love is continually offered and not returned, it is very difficult to keep on loving. If love is unreturned continually, persons tend to withdraw into themselves, to become closed, fearful to risk love again. A person can be knocked down only so often; eventually the person no longer struggles to stand up again. That happens to people in love, sometimes.

Can it be that God sometimes feels this way, when God's love is offered but not returned? What does God do when we fail to be faithful and loving? How can God's continuing, patient love for us be a model for our love for others? These are some of the questions behind today's study of the Scripture.

Selected Scripture

King James Version	**Revised Standard Version**
Isaiah 5:1-7	*Isaiah 5:1-7*
1 Now will I sing to my wellbeloved a song of my beloved touching his vineyard. My wellbeloved hath a vineyard in a very fruitful hill:	1 Let me sing for my beloved a love song concerning his vineyard: My beloved had a vineyard on a very fertile hill.
2 And he fenced it, and gathered out the stones thereof, and planted it with the choicest vine, and built a tower in the midst of it, and also made a winepress therein: and he looked that it should bring forth grapes, and it brought forth wild grapes.	2 He digged it and cleared it of stones, and planted it with choice vines; he built a watchtower in the midst of it, and hewed out a wine vat in it; and he looked for it to yield grapes, but it yielded wild grapes.
3 And now, O inhabitants of Jerusalem, and men of Judah, judge, I pray you, betwixt me and my vineyard.	3 And now, O inhabitants of Jeru- salem and men of Judah, judge, I pray you, between me and my vineyard.
4 What could have been done more to my vineyard, that I have not done in it? wherefore, when I	4 What more was there to do for my vineyard, that I have not done in it?

SECOND QUARTER

looked that it should bring forth grapes, brought it forth wild grapes?

5 And now go to; I will tell you what I will do to my vineyard: I will take away the hedge thereof, and it shall be eaten up; *and* break down the wall thereof, and it shall be trodden down:
6 And I will lay it waste: it shall not be pruned, nor digged; but there shall come up briers and thorns: I will also command the clouds that they rain no rain upon it.

7 For the vineyard of the Lord of hosts *is* the house of Israel, and the men of Judah his pleasant plant: and he looked for judgment, but behold oppression; for righteousness, but behold a cry.

Key Verse: **The vineyard of the Lord of hosts is the house of Israel ... and he looked for judgment, but behold oppression; for righteousness, but behold a cry. (Isaiah 5:7)**

When I looked for it to yield grapes,
why did it yield wild grapes?

5 And now I will tell you
what I will do to my vineyard.
I will remove its hedge,
and it shall be devoured;
I will break down its wall,
and it shall be trampled down.
6 I will make it a waste;
it shall not be pruned or hoed,
and briers and thorns shall grow up;
I will also command the clouds
that they rain no rain upon it.

7 For the vineyard of the Lord of hosts
is the house of Israel,
and the men of Judah
are his pleasant planting;
and he looked for justice,
but behold, bloodshed;
for righteousness,
but behold, a cry!

Key Verse: **The vineyard of the Lord of hosts is the house of Israel ... and he looked for justice, but behold, bloodshed; for righteousness, but behold, a cry. (Isaiah 5:7)**

As You Read the Scripture—Horace R. Weaver

Isaiah's call to prophecy/ministry came at a time when his heart was heavy with suffering—his beloved King Uzziah had died (about 739 B.C.). Isaiah records his call in chapter 6, which call logically and psychologically precedes chapters 1-5. Isaiah's personal experience of "seeing Yahweh [the Lord] sitting upon a throne, high and lifted up" was reinforced by an auditory experience:

> Holy, holy, holy is the Lord of hosts;
> and the whole earth is full of his glory.
> (Isaiah 6:3)

Isaiah, realizing his unworthiness, soon felt cleansed by the seraphim. He was called to speak:

> Go, and say to this people:
> Hear and hear, but do not understand;
> see and see, but do not perceive.

JANUARY 26   LESSON 9

The gross evil Israel is doing is keeping them from perceiving their evil ways. Making merry while neighbors cry for food, clothing, housing, fair wages, dulls the mind and heart. Israel cannot even hear God's cry! What does God want? More sacrifices for temple rituals? God is weary of them (Isaiah 1:14; 29:13). More money, and thus more pleasure? Minds dulled by sensuality and materialism? Wills infected by ostentation and self-indulgence, at the expense of the poor?

Isaiah 5:1. These verses constitute a parable. "Let me sing" (now hear me sing) is Isaiah's way of calling the crowd to his attention. The occasion is the celebration of the feast of Tabernacles, which is attended by great crowds of worshipers. It is possible, if not probable, that he was a priest. If so, he would have stood near the columns of the temple, which was a priestly prerogative.

The phrase "a love song for my beloved" raises a question: Who is "my beloved" in this case? He or she is certainly not a romantic interest, like that in the Songs of Solomon. Dr. G. G. D. Kilpatrick, the expositor for Isaiah in *The Interpreter's Bible* (pp. 196-97), suggests substituting the word "friend." The verse might read then:

> Now hear me sing on behalf of my friend,
> my friend's song about his vineyard.

Yet Dr. R. B. Y. Scott suggests in *The Interpreter's Bible* (pp. 196-97) that Isaiah meant what he says—that is, that Isaiah wrote with the intention of getting his male audience to listen to him. Hence,

> Let me sing for my beloved
>   a love song concerning his vineyard:
> My beloved had a vineyard
>   on a very fertile hill.

Verse 2. The vinedresser "digged it and cleared it of stones." Modern vinedressers and shepherds build small stone walls to indicate ownership. The owner "planted it with choice vines"; that is, he planted either red grapes or grapes from Sorek, a valley known for its fine vineyards. "He built a watchtower," a small eight-by-eight foot building, usually of stone. "And hewed out a wine vat in it" means he chiseled out an area into which workers could dump their loads of grapes and eventually stamp with their feet until the juices were separated from the skins.

> He looked for it to yield grapes,
>   but it yielded wild grapes.

Verses 3-4. "O inhabitants of Jerusalem and men of Judah" refers to those worshipers who were at the Feast of Tabernacles, in Jerusalem.

"Judge, I pray you between me and my vineyard." God has done all he could do with the vinedressers and their choice vines—what are the alternatives for a vinedresser?

Verses 5-6. "My beloved's" action must be:

> I will remove its hedge . . .
> ....
> I will break down its wall . . .

SECOND QUARTER

> I will make it a waste . . .
>
> I will also command the clouds
> that they rain no rain upon it.

Verse 7.

> For the vineyard of the Lord of hosts
> is the house of Israel,
> and the men of Judah
> are his pleasant planting;
> and he looked for justice,
> but behold, bloodshed;
> for righteousness,
> but behold, a cry!

The Scripture and the Main Question—William H. Willimon

Let Me Sing for My Beloved

Have you ever stopped to think how many love songs are sad songs? The other day, listening to my automobile radio, I noted that of the six or seven songs played in an hour, the majority were songs of sadness and lament. There were pleas for lost girlfriends to return, moans for wayward boyfriends, dirges for the end of a relationship. Evidently, love is no easy matter!

For the past few weeks we have been studying some of the great songs of the Bible. We have examined songs of praise and songs of hope and victory. Today we study a curious allegory found in the fifth chapter of Isaiah—the Song of the Vineyard.

Some of the great poetry of the Bible is found in the words of Isaiah. No wonder he was Jesus' favorite prophet. I remember the story of the first-year seminarian who, in an Old Testament course, was first introduced to Isaiah and, upon reading his words in chapter 9, exclaimed, "Look, Isaiah is quoting Handel!"

Sadly, most of us are more familiar with Isaiah through the music of Handel's *Messiah* than we are through reading Isaiah himself. But it is no wonder that when Handel wanted to set the mystery of Christ to music, he reached into the beautiful words of Isaiah.

The prophet begins a song that is an allegory, in which some things stand in place of other things. Does the prophet's allegorical poem remind you of that famous parable the prophet Nathan told King David (2 Samuel 12:1-12)? There the prophet says to the powerful king, "Let me tell you a little story about a rich man who took the one little lamb of a poor man."

The king was enraged at the terrible injustice. "That arrogant rich man ought to be punished."

Then the prophet explained that the story was not a newspaper account. It was an allegory. It was a story not about lambs but about the king's terrible marital infidelity with Bathsheba. "Thou art the man!" charged the prophet.

A similar dynamic is at work in today's Song of the Vineyard. Through a song, the prophet lures the listeners into his tale. The vinedresser has expended great effort to care for his beloved vineyard. Unfortunately, "it yielded wild grapes" (Isaiah 5:2). In great sadness, the owner of the vineyard abandoned the field and allowed the vineyard to remain exposed and unprotected.

Probably about this time, the allegory begins to hit home. "For the vineyard of the Lord of hosts is the house of Israel" (5:7). The tragedy of the vineyard is a story of God's love and Israel's infidelity. It is a story of love unreturned. Look at all that God has done for the Chosen People, and look at how they repaid God's love.

He Looked for Justice, but . . .

In one sense, Isaiah 5 is typical of much of the Bible—a long and rather sad record of God's fidelity and our infidelity. Time and again we rebelled and chose our way rather than God's way. In other words, the Bible, including this Song of the Vineyard, is a story of our sin.

When William Golding was given the Nobel Prize for literature, he was asked what he had learned in a lifetime of studying human nature. He replied, "I have seen that man produces evil as a bee makes honey." Golding's insight was not original. "I do not understand my own actions," confessed Paul, "for I do not do what I want, but I do the very thing I hate. . . . Sin . . . dwells within me. . . . I can will what is right, but I cannot do it. For I do not do the good I want, but the evil I do not want is what I do" (Romans 7:15, 17-19).

In the Bible, sin is always more than mere mistakes, slip-ups. Modern people reduce sin to psychological maladjustment, a problem of inadequate education, immaturity. But when the Bible speaks of sin, it does so in terms of lust, infidelity, prostitution, and other sexual imagery in order to convey the personal, deep sense of our sin. Sin is often compared to adultery, the violation of God's fidelity with our infidelity.

Here, in the Song of the Vineyard, the prophet tries to capture some of the deep, intimate sense of grief that God must feel when God is subjected to our infidelity.

So the Bible begins the story of humanity by telling of Adam and Eve, our primal parents who rebelled against God when given the first opportunity to do so. You and I, according to traditional Christian doctrine, never get beyond Adam and Eve. Our sin originates in us. The thoughts of our hearts are, according to Genesis, evil from our youth (8:21).

It is more than the mistakes we make; it is the way we are. We are born in rebellion, basing our lives upon what is false rather than what is true, preferring our wills to God's will. Among human beings, says Paul, "there is no distinction; since all have sinned and fall short of the glory of God." Original sin unites us with one another and is the gap between us and God.

We are, it would seem, like rather inept children. Children may know, in their heart of hearts, that their parents love them deeply and would do anything for them. But children sometimes so want to follow their own way, to do what they want to do rather than what their parents want, that they are unable to be obedient, unable to respond to their parents' love with their love.

That is quite sad.

SECOND QUARTER

A Love Song

This Song of the Vineyard would thus be ranked as one of the saddest of the sad songs in the Bible, just one more indication that we are utterly undeserving of the great love God has shown toward us. Did not we agree, at the beginning of this lesson, that nothing is sadder than unreturned love?

Yet there is more to this allegorical song than the sadness of unreturned love. Here is a God who not only sets a standard for justice and righteousness (5:7) but also comes back, again and again, to love. Even when we spurned God's faithfulness, God remained faithful.

My friend, Chad Davis, tells of standing at the gate of our state penitentiary and watching the fathers of prisoners come to the gate and ask to see their sons. The guard would go in and then come back to tell some of the fathers that their sons did not wish to see them. Still, every week, the fathers returned.

God is just like that father, only more so.

Jesus told the story of the prodigal son, in which the father, though his beloved son went into the far country and wasted his inheritance, still waited for and received the son. God is just like that father, Jesus said.

This why the Song of the Vineyard is more than just a sad, sad story of unreturned love. It is God who sends the prophet to tell Israel this story, to use all the poetic means at his disposal to reawaken Israel's love. Through this song, the prophet hopes to rekindle Israel's passion for righteousness and justice and thus return God's love through loving deeds.

As parents, wives, husbands, children, and church members, and in all the other relationships of our lives, we should mirror God's continual, never-failing love for us in our love for others. Even when our love is unreturned, we are called to love even as God has loved us.

Helping Adults Become Involved—Robert G. Rogers

Preparing to Teach

This lesson is the last in the series of five on "Songs from Festive Occasions." Lesson 5 presents a scenario wherein God's love for Israel is unreturned. Review the previous four lessons. You will notice that the series deals with relationships, between God and people, between man and woman.

Read Isaiah 5:1-7 carefully. Notice the imagery used. The "beloved" is God, and the "vineyard" is his people. What is your response to the people's refusal to return God's love? Have you experienced this situation in a human context? How do we feel when our love for another is not returned?

Your aim in this lesson is to help the class see the need to return God's love by loving and serving him. Also, in this process you will demonstrate an awareness of our human need to both give and receive love.

Introducing the Main Question

Offering love to others takes time and emotional effort. Most humans want responses from those to whom they offer love. Such responses prove that our love efforts have been worthwhile. Indeed, it is hard to love those who do not seem to care about our efforts in their behalf. Suggest, as does Dr. Willimon, that we can imagine God's feelings about the human community. His love for us is often unreturned.

Invite the class to think about unreturned love. Are there examples in their lives of this type of circumstance? How did they feel in the situation? What does it take to work through these feelings and continue to offer love even though it is unreturned?

Developing the Lesson

The Sons of the Vineyard describes God's way of dealing with unreturned love. To teach this lesson, you should develop the following three sections:

      I. The need to be loved
     II. Love and expectations
    III. Sharing God's love

I. The need to be loved

Begin by noting the basic human need to be loved. Each of us needs to feel important and accepted by others. Allude to Dr. Willimon's notion that every human wants his or her love to others to be returned. Perhaps even the Creator feels this way! Certainly the allegory entitled the Song of the Vineyard suggests it to be so.

Go over the biblical reading rather carefully. Point out the feelings of God that the biblical author suggests. Despite the time and effort God has devoted to his people ("vineyard"), they do not respond; he is rejected. What other divine emotions are portrayed in the vineyard imagery? Do words such as "disappointment" or "anger" fit here? One gets the impression in Isaiah that God has given and given, but there is little response from the human community to the gift of divine love.

Acknowledge that the same lack of response also prevails in human relationships. Tragically, it sometimes is the case in families that parents give, and receive little gratitude in return from their children. (Of course, the opposite is sometimes true.) How can one face continued rejection without becoming depressed? You may want to spend time here looking at the resources available to give us strength in such situations. Mention first that we can turn to God for aid. In the covenant relationship, the Creator returns our love, even when humans fail to do so. The other obvious resource is the love returned to us by members of the church family. Ask class members to list some examples of times when church members returned their love and gave them strength to continue in difficult situations. They may also want to list other resources, such as a favorite poem or book, that provided support to carry on.

II. Love and expectations

Most relationships of love carry expectations. Turn here to the biblical lesson and point out the divine expectations. The desire for faithfulness is obvious, as is the hoped-for expectation of gratitude. However, Isaiah 5:7 is a very important verse. God also expects that humans will be just and righteous as a sign of response to his love.

SECOND QUARTER

What sorts of things do we expect from our fellow humans? We anticipate that there will be a mutual giving in the relationship. Give the class opportunity to add other expectations they might bring to a relationship of love.

Those class members who are parents will remember times when they operated in a fashion similar to God. Because we love our children, we sometimes need to make demands that will help them respond to our love as they should. How can we assure the loved one that our love is still constant, despite either punishment or the threat of it? This is not an easy question to answer. Undoubtedly, each class member has his or her view.

III. Sharing God's love

The class has considered our need to be loved and the expectations that we bring to a relationship of love. Now it is appropriate to consider how we can take God's love and share it in the world. Develop this portion of the lesson as follows. First, suggest that we become equipped to share God's love by first returning it to him in our thanksgiving and praise. One of the purposes of worship is to give us the strength to go forth in ministry to the world. An equally strong theme in worship is the opportunity we have to demonstrate to God our love for him.

A second way to share God's love is by being his agent in the world. When presenting this aspect, you want to emphasize the support that comes through corporate witness. Here the church family is most helpful in supporting each individual's efforts to minister in the world. Acknowledge that such ministry may lead to a situation of "unreturned love." Not all to whom we offer friendship and love respond in kind. This is where the congregation provides a support group for our efforts. Spend a few moments listing some specific ways in which the church can help each member offer God's love to others. You might begin by listing several examples in which a church member helped you become a better agent of God's love.

Helping Class Members Act

Suggest that your people reflect in the coming week on specific instances when they might have been negligent about returning another person's offer of love. Perhaps they can learn from these memories and be more effective agents of God's love in the world.

Planning for Next Sunday

Next Sunday begins a new series, whose focus will be on prayer. The Lord's Prayer, found in Matthew 6:7-15, is the first prayer to be considered. The class should read it thoughtfully and notice that it has a twofold emphasis: God and his will for us and our human needs. They might also read another version, as found in Luke 11:2-4.

UNIT III: SONGS AND PRAYERS OF THE CHURCH
Horace R. Weaver

FOUR LESSONS **FEBRUARY 2–23**

Unit III offers an opportunity to study four liturgical texts from the New Testament. These include a prayer to guide disciples who await the dawning of God's reign, a prayer for the unity and mission of the church, and what many consider an early Christian hymn, recorded by the Apostle Paul. The unit concludes joyously with a study of the "Hallelujah Chorus" from the book of Revelation.

The individual lessons for this unit are as follows: "A Model for Prayer," February 2, calls for us to ask the Living Christ to "teach us how to pray." "Jesus' Prayer for Believers," February 9, suggests we are not alone when we pray—beside us, before us, among us, there is a force, a guide and friend, our priest (Jesus). "Being Servant of All," February 16, asks the question: What is the goal of our being Christian? Are we here to serve or to be served? To give or to receive? "Song of God's Victory," February 23, challenges us: What do we really want when we come to church on Sunday?

LESSON 10 **FEBRUARY 2**

A Model for Prayer

Background Scripture: 1 Chronicles 29:10-13; Matthew 6:7-15

The Main Question—William H. Willimon

Most people who study problems among human beings would agree that one of the most pressing human problems is that of communication. Marriages disintegrate because couples do not know how to talk to each other. Nations go to war because they refuse to sit down and talk out their differences.

It is no wonder that prayer is a major problem for believers. How ought we to pray? That is the question which lies behind today's study of the Lord's Prayer. We human beings are so inadequate. Our sins affect our judgment and cloud our speech. God is distant, righteous, and holy. When we pray, on Sunday in our worship or at any other time, are we really communicating, or are we just saying words? How do we talk to God?

Contemporary believers can take heart. Jesus' own disciples, those who communed with God every day through God's Christ, also had problems with prayer. "Teach us to pray," they asked Jesus.

"Pray then like this . . . " Jesus instructed his disciples in prayer by giving them a model prayer: "Our Father who art in heaven . . . " Tertullian calls the Lord's Prayer "an epitome of the whole gospel."

How can I pray? On Sundays we, like those disciples before us, come to Jesus asking, "Teach us to pray." By attending to the prayers in the Bible, we learn what it means to pray "in Jesus' name"—in the spirit of our Lord.

SECOND QUARTER

Selected Scripture

King James Version

Matthew 6:7-15

7 But when ye pray, use not vain repetitions, as the heathen *do:* for they think that they shall be heard for their much speaking.

8 Be not ye therefore like unto them: for your Father knoweth what things ye have need of, before ye ask him.

9 After this manner therefore pray ye: Our Father which art in heaven, Hallowed be thy name.

10 Thy kingdom come. Thy will be done in earth, as *it is* in heaven.

11 Give us this day our daily bread.

12 And forgive us our debts, as we forgive our debtors.

13 And lead us not into temptation, but deliver us from evil: For thine is the kingdom, and the power, and the glory, for ever. Amen.

14 For if ye forgive men their trespasses, your heavenly Father will also forgive you:

15 But if ye forgive not men their trespasses, neither will your Father forgive your trespasses.

Key Verse: **Now therefore, our God, we thank thee, and praise thy glorious name. (1 Chronicles 29:13)**

Revised Standard Version

Matthew 6:7-15

7 "And in praying do not heap up empty phrases as the Gentiles do; for they think that they will be heard for their many words. 8 Do not be like them, for your Father knows what you need before you ask him. 9 Pray then like this:

Our Father who art in heaven,
Hallowed be thy name.

10 Thy kingdom come,
Thy will be done,
On earth as it is in heaven.

11 Give us this day our daily bread;

12 And forgive us our debts,
As we also have forgiven our debtors;

13 And lead us not into temptation,
But deliver us from evil."

14 For if you forgive men their trespasses, your heavenly Father also will forgive you; 15 but if you do not forgive men their trespasses, neither will your Father forgive your trespasses."

Key Verse: **We thank thee, our God, and praise thy glorious name. (1 Chronicles 29:13)**

As You Read the Scripture—Horace R. Weaver

Jesus grew up in a large family—at least two girls, and four boys. Mary and Joseph would have taught them to participate in all the religious festivals and weekly sessions of worship on the sabbath (Saturday). After Jesus' baptism by his cousin John, Jesus began to teach whoever would listen, both men and women. Jesus' goal was not to help religious persons develop new religious institutions but to transform their minds and attitudes through his vivid consciousness of the power and omnipresence of the *living* God.

Matthew 6:7. The Greek word for "empty phrases" means "babble."

FEBRUARY 2 LESSON 10

Some Pharisees prayed long prayers. Sometimes they thought repeating the same prayer might gain God's attention and help. The great Roman senator Seneca (in the days when Paul ministered in Corinth) referred to those who "tire out the gods."

Verse 8. "Do not be like them," for God knows your needs. "Many words" are irrelevant!

Verse 9. Pray, then, like this:

> Our Father who art in heaven,
> Hallowed be thy name.

The word *Abba* ("father") was used by Jews in their prayer life, as it was by Jesus. It seems unlikely to me that Jesus used the word "Daddy" for "Father." This seems too sentimental.

"Who art in heaven" is a difficult phrase inasmuch as its interpretations are manifold. Is the Lord God the king of the universe? Or of the universe minus Planet Earth? Do God and Christ Jesus come to us on certain occasions? Are they with us always (as Moses heard God declare it, in Exodus 33), or on occasions when they visit Planet Earth?

"Our Father who art in heaven" really means a nonphysical deity whose presence is always with us, whether on airplanes (above the earth) or on terra firma.

Think: when Jesus metamorphosized after his death (so Paul) into a nonphysical being, was he (is he) no longer related directly to Planet Earth? Is Jesus Lord of Planet Earth? Such a claim requires Jesus to be both beyond and in space and time.

Verse 10.

> Thy kingdom come,
> Thy will be done,
>   on earth as it is in heaven.

The kingdom is central in Jesus' teachings. The kingdom comes as persons prepare for it by moral effort. Jesus would have it no other way! Jesus equates the kingdom with the doing of God's will on earth, as it is done in heaven.

Verse 11. "Give us this day our daily bread" is translated by many texts as "Give us our bread for the morrow." The reason: The word "daily" is not found in Greek writings.

Verse 12.

> And forgive us our debts [a Jewish figure for "*sins*"]
> As we also have forgiven our debtors.

Verse 13.

> And lead us not into temptation,
> But deliver us from evil.

Many ancient texts include the statement "for thine is the kingdom and the glory forever," which is from 1 Chronicles 29:10-13.

Verse 14. To "forgive persons their trespasses" may involve the moral and spiritual activity of three verbs: Daily we need to cancel our debts, to

SECOND QUARTER

mark our aims and rededicate ourselves to them, and to cleanse the whole practice of our life (*The Interpreter's Bible*, p. 316).

Verse 15. "if you do not forgive [persons] their trespasses, neither will your Father forgive your trespasses."

The Scripture and the Main Question—William H. Willimon

Pray Then like This

Sunday morning worship is a sort of "school for prayer." When someone says, "I don't know how to pray. I don't know what to say," we say, "Come to church. Pray for your sin, intercede for the needs of others, give thanks; you'll get the hang of it."

Yet what do people learn in this "school for prayer"? I had to ask myself that question a few years ago when a man in my church told me that he needed to talk about a terrible problem in his life.

"My supervisor is making my life miserable," he said. "At work he is on my back from the moment the whistle blows. He shouts at me, humiliates me, tries to make me look like a fool before the other workers. I hate him so much, I am fearful that one day he'll push me so far that I'll pick up a wrench and bash his brains out. What can I do?"

"Well," I said, "this is terrible. You must try something. Have you tried prayer?"

"Prayer?"

"Yes," I continued. "What if you prayed every morning before going to work, asking God to give you the inner peace and assurance you need to endure this person's insults? And pray for your supervisor. After all, Jesus tells us to 'pray for our enemies and to bless those who persecute us.'"

The man looked a bit baffled for a moment. Then he said, "I never heard us pray for our enemies before on Sunday morning."

It hit me. What sort of example had my prayers been for him? "O Lord, we thank you for the sun, and the birds, and the bees, and blah, blah, blah . . . "

As a preacher, as someone who leads prayer regularly, I must ask myself what I'm saying about prayer by the way I lead prayer; is it cliché-ridden goulash of conventional phrases and sweet-sounding platitudes, served up in a honey-throated voice, or an earnest attempt to lay ourselves open before God?

Note how the Lord's Prayer in Matthew 6:7-15 gets very specific about human needs—temptation, daily bread, debts, forgiveness. It isn't just beautiful, high-sounding words. It is an earnest effort to lay real life before a living God.

As Paul says, "We do not know how to pray as we ought" (Romans 8:26). Truly Christian prayer—prayer "in Jesus' name"—does not come naturally. It's not a matter of telling God what we want—that sort of thing comes quite naturally; any pagan can do that. No, *Christian* prayer is a matter of putting our wants alongside *God's* wants. Knowing that God's will may be different from our wills, our prayers must begin as Jesus' prayer did—"*thy* kingdom come, *thy* will be done"—and end with "Nevertheless, not *my* will, but *thine* be done."

FEBRUARY 2 — LESSON 10

Do Not Heap Up Empty Phrases

Because Christian prayer does not come naturally, prayer is a problem for many modern people. What are we doing here? For what are we supposed to ask? What to say?

For some, prayer has become little more than autosuggestion, self-therapy. In their view, prayer is mainly of value in helping us to get our heads straight about what we ought to do: Prayer is a time for quiet meditation so that we might enter ever more deeply into our own already inflated egos.

Note how many of our prayers are addressed to ourselves, rather than God. "Make us ever more mindful," we say. Our prayers become thinly disguised preaching, practical atheism in which God doesn't really matter because we are only talking to ourselves. This makes prayer seem silly, pointless.

Is God there or not? Is there anyone "out there" who hears and who cares? This frightening, fundamental question is at the heart of prayer. Everything depends upon the answer. It will not do to fudge and say things like "Prayer is mainly of value in putting us in the right frame of mind to solve the problems which beset us." No. Either we are speaking to a God who acts, or we are merely prattling on to ourselves.

Yet in asking God for things, we have said, "*Thy* will be done on earth as it is in heaven." Prayer is *conversation with God*, not magic. Prayer is not some magical formula through which we hope to entice an apathetic God to act in a way that pleases us. Our prayer is the worshipful recognition that God is continually acting in the world and the public signifying of our desire to be part of that activity. God will be working for good in the world, for order out of chaos, for justice and peace, whether we do so or not.

If we really want peace, food, justice, then we should resort not to prayer but to action. In prayer we ask for what God can and will do. But we also, in prayer, acknowledge "*Thy* will be done," realizing what God does not do. There are many things we ask God to do—feed the hungry, send rain, make peace, work reconciliation—that we are unwilling to do ourselves because of the sacrifice and struggle, the conversion and suffering, it might cause us. Yet there are things that God, for some reason, cannot or will not do. Why? We usually do not understand why we pray for badly needed rain and get none, or ask for a tumor to be healed and it becomes worse. Prayer does not usually answer the "Why"? But our prayer can give us *the faith to live with the absence of answers*. And for the Christian, that faith is considered a good deal more valuable even than answers.

A woman lay in a hospital bed, her body inflamed by the spread of cancer. Day after day we prayed for healing. Each day I could see her silent disappointment that she was not being healed.

Then one day she said, "Today let's not pray that I'll be healed. God knows that I hate this illness. God knows I want to be healed. Let's pray that, whether I'm healed or not, I'll feel close to God because even if I'm not healed—*especially* if I'm not healed."

When all is said and done, we want not simply peace, justice, health, bread. We want God. When we pray that God's will be done on earth as it is in heaven, this means that we want God as present to us on earth as God is present in heaven. In prayer we lay ourselves open to the presence of God, no matter what.

In prayer we ally ourselves with that will, making our desires more congruent with God's desires. We don't simply wish that the poor should be

SECOND QUARTER

fed, but that we should be participants in God's active love for the poor. We don't simply want peace; we want *God's peace, peace on God's* terms. We open ourselves up to new possibilities for participating in the reign of God. Prayer is *education in desire,* voicing our desires, placing them next to the desires of God as expressed in Scripture and in sacrament.

It is proper to be specific here, to get down to concrete particulars of what our hearts desire, even as Jesus models in the Lord's Prayer. In so doing, we bring these wants to the light of truth. Our wants are judged, purified, scrutinized. To pray "in Jesus' name" means to pray as he prayed in Gethsemane, ready to submit to the will of God, ready to be part of the coming kingdom, even if its advent means our suffering change.

Our rather infantile prayers of "give me" become "make me, make me." Prayer changes things—even us!

Helping Adults Become Involved—Robert G. Rogers

Preparing to Teach

This lesson begins a unit entitled "Songs and Prayers of the Church." It is not surprising that the Lord's Prayer is the first lesson to be studied. You might look briefly at the four lessons in the series and skim the following biblical passages: Matthew 6:7-15; John 17:1-11, 20-21; Philippians 2:1-11; and Revelation 15:2-4; 19:4-8.

Now examine the Lord's Prayer more closely. (You might compare Matthew's version with that found in Luke 11:2-4.) Notice how this prayer emphasizes both God's will for us and our human needs. Also consider the broader context for this prayer. Jesus is speaking about the nature of prayer itself. You should think of your own prayer life. What specific prayers help you?

Your aim for this lesson is to help the class understand the Lord's Prayer as a model for all prayer. In particular, you want them to understand that prayer helps us align human concerns with God's will.

Introducing the Main Question

Dr. Willimon suggests that prayer is a form of communication. Yet we moderns often have trouble communicating with one another, let alone with God. Some of your class members may feel uncomfortable praying. You need to address this concern initially.

Acknowledge that it is all right for people to have mixed feelings about the act of praying. Point out that the purpose of the four-lesson series is to help all class members become familiar with biblical prayers and therefore more comfortable with the idea of praying. Now spend a few moments sharing various concerns people have about prayer. Assure them that they should not feel guilty about their feelings. Some folks might find traditional "prayer language" difficult to use. Others may express concern about repeating the same prayer numerous times. You want to allow all who wish to state their concerns. Jot these down on a blackboard or flipchart.

Developing the Lesson

After spending some time letting your class state their concerns about prayer, you are now ready to develop the lesson in the following ways:

FEBRUARY 2   LESSON 10

        I. The mood of authentic prayer
       II. The Lord's Prayer as a model
     III. Prayer and decision making

I. The mood of authentic prayer

Direct the class's attention to the biblical reading for the day. Point out what Jesus emphasizes as necessary for prayer to be effective. He rejects the notion that one must use "lofty phrases." Also rejected is the idea that praying is designed to impress someone else. The key words you want to emphasize when speaking of prayer are "honesty" and "sincerity." In brief, all who pray simply have to be themselves before God. There is no need to stage a performance.

Try to help your class learn the nature of authentic prayer by conducting a brief exercise. Ask them to state, in the simplest terms, a basic human need. It might be a personal need or perhaps a community or world need. You might start it off by giving a simple sentence yourself. What you are trying to demonstrate is that prayer, as an expression of our inner feelings, need not be complicated. Indeed, the most basic statement often expresses best what we feel.

Close this section by noting the simplicity of the Lord's Prayer; it has been meaningful to Christians for centuries, but it is cast in everyday language. And, it expresses basic human needs.

II. The Lord's Prayer as a model

The beauty of the Lord's Prayer is that in a few short verses it praises God, seeks his will for us, and expresses human needs. Before considering this prayer in detail, point out that the familiar doxology ending ("For thine is the kingdom and the power and the glory, forever. Amen.") was added to the prayer after Matthew recorded his gospel.

Dr. Willimon believes that the purpose of prayer is to put "our wants" alongside "God's wants." Focus on Matthew 6:10 first; in this verse the framework for God's wants is listed. To pray that God's kingdom will come and his will be done is to acknowledge his rule over us. Suggest that this verse expresses the obligations that we have as members of a covenant. It is also an open-ended prayer. We must seek to discern God's will for us. This prayer opens up the line of communication between us and God.

Now turn to Matthew 6:11-13. Suggest that these verses express our need for daily sustenance, for forgiveness, for guidance. Note that they also are open-ended. Invite class members to suggest some specific examples of the general needs described in these verses—for example, the need to be forgiven (verse 12). Knowing that we are forgiven by God gives us a fresh start when we try to improve our relationships with him and our neighbor. Let class members suggest other specific examples of the petitions.

III. Prayer and decision making

Begin here by emphasizing that praying is not a substitute for acting. If we take the emphases in the Lord's Prayer seriously, praying should help us become better Christians. Remind class members how easy it is to state something and then forget about it. Prayer, if misused, can become a means of avoiding doing our work in the world.

In this section, you want to show the relationship between prayer concerns and possible human actions. Refer back to the "Prayer Needs" list

SECOND QUARTER

constructed earlier in the class and relabel it "Prayer Concerns." Beside this column, label another "Action Needed." Now ask for particular Christian deeds that might meet some of the needs and place them in the second column. After several minutes of discussion, it will become apparent that many human needs expressed in prayer implicitly demand action. As Christians, we express our need to God, but we also should make a decision to act when we know God's will for us.

End by suggesting that prayer is a "change agent." When we speak of our needs to God, we believe that he cares. We also must learn that we too must care. Prayer should express not only our needs but also our obligations.

Helping Class Members Act

For the coming week, ask the class to concentrate individually on their own prayer requests. What is the relationship between their requests and what they believe God's will is for them?

Planning for Next Sunday

Next Sunday's lesson is another prayer by Jesus. It is known as the "High Priestly Prayer," in which Jesus prays to God in behalf of his followers.

Class members should read John 17:1-11, 20-21. Ask them to notice the close relationship between Son and Father and the unity of all believers.

LESSON 11   FEBRUARY 9

Jesus' Prayer for Believers

Background Scripture: John 17

The Main Question—William H. Willimon

The questions which lie behind today's gospel are the anxious questions of the disciples who are about to be left behind by Jesus. Their questions are those of the church whom the departing Jesus is leaving behind in his ascension into glory. They are the questions of children as their parents put on their coats to go out for the evening: Where are you going? Who is going to stay with us? Can we go too? In response, Jesus tells them that he will not leave them alone. He will send a Comforter, a Counselor, a Helper who would dwell with them, never leaving them alone (John 14:16-17).

Even more, Jesus prays for them. He becomes for them the priest, the intercessor.

Behind our study of John 17 lies our questions: Does anybody out there care about me? How can I possibly be a faithful disciple despite my own weakness, ignorance, and inability to be faithful?

John 17, in its depiction of Jesus as the High Priest who intercedes for his disciples, is an immensely reassuring word: The living of this faith, the

FEBRUARY 9 LESSON 11

following of this Jesus, is not entirely left up to us. We are not alone. Beside us, before us, among us, there is a force, a guide and friend, our high priest.

There are many people in your adult class who come to church desperate for a word of reassurance and comfort. Life being what it is, the Christian faith being what it is, it is not easy to be a disciple of Jesus. Fortunately, we don't have to go it alone. It is not all left up to us and our own devices. A priest, someone very close to the altar of God, intercedes for us.

Who is this priest who prays for us?

Selected Scripture

King James Version

John 17:1-11, 20-21

1 These words spake Jesus, and lifted up his eyes to heaven, and said, Father, the hour is come; glorify thy Son, that thy Son also may glorify thee:

2 As thou hast given him power over all flesh, that he should give eternal life to as many as thou hast given him.

3 And this is life eternal, that they might know thee the only true God, and Jesus Christ, whom thou hast sent.

4 I have glorified thee on the earth: I have finished the work which thou gavest me to do.

5 And now, O Father, glorify thou me with thine own self with the glory which I had with thee before the world was.

6 I have manifested thy name unto the men which thou gavest me out of the world: thine they were, and thou gavest them me; and they have kept thy word.

7 Now they have known that all things whatsoever thou hast given me are of thee.

8 For I have given unto them the words which thou gavest me; and they have received *them*, and have known surely that I came out from thee, and they have believed that thou didst send me.

9 I pray for them: I pray not for the world, but for them which thou hast given me; for they are thine.

Revised Standard Version

John 17:1-11, 20-21

1 When Jesus had spoken these words, he lifted up his eyes to heaven and said, "Father, the hour has come; glorify thy Son that the Son may glorify thee, 2 since thou hast given him power over all flesh, to give eternal life to all whom thou hast given him. 3 And this is eternal life, that they know thee the only true God, and Jesus Christ whom thou hast sent. 4 I glorified thee on earth, having accomplished the work which thou gavest me to do; 5 and now, Father, *glorify* thou me in thy own presence with the glory which I had with thee before the world was made.

6 "I have manifested thy name to the men whom thou gavest me out of the world; thine they were, and thou gavest them to me, and they have kept thy word. 7 Now they know that everything that thou hast given me is from thee; 8 for I have given them the words which thou gavest me, and they have received them and know in truth that I came from thee; and they have believed that thou didst send me. 9 I am praying for them; I am not praying for the world but for those whom thou hast given me, for they are thine;

SECOND QUARTER

10 And all mine are thine, and thine are mine; and I am glorified in them.
11 And now I am no more in the world, but these are in the world, and I come to thee. Holy Father, keep through thine own name those whom thou hast given me, that they may be one, as we *are*.

20 Neither pray I for these alone, but for them also which shall believe on me through their word;
21 That they all may be one; as thou, Father, *art* in me, and I in thee, that they also may be one in us: that the world may believe that thou hast sent me.

Key Verse: **Neither pray I for these alone, but for them also which shall believe on me through their word; that they all may be one. (John 17:20-21)**

10 all mine are thine, and thine are mine, and I am glorified in them. 11 And now I am no more in the world, but they are in the world, and I am coming to thee. Holy Father, keep them in thy name which thou hast given me, that they may be one, even as we are one."

20 "I do not pray for these only, but also for those who are to believe in me through their word, 21 that they may all be one; even as thou, Father, art in me, and I in thee, that they also may be in us, so that the world may believe that thou hast sent me."

Key Verse: **I do not pray for these only, but also for those who are to believe in me through their word, that they may all be one. (John 17:20-21)**

As You Read the Scripture—Horace R. Weaver

Unlike Matthew, Mark, and Luke, John's Gospel does not "tell me the story of Jesus." John's concern in writing is theological and doctrinal, not biographical. John, writing at the close of the first century, faced heresy, opposition, and rivalry. John's Gospel therefore does not seek to win persons to Christ by the use of parables but rather by allegories, many of which are "I am" sayings.

John describes Jesus in terms of the logos (still in favor several centuries after the time of Herodotus), the light of the world, the life of men, the true knowledge of men, the real bread of life, the living water. The emphasis is not on legal codes of commandments but the revelations of God as grace and truth.

John 17:1-27. The title "The High Priestly Prayer" is derived from Jesus' self-consecration in this passage, before he offers his own life as the perfect sacrifice. Jesus then consecrates his twelve apostles, hoping they will offer their services in winning persons to faith in Christ.

Verse 1. "The hour has come" for Jesus to go to Gethsemane. Here Jesus asks the Father to glorify his son (Jesus) so that he might glorify the Father.

Verse 2. The purpose of glorifying Jesus is "to give eternal life to all whom (the Father) has given him." How different Jesus and Moses were: Moses feared looking into the face of God; Jesus "lifted up his eyes to heaven."

Verse 3. What constitutes eternal life? "That they know thee the only true God, and Jesus Christ" whom God has sent. Hosea cried out (chapter 4):

FEBRUARY 9   LESSON 11

"My people perish because they do not know God." Jesus came that people might know God in a personal way.

Verse 5. John, thinking of the first verses he wrote (1:1-14), considers the Messiah (Christ) as having been with God from the beginning. So Jesus asks, "Father, glorify thou me in thy own presence with the glory which I had with thee before the world was made." The passage from John 1:2-3 reads, "He was in the beginning with God; all things were made through him, and without him was not anything made that was made."

Verses 6-8. "They have kept thy word"—the apostles have received the Messiah's teachings, knowing full well that his message had come from God.

Verses 9-10. We are moved by Jesus' unmistakable pride in his disciples: "I am praying for them . . . for those whom thou hast given me, for they are thine; all mine are thine, and thine are mine, and I am glorified in them."

Verse 11. Jesus will soon leave his disciples, so he prays, "I am no more in the world . . . and I am coming to thee"—an event that will take place at the crucifixion twenty-four hours later. Even so, he prays to the Holy Father, "Keep them in thy name . . . that they may be one, even as we are one."

Verses 20-21. After praying for the disciples, Jesus prays for the church in the years ahead, "for those who believe in me through their word, that they may all be one." Jesus prays for the unity of the church, "that they may all be one; even as thou, Father, are in me, and I in thee, that they also may be in us, so that the world may believe that thou hast sent me."

Christ Jesus yearns for unity for all those who know the Holy Father, so that all may speak with one mind and one voice.

The Scripture and the Main Question—William H. Willimon

He Lifted Up His Eyes to Heaven

Was Jesus a priest? In one sense we know the answer to the question is no. Jesus was not a priest. He was often called "Rabbi," or teacher. But a rabbi was not a priest. He was a lay teacher of religion in the synagogue. Jesus was a layperson, not a priest in the temple.

And yet, on another and more profound level, Jesus was a priest. A priest is someone who mediates between God and God's people. The priest stands at the altar in the temple, the intermediary between humanity and God. The priest makes offerings at the altar and communicates the needs of the people to God. Jesus was a priest. As God's anointed one, he stood between earth and heaven, God and humanity, and interceded for us.

Most of us Protestants chose not to call our clergy priests. We speak of "pastor" or "preacher" or "minister," but not too often do we call our clergyperson a priest. For us, the term "priest" too closely denotes the hierarchical priesthood of the medieval church.

Yet clergy are still priests, in that they become the persons who help to mediate divine things on a human plane. Our clergy visit us in the hospital and pray for us. They preside in our worship, lead us in prayer on Sunday morning, baptize our young, serve the Lord's Supper. Our clergy are priests.

Every one of us needs a priest, that is, someone to present us to God, someone to stand between God and us and to bring our needs before God's throne. John 17 portrays Jesus as just this sort of priest. He was not going to leave his disciples all alone, but he would intercede for them.

SECOND QUARTER

Jesus, the priest still intercedes for us.

Of course, if your life is together, if you have power sufficient to meet all of your needs and to overcome all of your problems, then you really don't need a priest. But most of us are not like that. We need to know, when we are going through times of great difficulty, that someone is there for us, interceding, bringing our case before God, offering up our lives to the Lord and giver of life. Jesus is a priest.

I Am Praying for Them

Who needs a priest?

He had been born and bred, as they say, in North Carolina. Natural for him were two water fountains in stores, one marked "Colored," the other marked "White." The other people never had last names, only "Sam," or "Mary," "Sadie," or worse, "Buck," "Uncle," "Boy," "Girl." They never entered by the front door, sat only in the back of the bus, drank only from mayonnaise jars when they worked in your yard.

But that was yesterday, a long time ago, mistakes made by his parents, not him. He now lived in the New South, where things were done differently. Yes, differently, which means more subtly, covertly.

They sat in big, leather-bound chairs around the great oak table in the boardroom. He had worked hard to sit there, around that table.

"It's not that I dislike her," said his boss. "It's just that—it's just that she really doesn't quite fit in. She's not one of us, if you know what I mean."

Everybody knew what he meant. But nobody said it. Everybody reached down deep, deep in the past, to dredge up all those unstated, unwritten, but sealed-in-concrete customs and mores that told you who you were and defined the boundaries between us and them.

But for some reason, he reached even deeper, past the prejudices, past the folkways, and he said, "Jack, you know and we all know that's not right. She has done the work. She deserves the promotion. This company ought to set the standard for fair dealings with our people, regardless of the color of their skin."

Now how had someone like him mustered such courage in the face of so great an opposition? He was not by nature a courageous person. Later he said it was as if there was someone standing beside him, urging him on, giving him the strength to do what he knew to be right.

He had a priest.

She wanted, more than anything, love. She was so lonely, going every evening, at the end of every single evening, home to a place that didn't feel like home, a forlorn, empty, cold apartment. Out of her loneliness she began to visit bars, not to drink but out of desperation for a place to meet. There she met other lonely ones. At last she met someone and they talked and it was wonderful. They had so much in common. And she said to herself, "This is what it can be like. Two people, adult, sharing."

Then he said to her, in a way that did not say it but said it all, that they should share more than their opinions and conversation. And she was afraid. In that moment, she knew that she might risk losing him, a chance for companionship, love. But from somewhere, in the split-second moment, she found the means to say, "No. I'm not ready for that yet. We must have more time together."

She, as it turned out, was not alone. To her surprise, she had a priest,

FEBRUARY 9   LESSON 11

mediating divine power into her utterly human life, empowering her to be more than she could have been on her own.

The days following the funeral were like a dream. Martha ate. She slept. But she wasn't living. She didn't want to live. "What have I to live for?" she asked herself, quietly, in the deep recesses of her heart. "I can't go on without him. I have no point for living, no purpose. I need him. I can't make it by myself."

And then, not suddenly, but gradually, over the next days, it was as if there were a voice, not a loud voice but a still, small voice, that spoke quietly but resolutely: "Martha, you can make it. You are living. You must live. You can make it. Your life has not ended, it's just a new chapter which has begun." And then there was the morning in which she arose, put on her best suit, her favorite hat, and ventured forth to begin a new life, a liberated captive. A voice, speaking words to her she could have never spoken to herself.

The Glory Which Thou Hast Given Me, I Give to Them

Power. Spirit. Voice. In such holy moments we realize that we are being upheld, interceded for by the same Priest who prayed so earnestly for his first disciples. This One promised not to leave us desolate, and he keeps his promise. Without the help and intercession of this priest, how could we make it through life?

Last week, we studied how Jesus' disciples asked him to teach them to pray. In response he gave them a model prayer, the Lord's Prayer. This week, as we study John 17, we learn that Jesus is not only a teacher of prayer, but he also prays for us.

When life gets tough, it is a great comfort to know that the one who sits at the right of God the Father Almighty, the one who is so intimately linked with God that he is able to call God "Father," this one intercedes for us, presents us to God better than we could present ourselves.

When the going gets rough, it's good to know that we have a priest.

Helping Adults Become Involved—Robert G. Rogers

Preparing to Teach

This Sunday you and your class will study another prayer given by Jesus—the so-called High Priestly Prayer in the Gospel of John. Unlike the Lord's Prayer, this prayer is not one for the Christian community to imitate literally. Rather, Jesus offers it in behalf of his followers.

Read all of John 17 for the entire prayer that Jesus offers. Notice the themes of the prayer: the oneness of Jesus with God, Jesus' concern for his followers, his desire that his followers be unified. How might these themes provide meaning for the church today?

Spend some time thinking about the concept of intercession. The word describes the act of pleading in another's behalf. What value do you personally see in such activity?

Your aim with the class is to present another model of prayer offered by Jesus: intercessory prayer. You want the class to appreciate the value of praying in behalf of others.

SECOND QUARTER

Introducing the Main Question

Imagine the closeness that Jesus and his disciples felt. They had spent many days together, but now it was time for him to leave them. They were understandably anxious. Jesus, in turn, offered this prayer to help them in their time of anxiety.

We too are often anxious. We frequently feel forgotten or alone. What a comfort to know that someone else cares about us and is concerned about our welfare. Praying in behalf of someone else demonstrates that you are thinking about that person and that you are seeking God's blessing in his or her behalf.

How wonderful to have an example of Jesus' concern as found in the Gospel of John. He suggests a path for us to follow. We can be "priests," offering intercessory prayer to God for others. Spend a few moments citing ways that the church serves as intercessor. Cite such examples as prayers for national leaders or for the sick or bereaved. Class members may have other examples to suggest as well.

Developing the Lesson

Your class is now thinking about intercessory prayer as an active means of approaching God in behalf of other people. Now, develop the lesson in three parts:

> I. The value of intercessory prayer
> II. From Father to Son to us
> III. Unity in the church

I. The value of intercessory prayer

Dr. Willimon says that intercessory prayer lets us know that we do not have to face life's problems alone. Jesus offers his disciples (and modern followers) a practical example of sharing the burdens of others. As he prays in their behalf, he is sharing in their humanity, with all of its problems.

Present the benefits that come when we know others are aware of our situation. We know that they are taking time from their own life pursuits to think about us. Point out that we can offer intercessory prayer anywhere, at anytime. However, suggest that it would be thoughtful to let others know we are praying in their behalf. This would let them appreciate in a personal way our love for them.

A second value of intercessory prayer is that it gives us the courage to act. We know that we are not alone. Those who pray for us stand with us. Of course, you need to emphasize that we must finally decide to act as individuals, but it helps to know that others stand behind us.

At this point, ask if there are other values to intercessory prayer as seen by class members. Someone may mention that such prayer helps to bridge the miles that often separate family members or friends.

II. From Father to Son to us

In his role as High Priest, Jesus presents prayer as a two-way street. Prayer petitions go to God the Father from the human family. However, the High Priestly Prayer illustrates the blessing that comes from God in response. You want to lead the class in exploring how Jesus is the visible source of God's blessing. This will further expand the notion of Jesus as intercessor.

Point out some key words in the biblical passage. God's glory and love are manifested in the flesh in the person of Jesus. By living among us, Jesus gives the fullness of God's love to the human community. You can present Jesus as being both intercessor in our behalf and representative in God's behalf at the same time. This is part of the mystery that Christian theology has proclaimed: the divine and human nature of Jesus the Christ.

Now consider the role of the individual Christian in the world. Is it not possible for the believer to be both intercessor and representative, following in a modest way the model presented by Jesus? Suggest that Christians can be channels of God's blessing, even while serving as intercessors. Read John 17:18 to emphasize this role for Christians in the world.

III. Unity in the church

The dominant theme of John 17:20-21 is unity. Jesus affirms that he and God are one but then states that believers are also one with the Father and the Son. These verses provide a capstone for Jesus' intercessory activity.

What is the nature of this unity? Mention to the class that this is not based on a series of doctrines that every church member must affirm to be in "good standing." Rather, we are united in the knowledge of God's love for us. Further, there is unity in the commandment given us to be God's servants in the world. Point out that our unity in God and Jesus leads necessarily to the following way of life. We are to pray for, and act in behalf of, the world. This is our witness to God's love; this is our sign of unity.

Conclude the lesson by inviting class members to discuss ways in which they can serve both as intercessors before God and as representatives of God. In effect, you are asking them to examine a dominant theme of the Protestant Reformation, the priesthood of all believers.

Helping Class Members Act

Class members might spend time in the coming week thinking of several people in the community for whom they can serve as intercessors before God. They should pray for those individuals and try to determine specific ways to help them in the coming weeks.

Planning for Next Sunday

Next Sunday's biblical reading is a hymn or prayer celebrating Jesus' ministry in the world. The class should read Philippians 2:1-11. Ask them to note the central emphasis on helping others. Jesus came to serve, not to be served. Can this be a model for us today?

LESSON 12   FEBRUARY 16

Being Servant of All

Background Scripture: Philippians 2:1-11

The Main Question—William H. Willimon

In the past lessons of this series, we have studied some of the great hymns in Scripture. We have listened to the rhythms of some great biblical music. Today, we study another great hymn, the wonderful servant hymn of Philippians. However, I would suggest that Philippians 2 is more than a hymn; it is a dance, a movement of faith in an unexpected direction.

A few years ago I did research for a book on burnout among clergy and laity in the church. Why do people fall away from their initial commitment to the church? That was my question. The reasons are many. However, one reason that surfaced was this: Many people come to the Christian church not out of a deep commitment to the true purposes of the church but rather from a desire to receive "strokes"—to have all their needs met, to be affirmed by the pastor and the congregation. In other words, many people are attracted to the church for essentially selfish, self-centered reasons.

Sometimes, we in the church are to blame for this attitude. Sometimes our evangelism says, in effect, Is there something wrong with your marriage? Come to church and get that fixed. Are you having trouble with your children? Are you unhappy in life? Church is where you get all of your desires fulfilled and have all of your needs met.

When people then come to church, they are surprised to hear talk about self-sacrifice and self-giving rather than receiving. They feel betrayed. After all, they signed on to have their needs met, to receive strokes, not to give to others, so this becomes a reason for dissatisfaction with the church.

It's enough to make one ask, What is the goal of our being Christian? Are we here to serve or to be served? To give or to receive?

Selected Scripture

King James Version

Philippians 2:1-11

1 If *there be* therefore any consolation in Christ, if any comfort of love, if any fellowship of the Spirit, if any bowels and mercies,

2 Fulfil ye my joy, that ye be likeminded, having the same love, *being* of one accord, of one mind.

3 *Let* nothing *be done* through strife or vainglory; but in lowliness of mind let each esteem other better than themselves.

4 Look not every man on his own

Revised Standard Version

Philippians 2:1-11

1 So if there is any encouragement in Christ, any incentive of love, any participation in the Spirit, any affection and sympathy, 2 complete my joy by being of the same mind, having the same love, being in full accord and of one mind. 3 Do nothing from selfishness or conceit, but in humility count others better than yourselves. 4 Let each of you look not only to his own interests, but also to the interests of others.

FEBRUARY 16   LESSON 12

things, but every man also on the things of others.

5 Let this mind be in you, which was also in Christ Jesus:

6 Who, being in the form of God, thought it not robbery to be equal with God:

7 But made himself of no reputation, and took upon him the form of a servant, and was made in the likeness of men:

8 And being found in fashion as a man, he humbled himself, and became obedient unto death, even the death of the cross.

9 Wherefore God also hath highly exalted him, and given him a name which is above every name:

10 That at the name of Jesus every knee should bow, of *things* in heaven, and *things* in earth, and *things* under the earth;

11 And *that* every tongue should confess that Jesus Christ *is* Lord, to the glory of God the Father.

5 Have this mind among yourselves, which you have in Christ Jesus, 6 who, though he was in the form of God, did not count equality with God a thing to be grasped, 7 but emptied himself, taking the form of a servant, being born in the likeness of men. 8 And being found in human form he humbled himself and became obedient unto death, even death on a cross. 9 Therefore God has highly exalted him and bestowed on him the name which is above every name, 10 that at the name of Jesus every knee should bow, in heaven and on earth and under the earth, 11 and every tongue confess that Jesus Christ is Lord, to the glory of God the Father.

Key Verse: **Let this mind be in you, which was also in Christ Jesus. (Philippians 2:5)**

Key Verse: **Have this mind among yourselves, which is yours in Christ Jesus. (Philippians 2:5)**

As You Read the Scripture—Horace R. Weaver

The letter to the Philippians is the most affectionate letter Paul ever wrote to a congregation he established. Paul addresses the letter to Christians at Philippi, Macedonia. Philippi was a relatively small city, yet it was renowned for the high class of citizens who lived there. Octavius had declared Philippi a province, hence a city well cared for by Rome.

Paul had wonderful relations with the early Christians of Philippi. Those whom Paul converted were proud of him and loved him. This is shown by the gift of money that was gathered in Philippi to help him meet his expenses while incarcerated. The period of Paul's writings is uncertain, but they probably were written about A.D. 61-63.

Philippians 1:27-30. Paul urges his converts to "stand firm in one spirit, with one mind striving side by side for the faith of the gospel." They are to honor the gospel by demonstrating how their faith supports them in all kinds of disappointments. Paul may never see his friends again. Paul urges them "not to be frightened in anything by your opponents" (verse 28), who might arrest, beat, kill them. For it has been "granted to you that for the sake of Christ you should both believe in him but also suffer for his sake" (verse 29). What a privilege to be "engaged in the same conflict which you saw and now hear to be mine" (verse 30).

Philippians 2:1. Having expressed the special significance of his

SECOND QUARTER

imprisonment to the Christian mission, Paul then refers to how their love and sympathy has made them partakers in Christ's suffering. Paul uses "*so*" four times to make his points: (1) so if "there is any encouragement in Christ" (which of course there was!), (2) "any incentive of love" (which all had experienced), (3) "any participation in the Spirit" and, (4) "any affection and sympathy" (which was now basic to the nature of each)—if the above were true . . .

Verse 2. . . . "then complete my joy by being of the same mind, having the same love, being in full accord and of one mind." Are they not the marks of a Christian? And is not the Paraclete (one whom you call to your side) your Advocate, your Helper, your Comforter, your Strengthener? If, says Paul, each follower has the mind and heart and desire to know God and serve him that was in Jesus Christ, you "complete my joy."

Verse 3. "Do nothing from selfishness or conceit"; that is, seek to rid yourselves of motives that are self-seeking and zealous for your party advancement. "But in humility count others better than yourselves." Paul has written this letter to Philippi in part because of some verbal feuds within the fellowship. Paul sees and warns against trivial matters that can destroy their dedication to Christ. Obviously, Paul would feel terrible to have his first church in Europe be destroyed by trivial contentions.

Verse 4. Paul is anxious about the ambitions of little cliques that have developed, especially those led by two jealous women, Euodia and Syntyche, so he writes: "Let each of you look not only to [her] interests, but also to the interests of others."

Verse 5. What better way to deal with cliques than to seek together to "have this mind among yourselves, which you have in Christ Jesus." The need is for a moral gyroscope that helps persons remain steady.

Verses 6-11. To supremely exalt the Servant requires Paul's language to turn from prose to poetry, which should be seen/heard as a beautiful hymn of great artistry: Christ Jesus "who, though he was in the form of God, did not count equality with God a thing to be grasped, but emptied himself, taking the form of a servant, being born in the likeness of men" (verses 6-8). "Therefore God has highly exalted him and bestowed on him the name which is above every name, that at the name of Jesus [as with every king in every kingdom] every knee should bow, in heaven and on earth and under the earth, and every tongue confess that Jesus Christ is Lord, to the glory of God the Father" (verses 9-11).

The Scripture and the Main Question—William H. Willimon

Have This Mind Among Yourselves

Sometimes it bothers me that our Sunday worship is so passive. We come to church, plop down in the pew, and spend the rest of the service passively listening as the choir sings or the preacher speaks or prays. Recent worship innovations have attempted to get the congregation more actively engaged in worship, to give more acts of worship back to the congregation. Still, most of our services are far too passive.

This passivity in our times of prayer and praise is unfortunate, not only for liturgical reasons but also for biblical, theological reasons. What is the image of the Christian life that is given by such Sunday morning's passivity? The image conveys that the purpose of being a Christian is to sit, to listen, to be quiet while others speak, sing, pray, serve. That is an unfortunate picture of the Christian life that doesn't fit Scripture, such as today's lesson from Philippians 2.

Sometimes, when asked what worship means to them, people will sometimes use what I call the filling station analogy. They say something like "Sunday worship is like a service station. I come in empty and, through the preaching, the singing, and the praying, I get refueled and energized for the rest of the week." Certainly, that does happen to us on Sunday morning. But note how utterly passive this image is. Church is where you come to sit and be quiet, not to move forward and to serve.

Listen to today's lesson from Philippians, and you will be impressed by its movement. Follow the moves. "Though he was God, . . . [he] emptied himself, taking the form of a servant, . . . humbled himself, and became obedient unto death, even death on a cross. Therefore God has highly exalted him and bestowed on him the name which is above every name" (2:6-9).

Do you feel the movement? Jesus was like God, above/beyond everything. Yet he humbled himself, even as low as the ultimate humbling experience of all, even unto death, even death on a cross. You don't get any higher than God. You don't get any lower than a cross.

This movement, this emptying, is what Henri Nouwen has called "downward mobility." It is a gospel dance. Philippians 2:6-11 is an early Christian hymn. And you can still hear the beat embedded in this letter of Paul to the Philippians, catch the movement. It begins high. It ends low. Downward mobility.

And this is the movement, the dance, which Paul wants to fix in the brains of the church. "Have this mind among yourselves," Paul says. Make this movement part of you.

But Paul might say to her, "It's easier to teach history than to teach Christ." For the challenge is not simply to impart information *about* Jesus—there really isn't much information about Jesus in the Bible—but to teach the very *mind of Jesus*. Paul wants them not just to know the hymn, but to make this hymn so much a part of them that they hum it, tap their toes to it, can't get it out of their heads. Here, in our university, the department of religion will, like most departments of religion, teach you *about* religion. You can learn about Buddhism. About Christianity. They make Christianity into something that is academically acceptable—Christianity as sociology. The church as history. Jesus as a worthy subject for a master's thesis.

Nobody gets changed, no one's mind is blown from studying *about* Christ. Paul says church isn't Religion 101. Put your pencils and notebooks away today. There is no textbook, no exam. Worship is an attempt to get the mind of Christ in your mind until his mind, his movement, becomes so much a part of you, that it *is* you.

He Emptied Himself

It isn't easy, for here is a strange move. If it is odd for a god to empty himself—to take the form of a servant to wait on someone else's table, to wash someone else's wounds, to be rejected, to be slapped, to have someone else's spittle run down his cheeks, to be dressed up and mocked as a king, to be whipped, to be nailed to the cross with criminals—it is even more odd for us.

People don't come to study at universities in order to move down, to empty themselves. And people don't often come to church in order to engage in downward mobility. Our whole society, nearly everything we do, is geared toward enabling us to move onward and upward. In such a context, church becomes simply another means of getting on in the world, onward and ever upward.

The other day I was talking with a parent who had sent his son to our university. The father is a very successful person, in other words, a person who has been successful at being upwardly mobile. He had planned for his son to come to the university and then to join him, after graduation, in the family business. The father is now particularly unhappy with what has become of his son.

While at the university, the son became active in the local center for the homeless. First, he worked there one night a week as a volunteer. He became so concerned about the plight of the homeless that he began volunteering two nights a week, then three. His junior year of college, he dropped out of school and began working there full-time as a coordinator.

Now, the argument could be made that if the young man had finished school or perhaps gone on to law school, he could have done even more for the homeless. Perhaps. But my point is that here was someone who was well formed, well schooled, inculcated with the values of our upwardly mobile society. And yet he rejected those values and moved down a different and more narrow path. He, like Jesus, "emptied himself"; he "took the form of a servant." Here, I would submit, is an image of the Christian faith at its best because it is an image congruent with the movements of our Lord himself.

Admittedly, this is a difficult dance for you and me to learn, a tough procession with which to keep in step, a narrow way down, which ultimately leads us up.

Helping Adults Become Involved—Robert G. Rogers

Preparing to Teach

This lesson is based on a hymn by Paul that describes the activity of Jesus. It praises his life of self-giving and offers a model to the human community. Read Philippians 2:1-11. Notice the similarities to the High Priestly Prayer studied last week. (You might skim John 17 to refresh your memory.) In both, Jesus is sent by God to the human community. Further, his earthly ministry is a sign of God's presence.

As you read, also reflect on reasons why people join the church fellowship. Why did you join the church?

Your primary aim in the lesson is to demonstrate how Christians can model their lives after Christ. In particular, you will be emphasizing the life of service to others. In effect, you will be helping your class think again about why they belong to the church.

Introducing the Main Question

It seems to be fundamental to our human nature to want to be waited on by others. Many seem to be more skilled at receiving than at giving. Explore

FEBRUARY 16   LESSON 12

the basic belief of Dr. Willimon that folks often are mistaken about the true purpose of the church. He suggests that many see it as a place to have all of their troubles "fixed up." Some may even resent being told that the church needs them to give their time and financial resources.

How do members of your class respond to this? Assure them that it is all right to differ on the issue. After all, the purpose of an adult Sunday school is to think about the meaning of our faith as we strive to be better people.

Developing the Lesson

Undoubtedly, class members presented different opinions about why one should participate in the church fellowship. Now turn to the biblical lesson and use it to explore further what it means to follow Christ. The hymn in Philippians provides a marvelous way to explore the Christian life. Develop the lesson as follows:

    I. The act of choosing
   II. Self-giving as a life-style
  III. From humility to exaltation

I. The act of choosing

Refer back to Dr. Willimon's portion of the lesson. He claims that Christian worship (and, by implication, Christian life) seems passive. It is easy to let things go on around us without being actively involved. Indeed, it may be all too easy to let the professional staff do the work of the church.

Consider Philippians 2:5-7, where Jesus is described as being with God, the highest place in the universe to which one might aspire. Yet he voluntarily chose to accept the limitations of human life—the life of a servant at that! Jesus acted in behalf of the human family; he was not passive.

You want to help class members believe that they, too, can act. They can influence events and the direction of their lives by the choices that are made. As humans, we have a God-given freedom. (Of course, we do not always use this freedom wisely.) Ask members to tell about a particularly important choice in their lives that has made a significant difference. You might suggest that such choices as selecting a mate or accepting a particular job or even joining a particular church are significant ways of affecting our lives.

Conclude by reminding your people that Christianity is an active religion. It involves choosing to follow Jesus and electing to serve our fellow humans.

II. Self-giving as a life-style

The best way to open up this section is to consider the earthly life of Jesus. By being with God, he was participant in the divine power that governs the universe. However, he chose to limit himself in order to serve others. (Point out that God also limits himself in giving us freedom to act, even if we make the wrong choices.)

Self-giving, as a way of life, is not easy to achieve. Probably most of us would rather receive what Dr. Willimon calls "strokes." This word describes our own preoccupation with self. In focusing on our needs, we may be insensitive to the needs of others.

The challenge is to move beyond ourselves to consider what others need from us. Suggest that the church fellowship can help all of us be accountable

SECOND QUARTER

for the way we live our lives. Church members are not called to be judgmental of each other. However, ask how we can support personal efforts to be more self-giving. Give an example of how someone has gently helped you learn how to give more of yourself to others.

III. From humility to exaltation

Paul portrays Jesus as deservedly exalted and praised because of his humility. He was not exalted by God because he claimed it for himself, but rather, God saw that such a position was deserved. There is a great object lesson here for our relationship to God and for those with other people. God honors those who serve others. Is it not also the case that we reserve highest praise for those in the human family who give generously of themselves? What is it about the quiet giver that we so admire? As you ponder this question with the class, suggest the following. We appreciate the person who performs the needed task without fanfare; he or she does the job for its own sake, with no concern for reward or public acclaim. What other virtues of the truly humble person do we value? It could be helpful to the discussion if class members think about the characteristics of Jesus' earthly ministry that they most admire.

Conclude by emphasizing that anyone at any station of life can serve. It is not necessary to work at a particular job or to have a certain level of education or a particular status in the community to be an effective giver, one who is "exalted by God." Read aloud Matthew 6:1 as a reminder of humility: "Beware of practicing your piety before men in order to be seen by them; for then you will have no reward from your Father who is in heaven."

Helping Class Members Act

During the week class members should select a person in the church community whom they admire. How does that individual give of himself or herself? What special characteristics does the person exhibit? Are they worthy of imitation?

Planning for Next Sunday

The next lesson is the last in the series on Songs and Prayers of the church. It is a fitting conclusion for the series. The focus is once again on praising of God. Your people should read Revelation 15:2-4; 19:4-8. Ask them to notice especially the reasons given for praising God.

LESSON 13   FEBRUARY 23

Song of God's Victory

Background Scripture: Revelation 15:2-4; 19:1-8

The Main Question—William H. Willimon

It was meant to be a put down, a remark aimed to put me in my place. In a way, it did, but not as he intended. Why is Duke Chapel so often full when many university chapels or local churches are so often empty? He said, "Well, Duke Chapel puts on such a show on Sunday morning. And there are always those who want church to be nothing but a good show."

The buildings, the windows, the great choir, music from two organs, and sermons by two adorable ministers—Humph! It's all just a show. And I, not one to be put down without a fight, said, "So what's wrong with a show, if it is a very, very *good* show?"

I hesitate to speak for God—although I do so regularly from the pulpit—but I can't think of any reason why God should be opposed to a Sunday morning show, unless it's not a good show.

Tell me, when you leave the service of worship I have just led, "Good show!" I won't take offense. Our director of music will be positively pleased.

We're putting on a show for God. Why do you think we're all dressed up and the candlesticks are polished and the linen is pressed and the timpani are tuned? We're doing it for the benefit of a God who enjoys our prayers, our hymns, our trumpets and "loud clashing cymbals" (Psalm 150). If God didn't seek and enjoy our praise, thanksgiving, and petition, we wouldn't be here, and this building could be subdivided into faculty offices.

Why do you come to church on Sunday? After the prayers have been prayed and the songs have been sung, what good does it all do? These are the fundamental questions behind today's study of some of the great hymns in the book of Revelation.

Selected Scripture

King James Version	Revised Standard Version
Revelation 15:2-4	*Revelation 15:2-4*
2 And I saw as it were a sea of glass mingled with fire: and them that had gotten the victory over the beast, and over his image, and over his mark, *and* over the number of his name, stand on the sea of glass, having the harps of God.	2 And I saw what appeared to be a sea of glass mingled with fire, and those who had conquered the beast and its image and the number of its name, standing beside the sea of glass with harps of God in their hands. 3 And they sing the song of Moses, the servant of God, and the song of the Lamb, saying,
3 And they sing the song of Moses the servant of God, and the song of the Lamb, saying, GREAT AND MARVELLOUS *ARE* THY WORKS, LORD GOD ALMIGHTY; JUST AND TRUE *ARE*	"Great and wonderful are thy deeds, O Lord God the Almighty! Just and true are thy ways,

223

SECOND QUARTER

THY WAYS, THOU KING OF SAINTS.
4 WHO SHALL NOT FEAR THEE, O LORD, AND GLORIFY THY NAME? FOR *THOU* ONLY *ART* HOLY: FOR ALL NATIONS SHALL COME AND WORSHIP BEFORE THEE; for thy judgments are made manifest.

O King of the ages!
4 Who shall not fear and glorify thy name, O Lord?
For thou alone art holy.
All nations shall come and worship thee,
for thy judgments have been revealed."

Revelation 19:4-8
4 And the four and twenty elders and the four beasts fell down and worshipped God that sat on the throne, saying, Amen; Alleluia.
5 And a voice came out of the throne, saying, PRAISE OUR GOD, ALL YE HIS SERVANTS, AND YE THAT FEAR HIM, BOTH SMALL AND GREAT.

6 And I heard as it were the voice of a great multitude, and as the voice of many waters, and as the voice of mighty thunderings, saying, Alleluia: for the Lord God omnipotent reigneth.

7 Let us be glad and rejoice, and give honour to him: for the marriage of the Lamb is come, and his wife hath made herself ready.

8 And to her was granted that she should be arrayed in fine linen, clean and white: for the fine linen is the righteousness of saints.

Revelation 19:4-8
4 And the twenty-four elders and the four living creatures fell down and worshiped God who is seated on the throne, saying, "Amen, Hallelujah!" 5 And from the throne came a voice crying,
"Praise our God, all you his servants,
you who fear him, small and great."
6 Then I heard what seemed to be the voice of a great multitude, like the sound of many waters and like the sound of mighty thunderpeals, crying,
"Hallelujah! For the Lord our God the Almighty reigns.
7 Let us rejoice and exult and give him the glory,
for the marriage of the Lamb has come,
and his Bride has made herself ready;
8 it was granted her to be clothed with fine linen, bright and pure"—
for the fine linen is the righteous deeds of the saints.

Key Verse: **For the Lord God omnipotent reigneth. Let us be glad and rejoice, and give honor to him.** (Revelation 19:6-7)

Key Verse: **For the Lord our God the Almighty reigns. Let us rejoice and exult and give him the glory.** (Revelation 19:6-7)

As You Read the Scripture—Horace R. Weaver

The passages of scripture taken from Revelation affirm the certainty of the destruction of Rome. God is aware of the terrible persecutions under which Christians are living and will intervene in their behalf. From the time of Nero, Christians have been tormented in many horrible ways. During the current period (under the reign of Domitian), Christians, as well as all other

FEBRUARY 23   LESSON 13

people, were required to worship the emperor. Those who worshiped him were given a mark on their hands to indicate they had bowed down to Caesar. Without the mark, one could not make purchases in the marketplace, legally obtain marriage licenses, and so forth. Little wonder the faith of Christians was being stretched. The writer of Revelation assures them God will act!

Revelation 15:2. John, the visionary, sees a "sea of glass mingled with fire" (the same as he saw it in 4:6). "Those who had conquered the beast and its image [i.e., the chiseled image of the emperor] and the number of its name [666, which in Hebrew spells Nero Caesar] standing beside the sea of glass [sometimes known in hymnody as the crystal sea] with harps of God in their hands" were privileged to see and hear the marvelous music orchestrated by God himself.

Verses 3-4. And the martyrs "sing of Moses, the servant of God," who led Israel into the Promised Land, "and the song of the Lamb" (i.e., the song of Jesus, the savior), saying:

> Great and wonderful are thy deeds,
> O Lord God the Almighty!
> Just and true are thy ways,
> O King of the ages [or Nations]!
> Who shall not fear and glorify thy name, O Lord?
> For thou alone art holy.
> All nations shall come and worship thee.

Revelation 19:1-2. John heard "what seemed to be the mighty voice of a great multitude in heaven, crying, 'Hallelujah! [Praise the Lord!] Salvation and glory and power belong to our God.'"

Verse 4. "And the twenty-four elders [i.e., twelve leaders of antiquity and twelve apostles] . . . fell down [worshiped with heads to the earth as Muslims do] and worshiped God who is seated on the throne, saying, 'Amen. Hallelujah!'"

Verse 5.

> And from the throne came a voice crying,
> "Praise our God, all you his servants,
> you who fear him, small and great."

Verse 6. Then John heard what seemed to be the voice of an infinite number of people, "like the sound of many waters and like the sound of mighty thunderpeals [a cacophany of sounds], crying" in sheer wonder: "Hallelujah! For the Lord our God the Almighty reigns."

Verse 7. A time for rejoicing and exultation has come because "the marriage of the Lamb has come, and his Bride has made herself ready." This concept of a divine marriage is found in several places where Israel is the Bride (Isaiah 54:5-6; 62:5). Christians, probably following the Jewish ideas, taught that Christ became the bridegroom and the believers the bride (Matthew 22:1-14; 25:1-13). Later Christians interpreted this parable as Jesus being the bridegroom and the church being the bride.

Verse 8. The bride wears "fine linen, bright and pure," which contrasts with the purple and scarlet garb of the harlot, who is also bedecked with jewels (17:4; 18:16). The bride's fine linen costume is described as "the righteous deeds of the saints," which is a reminder of the white garments of the martyrs.

The Scripture and the Main Question—William H. Willimon

Let Us Rejoice, Exult, Give God the Glory

The Danish philosopher Kierkegaard once said that every time we gather to worship, our gathering is like a Sunday morning theater in which God is the admiring audience and we—choir, preacher, musicians, congregation—are on stage doing our best to make it a show worth watching.

But we're at a show in a twofold sense. For we are not only performing for God; *God is also performing for us.* The Germans have a word for worship: *Gottesdienst.* It means "God's service," in the twofold sense of the service we render to God and the service God renders to us. There are many Sundays when you are busy singing, praying, and listening to God, only to find that (surprise!) God is listening to you. You come depressed and leave exhilarated. You wander in and plop down in the pew, only to sail forth with new wings by the end of the service. You come, anxious because of the silence in your life, and leave reassured by a clear word. God has been serving you. You come to serve God so that God might have a better opportunity to serve you. And, as a preacher, I hope it will be a good show.

Which brings us to today's scripture from the book of Revelation. In chapter 15, verse 3, we hear victorious angels singing,

> Great and wonderful are thy deeds,
> O Lord God the Almighty!
> Just and true are thy ways,
> O King of the ages!

Then, from chapter 19, verses 1-3, a great voice of a huge heavenly multitude explodes into praise:

> Hallelujah! Salvation and glory and power belong to our God,
>   for his judgments are true and just
> ....
> Hallelujah!

Here is the probable congregational context for this sort of Sunday singing: This vision was addressed to a dispirited, disheartened church. The Easter exhilaration was past. There were persecutions by the emperor for some of the members of these churches. Others were simply ignored by their pagan neighbors. Now, it was the long haul. This vision was given to John who was on the island of Patmos, the Alcatraz of the Roman world. Was the whole Easter thing an idle tale? A dream? Wishful thinking?

Not what God offers for the post-Easter blahs: *God gives a vision, a show.*

The show opens when the curtain is raised in heaven itself (4:1). First we see the heavenly throne, surrounded by twenty-four elders seated upon their thrones (4:2). And what theatrical effects! There are flashes of lightning, peals of thunder. These announce that God himself is now on stage—heaven and earth quiver and shake before God.

FEBRUARY 23   LESSON 13

Encircling the throne are all sorts of wondrous creatures—a creature like a lion, a creature like an ox, a creature "with the face of a man," and a creature like an eagle—who shout unceasing praise to God on the throne and sing as the elders bow in unison. Whatever heaven is, it is a place of unrestrained singing and praise. Here is no sober, somber, buttoned-down place of respectable rhythms and restrained tempo. Here is a hymn of loud praise and exuberance.

Today's texts take place within this musical context. The chorus widens to include the voices of thousands of angels, animals, elders, all circling the throne, moving in concentric processional, singing, looking to the throne. "Praise to the Lamb!" they sing, "power, riches, wisdom, strength, honor, glory, blessing" (5:12). You've heard your choir do it when it sings Handel's *Messiah*, just like that.

It is a great choir that includes every single living creature "in heaven and on earth and under the earth and in the sea" (5:13). There is no corner of creation where some creature, some beetle or goldfinch or blue whale, is not singing for all it's worth.

The anthem heaps every accolade on the Lamb that can be sung: "power, riches, wisdom, strength, honor, glory and blessing" (5:12). The chorus prepares us for the breaking of the seals, and the scene ends with the Lamb and God seated together, center stage, backed by a loud, operatic "Amen."

O what a lovely Sunday show!

All Nations Come and Worship Thee

Remember our chief question, What does all of this mean? What does a wild vision like that mean for ordinary people like you and me? What difference does it make that the slaughtered Lamb sits beside exalted God, the Creator almighty on the golden throne at the center of heaven?

A few years ago, when the glorious Easter services in our chapel were completed and the show was over, I went to my office to disrobe and there was a note on my desk. The note said, "We are from South Carolina and were in the Chapel this morning because our twelve-year-old son is in Duke Hospital, paralyzed. Thanks for the beautiful service." Thanks for the beautiful service. Does a beautiful show explain a paralyzed twelve-year-old boy? What difference does it make?

Well, what word *do* you say to a paralyzed child and its parents? If there is a word, it must be bigger, grander, than our usual prosaic exhortations for self-help. It will have to be a word that's cosmic, poetic, outside, beyond the bounds of the expected, the conventional. It will be sung by a choir rather than argued by a preacher—that sort of word.

The Lamb, who one Good Friday was stripped, beaten, humiliated, and nailed on a cross to die, now sits enthroned in glory next to the Creator of the universe. Everything that God has—all wisdom, power, blessing and honor—now belongs to the Lamb, who knows what it's like to be helpless because he's been there.

And because the Lamb who has been here sits on the throne up there, we do have something to show the child dying of starvation in the African desert, the refugee perishing in the camp in Lebanon, the young man on death row in Atlanta, the child in Duke Hospital. What we show is a vision of a new heaven and a new earth, where the one who was slain in behalf of all those who are slain now rules in glory. We can take heart because, unlike

SECOND QUARTER

life, the one who rules makes judgments that "are true and just" (19:2). He gathers up all the hurt, all the injustice and pain, and sets it right. Therefore, we rightly sing, "Hallelujah!"

Through our hymns, here is our Sunday morning message: "O gentle, hurting, baffled, tearful ones, wherever you languish within the sound of my voice, peer through the bars of your cell, turn your head to catch the light through your hospital window, see the vision and hear the song, sung by hosts in heaven and choirs on earth, 'Worthy is the Lamb who was slain!'"

Hallelujah! Praise ye the Lord!

Helping Adults Become Involved—Robert G. Rogers

Preparing to Teach

This is the last lesson in the series on songs and prayers of the church. As you have done with the other final lessons in a series, look over the past thirteen lessons. Are there any issues that are worthy of consideration again in this week's class?

Read Revelation 15:2-4; 19:4-8. These verses are a fitting climax to the four-lesson unit. They celebrate the Creator of the universe as the being most worthy of our praise and devotion. Notice carefully what the verses tell us about God. They especially celebrate his gifts to the human community: the created order itself, his son Jesus Christ, and the numerous acts of salvation throughout history. Are there any specific acts of God that you would deem especially worthy of praise?

Your central aim in this lesson is to focus on the act of praising God. You want to help the class both celebrate the person of God as creator and sustainer and meditate on those divine gifts that merit praise and thanksgiving.

Introducing the Main Question

The experience of worship traditionally has been an occasion for inspiration and renewal. There are clear benefits for the worshiping community, and believers affirm that God is pleased with worship as well.

Dr. Willimon presents the worship service as a show in the best sense of the word. By this he means that we do our best to show God our highest esteem and affection. The word "worship" comes from an Old English word that means "worthiness," "esteem," and "respect." Worship, then, is a "show" in the sense that it demonstrates great respect for the Creator of the universe.

Spend a few moments reflecting on those things that God has done and continues to do that are most worthy of our respect and praise. You might use the blackboard in this exercise. Begin by suggesting a few that you thought about when preparing for class. Invite class members to add their own thoughts.

Developing the Lesson

After a brief discussion on some of the reasons that we praise God, you are ready to guide the class in discovering the full meaning of the scriptural lesson. Develop it as follows:

FEBRUARY 23　　　　　　　　　　　　　　　　　　　　　　LESSON 13

    I. The singing of the universe
   II. Worship and communication
   III. Equipping the saints

I. The singing of the universe

Begin by considering the biblical reading in its entirety. The setting emphasizes the "heavenly choir" as it celebrates God's acts of salvation in behalf of his people. Point especially to the Song of Moses, which is mentioned. Remind the class that this was studied in a previous lesson in this quarter. Suggest that there is a link between praises sung in heaven and those sung on earth. Both in the realm of nature and in the community of faith, songs of praise are "like the sound of many waters and like the sound of mighty thunderpeals" (Revelation 19:6).

Consider briefly the world of nature. Each creature responds to the Creator by being its best. You might suggest the example of the bird that sings joyously during the nesting season. Can we not listen and give thanks to God for the melody that we enjoy?

Now turn to the human creature. Think of those times that we feel unrestrained joy. What experiences lead to those feelings? Perhaps a son or daughter has just announced an engagement to a wonderful young person with whom to share adult life. Or perhaps a dear friend has been cured of a serious illness. Suggest that our feelings of elation and thanksgiving in these situations are also part of the "singing of the universe." Now spend a few moments analyzing the worship service in your own congregation. Are the hymns sung with fervor? Are they as joyful as the voice of a bird? Does the service of praise and thanksgiving capture the emotional high that we feel in times of personal happiness? If so, then the church too is singing with the "heavenly choir" and the natural world.

II. Worship and communication

In his exposition, Dr. Willimon affirms that worship is both our praising of God and God's opportunity to respond to us. In short, the worship setting provides opportunity for dialogue between God and us. We speak to God through song and prayer. In turn, Scripture and the sermon provide ways for God to reach out to us through his Word.

You might develop this section by referring to the author of the book of Revelation. He presents his mystical vision throughout as a dialogue between himself and God. Worship at its best provides just this type of interchange. In a dialogue, both partners give and receive. It is a mutually enriching experience.

Close this section by referring to the covenant relationship between God and people celebrated throughout the Bible. In the worship experience this relationship is renewed and strengthened.

III. Equipping the saints

Read aloud Revelation 19:7-8. The imagery presented here is rich in meaning for the worship setting. Such terms as "Lamb," "Bride," and "fine linen" represent the relationship between Christ, the church, and the life-styles of Christians. You should emphasize that there is a conscious link between praise and celebration and the commandment to do righteous deeds. Perhaps your church's worship service consciously includes a

SECOND QUARTER

"commissioning," in which the congregation is reminded of the obligation to serve others in the world.

The "Hallelujah Chorus" celebrates God's reign, the coming of Jesus, the gift of the church, and righteous deeds performed by the faithful. What an appropriate way to conclude this series on songs and prayers of the church. God, Christ, church, and individual parishioners are yoked together. Further, Christians in the present are joined to those "saints" who have gone before, whose very lives were an act of praise to God. Suggest that we, too, are called to affirm lives of praise and thanksgiving.

Helping Class Members Act

Your people might allow their creativity to be expressed. How would they assemble a "Hymn to the Creator"? What component parts would their hymn contain? They might consider the models presented in the book of Revelation and then develop their own hymn.

Planning for Next Sunday

The lesson for March 1 is "Entering God's Kingdom." The background scripture is Mark 1:15. This lesson begins the first of eight lessons based on the Gospel of Mark. Read Mark 1:1-11, which introduces Jesus' cousin, John.

THIRD QUARTER

COURSE 1: The Strong Son of God

UNIT I: MISSION AND MESSAGE
Horace R. Weaver

FOUR LESSONS   MARCH 1–22

There are two courses of study in this quarter, as noted in the above titles: The first course is "The Strong Son of God" and has two units of study, with a total of eight lessons. The second course is "God's People in the World" and has one unit of six lessons.

The first course is a study of the Gospel of Mark. The study emphasizes Mark's depiction of Jesus as a man of action—strong, vital, and willing to suffer. This unique understanding of Jesus permeates the selected texts. The full redemptive power of God is displayed against the constant threat of opposition, persecution, and death. All the events point toward Jerusalem. The basic conflict eventually finds its resolution in the crucifixion and its vindication in the story of the empty tomb.

The four lessons of unit 1 focus on Jesus' ministry in and around Galilee. They depict his mission on earth as moving toward fulfillment despite rejection, opposition, and misunderstanding. The four lessons of unit II, "Confession and Crucifixion." begin with the decisive point when Jesus is recognized as the Christ and move directly to the culmination of his mission in Jerusalem.

The lessons of unit 1 may be described as follows: "Entering God's Kingdom," March 1, asks, What are we going to do with the rest of our lives? "Affirming the Priority of People," March 8, challenges us to discover the positive principle that lies behind all restriction and regulation, in order that we may learn to live celebrative lives. "Ministering in Spite of Rejection," March 15, helps us learn to deal effectively with our frustrations and disappointments as we seek to follow Jesus. "Jesus Meets Needs," March 22, helps us understand that the mission and message of Jesus is to all persons.

Contributors to the third quarter:
Ralph W. Decker, former Professor, Boston University School of Theology; retired Dean and Professor, Scarritt College; former Director of Department of Educational Institutions, The United Methodist Church, Nashville, Tennessee.
Barbara Derrick, Pastor, Goose Creek United Methodist Church, Goose Creek, South Carolina.
Pat McGeachy.
Roy H. Ryan, Methodist Minister, Director of Education and Ministry for Older Adults, Board of Discipleship, United Methodist Church, Nashville, Tennessee.

The Gospel of Mark
BARBARA DERRICK

The earliest account of the life of Jesus has come down to us from Mark. Mark tells his story in 661 verses, only 24 of which do not occur somewhere in Matthew and Luke.

Clearly, Matthew and Luke had Mark's Gospel before them as they wrote and used his work as the basis into which they fitted the extra material they wished to include. Of Matthew's 1,068 verses, 51 percent come from Mark. Of Luke's 1,149 verses, 53 percent come originally from Mark. Matthew uses 606 of Mark's 661 verses. Luke reproduces 320 of Mark's 661.

Written in an on-the-spot manner, this Gospel mostly tells of things Jesus did rather than things he said.

If we wish to discover something about a person, we have only to read that person's account of an event. What, then, are some of Jesus' traits, as recorded by Mark?

First, *Jesus was a man of action*, unrestrained by the mores of the day—an independent thinker who did not mind upsetting the status quo.

Once there was a Syrophoenician woman who asked Jesus to heal her daughter. Jesus reminded her that she was not a Jew. But Jesus, unlike other Jews, respected this woman, saw in her a wit, an energy, a vitality that he admired. "It is not right to take the food that belongs to the children and throw it to the dogs," Jesus told the woman. Jesus was talking with her, something a strict Jew would not do.

The woman replied, "I know the children are fed first, but can't I even get the scraps the children throw away?" The woman knew that in those days people did not use knives or forks or table napkins. They ate with their hands, then wiped them on chunks of bread and flung the bread away for the house-dogs to eat. Jesus must have smiled. Here was a woman who knew what she wanted and was willing to risk her own self-esteem to get it.

Jesus took action, even though that action got him into hot water, and healed the woman's daughter.

Second, *Jesus was decisive*. Go and preach and teach, he told his disciples, but if you are not received well, shake the dust from your feet. Turn to something more fruitful. Don't waste your time. The responsibility of preaching was the disciples', but heeding the Word was the responsibility of the hearer.

Third, *Jesus was a man of consideration*. A deaf man came to Jesus, and Jesus took him aside from the crowd. The two of them were all alone. Jesus respected this man's feelings. Deaf people are often a little embarrassed. Jesus used pantomime to let the man know what he was going to do. He placed his hands in the man's ears, showing he was going to be involved with the man's ears. Next, he touched his tongue to indicate spittle, knowing everyone knew spittle was thought to be curative. Finally, he looked to heaven, indicating that healing came from God.

Jesus dealt with the man tenderly. The man had a special need and a special problem, and in his tenderness Jesus dealt with him in a way that spared his feelings, in a way that he could understand.

Again: There was a man with a withered hand. He was a stonemason and sought help because his livelihood was in his hands. He did not want to accept charity. He wanted to work. This man came to Jesus on the sabbath. Jesus could have allowed himself to be powerless to help this man by being enslaved by the rules and regulations that were enforced by the Jews. On

MARCH 1   LESSON 1

the sabbath, the most that could be done would be to keep the injury from getting worse. It must not be made better. A fracture could not be relieved by so much as pouring cold water over it, nor could ointment be placed on a cut finger. A strict Jew would not even defend his life on the sabbath. Sabbath regulations were so strict that orthodox Jews allowed themselves to be burned to death in the War of the Maccabees rather than defend themselves on the sabbath. But Jesus felt secure enough within himself that he was willing to accept displeasure in exchange for the man's wholeness.

Mark's Gospel gave us a more human idea of Jesus than any other Bible book. Mark made Jesus real and highlighted his special traits in a crisp, vigorous way.

Mark was the son of a well-to-do lady of Jerusalem whose name was Mary and whose house was a rallying point of the early church. It was to her home that Peter came after he was freed from prison.

As a nephew of Barnabas, Mark set out with Paul and his uncle when they left on their first missionary journey, but Mark turned back. Later, on his second missionary journey, Paul refused to take Mark with him. Some twelve years after that, Mark appeared in Rome with Paul. And some four or five years still later, Paul asked for Mark as he faced martyrdom. At some point between abandoning that first missionary trip and meeting up with Paul in Rome, Mark had regained Paul's respect. You can be sure this involved Mark's making a decision for Christ.

When Jesus began to preach, he addressed multitudes. But these multitudes dwindled as the message became more difficult to follow. They shrunk to seventy, then to twelve, then to three, and finally to one—Jesus himself, who suffered alone on the cross.

The message seems to be clear: Each individual has a responsibility. Mark had a decision to make, Jesus had a decision to make, and ultimately, so do we.

LESSON 1   MARCH 1

Entering God's Kingdom

Background Scripture: Mark 1:1-15

The Main Question—Pat McGeachy

What are you going to do with the rest of your life? Many of us never even raise the question; we just go on doing whatever it is we do, day after day, without reflecting on it. This is not always bad; once we have charted a course, it may be best to put our blinders on and stick to that task, come heaven or high water. There were times in Jesus' life when he had to set his face like a flint to do what must be done (Luke 9:51; the word used literally means that he "made solid his face"). But that was *after* the great decision had been made. The question for this week has to do with the beginning of his ministry (Mark 1:1).

THIRD QUARTER

For some of us, the moment of decision is one great hour, a watershed, before which we are one person and afterward another. Perhaps you can name the day; I can for myself. In Herman Wouk's 1951 novel *The Caine Mutiny*, Willie Keith, the young lieutenant, has such a moment the day his ship survives a kamikaze attack.

> With the smoke of the dead sailor's cigar wreathing around him, Willie passed to thinking about death and life and luck and God. Philosophers are at home with such thoughts, perhaps, but for other people it is actual torture when these concepts—not the words, the realities—break through the crust of daily occurrences and grip the soul. A half hour of such racking meditation can change the ways of a lifetime. Willie Keith crushing the stub in the ashtray was not the Willie who had lit the cigar. That boy was gone for good. (p. 533)

Perhaps such a watershed moment stands out in your memory.

But perhaps, even more likely, you find yourself making course corrections all along the way, like a guided missile, all the while honing in on the target you have set. In either case—a major lifetime decision or a daily change of direction—the question remains: What shall I now do?

Selected Scripture

King James Version

Mark 1:1-15

1 The beginning of the gospel of Jesus Christ, the Son of God;

2 As it is written in the prophets, Behold, I send my messenger before thy face, which shall prepare thy way before thee.

3 The voice of one crying in the wilderness, Prepare ye the way of the Lord, make his paths straight.

4 John did baptize in the wilderness, and preach the baptism of repentance for the remission of sins.

5 And there went out unto him all the land of Judaea, and they of Jerusalem, and were all baptized of him in the river of Jordan, confessing their sins.

6 And John was clothed with camel's hair, and with a girdle of a skin about his loins; and he did eat locusts and wild honey;

7 And preached, saying, There cometh one mightier than I after me, the latchet of whose shoes I am

Revised Standard Version

Mark 1:1-15

1 The beginning of the gospel of Jesus Christ, the Son of God.

2 As it is written in Isaiah the prophet,
"Behold, I send my messenger
  before thy face,
who shall prepare thy way;
the voice of one crying in the
  wilderness:
Prepare the way of the Lord,
  make his paths straight—"

4 John the baptizer appeared in the wilderness, preaching a baptism of repentance for the forgiveness of sins. 5 And there went out to him all the country of Judea, and all the people of Jerusalem; and they were baptized by him in the river Jordan, confessing their sins. 6 Now John was clothed with camel's hair, and had a leather girdle around his waist, and ate locusts and wild honey. 7 And he preached, saying, "After me comes he who is mightier than I, the thong of whose sandals I am not worthy to stoop down and untie. 8 I have baptized you with

not worthy to stoop down and unloose.

8 I indeed have baptized you with water: but he shall baptize you with the Holy Ghost.

9 And it came to pass in those days, that Jesus came from Nazareth of Galilee and was baptized of John in Jordan.

10 And straightway coming up out of the water, he saw the heavens opened, and the Spirit like a dove descending upon him:

11 And there came a voice from heaven, *saying*, Thou art my beloved Son in whom I am well pleased.

12 And immediately the spirit driveth him into the wilderness.

13 And he was there in the wilderness forty days, tempted of Satan; and was with the wild beasts; and the angels ministered unto him.

14 Now after that John was put in prison, Jesus came into Galilee, preaching the gospel of the kingdom of God,

15 And saying, The time is fulfilled, and the kingdom of God is at hand: repent ye, and believe the gospel.

Key Verse: **Thou art my beloved Son in whom I am well pleased. (Mark 1:11)**

water; but he will baptize you with the Holy Spirit."

9 In those days Jesus came from Nazareth of Galilee and was baptized by John in the Jordan. 10 And when he came up out of the water, immediately he saw the heavens opened and the Spirit descending upon him like a dove; 11 and a voice came from heaven, "Thou art my beloved Son; with thee I am well pleased."

12 The spirit immediately drove him out into the wilderness. 13 And he was in the wilderness forty days, tempted by Satan; and he was with the wild beasts; and the angels ministered to him.

14 Now after John was arrested, Jesus came into Galilee, preaching the gospel of God, 15 and saying, "The time is fulfilled and the kingdom of God is at hand; repent, and believe in the gospel."

Key Verse: **A voice came from heaven, "Thou art my beloved Son; with thee I am well pleased." (Mark 1:11)**

As You Read the Scripture—Ralph W. Decker

Mark 1:1. This is the author's title for his book. The key word is "gospel," which is derived from the Anglo-Saxon words *god spel*, which in turn translate the Greek word *euangelion*, which means "good news." The designation of Jesus is made up of his personal name, which is the Greek form of the Hebrew name Joshua (that is, Yeshua) and the title Christ, from the Greek word meaning "anointed one." As used by Mark, the two words form a proper name.

Verses 2-3. The Gospel opens with a brief account of the work of John the Baptizer. The early church saw John as the forerunner of Jesus, preparing the way for him. Although the entire quotation given here is credited to Isaiah, the part in verse 2 is from Malachi 3:1. Verse 3 is from Isaiah 40:3.

Verse 4. Most probably John's baptism was by immersion. It was an act that allowed persons to declare publicly their turning away from the past and their commitment to a new way of life.

THIRD QUARTER

Verse 5. The response of the people of Jerusalem and the rest of Judea suggests that John was preaching somewhere near the place where the Jordan River empties into the Dead Sea.

Verse 6. The austerity of John's life is shown by his food and clothing. The locusts mentioned were actual insects, not seeds of the carob tree, as some have suggested. Locusts are eaten in some places today, even in the United States.

Verse 7. The heart of John's message was the approaching advent of the long-awaited Messiah, redeemer of Israel.

Verse 8. John contrasted his baptism, an outward and symbolic washing, with that of the Coming One, which would be an inner, spiritual cleansing.

Verse 9. Mark gives no hint as to why Jesus was baptized. Matthew (3:13-15) reports that John protested that he was not worthy to baptize Jesus. As a cleansing from sin, the baptism of Jesus presents a problem. Seen, as a more careful look suggests, as a commitment to the kingdom of God, there in no problem. By accepting John's baptism, Jesus declared he was ready for God's kingdom to come on earth.

Verse 10. "Immediately" is one of Mark's favorite words. It occurs forty-nine times in his Gospel and makes it a fast-moving account. In Mark's report events following the baptism were experienced by Jesus only. He alone saw the dove and heard the voice. There is no indication that anyone else saw or heard anything unusual. This suggests an inner personal experience through which Jesus became fully aware of a special relationship with God, an experience he later described to his disciples in the picture language used here.

Verse 11. In Mark's Gospel this is the point at which Jesus became fully aware of his special relationship with God.

Verse 12. Since Jesus was already in the wilderness with John, the word here suggests withdrawal from all human companionship and the loneliness of the temptation experience. The word "drove" is much more forceful than "led," which is used by Matthew (4:1) and Luke (4:1). It is characteristic of Mark's vigorous style and suggests the impact made by the baptismal vision.

Verse 13. Mark's account of the temptations gives none of the details reported by Matthew (4:1-11) and Luke (4:1-13). Brief as it is, it pictures the struggle between evil (Satan) and good (the angels) that accompanies every major decision.

Verse 14. This verse may imply that Jesus associated himself with John for a time, or that he carried on a ministry in Judea parallel to that of John. When John was imprisoned, Jesus returned to his home territory of Galilee and there began his public ministry.

Verse 15. Jesus' first preaching, as reported here, closely paralleled that of John, as reported by Matthew (3:2). Its emphasis was upon the approaching kingdom of God and the urgency of preparing for it.

The Scripture and the Main Question—Pat McGeachy

Begin at the Beginning

Three of the four Gospels (Mark, Luke, and John), like the book of Genesis, have the word "beginning" in their first sentence. And Matthew

MARCH 1   LESSON 1

begins with the very word *genesis* itself, translated "genealogy" and meaning, of course, a beginning of sorts. That is because all four of these books are about something radical, new, and different. Whereas the Old Testament era came to a close with the cynicism of Ecclesiastes ("There is nothing new under the sun"), the new Testament ushers in something utterly unexpected (Revelation 21:5). All four of the Gospels reflect this excitement.

But they each have their own idea about where the beginning is. Luke starts with those who were eyewitnesses and tells of the birth of a baby. Matthew begins with that baby's pedigree, going all the way back to Abraham. And John goes all the way back to the dawn of creation itself, where the Word broods over the primordial chaos. But our storyteller, Mark, the earliest of the four, begins with an old passage of Scripture, a country preacher who embodies it, and a young (30-year-old) man named Jesus. No philosophizing, no throat clearing, no pencil sharpening—Mark just begins. Perhaps this is best; it is certainly the simplest. How many times have you heard someone say, "I just don't know where to begin?" If you ever say that, follow Mark's advice: Begin at the beginning, go till you come to the end, then stop. We have to do with a Gospel that is, of the four, the first, the shortest, and, for many, the best.

The Voice in the Wilderness (Mark 1:1-4)

Mark begins his Gospel with a text, or, more accurately, with two texts. The first (Malachi 3:1) is a promise that comes at the very end of the Hebrew Scriptures. That prophecy ends with bad news and good news.

The bad news is

- God is coming like a refiner's fire (Malachi 3:2).
- God is coming like a burning sun (Malachi 4:1).

The good news is

- God will purify Israel (Malachi 3:3-4).
- The sun of righteousness brings healing to those who fear the Lord (Malachi 4:2).

And in the spirit of that ancient bad news/good news, John the Baptizer comes, calling for both repentance and rejoicing (Mark 1:4).

Mark's second text comes from the great prophet of the return from captivity, whose words are recorded in the book of Isaiah. Jesus quotes more from this writing than from any other part of Scripture. (Second in number of quotes is the book of Psalms.) Isaiah was Jesus' spiritual teacher and guide. When he preached his first sermon in Nazareth (Luke 4:16-30), Jesus chose as his text one of the servant passages (Isaiah 61:1-2) to describe the shape of his ministry.

Chapters 40–66 of Isaiah are clearly written about the time when the Babylonian captivity was coming to an end and a new Exodus was taking place. So it is very appropriate that Mark should, at the very beginning of his writing, choose a portion of the opening words of this prophecy. We have here to do with a curious fact: Mark slightly alters the meaning of the Old

THIRD QUARTER

Testament scripture and finds in it a deeper meaning than Isaiah himself meant.

Let me explain. You are certainly familiar with the fact that Hebrew poetry is generally written with parallel ideas, such as in Psalm 19:1-2:

> The heavens are telling the glory of God;
> And the firmament proclaims his handiwork.
>
> Day to day pours forth speech,
> And night to night declares knowledge.

Almost certainly, in its original form, the words of the prophet (Isaiah 40:3) were spoken (and written) in parallel form, as the Old Testament has them:

> A voice cries:
> "In the wilderness prepare the way of the Lord,
> Make straight in the desert a highway for our God."

The imagery is that of the desert journey made long ago by Israel, out of slavery in Egypt, straight through the Red Sea, past Mount Sinai, and across the Arabian Desert to the land of promise. Isaiah is singing of a new Exodus, this time from the captivity in Babylon. And Marks sees a *third* Exodus, this time from slavery to sin through the desert of our separation from God. But by translating it with a slight difference, concentrating not so much on the highway as on the prophet, he adds to Malachi's prediction of the messenger Isaiah's wilderness setting, so that we are given a vivid picture of the desert wildman, standing in a vast wasteland, his voice echoing through the canyons, calling people back to God.

John the Baptizer (Mark 1:4-8)

John the Baptist would have fit in very well among the hippies of the sixties in America. He dressed in primitive, simple clothing (a camel's-hair poncho, cinched at the waist with a leather belt) and subsisted on a simple high protein and natural sugar diet (locusts and wild honey). Even to the relatively primitive society of ancient Judea, he was a curiosity, for they all made an expedition into the wilderness to see for themselves. And having gotten their attention, John proceeded to preach to them.

John the Baptist, for all his crowd-attracting strangeness, did not come to call attention to himself but to another. (In addition to Mark 1:7-8, see also John 1:8 and 3:30, and similar verses in Matthew and Luke.) In a world where all the voices tell you to honor yourself, to cover your escape, to look out for number one, the attitude of John is a breath of fresh wind on a sultry afternoon. It is also the teaching of Jesus (see Mark 8:34-36). Self-denial is self-discovery.

God's Servant Son (Mark 1:9-11)

Although it is not so evident, this passage ends with a text, as it began. When Jesus was baptized in the river, the voice from heaven echoed two more Hebrew verses: Psalm 2:7 and Isaiah 42:1.

The second Psalm is about the conquering Son of God, who overthrows the enemy with a rod of iron in spite of their haughty ways. It is God's derisive laugh (Psalm 2:4) at human pretense. By contrast, Isaiah 42:1-4 is one of a number of passages describing God's Chosen One as a suffering servant, gentle and tender. See also Isaiah 49:1-6; 50:4-9; and especially 52:13–53:12; the picture we get in these verses is an almost photographic description of Jesus. He was indeed the conquering Son promised in Psalm 2, but the method that he chose for his conquest was that of the Servant.

This pattern is to be found throughout Jesus' ministry. He spoke with stern authority (Mark 1:27-28), as one who truly believed in his power, but he was careful not to blow his own horn. Instead, he seemed to be trying to keep his messiahship a secret (Mark 1:44; 7:36; 8:30; 9:9; and many other verses in the other Gospels). Jesus' two-way understanding of his mission can be summed up in this dictum:

> Trust God entirely;
> Don't worry about your own glory.

Or, if you prefer, Proverbs 3:5-6.

The Temptation (Mark 1:12-13)

Mark gives us none of the details of this struggle; for that you will want to look carefully at Matthew 4:1-11 and Luke 4:1-13. But we can be sure, from what we have already learned about John and Jesus, that Satan tempted him to seek his own glory and security. Instead, Jesus chose the way of humility and vulnerability. And so should we, as we ask ourselves, "What will I do with the rest of my life?" The thirty-year-old Jesus is our model as we seek to give our own answers, whatever our age.

Helping Adults Become Involved—Roy H. Ryan

Preparing to Teach

With this lesson we begin a new quarter and a new course of study, which has two units of study.

You will want to take a careful look at the first unit and get its themes clearly in mind. Remember, we are dealing with "The Strong Son of God" and considering his mission and message.

The aim of our lesson is to help us respond to the question, What will I do with the rest of my life?

As you prepare to teach, it will be important to study Mark 1:1-15, along with other passages referred to in the section on "The Scripture and the Main Question." A good commentary will be helpful. Dr. Decker's section "As You Read the Scripture" will also be helpful in understanding the text material.

Think of what resources and supplies you will need in the classroom and make arrangements to have those supplies on hand. Your preparation for teaching also involves your own spiritual preparation and meditation. Pray for your students.

A possible outline for the lesson might include these points:

    I. Introduction
   II. A voice in the wilderness
  III. God's Servant Son
  IV. The temptation of Christ

THIRD QUARTER

Introducing the Main Question

What is the main question confronting us in this lesson? Read carefully Dr. McGeachy's exposition on the main question. If it is indeed the question, What will I do with the rest of my life? then it is a question of life-changing proportions!

We Christians believe that hearing and responding to the call of Christ upon our lives is life-changing. Jesus Christ preached the same sort of message that John the Baptist had been preaching, "Repent, and believe the gospel" (Mark 1:15).

Where are members of your class in their Christian pilgrimage? Are some of them new Christians? Perhaps you teach an older adult group, and most of your class members have been on their Christian journey a long time. Dr. McGeachy suggests that it is likely that such followers find themselves "making course corrections all along the way." Is that descriptive of members of your class?

You will want to help persons respond anew to the call of Jesus Christ upon their lives as they enter the kingdom or as they continue their daily journey with Christ as Savior and Lord.

Developing the Lesson

I. Introduction

Take a few minutes at the beginning of the session to give a brief overview of the first unit of four lessons on the mission and message of Christ. Share some of your hopes and expectations for the unit. What do you hope will result in the lives of persons as a result of this study?

II. A voice in the wilderness

Read Dr. McGeachy's exposition in regard to the beginning of Jesus' ministry and the message that John the Baptist was proclaiming in the wilderness. Give a description of John and what role he played in preparing the way for Jesus and in launching Jesus' ministry. He baptized Jesus and proclaimed him Messiah. He admitted that he was merely a "voice crying in the wilderness," calling attention to Jesus, who was far greater than he. Help members of the class to see that the message of John and the prophets contained both bad news and good news.

III. God's Servant Son

"Thou art my beloved Son" was the message that came down from God at the time of Jesus' baptism. This was the simple yet profound truth that Jesus Christ was different, unique—he was the Savior. He was God's own Son come to live among us, to show us the Father.

God was well pleased with his Son (Mark 1:11). Jesus did not seek to call attention to himself, but because of who he was and his unique mission, God's love was made manifest in him. He was the Suffering Servant who was willing to lay down his life for his friends.

In what way is Jesus different from other preachers or prophets? What difference does Christ make in our lives?

IV. The temptation of Christ

Jesus Christ was tempted. Mark does not give us any details. Look at Matthew 4:1-11 and Luke 4:1-13 for more help on how Christ was tempted.

MARCH 8   LESSON 2

He was tempted in all points, as you and I are tempted. He knows our struggle. He gives us the power to overcome temptation. He also forgives our sins when we succumb to our temptations. He is a wonderful Savior.

Why was it important for Jesus Christ to be tempted even as we are tempted? What enabled him to overcome temptation?

Helping Class Members Act

This lesson affords class members an opportunity once again to be confronted with the good news of Jesus Christ and to make appropriate and faithful responses to his call upon their lives.

As teacher, you are in a position to help persons deal with where they are in their faith pilgrimage. Help them to see that they need to continue to make decisions to follow Christ and to seek his guidance in their lives.

Ask them to reflect upon their own commitments and to let Jesus Christ come anew into their daily lives.

Join with the class in this prayer: Dear God and Father of our Lord Jesus Christ, have mercy upon us and grant us new life in Christ. Amen.

Planning for Next Sunday

Ask members to read Mark 2:23–3:6 and the lesson, "Affirming the Priority of People."

LESSON 2   MARCH 8

Affirming the Priority of People

Background Scripture: Mark 2:23–3:6

The Main Question—Pat McGeachy

Someone once asked a little boy, "What do you think God is like?" He thought for a moment and then answered, "God is sort of like a policeman who goes around seeing if people are having any fun, and if they are, God tells them to stop." Now, sometimes wisdom comes from the mouths of babes, but not always. Here we have an example of bad theology, though I suspect it did not originate with that little boy; he probably learned his theology from the adults in his world.

This childish (not childlike) belief we may describe as Negative Theology, whose God's name is NoNo. And I suspect many adults really do believe it; that certainly seems to be clear from the way they practice their faith. One of its proverbs is the old saw, "If anything is any fun, you know it must be either illegal, immoral, or fattening."

But this is not what Jesus taught! When he summarized the Ten Commandments, most of which begin with "You shall *not*," he gave what we sometimes call the Two Great Commandments (Mark 12:28-34), both of

THIRD QUARTER

which begin with "You *shall*." In our scripture for today we have to do with laws about sabbath observance, which were very important to the pious Hebrew in Jesus' day. (Indeed, they are important in our own time.) We will see that the law was not arbitrarily imposed just to keep us from having fun but was given to us with a positive blessing. And the discovery of this principle should lead us to find that all good rules and regulations have positive, not negative, purposes. Contrary to what the small boy mentioned above thought, God is actually more like a doorkeeper, who looks for those who are shut out from joy and opens doors for them.

The question, then, for us in this lesson is, How can we discover the positive principle that lies behind all restriction and regulation, in order that we may learn to live celebrative lives?

Selected Scripture

King James Version

Mark 2:23-28

23 And it came to pass, that he went through the corn fields on the sabbath day; and his disciples began, as they went, to pluck the ears of corn.

24 And the Pharisees said unto him, Behold, why do they on the sabbath day that which is not lawful?

25 And he said unto them, Have ye never read what David did, when he had need, and was an hungred, he, and they that were with him?

26 How he went into the house of God in the days of Abiathar the high priest, and did eat the shewbread, which is not lawful to eat but for the priests, and gave also to them which were with him?

27 And he said unto them, The sabbath was made for man, and not man for the sabbath:

28 Therefore the Son of man is Lord also of the sabbath.

Mark 3:1-6

1 And he entered again into the synagogue; and there was a man there which had a withered hand.

2 And they watched him, whether he would heal him on the sabbath day; that they might accuse him.

3 And he saith unto the man which had the withered hand, Stand forth.

Revised Standard Version

Mark 2:23-28

23 One sabbath he was going through the grainfields; and as they made their way his disciples began to pluck ears of grain. 24 And the Pharisees said to him, "Look, why are they doing what is not lawful on the sabbath?" 25 And he said to them, "Have you never read what David did, when he was in need and was hungry, he and those who were with him: 26 how he entered the house of God, when Abiathar was high priest, and ate the bread of the Presence, which it is not lawful for any but the priests to eat, and also gave it to those who were with him?" 27 And he said to them, "The sabbath was made for man, not man for the sabbath; 28 so the Son of man is lord even of the sabbath."

Mark 3:1-6

1 Again he entered the synagogue, and a man was there who had a withered hand. 2 And they watched him, to see whether he would heal him on the sabbath, so that they might accuse him. 3 And he said to the man who had the withered hand, "Come here." 4 And he said to them, "Is it lawful on the

4 And he saith unto them, Is it lawful to do good on the sabbath days, or to do evil? to save life, or to kill? But they held their peace.
5 And when he had looked round about on them with anger, being grieved for the hardness of their hearts, he saith unto the man, Stretch forth thine hand. And he stretched *it* out: and his hand was restored whole as the other.
6 And the Pharisees went forth, and straightway took counsel with the Herodians against him, how they might destroy him.

sabbath to do good or to do harm, to save life or to kill?" But they were silent. 5 And he looked around at them with anger, grieved at their hardness of heart, and said to the man, "Stretch out your hand." He stretched it out, and his hand was restored. 6 The Pharisees went out, and immediately held counsel with the Herodians against him, how to destroy him.

Key Verse: **He said unto them, The sabbath was made for man, and not man for the sabbath: Therefore the Son of man is Lord also of the sabbath. (Mark 2:27-28)**

Key Verse: **He said to them, "The sabbath was made for man, not man for the sabbath; so the Son of man is lord even of the sabbath." (Mark 2:27-28)**

As You Read the Scripture—Ralph W. Decker

The sabbath was the great religious institution of the Jewish religion. Mark indicates that early in his ministry Jesus came into conflict with the Pharisees concerning its proper observance and use. The Pharisees formed the leading religious group within Judaism. Their main characteristic was their narrow interpretation of the law and their rigid observance of it. The two incidents reported in Mark 2:23–3:6 indicate that Jesus placed response to human need before rigid observance of the Pharisaic interpretation of the law concerning the use of the sabbath.

Mark 2:23. The way in which Mark put his material together by topic rather than dating is seen in the vague reference to "one sabbath." This incident may have had no time relationship to the next one, but together they reflect growing opposition to Jesus.

Verse 24. The charge against the disciples was not one of theft. The law provided that any passerby could help himself to a few handfuls of grain or grapes (Deuteronomy 23:24-25). The charge was violation of the sabbath by working—harvesting (plucking grain), threshing (rubbing the kernels together), and winnowing (blowing the chaff away).

Verse 25. The Pharisees were given to quoting Scripture to support their positions. So Jesus answered their question with a Scripture reference. He defended his disciples by recalling that King David had violated ritual law to satisfy the hunger of his men.

Verse 26. Mark mistakenly names the priest as Abiathar. The original account (1 Samuel 21:1-6) names Abiathar's father (Ahimelech. The bread of the Presence, or showbread, consisted of twelve small loaves made from fine flour and set before the Lord in the Tent of Meeting. Each day fresh loaves replaced the older ones, which were then eaten by the priests.

Verse 27. Jesus asserts that the sabbath was instituted to serve human

THIRD QUARTER

welfare and that man was not to be a slave to sabbath regulations. This important saying appears only in Mark.

Verse 28. Combined with verse 27, this statement seems to apply to humans. The parallels in Matthew (12:8) and Luke (6:5) clearly refer to Jesus.

Mark 3:1-6. A second dispute concerning sabbath observance results from Jesus' healing of a man's crippled hand. In the incident of the grain the disciples were accused of sabbath breaking. Here, Jesus himself is accused.

Verse 1. This controversy shows that Jesus valued the sabbath and observed it with customary attendance at his synagogue.

Verse 2. The "they" of this verse are the Pharisees referred to in verse 6. The fact that they were closely watching Jesus suggests a planned attempt to put him in an embarrassing position.

Verse 3. Jesus recognized their intention and accepted the challenge.

Verse 4. Jesus' question was a very pointed one. By healing he was promoting health and life. By plotting against him, his enemies were plotting to destroy life. Jesus' question deals with the intentions of his opponents. It placed his opponents in a dilemma—a situation where either a positive or a negative answer would seem wrong.

Verse 5. Neither Matthew nor Luke mentions Jesus' anger. The idea of an angry Jesus is disturbing to some. Apparently, Mark felt that no other word was adequate. Jesus' distress and anger arose from the Pharisees' use of the cripple's misfortune to achieve unworthy ends.

Verse 6. Mark adds that the Pharisees enlisted the support of the Herodians for their plan to destroy Jesus. Nothing certain is known about this group, mentioned only by Mark (3:6; 12:13) and Matthew (22:16). One strong possibility is that they were officials of the court of Herod Antipas, ruler of Galilee.

The Scripture and the Main Question—Pat McGeachy

Doing Good

Mark's Gospel is such a concise literary whole that it is painful to have to skip any parts of it. In the last lesson we dealt with John the Baptist, Jesus' baptism, and Jesus' temptation in the wilderness. Now we skip a few months, to find him going busily about God's work and getting into trouble with the authorities over it. We have vaulted over the following:

- Jesus' preaching (1:14-15)
- The calling of Simon, Andrew, James, and John (1:16-20)
- An exorcism (1:21-28)
- The healing of Simon's wife's mother (1:29-31)
- Jesus' popularity (1:32-38)
- A leper cleansed (1:40-45)
- A paralytic healed and forgiven (2:1-12)
- The call of Matthew (2:13-14)
- A controversy over eating with sinners (2:15-22).

In order to set the stage for what we are studying this week, it would be a good idea to read over those verses. They depict a compassionate Jesus, popular with the crowds whom he is healing and helping but beginning to develop some problems with the religious authorities whose turf he seems to be invading. Although Jesus went about doing good (Acts 10:38), they thought of him as bad, partly because he didn't do things "the way we've always done it" and partly because his very goodness points up the narrow vision of most of the Pharisees. With the sabbath question, all this simmering hostility comes to a rolling boil.

In the Cornfield (Mark 2:23-28)

Jesus and his disciples were hungry (see Matthew 12:1), probably because they had been to church all morning; the pious Jew usually fasted until after the sabbath worship. It must have been springtime, for the grain was ripe enough to eat but not yet harvested. The King James Version says "corn," but the Hebrew word in question is a generic term for all the cereal foods grown in Palestine, including wheat, barley, spelt, and millet. All of these may be eaten raw, straight from the fields, though to an urban palate they might taste rather strange.

The Pharisees immediately went on the attack on the technical point of the disciples' violation of the rules. No sort of work was allowed on the seventh day, but how do you define what is work? One rabbi wrote, "He that reaps on the sabbath, though never so little, is guilty. And to pluck the ears of corn is a kind of reaping." If this seems strange to us, we must remember that the Pharisees were not wicked people; they were deeply devout. They valued the keeping of the law above all things and would be greatly admired in our day as those who believed in personal piety and social righteousness. But, as in this case, they tended to neglect general principles in favor of the fine details of the rules (see Matthew 23:23-24). It was even said among some of them that a tailor would be violating the sabbath if he left a needle in the collar of his robe, for he would then be carrying the tools of his trade. Or, if a householder dragged a piece of furniture and scraped a furrow in the dirt floor of his home, that would be plowing on the sabbath!

Jesus could have replied to their criticism that they were not violating the fourth commandment, only some scholar's *interpretation* of that rule, but instead he went even further into the heart of the law (compare Matthew 5:17-20), suggesting that even the commandment itself, when it is purely ceremonial in purpose, can be violated to serve a higher human purpose. This he illustrated by reminding them of the story found in 1 Samuel 21:1-6, of how David violated the rules with the blessing of a priest, when his men were hungry. From this he drew the general principle: The sabbath was made for human use, not the other way around. And from that there follows this: Therefore, the Human One (Jesus, the Son of man) is Lord of the sabbath.

There are two positive forms of the rule. The first is, God gave us the sabbath not simply to be a restrictive requirement ("Don't do this and don't do that") but for our positive good, to keep a healthy rhythm in our lives. And the second is, Jesus is more important than all the rules there are.

In the Synagogue (Mark 3:1-6)

That very same day, as Mark has it (but see Luke 6:6), they encountered in the house of worship a man with a withered hand. According to one ancient tradition, this man was a mason, who said to Jesus, "I used to earn my living with my hands; restore me, that I may not be disgraced by begging." One almost suspects that the authorities put him up to speaking to Jesus, for they were all watching him like hawks, to catch him violating the sabbath (verse 2).

It is hard by any stretch of the imagination to see how simply saying "Stretch out your hand" could be a violation of the law, particularly when a great good is being accomplished. Even the ancient rabbis recognized an emergency when they saw one. They taught that "all danger to life or limb abrogates the sabbath." And Matthew (12:11-12) has Jesus making reference to another exception: When a sheep falls into a pit (see also Luke 14:5).

The point here is the same as that above: God's rules were given for good, not harm—to save life, not to kill (Mark 3:3). The sabbath rule is not so much a negative restriction as a positive release.

The Positive Law

The same thing can be said of all laws. When Jesus summarized the law, he chose two positive statements: Love God with your whole being and love your neighbor as yourself (Matthew 22:34-40; Mark 12:28-34; Luke 10:25-28; see also Deuteronomy 6:4-5 and Leviticus 18). Indeed, all of the Ten Commandments, though they are usually expressed as "Thou-shalt-nots," can be said in positive form with a little spiritual imagination:

1. Put God first.
2. Keep symbols in their place.
3. Honor God's name.
4. Keep the sabbath.
5. Honor your parents.
6. Respect life.
7. Keep your promises.
8. Respect the property of others.
9. Tell the truth.
10. Rejoice in your neighbor's success.

It is significant that as I write these words, there is a campaign all across America to put a stop to drug abuse by encouraging everyone, especially schoolchildren, to "just say no." I am heartily in favor of this campaign, and I even have a "just say no" button and tee shirt. But there is a piece of me that wonders if "just say yes" might be a more effective slogan in the war against controlled substances. I have found in the raising of my own children that constant negatives sometimes tempt us to rebellion. The surest way to make a motion picture popular is to give it a negative rating. I am told that being banned in Boston was at one time a real help to an author in selling books. But what if we could learn to say yes? Yes to clean living and safe driving, yes to sober celebrations, yes to a cool mind and a healthy liver, yes to all that a drug- and alcohol-free life can mean—that might be motivation indeed.

Because of the gospel of Jesus Christ, we now know that the law was made for us, not we for the law. In Jesus, all the nos of the law are turned into yesses. As Paul puts it in the first chapter of 2 Corinthians (verses 19-20):

MARCH 8   LESSON 2

"The Son of God, Jesus Christ, whom we preached among you . . . was not Yes and No; but in him it is always Yes. For all the promises of God find their Yes in him."

All this means that we are to have deeper respect for our fellow human beings, just as God has given such respect to us in creating the commandments for our own good. While we are to go on hating sin, we are to love the sinner.

Helping Adults Become Involved—Roy H. Ryan

Preparing to Teach

We continue in this lesson to look at the mission and message of Jesus. According to Mark, Jesus had been going about doing good (see Dr. McGeachy's section "Doing Good"). Our lesson today takes a different turn. Jesus begins to run into opposition.

The aim of this lesson is to help us discover the positive principle that lies behind rules and restrictions, in order that we may learn to live celebrative lives.

Study carefully the section "As You Read the Scripture." Dr. Decker provides a helpful exegesis of these verses about sabbath observance. You may also want to read additional commentary on Mark 2:23–3:6.

Another good way to prepare to teach is to read the scripture in several translations or paraphrases. You may even wish to use a different translation from that printed in the student material.

Take an inventory of the supplies you will need. Do you have a chalkboard or newsprint on which to post an outline of the lesson?

A possible outline for the lesson might be the following:

                 I. Introduction.
                II. The disciples pick grain.
               III. Jesus heals in the synagogue.
               IV. The positive side of law.

Introducing the Main Question

The main question centers around what we think about God. But it focuses in this lesson on the sabbath observance and how Jesus dealt with it. Dr. McGeachy has framed the main question as "How can we discover the positive principle that lies behind all restriction and regulation, in order that we may learn to live celebrative lives?"

How will you help members of your class get in touch with the question? How will it connect with where they live?

Be prepared to lead the group in thinking about the question. You might pose one or more of the following questions after you read the scripture and are ready to begin considering the lesson:

1. What purpose do rules and regulations serve?
2. Do you think being a Christian is primarily a matter of keeping the commandments? Why or why not?

THIRD QUARTER

What caused the Pharisees to turn against Jesus? He had been well received by most of the people and praised for his work of healing and his teaching. It would seem that Jesus did put a priority on persons, rather than on keeping all the rules.

Developing the Lesson

I. Introduction.

This lesson is about sabbath observance. It deals with one of the central issues for faithful Jews of Jesus' day, keeping the law. Jesus seemed to have an interpretation of the laws governing the sabbath different from that of most of the Pharisees. He was more concerned about the well-being of persons than about following traditional narrow rules that had become burdensome of the people.

II. The disciples pick grain.

Any work was forbidden on the sabbath. Even though the disciples were hungry, they were not supposed to break the sabbath rules just to satisfy that hunger. The law took priority over people's needs. The Pharisees were not bad people; they simply had become so rigid in interpreting and keeping the laws that they sometimes forgot the ultimate purpose of law—to serve the well-being of persons and society.

Jesus defended his disciples. When the Pharisees confronted him with the charge of breaking the sabbath, Jesus quoted Scripture to prove his point (much like the Pharisees tended to do). He reminded them of what King David did to satisfy the hunger of his men (1 Samuel 21:1-6). See Dr. Decker's exegesis of these verses. Jesus knew how King David was revered by all good Jews. He could not have chosen a better example to carry his point that human need should take priority over keeping the rules (especially if those rules are not dealing with life-and-death issues).

III. Jesus heals in the synagogue.

A man with a withered hand became the occasion for Jesus to again test the principle of persons versus rules. It was against the law to heal on the sabbath, yet Jesus did it very openly. It is hard to understand, as Dr. McGeachy comments, how simply saying "Stretch out your hand" could be a violation of the law. But it was interpreted as such by the Pharisees.

God's rules were given for good, not harm—at least, that was the way Jesus interpreted it. He confronted his accusers by asking, "Is it lawful on the sabbath to do good or to do harm, to save life or to kill?" In the face of that question, "they were silent" (Mark 3:4).

IV. The positive side of law.

"Love God and your neighbor"—Jesus summarized the Law and the Prophets with that simple statement. Love is a positive force that generates that which is good and lovely, that which builds up and does not destroy. If any law detracts from love of God or love of neighbor, then it misses the mark.

The Golden Rule ("Do unto others as you would have them do unto you") is well grounded in Christian Scripture. The mission and message of Jesus certainly affirmed it as a basic rule for the good life, the life of faith. That which harms persons is on the face of it bad or evil. That which serves

MARCH 15   LESSON 3

persons is good. Read Matthew 25 to remind yourself and the class that the true test of love of God and true discipleship to Jesus Christ is to be found in the way we behave toward others.

Jesus put persons first. He was concerned that they experience the wholeness of life. He came to give abundant life. Therefore, those who follow Jesus are bound to place a priority on persons.

Helping Class Members Act

What are some concrete ways you and your class members can put this principle into effect? How can you make people your priority? What about some of the following:

- Help feed the hungry.
- Provide shelter for the homeless.
- Get involved in justice ministries.
- Visit those who are sick.
- Get involved in prison ministry.

Conclude the lesson with this prayer: God of all Creation, we know that you are concerned for your whole creation. We thank you that you are concerned for the well-being of all your children. Help us get our priorities straight by putting persons first. In Jesus' loving name, Amen.

Planning for Next Sunday

Ask persons to read the scripture and lesson material. Also ask them to be prepared to report on any ways they have been involved in direct ministry to persons (as a follow-up to today's lesson).

LESSON 3   MARCH 15

Ministering in Spite of Rejection

Background Scripture: Mark 6:1-13

The Main Question—Pat McGeachy

A woman told me that when her first baby was born, she halfway expected that something would come over her called "motherhood," and she would be gifted with all the instincts needed to raise her child. But she found that she had to learn how to be a mother as she went along. Not even *her* mother knew all the answers. In a similar way, I think I sort of expected a kind of divine electricity to charge through me when I was ordained to the ministry, empowering me to dispense the grace of God. But sad to say, it has taken me many years to admit the truth that I don't know any more than you do about how to do ministry, in spite of my calling.

THIRD QUARTER

How do you suppose Jesus felt? Do we think of him as a kind of indestructible cartoon superman, who could not be ruffled? No, we can discover dozens of Bible verses describing his human frailties: grief (John 11:35), disappointment (Luke 19:41), anger (John 2:15), weariness (John 4:6), hunger (Luke 4:2), thirst (John 19:28), anxiety (Mark 14:33), reluctance (Mark 14:35), and even doubt (Mark 15:34). He was the most gifted person who ever lived, but he could not do everything.

In today's scripture we find Jesus frustrated because of the unbelief of those he was trying to reach, and some counsel that he gives to us for those times when we too will encounter disappointment as we seek to fulfill our Christian duty. The question for us this week is this: How does a Christian deal with frustration? If it happened to our Lord, we can be sure it will happen many times more to us. But we can learn from Jesus, by both the way he dealt with disappointment and the advice he gives us, how to deal with it when it comes our way. The principles we find here will help us with everything from evangelistic witnessing to attempts to teach our children, improve our government, and clean up our environment. Of course we're frustrated; so was Jesus. Now, what shall we do about it?

Selected Scripture

King James Version

Mark 6:1-13

1 And he went out from thence, and came into his own country; and his disciples follow him.

2 And when the sabbath day was come, he began to teach in the synagogue: and many hearing *him* were astonished, saying, From whence hath this *man* these things? and what wisdom *is* this which is given unto him, that even such mighty works are wrought by his hands?

3 Is not this the carpenter, the son of Mary, the brother of James, and Joses, and of Juda, and Simon? and are not his sisters here with us? And they were offended at him.

4 But Jesus said unto them, A prophet is not without honour, but in his own country, and among his own kin, and in his own house.

5 And he could there do no mighty work, save that he laid his hands upon a few sick folk, and healed *them*.

6 And he marvelled because of their unbelief. And he went round about the villages, teaching.

Revised Standard Version

Mark 6:1-13

1 He went away from there and came to his own country; and his disciples followed him. 2 And on the sabbath he began to teach in the synagogue; and many who heard him were astonished, saying, "Where did this man get all this? What is the wisdom given to him? What mighty works are wrought by his hands! 3 Is not this the carpenter, the son of Mary and brother of James and Joses and Judas and Simon, and are not his sisters here with us?" And they took offense at him. 4 And Jesus said to them, "A prophet is not without honor, except in his own country, and among his own kin, and in his own house." 5 And he could do no mighty work there, except that he laid his hands upon a few sick people and healed them. 6 And he marveled because of their unbelief.

And he went about among the villages teaching.

MARCH 15   LESSON 3

7 And he called *unto him* the twelve, and began to send them forth by two and two; and gave them power over unclean spirits;

8 And commanded them that they should take nothing for *their* journey, save a staff only; no scrip, no bread, no money in *their* purse:

9 But *be* shod with sandals; and not put on two coats.

10 And he said unto them, In what place soever ye enter into an house, there abide till ye depart from that place.

11 And whosoever shall not receive you, nor hear you, when ye depart thence, shake off the dust under your feet for a testimony against them. Verily I say unto you, It shall be more tolerable for Sodom and Gomorrha in the day of judgment, than for that city.

12 And they went out, and preached that men should repent.

13 And they cast out many devils, and anointed with oil many that were sick, and healed *them*.

Key Verse: **A prophet is not without honour, but in his own country, and among his own kin, and in his own house. (Mark 6:4)**

7 And he called to him the twelve, and began to send them out two by two, and gave them authority over the unclean spirits. 8 He charged them to take nothing for their journey except a staff; no bread, no bag, no money in their belts; 9 but to wear sandals and not put on two tunics. 10 And he said to them, "Where you enter a house, stay there until you leave the place. 11 And if any place will not receive you and they refuse to hear you, when you leave, shake off the dust that is on your feet for a testimony against them." 12 So they went out and preached that men should repent. 13 And they cast out many demons, and anointed with oil many that were sick and healed them.

Key Verse: **Jesus said to them, "A prophet is not without honor, except in his own country, and among his own kin, and in his own house." (Mark 6:4)**

As You Read the Scripture—Ralph W. Decker

The sixth chapter of Mark opens a new phase in the ministry of Jesus. Up to this point Jesus' activities have centered in and around Capernaum, with one brief tour of Galilee (1:39) and one trip across the lake and back (4:35–5:21). Jesus now becomes more of a wandering teacher, returning to Capernaum twice (9:33) before his final journey to Jerusalem. Much of the activity in chapters 6 through 9 takes place outside Galilee and beyond the jurisdiction of Herod Antipas.

Mark 6:1. The events reported in the previous chapter took place somewhere on the western shore of the Sea of Galilee. A new phase of Jesus' ministry began when he left that area and moved westward. While both Mark (6:1) and Matthew (13:54) give only the general location ("his own country"), Luke pinpoints it as "Nazareth, where he had been brought up" (4:16). That his disciples went with him indicates that he went there to evangelize rather than to visit his family. His was a preaching mission.

Verse 2. Any adult male Jew could speak in the synagogue. As Jesus spoke many who had known him previously were astonished. This suggests

THIRD QUARTER

that a decided change had taken place in his manner and actions. That his reputation as a healer had preceded him is shown by the reference to his mighty works, none of which occurred in Nazareth.

Verse 3. Mark alone tells that Jesus had been a carpenter. The actual Hebrew word used here many mean either a builder or a woodworker. Matthew (13:55) refers to him as "the carpenter's son." It was customary for sons to follow the trades of their fathers. The fact that Mark calls Jesus the son of Mary rather than the son of Joseph suggests that Joseph was dead. Joseph is not mentioned in the naming of family members, nor is he shown to be present during the ministry of Jesus. This too suggests that he had died before Jesus began his public ministry. The reason for the public's anger is not clear in Mark. Luke (4:25-29) indicates that it was due to Jesus' unfavorable comparison of his Jewish hearers with believing foreigners.

Verse 4. This saying may have been a familiar proverb. In any case, Jesus is not claiming to be a prophet. He is pointing out that familiarity tends to lessen respect.

Verse 5. Mark clearly states that faith on the part of the patient was a requisite for Jesus' healing. Unbelief definitely interfered with Jesus' ability to heal. Earlier, Jesus had said that the faith of the patient was the key factor in healing (5:34).

Verses 7-8. After spending some time in the villages around Nazareth, Jesus made a significant change in his work. He began to send the Twelve on special missions. These probably lasted only a few days each. Jesus' instructions were not for the long-range work of the church or even for a single long missionary campaign. They fit only a short, intensive effort. Going in pairs, the disciples could encourage each other.

Verse 9. The apostles were to go without baggage that would impede their work.

Verse 10. They were to rely upon the hospitality of their hearers and to avoid unnecessary changes of lodgings.

Verse 11. They were to avoid wasting time in unreceptive situations. The reference to Sodom and Gomorrah found here in the King James Version is omitted from the Revised Standard Version because it is absent from the earliest and best manuscripts.

Verses 12-13. The work of the apostolic teams was threefold: peaching repentance for sins, casting out demons, and healing the sick by anointing them.

The Scripture and the Main Question—Pat McGeachy

The Difficulties Increase

Again, on our swift journey through Mark's story, we pass over great things: the appointing of the Twelve, many healings, and much teaching through the use of parables. When we come to chapter 6, we find that all is not completely rosy for the popular young preacher. As the Fourth Gospel says it, "He came to his own home, and his own people received him not" (John 1:11).

You Can't Go Home Again (Mark 6:1-6)

"He went away from there and came to his own country" (1:1). Of course, the reference is to Nazareth, where Joseph and Mary lived and where Jesus had been brought up. A town is still there, containing one of those rare things, a site that we can probably say for certain is much the same as it was in Jesus' own day, that is, Mary's Well, a spring from which the town gets its water and to which the boy Jesus must have gone daily, as would have all the city. It is surrounded by gardens, olive groves, fig trees, and cypresses. One can infer that Jesus loved his home town, for there he learned to appreciate the natural world and to ply the trade of his father.

He must have been looking forward to showing his "own country" to his disciples, who were following him on his swift homeward march (6:1). Jesus was evidently well liked by his town's people (see Luke 2:52; 4:16). He had been accustomed to going regularly to the synagogue there with his parents, and when he returned as a popular young rabbi, it was natural that he was invited to read from the Scripture and to teach. And at first, both as Mark records it here, (verse 2) and as Luke tells it (4:22), they were pleased, surprised, and impressed at their "local lad made good."

But it didn't last long. I think I can really identify with Jesus at this point, at least to some extent. I had preached with some success before the faculty of my seminary, and in some churches here and there, but the hardest sermon I ever had to preach was the time when I spoke to the folks at the Wednesday night prayer meeting in the church where I grew up as a boy. Unlike Jesus, I hadn't always been in favor with God and everybody. These were people who knew all about my boyhood scapes and had no reason to be impressed with my newfound knowledge. The only person impressed with me that night was me, and I fell flat on my face. It's pretty hard to fool the people who knew you when!

And those who remembered Jesus as a youth had a hard time accepting him as a prophet in their midst. "Is this not the carpenter?" they asked (Mark 6:3). "Don't we know his folks?" (Here, happily, we are given a list of Jesus' male siblings: James, Joses [Joseph], Judas, and Simon. These were all like Jesus, fairly common names in those days. We are also given to understand that Jesus had several sisters too.) Somehow it's hard to accept someone we *know* as being very special. I can remember shaking my head once when a high school friend was elected to the United States Senate. "What can they see in him?" I wondered. "He's got feet of clay just like everybody else." But of course! Senators aren't superheroes. They are ordinary people whose gifts have been put at the disposal of their country. And if one of them, or you, or I, could put our gifts completely at the disposal of God, as Jesus did, what astonishing things might we accomplish (John 1:12).

We needn't put much weight on the fact that they seemed to criticize Jesus for being a carpenter (verse 3). This does not mean that they looked down upon those who practiced manual trades. No, the rabbis of ancient Israel taught people to respect and practice the honest trades. (By the way, the Greek word rendered "carpenter" can also be translated "smith," and there is a very old tradition that Jesus made plows and yokes.) The point is simply that it is hard to recognize greatness in that which is familiar to us.

And "they took offense" at him (Mark 6:3). The Hebrew word that occurs here literally means "they stumbled" over him. I don't think we should be too hard on them. If you and I had been there, do you think we would have readily accepted this carpenter's son as a prophet? Or, to put it in what is perhaps even sharper focus, imagine a young person in your community whom you know—a high school honors student, a young athlete, a

THIRD QUARTER

schoolteacher, someone in business. Could you think of him or her as a prophet? Can you think of yourself as one?

In reply, Jesus quoted a proverb to them: "Everybody honors the prophet, except the next-door neighbors." And (is this not astonishing?) "he *could do no mighty works*" (6:5). Matthew (13:58) simply says that he "did not do many mighty works there." But Mark clearly says that he couldn't. And Jesus himself marveled at it (Mark 6:6). He was able to heal a few folks and to get in some teaching, but on the whole this was not a very successful mission. Luke's account (4:16-30) tells us that they were so hostile toward him that they tried to kill him.

What are we to make of this? Clearly, not even Jesus can give gifts to those who will not receive them. God is ever ready to help us, but unless we ask for help (repent and believe), not even God will force that help on us. The wind of the spirit may blow (John 3:8), but unless we set our sails, it won't get us anywhere. Jesus may knock (Revelation 3:20), but we have to open the door.

Instructions (Mark 6:7-13)

Almost, it seems, as a response to his own failure in Nazareth, Jesus begins to help his apostles understand what obstacles they will confront. (It will get even worse; see Matthew 10:17-18.) Here are his instructions, as Mark records them:

1. Go in pairs (verse 7); we mustn't try to do it alone, as though we were depending on our own strength.
2. Go with Christ's authority (verse 7); we cannot cast out demons without an intimate relationship with the Lord. (Note the wonderful funny story about the seven exorcists who got stripped and beaten for using an authority they did not really understand or believe, recorded in Acts 19:13-16.)
3. You don't need a lot of supplies and equipment; God will provide (verses 8-9).
4. Accept the hospitality of those to whom you minister (verse 10).
5. If it doesn't work, forget it and go on. Jesus almost seems to be saying, "Tell them to go jump in the lake," but to "shake off the dust" simply means "put all that behind you."

It's that last instruction that is relevant here. We are not to worry about our failures, any more than Jesus should worry about his lack of success in Nazareth. It may be Paul who plants and Apollos who waters, but it is God who gives the growth (1 Corinthians 3:6). We do not convert other people; the Holy Spirit does. We cannot teach other people if they are unwilling to learn. As the old saw has it, you can lead a horse to water, but you can't make it drink.

This is a very liberating rule. We are not responsible for the outcome; instead, we are to do our best. This applies not only to evangelistic visitation but also to raising our own children, teaching a class, pastoring a church, or attempting to persuade a city council of a more effective way of doing things. For one thing, when we don't have to worry about the outcome, we can relax and enjoy what we are doing. We can live joyfully *with* our children, rather than against them in hostility. We can learn to be like the patient father in Jesus's wonderful story (Luke 15), who waited, looking

MARCH 15　　　　　　　　　　　　　　　　　　　　　　LESSON 3

expectantly down the road, for his prodigal son to come home. Of course, we are responsible for doing our best, but we don't have to tear out our hair, wring our hands, or have a fit. Ministry is even fun when we can let go and let God take charge of it. When the disciples went out, armed with Jesus' instructions, they did very well (Mark 6:12-13; see also Luke 9:1-5). It's an exciting thing to engage in the spreading of the good news. It takes no special equipment, and we are not alone. You and I can make a real difference in the world if we can learn to follow the example of our Lord in our own home town.

Helping Adults Become Involved—Roy H. Ryan

Preparing to Teach

Read your student and teacher material, then read the section "As You Read the Scripture" and Dr. McGeachy's exposition of the text of Mark 6:1-13. In addition, you may wish to read a commentary.

The aim of this lesson is to help us learn to deal effectively with our frustrations and disappointments as we seek to follow Jesus.

In the lesson last week we got a glimpse of how Jesus dealt with persons in the face of opposition from the Pharisees, who felt that the law should take precedence over persons. He took an unpopular stand and began to rile the Pharisees and those who agreed with them.

Today's lesson deals with a different kind of opposition, opposition from those who were his "own people." He goes back to Nazareth where he grew up and found that "he could do no mighty work there." This must have hurt him more deeply than the opposition of the Pharisees. After all, he expected that. But the opposition of his own neighbors and kinsfolk?

A possible outline for the lesson could be as follows:

      I. Introduction.
      II. The difficulties increase.
      III. You can't go home again.
      IV. Instructions for the disciples.

Introducing the Main Question

How do you deal with disappointments and frustrations, especially when you feel you are doing God's work? Jesus knew he "was about his Father's business." It would seem to follow, then, that all religious folk would be interested in what he had to say. He had been proclaimed by John the Baptist to be the Son of God, and his faithful disciples had come to know him as Savior and Lord. Why would people continue to doubt or ridicule him?

Dr. McGeachy suggests that we as Christians can expect to meet with frustration and disappointment, just as Jesus did. He was not immune from it; we certainly will not be. How, then, do we deal with it? That is the question.

You may want to ask members of the class to do some sharing around that question. How do they deal with frustrations and disappointments as they seek to live Christian lives?

If you gave them the assignment last week to report on ways they were

THIRD QUARTER

involved in "putting a priority on persons" during the week, you will want to provide for some time for them to report. It may be that some of them did experience frustration or disappointment as they sought to put people first.

Developing the Lesson

I. Introduction.

Spend a few minutes setting the stage for this lesson from Mark 6. Tell a little bit about what has happened between 3:6 (the end of last week's scripture lesson) and the end of chapter 5. Dr. Decker's exegesis will also be helpful as you set the stage.

Point out the main question as you begin the session, and call for a discussion or reports as indicated above.

II. The difficulties increase.

The question of authority arose when Jesus addressed his hometown synagogue, as it often does when any great teacher or leader goes back home. "Where did Jesus learn this?" the townspeople wondered. "Who gave him the authority to tell us what we ought to believe and do? After all, we have had the prophets for centuries, who have done just that. Is he some kind of prophet?"

There were also questions about his true identity. "Is not this Mary's son? Do not his brothers and sisters still live among us? I thought he was a carpenter." It probably seemed strange to the people of Nazareth that "any good thing could come out of Nazareth." After all, it was just a small town, and no one ever paid any attention to them. Jesus' identity was tied up with his earthly family and the place where he grew up, and some of the people could never get beyond that.

III. You can't go home again.

"A prophet is not without honor, except in his own country, and among his own kin, and in his own house." Jesus knew what he was up against. Prophets and great leaders have always faced that problem. When a local boy or girl makes good, it is sometimes a matter of pride for the community that nurtured him or her, but it is indeed very difficult for such a person to go home again and get a fair hearing. There will always be petty jealousies, doubts, suspicions of how he or she made it, and the like. Jesus' reputation should have preceded him, but according to Mark, this was the first time he went home after his public ministry began. We do not know how long a period of time had elapsed between his departure from home and this return.

"He could do no mighty work there." He was able to heal a few persons, but for the most part his ministry among his own homefolk was a big disappointment. Unless persons have faith in Christ, his works are hampered. It has always been that way. People were healed by faith, not by their doubts. The people in his home town obviously had too many doubts.

IV. Instructions for the disciples.

He gave them simple instructions for the road. Read Mark 6:7-11 for a summary of his instructions. Note what Dr. Decker says about these instructions in his exegesis of verse 7. We should not take these instructions literally for the work of Christian evangelism and mission for our day.

However, we can learn from what he told his disciples and can thus be better prepared to be his witnesses.

They went out and preached and cast out demons (verses 12-13). They seem to have gotten the results that Jesus wanted. He had prepared them for their ministry. They were men of faith who went out in faith. We, like those early disciples, can do great things for God if we go in the spirit of Jesus Christ and in a deep faith in his leadership.

Helping Class Members Act

Encourage class members to keep on keeping on in their efforts to witness for Christ, even though they may run into difficulties. Some persons will not be responsive to the claim of Christ upon their lives. Some people may even make fun of those who take their faith seriously by becoming involved in ministering to persons. Ask members to think about one or two ways they will witness to their faith during the coming week.

Finish up the lesson by praying together: Dear God, give us grace and strength to follow you. Give us wisdom to know what you want us to be and do and the courage to accomplish great things for your kingdom. In the strong name of Jesus, Amen.

Planning for Next Sunday

Ask each person to invite someone else to come to class next week and to pray for other members of the class. Each should also read Mark 7:24-37.

Jesus Meets Needs

Background Scripture: Mark 7:24-37

The Main Question—Pat McGeachy

At other times in these lessons I have suggested that the main question was, Where do you draw the line? In fact, I have a notion that this may be the main question for all lessons.

You shall not kill . . . Yes, but what about self-defense? Where do you draw the line?

You shall not commit adultery . . . yes, but what about lustful thoughts? Where do you draw the line?

Love your enemies . . . yes, but suppose they are blasphemers? Where do you draw the line?

How many times must I forgive?
When have I done enough?
How often should I pray?

THIRD QUARTER

I love my country, but what if my country is acting immorally? Where do you draw the line?

In this lesson, the line has to do with the question, How far shall we go in taking the gospel and its healing message? In this brief passage we are told that Jesus broke out of his usual routine and went in to the pagan lands to the north: to Tyre and Sidon, Phoenecian territory, and then back through the headwaters of the Jordan and into the predominantly Greek area known as the Decapolis ("ten cities"). There he astonished his disciples by offering his gospel to those who were considered "dogs" by pious Jews. Jesus was teaching them to draw their line in an ever-widening circle, which would eventually take in not merely the unbelievers of Tyre and Sidon but even idolatrous Athens and impious Rome. Indeed, it will go further than that, for as John has told us (1 John 2:2). Christ "is the expiation for our sins, and not for ours only but also for the sins of the whole world."

Then our question becomes, In the missionary task of the church, in our own friendships and reachings out, where do we stop? Do we go to the uttermost parts of the earth? To outer space? How do you answer?

Selected Scripture

King James Version

Mark 7:24-37

24 And from thence he arose, and went into the borders of Tyre and Sidon, and entered into an house, and would have no man know *it:* but he could not be hid.

25 For a *certain* woman, whose young daughter had an unclean spirit, heard of him, and came and fell at his feet:

26 The woman was a Greek, a Syrophenician by nation; and she besought him that he would cast forth the devil out of her daughter.

27 But Jesus said unto her, Let the children first be filled: for it is not meet to take the children's bread, and to cast *it* unto the dogs.

28 And she answered and said unto him, Yes, Lord: yet the dogs under the table eat of the children's crumbs.

29 And he said unto her, For this saying go thy way; the devil is gone out of thy daughter.

30 And when she was come to her house, she found the devil gone out, and her daughter laid upon the bed.

Revised Standard Version

Mark 7:24-37

24 And from there he arose and went away to the region of Tyre and Sidon. And he entered a house, and would not have any one know it; yet he could not be hid. 25 But immediately a woman, whose little daughter was possessed by an unclean spirit, heard of him, and came and fell down at this feet. 26 Now the woman was Greek, a Syrophoenician by birth. And she begged him to cast the demon out of her daughter. 27 And he said to her, "Let the children first be fed, for it is not right to take the children's bread and throw it to the dogs." 28 But she answered him, "Yes, Lord; yet even the dogs under the table eat the children's crumbs." 29 And he said to her, "For this saying you may go your way; the demon has left your daughter." 30 And she went home, and found the child lying in bed, and the demon gone.

31 And again, departing from the coasts of Tyre and Sidon, he came unto the sea of Galilee, through the midst of the coasts of Decapolis.
32 And they bring unto him one that was deaf, and had an impediment in his speech; and they beseech him to put his hand upon him.
33 And he took him aside from the multitude, and put his fingers into his ears, and he spit, and touched his tongue;
34 And looking up to heaven, he sighed, and saith unto him, Ephphatha, that is, Be opened.
35 And straightway his ears were opened, and the string of his tongue was loosed, and he spake plain.
36 And he charged them that they should tell no man: but the more he charged them, so much the more a great deal they published *it;*
37 And were beyond measure astonished, saying, He hath done all things well: he maketh both the deaf to hear, and the dumb to speak.

Key Verse: **And were beyond measure astonished, saying, He hath done all things well: he maketh both the deaf to hear, and the dumb to speak. (Mark 7:37)**

31 Then he returned from the region of Tyre, and went through Sidon to the Sea of Galilee, through the region of the Decapolis. 32 And they brought to him a man who was deaf and had an impediment in his speech; and they besought him to lay his hand upon him. 33 And taking him aside from the multitude privately, he put his fingers into his ears, and he spat and touched his tongue; 34 and looking up to heaven, he sighed, and said to him, "Ephphatha," that is, "Be opened." 35 And his ears were opened, his tongue was released, and he spoke plainly. 36 And he charged them to tell no one; but the more he charged them, the more zealously they proclaimed it. 37 And they were astonished beyond measure, saying. "He had done all things well; he even makes the deaf hear and the dumb speak."

Key Verse: **They were astonished beyond measure, saying, "He has done all things well; he even makes the deaf hear and the dumb speak." (Mark 7:37)**

As You Read the Scripture—Ralph W. Decker

Following his unhappy visit to Nazareth (Mark 6:1-6), Jesus continued his ministry in Galilee. He sent his disciples out in pairs to preach, teach, and heal. While the crowds were eager to hear him (6:33), the Pharisees were becoming openly hostile (7:1-8).

Mark 7:24. No word is given as to why Jesus withdrew from Jewish territory into the Gentile area of Syrophoenicia. He may have been seeking for himself and his disciples the rest that was denied them in Galilee (6:31-33). Or, he may have been seeking time to evaluate the ministry that had brought him into open conflict with civil (Herod Antipas) and religious (the Pharisees) authorities. The latter is suggested by Mark's report that Jesus tried to keep his whereabouts unknown. Tyre was a Syrian town on the northern border of Galilee. Sidon was about 30 miles farther north. Both were seaports.

Verse 25. Jesus' reputation as a healer had preceded him. His attempt at seclusion was interrupted by the insistent mother of a sick child.

Verse 26. The woman is identified as a Greek, which probably means that she was a Greek-speaking Gentile, not necessarily a citizen or native of Greece. Mark identifies her as a Syrophoenician, a native of Phoenicia, which was part of the Roman province of Syria. Matthew (15:22) calls her a Canaanite, a descendant of the people who occupied Palestine before the Israelites. That she was not Jewish is important to Mark's report of the incident.

Verse 27. Jesus' response to the woman's plea seems harsh and uncharacteristic. It has been suggested that Jesus was using a folk saying and repeating it to test the woman's faith.

Verse 28. Some have read the woman's response as a clever retort. It should be seen as a humble plea for help.

Verse 29. Matthew's account of the incident (15:26) makes it clear that Jesus responded because of the woman's humility, not because of her clever reply.

Verse 31. Although both Matthew (15:21) and Mark (7:24) report Jesus' brief withdrawal into Syrophoenicia, only Mark reports the roundabout way in which he returned to Galilee. He reports that Jesus skirted the northern boundary of Herod Antipas's territory (Galilee), crossed the Jordan above the Sea of Galilee, and spent consider time in the region of the Decapolis before returning to his home territory below the Sea of Galilee. The Decapolis was a federation of Greek cities, nine of which were east of the Jordan River. They were definitely Gentile in population and character.

Verse 32. Upon his return to home territory, Jesus was immediately met with a request to heal a deaf mute.

Verse 33. That Jesus took the afflicted man apart from the crowd suggests that he was trying to deemphasize healing as against teaching. Since the man was deaf, Jesus used pantomime to communicate with him.

Verse 34. Ephphatha, the one word Jesus spoke, is an Aramaic word meaning "open" or "be opened." Aramaic was the language of the Palestinian Jews in Jesus' day. This is one of the four Aramaic words or phrases spoken by Jesus and preserved in the Greek Gospels. The four, three of which appear only in Mark, are *talitha cumi* ("little girl, arise," Mark 5:41), *ephphatha* ("be opened," Mark 7:34), *Abba* ("Father," Mark 14:36), and *"Eloi, eloi, lama sabachthani"* ("My God, my God, why hast thou forsaken me?" Mark 15:34; Matthew 27:46).

Verse 36. Jesus' admonition to the man and his friends indicates that he did not wish to be known primarily as a healer or to have his teaching ministry sidetracked by requests for healing. Their reaction as reported was a very human one. They immediately set about spreading reports of the cure.

Verse 37. Jesus was more readily accepted for his healing than for his teaching.

The Scripture and the Main Question—Pat McGeachy

A Trip into Lebanon (Mark 7:24, 31)

If, as we have seen (Mark 6:4), a prophet has little honor in his own country, it is now made clear that the converse is true. Jesus makes his only foray (that we know about) onto foreign soil, and there is received with enthusiasm. Tyre and Sidon are famous cities; I count over sixty references to one or the other from Genesis to Acts. Quite often they are mentioned together. In the time of the Judges they were strong places (Joshua 19:28-29), and during the preaching of the later prophets they figure prominently, coming under the judgment of Amos (1:9), Isaiah (23:12), Joel (3:4-6), Jeremiah (27:1-11), and Ezekiel (26-29).

In ancient times, Tyre and Sidon, which are only about twenty-four miles apart, were major cities of Phoenicia. They are mentioned in Homer and in other secular literature. More than once they have been laid waste by conquerors. It took Nebuchadrezzar thirteen years to conquer Tyre in 572 B.C., and it took Alexander the Great nearly a year to do it a couple of centuries later. And out of defeat they have risen to become once more centers of commerce, exploration, and military significance. So synonymous with empire did they become that Rudyard Kipling, around the beginning of our century, in a poem called *Recessional* about the evils of imperialism, used one of them as a metaphor:

> Lo, all our pomp of yesterday
> Is one with Nineveh and Tyre!

And, what may be most amazing, they are still in the news! In the modern country of Lebanon, Tyre and Sidon are known as Sur and Sayda, but they are built on the ruins of the former mighty cities. And I have seen them called by their ancient names within the past year. The pagan world continues to rear its head in our day, as it did in the time of Jesus, and there is yet mission work to be done there.

We don't think of Jesus as a traveler, and indeed, this journey did not take him far. Tyre is only a little over a hundred miles from Jerusalem. But how long would it take you to make a journey of a hundred miles on foot? Why did he go such a distance? Could it have been a journey of discovery for Jesus? Or could he have been signaling the beginning of the missionary movement that would take the news of the God of Israel to the Gentile world?

A Greek Woman and Her Child (Mark 7:24-30)

This is a difficult passage for Christians because it reports a very disturbing statement by Jesus. Mark makes it clear (verse 26) that the woman was a foreigner, "a Greek, a Syrophoenician by birth." Devout Jews were accustomed to calling such people "Gentile dogs" (Psalm 22:16, 20; Philippians 3:2). One ancient rabbi has written, "The nations of the world are compared to dogs." But would Jesus use such an expression? Apparently he did, though some commentators point out that he softened it a little by using a word that actually means "doggies," an affectionate diminutive ordinarily applied to housepets. Why would he do so? Some possible explanations:

Perhaps he wished to keep his identity as a Jew clear, not being ready to reveal his radical universalism just yet. The hour had "not yet come" when he was ready to reveal that the gospel was for all the world. (Compare Matthew 10:5-6 and Matthew's account of this same event in 15:21-28 with later sayings such as Matthew 28:19, Luke 24:47, and Acts 1:8.)

Perhaps Jesus was testing the strength of the Syrophenician's faith, or teaching her the lesson of persistence and importunity in prayer (see the parable of the judge and the widow (Luke 18:1-8).

THIRD QUARTER

Or perhaps he was demonstrating to the disciples that greater faith was often to be found among the heathen than among Israel (see Matthew 8:10).

It has even been suggested that Jesus' own understanding of the breadth of his ministry had not yet come to its full development, and that this non-Jewish woman may have influenced him to see how far-reaching the good news was to be. But I have problems with this interpretation, especially since Luke's account of Jesus' first sermon in his home town (Luke 4:16-30) clearly indicates that he was thinking beyond the borders of Israel very early in his career; note the reference there to Naaman the Syrian and the widow from Sidon. Perhaps the extremely negative reaction of the people of Nazareth (Luke 4:28-29) was one of the reasons he decided to go slow with such radical good news.

Whatever Jesus' reluctance may have been, it was won over by the woman's persistent spirit. With good humor, seemingly taking no offense, she picked up on his image, arguing that if she's a household pet, then she has a right to the crumbs. Jesus' disciples apparently stayed long enough to learn the end of the story, that the child in fact was healed of its demon.

A Person with Speech and Hearing Impairment (Mark 7:31-37)

Jesus took the long way home from Tyre. If you will look at your map, you will see that he went further north to Sidon, then swung round the shoulder of Mount Hermon (its snows are the source of the Jordan at Caesarea Philippi) and down into the Decapolis. This would bring him up to the sea of Galilee from the east, through what is today called the Golan Heights.

In that region some people encountered him with a man who was "deaf and had an impediment in his speech." For obvious reasons, these two problems often come together. Jesus seems to have communicated with the man by sign language, to indicate what he was about to do, by touching his own ears and tongue. This took place away from the crowd (verse 33), though there were apparently witnesses, for Mark records the healing in some detail. It is clear that Jesus took special pains with this man, perhaps because, like the Syrophoenician woman, he was a Gentile, or perhaps simply because he was deaf. Deafness is a much more serious handicap than most of us realize. Blindness we clearly understand as a calamity, but blind people usually function in society pretty well because they can communicate well. For the deaf it is another matter. We make jokes about the hard of hearing, and if we start going deaf we tend to try to hide it and sometimes end up feeling pretty paranoid, or at least left out of things. If you want to test this, try watching a television program without the sound and then listening to it without the picture, and see which one is easier to follow!

In any event, Jesus took considerable pains to help this man understand what he was doing, and perhaps to nurture the man's faith. Finally, perhaps using his saliva as a healing ointment (see John 9:6), he said, "Ephphatha!" (an Aramaic word meaning "be opened"). Mark likes to preserve examples for us of Jesus' native tongue, indicating that his sources (Peter?) were close at hand. (See also Mark 5:41 and 15:34.) Again (verse 36), he tried to keep his power a secret, but the word spread like wildfire.

MARCH 22   LESSON 4

Where Do We Draw the Line?

Of course, you have had no trouble answering the question this week. As we are to forgive seventy times seven times (that is, indefinitely, Matthew 18:22), we are to go the second mile in carrying the good news to others. We are to take it to "dogs," those whom the world sees as unworthy. We are to take special care of the handicapped, those whom the busy world ignores. The fields are white with harvest, and we are not to rest till every knee has bowed and every tongue confessed that Jesus is Lord (Philippians 2:10-11). It is God's will (Ephesians 1:10) that everything in heaven and earth one day be united in Christ. Of course, not even Jesus could go to everybody in the world. He had to stop a hundred miles from home. And you and I cannot witness to the whole world. But we can be a part of the "good infection" that spreads wherever people discover the joy of life in Christ and will eventually leaven the whole lump (Matthew 13:33; 24:14).

Helping Adults Become Involved—Roy H. Ryan

Preparing to Teach

This lesson will conclude the first unit, "Mission and Message." It deals with Jesus' visit into Gentile territory and an account of healing while he is there. This account continues the theme of helping persons and placing the needs of persons above convention and tradition. It ought to be clear by now to Jesus' disciples and to those interested in his ministry that he is not just a local prophet and teacher. His mission is not limited to the Jews.

The aim of this lesson is to help us see and understand that the ministry, message, and mission of Jesus is to all persons. God loves the whole world. Jesus is God's Son (John 3:16).

Study Dr. Decker's comments in the section "As You Read the Scripture" for a fuller explanation of the geographical and social setting in which Jesus' visit occurs. Also, Dr. McGeachy's exposition gives some helpful information on the same subject.

This lesson has profound implications for our view of Christianity and what our obligation may be to those who are outsiders. It is easy for us to become provincial in our beliefs and view of mission. This lesson should help us broaden our vision of what we are called to do as followers of Christ.

A possible outline for the lesson might look like this:

      I. Introduction.
     II. A trip outside Israel.
    III. A Greek woman asks for help.
   IV. A deaf person is healed.

Introducing the Main Question

What is the main question confronting us in this lesson? It seems to be quite clear. What are the boundaries of our witness and concern as Christians? How far shall we go in carrying the gospel to the rest of the world?

Most members of your class will probably have no difficulty in affirming our need to send missionaries to all parts of the world, though they may

THIRD QUARTER

indeed disagree on what those missionaries should attempt to do. (Is their mission primarily evangelism, or is it also development and healing?) But what about our personal obligation? Where do our concerns end? What are the limits of our witness? How far should we go in reaching out to persons and seeking to meet their needs in the name and spirit of Jesus Christ?

This question hits home to all of us at some level. You may want to probe a little with your class to see where they are in their thinking about the scope of the mission and message of Christ.

Developing the Lesson

I. Introduction.

Tell the story of Jesus' trip into the foreign territory. It is interesting to note that he ventured into what is modern Lebanon. Does that have any symbolic meaning? Also, the two cities mentioned, Tyre and Sidon, were major seaport cities in that part of the world.

This visit follows on his less than successful visit to his home base of Galilee. Why would he make this relatively long trek at this particular point in his ministry?

II. A trip outside Israel.

Jesus is probably seeking rest. After all, they had just come away from a disappointing experience. Maybe they needed to withdraw into an area where Jesus was not well known. We can all appreciate the need to get away at times. We need it to get our bearings.

He was facing more conflict from political and religious authorities in his homeland. Why not go outside for a brief respite?

Jesus' reputation preceded him. He discovered that the word had spread about his healing ministry. He was becoming known outside the borders of his own country.

Even though communication then was primitive compared to our day, when someone does the things he had been doing, the word gets around. It is hard to keep secret such good news as he was proclaiming and practicing through his ministry of healing.

III. A Greek woman asks for help.

She had heard of his power to heal. She came pleading with him to help her daughter. She did not care about geographic or political boundaries. Her daughter was ill. When we are confronted with a severe illness, we look wherever we can for a cure. She did not speak the same language or share the same religious heritage as Jesus, but she did share in a common humanity.

Jesus says a strange thing to her. It is difficult for us to believe what we read! Why would Jesus compare her to a dog (or "doggie," as Dr. McGeachy suggests)? Consider the comments by Dr. McGeachy and Dr. Decker and compare them with your own commentary. Be prepared to help the class understand what was going on here.

IV. A deaf person is healed.

Jesus is back in his home territory. It is interesting to note that Jesus takes the man aside. We do not know for sure why he chose to do so. Dr. Decker suggests that perhaps it was to deemphasize healing as against teaching

CONFESSION AND CRUCIFIXION

(verse 23). With his power to heal, it was probably difficult for him to do the kind of teaching he felt was needed. If healing the sick took all his time and energy, what would be left for teaching the important truths of God?

Jesus heals the man of his deafness and muteness. He seems to have communicated with the man by pantomime or sign language.

Though Jesus clearly wanted to be teaching, he could not turn aside from the hurts of persons. His mission and message go hand in hand. He came as teacher and healer. He came to bring wholeness of life—that does not leave out any part of our existence.

Helping Class Members Act

What could your class do as a group to express outreach and concern in your community? In the world? What projects could you adopt that would require personal involvement in mission and ministry, not just sending money? See if you can help the class members come up with one or two new ways of expressing their concern for persons outside their local church.

Individual class members could also be challenged to think of ways they could reach out to the stranger or the foreigner with a hand of friendship and love. What about persons in your community who have come from other countries, who are from other cultures or religions and who speak a different language. How will you show forth your love of Christ as you seek to "love the neighbor in need"?

End the class time with a prayer: God of all people, save us from narrowness and provincialism. Give us grace and love so that we may love all persons and seek to help all who are in need. In Jesus' name, Amen.

Planning for Next Sunday

Briefly introduce the new unit and ask members to study the scripture (Mark 8:27–9:13) and the lesson material.

UNIT II: CONFESSION AND CRUCIFIXION
Horace R. Weaver

FOUR LESSONS **MARCH 29–APRIL 19**

The four lessons of unit II begin with the decisive point when Jesus is recognized as the Christ and move directly to the culmination of his mission in Jerusalem.

Unit II is composed of the following four lessons: "A Price to Pay," March 29, asks two questions: Who do you think Jesus is? And who do you think you are? "Love Says It All," April 5, asks: Which commandment ranks first place? "Christ Died for You," April 12, raises these questions: Can a scaffold be a throne? Is there any hope for your tragic life, and mine? "Death Is Not the End," April 19, opens new vistas: How can you and I confront death as the followers of the Lord of Life?

LESSON 5   MARCH 29

A Price to Pay

Background Scripture: Mark 8:27–9:13

The Main Question—Pat McGeachy

In the last lesson I tried to say that the question, Where do you draw the line? lies at the heart of most of our questions. That is certainly true of matters of ethics and practice. But there is another, more subtle and more powerful question, never more clearly raised than in this passage for today, which everyone must answer if life is to have meaning, purpose, and satisfaction: How can I be a strong person, with dignity, genuine pride, and self-respect, without falling into the ego trap of false pride, the sort that goes before a fall (Proverbs 16:18)? In one sense, every thought and action of our lives is a battle between self-assertion and withdrawal. Do I speak or remain silent? Do I fight or flee?

The wonderful life and example of Jesus of Nazareth provide for us the best way I know of answering that question. When he asked the disciples, "Who do you think I am?" he was also asking them, "Who do you think you are?" We cannot come to understand Jesus without coming to a better understanding of ourselves. And the very way in which he approaches this basic faith question (What do you think of Jesus?) contains the beginnings of our answer.

Jesus does not tell the disciples who he is (Matthew 16:17), but like a Socrates drawing on the minds of his pupils, Jesus elicits from their own hearts the response of faith: "You are the Christ." So are we to approach the business of being Christian witnesses. We are not to *win* the world. We are not to *tell* the world the truth. We are not to *argue* people into salvation. Our task, after the example of our Lord, is to witness, by word and deed, who Jesus is, so that others will come to see, as Peter did, that he is the answer to life's greatest question.

The question then is, What do you think of Jesus? But it is also, Who are you, and how will you live your life?

Selected Scripture

King James Version

Mark 8:27-38

27 And Jesus went out, and his disciples, into the towns of Caesarea Philippi: and by the way he asked his disciples, saying unto them, Whom do men say that I am?

28 And they answered, John the Baptist: but some *say*, Elias; and others, One of the prophets.

29 And he saith unto them, But

Revised Standard Version

Mark 8:27-38

27 And Jesus went on with his disciples, to the villages of Caesarea Philippi; and on the way he asked his disciples, "Who do men say that I am?" 28 And they told him, "John the Baptist; and others say, Elijah; and others one of the prophets." 29 And he asked them, "But who do you say that I am?" Peter answered

MARCH 29

whom say ye that I am? And Peter answereth and saith unto him, Thou art the Christ.

30 And he charged them that they should tell no man of him.

31 And he began to teach them, that the Son of man must suffer many things, and be rejected of the elders, and *of* the chief priests, and scribes, and be killed, and after three days rise again.

32 And he spake that saying openly. And Peter took him, and began to rebuke him.

33 But when he had turned about and looked on his disciples, he rebuked Peter, saying, Get thee behind me, Satan: for thou savourest not the things that be of God, but the things that be of men.

34 And when he had called the people *unto him* with his disciples also, he said unto them, Whosoever will come after me, let him deny himself, and take up his cross, and follow me.

35 For whosoever will save his life shall lose it; but whosoever shall lose his life for my sake and the gospel's, the same shall save it.

36 For what shall it profit a man, if he shall gain the whole world, and lose his own soul?

37 Or what shall a man give in exchange for his soul?

38 Whosoever therefore shall be ashamed of me and of my words in this adulterous and sinful generation; of him also shall the Son of man be ashamed, when he cometh in the glory of his Father with the holy angels.

Mark 9:1

1 And he said unto them, Verily I say unto you, That there be some of them that stand here, which shall not taste of death, till they have seen the kingdom of God come with power.

Key Verse: And when he had called the people unto him with his

LESSON 5

him, "You are the Christ." 30 And he charged them to tell no one about him.

31 And he began to teach them that the Son of man must suffer many things, and be rejected by the elders and the chief priests and the scribes, and be killed, and after three days rise again. 32 And he said this plainly. And Peter took him, and began to rebuke him. 33 But turning and seeing his disciples, he rebuked Peter, and said, "Get behind me, Satan! For you are not on the side of God, but of men."

34 And he called to him the multitude with his disciples, and said to them, "If any man would come after me, let him deny himself and take up his cross and follow me. 35 For whoever would save his life will lose it; and whoever loses his life for my sake and the gospel's will save it. 36 For what does it profit a man, to gain the whole world and forfeit his life? 37 For what can a man give in return for his life? 38 For whoever is ashamed of me and of my words in this adulterous and sinful generation, of him will the Son of man also be ashamed, when he comes in the glory of his Father with the holy angels."

Mark 9:1

1 And he said to them, "Truly, I say to you, there are some standing here who will not taste death before they see the kingdom of God come with power."

Key Verse: He called to him the multitude with his disciples, and

disciples also, he said unto them, Whosoever will come after me, let him deny himself, and take up his cross, and follow me. (Mark 8:34)

said to them, "If any man would come after me, let him deny himself and take up his cross and follow me." (Mark 8:34)

As You Read the Scripture—Ralph W. Decker

This lesson marks the great divide in Mark's Gospel. What has one before paved the way for Peter's recognition of Jesus' messiahship and for Jesus' acknowledgement of it. What follows traces Jesus' movement toward the cross.

Mark 8:27. Jesus, with his disciples, was avoiding the area governed by Herod Antipas, who had caused the death of John the Baptizer. Mark reports that he carried his ministry into the villages around Caesarea Philippi, a city in the northernmost part of Palestine. There was another Caesarea on the Mediterranean coast south of Mount Carmel. This one, on the southern slope of Mount Hermon, was an older city rebuilt and renamed by Philip, son of Herod the Great. He named it in honor of Caesar and himself. At this point Jesus asked his disciples what people were saying about him.

Verse 28. Their answers indicate a widespread belief that Jesus was either John the Baptizer or one of the older prophets come back to life.

Verse 29. Having set the disciples to thinking, Jesus asked their own opinions. Peter, the most outspoken disciple, replied, "You are the Christ." He undoubtedly spoke in Aramaic, calling Jesus the Messiah.

Verse 30. Jesus charged his disciples to keep this knowledge to themselves, probably because the popular expectation of a military messiah was so different from his own concept of a servant messiah that misunderstanding would have resulted.

Verse 31. The disciples shared the popular idea of a conquering messiah. Jesus set about changing their view.

Verse 32. Peter objected to Jesus' idea of messiahship. Matthew (16:23) reports his objection more fully.

Verse 33. Jesus tells Peter that he is acting like Satan, the tempter, in trying to turn him from his mission.

Verses 34-37. Jesus points out that his followers must be ready to share his sufferings. He promises that those who do will share his glory.

Verse 34. With his announcement that he was to be a suffering messiah, Jesus called his disciples to self-denial. This is Mark's first mention of a cross. A condemned person was forced to carry his cross to the place of execution. Jesus here asks his followers to assume voluntarily that which would lead to conflict, rejection, and suffering.

Verse 35. While he spoke of death, Jesus offered life. Letting go of an old life makes way for living a new one.

Mark 9:1-13. This report of the transfiguration is probably based on Peter's memory of it. He was one of the three disciples present and the only one reported to have said anything.

Verse 2. Peter, James, and John formed an inner circle among the Twelve. They alone were present at the most personal and important events in Jesus' life and ministry.

Verse 3. In the disciples' vision, even Jesus' clothing was glorified.

Verse 4. Moses and Elijah represented the Law and the Prophets—the

MARCH 29   LESSON 5

entire religious history of Israel. They both had faced rejection and suffering. Moses had experienced the revolt of the Israelites. Elijah had fled the length of Palestine to save his life.

Verses 6-8. The transfiguration was primarily an experience in which Jesus' mission and ministry were confirmed. The three disciples were confused and shaken but assured of one thing—what Jesus was doing was in keeping with the Law and the Prophets.

Verses 9-13. The discussion here is not easy to follow. Jesus told the disciples not to talk about the transfiguration until he had risen from the dead. They were puzzled because they did not expect the messiah to die. This raised the question of whether Jesus really was the messiah. In their search for evidence, they recalled that Malachi (4:5-6) said that Elijah would return before the messiah came. In effect, they asked Jesus, "If you are the messiah, why did not Elijah return?" Jesus replied that he had come. Matthew (17:13) adds that the disciples understood Jesus to refer to John the Baptizer.

The Scripture and the Main Question—Pat McGeachy

What Do You Think of the Christ? (Mark 8:27-30)

That question will serve as a title for this section of Mark's Gospel. As we study this paragraph, you may want to keep one finger in your New Testament at Matthew 16:13-20, which is an expanded version of the same incident; will we look at it from time to time.

First, a word about Caesarea Philippi. It has the distinction of being named after two famous rulers: Philip of Macedonia, father of Alexander the Great, and Tiberius Caesar. There is no more beautiful spot in the world. A number of religious structures have been built there, by the Romans, who worshiped the nature god Pan, by Herod the Great, and by Agrippa II, who tried to name it after still another emperor, Nero. But only a small town remains there today, called Banias, a name that still hints of Pan. And that is not inappropriate, for nature has finally conquered Caesarea Philippi. The ancient ruins are gone, and what is left is the lovely grove of trees around the cold mountain stream that is the principal source of the Jordan River.

The river there is no more than thirty feet wide—really no more than a creek. Fed by the snows of Mount Hermon, it flows cheerfully over smooth stones under eucalyptus trees. Though the structures human beings have built throughout the Holy Land are long since gone, the hills and streams really are very much as they must have been two thousand years ago. I like to picture Jesus and his disciples halting their journey there on the banks of the Jordan, laughing with one another, not frivolously but as those experiencing a deep joy. They have been together for a couple of years now, and the little band is maturing in their understanding, though there is one rather sizeable leap of faith they have not yet made. I imagine Jesus looking around at his friends and saying to himself, "Well, I believe the time has come to deal with the great question." At any rate, perhaps with a sigh of resignation, or even an uneasy clearing of his throat, he asked it: "Who do they say that I am?"

There are a number of answers. Some say John the Baptist. Jesus' cousin is now dead, having been killed by Herod due to a rash promise made to his

THIRD QUARTER

stepdaughter, Salome the dancer. See Mark 6:14-29, noting especially verses 14-15, which support the answers given by the disciples in our lesson. Does it surprise you that so soon after John's murder there are those who believe he is alive? As I write this, I am informed that a contemporary American folk hero, Elvis Presley, has recently been sighted in Cleveland, Ohio, although he has been dead for a good many years. Popular legends die hard, and John had become one.

Some say Elijah. The Hebrew Scriptures end with the prediction that this most famous of the early prophets would come again to precede "the great and terrible day of the Lord" (Malachi 4:5). Even today there is a pious hope among Jews that Elijah may come to their Passover feast. In the closing verses of this lesson, Jesus will claim that John the Baptist *is* this promised Elijah (Mark 6:13; see also Matthew 17:13 and 11:13-14).

Others say "one of the prophets," perhaps Jeremiah (Matthew 16:14), who was considered in some rabbinical traditions as another who would appear as a forerunner to the coming messiah. It was claimed that he and Elijah would find the lost Ark of the Covenant, which Jeremiah had hidden in a cave at the time of the Babylonian captivity, and restore it to the Holy of Holies. Or perhaps a new, as yet unnamed prophet might emerge (see John 1:25), who would clear the way for the coming of the messianic age.

All three of these—John the Baptist, Elijah, another prophet—are penultimate figures: the last but one. And they are not enough to describe the office Jesus of Nazareth has come to fill. So (verse 29) Jesus pushes them one step further, by asking in effect, "Yes, but what do *you* say?" And at this point, inspired beyond his simple fisherman's insight, Peter blurts out, "You are the Christ!" Luke (9:20) expands Peter's words to say "the Christ of God," and Matthew (16:16) still further: "You are the Christ, the Son of the living God." (Although John does not exactly describe this incident, he records a very similar confession by Peter in 6:66-69.)

Christ is the Greek form of the Hebrew word *messiah*. They both have "oil" as their root meaning and mean "the anointed" or "chosen one." (See Psalm 133:2; Exodus 29:7; 1 Samuel 16:1, 12-13; and many other references.) In Jewish and Christian belief, the messiah is the one anointed, that is, empowered by the pouring out of God's Spirit to deliver God's people and establish the kingdom. It is still the hope of pious Jews that this day will come, and Christians share a similar expectation in the form of the anticipated return of the Christ.

How did Peter know that Jesus was the Messiah? No human being ("flesh and blood," Matthew 16:17) had told him. But the days, months, and years he had spent with Jesus had begun to bear fruit. With a sudden rush of God-given insight, Peter has come to see who Jesus really is. It is the greatest "Eureka!" the greatest "Aha!" experience in human history. And it is one that must come to all who call themselves Christians. Our parents, our preachers, our teachers can tell us, but only when we come, by the grace of God, to see it for ourselves can we lean our whole weight on this Galilean.

"And he charged them to tell no one about him" (verse 30). A strange sort of evangelism, isn't it? But it must be this way. We cannot cram Christ down another's throat. We can witness to these things by what we say and do and by our life-style as Christians, but we cannot convince and convict. Only the Spirit of God can do this.

MARCH 29   LESSON 5

The Hard Facts (Mark 8:31–9:10)

The truth is that even after we have made our profession of faith, we are not fully educated. There is much that we, like the disciples, have still to learn: Jesus is not the sort of "happy ending" Messiah we have been wishing for. The road is hard. Like Peter, we don't want to face this (verse 32), and we must learn that we cannot have Easter without going through Good Friday.

Moreover, we too must die. We must suffer the death of our own egos, take up our own crosses, and lose our lives. Satan doesn't want us to believe this either. The world jeers at us when we follow Christ, saying, "If you were really doing God's will, you would be rich, successful, happy, and a television star." But we are promised no such rose garden. Read again the Beatitudes (Matthew 5:3-12). The world calls us to be rich, powerful, laughing, and proud, but Jesus calls us to be poor, weak, mournful, and persecuted. Like Peter, we have a hard time accepting this.

The Transfiguration (Mark 9:6-13)

Our lesson concludes with a note of power and hope. Yes, Christ must suffer. Yes, Christ's followers must take up their crosses and lose their lives. But all the Law (Moses) and the Prophets (Elijah) testify that this is the way to eternal life. In what must be one of the strangest stories in all history, we are given a brief glimpse of the glorified Christ. We began by looking at Caesarea Philippi, under the slopes of Mount Hermon. We must conclude at another beautiful spot, Mount Tabor, the traditional scene of the transfiguration. It rises nearly two thousand feet right up out of the plain, not far from Nazareth, and offers a commanding view in all directions. For those who have come to claim that Jesus is the Christ, there is this added vision of that Christ in all his glory. This vision is fleeting; no booths can contain it (verses 5-6); we must come down the mountain into the real world where the Messiah must suffer and where we must suffer with him. But we need never forget the glory (Revelation 21:22-26) that will one day be revealed.

Helping Adults Become Involved—Roy H. Ryan

Preparing to Teach

With today's lesson we begin a new unit entitled "Confession and Crucifixion." You will want to scan the entire unit of four lessons and be familiar with the content of the lesson material and the Scripture passages to be studied. This unit deals with some hard issues and some crucial questions faced by those who would follow Jesus.

The aim of this lesson is to help us respond in faith to the question, Who is Jesus Christ? A secondary aim is also to help us answer the question, Who am I? How we answer the first question will affect our answer to the second!

Dr. Decker writes that "this lesson marks the great divide in Mark's Gospel." What has happened before helps prepare the disciples to answer the question about who Jesus is. What will follow traces the movement of Jesus toward the cross.

Jesus does not tell the disciples that he is the promised messiah. He wants

THIRD QUARTER

them to figure that out for themselves. "Who do you say I am?" becomes a key question for every person who is ever confronted with the message of Jesus Christ.

Make sure you have the necessary resources and supplies you need before the class meets.

A possible outline for the lesson would be this:

> I. Introduction.
> II. Who do you say Jesus is?
> III. After you answer the question, what then?
> IV. The transfiguration.

Introducing the Main Question

The main question of the lesson is in fact the question asked by Jesus of his disciples, "Who do you say I am?" It is not enough for us to speculate about who other people say Jesus is. He comes to be the Christ for us only when we can answer the question ourselves. Christianity is not a secondhand religion. Though the tenets of faith can be taught and handed down from one generation to the next, the faith becomes real for us personally when we can answer Jesus' question with conviction. Is he the Christ for me?

How will you help members of the class connect this lesson with their lives? How can you help them answer Jesus' question for themselves?

Most persons in your class are already Christians. They have made a profession of their faith in Christ and united with the church. However, this question continues to haunt each of us because it is recurring. All through life, we will be answering that question. And the way we answer it will have a profound influence on the way we live our lives.

Developing the Lesson

I. Introduction.

As indicated above, you will want to give a brief introduction or overview of the unit before you begin today's lesson.

You might start the lesson with the question, Who is Jesus Christ? You might post the question on a chalkboard or newsprint for all to see as they enter the room. One way to begin would be to ask the question and take a few minutes to receive responses from class members. How would they answer the question?

II. Who do you say Jesus is?

What are others saying about Jesus? Jesus started with a more general question of the disciples: "Who do people say that I am?" That was easy. The disciples began to recite all they had heard from others. Some thought he was John the Baptist come back to life. Others thought he might be Elijah (after all, faithful Jews did expect Elijah to return). Still others thought that he was certainly one of the prophets returned.

What do you say? The question became more focused and personal. Now the disciples were going to have to speak for themselves. Peter, the outspoken one, answered, "You are the Christ." Regardless of what others think, I know you are the promised messiah of God! Peter's proclamation of faith became the very cornerstone of the church. The covenant community that was to come into being, the church, would be founded upon that affirmation.

III. After you answer the question, what then?

You have committed yourself to a way of believing and being in the world. There is no turning back. You have acknowledged that Jesus of Nazareth is indeed the "only begotten son of God," and having made that decision you must move with faith with him into the unknown future.

The way may be hard. Jesus did not promise his disciples a rose garden but rather a different kind of garden of testing and trial. "If any man would come after me, let him deny himself and take up his cross and follow me" (verse 34). It does not get any plainer than that. To follow him will bring suffering.

When we make our commitment to follow Christ, we still have much to learn. We cannot know what the future will bring. But we do know that he will be with us. That makes the suffering bearable.

IV. The transfiguration.

In the midst of suffering, there is hope. God is in Christ bringing about reconciliation. God is in Christ giving us the assurance that we are not alone in our struggle. If we come to trust Jesus Christ, we have God's word that Jesus Christ is real, that he is who he said he was, that he will make good on his promises.

Life is transformed when Jesus Christ comes into it. We have seen it happen. It has happened to us. We know the power of this transfigured one. We are given new life and hope, even as we take up our crosses.

Helping Class Members Act

When we are confronted with the question, Who do you say I am? it becomes a life-changing possibility. If we confess that Jesus Christ is Lord, then we take his mission and message upon ourselves and become his representatives in the world. We come to see ourselves as "the body of Christ," called to be an extension of his ministry of love and healing.

Having said yes to Christ, how will our lives be different? What evidence will we have to let the world know that we have decided to follow Jesus? How will we bear up under our suffering? How will we show forth the love of Christ in the way we relate to others?

Help class members reflect on these and other questions as you conclude the lesson. Send class members on their way with this prayer: Lord, we believe. Help thou our unbelief. For Christ's sake, Amen.

Planning for Next Sunday

Read Mark 12:28-37. Make any assignments you think appropriate.

LESSON 6   APRIL 5

Love Says It All

Background Scripture: Mark 12:28-37

The Main Question—Pat McGeachy

This is one of those lessons where finding the main question is absurdly easy; our friend the scribe (Mark 12:28) asks it for us: "Which commandment is the first of all?" We might have phrased it a little differently. A philosopher might have asked, "What is the supreme good in life?" A military commander might have asked, "What is our objective?" A person in business might have asked, "What will profit us?" There are lots of ways to say it: "What is our chief end?" "How should we arrange our priorities?" "What's the point?" "Where is our true home?" "What is the bottom line?" But I think we all know what the question is.

However, we often don't ask it. Many of us go through life just making the motions; as one philosopher said, "We may be alive, but we don't really *exist!*" That is, we are not filled from day to day with the rich assurance that we are seeking the right ends, doing what we were meant to do. And this is important. You can use a clock to drive nails if you want to, but it does not drive the nails very well, and the whole process is not very good for the clock. So it is with a human life that does not have its uses all straightened out. We need to ask this question.

And we need to listen very carefully to the answer. It is a simple one, and we all know it: Love God, and love your neighbor. What could be plainer? And yet love is often misunderstood. Love is, as some wag has said, a many *splintered* thing. We use the same word love to describe our feelings for everything from art to apple pie. We say both "I love water skiing" and "Love your neighbor." We have much to learn from Jesus at this point. He is not even being original. The first commandment is already there in Deuteronomy 6:5, and the second is already there in Leviticus 19:18. But the genius of Jesus is that he puts the two together, and by his very life shows us what they mean.

Selected Scripture

King James Version	Revised Standard Version
Mark 12:28-37	*Mark 12:28-37*
28 And one of the scribes came, and having heard them reasoning together, and perceiving that he had answered them well, asked him, Which is the first commandment of all?	28 And one of the scribes came up and heard them disputing with one another, and seeing that he answered them well, asked him, "Which commandment is the first of all?"
29 And Jesus answered him, The first of all the commandments *is*, Hear, O Israel; The Lord our God is one Lord:	29 Jesus answered, "The first is, 'Hear, O Israel: The Lord our God, the Lord is one; 30 and you shall love the Lord your God with all your heart, and with all your soul,

APRIL 5　　　　　　　　　　　　　　　　　　　LESSON 6

30 And thou shalt love the Lord thy God with all thy heart, and with all thy soul, and with all thy mind, and with all thy strength: this *is* the first commandment.
31 And the second *is* like, *namely* this, thou shalt love thy neighbour as thyself. There is none other commandment greater than these.
32 And the scribe said unto him, Well, Master, thou hast said the truth: for there is one God; and there is none other but he:
33 And to love him with all the heart, and with all the understanding, and with all the soul, and with all the strength, and to love *his* neighbour as himself, is more than all whole burnt offerings and sacrifices.
34 And when Jesus saw that he answered discreetly, he said unto him, Thou art not far from the kingdom of God. And no man after that durst ask him *any question.*
35 And Jesus answered and said, while he taught in the temple, How say the scribes that Christ is the son of David?
36 For David himself said by the Holy Ghost, The Lord said to my Lord, Sit thou on my right hand, till I make thine enemies thy footstool.
37 David therefore himself calleth him Lord; and whence is he *then* his son? And the common people heard him gladly.

Key Verse: **Thou shalt love the Lord thy God with all thy heart, and with all thy soul, and with all thy mind, and with all thy strength. ... Thou shalt love thy neighbour as thyself. There is no other commandment greater than these. (Mark 12:30-31)**

and with all your mind, and with all your strength.' 31 The second is this, 'You shall love your neighbor as yourself.' There is no other commandment greater than these."
32 And the scribe said to him, "You are right, Teacher; you have truly said that he is one, and there is no other but he; 33 and to love him with all the heart, and with all the understanding, and with all the strength, and to love one's neighbor as oneself, is much more than all whole burnt offerings and sacrifices." 34 And when Jesus saw that he answered wisely, he said to him, "You are not far from the kingdom of God." And after that no one dared to ask him any question.

35 And as Jesus taught in the temple, he said, "How can the scribes say that the Christ is the son of David? 36 David himself, inspired by the Holy Spirit, declared,
'The Lord said to my Lord,
Sit at my right hand,
till I put thy enemies under thy feet.'
37 David himself calls him Lord; so how is he his son?" And the great throng heard him gladly.

Key Verse: **"You shall love the Lord your God with all your heart, and with all your soul, and with all your mind, and with all your strength. ... you shall love your neighbor as yourself." There is no other commandment greater than these. (Mark 12:30-31)**

As You Read the Scripture—Ralph W. Decker

Deuteronomy 6:4-9. These verses form a basic creed or statement of faith of the Hebrew religion. Many ancient rabbis considered this commandment

THIRD QUARTER

to be the most important of the 613 they found in their Scriptures. Jesus, when asked which commandment was the most important, replied, apparently without hesitation, by quoting from this passage (Matthew 22:24-40; Mark 12:29-34; Luke 10:27-28). Thus for both Jew and Christian, it is considered God's basic requirement. In Jewish practice it is known as the Shema, from its first word in Hebrew, which is translated "Hear."

Verse 4. As indicated in the margin of the Revised Standard Version, this statement is not readily translated. Literally, it consists of four words: "Yahweh, our God, Yahweh, one." The meaning, however, seems clear. There is one God, and that God is to receive all of Israel's devotion and worship.

Verse 5. The word "love" as used here is not to be confused with its use to denote the affection that exists between humans. It involves respect and reverence, but more than obedience based on duty and fear. It expresses wholehearted and obedient service.

Verse 6. The heart was considered to be the seat not only of affection and devotion but also of the human will.

Verse 7. Commitment to the will of God is to be the constant and decisive guide of life. Love toward God, expressed in obedience and reverence, is to be the central and constant aim of life.

Verse 8. These words were intended to urge constant attention to God's will. Many Jews take them literally and wear small leather, wood, or rock boxes containing small scrolls lettered with Deuteronomy 6:4-9 and other Scripture passages while they recite this passage.

Verse 9. Likewise, some Jews attach small containers of Scripture passages (called *mezzuzah*) to the frames of their main doors and touch them when entering or leaving the house.

Mark 12:28-37. This episode concerning the greatest commandment appears in the first three Gospels. However, Matthew (22:32-40) and Luke (10:25-28) treat it very differently from Mark. In those Gospels, the scribe, himself an interpreter of the law, is shown trying to trick Jesus into an unacceptable answer. In Mark he is presented as being impressed with Jesus' answers to the trick questions of the Sadducees and sincerely asking Jesus' opinion on a much-discussed question.

Verse 28. The scribes were professional interpreters and teachers of the law. This one, impressed by Jesus' answers to the difficult questions of the Sadducees, asked Jesus' opinion on a matter frequently discussed among the rabbis.

Verse 29. Jesus began his answer with the great creedal statement of Judaism (Deuteronomy 6:4-5), which expresses the unity of God.

Verse 30. It also calls for undivided loyalty to him. Jesus made a significant addition to the Deuteronomic command. It calls for loving God with one's heart, soul, and might; Jesus added "with all your mind."

Verse 31. It is widely accepted that Jesus was the first to link the command about loving one's neighbor (Leviticus 19:18) with the Deuteronomy passage.

Verses 32-33. The scribe responded favorably to Jesus' answer, calling him Teacher and restating his quotations from Deuteronomy and Leviticus.

Verse 34. Jesus commended the scribe upon his position. The discussion seems to have silenced the questioners.

APRIL 5   LESSON 6

Verses 35-37. Jesus now takes the offensive, challenging the questioners with questions. They taught that the messiah would be a descendant of David. Jesus quotes from Psalm 110, commonly attributed to David, in which the author calls the messiah his Lord. Jesus' messiahship does not depend upon a family relationship to a human king.

The Scripture and the Main Question—Pat McGeachy

A Test Question (Mark 12:28)

A scribe asked Jesus a question. The root meaning of the word "scribe" is "to write"; we spot it easily in words such as "inscribed" or "scribble," and perhaps less obviously in "prescription" and "scripture." In ancient times, before the invention of printing, scribes played a role of great importance, for all manuscripts had to be handwritten. Such copiers were highly prized because few people knew how to write. Much of their work was tedious and boring, but because they laboriously copied the important writings over and over, they eventually became deeply knowledgeable about them, even to the minutest details.

There were scribes among both the Sadducees and the Pharisees in Jesus' time, and they often hotly debated the fine points of the law. The question our particular scribe asked Jesus (which is the greatest commandment) was not an unusual one; it had been debated before, and no doubt will be in centuries yet to come. But it was a difficult and technical matter. To pick one of the Ten Commandments over the others was bound to produce a fierce debate that no one could win. Matthew (22:35) identifies this man as a lawyer (he could have been both a lawyer and a scribe) and tells us that he was deliberately trying to test Jesus.

But instead of picking one of the Ten Commandments, Jesus went to two other sources, both familiar to the Jews of his day: Deuteronomy 6:5 and Leviticus 19:18. In so doing, he completely avoided the trap of the trickster and opened instead a new line of understanding about the faith, which turns on our understanding of the word "love."

Vertical Love (Mark 12:29-30)

The first commandment is the one that goes up and down, like Jacob's ladder, between us and God, and might be seen as the upright post of Christ's cross. It calls us to right theology, right beliefs. The second commandment can be seen as the arms of the cross, reaching out on either side to neighbor and calling us to right practice, to ethical behavior. Together they form one great whole.

Mark's account of Jesus' answer, like Luke's (10:27), includes four words, whereas in the other references (Deuteronomy 6:5, Matthew 22:34) there are only three. But in all four cases the words mean "with your whole being." Sometimes we divided ourselves two ways (body and soul, cerebral and visceral) and sometimes three (body, mind, and spirit; thinking, feeling, willing). Mark's four-part division is

- Heart (the inner person)
- Soul (psyche; often translated "life")
- Mind (understanding)
- Strength (might, power, ability)

THIRD QUARTER

In short, there is no part of our lives that ought not to be dedicated wholly to the praise and service of God.

Horizontal Love (Mark 12:31)

This commandment is also found elsewhere in the Scriptures—in the other Gospel accounts of this testing, in Leviticus 19:18, of course, but also in Romans 13:9; Galatians 5:14; and James 2:8. It is clearly directed toward neighbor, but that word must be defined in very broad terms. In Luke 10:29-37, Jesus enlarges on the definition with a story known to every Sunday school student and makes sure we include even the despised Samaritan. But in this also he is not departing from the Hebrew Scriptures. We don't often notice Leviticus 19:34, which tells us that we should love *strangers* as ourselves.

Actually, a more literal translation of these words might be "You shall love your neighbor and the stranger *as one of your own.*" In other words, we are to treat all persons as part of our extended family under God. Sometimes you will hear this verse cited as evidence that we are to love ourselves, and certainly we should do that, for God loves us, and we should not treat ourselves any worse than God does, but that is not exactly what the old law is saying.

The Two Laws Hang Together

In summary, the two laws tell us that we are to love both God and our fellow human beings, with all our powers. They cannot be separated. This is most clearly stated in the simple language of 1 John 4:20-21: "If any one says, 'I love God,' and hates his brother, he is a liar; for he who does not love his brother whom he has seen, cannot love God whom he has not seen. And this commandment we have from him, that he who loves God should love his brother also." It doesn't get any plainer than that.

What, Then, Is Love?

There are four Greek words for love, known to many of us because of C. S. Lewis' helpful book, *The Four Loves.* To refresh your memory, they are:

1. *Storge,* affection, the natural love between puppies in the same litter, between parent and child, or between an elderly couple who have been together so long they have even begun to look like each other: You can't make this kind of love happen; it is something you are born with, or that comes along in its own time. A southern waitress, when told by the customer that he hadn't ordered grits with his breakfast, replied, "You don't order grits; grits jest comes." *Storge* is like grits.

2. *Philia,* friendship: (Some of the derivatives of this word include Philadelphia, "city of brotherly love," and all the words that end in "phile," such as "bibliophile" ("book-lover"). It's a little like grits too. Most of our deep friendships seem to happen *to* us, rather than the other way around. We naturally love those who are like us, those with whom we enjoy working and playing or those whose opposites complete ours (like Jack Spratt and his wife). It is true that in some sense we can try to "make" friends, but in fact, the best way to do this is to "be" friendly and take whatever gift of friendship comes our way.

3. Eros, passion or appetite: This comes like grits too, or maybe more like hot fudge cake or apple pie! The Romans personified it as Cupid and thought he went about shooting us with arrows. (Well, can you give a better explanation of why people fall in love?) As with friendship, we have some control over this passion; it is possible to make it happen, and sometimes necessary to cool it down, but in many cases it comes over us like a force from without.

4. Agape, charity: Here at last is love that is an act of the will. We have for the objects of our charity neither natural affection, companionship, nor passion. It is the one love we can control. And it is this that God commands of us. *Agape* is the word Jesus uses here. We are not commanded to like people, or to *feel* toward them any way in particular. We are commanded to will good for them, to wish them well, and to give them the gift of our selves, body, mind, and spirit.

On the surface it sounds sort of coldblooded. But to those who practice it, Christian charity soon passes into realms of joy that surpass even the delights of Venus. To those of you who have not yet experienced it, that may seem hard to believe. And it *is* difficult to explain. As the old hymn has it, "the love of Jesus, what it is, none but his loved ones know." And yet, to those who learn to love God and neighbor with genuine charity, like the charity with which God in Christ has first loved us (Romans 5:8; 1 John 4:10), the other three loves become transformed and deepened. Ordinary human relations between parent and child become symbols of God's relationship to us; so Jesus called God father. Human community is a symbol of God's relationship to us; so Jesus called us his friends (John 15:13-15). Even sexual love is such a symbol; so Jesus is called the bridegroom. And don't forget Hosea and his wife, or Jeremiah 31:32, or the happy ending to the love story in Revelation 21:2.

The great question is, What is more important than anything else? And the answer is, love. And if you want to know what kind of love, the answer is to be found in Jesus of Nazareth, who showed us what love is and enables us to love because he first loved us.

Helping Adults Become Involved—Roy H. Ryan

Preparing to Teach

Review the assignments you gave class members last week. Make sure to incorporate those assignments into today's lesson plan.

This lesson really gets at the heart of what Christianity is all about; love of God and love of neighbor are the centerpieces of Christian faith.

The aim of this lesson is to help us to answer rightly the question, Which is the first commandment? In other words, What is the essence of Christianity? If that law of love is written upon our hearts, all else will fall into place.

This law of love is built into the very heart of the universe. Love builds; hate destroys. If God is love, then we are called to be "in love" with God and our neighbors.

Think about what you will need before the class meets. Are there special supplies or resources that would help you teach more effectively? Make sure you have what you need.

Remember, your preparation has to be more than mental. If we are to

THIRD QUARTER

love God with heart, mind, soul, and strength, then your preparation to teach needs to incorporate all these dimensions of love. Put your mind into the preparation, but also put in your heart (emotions), your soul (inner being), and your strength (wisdom and physical energy).

A possible outline of the lesson could be as follows:

        I. Introduction.
       II. Loving God.
     III. Loving neighbor.
    IV. What is love?

Introducing the Main Question

Again, as in the previous lesson, the main question is quite obvious: Which commandment is first of all? How do you help members of the class face up to that profound question?

Try some of the different ways of stating the question, as suggested by Dr. McGeachy. How would a philosopher phrase it? A military person? A business person? Ask members of the class to share some ways they might ask the same question.

Try some of the different ways of stating the question, as suggested by Dr. McGeachy. How would a philosopher phrase it? A military person? A business person? Ask members of the class to share some ways they might ask the same question.

Share the information about how faithful Jews reminded themselves of the Shema. See Dr. Decker's exegesis of Deuteronomy 6:8-9. In what ways might we be constantly reminded of the centrality of this first great commandment for our lives?

Developing the Lesson

I. Introduction.

You might again have the main question posted in plain view for all class members to see as they enter the room: Which commandment is first of all?

Begin by asking the participants to think about what they put first in their lives. What, for each person in the class, is the greatest value in life? Perhaps some persons might be willing to share their responses. You could then lead a discussion about how we can know what really comes first in people's lives by the way they live.

II. Loving God.

Love of God necessarily comes first. Getting our "vertical" relationship in proper order then enables us to get our "horizontal" relationships straight. Loving God involves our whole being—mind, heart, soul, and strength. It means so ordering our lives that everything we say, think, or do shows forth our belief in God and our love for God.

If we love God, we will love that which comes from God. We will love all of God's creation, the earth and all that is in it, both human and animal life.

What are some ways we can show our love to God? Or, how can you tell if someone really loves God?

III. Loving neighbor.

Our horizontal relationships also give off signals about our real love of God. First John has stated it rather plainly: "How can you say you love God whom you have not seen if you do not love the brother [neighbor] whom you have seen?" It works both ways. We love God, and that enables us to love our neighbors. We love our neighbors, and that shows that we do indeed love God who created us all.

Who is our neighbor? That question is always being asked, even though we have a definitive answer in Scripture. It was asked of Jesus by a lawyer who wanted to put him to the test. See Luke 10:29-37, the famous story of the good Samaritan. That story tells us plainly who our neighbor is and how we ought to behave toward him. It is clear that our neighborhood takes in the whole of humankind. We are citizens of a global village in which every other human being is our neighbor in the spiritual sense.

How do we show love for our neighbor? Does this command also include strangers, the homeless, the foreigner?

IV. What is love?

Even if we know the answer to "who is my neighbor?" surely there must be some confusion about what love is. Love used in this passage is certainly more than affection or a sentimental feeling toward others. Read Dr. McGeachy's commentary on the four types of love. Help the class members understand the differences involved when we love with *agape* love. On our own we do not have the ability to love all persons. We like to pick and choose whom we will love. We do not find all persons attractive. We certainly do not find all persons likeable. How, then, can we truly love, even the unlovable? Is it humanly possible to love all persons?

Helping Class Members Act

Ask class members to identify in their own minds one individual (or group of persons) whom they do not like. Ask them to list for themselves all the reasons they do not like that person or group of persons. Then ask them to take a few minutes to pray for that person or group.

Finally, ask them if they will agree to take some positive step in the coming week to set their relationship right with that person or group, or if they will pray for them each day during the coming week.

Conclude the session with this prayer: Dear God, some persons are not easy to love. You never told us it would be easy to be one of your faithful disciples. Give us grace and strength to love even the unlovable. In Christ's name, Amen.

Planning for Next Sunday

Ask class members to be ready to report on some of their feelings as they carried out the assignment described above. Encourage them to read and study next Sunday's lesson.

LESSON 7   APRIL 12

Christ Died for You

Background Scripture: Mark 15:1-41

The Main Question—Pat McGeachy

A wonderful thing happened to me when I was a small boy—I got the measles. Maybe that doesn't sound very wonderful to you, but you must understand that as a boy I liked nothing so much as to be sick during the school term (provided it wasn't something itchy like chicken pox, or miserable like whooping cough). I could lie in bed all day, like a king, and read and draw and listen to soap operas. (Yes, we had them in the days before television, and they were better, I think, on the radio because your imagination could make them so real.) So I stayed home from school with a quarantine sign on the front door of my house, to keep out all pests, and looked forward to days and days of wonderful, luxurious leisure.

But suddenly it was all destroyed. The doctor came to call (they used to do that) armed with the biggest, ugliest needle I ever saw. How I hated needles! I broke into tears, sobbing to my mother, "It's not fair! You never told me there was going to be a shot!" All my fantasies about lazy luxury were transformed into a stabbing nightmare, and I would not be comforted.

And so the glad story of Jesus was turned from the joy of Christmas angels into the horror of that black Friday. Our advent has come to naught. We had thought and hoped (Luke 24:21) that he was the one to redeem Israel. But now look at the unfair trial, the brutal mocking of the innocent one, and the terrible execution. If I thought my selfish boyhood dreams had been shot down by a mere needle, how much more were all the dreams of humankind shot down by that hideous cross.

And yet we call that day *Good* Friday. How can that be? How could death ever be a good thing, even a peaceful one? "Where is the good in goodbye?" And that is our question: Can a scaffold be a throne? Or more personally: Is there any hope for your tragic life, and mine?

Selected Scripture

King James Version

Mark 15:22-39

22 And they bring him unto the place Golgotha, which is, being interpreted, The place of a skull.

23 And they gave him to drink wine mingled with myrrh: but he received *it* not.

24 And when they had crucified him, they parted his garments, casting lots upon them, what every man should take.

Revised Standard Version

Mark 15:22-39

22 And they brought him to the place called Golgotha (which means the place of a skull). 23 And they offered him wine mingled with myrrh; but he did not take it. 24 And they crucified him, and divided his garments among them, casting lots for them, to decide what each should take. 25 And it was the third hour, when they crucified him.

25 And it was the third hour, and they crucified him.
26 And the superscription of his accusation was written over, THE KING OF THE JEWS.
27 And with him they crucify two thieves; the one on his right hand, and the other on his left.
28 And the scripture was fulfilled, which saith, And he was numbered with the transgressors.
29 And they that passed by railed on him, wagging their heads, and saying, Ah, thou that destroyest the temple, and buildest *it* in three days,
30 Save thyself, and come down from the cross.
31 Likewise also the chief priests mocking said among themselves with the scribes, He saved others; himself he cannot save.
32 Let Christ the King of Israel descend now from the cross, that we may see and believe. And they that were crucified with him reviled him.
33 And when the sixth hour was come, there was darkness over the whole land until the ninth hour.
34 And at the ninth hour Jesus cried with a loud voice, saying, Eloi, Eloi, lama sabachthani? which is, being interpreted, My God, my God, why hast thou forsaken me?
35 And some of them that stood by, when they heard *it*, said, Behold, he calleth Elias.
36 And one ran and filled a sponge full of vinegar, and put *it* on a reed, and gave him to drink, saying, Let alone; let us see whether Elias will come to take him down.
37 And Jesus cried with a loud voice, and gave up the ghost.
38 And the veil of the temple was rent in twain from the top to the bottom.
39 And when the centurion, which stood over against him, saw that he so cried out, and gave up the ghost, he said, Truly this man was the Son of God.

26 And the inscription of the charge against him read, "The King of the Jews." 27 And with him they crucified two robbers, one on his right and one on his left. 29 And those who passed by derided him, wagging their heads, and saying, "Aha! You who would destroy the temple and build it in three days, 30 save yourself, and come down from the cross!" 31 So also the chief priests mocked him to one another with the scribes, saying, "He saved others; he cannot save himself. 32 Let the Christ, the King of Israel, come down now from the cross, that we may see and believe." Those who were crucified with him also reviled him.

33 And when the sixth hour had come, there was darkness over the whole land until the ninth hour. 34 And at the ninth hour Jesus cried with a loud voice, "Eloi, Eloi, lama sabachthani?" which means, "My God, my God, why hast thou forsaken me?" 35 And some of the bystanders hearing it said, "Behold, he is calling Elijah." 36 And one ran and, filling a sponge full of vinegar, put it on a reed and gave it to him to drink, saying, "Wait, let us see whether Elijah will come to take him down." 37 And Jesus uttered a loud cry, and breathed his last. 38 And the curtain of the temple was torn in two, from top to bottom. 39 And when the centurion, who stood facing him, saw that he thus breathed his last, he said, "Truly this man was a son of God!"

THIRD QUARTER

Key Verse: **When the centurion, which stood over against him, saw that he so cried out, and gave up the ghost, he said, Truly this man was the Son of God. (Mark 15:39)**

Key Verse: **When the centurion, who stood facing him, saw that he thus breathed his last, he said, "Truly this man was a son of God!" (Mark 15:39)**

As You Read the Scripture—Ralph W. Decker

Following the events of the previous lesson, the priests and scribes agreed that Jesus must be prevented from continuing his teaching (Mark 14:1). The cooperation of Judas made it possible to arrest Jesus at night in the Garden of Gethsemane. He was brought before an unofficial nighttime meeting of the Sanhedrin, the supreme court of Judaism. False witnesses failed to support the charge that Jesus had threatened to destroy the temple. The high priest then demanded to know if Jesus claimed to be the messiah. Although Jesus' affirmative answer was not blasphemous, Mark reports unanimous conviction on that charge, with a sentence of death.

Mark 15:1. The morning session of the Sanhedrin was official. Mark treats it as a consultation rather than as a trial. It was probably held to legalize the actions of the previous night. Deprived by Rome of the power to impose the death sentence, the court sent Jesus to Pilate as one accused, not condemned. The charge before Pilate was based on politics, not on religion.

Verse 2. Jesus was accused of claiming to be king of the Jews, a rival of the Roman emperor for the rule of Palestine. Jesus' reply to Pilate is hard to interpret. It may have been either the question "Do you say so?" or the comment "You said that, I didn't." In any case, it was ambiguous.

Verses 3-5. Pilate found himself with an innocent prisoner who refused to defend himself.

Verse 7. Nothing is known of Barabbas outside what is given here and in parallel sections of the other Gospels. He had participated in a revolt against Rome, killing one or more persons.

Verses 8-10. Pilate thought he could both honor the crowd's request and get rid of an innocent prisoner.

Verses 11-15. The demand for Barabbas put him in an awkward position. Fearing mob violence, he ordered Jesus' death.

Verses 16-20. A condemned prisoner had no civil rights. The soldiers could mistreat him as they wished. The palace was the Tower of Antonia, located in one corner of the temple court. It served as a barracks for Roman troops brought into Jerusalem in anticipation of trouble during Passover. A battalion was six hundred men.

Verse 17. The mistreatment of Jesus, "King of the Jews," was a mockery based on honors given a Roman emperor.

Verse 20. Crucifixion was a Roman punishment for slaves and rebels. It was primarily death by exposure, accompanied by hunger and thirst.

Verse 21. A condemned person was compelled to carry his own cross to the place of execution. Jesus, exhausted by mistreatment (verse 15), was unable to carry his. Simon was a Passover pilgrim from the Jewish colony in North Africa. The mention of his sons shows they were well known when Mark wrote.

Verse 22. Golgotha is the English form of an Aramaic word for skull. Its Latin form is *calvaria,* from which comes the English word "Calvary."

APRIL 12   LESSON 7

Verse 23. The myrrh mixed with wine would deaden pain. Jesus refused to die in a drugged condition.
Verse 24. Roman soldiers, not Jews, did the actual crucifying.
Verse 25. The third hour was 9:00 A.M.
Verse 26. The charge upon which Jesus was crucified was posted above his head.
Verse 27. It was customary to execute condemned prisoners in groups.
Verses 28-32. The mob that had called for crucifixion, including scribes and priests, witnessed the event and taunted Jesus while he was on the cross.
Verse 34. Jesus' cry is the opening line of Psalm 22, which begins with this cry of despair but closes with a word of confidence in God's goodness.
Verse 36. Scholars disagree about the soldier's intent. Pure vinegar would be another torture. A vinegar-based beverage, popular among Roman troops, would be an act of mercy.
Verse 37. The nature of the loud cry is uncertain. It could have indicated either despair or victory.
Verse 38. The destruction of the curtain that had kept people out of the Holy of Holies was a symbol that Jesus had direct access to God.
Verses 40-41. The three women who witnessed the death of Jesus are later named as the first to see the empty tomb and receive word of the resurrection (16:1).

The Scripture and the Main Question—Pat McGeachy

This familiar chapter speaks for itself. I am going to suggest that we let the Bible be its own commentary for these stark events by looking at the other parts of Scripture that cast light on them.

The Trial Before Pilate (Mark 15:1-5)

All night, as chapter 14 has told us, Jesus has been a prisoner of the Jewish authorities. In modern Jerusalem, beneath a building called the Church of the Crowing Cock, where some say the house of the high priest stood, guides will show you a dungeon into which the Lord is said to have been lowered for the night. But Mark's account seems to indicate that the trial before the high priest took place after it was very late, perhaps in the wee hours of the morning, so that Jesus may have been up all night, alternately held before the religious authorities and being ridiculed and beaten by their armed guards.

At any rate, when morning finally came (15:1), heralded by the crowing cock that confirmed Peter's shame, the whole assembly moved to the official residence of Pilate. The purpose of this second trial was clear: Capital punishment could only be carried out by Roman authority (John 18:31), and the religious leaders wanted Jesus dead. From what we know of Pontius Pilate, he was an essentially selfish person. He could be persuaded to stand for justice when it was politically helpful for him to do so, but he inclined to do whatever would win him favor in the eyes of the emperor Tiberius, who had appointed him, or the Jewish authorities, without whom he could not keep the peace in his province. In short, he was the kind of person who is always asking, "What's in it for me?"

But he was not without some sense of morality, because he did not accept the accusations of the religious leaders at face value. Instead, he puzzled

THIRD QUARTER

over their motives and was strangely moved by the man Jesus, as indicated by verse 5. The conversation between Jesus and Pilate, as Mark gives it, is very brief, consisting of only one terse comment by Jesus, followed by silence to all of Pilate's questions. Although we can never be sure just what order to arrange things in, it is interesting to try to reconstruct the whole conversation by quoting from all four of the Gospels. Perhaps the encounter went like this:

Pilate: Are you the king of the Jews?
Jesus: You have said so. (Mark 15:2)
Chief Priests: [Additional charges] (Mark 15:3)
Pilate: Are you the king of the Jews? (John 18:33)
Jesus: Do you say this of your own accord, or did others say it to you about me? (John 18:34)
Pilate: Am I a Jew? Your own nation and the chief priests have handed you over to me; what have you done? (John 18:35)
Jesus: My kingship is not of this world; if my kingship were of this world, my servants would fight, that I might not be handed over to the Jews; but my kingship is not of the world. (John 18:37)
Pilate: So you *are* a king?
Jesus: You say that I am a king. For this I was born, and for this I have come into the world, to bear witness to the truth. Everyone who is of the truth hears my voice. (John 18:37)
Pilate: What is truth? (John 18:38) [addresses the religious leaders again] I find no crime in him. But you have a custom that I should release one man for you at the Passover; will you have me release for you the king of the Jews? (John 18:38-39)
Religious leaders: Not this man, but Barabbas.
Pilate (to Jesus): Have you no answer to make? See how many charges they bring against you. (Mark 15:4)
Jesus: [Silence] (Mark 15:5)
Pilate: [Filled with wonder] (Mark 15:5)

Pilate and the Multitude (Mark 15:6-20)

Again, let us try to reconstruct the dialogue, using all four of the Gospels:

Pilate's Wife (Procla is her traditional name): Have nothing to do with that righteous man, for I have suffered much over him today in a dream. (Matthew 27:19)
Pilate (to the multitude): Do you want me to release for you the king of the Jews?
Multitude: Away with this man, and release to us Barabbas! (Luke 23:18)
Pilate: Then what shall I do with the man whom you call the king of the Jews? (Mark 15:12)
Multitude: Crucify him!
Pilate: Why, what evil has he done? I have found in him no crime deserving death; I will therefore chastise him and release him. (Luke 23:22)
Multitude: Crucify him!
Pilate: Take him yourselves and crucify him, for I find no crime in him! (John 19:6)

APRIL 12   LESSON 7

Religious Leaders: We have a law, and by that law he ought to die, because he has made himself the Son of God. (John 19:7)
Pilate (to Jesus): Where are you from? (John 19:9)
Jesus: [Silence] (John 19:9)
Pilate: You will not speak to me? Do you not know that I have power to release you and power to crucify you? (John 19:10)
Jesus: You would have no power over me unless it had been given to you from above; therefore he who delivered me to you has the greater sin. (John 19:11)
Pilate (washing his hands): I am innocent of this man's blood; see to it yourselves. (Matthew 27:24)
Multitude: His blood be on us and on our children! (Matthew 27:23) If you release this man you are not Caesar's friend; everyone who makes himself a king sets himself against Caesar. (John 19:13)
Pilate (indicating Jesus): Here is your king.
Multitude: Away with him! Crucify him!
Pilate: Shall I crucify your king?
Priests: We have no king but Caesar.

Then Pilate handed Jesus over to them to be crucified, and after being mocked, spit upon, and beaten, they led him away. According to John, there was one final word spoken by Pilate, after a complaint was made about the sign he had ordered placed on the cross: "What I have written, I have written." Tradition has it that he was never afterward able to feel that his hands were clean. There is a stronger tradition that soon after this, he committed suicide. In any case, for all his scheming, Pilate has been remembered throughout subsequent history whenever the Apostles' Creed is recited. Not even Judas has suffered such calumny.

The Crucifixion

According to Mark (and Matthew), the only other thing said by Jesus after this was the opening sentence of Psalm 22, followed by a loud cry just before he died. You may wish to read that Psalm, especially verses 7-8 and 16-18. It seems almost that the psalmist was a witness of these events. A psychologist once told me that Psalm 22 contains all of the symptoms of acute classical depression.

But you may also wish to read the other things said by Jesus as recorded in John (19:26-27, 28, 30) and Luke (23:28-31, 34, 43, 46). The last of those is also for a psalm, 31:5: "Father, into your hands I commit my spirit." In the language of the same Bible prayer book with which he had expressed his despair and agony, Jesus also expressed his hope and confidence.

Facing Death

As we have seen, Jesus, instead of having a tantrum, like I did over a silly shot, or as Dylan Thomas said we should ("Rage, rage against the dying of the light!"), faced his death in all the right ways, without hostility or defensiveness. Instead, he faced it with an honest admission of his own fears and doubts, with silence when it was appropriate (see Isaiah 53:7), with concern for others, with total disregard for his own safety, with complete courage in the presence of authority (see Matthew 10:17-20), and with utter

THIRD QUARTER

confidence in God. If you and I can confront our own mortality with such equanimity, we will not only die well but will have a foretaste of the Easter that lies beyond Good Friday, to which we will turn in our next lesson.

Helping Adults Become Involved—Roy H. Ryan

Preparing to Teach

This may be one of the most difficult lessons to teach in the whole of Scripture. The crucifixion of our Lord was the darkest day in human history. The Son of God was being killed like a common criminal.

As we approach Holy Week, we usually begin to sense both the tragedy and the triumph of the events that took place almost twenty centuries ago. For those of us who live on "this side of Calvary and the resurrection", the whole week is brought into proper perspective. But what about those contemporaries of Jesus, especially his followers and disciples, who had to experience the agony and the defeat, not knowing for sure that victory would be wrought?

How can you prepare yourself mentally and spiritually for teaching today's lesson? Give attention to that issue, and prepare yourself accordingly.

The aim of today's lesson is to help us understand how a scaffold can become a throne, how tragedy can be turned into triumph. We see this in the scripture lesson, and hopefully we can begin to see it in our own lives. There is hope, even in moments of tragedy and despair.

Give some thought to how you will incorporate any assignments you gave last week. Will you call for reports on what persons did in regard to ways they might learn to love and serve those whom they do not like?

Think about any supplies or equipment you may need. Be sure your room is prepared appropriately for your method of teaching (arrangement of chairs, etc.).

A possible outline for the lesson would be as follows:

      I. Introduction
     II. The trial before Pilate
    III. Pilate and the multitude
    IV. The crucifixion

Introducing the Main Question

It may be a little more difficult to identify the main question in this lesson as compared to recent ones. Dr. McGeachy suggests that the main question is twofold: (1) Can a scaffold be a throne? and (2), Is there any hope for your tragic life, and mine?

How will you help class members face the main question? How shall it be posed? What will speak to their innermost beings as they are confronted with the death of Jesus Christ?

Ask: How do you feel when you hear of an innocent person who has been imprisoned? Or: How do you feel when a perfectly good person has to suffer humiliation and pain that seem so unjust? Involve the class members in facing the question at a "feeling" level, not just a rational level.

APRIL 12   LESSON 7

Developing the Lesson

I. Introduction

You may want to put into your own words the story of those last two tragic days of Holy Week. Mark 15:1-41 gives a rather detailed account.

Another possibility would be to ask someone from the class (whom you have asked in advance) to briefly recount what happened. If you have a good storyteller in your class, you might enlist his or her help.

You might share some of your deep feelings out of your experience of living with this scripture and of preparing to teach it. Let the class members know what has been going on with you as you have prepared for today's lesson.

II. The trial before Pilate

The Sanhedrin conducted a trial before they turned Jesus over to Pilate. Why did they turn him over to Pilate? Basically because they wanted him dead, and they did not have the power to execute anyone. That was left to the civil authority of Rome. The religious council (Sanhedrin) accused him of blasphemy because he had claimed to be the messiah. They found him guilty. That was deserving of the penalty of death under their laws, but they had no power to execute the law because the law of Rome prevailed.

Pilate tried to escape responsibility for Jesus. He really wanted nothing to do with him. He would have much preferred the religious leaders to take care of him themselves. But he is thrust in the middle of a religious conflict. In order for Pilate to take the case, the leaders had charged Jesus with sedition (claiming to be king). Everyone knew that the emperor was king!

What was Pilate's part in this whole nasty event? Why did he not want to become involved?

III. Pilate and the multitude

Pilate turned to the crowd, hoping they would help him get out of a sticky situation. It was his custom to release one prisoner at the time of Passover. He hoped they would call for the release of Jesus. They did not, however. They called for his crucifixion.

Pilate tried to wash his hands of the affair, both literally and figuratively. He did not want innocent blood on his hands. He was accustomed to dealing with common criminals, and he did not mind meting out justice where it was due. But he saw no justice in crucifying Jesus. He was now caught in a no-win situation. He gave in to the cry of the crowd instead of being guided by his own instincts and better judgment. He was, in that sense, not unlike a lot of us.

If you had been in Pilate's place, what would you have done?

IV. The crucifixion

It was a humiliating, agonizing way to die—suspended on a cross, between two common thieves, crowned with a plait of thorns, called "King of the Jews" in derision, scoffed at by the soliders, mistreated, killed.

What about out own death? How will we face it? Will we be like Jesus and commit ourselves into the hands of God?

THIRD QUARTER

Helping Class Members Act

What is our response to what Jesus Christ has done for us? As Christians, we believe that "his sacrifice on the cross was sufficient for the sins of the whole world." That includes us, so we can truly say, "Christ died for me."

Ask class members to reflect on what Jesus' death means to them personally. Also, have them think about how they will face their own death, what role their faith will play in that final act of life's drama.

End the lesson with this prayer: We thank you, God, for Jesus Christ, who loved us and gave himself for us. Help us to be worthy of his love and sacrifice. Amen.

Planning for Next Sunday

Ask class members to concentrate on their devotional lives this week and to come next Sunday prepared to join in celebrating the victory we have in Christ.

LESSON 8　　　　　　　　　　　　　　　　　　　　　　　　APRIL 19

Death Is Not the End

Background Scripture: Mark 15:42–16:8

The Main Question—Pat McGeachy

Do you remember how old you were when it first dawned on you that you were not immortal? As a baby, you were an emperor with absolute powers: When you were uncomfortable, all you had to do was yell, and someone hurried to feed you or hold you or change you. Only gradually did you discover that there were limits to your authority. You must wait for supper, you must share your toys, you may not shout "Fire!" in a crowded theater. Finally, at some moment in your life, it dawns on you that the universe really doesn't care much about you at all. You are an antlike creature on a tiny planet. Soon you will be gone, and eventually forgotten. It is a chilling thought.

Such a thought first came to me when I was about ten years old, riding to school on my bicycle. I went blithely along, cheerful, oblivious, and immortal. Suddenly, as I turned a corner, I heard the terrifying screech of brakes and a car whizzed by me with inches to spare, its driver cursing, more in fright than anger. I ended up in a ditch beside the road, unhurt but never to be the same again. From that moment on, the ominous thought began to grow within me: One day, Pat, you will be dead.

And yet I have to remind myself of it, even now. It is so hard to face that I don't want to think about it. It's not fair! I don't want it to happen. But I know it will. So I have another question to ask, and it is the main question of

APRIL 19　　　　　　　　　　　　　　　　　　　　　LESSON 8

this lesson. If death lies inevitably at the end of your life and mine, then what is the point?

"I came," said Jesus (John 10:10), "that they may have life, and have it abundantly." But if we are honest, isn't death all around us? How can Jesus' promise be taken seriously? How shall you and I confront death as the followers of the Lord of Life?

Selected Scripture

King James Version

Mark 15:42-47

42 And now when the even was come, because it was the preparation, that is, the day before the sabbath,

43 Joseph of Arimathea, an honourable counsellor, which also waited for the kingdom of God, came, and went in boldly unto Pilate, and craved the body of Jesus.

44 And Pilate marvelled if he were already dead: and calling *unto him* the centurion, he asked him whether he had been any while dead.

45 And when he knew *it* of the centurion, he gave the body to Joseph.

46 And he bought fine linen, and took him down, and wrapped him in the linen, and laid him in a sepulchre which was hewn out of a rock, and rolled a stone unto the door of the sepulchre.

47 And Mary Magdalene and Mary *the mother* of Joses beheld where he was laid.

Mark 16:1-8

1 And when the sabbath was past, Mary Magdalene, and Mary the *mother* of James, and Salome, had bought sweet spices, that they might come and anoint him.

2 And very early in the morning the first *day* of the week, they came unto the sepulchre at the rising of the sun.

3 And they said among themselves, Who shall roll us away the

Revised Standard Version

Mark 15:42-47

42 And when evening had come, since it was the day of Preparation, that is, the day before the sabbath, 43 Joseph of Arimathea, a respected member of the council, who was also himself looking for the kingdom of God, took courage and went to Pilate, and asked for the body of Jesus. 44 And Pilate wondered if he were already dead; and summoning the centurion, he asked him whether he was already dead. 45 And when he learned from the centurion that he was dead, he granted the body to Joseph. 46 And he bought a linen shroud, and taking him down, wrapped him in the linen shroud, and laid him in a tomb which had been hewn out of the rock; and he rolled a stone against the door of the tomb. 47 Mary Magdalene and Mary the mother of Joses saw where he was laid.

Mark 16:1-8

1 And when the sabbath was past, Mary Magdalene, and Mary the mother of James, and Salome, bought spices, so that they might go and anoint him. 2 And very early on the first day of the week they went to the tomb when the sun had risen. 3 And they were saying to one another, "Who will roll away the stone for us from the door of the tomb?" 4 And looking up, they saw that the

stone from the door of the sepulchre?

4 And when they looked, they saw that the stone was rolled away: for it was very great.

5 And entering into the sepulchre, they saw a young man sitting on the right side, clothed in a long white garment; and they were affrighted.

6 And he saith unto them, Be not affrighted: Ye seek Jesus of Nazareth, which was crucified: he is risen; he is not here: behold the place where they laid him.

7 But go your way, tell his disciples and Peter that he goeth before you into Galilee: there shall ye see him, as he said unto you.

8 And they went out quickly, and fled from the sepulchre; for they trembled and were amazed: neither said they any thing to any *man;* for they were afraid.

stone was rolled back; for it was very large. 5 And entering the tomb, they saw a young man sitting on the right side, dressed in a white robe; and they were amazed. 6 And he said to them, "Do not be amazed; you seek Jesus of Nazareth, who was crucified. He has risen, he is not here; see the place where they laid him. 7 But go, tell his disciples and Peter that he is going before you to Galilee; there you will see him, as he told you." 8 And they went out and fled from the tomb; for trembling and astonishment had come upon them; and they said nothing to any one, for they were afraid.

Key Verse: **He saith unto them, Be not affrighted: Ye seek Jesus of Nazareth which was crucified: he is risen; he is not here: behold the place where they laid him. (Mark 16:6)**

Key Verse: **He said to them, "Do not be amazed; you seek Jesus of Nazareth, who was crucified. He has risen, he is not here; see the place where they laid him." (Mark 16:6)**

As You Read the Scripture—Ralph W. Decker

Mark 15:42. Since the Jewish sabbath coincides with our Saturday, the Day of Preparation would coincide with out Friday. According to Mark, Jesus was crucified about 9:00 A.M. ("the third hour," 15:25), hung on the cross about six hours, and died about 3:00 P.M. ("the ninth hour," 15:33). The Day of Preparation ended at sunset on Friday, at which time the sabbath began. It was contrary to Jewish law for the bodies of executed criminals to remain unburied on the sabbath. The Romans had no such regulation and allowed dead bodies to remain on their crosses until they rotted away. Because of the earlier demonstrations by the Passover crowds (15:11-14), Pilate may have granted Joseph's request to avoid trouble.

Verse 43. Joseph of Arimathea is generally regarded as a member of the Sanhedrin, but it is difficult to reconcile his gracious act with the vote of that body, reported to be unanimous (14:64). Differences of opinion have led some to suggest that Joseph was a member of a lesser council in his home town, and others to suggest that the manner of Jesus' dying had changed his mind. At the very least, he may have been acting as a devout Jew who wished to save the area from the ritual pollution of an unburied body on a sabbath that was also a feast day.

APRIL 19 LESSON 8

Verse 44. That Pilate should have questioned the report that Jesus was already dead is no surprise. Crucifixion was basically death by prolonged exposure and suffering on a cross; it often took several days for the person to die.

Verse 45. Pilate granted Joseph's request, probably as a step toward preventing violent demonstrations among the hundreds of pilgrims in Jerusalem for the Passover. John reports that the Roman soldiers made sure their victims were dead by breaking the legs of the two thieves and stabbing Jesus in the side.

Verse 46. By entombment of the body of Jesus, even though hurried and incomplete, Joseph saved the area from pollution by a dead body on a sabbath that was also a feast day.

Verse 47. Mary Magdalene and Mary the Mother of Joses are identified as eyewitnesses to the burial of Jesus. (Earlier, in 15:40, they were named as eyewitnesses to the burial of Jesus. (Earlier, in 15:40, they were named as eyewitnesses of the crucifixion, along with Salome). That they were such is important in view of the suggestion that they had gone to the wrong tomb in the semidarkness of early morning.

Mark 16:1-2. On the morning of the first day of the week (our Sunday), three of the women who had witnessed the crucifixion went to the tomb to complete the hurried burial of Friday afternoon. The sabbath had ended at sunset the evening before.

Verses 3-4. The women's concern about being able to open the tomb is underlined by Mark's report that the stone that closed it was "very large."

Mark's account of their discovery is very brief. It describes only the empty tomb, not the resurrection. But the words of the young man in the tomb (Matthew 28:5 identifies him as an angel) are clear and conclusive.

Verse 6. As evidence of the resurrection, the young man said, in effect, "You are looking for Jesus. He was here. He is not here now. See for yourselves." His explanation, "He is risen," is given in one dramatic word in Greek. It has become the basis for the Christian faith.

Verse 7. Although a reunion of the risen Christ with his disciples in Galilee is promised, no resurrection appearances of Jesus are reported by Mark.

Verse 8. In the oldest manuscripts the Gospel according to Mark ends abruptly, possibly in the middle of a sentence, indicating that the final section has been lost. Two endings, one much shorter than the other, have been attached to make up the loss.

The Scripture and the Main Question—Pat McGeachy

The Tomb (Mark 15:42-46)

In all cultures the burial of the dead is an important rite. There are variations of it, of course: entombment of the body above ground, after the custom of the Egyptians, or the burial of ashes after cremation, but whatever the details, no culture is without its traditions of respect for the dead and the proper disposal of their bodies. Most of them began as a matter of necessity: to keep away wild beasts and to prevent odor and disease. But always there has been attached to them a sense of tender care for the dead. Most cultures instinctively cover bodies at once; if there is not a sheet or blanket available, someone will donate a shirt or jacket. Even with

THIRD QUARTER

regard to criminals it was considered unlawful by the Hebrews to leave a dead body hanging in a tree overnight (see Deuteronomy 21:22-23). Strictly speaking, Jesus, being crucified as a criminal, was not entitled to honorable burial.

But there was a wealthy man among the disciples, one Joseph of Arimathea, who cared deeply about what would be done with the body. This Joseph is mentioned in each of the four Gospels, and in all four only at the account of Jesus' burial. Apparently he had been quiet up until now, being a respected member of the Sanhedrin, but a believer. Luke (23:51) tells us that he had not consented to the death of Jesus. Now that the deed has been done, when you would expect him to give up and write Jesus off, something gave him the courage to go to Pilate and risk his reputation by asking for the body. And when Pilate learned from the centurion that Jesus was dead, he granted the body to Joseph, who laid him in a rock tomb.

Matthew (27:60) tells us that it was Joseph's own brand new tomb, and John (19:39) that Nicodemus, also a wealthy secret disciple, assisted him with the burial, using an enormous quantity of spices. The anointing of bodies surely had it beginnings for the most earthy reasons, but it had come to be a sign of respect, or even of a hoped-for miraculous recovery through healing. Consider the present-day practice of some Christians to anoint with oil in the giving of last rites, and remember what Jesus said to the woman who poured the expensive nard upon his head (Mark 14:8). As we shall see in the next chapter, there was further anointing to take place.

The courageous act of Joseph, in taking his stand with the dead Christ, is seen as a fulfillment of the prophecy in Isaiah 53:9, "And they made his grave . . . with a rich man in his death." But beyond that, it leaves us with hope. Most of those who will be reading these words are, by the world's standards, as wealthy as Joseph was. May God grant that we too will have the courage to follow Jesus, even when all seems to be lost, and to do the right thing with no hope of reward (Luke 6:35).

The Women (Mark 15:47–16:1)

Women have been prominent in Jesus' ministry all along (Luke is good at reporting about them; see Luke 8:2-3), but all four Gospels make it clear that they were especially present at Jesus' death. Indeed, it was because of their participation in his death that they became witnesses to his resurrection (Philippians 3:10-11). The women mentioned here are

- Mary Magdalene (see Luke 8:2).
- Mary the mother of James the less (which may refer either to his age or his stature), one of the twelve, and his brother Joses.
- Salome, wife of Zebedee and mother of John and the other apostle James.

In addition, Luke 24:10 mentions Joanna, wife of Chuza, Herod's steward, who was one of the well-to-do women of Luke 8:3, plus other unidentified women.

In his account John describes a major role for Mary Magdalene, ignoring the others (John 20:1-18). In John's version she really becomes the first of the apostles, if by that word we mean "one sent to bear testimony to the risen Christ" (John 20:17). It is because of that passage that she had been

APRIL 19 LESSON 8

depicted ever since in Christian art as one who is weeping, and her very name has given us the English word "maudlin," meaning "lugubrious" or "overly tearful."

Whichever of the four Gospel accounts you like best, the total picture is one in which women play a primary role, both in grieving over the death and rejoicing over the resurrection. One of the radical things about Jesus was his attitude toward women, whom he included fully among his friends (remember the Mary and Martha stories, and also Galatians 3:28). Because of the times in which they lived, women had to stay in the background for much of the story, but here at the end, as is often the case, it is the women, not the men, who are with Jesus in his last bitter hours. And because of their faithfulness, it is they who discover the empty tomb and are entrusted with the good news of the resurrection (Mark 16:8).

The Empty Tomb (Mark 16:2-8)

Mark's Gospel is strange in some ways. Almost certainly the earliest of the four, it both begins and ends abruptly. At the beginning it says nothing of the birth stories but starts with John the Baptist. It contains no mention of a miraculous birth and no details of Jesus' baptism and temptation. By the time we get to verse 14 of the first chapter, we are already dealing with Jesus' preaching ministry. And if it does in fact end at 16:8 (almost all scholars agree that the remaining verses, which do not appear in the earliest manuscripts, are the work of another writer), it leaves us hanging with the strange words, "and they said nothing to any one, for they were afraid."

But that is the way the Christian life always seems to be. It is never neat as we would want it to be. Rare is the person who grows up normally in a good Christian home, is baptized in the nurture and admonition of the Lord, goes to Sunday school every week, is confirmed during a trouble-free adolescence, and goes on to live a model Christian life. That may be the ideal we all should strive for, but nearly every Christian I know, like Bunyan's Pilgrim, is beset along the way with doubts and difficulties. Instead of the neat pattern described above, we experience broken homes, adolescent rebellion, dramatic conversions, prodigal journeys into far countries, bad marriages, and untimely ends.

If we are honest, we know that we have doubts and difficulties. However, with the little Gospel according to Mark, we can come to understand how to deal with these. When times get tough and things grow dark, God seems far away and our prayers bounce off the ceiling, that is the time to get up early, and, against all logic, collect our spices and go with the women to the tomb. As we go, we may well ask, "Who will roll away the stone for us from the door of the tomb?"

But that is because we reckon without the power of God. When we arrive, we will find the stone rolled away and a young man in white standing within. "Do not be amazed," he will say. "You seek Jesus of Nazareth, who was crucified. He has risen, he is not here; go and tell others." This vision is promised to all those who follow Jesus. If you do not see it at first, get up and go anyway. Go to dark Gethsemane and learn from Jesus how to pray. Go to the judgment hall and learn from him how to bear the cross. Go to Calvary and learn from him how to die.

THIRD QUARTER

> Early hasten to the tomb
> where they laid his breathless clay;
> All is solitude and gloom;
> Who hath taken him away?
> Christ is risen! He meets our eyes.
> Saviour, teach us so to rise.
> ("Go to Dark Gethsemane")

The burial of our dead is important, for we must come to terms with reality. But we must not concentrate on plastic flowers and artificial grass. We must face death with all the honesty we can muster, for only through Good Friday can we come to Easter. May God give us the courage of Joseph of Arimathea, and those women.

Helping Adults Become Involved—Roy H. Ryan

Preparing to Teach

This, the most glorious day of the Christian year, affords a wonderful opportunity to affirm our deepest belief that Jesus is risen from the dead. This affirmation is at the center of our faith as Christians. If Christ had not been raised, as Paul said, "then our faith would be vain and we of all people would be most miserable."

As you prepare to teach, you will want to read and meditate on the Easter story. You may want to read the story in Matthew 28:1-10 and Luke 24:1-12. These accounts are longer than Mark's and give a few more details that we have come to associate with the Easter story.

The title of our lesson today, "Death Is Not the End," is the most wonderful news human beings could ever hear. Be prepared to help class members celebrate this good news. You might ask a few of them to share what Easter means to them.

The aim of this lesson is to enable us to confront life and death as those who have faith in Jesus Christ as Lord and who believe his promises.

A possible outline might be as follows:

> I. Introduction
> II. The tomb
> III. The women
> IV. The empty tomb

Introducing the Main Question

By the time we become middle aged, most of us have finally come to grips with the reality that we are not immortal, that we will some day die. There will be an end to our earthly existence. Most people prefer not to think about that too much, and with good reason; it can be very depressing—unless we believe that God did not create us to die but to live. In Jesus Christ we hear God's word of hope, and we see it evidenced in his resurrection from the dead.

Since your class is made up of adults, it should not be too difficult to confront the main question, How shall you and I confront death as the followers of the Lord of Life?

APRIL 19 — LESSON 8

Some members of your class may have had some close calls with death and can share firsthand experience of what that feels like. By now, all of us as adults have experienced death in our families and among close friends. Death is no stranger to us, even if we have not faced up to our own death.

However, this is not a day to be morbid about death but to celebrate life in the midst of death.

Developing the Lesson

I. Introduction

Much of the material in the two sections above could be used to help you introduce the lesson. Do not dwell on death, acknowledge it and move on to the meaning of this day for Christians. Today the subject is *life*!

II. The tomb

The first thing we note in the Scripture lesson is the kindness of Joseph of Arimathea. Whatever his motive (see Dr. Decker's exegesis of these verses), the fact remains that he did a very decent thing. He was a man of some note among the Jews, perhaps a member of the Sanhedrin. He must have had some sympathy with what Jesus had taught. He may have also been impressed with the way he died.

Jesus had told his disciples early in his ministry that "the Son of Man has no place to lay his head." This was obviously true for him in death as well as in life. He is laid to rest in a borrowed tomb. Joseph has his body wrapped in a linen cloth, puts the body in a hewn-out tomb, and rolls a large rock against the door.

What do you think prompted Joseph to request the body of Jesus and to go to a great deal of trouble to entomb it?

III. The women

Three women, according to Mark, came to the tomb early Sunday morning to anoint his body and to thus complete the preparation for burial. These same women were reported to have been present when Jesus was crucified.

These faithful women became the first eyewitnesses to the empty tomb. (Again, you may want to read the parallel accounts in Matthew and Luke in order to get more details.) It is important to note that women played an important role in early Christianity. That fact is sometimes overlooked.

How must these faithful women have felt when they discovered the tomb was empty?

IV. The empty tomb

Mark's account is sketchy. Many scholars believe that Mark's Gospel ends with 16:8 and that what follows in our version was added centuries later. In any case, Mark gets to the point. The tomb was empty. Jesus' body was not there. Our faith is not based simply on an empty tomb, because that does not guarantee resurrection. We do not say in our creed, "I believe in an empty tomb"; rather, we affirm, "I believe in the resurrection of the body."

When we come up against hard times, when death and defeat seem to be our lot, God comes into the human equation and turns it in our favor. We are not born to die but to live. We are not born to merely exist—we are born to experience "abundant life." God has created us for life, and the

THIRD QUARTER

resurrection of Jesus is God's sure sign that we too have the promise of life in him.

What is the basis of our hope as Christians?

Helping Class Members Act

It would be appropriate to take a few minutes to reflect on the unit of study that concludes today. Ask class members to share some of the learnings or new insights they have gained from this unit.

The message of today's lesson is about life, about celebration, about abundant living in the midst of all kind of difficulties.

Help the class members assess what they each have to celebrate on this special day.

Lead the class in a prayer of thanksgiving. You might use the following prayer (or one that comes out of your own heart and experience): God of life, we thank you for Jesus Christ, for his victory over death. We thank you for the promise of life in him. We praise you for your wonderful works of creation and for the joyful hope you have placed in our hearts today. In the name of the resurrected Lord, even Jesus Christ, Amen.

Planning for Next Sunday

Briefly introduce the new course, "God's People in the World," which begins with next Sunday's lesson. The scripture lesson is 1 Peter 1:3-9, 13-21. The topic, "The Gift of Living Hope," builds on the topics of previous lessons.

COURSE 2: God's People in the World
Horace R. Weaver

SIX LESSONS   **APRIL 26–MAY 31**

There are six lessons in this course, and they provide a series of post-Easter lessons based on 1 and 2 Peter. As the first course of two units provided a study of the Gospel of Mark, so this second course is a study of the gospel of Peter.

A description of each of the six lessons follows: "The Gift of Living Hope," April 26, asks: What are we to believe and do as followers of Jesus Christ? "Called to Be God's People," May 3 asks: Who am I meant to be? "Witnessing in Suffering," May 10, seeks to help class members come to some witness to their faith in Christ through suffering. "Excellent Exhortations," May 17, offers a great challenge: How can adults exert leadership in the church but at the same time remain humble servants of Christ? "Growing in Grace," May 24, helps adult Christians see the need for continuing growth and helps them consider some practical ways to continue their spiritual quest. "Living in Light of the Future," May 31, suggests that Christian adults think about their view of history in light of God's will and purpose.

LESSON 9   APRIL 26

The Gift of Living Hope

Background Scripture: 1 Peter 1:1-25

The Main Question—Pat McGeachy

I have been writing United Methodist Bible study helps for more than fifteen years, so perhaps it is time to confess that I was not born a Methodist but a Presbyterian. The difference between the two is not so great, but, whereas John Wesley was strangely warmed at Aldersgate, I think John Calvin must have been strangely chilled in Geneva. At any rate, the two denominations have long had a traditional argument with each other about the place of faith and works in the Christian life.

It has been good for me to become an honorary Methodist, because I have come to believe that such an argument is largely a waste of time. We can cite verses that seem to side with works (James 2:17-18) and those that seem to side with faith (Ephesians 2:8-9). But we can also find plenty that seem to include both, such as Philippians 2:12-13: "Work out your own salvation with fear and trembling; for God is at work in you, both to will and to work for his good pleasure."

The truth is, I think, that the Christian life is not so much a matter of believing or doing as it is of *being*. As we begin this study of 1 and 2 Peter, we are dealing with instructions to struggling Christians, suffering under persecution and wondering how they are to cope. The question that they are asking is "What are we to believe and how are we to act, in order to survive in this wicked world?"

It is a good question, and just as relevant in our time as in the days of the New Testament church, and now, as then, I believe the answer will come to us not so much in terms of right doctrine, though that is certainly what we desire, or right behavior, though that is certainly what we ought to have, as in terms of *being the people of the resurrection*. So I will rephrase our question in that way: How are you and I to live, as disciples of the risen Lord? Let us see what the Big Fisherman will advise us.

Selected Scripture

King James Version

1 Peter 1:3-9, 13-21

3 Blessed *be* the God and Father of our Lord Jesus Christ, which according to his abundant mercy hath begotten us again unto a lively hope by the resurrection of Jesus Christ from the dead,

4 To an inheritance incorruptible, and undefiled, and that fadeth not away, reserved in heaven for you,

Revised Standard Version

1 Peter 1:3-9, 13-21

3 Blessed be the God and Father of our Lord Jesus Christ! By his great mercy we have been born anew to a living hope through the resurrection of Jesus Christ from the dead, 4 and to an inheritance which is imperishable, undefiled, and unfading, kept in heaven for you, 5 who by God's power are guarded through faith for a salvation ready

THIRD QUARTER

5 Who are kept by the power of God through faith unto salvation ready to be revealed in the last time.

6 Wherein ye greatly rejoice, though now for a season, if need be, ye are in heaviness through manifold temptations:

7 That the trial of your faith, being much more precious than of gold that perisheth, though it be tried with fire, might be found unto praise and honour and glory at the appearing of Jesus Christ:

8 Whom having not seen, ye love; in whom, though now ye see *him* not, yet believing, ye rejoice with joy unspeakable and full of glory:

9 Receiving the end of your faith, *even* the salvation of *your* souls.

....

13 Wherefore gird up the loins of your mind, be sober, and hope to the end for the grace that is to be brought unto you at the revelation of Jesus Christ;

14 As obedient children, not fashioning yourselves according to the former lusts in your ignorance:

15 But as he which hath called you is holy, so be ye holy in all manner of conversation;

16 Because it is written, Be ye holy; for I am holy.

17 And if ye call on the Father, who without respect of persons judgeth according to every man's work, pass the time of your sojourning *here* in fear:

18 Forasmuch as ye know that ye were not redeemed with corruptible things, *as* silver and gold, from your vain conversation *received* by tradition from your fathers;

19 But with the precious blood of Christ, as of a lamb without blemish and without spot:

20 Who verily was foreordained before the foundation of the world, but was manifest in these last times for you,

to be revealed in the last time. 6 In this you rejoice, though now for a little while you may have to suffer various trials, 7 so that the genuineness of your faith, more precious than gold which though perishable is tested by fire, may redound to praise and glory and honor at the revelation of Jesus Christ. 8 Without having seen him you love him; though you do not now see him you believe in him and rejoice with unutterable and exalted joy. 9 As the outcome of your faith you obtain the salvation of your souls.

....

13 Therefore gird up your minds, be sober, set your hope fully upon the grace that is coming to you at the revelation of Jesus Christ. 14 As obedient children, do not be conformed to the passions of your former ignorance, 15 but as he who called you is holy, be holy yourselves in all your conduct; 16 since it is written, "You shall be holy, for I am holy." 17 And if you invoke as Father him who judges each one impartially according to his deeds, conduct yourselves with fear throughout the time of your exile. 18 You know that you were ransomed from the futile ways inherited from your fathers, not with perishable things such as silver or gold, 19 but with the precious blood of Christ, like that of a lamb without blemish or spot. 20 He was destined before the foundation of the world but was made manifest at the end of the times for your sake. 21 Through him you have confidence in God, who raised him from the dead and gave him glory, so that your faith and hope are in God.

APRIL 26   LESSON 9

21 Who by him do believe in God, that raised him up from the dead, and gave him glory; that your faith and hope might be in God.

Key Verse: Blessed be the God and Father of our Lord Jesus Christ, which according to his abundant mercy hath begotten us again unto a lively hope by the resurrection of Jesus Christ from the dead. (1 Peter 1:3)

Key Verse: Blessed be the God and Father of our Lord Jesus Christ! By his great mercy we have been born anew to a living hope through the resurrection of Jesus Christ from the dead. (1 Peter 1:3)

As You Read the Scripture—Ralph W. Decker

First and Second Peter belong to a group of New Testament books known as catholic (universal) or general letters, written to the entire church rather than to a single church or individual.

1 Peter 1:1. Following the crucifixion and resurrection of Jesus, Peter became leader of the Christian community during the critical period of its early existence (Acts 1–12). After a brief imprisonment in Jerusalem, he disappears from the Scripture record (Acts 12:17). Tradition says he preached in Syria, Asia Minor, Greece, and finally in Rome, where he was martyred during the persecutions under Nero (A.D. 64–65). In calling himself an apostle, the author gives his authority for writing. The intended readers were exiles in the sense that they were residents of earth whose true homeland was heaven. They were the Christian Dispersion, analogous to the Jewish Dispersion, Jews who had scattered (dispersed) from Palestine throughout other lands. The five place names are those of Roman provinces, together comprising Asia Minor.

Verse 2. The reference to Jesus' blood reflects the custom of sprinkling the Ark of the Covenant with animal blood as a sign of the repentance of the Israelites. This verse contains the elements of the doctrine of the Trinity—Father, Spirit, Jesus Christ. Greeks usually began letters with the word "greeting" (Acts 15:23; 23:26; James 1:1). Peter substitutes words with religious meaning: grace (the unmerited love of God) and peace (the proper relationship with God).

Verses 3-9. The complex doctrinal statements of this paragraph may be summarized in two points: (1) Jesus' resurrection gives hope that the faithful will obtain a heavenly salvation and (2) sufferings test and purify the faith by which persons enter that salvation.

Verse 3. The combination of two titles with his name shows the belief of the early church concerning Jesus. "Christ" is the English form of the Greek *Christos,* which translates the Hebrew "Messiah." "Lord" throughout the Old Testament refers to God. The phrase "born anew" reflects the experience of Peter. He was a different person following the resurrection.

Verse 4. The land of Canaan was the inheritance of Israel (Deuteronomy 15:4; 19:10). The author promises a better one for Christians—an eternal one.

Verse 5. Early Christians believed the end of the age was near at hand.
Verse 6. The phrase "may have to suffer" suggests that Asia Minor

THIRD QUARTER

Christians were not yet being persecuted but that the trouble at Rome would spread to them. This would date the letter at about A.D. 62–63.

Verse 7. Perseverance under persecution will win the favor of God.

Verse 8. The readers had not known Jesus in the flesh.

Verse 9. The present tense of "obtain" indicates that salvation can be experienced here and now.

Verses 10-12. Early Christians found many references to Christ and his saving act in the Old Testament. Here, Peter says that predictions concerning a savior have been fulfilled.

Verses 13-21. This is a call to holy living. Girding is related to the loose ankle-length robes worn by men. When more than usual movement was desired, the robe was pulled up and tucked around a belt worn at the waist. The exhortation to be sober is a call for calm and serious thinking.

Verse 14. This is a hint that the letter was addressed to Gentile Christians. Their former ignorance would have been lack of knowledge of the will of God, given to the Jews in the Mosaic law.

Verses 15-16. Leviticus 11:44-45 is quoted. The root meaning of "holy" is "set apart" or "separate because different."

Verse 17. The word "fear" here connotes awe and reverence rather than cringing.

Verse 18. Terms from the slave market and the temple are used to show that the salvation of humankind was costly.

The Scripture and the Main Question—Pat McGeachy

A Circular Letter (1 Peter 1:1-2)

The regions mentioned in verse 1 are in the northern part of Asia Minor, what is now Turkey. Perhaps the messenger who delivered this letter from Rome journeyed through them, more or less in the order given, reading them to the churches along the way. The language of these two verses makes it sound almost as though Peter was writing to Jews. The word "Dispersion" was characteristically used to describe communities created by the scattering of the Jews under the Assyrians and the Babylonians; there were also considerable migrations during the Greek and Roman conquests. To such communities Paul and the other early missionaries had gone, preaching first to the Jews and then the Gentiles in the various cities of Asia Minor, Greece, and so forth.

But this letter is clearly written to Christians. Peter naturally uses the term "the new Israel" to describe the disciples of Jesus (not once does he use the word "church"), for so they had begun to think of themselves. And when he speaks (verse 2) of the sprinkling of Jesus' blood, he is clearly saying that the atoning work of Christ has taken the place of the ancient Jewish sacrificial system (see Hebrews 9:13-14). These are Christian congregations to which he is writing, but we are to think of them in a very real sense as God's new Israel (see Galatians 6:16).

A New Way of Looking at Life (1 Peter 1:3-9)

With a wonderful outpouring of joy, he begins the main body of his letter. Peter can hardly contain himself. Perhaps he is remembering the old days when he would have taken sword in hand and fought to keep Christ from suffering (John 18:10-11), the old days when he had tried to dissuade Jesus from his destiny (Matthew 16:21-23). But no more. Here he is practically bubbling over with enthusiasm (that word means "filled with God"), confident of the resurrection and ready to face the difficulties and dangers of a Christian in the world. Listen to the rolling words: imperishable, undefiled, unfading, kept in heaven, genuine, precious, unutterable, and exalted joy. This is not the Peter muttering his denial or weeping for his disloyalty (Luke 22:62), but the Peter running toward the empty tomb (John 20:4). In contrast to this genuine faith, tested in trial and found to be pure, the troubles of the world seem almost inconsequential. It's the difference between a small child dreading the huge and horrible needle in the hands of a tormentor and a mature adult facing the pinprick of the healer.

Let me describe that difference in terms of a contemporary person. Think of someone (perhaps yourself at one time) who is afraid of everything. Whatever you eat is fattening (if not carcinogenic), every new idea contains a heresy, and every dark alley a mugger. Such a person can hardly wake up in the morning for fear of getting through the day. But on the other hand, think of someone who *really* believes in the power of God to bring about resurrection. The troubles that person confronts are just as real, but they are somehow manageable. The ringing of the telephone spells not crisis but opportunity; the headline in the newspaper, ominous as it may be, can never dampen the ultimate optimism of one who believes in the power of God to bring in the kingdom in the Lord Jesus Christ. It's hard to read 1 Peter 1:3-9 without being recharged, filled with "unutterable and exalted joy," and made ready to face whatever life may bring.

Prophecy Fulfilled (1 Peter 1:10-12)

We must not suppose that this exaltation is ours alone. It was prepared for us from the beginning of time. As the prologue to the Fourth Gospel makes clear, Christ, the Word, was present in the creation with God (John 1:1-3). In spite of the sin of Adam and Eve, in spite of the babbling divisions of the human race (Genesis 11:9), in spite of the failure of Israel to live up to its prophetic destiny (Amos 3:1-2), in spite of all the legalism and the mysterious rituals of the Old Testament, there shines a prophetic light (Isaiah 9:2), pointing to the coming messiah. As Peter makes it clear (1:11), the time when these things should be fulfilled was uncertain. But they knew that it would one day come, as sure as God keeps promises (see Habakkuk 2:1-4). Indeed, for you and me, in our day, the times are yet uncertain. Much of the war is yet to be fought; the world is still full of great anguish. Nevertheless, we are confident that the decisive beachhead has been established, and that the outcome of the war is sure. Christ has won the battle over the forces of darkness, and we can join in the fight (Ephesians 6:10-20) with gusto and confidence. Even the angels (1 Peter 1:12) are watching from the ramparts of heaven for the expected triumph.

It's a Great Time to Be Alive (1 Peter 1:13-21)

Because of what we believe about the power of God to bring about resurrection, the actions of our lives are to be changed. We are to live sober, godly lives, as obedient children. Contrary to popular belief, the grace of

THIRD QUARTER

God produces not libertinism but obedience. Consider the two opposites depicted here:

- One who believes that all is lost and that no human effort can do any good says, "To hell with it. I'll eat, drink, and be merry, for tomorrow we die."
- One who believes that God in Christ has the power to win the victory, in spite of his own failures, is moved to say, "Life is worth living. I will do my best."

Predestination (if that is the right word) is clearly not fatalism. First Peter 1:20 was written not to lock us into a certain destiny but to free us up for victorious living. When I believe that it all depends on me, I am crushed by the insurmountable burdens of the world and unable to face tomorrow. But when I believe, as Peter clearly does, that it all depends upon God, who raised Jesus Christ from the dead, then I am set free to tackle the burdens of living with hope, joy, and promise. It's a great time to be alive. Let's get on with living!

The Imperishable Word (1 Peter 1:22-25)

Strange and incomprehensible are the ways of God! In order for us to discover that we have power, we must come to terms with our weakness. In order for us to be optimistic, we must face the truth of Isaiah's gloomy prophecy that all flesh is like grass. Isaiah 40, from which Peter is quoting here, is one of the most optimistic passages in all the Bible. It is a word of comfort to captive Israel, promising that God will make a new Exodus in the desert, that they may be restored. But that optimism is based entirely upon the grace of God. Human efforts have failed; the grass has withered, and the flower has failed. Now it is possible for us to accept the work of God. As long as we depend on our own righteousness, pride keeps us from receiving the good gift, but when the plant falls to the ground and dies (John 12:24; 1 Corinthians 15:36, 42), its seed is ready to be born as a new plant of a different order. When we have lost our lives (Luke 9:24), then, and only then, will we find them. If we wish to become great in the kingdom, we must become small. If we wish to be honored at the head table, we must take a seat at the foot. If we want to wear a crown, we must take up a cross.

All through this chapter we have been reminded, again and again, by the apostle that neither our works (however holy) nor our faith (however sincere) will bring in the kingdom. That will be accomplished "not by might, nor by power" but by the Spirit of God (Zechariah 4:6). If we thought it was our own doing, we should be forever trying to do that one more thing or forever trying to squeeze one more drop of fervor from our faith. But there is no perfect piety, not for you and me. Our task is not to bring in the kingdom. It is our Father's good pleasure to give us that (Luke 12:32). Our task is to be the people of God, those who live as though they believe in the resurrection, the resurrection of our Lord long ago, and our own today!

Helping Adults Become Involved—Roy H. Ryan

Preparing to Teach

We begin a new course of study with today's lesson. The biblical material will come from 1 and 2 Peter. The course is entitled "God's People in the

World." It follows logically the lessons from Mark in which we considered the life of Jesus and his message and mission. We are a people of the resurrection. So, how does that affect the way we live in the world?

It would be well for you to read 1 and 2 Peter before you teach this lesson. Look at the unit as a whole, and try to get a mental picture of where you are going in these next six lessons.

Dr. Decker's exegesis of today's scripture lesson, along with the exposition by Dr. McGeachy, should be especially helpful as you introduce the unit and this first lesson.

A good study Bible (with marginal notations) or a commentary will give you additional help as you study these two important epistles.

The aim of today's lesson is to help adult Christians better understand how they are called to live as disciples of the risen Lord.

Make sure you have the resources and supplies you need for your classroom. As you develop your teaching plan, note any special materials needed for teaching, and plan to make those available.

A possible outline for the lesson would be as follows:

      I. Introduction.
     II. A new way of looking at life.
    III. Prophecy fulfilled.
    IV. It's a great time to be alive.

Introducing the Main Question

How is a Christian supposed to live? Dr. McGeachy appropriately states the question in a positive way: "The truth is, I think, that the Christian life is not so much a matter of believing or doing, as it is of *being*." This writer agrees; what do you think?

Sometimes we spend a lot of energy dealing with what we "ought" to do (and there is no doubt that what we do is important), or what we "ought" to believe (and belief is rather critical, because it does make a difference what we believe). But the critical question has to do with being. We are called to be. Our actions will then flow out of our being. We will do good work because of who we are. We will seek to increase our faith and get our beliefs straight because we want to be the best Christians we can be.

The question, then, is this: How are you and I to live (be) as disciples of the risen Lord?

Help the class understand the difference between doing good, right belief or doctrine, and being a Christian. Dr. McGeachy's comments will be helpful.

Developing the Lesson

I. Introduction.

Introduce the lesson with the material given above in the "Introducing the Main Question" section. Spend some time helping clarify the difference between doing, believing, and being. Dr. McGeachy's comments about his being raised a Presbyterian (Calvinist) but also being an adopted Methodist (Wesleyan) can help to clarify some of the shades of difference and points of emphasis in different Christian traditions.

Where do you come down on this matter?

THIRD QUARTER

II. A new way of looking at life.

The old way has passed away. As Peter shares his joy of the new life found in Jesus Christ, he is likely remembering the old days when there was not much hope. At one point, the disciples had lost hope (at the crucifixion of Jesus). They thought their "movement" had died with Jesus. They wondered about all his wonderful teaching. Had it come to naught with his death?

We rejoice in the new life that comes from faith in Christ. Peter pours out the joy in his heart as he shares this good news. "We have been born anew to a living hope through the resurrection of Jesus Christ from the dead" (verse 3).

What are some differences in the life of Peter before the resurrection and after the resurrection? What are some differences in your life since you became a Christian?

III. Prophecy fulfilled.

This joy we have experienced was prepared for us "from the beginning" (John 1:1-3). The prophetic word had always included a note of hope. The prophets could not know the fullness revealed in Jesus Christ, but they looked for his coming. God had always been concerned about the salvation of his whole creation. In Christ we see that hope culminated.

It has come to us as a gift—"God so loved the world" (John 3:16). We have not earned this wonderful gift of new life. We are not born anew by our own good works. We are not saved by our right belief. We are born anew through the resurrection of Jesus Christ.

Why are the birth, life and teachings, death, and resurrection of Jesus Christ so important in God's work of salvation?

IV. It's a great time to be alive.

Our lives are made rich and full through faith in Jesus Christ. "The old has passed away and all things have become new." We see life differently. We act differently. We believe differently. Jesus Christ has made a radical difference in the world and in our own individual lives. Because of this hope we have within us, we have power to live more wholesome and fulfilling lives.

Helping Class Members Act

Maybe the emphasis should be on helping the class members *be!* However, since we believe that our behavior or actions flow out of our being, it is appropriate to talk about how we are to behave as Christians.

Having been reminded that we are a people of hope, how will our lives be different in the coming week? Will we be able to deal more adequately with our disappointments? Will we seek ways to witness to what Jesus Christ has done for us? Will we witness to someone, a friend perhaps, who does not have this hope?

Join with your class in this prayer: We thank you God for the living hope we have in Jesus Christ. We pray for your guidance as we seek to live lives worthy of him. Amen.

Planning for Next Sunday

The lesson next Sunday deals with the topic "Called to Be God's People." The scripture lesson is 1 Peter 2:1-10. Give any assignments needed.

LESSON 10   MAY 3

Called to Be God's People

Background Scripture: 1 Peter 2:1-25

The Main Question—Pat McGeachy

If I were making a list of the "great" passages of Scripture, that is, those I would like to have memorized before I am cast away on the proverbial desert island, my list would certainly include 1 Peter 2:4-10. Indeed, the whole chapter is a gem; it is a sort of "little Epistle." Verses 1-10 describe what Christians believe, verses 11-20 describe how Christians should behave, and verses 21-25 issue a call to the renewal of our belief.

If I were to sum up this chapter in the form of a question, that question would be, Who are you? On the face of it, you would think most of us would already know who we are. But strange (and sad) as it seems, most of us cannot answer this basic question. I have seen this demonstrated as a parlor game. You give everyone a card and a pencil and ask him or her to give three possible answers to the following:

I am a(n) _____,

I am a(n) _____,

and I am a(n) _____.

You might try it on yourself now. What did you list first? Your vocation? And avocation? A family connection? A name? The name of a religious affiliation? A political party? What do you think others would list about you if they were given your card to fill out?

All this is to say, with Laertes, "Know thyself." Now we only know in part, Paul says (1 Corinthians 13:12), as a reflection in an imperfect mirror, but we look forward to the day when we will be fully known. A look at 1 Peter, chapter 2, will hasten the coming of that vision. Our question is, then, Who am I? Or, perhaps better, Who am I meant to be? For the process is not ended. As the bumper sticker has it, "Be patient with me, God isn't through with me yet!"

Selected Scripture

King James Version

1 Peter 2:1-10

1 Wherefore laying aside all malice, and all guile, and hypocrisies, and envies, and all evil speakings,

2 As newborn babes, desire the sincere milk of the word, that ye may grow thereby:

3 If so be ye have tasted that the Lord *is* gracious.

Revised Standard Version

1 Peter 2:1-10

1 So put away all malice and all guile and insincerity and envy and all slander. 2 Like newborn babes, long for the pure spiritual milk, that by it you may grow up to salvation; 3 for you have tasted the kindness of the Lord.

THIRD QUARTER

4 To whom coming, *as unto* a living stone, disallowed indeed of men, but chosen of God, *and* precious,

5 Ye also, as lively stones, are built up a spiritual house, an holy priesthood, to offer up spiritual sacrifices, acceptable to God by Jesus Christ.

6 Wherefore also it is contained in the scripture, Behold, I lay in Sion a chief corner stone, elect, precious: and he that believeth on him shall not be confounded.

7 Unto you therefore which believe *he is* precious: but unto them which be disobedient, the stone which the builders disallowed, the same is made the head of the corner,

8 And a stone of stumbling, and a rock of offence, *even to them* which stumble at the word, being disobedient: whereunto also they were appointed.

9 But ye *are* a chosen generation, a royal priesthood, an holy nation, a peculiar people; that ye should shew forth the praises of him who hath called you out of darkness into his marvellous light:

10 Which in time past *were* not a people, but *are* now the people of God: which had not obtained mercy, but now have obtained mercy.

Key Verse: **Ye are a chosen generation, a royal priesthood, an holy nation, a peculiar people; that ye should shew forth the praises of him who hath called you out of darkness into his marvelous light. (1 Peter 2:9)**

4 Come to him, to that living stone, rejected by men but in God's sight chosen and precious; 5 and like living stones be yourselves built into a spiritual house, to be a holy priesthood, to offer spiritual sacrifices acceptable to God through Jesus Christ. 6 For it stands in scripture:

"Behold, I am laying in Zion a stone, a cornerstone chosen and precious,
and he who believes in him will not be put to shame."

7 To you therefore who believe, he is precious, but for those who do not believe,

"The very stone which the builders rejected
has become the head of the corner,"

8 and

"A stone that will make men stumble,
a rock that will make them fall";

for they stumble because they disobey the word, as they were destined to do.

9 But you are a chosen race, a royal priesthood, a holy nation, God's own people, that you may declare the wonderful deeds of him who called you out of darkness into his marvelous light. 10 Once you were no people but now you are God's people; once you had not received mercy but now you have received mercy.

Key Verse: **You are a chosen race, a royal priesthood, a holy nation, God's own people, that you may declare the wonderful deeds of him who called you out of darkness into his marvelous light. (1 Peter 2:9)**

As You Read the Scripture—Ralph W. Decker

1 Peter 2:1. The sins listed are neither major crimes nor outward actions. They are wrong feelings and attitudes.

Verse 2. Being born again is a first step, not a final one, in a person's salvation. A newborn needs nourishment to develop and grow. Peter urges new Christians to reach after spiritual nourishment in order that they might grow into spiritual maturity.

Verse 3. The verse echoes the invitation of Psalm 34:8 to "taste and see that the Lord is good."

Verse 4. Peter urges his readers to be active in the service of God. He pictures the church as the new temple and Christ as its cornerstone. The cornerstone that determines the size and shape of a building. Seeing Jesus as determining the design of the church, Peter urges his readers to build themselves into it. He also speaks of Christians as offering themselves in sacrifice.

Verse 6. This echoes Isaiah 28:16.

Verse 7. This quotes Psalm 118:22.

Verse 8. This echoes Isaiah 8:14. A good stone can cause harm. So, Christ is a stumbling block for unbelievers.

Verse 9. Peter here transfers to the church several titles that had been given the Jewish people—"chosen people" (Isaiah 43:20), "a kingdom of priests and a holy nation" (Exodus 19:6). This reflects the early church teaching that Christians were a new Israel or people of God.

Verse 10. This may be an echo of Hosea 2:23. This verse suggests that Peter was writing to Christians of Gentile background. They are being gathered into a new nation. Formerly they had no relationship; now they are bound-together in a common faith.

Verse 11. The characterization of the Christian readers as aliens and exiles suggests they were a minority. Much of this letter is concerned with Christian living in a pagan world. Christians are aliens on earth because their citizenship is in heaven. Peter calls for them to live by the standards of their home country, not of earth.

Verse 12. Early Christians were accused of many crimes, sometimes through malice, sometimes through misunderstanding of their teachings and practices. The accusations involved sedition, immorality, ritual murder, and cannibalism. Peter urges that the best defense will be a stainless record.

Verse 13. When this letter was written, all civil authorities to whom its intended readers were subject were pagan. Even so, Peter urges respect for them. They have a place in God's plan, maintaining order and promoting welfare.

Verse 15. Obedience to law forestalls criticism and answers charges of sedition.

Verse 16. Christians are to obey civil authorities as free persons who choose to do so. Peter warns against abuse of Christian freedom. It is not freedom to do as one pleases but freedom to serve God.

Verse 17. These admonitions unite citizenship with Christian character.

Verses 18-25. Peter here deals with the way Christians should act within their own households, especially those in which some members are Christian and some are not. He first deals with the conduct of Christian slaves toward pagan masters. Slavery was an institution deeply embedded in the Greek and Roman cultures of the first century. Neither Peter nor any other Christian New Testament author attempted to abolish slavery. But both Peter (2:18–3:7) and Paul (Galatians 3:28) opened the way for later

THIRD QUARTER

changes in attitudes and practices by proclaiming all persons equal in the sight of God.

Verse 18. In the Greek the opening word means household slaves—tutors, physicians, musicians, house managers—as well as those who do menial work. The fact that both Peter and Paul (Colossians 3:22-24) undertook to instruct slaves suggests that many early Christians were of that social class.

The Scripture and the Main Question—Pat McGeachy

A Conclusion and Introduction (1 Peter 2:1-3)

The chapter and verse numbers in your Bible have nothing to do with the original message. They were added in the Middle Ages as an invention to make it easier to refer to a particular passage. The first "chapter and verse" Bible was printed about four hundred years ago, and unfortunately, whoever added the numbers was not always careful. There are some places where they obscure the sense of the passage or interrupt it. (One legend has it that the versifier did the work while riding on a lame mule: Whenever the mule took a step, a verse number was put in, and whenever the mule stumbled a chapter!) Anyway, the first two verses of chapter 2 clearly belong to the material we were discussing in our last lesson. They effectively conclude the section on the celebration of the risen Christ with a call to renewal and Christian growth, ending with the lovely expression, "For you have tasted the kindness of the Lord."

But we can't blame the medieval monk too much, for these verses also make a proper introduction to the material of chapter 2. Peter says, in effect, "Since you have tasted the kindness of the Lord" (the wonderful resurrection story), "you now have some growing up to do." And this he follows with an invitation to active participation in the life of the church.

But there is still another way to divide this material, which makes even more sense: Why not put the beginning of chapter 2 right before 2:11? In my Revised Standard Version, the editors have left a double-space there to indicate an important division. Their other main division comes between 4:19 and 5:1, but if I were in charge, I would have put it after the Amen in 4:11. The point of all this is that you will want to decide for yourself how to outline 1 Peter, so that you can better understand and remember its contents. My way of dividing it would be this:

1. Introduction (1:1-2)
2. What we believe (1:3–2:10)
3. How we should live (2:11–3:12)
4. The suffering to come (3:13–5:11)
5. Conclusion (5:12-14)

But it is better for you and your class to decide.

Invitation to Community (1 Peter 2:4-10)

In verse 3, Peter has alluded to tasting the Lord's kindness, promised in Psalm 34:8 (see also Psalm 27:13 and Hebrews 6:4-5). He clearly believes, as was hinted at in the last chapter, that the Christian church is the continuation of Judaism, a new Israel founded on Christ. The new Israel will not be based on racial and ethnic ties but on the new tie of obedience to the Lord. Thus the Gentiles to whom he is writing, though they at one time had no sense of belonging to the people of God (verse 10), are now fully included in the new structure.

The metaphor is that of building blocks, founded on Christ, the chief cornerstone. Can it be an accident that Peter's own name is "Stone" and that Jesus once called him a sort of cornerstone on which the church would be built (Matthew 16:18)? He invokes ancient prophecies here to establish Jesus as the fulfillment of Israel's destiny as the foundation of a new order in the world (verse 6; Isaiah 28:16). Then he uses other ancient texts to point out the dual nature of a rock. It can be something one stumbles over (verse 8; Isaiah 8:14-15) or the chief cornerstone (verse 7; Psalm 118:22). The stone remains the same; it depends on how you come to it. You can build on it or trip over it; it is up to you. This is also said by Paul (1 Corinthians 1:23-24): "We preach Christ crucified, a stumbling block to Jews and folly to Gentiles, but to those who are called, both Jews and Greeks, Christ the power of God and the wisdom of God."

Please note that it is important to Peter that we not take his rocky metaphors *too* literally. He is not speaking of a static stone structure here but of a living, breathing church. Christ is a *living* stone (verse 4), and we ourselves (verse 5) are to be flesh and blood bricks in this building we call the church. The spiritual temple is to take the place of the physical temple in old Jerusalem (Zion), and the new priesthood is to be the priesthood of all believers.

Before we leave this beautiful passage, let me point out one other comparison. The image of a people once separated from God who are now included in the inner circle is to be found in lots of places. I think of Ephesians 2:11-22, which contains the saddest sentence in the Bible (2:12) but ends with the very same metaphor that Peter is using here: the building of a new temple in Christ Jesus in which all God's children are included. And I think also of Hosea, who named one of his children Lo-ammi, which means "not my people," to symbolize the fact that Israel herself had been cut off from the family of God (Hosea 1:8). That ancient prophet believed in the coming of the day when the child's name should be changed (Hosea 2:23) to "You are my people," when Israel would return to her true calling. So we are not to think that the Jews are excluded from the new temple described by Peter in our passage this week. They too are to be part of the new order. In the last book of the Christian Scriptures, Revelation, there are twenty-four elders around the throne of God (Revelation 4:4). I take this to symbolize the ultimate reunion of Jews and Christians: The twelve tribes and the twelve apostles represent the new priesthood, forever united at last and able to say to God, "You are my God" (Revelation 21:3). There are great days ahead, and 1 Peter 2:2-10 is an invitation to all of us to join in. If we want to answer the question, Who am I? we will need to ask a prior question, *Whose* am I? It is in the community of living stones, the church, that I will find this out.

The Church and the World (1 Peter 2:11-25)

The basic drive of this part of the letter (and, as I indicated earlier, we need to include 3:1-12 in this section) has to do with our relationship to

THIRD QUARTER

human institutions. We are indeed a revolutionary new kingdom, but it does not get its authority from this world (John 18:36). Conversely, it is not intended to overthrow the institutions of this world but to remake them from within. Peter proceeds to describe how the Christian ought to relate to

- Government (2:13-17)
- Business (employee relations, 2:18-25)
- Marriage (3:1-7)
- Church (3:8-12)

Peter's thought is clearly governed by the mores and patterns of his time; we must not read into these verses instructions as to how our ancestors ought to have related to King George the Third and the American Revolution, or to ancient notions about women being the "weaker sex." But there are general principles here that can guide us in all our relationships. Let's list just a few:

- Live as free people but not as libertines (2:17).
- Seek approval from God, not fallible humans (2:19).
- Find your true beauty within (3:4).
- Have unity of spirit for all (3:8).

Because we are truly the new priesthood, we are to relate to all people as though Christ's sacrifice had reconciled us all to one another and to God. We are free to live in loving service even to those who are sometimes cruel and unfair. Let me sum it up in the form of an answer to our basic question, Who am I? In the positive form I would say, "Because I know who I am (whose I am), I am afraid of no one. No one can harm me. My life is hid with Christ in God. Therefore I am free to relate to you, and to everyone else I encounter, in the loving spirit of Christ."

Helping Adults Become Involved—Roy H. Ryan

Preparing to Teach

Read 1 Peter 2 with a good commentary in hand. You will also want to read very carefully the exegesis and exposition in the preceding sections of this lesson.

This lesson gives some warnings about what Christian believers should avoid as well as admonitions about their relationships to political and civic leaders.

The aim of the lesson is to help adults recognize their identity in Christ and to grow toward maturity in him.

A major objective of adult Christian education is to help persons continue to grow in their discipleship. This lesson will help to focus that concern as you help members of the class see themselves within the context of the church. Peter uses several images or metaphors to describe what the church is.

If we are called to be God's people, as the title of our lesson suggests, how do we live into that calling?

Make sure you have the resources and supplies needed in the classroom. Also, plan to arrange the room in accordance with your teaching plan. Is it a lecture? A discussion? A combination of both?

A possible outline for the lesson could be as follows:

   I. Introduction.
   II. Jesus Christ, the Living Stone.
   III. Living as responsible Christians.
   IV. Jesus Christ is our example.

Introducing the Main Question

What is the question or issue this lesson seeks to address? One of the commentators suggests it is about the questions, Who am I? Who am I meant to be? How do we define ourselves? If someone asks, "Who are you?" what would your response be?

You might try this out with your group. Have each person think about the question, Who am I? and then turn to one other person in the group (preferably not one's spouse) and discuss their answers. After a few minutes, ask group members to share with the total group a little of what they talked about. How did they describe who they were? What were the most important criteria they used in identifying themselves? Was it name? Profession or occupation? Where they came from? Their church connection?

Did anyone say "I am a Christian" as a first response? Is it possible that such a response is basic to whatever else we say about ourselves? We are called to be Christians—that is our vocation (from the Latin word meaning "to be called"). Everything else we are and do grows out of that basic vocation or calling.

Developing the Lesson

I. Introduction.

Use some or all of the suggestions contained in the two sections above.

This approach suggests more informal methods than you may normally use in teaching. If you are accustomed to lecturing, do not be afraid to try some new methods.

If you can get the class members involved in thinking about the lesson in personal terms, help them to see where it relates to where they live, they are more likely to be helped by it.

II. Jesus Christ, the Living Stone.

Jesus is the cornerstone of the church. He is also its foundation. Peter uses "living stone" in a dynamic sense; Jesus generates life and vitality. The church of which he is the head is also a dynamic body, always changing and growing. Those of us who are followers of Jesus are also like living stones, being built into a spiritual house (verses 4-5).

Peter uses a variety of citations from the Hebrew Scriptures to describe God's people (Israel), these living stones. Peter and the early apostles and disciples wanted all to know that Jesus Christ had brought into being a new Israel. Thus Peter uses "chosen race," "a royal priesthood," "a holy nation," and "God's own people" to describe this new spiritual reality.

What image best describes the church for you?

THIRD QUARTER

III. Living as responsible Christians.

Peter urges Christians to maintain good conduct. They should be models of good behavior so that unbelievers will observe them and glorify God. Some people believe that the best way to witness to non-Christians is to live with high moral standards.

But this may bring us a little trouble. How far should we carry out loyalty? In a democratic society, we put a great deal of trust and confidence in our elected leaders, but they sometimes disappoint us. Does this mean that we should never question their judgment or authority? Are they really God's representatives? What does this passage really mean?

Slavery was an accepted institution in the Greek and Roman world. Thus Peter's admonitions to slaves fit with his other notions of submitting oneself to the authorities. But how do these recommendations fit into our world today?

What are some signs of responsible Christian living? How ought we to think about and relate to our elected officials?

IV. Jesus Christ is our example.

We need to pattern our lives after Christ. One of the great verses of Scripture is from today's assigned reading: "Christ also suffered for you, leaving you an example, that you should follow in his steps" (verse 21). What would it mean if we took that admonition seriously?

Helping Class Members Act

In his book *In His Steps*, Charles Sheldon tells the story of a group of church members who covenanted together for one year to try to follow in Jesus' steps. They would always ask, "What would Jesus do?" before they made any decisions or took any action. They found it difficult! Some would argue that it is unrealistic to try "to be like Jesus." What do you think?

Challenge class members to try such an experiment for next week. Ask them to very consciously seek to follow Jesus in everything they do (as they understand the mind and spirit of Jesus).

Planning for Next Sunday

If you challenge class members as indicated above, be ready to have some of them report on what happened next Sunday. Read 1 Peter 3:13–4:11.

LESSON 11   MAY 10

Witnessing in Suffering

Background Scripture: 1 Peter 3:13–4:11

The Main Question—Pat McGeachy

Escapism, someone has said, is a dirty word, but not if you are in prison! If that is the case, then most of us must be prisoners of some sort, because most of us have several means of escape. Some of them are not so bad. Here's a list of some of the things I do to escape: sleep, eat, draw doodles on my church bulletin, do crossword puzzles and logic problems, play solitaire, daydream, pretend to be funny. . . I'd better quit before the list gets too long! Taken by themselves, none of the above are all that heavy, but together they can add up to some real problems. In fact, any one of them, if carried to extremes, is bad news.

Then, of course, there are those escapes that we all recognize as really dangerous: the misuse of alcohol and other drugs, compulsive gambling, sexual misconduct, and the like. Some forms of mental illness involve withdrawal from the real world and the creation of imaginary worlds that seem to the patient to be easier to handle. Most of us are willing to suffer a certain amount of pain if we feel it is accomplishing something and that we can see light at the end of the tunnel. But what about those who go through life in constant fear or hurt? How much of that can we stand?

Karl Marx, the father of Communism, said that religion is an escape. He called it the opium of the people, meaning that instead of helping people face the truth about the world, Religion tells people to pretend that everything will be all right "in the sweet by and by." In the meantime, Marx claimed, we misuse people for our own selfish ends. For example, some people get rich from cheap labor, claiming that since the laborers will get their reward in heaven we don't have to worry about them here. But Marx notwithstanding, Christ does not call us to escape; Christ calls us to suffer, to take up a cross. Our question then becomes, How can this possibly be good news?

Selected Scripture

King James Version	Revised Standard Version
1 Peter 3:13-18	*1 Peter 3:13-18*
13 And who *is* he that will harm you, if ye be followers of that which is good?	13 Now who is there to harm you if you are zealous for what is right?
14 But and if ye suffer for righteousness' sake, happy *are ye:* and be not afraid of their terror, neither be troubled;	14 But even if you do suffer for righteousness' sake, you will be blessed. Have no fear of them, nor be troubled, 15 but in your hearts reverence Christ as Lord. Always be prepared to make a defense to any one who calls you to account for the hope that is in you, yet do it with
15 But sanctify the Lord God in your hearts: and *be* ready always to *give* an answer to every man that	

THIRD QUARTER

asketh you a reason of the hope that is in you with meekness and fear:

16 Having a good conscience; that, whereas they speak evil of you, as of evildoers, they may be ashamed that falsely accuse your good conversation in Christ.

17 For *it is* better, if the will of God be so, that ye suffer for well doing, than for evil doing.

18 For Christ also hath once suffered for sins, the just for the unjust, that he might bring us to God, being put to death in the flesh, but quickened by the Spirit:

1 Peter 4:1-2, 7-11

1 Forasmuch then as Christ hath suffered for us in the flesh, arm yourselves likewise with the same mind: for he that hath suffered in the flesh hath ceased from sin;

2 That he no longer should live the rest of *his* time in the flesh to the lusts of men, but to the will of God.

....

7 But the end of all things is at hand: be ye therefore sober, and watch unto prayer.

8 And above all things have fervent charity among yourselves: for charity shall cover the multitude of sins.

9 Use hospitality one to another without grudging.

10 As every man hath received the gift, *even so* minister the same one to another, as good stewards of the manifold grace of God.

11 If any man speak, *let him speak* as the oracles of God; if any man minister, *let him do it* as of the ability which God giveth: that God in all things may be glorified through Jesus Christ, to whom be praise and dominion for ever and ever. Amen.

Key Verse: **It is better, if the will of God be so, that ye suffer for well doing, than for evil doing. (1 Peter 3:17)**

gentleness and reverence; 16 and keep your conscience clear, so that, when you are abused, those who revile your good behavior in Christ may be put to shame. 17 For it is better to suffer for doing right, if that should be God's will, than for doing wrong. 18 For Christ also died for sins once for all, the righteous for the unrighteous, that he might bring us to God, being put to death in the flesh but made alive in the spirit.

1 Peter 4:1-2, 7-11

1 Since therefore Christ suffered in the flesh, arm yourselves with the same thought, for whoever has suffered in the flesh has ceased from sin, 2 so as to live for the rest of the time in the flesh no longer by human passions but by the will of God.

....

7 The end of all things is at hand; therefore keep sane and sober for your prayers. 8 Above all hold unfailing your love for one another, since love covers a multitude of sins. 9 Practice hospitality ungrudgingly to one another. 10 As each has received a gift, employ it for one another, as good stewards of God's varied grace: 11 whoever speaks, as one who utters oracles of God; whoever renders service, as one who renders it by the strength which God supplies; in order that in everything God may be glorified through Jesus Christ. To him belong glory and dominion for ever and ever. Amen.

Key Verse: **It is better to suffer for doing right, if that should be God's will than for doing wrong. (1 Peter 3:17)**

MAY 10   LESSON 11

As You Read the Scripture—Ralph W. Decker

First-century Christians often faced persecution because they were misunderstood. Their withdrawal from worldly activities, combined with their talk of partaking of the body and blood of Christ, led to charges of cannibalism and other inhuman practices. The writer of 1 Peter tried to prepare his readers to meet such charges and to live righteously in a hostile world.

1 Peter 3:13. He taught that the best way to meet false charges is to live a completely blameless life, leaving persecutors without a valid reason for their actions. His word "zealous" is a strong one, suggesting enthusiastic commitment to righteous living.

Verse 14. His promise of blessing in return for undeserved suffering echoes Jesus' beatitude "Blessed are you when men revile and persecute you . . . on my account" (Matthew 5:11).

Verse 15. He urges Christians under persecution to remain loyal to Christ, to answer charges intelligently, and to act courteously toward their accusers.

Verse 16. An upright life and a clear conscience are the best defenses against false accusations.

Verse 17. Right living does not guarantee freedom from suffering. It does enable one to suffer victoriously.

Verses 18-22. This is the most difficult passage to follow in this letter. It deals with several different topics. They are loosely related and can be treated separately.

Verse 18. The author says that Christ died because of the sins of others, that his action need not be repeated, that he died for the unrighteous and to reconcile humans and God.

Verse 19. This verse, along with 4:6, has been interpreted as meaning that in the time between his death on the cross on Friday and his resurrection appearances on Sunday, Jesus went to the abode of the dead and preached salvation to the souls imprisoned there. This answers the question of the whereabouts of Jesus' spirit between Good Friday afternoon and Easter morning.

Verse 20. Among those offered salvation during his visit to Hades were those who had refused to heed Noah's call to repentance and who perished in the Flood. The eight persons who escaped the Flood were Noah, his wife, his three sons (Ham, Shem, Japheth), and their wives. In the ark they were saved by the water that destroyed others.

Verse 21. The saving of Noah and his family by means of water suggests to the writer the salvation of others by baptism. Yet he points out that the effect of baptism is not physical but spiritual.

Verse 22. As to the whereabouts of the risen Christ, Peter tells of his ascension into heaven, his position of highest honor there, and his present authority over spiritual forces.

1 Peter 4:1-6. In this passage, which is difficult to follow, Peter says that Christians are under obligation to rid themselves of all traces of their former pagan lives.

Verses 1-2. Since they have the example of Christ's triumphant suffering, Christians are to see their suffering as evidence of freedom from sin.

Verse 3. This call to let go of a pagan past is evidence that Peter was writing to Christians of Gentile background. Apparently, he regarded the six listed sins as the most prevalent.

Verse 4. Refusal to participate in the vices of one's time and place may bring abuse.

Verse 5. Although it is not clear whether Peter meant that Christ will judge, or God, this verse reads like the Apostles' Creed statement "Jesus Christ . . . will come to judge the quick and the dead."

Verse 7. Like most early Christians, Peter believed the end of the world was at hand. He instructs his readers to prepare for it by remaining calm, loving one another, and serving God.

Verses 8-9. The author gives specific examples of such service and closes this part of his letter with a doxology.

The Scripture and the Main Question—Pat McGeachy

Purification (1 Peter 3:13-22)

Invariably, when you and I suffer discomfort, pain, or hardship, there sneaks into the back of our minds a little voice that says, "It's not fair!" We have the notion that having behaved ourselves, we ought to be rewarded, not persecuted. We're like the schoolchild who said, "I studied hard, and the teacher asked questions on stuff we hadn't been told to study. No fair!" And we would be right to have such feelings. About 60 percent of the book of Psalms seems to be given over to wailing, lamenting, and cursing about the unfair treatment that God's people are getting, and to wondering if God is asleep or something (see Psalm 44:23-24, for example). Even Jesus wanted to get out of his sufferings (Mark 14:36).

But the plain fact is that life *isn't* fair, no matter how much we wish it were. And the deepest truth that we Christians know about life is that it is the innocent who suffer. Think about those poor babies that Herod was afraid might be competition for him (Matthew 2:16). Or worst (best?) of all, think about the fact that Jesus, the purest and best person who ever lived, was put to death as a common criminal. He did this not for the good guys but for the bad guys! Christ died for the ungodly (Romans 5:6). Or, as Peter puts it in 3:18, "Christ died for sins once for all, the righteous for the unrighteous." Talk about unfair! And if you and I choose to follow Christ, we can expect to encounter some of the same sufferings ourselves. Jesus may have promised us a rose garden, but he didn't say it would be free of thorns. He clearly told us that if we would come after him, there would be a cross to bear (Luke 9:23).

Now, not all suffering is cross-bearing. Peter clearly makes a distinction (3:17) between suffering that is a result of obedience to Christ and suffering that is the natural consequence of sin. And there is, of course, a third sort of suffering, that which seems to be a kind of natural part of living in this world; I mean things like mosquitoes and sinus trouble, or worse. This is not the place to get into a discussion of that sort of suffering. We'll deal with that when we next take up the book of Job. But for now, let's make it clear that in this lesson we are dealing with the kind of suffering that purifies and cleanses, the sort that is a natural part of our belonging to Christ, the suffering Messiah.

Let me tell you a story that came to me from the mission fields of the Congo (now Zaire), which illustrates how natural suffering can be confused with spiritual suffering. A missionary was baptizing an African chieftain who had made a profession of faith. This took place in a tributary of the Congo, and the missionary found it necessary to borrow a spear to lean on against the swiftness of the current. To his horror, when they came out of the river, he discovered that he had set the point of the spear on the foot of the man he had been baptizing, so that it was painfully wounded. "Good Lord, man!" he cried, "You never even changed your expression! Why didn't you tell me?" "I thought it was part of the ceremony," replied the stoical African.

I can understand how, coming from an African tradition of painful rituals, the man might have expected pain to be associated with baptism. But if I understand the sacrament, it is supposed to be associated with a different sort of pain: not accidental injury from a spear point but the purposeful injury to the ego that comes from undergoing such a humbling experience. At this point I am a little jealous of my Baptist friends, who truly understand the essential *embarrassment* of baptism. We take it almost too casually, a little tap of a few droplets on the head (sometimes even warm so as not to shock the baby), but with no sense of washing as indicated by 1 Peter 3:21, or the overwhelming flood of Noah's time (1 Peter 3:20). Entry into the Christian life is an awkward thing. Our dignity has to go. That is why it is so very difficult for a grown person to join the church. We have been taught all our lives that we are to be dignified, and now the preacher is making us say, "I am a low-down sinner, and I need help." It is like the first step in AA. It is like a spear point in your foot.

There is, then, legitimate suffering, which Christians can expect to encounter. Let me make a partial list of some that occur to me; you and your class may wish to discuss others.

- Ridicule from non-Christians who do not understand our faith and practices
- Weariness from long labor in the Lord's name
- Imprisonment for our faith (This not confined to "our fathers chained in prisons dark" but is a very real possibility in today's world.)
- Illness or even death (I know a physician dedicated to ministry to AIDS victims who contracted the disease himself.)
- Poverty

But I must tell you that Peter is right (verse 14): If you do suffer for righteousness' sake, you will be blessed. He got these words from the Lord himself (Matthew 5:10).

New Life in Christ (1 Peter 4:1-11)

Yes, there are thorns in this rose garden, but there are also roses. Suffering is painful, but good suffering has the result of taking our minds off of sin and frees us to think of what true goodness really means. This is a very difficult mental attitude to achieve. We might consider two ways of looking at this:

- Bad suffering: Oh, how I wish I could have some chocolate cake!
- Good suffering: How great it is to be getting thin again!

THIRD QUARTER

- Bad suffering: I wish I could take a drink and forget my troubles.
- Good suffering: How great it is to feel alive, alert, and not have a hangover.

The end of all things is at hand (4:7). This is the very time when those who do not understand the true nature of the Christian life would think about going on a binge. But Peter tells us this is the very time to live a godly, righteous, and sober life. (You might want to memorize 4:8-11 or write it on a card to carry in your wallet. It's a good description of living the good life.)

There is a legend that someone once interrupted Francis of Assisi as he was hoeing his garden to ask him, "What would you do if you knew the end of the world was coming tonight?" The good saint is said to have answered, "Well, first I would finish hoeing my garden." Just so does Saint Peter want us to live, in the expectation of the sudden return of Christ. It is not a time for libertinism but for doing our duty. When the end of the world comes, we want to be found at our posts. (Check Luke 12:32-40 for our Lord's description of the way to live in anticipation of the end.) There are stories of people who, confronted with their own mortality (say, by a heart attack, or some other emergency), have altered their whole life-style and begun to stop and smell the roses, spend more time with their children, or devote themselves to less selfish and more lasting pursuits. You may wish to test yourself: What would you say if you were asked the same question as Saint Francis?

If you want other suggestions as to how to live in anticipation of the last things, consider Romans 12:3-21 and 1 Thessalonians 5:1-22, and, for that matter, the Sermon on the Mount too (Matthew 5–7). A good case can be made that the entire New Testament is a document written for those who are living near the end of time (or ought to act as though they are), and so is good advice for us all. But in all of this, what about the suffering? Will we be able to bear it? The testimony of the saints throughout the history of the church answers yes to this. It will hurt, but it will be a good hurt, and we will be given strength to bear it. Such suffering will produce growth (Romans 5:3-5) and renewed hope. Moreover, it will not last forever (2 Corinthians 4:17-18), and the reward for which we are waiting will make it all worthwhile. This is not a "pie in the sky by and by" promise, of the sort ridiculed by Marx when he called religion an opium. It is the suffering that purifies and rewards.

Helping Adults Become Involved—Roy H. Ryan

Preparing to Teach

You may find this a difficult lesson to teach. It is not easy to understand the age-old question, Why must we suffer? Most persons seem to try to avoid suffering. Think about ways you can approach this topic helpfully as you begin to prepare.

Read 1 Peter 3:13–14:11. Make use of whatever different translations or paraphrases you have available. Also consult a Bible commentary for help. You might find it helpful to make notes as you read the scripture. Some find it helpful to write their own commentary as they read.

MAY 10   LESSON 11

Think about the members of your class. You probably know them well enough to have some idea of the kind of suffering they have experienced in their lives. Do you have persons in your class who have suffered because of beliefs or stands they have taken that were unpopular? Do some of them work in environments that are not conducive to godly living? Are some of them business persons who have taken ethical stands that adversely affected the bottom line of their businesses?

The aim of this lesson is to help adult Christians better understand the place of suffering in the Christian life and be prepared to "suffer for Christ's sake."

An outline of the lesson would be as follows:

        I. Introduction.
       II. Suffering brings purification.
      III. Living by the will of God.
      IV. Be prepared for the end.

Introducing the Main Question

Christ calls us to suffer. How can that possibly be good news? asks Dr. McGeachy in his exposition of this passage. Who wants to suffer?

Note that the topic for today is "Witnessing in Suffering." This is related to how we deal with suffering as well as to the causes of suffering. Regardless of what causes suffering, how do we face it and live victoriously in spite of it?

What does it mean to suffer for Christ's sake? Is that different from just plain old everyday suffering? Is all physical pain and suffering to be equated with suffering for Christ's sake? What about those who look upon their physical pain as bearing a cross?

Physical pain and suffering come to all of us to some degree at some point in life. This is certainly not to be voluntarily taken on in order to honor Christ. The suffering that Peter is talking about is that which we take on because we belong to Christ. How will you get members of the class involved in this question?

Developing the Lesson

I. Introduction.

Start by asking one or both of the following questions: What does it mean to suffer for Christ's sake? How should Christians deal with suffering, no matter what its cause? You are attempting to help class members come to some new insights and understand ways they can witness to their faith in Christ through suffering.

II. Suffering brings purification.

Do right, even if you have to suffer for it. Paul told the Romans, "Do not be conformed to this world, but be transformed by the renewing of your minds." A paraphrase of that passage has it, "Don't let the world squeeze you into its own mold." Peter urges Christians to do right and stand up for the right even if it means suffering. In so doing, you will be blessed.

Always be ready to give a reason for the faith within you. If you know

THIRD QUARTER

what you believe and in whom you believe, you will be given courage to stand against those who dishonor Christ. Do not fear those who might harm you if you do not think or act the way they do. Do not be swayed by crowd psychology or be trapped by whatever happens in vogue. That is precisely why so many people in our day are in trouble with drugs and other addictive forms of behavior.

How does it feel when you attempt to do the right thing and your friends or colleagues strongly disagree with you? How well prepared are you "to give a defense of your faith"?

III. Living by the will of God (4:1-6).

We are called to live in some new ways. Look at the list Peter gives of things to avoid. Are any of these behaviors still a problem today? Are we tempted to live like the crowd because it seems the easy way out? What a difference it makes in our lives when we take the will of God seriously. (It would be helpful for you to read Leslie Weatherhead's classic book, *The Will of God*).

God's judgment is upon those who live by their own rules and disregard God's love and justice. The whole purpose of the gospel is to empower persons to live as God intended us to live. Justice and mercy are what God requires of us. (Jesus and Micah both gave us this counsel.)

How do we discern the will of God? How can we be empowered to live by God's will?

IV. Be prepared for the end.

The end of all things is at hand. This has been a recurring theme in the Bible. God will have a day of calling us into account. History seems to be moving toward some kind of culmination. God has time in his hands, and we can never know fully when the end time will be. The message of Peter is "Be prepared." Jesus seemed to also preach this same message of preparedness (see, for example, the parable of the wise and foolish virgins).

Love one another, practice hospitality, be good stewards of God's grace. Dr. McGeachy suggests that this passage would be a good one to memorize and store away in your heart and mind. What do you think?

How can we be prepared for the end of time? Or for the end of our personal history (death)?

Helping Class Members Act

See if some of the following suggestions would be helpful as you seek to help class members put their faith into practice:

- Evaluate your attitude toward suffering.
- See what you can do this week to seek God's will for you.
- Ponder what you would do if you knew this would be the last week of your earthly life.

Conclude the session with this prayer: Dear God, help us discern your will for our lives and give us courage to live it. Help us to be good witnesses for you in our suffering. Amen.

MAY 17   LESSON 12

Planning for Next Sunday

Make appropriate assignments. Ask members to read 1 Peter 5:1-11 and the lesson material in their student book.

LESSON 12   MAY 17

Excellent Exhortations

Background Scripture: 1 Peter 5:1-11

The Main Question—Pat McGeachy

Last week we studied about suffering and reminded ourselves of Jesus' call to take up our daily cross. We are told that to lose our lives for Christ's sake means ultimately to find them. But there is a catch to it. I call it Catch One, because I believe it lies near the heart of the meaning of life: You must *really* lose your life; you can't *pretend* to lose it, knowing that Jesus will reward you. You can't jump only when you know that the bottom is really only a few feet down. You have to jump knowing that you are in for a real fall. Another way to put it is this: You can't wear your humility button! Because the minute you put it on, you are no longer humble.

There is no better way in which this is illustrated than in the matter of leadership. If a person truly wants to be president of the United States, we are suspicious, because that person may be merely wanting power and prestige. But if we wait for a president who doesn't want to be president, how are we going to get anybody to run? We want our pastors, and other church leaders, to have real leadership ability, but at the same time we want them to be humble servants. In fact, the word "minister," which we commonly use for such leaders, literally means "servant." That's the way Jesus used it (see Mark 10:45, especially in the King James Version). We put ministers on a pedestal and then fuss at them for being there. We do the same with laypeople: We say, "Why don't more people take an active part in our church?" But when somebody does, we fuss about how they are "trying to run things."

The question, then, for this week's lesson is, How can Christians combine both humility and visibility, both leadership and service, both banner-waving and cross-bearing? Or, to put it another way, What's the difference between humility and low self-esteem?

Selected Scripture

King James Version	**Revised Standard Version**
1 Peter 5:1-11	*1 Peter 5:1-11*
1 The elders which are among you I exhort, who am also an elder,	1 So I exhort the elders among you, as a fellow elder and a witness

THIRD QUARTER

and a witness of the sufferings of Christ, and also a partaker of the glory that shall be revealed:

2 Feed the flock of God which is among you, taking the oversight *thereof*, not by constraint, but willingly; not for filthy lucre, but of a ready mind;

3 Neither as being lords over *God's* heritage, but being ensamples to the flock.

4 And when the chief Shepherd shall appear, ye shall receive a crown of glory that fadeth not away.

5 Likewise, ye younger, submit yourselves unto the elder. Yea, all *of you* be subject one to another, and be clothed with humility: for God resisteth the proud, and giveth grace to the humble.

6 Humble yourselves therefore under the mighty hand of God, that he may exalt you in due time:

7 Casting all your care upon him; for he careth for you.

8 Be sober, be vigilant; because your adversary the devil, as a roaring lion, walketh about, seeking whom he may devour:

9 Whom resist stedfast in the faith, knowing that the same afflictions are accomplished in your brethren that are in the world.

10 But the God of all grace, who hath called us unto his eternal glory by Christ Jesus, after that ye have suffered a while, make you perfect, stablish, strengthen, settle *you*.

11 To him *be* glory and dominion for ever and ever. Amen.

Key Verse: **Humble yourselves therefore under the mighty hand of God, that he may exalt you in due time: Casting all your care upon him; for he careth for you. (1 Peter 5:6-7)**

of the sufferings of Christ as well as a partaker in the glory that is to be revealed. 2 Tend the flock of God that is your charge, not by constraint but willingly, not for shameful gain but eagerly, 3 not as domineering over those in your charge but being examples to the flock. 4 And when the chief Shepherd is manifested you will obtain the unfading crown of glory. 5 Likewise you that are younger be subject to the elders. Clothe yourselves, all of you, with humility toward one another, for "God opposes the proud, but gives grace to the humble."

6 Humble yourselves therefore under the mighty hand of God, that in due time he may exalt you. 7 Cast all your anxieties on him, for he cares about you. 8 Be sober, be watchful. Your adversary the devil prowls around like a roaring lion, seeking some one to devour. 9 Resist him, firm in your faith, knowing that the same experience of suffering is required of your brotherhood throughout the world. 10 And after you have suffered a little while, the God of all grace, who has called you to his eternal glory in Christ, will himself restore, establish, and strengthen you. 11 To him be the dominion for ever and ever. Amen.

Key Verse: **Humble yourselves therefore under the mighty hand of God, that in due time he may exalt you. Cast all your anxieties on him, for he cares about you. (1 Peter 5:6-7)**

MAY 17 LESSON 12

As You Read the Scripture—Ralph W. Decker

The First Letter of Peter closes with several paragraphs of advice and exhortation directed to both church leaders and church members.

1 Peter 5:1. The second verse makes it clear that the elders here addressed were not only older persons but also church officials who exercised considerable authority in the local congregation. Peter lists three things that give him the right to instruct and direct his readers, including the elders: (1) He too is an elder (he humbly refrains from proclaiming his superior position of apostle, although he has stated it in the opening sentence of the letter); (2) he was an eyewitness of the crucifixion; (3) in witnessing the transfiguration (Matthew 17:1-8; Mark 9:2-8; Luke 9:28-36) he had a glimpse of the glory of Christ, which will be fully revealed in the Second Coming, which is now approaching.

Verse 2. The opening words of this verse read like those of the risen Christ to Peter as reported in John 21:15-17 "Feed my lambs.... Tend my sheep.... Feed my sheep." Both passages may echo words of Jesus spoken to Peter many years before either book was written.

Verses 2-3. Church leaders are to serve willingly, not because they are pressured to do so. Nor, although they are paid, are they to serve primarily for gain. They are to serve joyfully and eagerly, primarily by setting good examples. Peter here forbids greed, not acceptance of reasonable support.

Verse 4. This is another reference to the Second Coming. It is the only place in the New Testament where Jesus is called "the chief Shepherd," although he is called "the good shepherd" in John 10:11, 14 and "the great shepherd of the sheep" in Hebrews 13:20. That he is here called "chief Shepherd" suggests that the elders were being referred to as shepherds. The Greek words translated "crown of glory" refer not to a metal crown worn by a monarch as a symbol of power and rule but to a wreath of laurel leaves placed on the head of an athlete as a symbol of victory. The Christian who lives victoriously will win an unfading crown, in contrast to the perishable garlands awarded in athletic contests.

Verse 5. This may be an echo of the occasion, reported in John 13, upon which Jesus girded himself with a towel and performed a servant's work in washing the feet of his disciples. Not only the younger church members but all believers are to defer to one another. Humility is a major Christian virtue.

Verses 6-8. Peter gives further instructions for church members. They are to be humble, trustful toward God, sober (serious), and ever alert to sin. Even though they are urged to cast all their worries on God, they are not excused from responsibility for their choices and actions.

Verse 6. Egotism and self-satisfaction stand in the way of God's help. Humility opens the way for him to help.

Verse 7. Caring means sharing, even when a caring God relieves a worried human of anxieties.

Verse 8. Reliance upon God does not release a person from accountability. Even though under his care, one must remain alert. Satan, the tempter, is here likened to a hungry lion ready to pounce upon careless humans.

Verse 9. Peter calls for a firm faith as the best resistance to evil. He also points out to his readers that they have plenty of company in their troubles.

THIRD QUARTER

He advises unity and mutual support as defenses against the common enemy. He that is hunting for human souls must be met with a united resistance.

Verse 10. The phrase "a little while" suggests that Peter expected an early end to the present age and its problems, as did many first-century Christians.

Verse 11. The major part of the letter closes with an ascription of praise similar to the one in 4:11.

The Scripture and the Main Question—Pat McGeachy

True Leadership (1 Peter 5:1-5)

Outside of the Bible, I think the best paragraph I ever read on humility is that of C. S. Lewis in *Mere Christianity*:

> Do not imagine that if you meet a really humble man he will be what most people call "humble" nowadays: he will not be a sort of greasy, smarmy person, who is always telling you that, of course, he is nobody. Probably all you will think about him is that he seemed a cheerful, intelligent chap who took a real interest in what *you* said to *him*. If you do dislike him it will be because you feel a little envious of anyone who seems to enjoy life so easily. He will not be thinking about humility: he will not be thinking about himself at all.
>
> If anyone would like to acquire humility, I can, I think, tell him the first step. The first step is to realise that one is proud. And a biggish step, too. At least, nothing whatever can be done before it. If you think you are not conceited, it means you are very conceited indeed. (p. 114)

That will serve as a very good introduction to the last chapter of 1 Peter. It has to do with leadership, a knotty problem for all of us, followers as well as leaders. One day, just about sunset, I saw a flight of wild ducks pass a church steeple in single file. The procession went on for nearly an hour; I lost count of how many hundreds of ducks their were. But as the light faded, I thought to myself, "I sure am glad I'm not the front duck in that lineup. I wonder if he knows where he is going." Leadership is not easy. You have to know where you are going, but you also have to be free from conceit about your knowledge. To switch metaphors, the mule has to be in front of the wagon to pull it, but it must stay within the traces. Let's take a verse by verse journey through this chapter, and see what Peter, one of the great leaders of the church, has to say about the art of being the front duck.

1 Peter 5:1—Here the apostle identifies himself as a person with leadership abilities. He was there at the beginning, an eyewitness to the great events in Jesus' life, but he does not use this as an excuse to lord it over them; rather, he identifies himself as a "fellow elder." It is incumbent upon all leaders that they stay in fellowship with their followers. The most successful thing I ever did in the pastorate was in a rural congregation I once served. I hired myself as a hand to all the families in the church and learned to drive a tractor, build a fence, and cut a horse. The bond between leader and people became close because we came to know each other intimately.

The word "elder" deserves some attention. It is an Old Testament church word, as well as New, occurring first in Genesis 50:7 and often in the rest of the Pentateuch where matters of government are raised. See, for instance, the homely account of the place of the elders in the time of the Judges as described in Ruth 4:1-12. In the New Testament the Greek word (which at root simply means "an older person") is *presbuteros*. The word "priest" comes from this same root. In the New Testament, the word seems to be used interchangeably with *episcopos*, "bishop." This is because church government did not have firmly fixed forms until after the New Testament was written. But as we will see in the next verse, by using it Peter clearly meant to indicate his position of leadership, perhaps over a particular congregation.

1 Peter 5:2—Tend the flock. Compare this with the words spoken to Peter himself by the Lord in John 21:16. There is, of course, only one Shepherd (John 10:16), but the role of the undershepherd is depicted in many parts of the Bible (1 Chronicles 11:2; Ezekiel 34:1-17) and is understood here (see 1 Peter 5:4). The church leaders are not to grow fat because of their position, though this sometimes happened then, and still does in our time.

1 Peter 5:3—Don't be domineering; literally, don't "lord it over" those who are in your charge (the Greek word here is *kleron*, from which our word "clergy" comes). The best way to lead is by example.

1 Peter 5:4—The Chief Shepherd will reward you. Here is reference to 1 Peter 2:25 and John 10:11. It is similar also to Jesus' saying that one who has been faithful in little things will be given more authority (Matthew 25:21). We are not to seek the glory of this world but to do our duty, knowing that God will reward us in good time. Another dimension to this is the fact that virtue is its own reward.

1 Peter 5:5—Successful leadership requires the support of those who are led. If we all humble ourselves, clergy and laity alike, we can expect to make real progress as a church. But if we are all power hungry or full of false pride, we can expect trouble. Peter concludes with a quotation from Proverbs 3:34, which leads him into his next section.

True Humility (1 Peter 5:6-11)

1 Peter 5:6—Humility begins when we put ourselves under the authority of God. Only then can we hope to exercise leadership over others. It is said that when the Episcopal bishop James Pike was being tried for heresy, he announced, "No one possesses authority who is not *under* authority." This is especially true of leadership in the church, but also of secular leadership. What made George Washington a great president was his obedience to a higher calling. Great scientists must be committed to a truth that is larger than themselves. I can be a better husband and father if I put God first in my life.

1 Peter 5:7—This means above all that I must trust God. I cannot bear the responsibilities of leadership unless I am willing to cast my anxieties on God. If I am preoccupied with them, I will not be able to help others. When I left for college, my parents wrote in the front of the Bible that they gave me "Proverbs 3:5-6." If you check these verses, they will help you as much as they did me.

1 Peter 5:8—The real enemy is not people but the principalities and powers (see Ephesians 6:10-20). Their principal weapon against us is fear, but if we continue to trust in God, casting our cares on the God who cares, none of those fears can destroy us.

1 Peter 5:9—We can take considerable comfort from the fact that we are not alone. If Peter could feel this way in the first century, how much more can you and I feel it, seeing that we have nearly twenty centuries of martyrs and witnesses who have gone before us, whose examples can give us comfort. That is why we belong to a connectional church. When one of us suffers, we all suffer (1 Corinthians 12:26). The secular way of saying this is "A sorrow shared is half the sorrow, a joy shared is twice the joy."

1 Peter 5:10—Best of all, there is light at the end of the tunnel. This suffering is for a brief time (2 Corinthians 4:17), and the promise is that God will set things right in due time. I don't know about you, but I can stand almost anything if I feel that it has a purpose and I can see some eventual relief from it.

1 Peter 5:11—This is a brief ascription of praise to God, but it sums up the whole matter of leadership and humility. It gives the Lordship wholly and entirely to God. One who can turn the dominion over to God has no power needs to interfere with a life of genuine service to others. As long as we are seeking gratification in our position over other human beings or toadying up to those in leadership assignments, we will always be struggling to be top dog. But the minute we can turn loose of this, the minute we can lose our lives, in that minute we suddenly become humble, and, by the mystery of God, great.

Helping Adults Become Involved—Roy H. Ryan

Preparing to Teach

This passage contains a series of exhortations to the elders (the leaders) in the church. It also provides some advice for younger members of the church. As Dr. Decker points out, "The elders here addressed were not only older persons but also church officials who exercised considerable authority in the local congregation." In the one instance (verse 5), Peter does admonish those who are younger and likely do not have leadership roles in the congregation. As adult church members and leaders, the lesson is certainly directed to us.

Read both Dr. Decker's exegesis and Dr. McGeachy's commentary on this passage.

Think about members of your class as you prepare. How might the message of 1 Peter 5:1-11 influence their lives? How can it be made relevant?

The passage is really about Christian leadership. What ought Christian leaders be like? How should they lead? You will undoubtedly have some of your congregation's leaders in your class; this lesson will have special relevance for them.

The aim of the lesson is to help adults better understand how they can exert leadership in the church but at the same time remain humble servants of Christ.

A possible outline for the lesson might be as follows:

I. Introduction.
II. Tend the flock of God.

MAY 17   LESSON 12

    III. Humble yourselves.
    IV. Resist evil.

Introducing the Main Question

What is the real question confronting us in this lesson? I like the way Dr. McGeachy has stated it: "How can Christians combine both humility and visibility, both leadership and service, both banner-waving and cross-bearing?"

How do Christian persons (especially leaders in the church) live out their role as both leaders and as humble servants? It is often difficult to keep these two roles in balance. If one is too aggressive in one's leadership style, where is the humility? If one is too "laid back," too passive (which we sometimes equate with humility), how will anything get done?

Plan to engage members of the class in a discussion around the question, What is the role of a Christian leader? Or, What are the qualities you look for in our church leaders?

Developing the Lesson

I. Introduction.

A good way to begin the lesson would be to (1) ask one of the questions suggested above and engage in class discussion, (2) select a church leader you think embodies both leadership skills and a humble attitude and describe that person to the group.

You might post on newsprint one or more key questions relating to the lesson around the room. These questions should provoke class members to think about what a Christian leader ought to be like.

II. Tend the flock of God.

This image of the Good Shepherd may seem a little foreign to most of us today, but it can likely be understood with a little explanation. Jesus used this same image when he told Peter, "Feed my sheep." In the church we sometimes refer to the congregation as a flock (a term used for a group of sheep). A pastor is sometimes even considered a shepherd of the flock of God. We may not use this exact term, but most adults will know what it means.

Christian leaders are to look after those in their charge. Mr. Wesley, the founder of the Methodist movement, believed in organizing persons into small groups (classes) so they could watch out for one another and be accountable to one another. Each class had a leader who was a kind of shepherd for the class. What about your adult class? Do you also tend to one another's needs, look out for one another, care for one another? That is shepherding in the New Testament sense. How do we tend the flock of God?

III. Humble yourselves.

Show humility toward one another. We are called as Christians to show no favoritism but to count all persons as worthy of our love and concern. We do not help other persons in order to gain favor with anyone. We are reminded of Jesus' teaching, "Whoever would be great among you must be servant of all."

THIRD QUARTER

Humble yourselves before God. Again we are reminded of Jesus' teaching about our humility before God. In Luke 18:9-14, the parable of the Pharisee and the publican, Jesus concludes with these words: "Every one who exalts himself will be humbled, but he who humbles himself will be exalted." Is humility something one can learn? What are some signs of true humility?

IV. Resist evil.

Be sober, be watchful (1 Peter 5:8). This is a clear warning for Christians to be on guard against all forms of evil. However we may think about evil, whether we see it as personalized in a devil or as some negative force, we know it exists. Martin Luther, the great reformer, sought to ward off evil by always reminding himself "I have been baptized," that is, "I belong to Christ." If we see ourselves as belonging to Christ, that will give us strength to be sober and watchful.

Resist your adversary, the devil (verses 8*b*-9). Stay firm in your faith. Do not yield to the temptation to go back to your old ways. How do we deal with evil in the world? How do we confront the evil in our own lives?

Helping Class Members Act

Discuss ways you could care for one another more helpfully in your class. Ask persons to reflect prayerfully on the way they exercise leadership. Ask persons to consciously remind themselves, as they confront any temptation, "I have been baptized."

Finish up the lesson time with this prayer: Dear God, give us grace to be humble servants of yours in all areas of our lives. In the name of Christ who came to serve, Amen.

Planning for Next Sunday

Read 2 Peter 1:1-14. The topic will be "Growing in Grace." Also read Ephesians 4. It will help you with the issue of "growing up" toward maturity in Christ. As you plan, consider the "means of grace which the church supplies," such as worship, Bible study, sacraments, prayer, service, and so forth.

LESSON 13　　　　　　　　　　　　　　　　　　　　MAY 24

Growing in Grace

Background Scripture: 2 Peter 1:1-14

The Main Question—Pat McGeachy

The tiny capsules in which the first astronauts went up had no windows, and when they were in zero gravity it was hard to tell if they were moving or not. Sometimes, when the retro rockets fired to slow them down, it *felt* as though they were being propelled in the opposite direction from the one in which they were supposed to be going. So they had to depend on their instruments to make sure that they were on track. In the same way, sometimes it is hard for Christians to know where we are headed.

Regardless of whether you believe in the theory of evolution associated with Charles Darwin, you will surely concede that evolution has a place in the Bible. What I mean is this: It is clear that things started out incomplete. "The earth was without form and void" (Genesis 1:2) before God brought order and life to it. The history of God's relationship with us has gone through some changes: Once we followed ancient rules and rituals; today we live with a sense of freedom (Galatians 5:1); once we were no people, now we are God's people (1 Peter 2:10).

Of course, not all change is good. When we find it happening to an egg, C. S. Lewis said, we call that "going bad." The Scriptures provide for us measures of our change, that we may make sure that our evolution is indeed progress and not deterioration. One such standard is set forth in Ephesians 4:15-16, which thinks of the church as a body, growing in love under the leadership of Christ, our head. (There are others: Matthew 5:21-22, 27-28, 33-34, 38-39, 44-45; Philippians 3:12-16.) But 2 Peter is a good place to look for the steppingstones that will lead us to growth in Christ, especially chapter 1, verses 5-11. Let us turn there to find an answer to the question, How can you tell if you are making progress? And one related to it: How shall the Christian continually grow in grace?

Selected Scripture

King James Version

2 Peter 1:1-14

1 Simon Peter, a servant and an apostle of Jesus Christ, to them that have obtained like precious faith with us through the righteousness of God and our Saviour Jesus Christ:

2 Grace and peace be multiplied unto you through the knowledge of God, and of Jesus our Lord,

3 According as his divine power hath given unto us all things that

Revised Standard Version

2 Peter 1:1-14

1 Simon Peter, a servant and apostle of Jesus Christ,

To those who have obtained a faith of equal standing with ours in the righteousness of our God and Savior Jesus Christ:

2 May grace and peace be multiplied to you in the knowledge of God and of Jesus our Lord.

3 His divine power has granted to us all things that pertain to life

THIRD QUARTER

pertain unto life and godliness, through the knowledge of him that hath called us to glory and virtue:

4 Whereby are given unto us exceeding great and precious promises: that by these ye might be partakers of the divine nature, having escaped the corruption that is in the world through lust.

5 And beside this, giving all diligence, add to your faith virtue; and to virtue knowledge;

6 And to knowledge temperance; and to temperance patience; and to patience godliness;

7 And to godliness brotherly kindness; and to brotherly kindness charity.

8 For if these things be in you, and abound, they make *you that ye shall* neither *be* barren nor unfruitful in the knowledge of our Lord Jesus Christ.

9 But he that lacketh these things is blind, and cannot see afar off, and hath forgotten that he was purged from his old sins.

10 Wherefore the rather, brethren, give diligence to make your calling and election sure: for if ye do these things, ye shall never fall:

11 For so an entrance shall be ministered unto you abundantly into the everlasting kingdom of our Lord and Saviour Jesus Christ.

12 Wherefore I will not be negligent to put you always in remembrance of these things, though ye know *them*, and be established in the present truth.

13 Yea, I think it meet, as long as I am in this tabernacle, to stir you up by putting *you* in remembrance;

14 Knowing that shortly I must put off *this* my tabernacle, even as our Lord Jesus Christ hath shewed me.

Key Verse: **His divine power hath given unto us all things that pertain unto life and godliness, through the knowledge of him that hath**

and godliness, through the knowledge of him who called us to his own glory and excellence, 4 by which he has granted to us his precious and very great promises, that through these you may escape from the corruption that is in the world because of passion, and become partakers of the divine nature. 5 For this very reason make every effort to supplement your faith with virtue, and virtue with knowledge, 6 and knowledge with self-control, and self-control with steadfastness, and steadfastness with godliness, 7 and godliness with brotherly affection, and brotherly affection with love. 8 "For if these things are yours and abound, they keep you from being ineffective or unfruitful in the knowledge of our Lord Jesus Christ. 9 For whoever lacks these things is blind and shortsighted and has forgotten that he was cleansed from his old sins. 10 Therefore, brethren, be the more zealous to confirm your call and election, for if you do this you will never fall; 11 so there will be richly provided for you an entrance into the eternal kingdom of our Lord and Savior Jesus Christ.

12 Therefore I intend always to remind you of these things, though you know them and are established in the truth that you have. 13 I think it right, as long as I am in this body, to arouse you by way of reminder, 14 since I know that the putting off of my body will be soon, as our Lord Jesus Christ showed me.

Key Verse: **His divine power has granted to us all things that pertain to life and godliness, through the knowledge of him who called us**

	LESSON 13
called us to glory and virtue. (2 Peter 1:3)	to his own glory and excellence. (2 Peter 1:3)

As You Read the Scripture—Ralph W. Decker

The usual questions about who wrote this book and when, where, and to whom it was written are not easily answered. The opening verse says it was written by Peter, but only the most conservative scholars now take that claim literally. The doubts as to Peter's being the author are not new. The letter is not quoted or even mentioned in the existing writings of church leaders of the first two centuries. Nor is it mentioned in any of the lists of accepted Scriptures that have come down from the second century. The oldest known mention is in a writing of Origen, a Christian teacher who lived about A.D. 185–254.

Indications of a late date are found within the letter itself. "The fathers" have died (3:4). The long delay of Christ's return has become a problem (3:3-9). Being a Christian has become sufficient cause for official persecution (1 Peter 4:16). Peter died in a localized persecution in A.D. 64–65. Many scholars believe this letter reflects the more general persecutions of A.D. 125–150.

2 Peter 1:1. The opening of this letter differs from the openings of other New Testament letters in that it does not mention the readers' place of residence, national origin, or relationship to the writer. This is clearly a general letter. The Hebrew name Simeon (Simon is its Greek form) occurs only here and in Acts 15:14. It has been used both in support and in opposition to the theory that Peter is this epistle's author. Some who support Peter as being the author see him using the Jewish form of his Greek name, by which he was known among family and close friends. Others think someone, not Peter, used it to "prove" that he was a Jew who became an apostle.

Verse 2. The last six words in verse 1 refer to one person—Simon Peter. The last six in this verse refer to two persons—"our *God* and Savior *Jesus Christ.*" Together they reflect the beginnings of the doctrine of the Trinity—one God in three Persons.

Verses 3-4. Through knowledge of Christ, believers obtain everything necessary for salvation. Salvation consists of escaping the world's evil and sharing in Christ's divine nature. The corruption to be escaped is the moral decay of human society. That decay is caused by passion or lust, uncontrolled desire for forbidden things.

Verses 5-8. What is given by Christ's divine power must be accepted and developed by the individual in order that salvation may be complete. We must do all that we can to bring our lives into line with our knowledge of Christ. Starting with faith, the belief that Jesus is the Christ, the Son of God, the believer must develop an ethical and moral life, nurtured by seven characteristics: virtue, knowledge, self-control, steadfastness, godliness, brotherly affection, and love. This list is a progression. Each virtue adds to the one preceding it. The list starts with faith and climaxes with love (Compare 1 Corinthians 13).

Verse 8. Salvation involves not only possession of these virtues but also continuing growth in them.

Verse 9. Salvation is not a static condition. It involves not only release from old sins but also development in Christian character.

THIRD QUARTER

Verses 10-11. Honest efforts to confirm one's call and faith response through practicing the Christian virtues (verses 5-7) will result in steadfastness and entrance into Christ's kingdom.

Verses 12-15. This might be called Peter's last will and testament. The author expresses concern that the gospel as he has preached it will be preached after his death, which he expects soon.

Verse 12. The truth the readers have is the teaching of the apostles and their accounts of the ministry of Jesus, their witness to his resurrection, and their proclamation of his lordship.

Verse 14. The prediction of an early death may refer to the risen Christ's statement to Peter in John 21:18 and to John's interpretation of it as a prediction of Peter's martyrdom (John 21:19).

The Scripture and the Main Question—Pat McGeachy

A Problem for Scholars

We might as well begin our two-lesson look at 2 Peter by facing a very real problem in scholarship. Frankly, most scholars think it wasn't written by Peter himself but by a disciple some years later, who used (not deceitfully—this was appropriate in those days) Peter's name. One of the reasons that we think it must have been later is that parts of it (most of chapter 2) are clearly dependent on the letter of Jude. You will want to compare the two. Of course, it could have been the other way around—Jude copying from Peter—but for various reasons most scholars don't think so. For a long time doubts have been expressed about its inclusion in the Bible, and there is no record of its existence in Christian literature before A.D. 200. Jude, however, was widely in use at this time.

One answer to this question will not affect the way in which we study these two lessons, but it is important that we realize that in 2 Peter we do not have a clear sequel to 1 Peter. It may have been written a good many years later, probably in response to a danger confronting the early church, the same one that was bothering Jude. I don't want to make too big a deal about this, but it is only fair that we be straight with each other about these lessons. So, having said all that, lets proceed to look, first of all, 2 Peter 1:1-14.

Greeting (2 Peter 1:1-2)

2 Peter 1:1—The letter begins with the writer's name, as was the custom for letters in those days, though as we have said, this may have been written by a disciple (such as Sylvanus) rather than by Peter himself. A number of other early letters were so designated, but this one, if it is one, is the only one to have been included in the canon of the New Testament. It is clear from the first verse that it is a circular letter, not intended for a particular congregation but for Christians in all churches who share the writer's convictions.

2 Peter 1:2—He begins with a benediction. Contrary to popular belief, a benediction does not mean a prayer at the end of the service but a blessing appropriate at any time in worship. The shortest benediction that I know is "Goodbye," which usually does come at the end, though it doesn't have to. It doesn't mean "ten-four" or "signing off." It means, as we all know when we stop to think, "God be with you." It is certainly appropriate at the beginning of a conversation. Indeed, some churches begin their service with such a greeting:

> Leader: The Lord be with you.
> People: And also with you.

"Hello" is also a benediction, meaning "health and wholeness to you." And we are used to saying it at the beginning of conversations.

Keep the Faith (2 Peter 1:3-11)

2 Peter 1:3—God has given us all that we need to know to live a faithful Christian life.

2 Peter 1:4—The promises of God give us the courage to face all the difficulties of this life, and to lay hold of part of God's own self, the divine nature. Compare this with John 1:12.

2 Peter 1:5—This verse is the start of a long sentence that builds and builds. It starts with faith and adds virtue, then knowledge. Faith alone, without virtue, is dead (James 2:17), and without knowledge it can be blind and meaningless. It is not enough merely to have faith. It must be faith *in* that which we have come to know and understand.

2 Peter 1:6—To these we must add self-control, steadfastness, and godliness. (Our list is beginning to sound like the fruit of the Spirit (Galatians 5:22-23) and some other New Testament collections of virtues, such as Romans 5:1-5).

2 Peter 1:7—The list goes on. We add brotherly affection and love. Here we have in one sentence the two New Testament root words translated as "love," *philia* and *agape*. They quite properly belong together, but are in the right order if we are progressing from lesser to greater gifts, from faith to love. Brotherly love means friendship, but *agape* means charity, love that is akin to the divine love by which, while we were yet sinners, God first loved us (Romans 5:8).

2 Peter 1:8—When these things are second nature to us, they make it certain that we will be effective and fruitful in keeping the faith and passing on the knowledge of our Lord Jesus Christ. We cannot pass on a gospel that we have not made our own. If we *have* made it our own, we can hardly help passing it on by word and by example.

2 Peter 1:9—Not to have these virtues is to have forgotten the grace in which we were called. Not to have these virtues is to depend on myself and my own righteousness, to my eventual failure.

2 Peter 1:10—The way to keep from falling is to keep hammering away at the realization that we were called by the grace and power of God and not by our own righteousness (Ephesians 2:8-9). It is strange to say that one has to work at grace, since grace is a free gift. Perhaps it would be better to think of this as actively participating in the "means of grace," not so that we can create it but so that we can make ourselves receptive to it, as a sailor by hoisting sails is receptive to the wind, whenever God chooses to make it blow (John 3:8).

2 Peter 1:11—This section is concluded with a firm promise that if we do persevere, there will be a rich reward in the eternal kingdom of Christ.

THIRD QUARTER

The Apostle's Testimony (2 Peter 1:12-15)

2 Peter 1:12—The writer does not intend to nag. He knows that his hearers already know much of what he is saying. Surely this is true of most of the people who come to our church services Sunday after Sunday, year after year. But it is good to hear the old words over and over again. Sometimes, perhaps, we say them too often, so that they lose something in becoming repetitive. And sometimes their very familiarity makes them hard to hear. But most of the time, it is the old words that heal and help. Consider a funeral: That is no time to say something cute and different. In such an hour we take comfort from the same words that have comforted our ancestors for generations. And is not every moment a time when we should be conscious of our impending death?

2 Peter 1:13—As long as I am in the body, I'm going to keep on telling you. A friend of mine, at age 103, sometimes would say, "I wonder why God keeps me around." But I knew why. She was there to remind me of the old truths, delivered to the saints, as long as she was in the body.

2 Peter 1:14—The writer knows that he will die soon. Perhaps he is in prison, awaiting execution. (If it really was Peter, that is the likely explanation.) Or perhaps he is simply conscious that he is getting old. In either case, he considered his premonition a word from Christ.

2 Peter 1:15—The writer concludes, "I want you to keep on thinking of what I have told you." You and I could ask for nothing more than to be remembered for the good counsel that we have passed on, both by the words we have spoken, the deeds we have done, and the life-style that we have demonstrated.

Growing in Grace

How do you grow in grace? You just keep on practicing the Christian life, developing good habits, and saying over and over the old words that have been passed down through the leaders who have gone before. You can't *make* grace happen, of course, but what Brother Lawrence of the Resurrection called the practice of the presence of Christ develops in us such spiritual systems that from day to day we continue to become more and more secure in the faith.

Helping Adults Become Involved—Roy H. Ryan

Preparing to Teach

What does it mean to grow in grace? We have probably heard that phrase quite a lot in the church. This lesson should help us better understand what it means. If you have read Ephesians 4, you should have some good background help on what it means to keep on growing as a Christian person. Giving thought to the ways we can grow in our Christian life by participating in the life and ministry of the church should also help you in your preparation.

Most adults want to keep on growing. We have come to know that if we stop growing we will deteriorate. Continuing education is now the "in" thing in most professions and occupations. What about growth in our spiritual life? Are we as concerned there as we are in our professional or

MAY 24   LESSON 13

vocational pursuits? Many adults are. That is one reason they come to Sunday school classes.

The aim of this lesson is to hold before adult Christians the need for continuing growth and to help them consider some practical ways to continue their spiritual quest.

You will want to give some thought to how you will deal with the scholarly question, Who wrote 2 Peter? It may not be an issue you want to deal with in class, but you need to at least be aware of the dispute about the authorship and time of writing of this letter. Dr. Decker and Dr. McGeachy each have helpful comments about the controversy. A good commentary will give you additional information, if you desire it.

An outline for the lesson could be as follows:

        I. Introduction
       II. A greeting and a benediction
      III. Keep the faith
      IV. Growing in grace

Introducing the Main Question

How can we keep on growing as Christians? You may want to post that question on the chalkboard or newsprint for all to see.

You may want to engage class members in a discussion of a question such as, What have you found helpful in your own growth as a Christian? You may expect some of the following responses: worship, prayer and Bible study, spiritual life retreats, the sacrament of holy communion, doing works of love and mercy, and giving money to worthy causes. You may think of other means of grace by which persons are helped to move toward maturity in Christ.

Developing the Lesson

I. Introduction

A good way to introduce the lesson is suggested above. An alternate method would be to take some time to talk about the authorship and time of writing of 2 Peter. The difficulty with taking this approach is the danger of becoming sidetracked from the real topic, Christian growth.

II. A greeting and a benediction

The writer greets the readers or hearers of his epistle as equals in faith. He is not writing or speaking down to them. He acknowledges the integrity of their faith and commitments. When we talk about the need to grow in our discipleship, that does not denigrate where people are in their faith journey. It is simply a recognition that no matter how far along we are toward maturity, we always have room to grow.

"May grace and peace be multiplied to you." That sounds more like a benediction. Dr. McGeachy has some helpful comments about the proper place of benedictions in our Christian worship and our vocabulary. Do you find it meaningful when someone gives you a blessing?

III. Keep the faith

Faith is basic to our lives as Christian disciples. That is how it all begins; "we are saved by grace through faith." The writer begins a long litany of qualities that ought to characterize our lives as Christians. Faith is the very foundation upon which we build lives as disciples. We start as "babes in Christ," with a very immature faith, but with God's help we can "feed on the meat of the gospel" as Paul suggested and thus be strengthened. Only by growing up can we avoid being swayed "by every wind of doctrine" (Ephesians 4:14).

By taking on other virtues, we can finally become able to love (verse 7). Love (*agape*) is the greatest of all gifts (see I Corinthians 13:13). Take a look at all the qualities or virtues mentioned in verses 5-7. If we take on these qualities of life, we will be effective and fruitful as followers of Jesus Christ. Discuss some ways we can begin to claim these virtues.

IV. Grow in grace

Grace is the unmerited favor of God. How, then, can one grow in grace if it is a gift? Grace is God's gracious offer but is appropriated only when we take advantage of it. Therefore, we want to put ourselves into settings and situations that will enable us to receive God's grace. As mentioned above, one good example of such a setting is worship. Some people seem to feel that worship is optional for Christians. What do you think?

We are called to avail ourselves of every means of grace offered through the church. If we are to continue to grow, we need to give attention to our participation in the total life and ministry of the church. The grace of God is not limited to the church, but our experience seems to validate the fact that the church is our greatest source of spiritual nurture and guidance. How might you give more attention to your growth as a Christian?

Helping Class Members Act

What about asking the members to make some new commitments for themselves? For instance, ask each person to identify one additional way they would be willing to work on spiritual growth. It might be prayer or Bible study on a regular basis. It might be through regular attendance at worship. Some might be willing to attend a spiritual life retreat. Challenge your class to come up with some ways you can together keep on growing.

Join together in this prayer: We thank you, God, for the gift of your grace. We ask for help in our continuing growth in order that we will not always be "babes in Christ" but will mature in Christian life. In his Name, Amen.

Planning for Next Sunday

The lesson next week concludes the quarters study. Ask members to read 2 Peter 3:3-14. Plan for a time of evaluation at the end of next week's lesson. Help will be provided for such an evaluation in this section of that lesson.

LESSON 14   MAY 31

Living in the Light of the Future

Background Scripture: 2 Peter 3:3-14

The Main Question—Pat McGeachy

When I was a young man I decided that I did not believe in the teachings that had been handed down to me by my parents. I thought I could prove that they were wrong because they did not make logical sense. What, I thought, could the death and resurrection of a man nearly two thousand years ago have to do with my life today? And what good would it do me, even if it were true? As I understood it, I would then go to heaven, where I would have to play a harp (an instrument I heartily detested, for, except for Harpo Marx, it was always played by ladies in evening dresses at very stiff occasions) for ever and ever and ever. Which is a long time to be doing anything, even if you are enjoying it.

But my problem, as I came to discover on getting a little older, was based on a kind of arrogance. I had supposed that reality was the way *I* saw it. It did not occur to me that God might see reality in a very different way. According to 2 Peter 3:8, God doesn't see the two thousand years separating me from Jesus as a large interval at all. God doesn't seem to think eternity is a very long time, or that there isn't plenty of time in a brief moment for many wonderful things to happen.

The great question for me, then, in this lesson is, How should the Christian view history? How should we think of space and time? How, in other words, does God see these things, and can we begin to look at the world through eyes not of skepticism but of faith? The answer to those questions, as 2 Peter gives it, so alters my view of reality that I find myself once more as full of excited anticipation as a child waiting for Christmas, and eager to do justice, love mercy, and walk humbly before God.

Selected Scripture

King James Version

2 Peter 3:3-14

3 Knowing this first, that there shall come in the last days scoffers, walking after their own lusts,

4 And saying, Where is the promise of his coming? for since the fathers fell asleep, all things continue as *they were* from the beginning of the creation.

5 For this they willingly are ignorant of, that by the word of God the heavens were of old, and the earth standing out of the water and in the water:

Revised Standard Version

2 Peter 3:3-14

3 First of all you must understand this, that scoffers will come in the last days with scoffing, following their own passions 4 and saying, "Where is the promise of his coming? For ever since the fathers fell asleep, all things have continued as they were from the beginning of creation." 5 They deliberately ignore this fact, that by the word of God heavens existed long ago, and an earth formed out of water and by means of water, 6 through which

THIRD QUARTER

6 Whereby the world that then was, being overflowed with water, perished:

7 But the heavens and the earth, which are now, by the same word are kept in store, reserved unto fire against the day of judgment and perdition of ungodly men.

8 But, beloved, be not ignorant of this one thing, that one day *is* with the Lord as a thousand years, and a thousand years as one day.

9 The Lord is not slack concerning his promise, as some men count slackness; but is longsuffering to us-ward, not willing that any should perish, but that all should come to repentance.

10 But the day of the Lord will come as a thief in the night; in the which the heavens shall pass away with a great noise, and the elements shall melt with fervent heat, the earth also and the works that are therein shall be burned up.

11 *Seeing* then *that* all these things shall be dissolved, what manner *of persons* ought ye to be in *all* holy conversation and godliness.

12 Looking for and hasting unto the coming of the day of God, wherein the heavens being on fire shall be dissolved, and the elements shall melt with fervent heat?

13 Nevertheless we, according to his promise, look for new heavens and a new earth, wherein dwelleth righteousness.

14 Wherefore, beloved, seeing that ye look for such things, be diligent that ye may be found of him in peace, without spot, and blameless.

Key Verse: **Nevertheless we, according to his promise, look for new heavens and a new earth, wherein dwelleth righteousness. (2 Peter 3:13)**

the world that then existed was deluged with water and perished. 7 But by the same word the heavens and earth that now exist have been stored up for fire, being kept until the day of judgment and destruction of ungodly men.

8 But do not ignore this one fact, beloved, that with the Lord one day is as a thousand years, and a thousand years as one day. 9 The Lord is not slow about his promise as some count slowness, but is forbearing toward you, not wishing that any should perish, but that all should reach repentance. 10 But the day of the Lord will come like a thief, and then the heavens will pass away with a loud noise, and the elements will be dissolved with fire, and the earth and the works that are upon it will be burned up.

11 Since all these things are thus to be dissolved, what sort of persons ought you to be in lives of holiness and godliness, 12 waiting for and hastening the coming of the day of God, because of which the heavens will be kindled and dissolved, and the elements will melt with fire! 13 But according to his promise we wait for new heavens and a new earth in which righteousness dwells.

14 Therefore, beloved, since you wait for these, be zealous to be found by him without spot or blemish and at peace.

Key Verse: **According to his promise we wait for new heavens and a new earth in which righteousness dwells. (2 Peter 3:13)**

MAY 31   LESSON 14

As You Read the Scripture—Ralph W. Decker

The final chapter of 2 Peter emphasizes the certainty of God's punishment of heresy, immorality, and false teaching. Its main theme is the return of Christ, which the author associates with a fiery destruction of the earth and everything in it (3:10). He reminds his readers that the end of the age has been predicted by prophets and apostles, and he urges them to prepare for it.

2 Peter 3:3. In preceding verses the author had reminded his readers that he has tried to prepare them for the end of the age. Now he warns unbelievers who deny and ridicule his predictions. The "last days" were not the end of the world but a period of time of undisclosed length that would precede it. Those day would be filled with catastrophe and affliction. That concept was widely believed by both Jews and Christians (Matthew 24:7-8; 1 John 2:18).

Verse 4. Early Christians expected to live to see the end of the age and the return of Christ. As time passed, questions began to arise. Paul had to deal with the problem of those who had been promised they would witness Christ's return but who had died without its taking place (1 Thessalonians 4:15-17; 1 Corinthians 15:51-52). The scoffers of whom Peter wrote seem to have been challenging the whole idea of a return, saying that nothing had changed since creation.

Verses 5-7. The author claims that they ignore the Flood. He offers it as proof of one complete change since creation and of the possibility of another.

Verse 7. The "heavens and earth that now exist" are what remained after the Flood, which was destruction by water. The idea that the next great change would come through destruction by fire had been predicted by several Old Testament prophets (Isaiah 30:30; 66:15-16; Nahum 1:5-6; Malachi 4:1).

Verse 8. The word "beloved" indicates that the author is addressing the faithful. He is concerned that they not be persuaded by the argument of the heretics that long delay is proof that Christ will not return. In answer he draws support from Psalm 90:4. Although he does not quote it exactly, he uses it as basis for his argument that God's time differs from human time. To humans a thousand years are an eternity. To God a thousand years are as one day.

Verse 9. His second explanation for the delay is God's patience. While some might count his slowness to act as indifference or impotence, the author counts it as forbearance and mercy. The delay provides more time for persons to repent and respond.

Verse 10. The idea that "the day of the Lord will come like a thief in the night" is found also in Matthew 24:43-44; Luke 12:39-40; 1 Thessalonians 5:2, 4; and Revelation 3:3; 16:15. It reflects a widely held belief that may have originated with Jesus himself. Peter, with other New Testament writers, believed that the return of Jesus would coincide with the long-awaited Day of the Lord, foretold by Hebrew prophets. Therefore, he describes it in terms drawn from their descriptions of that "great and terrible day" (Joel 2:31). He saw it as involving all things—the heavens, the elements, the earth. Whether or not he expected the world literally to end in fire, he foresaw a time of terror and awful punishment for the wicked.

Verse 11. The delay is not a time for laxity but for holy, godly living.

THIRD QUARTER

Verse 12. The writer seems to think believers can hasten the day of Christ's return through such living.

Verse 13. He looks beyond the purifying fire to a new heaven and a new earth.

Verse 14. He calls for righteous living in the meantime. His exhortations may be read as addressed to either the church in general, urging it to get rid of heresy and live in harmony, or to individual Christians, urging them to get rid of personal sins and dwell in peace.

The Scripture and the Main Question—Pat McGeachy

The World's Skepticism (2 Peter 3:3-7)

2 Peter 3:3—We shouldn't be surprised, 2 Peter tells us, that the beliefs we Christians hold dear are not shared by everyone else in the world. Just as the neighbors of Noah were surely skeptical of his building an ark in his backyard, so the secular realists of our time will be skeptical of Christian claims that this world will pass away. It is hard to understand this, for if anything is certain both to science or psychology, it is that things don't last forever. The universe itself, the physicists tell us, is rapidly declining toward entropy. And we only have to listen to our own scriptures to have this idea reinforced:

> The years of our life are seventy,
>   or, in special cases, eighty;
> Yet they are only toil and trouble;
>   they are soon gone, and we fly away.
>   (Psalm 90:10, freely translated)

(Keep this psalm handy; it is an important companion to 2 Peter).

Even at the end of all things, there will be those who, caught up in their own passions, will continue to deny what is the plain truth to those who have eyes to see: The doom is coming.

2 Peter 3:4—What they say is "No Messiah is coming; what's the use." They would prefer to go down partying in the ship's bar or peering into the gloom from the bridge with heroic nihilism, rather than accept the good news that a lifeboat is available.

2 Peter 3:5—These scoffers ignore the fact that God formed the earth out of chaos. (Read Stephen Hawking's remarkable book, *A Brief History of Time*, if you are interested in the physicist's viewpoint. What we call God, saying, "Let there be light!" the physicists call the Big Bang.)

2 Peter 13:6—They also ignore the fact that the God who brooded on the face of the waters (Genesis 1:2) can (and has) destroyed the world by those same waters.

2 Peter 13:7—Next time it will be by fire, but the earth and the things of the earth were not made to last forever. Therefore, be prepared for the great judgment that is to come.

It is hard to understand how the skeptical world can fail to see this. But it goes on fiddling while Rome burns, a grasshopper who denies that winter will ever come. There was a commercial a few years ago, designed to wake people up, which went something like this:

MAY 31 LESSON 14

Voice: Come to church with me today.
Skeptic: Sorry, I have a conflict.
Voice: Then how about next week.
Skeptic: I'll be busy then, too.
Voice: Three weeks then, maybe?
Skeptic: Oh, I never make appointments that far in advance. You never know what will happen. The whole world could come to an end by then.

Long, loud silence.

God and Time (2 Peter 3:8-10)

2 Peter 3:8—This verse is a variation on Psalm 90:4. That psalm, which should be read aloud, sounds at first like a very gloomy message of doom. Yet Isaac Watts saw in it a word of comfort and wrote it in the form of the hymn, "O God, Our Help in Ages Past." It contains the stanza

> A thousand ages in thy sight
> are like an evening gone,
> Short as the watch that ends the night
> before the rising sun.

How did Watts see any comfort in that? I think maybe like this: You an I see history from within, as points along a line. But God, who dwells in eternity, surrounds the time-line of history and can enter it at any point. Indeed, the Christian gospel says that God *did* enter history, in the person of Jesus of Nazareth, so that ever since we have divided time into B.C. and A.D. But we are only separated from the historical Jesus by a couple of night watches, as God measures time. Indeed, for God, time doesn't exist at all. God is everywhere at all times, and is not "waiting" in the same sense that you and I long for a coming event. All times are alike to God, who is the Alpha and the Omega, the beginning and the end (Revelation 1:8), who was and is and is to come. When Moses asked for God's name at the burning bush, he was told, "I AM WHO I AM" (Exodus 3:14), and Jesus echoed these words in his own day, saying, "Truly I tell you, before Abraham was, I am" (John 8:58). Only a God who transcends space and time can enter it at all points. Only the author of the book can stop time, enter into the book, and change the plot, if need be, to suit the writer's ends. And God is the Author of our story.

2 Peter 3:9—It may seem to you that God is slow in acting, but that is not true (see Habakkuk 2:1-4); it only seems that way because you see history through temporal human eyes, not the divine eyes of eternity. If God is being "patient," it is to give the whole creation a chance to repent, because God does not want anyone to perish (see Matthew 18:14).

2 Peter 3:10—Of this you can be sure: You do not know when the day will come; it will be like a thief in the night (Matthew 24:43; Luke 12:39; 1 Thessalonians 5:2-4; Revelation 3:3; 16:15), but that day will surely come, and when it does, it will be with a terrible noise and a burning destruction. It is hard not to read this without thinking of the unthinkable event of a nuclear holocaust. But does it really matter whether you think of a cosmic cataclysm or the cessation of your own heart? Either scenario is just as certain, just as unpredictable, and leaves you just as dead.

THIRD QUARTER

Warning and Promise (2 Peter 3:11-14)

2 Peter 3:11—Knowing that these things are sure to come, what sort of people are we to be? For it is clear that while *things* will be destroyed, people are intended for resurrection, life out of and beyond death. We therefore must live lives that will ensure our survival (see 1 Corinthians 3:10-15). It is not that we will be saved by our works, but that we are to practice putting our trust in those things that will never be destroyed, rather than laying up for ourselves the rusty and corruptible treasures that the world offers (Matthew 6:19-21).

2 Peter 3:12—We are to wait expectantly for that day, even longing for it. Every day, somewhere in the world, there is a person praying to God, "Thy kingdom come." But do we really want it to come? I suspect that most of us really don't, especially not in a form that will "melt all the elements." And yet when you consider the sickness, pain, and hunger of the world, do you not want it all to be set right?

2 Peter 3:13—And set right it will be. According to God's promise, we are going to see a new sky (heavens) and a new earth, where justice at last is done (see Revelation 21:1).

2 Peter 3:14—Therefore, clean up your act, so that you will be found, when the time comes, ready to move into that new world. If, when the time comes, you still don't want to sit next to a person of another race, you're going to have to learn to do that. If you don't know how to sing, you're going to have to learn. There is no temple in that city (Revelation 21:22), so you won't have to go to church, and its gates will always be open (Revelation 21:25), so there is no danger of your being left out. But all that is ugly and filth (Revelation 21:27) will be left out, so you may have to discard a lot of habits, even your right eye and hand (Matthew 5:29-30), when you enter. It will be far better, when that time comes, for you to have made your peace with God's righteousness and begun to learn the discipline of leading the heavenly life, here on earth. Perhaps that is why we were put here: to prepare us for heaven. If so, and in any event, let us be getting ready.

Helping Adults Become Involved—Roy H. Ryan

Preparing to Teach

This lesson concludes our study of 1 and 2 Peter. It also brings the quarter to a close. Therefore, you will want to think about ways of helping the members evaluate what they have learned or ways in which they have grown during this study.

First, give attention to a study of 2 Peter 3:3-14. Read the comments by Dr. Decker and Dr. McGeachy. You may also want to read a good commentary on this passage.

Think about the members of your class. How will they respond to this matter of the end of history and their own accountability to God?

Give attention to the supplies you may need for this session. Will you have a written form of evaluation? If so, have paper and pencils available.

Here are some suggested questions you might use for evaluating this second course of study as you come to the close of your session. (You will be reminded of the evaluation under the section "Helping Adults Become Involved.")

MAY 31   LESSON 14

1. What are some concerns or issues that have become clearer to you in this study of 1 and 2 Peter?
2. Have these six lessons helped you to better understand what it means to be a Christian in today's world? How?
3. As a result of this study, what changes will you make in your own life?

The aim of today's lesson is to help Christians think about their view of history in light of God's will and purpose.
A possible outline of the lesson would be as follows:

> I. Introduction
> II. The world's skepticism
> III. God and time
> IV. Warning and promise

Introducing the Main Question

Do members of your class believe that Jesus Christ will come again? Do they believe there will be an end to history? Do they believe God will destroy the earth by fire, just as it was almost destroyed (radically changed) by water in the time of Noah? Will humankind self-destruct? Will there be a great war that will bring about ultimate destruction of humankind?

These are some of the issues and questions being addressed by large numbers of Christians in our day. It has been true in every generation. We hear all kinds of speculations and conjectures. Some so-called prophets have even gone so far as to predict the time of the end.

You may wish to get some reaction from members of the class on these and similar questions. Help them see that the lesson today provides some guidance on some of these questions.

Developing the Lesson

I. Introduction

You may want to begin with your own personal view of what the Day of Lord or the end of time means. (Your view, I hope, will be shaped by the biblical witness and not just your personal opinion.)

Another way to introduce the lesson would be to pose some of the questions listed above and provide opportunity for some discussion.

II. The world's skepticism

Where is the promise of his coming? One reason most scholars date 2 Peter at sometime toward the end of the second century (A.D. 150–200) is because of this passage. The writer acknowledges that the "fathers" have all died (verse 4). Those early apostles who had predicted that Jesus would be coming again were all gone. What happened to their predictions? If Jesus was supposed to come again, why has he waited so long? Many are still skeptical, and is it any wonder? After all, we are constantly hearing preachers (televangelists seem especially to dwell on it a lot) talk about the imminent second coming or the end of the world.

Don't forget, the writer of 2 Peter warns, God did it once, he will do it again. It will not be by water (as with Noah) but with fire. That metaphor of "fire" is a much-used biblical term when talking about the end time.

THIRD QUARTER

What are we to believe? Is there any way for us to know for sure how or when God will consummate history?

III. God and time

As we see time, we are caught up in history. We measure time with minutes, hours, days, years. We live by watches and calendars. A lifetime of 70 to 80 years seems a long time (except when we get there ourselves). We are basically impatient people. We want instant gratification. We like to make things happen.

But God is not limited by time, as we are. Eternity is not simply the extension of time. It is a different realm of being. God is the God of the past, present, and future. He is the beginning and the end. We can have no sure knowledge of what God's plan may be for creation. We are caught in time; God is outside and beyond it. It is literally beyond our ability to reason.

If we are in God's love and care, should we be concerned about how and when God will bring the kingdom into fullness?

IV. Warning and promise

The Day of the Lord will be hard on those who have been wicked and disobedient. Judgment is sure. God is a righteous God. Do not be fooled or lulled into unrighteousness by those who are skeptical, who do not believe either the warning or the promise.

The promise is a generous one for those who have been faithful. A new heaven and a new earth will come where God's righteousness will dwell (prevail). How do Christians prepare for this great day? By living lives of faithful obedience to the will of God.

Do you believe that each person will be held accountable for his or her life? Do you believe that God is preparing a new heaven and a new earth for all his faithful people?

Helping Class Members Act

Spend a few minutes talking about how we can live in such a way as to be ready when our time comes or when God's time comes.

If you decide to evaluate this course, you will need to allow several minutes. Use questions similar to those mentioned in the section "Preparing to Teach," or come up with some you think more helpful or appropriate. If you decide to have a written evaluation, be sure you have paper and pencils available.

Conclude your time together with a prayer: Dear God, help us to live lives of faithfulness every day so that we will always be prepared for the coming of your kingdom. In the name of Christ who gives us new life every day and for eternity, Amen.

Planning for Next Sunday

Your next quarter's material is also divided into two courses. The first course is entitled "God's Judgment and Mercy"; it deals with several little-studied prophets. The first one that will be considered is Obadiah.

FOURTH QUARTER

COURSE 1: God's Judgment and Mercy

UNIT I: WARNINGS AND PROMISES FROM GOD
Horace R. Weaver

FIVE LESSONS   JUNE 7–JULY 5

There are thirteen lessons in this quarter. The thirteen lessons are divided into two distinct courses of study, "God's Judgment and Mercy" (seven lessons) and "Guidelines for Ministry" (six lessons).

The first course of study consists of seven lessons based on the books of Obadiah, Jonah, Nahum, Habakkuk, and Zephaniah. The agony of the prophets is apparent, as they plead with God and his people. The seven lessons consist of two units of study: "Warnings and Promises from God" (five lessons) and "A Remnant Is Saved," (two lessons).

Unit I, "Warnings and Promises from God," consists of five lessons. Lesson one focuses on Obadiah's promise that God would judge Edom and restore Judah. The following two lessons consider Jonah's response to God's call for him to preach to the hated people of Nineveh. Lesson four deals with Nahum's message that God will break the Assyrians' yoke and set the people of Judah free. The final lesson of unit I considers Habakkuk's question about God's actions and his decision to wait on God for fuller understanding.

The titles and concerns for each lesson are as follows: "God's Justice Will Prevail," June 7, seeks to help adults face squarely the question, Why do the innocent suffer, and how can we believe the justice of God will ultimately triumph? "Running Away from God," June 14, is a magnificent parable of our efforts to avoid responding to the loving, seeking God. "Disturbed by God's Grace," June 21, asks: Why is God's grace sometimes so disturbing? "Good News for God's People," June 28, challenges us to participate with God in the struggle to be free from forces that oppress us. "Faithfulness in Crisis," July 5, helps adults reflect prayerfully on life crises and deepens their trust in the God who stands with us in those crises.

Contributors to the fourth quarter:
  Charles T. Klinksick.
  Horace R. Weaver.
  William H. Willimon.
  Douglas E. Wingeier, Professor of Practical Theology, Garrett-Evangelical Theological Seminary, Evanston, Illinois.

LESSON 1   JUNE 7

God's Justice Will Prevail

Background Scripture: Obadiah

The Main Question—William H. Willimon

Someone has said that the great question of our day is the question of fairness. Is it fair that, in a country so rich in resources, the poor must perish from too little while the rich perish from too much? Is our system of taxation fair to every economic segment of our society? Are women fairly paid for the work they do?

A number of years ago the best selling book was Rabbi Harold Kushner's *When Bad Things Happen to Good People*. It was a book that treated many important subjects, the chief of which was fairness. Behind every "Is this fair?" question is the "Is this just?" question. Aristotle defined justice as "giving each person his due." Justice is getting what you deserve. Unfortunately, Aristotle's definition of justice fails to advance the discussion. After all is said and done, what do we deserve? Not simply what do we deserve from our personal point of view, but what do we deserve from *God's* point of view?

Behind Rabbi Kushner's question "Why do bad things happen to good people?" is the assumption that the people to whom these bad things are happening are good, undeserving of a bad fate. Of course, that is often the case in life. There is clearly undeserved, unmerited suffering.

But what about the reverse? How do you feel when good things happen to bad people? "Why do the wicked prosper?" asks the psalmist. Behind these deep questions is an even deeper one: Is God just? Much in life contradicts the assertion of the justice of God; much in the Bible continues to affirm that God is good and wills good for God's creatures. Has God created the sort of world where the good get what they deserve and the bad get punished?

Get ready for some deep questions and some invigorating discussion in today's lesson!

Selected Scripture

King James Version

Obadiah 1:4, 10-11, 15, 17, 21

1 The vision of Obadiah. Thus saith the Lord God concerning Edom; We have heard a rumour from the Lord, and an ambassador is sent among the heathen, Arise ye, and let us rise up against her in battle.

Revised Standard Version

Obadiah 1-4, 10-11, 15, 17, 21

1 The vision of Obadiah.

Thus says the Lord God concerning Edom:
We have heard tidings from the Lord,
    and a messenger has been sent among the nations,
"Rise up! let us rise against her for battle!"

JUNE 7   LESSON 1

2 Behold, I have made thee small among the heathen: thou art greatly despised.	2 Behold, I will make you small among the nations, you shall be utterly despised.
3 The pride of thine heart hath deceived thee, thou that dwellest in the clefts of the rock, whose habitation *is* high; that saith in his heart, Who shall bring me down to the ground?	3 The pride of your heart has deceived you, you who live in the clefts of the rock, whose dwelling is high, who say in your heart, "Who will bring me down to the ground?"
4 Though thou exalt *thyself* as the eagle, and though thou set thy nest among the stars, thence will I bring thee down, saith the Lord.	4 Though you soar aloft like the eagle, though your nest is set among the stars, thence I will bring you down, says the Lord.
10 For *thy* violence against thy brother Jacob shame shall cover thee, and thou shalt be cut off for ever.	10 For the violence done to your brother Jacob, shame shall cover you, and you shall be cut off for ever.
11 In the day that thou stoodest on the other side, in the day that the strangers carried away captive his forces, and foreigners entered into his gates, and cast lots upon Jerusalem, even thou *wast* as one of them.	11 On the day that you stood aloof, on the day that strangers carried off his wealth, and foreigners entered his gates and cast lots for Jerusalem, you were like one of them.
15 For the day of the Lord *is* near upon all the heathen: as thou hast done, it shall be done unto thee: thy reward shall return upon thine own head.	15 For the day of the Lord is near upon all the nations. As you have done, it shall be done to you, your deeds shall return on your own head.
17 But upon mount Zion shall be deliverance, and there shall be holiness; and the house of Jacob shall possess their possessions.	17 But in Mount Zion there shall be those that escape, and it shall be holy; and the house of Jacob shall possess their own possessions.
21 And saviours shall come up on mount Zion to judge the mount of	21 Saviors shall go up to Mount Zion

Esau; and the kingdom shall be the Lord's.

to rule Mount Esau: and the kingdom shall be the Lord's.

Key Verse: For the day of the Lord is near upon all the heathen: as thou hast done, it shall be done unto thee: thy reward shall return upon thine own head. (Obadiah 15)

Key Verse: For the day of the Lord is near upon all the nations. As you have done, it shall be done to you, your deeds shall return on your own head. (Obadiah 15)

As You Read the Scripture—Charles T. Klinksick

Obadiah is the shortest of the Old Testament books. It is a terse one chapter, two-sided prophecy of warning against the Edomites and a promise of hope for the assaulted Israelites. Edom was south of the Dead Sea, on the trade route to Arabia, the Gulf of Aqabah, and the Red Sea. Copper and iron mining, trade, and mountainous living sustained the Edomites in power from the thirteenth to the eighth century B.C. Little remains of their history. They are identified as rugged descendants of Esau, twin brother of Jacob. Obadiah himself was an obscure prophet writing earlier than or near the time of the fall of Jerusalem, which occurred shortly after 600 B.C. Obadiah in various spellings was a common name in some Old Testament writings.

Obadiah 1-4. "We" is Obadiah speaking for himself, other prophets of his day, and his people, whom Edom hated vengefully. Jeremiah (49:7-16) quotes Obadiah's prophecy against Edom word for word in some verses. He paraphrases some of the ideas in his own words. He also adds descriptions not included in Obadiah (see Jeremiah 49:17-22). The Lord's message in both texts is a call for battle and a declaration of war against the high and mighty rock dwellers. Your pride will lead to your destruction, says the Lord.

Verse 10. Israel is referred to as "your brother Jacob." The statement indicates how shamefully the Edomites have dealt with their kinsmen.

Verse 11. Edomites offered no help but stood by as observers when the Chaldeans destroyed Jerusalem. Jeremiah describes the invasion (chapter 39) with no reference to Edom.

Verse 15. "The day of the Lord" is a term often used in the Old Testament to indicate a pending day of reckoning. "As you have done, it shall be done to you" is the flip-side of the Golden Rule, a promise of a boomerang returning to hit the Edomites.

Verse 17. Obadiah now offers hope. The temple hill shall be a place of sanctuary for some. Mount Zion was the holy hill on which the temple had been built in Jerusalem. "The house of Jacob" means Israelites. Some, the exiles with their possessions, will be physically moved hundreds of miles to Babylon. The Israelites will not lose everything.

Verse 21. Two mountains are mentioned in contrast: Zion in Jerusalem, the sacred and central symbol of Jewish religious life, and Seir (Mount Esau), a symbol of the irreligious conduct of the Edomites. Mount Esau runs the length of Edom; it is a high plateau whose edges are rugged and nearly impassable. "Saviors," heroes, shall go up to God's mountain and rule over the Edomites and their mountain. The Lord God shall be king, and his shall be the kingdom. Obadiah's message ends with a promise of hope and justice. The language is broad and figurative, but the message is clear: Despite the desperate dealings of the enemy, God's justice will ultimately prevail.

The Scripture and the Main Question—William H. Willimon

The Vision of Obadiah

How often do we deal with a book of the Bible that can be read in one sitting? For that matter, the book of Obadiah can be read in one standing! This shortest of short biblical books, although short on verses, is very long on content because, in Obadiah, we are coming face-to-face with some very deep subject matter.

The context of Obadiah is revealed within the first verses of the vision. Edom and its inhabitants stood by and did nothing when their brothers and sisters in Israel were in peril. Like the prophet Joel, Obadiah predicts that God will punish Edom for its cowardice and complicity with the aggressors from the north (verses 1-4). Before the book ends, Obadiah also foretells the day when Israel shall be returned from its terrible exile to the Promised Land and shall rule over Edom (verses 19-21). In other words, eventually, when God works it all out, the good shall get what they so richly deserve and the bad shall get what they deserve. God is just.

The questions behind today's scripture, although probably spoken sometime in the sixth century B.C., are as contemporary as today's newspaper headlines. They are the questions of the suffering mother in the Palestinian refugee camp, or the child in Lebanon. Just this morning I picked up my local newspaper and read of a trial in our town in which a man was acquitted, on a technicality, of murdering another man. When the jury's verdict was read, the mother of the murdered man screamed out in the courtroom, to the attorneys, the judge, and the jury, "I hope that your children are murdered like that man murdered my son!"

She was overcome with anger, not only at the loss of her son but also at the injustice of it all. Her son had been murdered. Someone ought to pay for the act. But here his murderer was being let free. Was this just?

My church now has a new hymnal. In the old hymnal, we had the major portions of most of the Psalms, but not all of them. One bit of Psalms that never made it into our previous hymnals was the last verses of Psalm 137. Do you remember how that Psalm ends?

> O daughter of Babylon, you devastator!
> Happy shall he be who requites you
> with what you have done to us!
> Happy shall he be who takes your little ones
> and dashes them against the rock!
> (137:8-9)

Now I ask you, are such sentiments Christian? It's not nice to say that about other people's children. Thus John Wesley once said that "there are some Psalms which are unfit for Christian ears." Presumably Wesley had these verses of Psalm 137 in mind.

It is relatively easy for you and me to sit back and condemn the writer of Psalm 137 for such unkind thoughts toward those Babylonian babies. I can also be a bit condescending toward the anger expressed in the first verses of Obadiah toward the Babylonians and their Edomite collaborators. It is easy for me because I have never seen (as did those Israelites) foreign invaders who raped and pillaged, who destroyed my town and carried off my family into exile. I have never had my children led to the gas chambers. Therefore, my thoughts are always pleasant and good natured.

But let us be reminded that there are still vast numbers of human beings who are suffering much the same fate as those sixth-century Israelites. They are encountering circumstances in life that cause them to call out to God for justice, for the setting right of terrible wrong and recompense for injustice.

Obadiah asserted, all present evidence to the contrary, that the ways of God would not be mocked, that although present circumstances did not confirm the justice of God, the future would be a time for setting things right. "Saviors shall go up to Mount Zion to rule Mount Esau; and the kingdom shall be the Lord's" (verse 21).

The Day of the Lord Is Near

Why do bad things happen to good people? Why do good things happen to bad people? I do not know how a nonbeliever would frame such a question. If you do not believe in the existence of a God who is good, then presumably it is pointless to ask such questions. Without a good God, then the world is a place where merely natural forces rule, where everything is a matter of chance, sheer luck, or random reaction of this bumping into that.

However, Christians share with Israel the belief that God is good, that while God is not responsible for every single thing that happens in life, God is ultimately responsible for the outcome of the world, constantly, although sometimes silently and unrecognizably, working out divine purposes in the world. This, I believe, was the assertion of Obadiah.

The great British preacher, Leslie Weatherhead, wrote a wonderful little book called *The Will of God*. In his book, Weatherhead pondered the significance of the expression, often heard when there is some tragedy or misfortune, "This is God's will."

What do we mean by this? Do we really mean to say that everything that happens in life happens because God wants it to happen that way? I have met some people who do say that, although I could not. There is too much unadulterated evil in the world, too many pointless tragedies, too much undeserved suffering to ascribe everything that happens to the will and workings of God. How could God in any sense be said to be good if every single event that happened in this world were the result of God's will?

However, said Weatherhead, we need to take a somewhat more expansive view of God's will. In the immediate, momentary situation, this circumstance may *not* be the will of God. This situation may be absolutely contrary to what God wants in the world. God may be just as grieved by this event as we are. Yet in the long run, over the course of the years, ultimately, God will not be mocked. God's will is being accomplished in the world despite the tragedies, accidents, evil, and sin that often occur in this world.

To the ones in Edom who thought that they had gotten away with irresponsibility, Obadiah could say, "the day of the Lord is near" (verse 15), "your deeds shall return on your own head." These words were threat to the Edomites but promise to the suffering Israelites. God's will would be accomplished. Perhaps not today, maybe not even tomorrow, but ultimately there would be a day that would be God's day, in which God's will for Israel would be done.

The Kingdom Shall Be the Lord's

Whenever there is injustice, oppression, suffering, people who believe in a good God want to know, Why? Encounters with injustice are the ultimate threat to faith in a good God. So contemporary believers, just as Israel in the sixth century B.C., ask questions like, "Why did this happen to me?" "When shall my suffering end?" "How will things be set right?"

Sometimes, to be honest, we can't come up with quick, ready answers. Often, we cannot tell such sufferers that God will set things right in the immediate situation. However, Obadiah does remind us that we do have something to say to such questions. God's prophet asserts that God's way will triumph. He does not give specifics. He speaks poetically, in a stirring, visionary way. But still he speaks. He asserts that in the long run, God will have God's way, and the justice of God will be vindicated. The kingdoms of this world, which have often gone their own way and committed deeds as offensive to God as they are to us, shall be punished. And the righteous shall be redeemed, all kingdoms shall now be God's kingdom, our questions will be answered by the most irrefutable, undeniable answer of all—the ultimate triumph of the justice of God.

Helping Adults Become Involved—Douglas E. Wingeier

Preparing to Teach

Be in prayer for your class members and your church, and for yourself as an instrument for transmitting God's message. Read through the entire unit to get a clear overview.

Excellent background on the Old Testament prophets may be found in articles on "Prophet/Prophecy" in *The Interpreter's Dictionary of the Bible* and *Harper's Bible Dictionary*, and in Walter Brueggemann, *The Prophetic Imagination*, and Gerhard von Rad, *The Message of the Prophets* (especially his chapter on "The Day of Yahweh" and pp. 255-57 on Jonah).

For this lesson on Obadiah, study the background scripture and its exposition in commentaries like *The Interpreter's Bible, The Interpreter's One-Volume Commentary on the Bible, Peake's Commentary on the Bible,* and *Harper's Bible Commentary*.

Think of instances of unfairness or injustice in your life or community, the daily news, Third World countries, and/or elsewhere in the Bible (e.g., the crucifixion). What word of hope do you have to offer to persons in these circumstances?

For insight on the problem of innocent suffering read Harold Kushner, *When Bad Things Happen to Good People*, and Leslie Weatherhead, *The Will of God*.

Your aim is to enable persons to face squarely the question of, Why do the innocent suffer and the unrighteous prosper? and to consider Obadiah's response that the justice of God will ultimately triumph.

Outline the lesson as follows:

FOURTH QUARTER

    I. Injustice—in Obadiah's time and ours.
    II. The vision of Obadiah.
    III. The Day of the Lord is near.

Introducing the Main Question

Begin by asking class members to name instances of injustice in their own lives, families, community, or current events. You may need to prime the pump with examples from your preparatory reflection. Illustrations might include the birth of a Down's syndrome baby, one child's being punished for the disobedience of another, the conviction of an innocent man, a teenager dying of leukemia, victims of natural disasters, apartheid in South Africa, or the exploitation of the poor by the wealthy elite in Central America and other Third World countries.

Ask: why sometimes do the innocent suffer and the guilty get off scot free? Develop this issue with ideas from Dr. Willimon's "The Main Question." This lesson on Obadiah addresses this troubling question.

Developing the Lesson

I. Injustice—in Obadiah's time and ours.

Draw on the accounts in "As You Read the Scripture," "The Vision of Obadiah," and the commentaries to describe Obadiah's historical context. The kingdom of Judah has fallen to Babylon, the people have been taken into exile, and the neighboring Edomites (descendants of Esau) have not lifted a hand to help their kinsmen. They have even gloated over their misfortune and occupied their territory (see Ezekiel 35:3-15; Psalm 137:7). From the prophet's vantage point, the righteous people of Judah have suffered unjustly, while the wicked Edomites have benefited.

Return to the instances of innocent suffering mentioned earlier. Distinguish between those where the suffering can be traced to human responsibility (exploitation, judicial inequities, parental error) and those due to an imperfect natural order (birth defects, natural disasters).

Ask: Why do these things happen? Who is responsible? Are they God's will? If so, why does a good God permit them? If not, what causes them? Is God unable to prevent them? Let the class ponder these big questions as a way of introducing Obadiah's vision.

II. The vision of Obadiah.

Have the entire chapter read aloud. Point out the structure of the book:

    A. Judgment on Edom (verses 1-14)
        Verse 1a: The title, Obadiah's Vision
        Verses 1b-4: Warning of Edom's doom
        Verses 5-9: Completeness of Edom's downfall
        Verses 10-14: Reasons for Edom's punishment
    B. The Day of Yahweh (verses 15-21)
        Verses 15-16: The judgment on all nations
        Verses 17-21: The restoration of Israel

Raise the question discussed by Willimon of the appropriateness of the vengeful vindictiveness, found here and in Psalm 137:8-9, compared with the forgiving spirit of Christ on the cross. Ask: Can you understand why people who suffer unjustly would feel this way? Have you ever had such feelings? Expressed them? Do you agree with John Wesley, who removed Psalm 137:8-9 from the Psalter because they were "not fit for the mouths of a Christian congregation"? Is it all right to tell God exactly how we feel? What is the alternative?

III. The Day of the Lord is near.

Having expressed his people's anger and resentment, the prophet now offers the promise that gives God's people hope. God is good and will not leave the people of God to suffer indefinitely. History's outcome is in God's hands; the Day of Yahweh will come, when wrongs will be righted and the just will be rewarded.

Discuss Leslie Weatherhead's distinction between God's *intentional* (God's original plan for the well-being of all people), *circumstantial* (what God allows to happen in a situation shaped by human evil), and *ultimate* wills (the goal God will reach in the end). What would each of these have been in Obadiah's situation? In the case of Christ on the cross? In the examples of innocent suffering discussed earlier?

Ask the class if the biblical promise of the ultimate triumph of God's righteousness is sufficient to sustain them through times of pain and discouragement. What more might we need? Suggest that the awareness of God's presence, as conveyed by the care and support of fellow Christians, often augments the promise of future vindication in strengthening us to endure and live victoriously.

Helping Class Members Act

Drawing on Dr. Willimon's "The Kingdom Shall Be the Lord's" section, assert with Obadiah that no matter how dark present circumstances appear, in the long run God's purpose will be achieved and God's justice will be done.

To help that happen, have the class select two injustices from those mentioned earlier—one individual and one global—and decide on action steps to address them.

Whether the individual involved is local or distant, determine what kind of aid and support—an offering, advocacy, companionship, prayer—would be most helpful. Set up a committee to coordinate the assistance.

For the social injustice, have another group gather information on the issue and the avenues for action. These may include letter writing to Congress or newspapers, collection of clothing or medical supplies, sending a work team to a disaster area, or participating in a demonstration.

A possible follow-up on the issue of innocent suffering would be to invite those interested to engage in a short-term study of the books by Harold Kushner and Leslie Weatherhead. Include your pastor in these discussions.

In closing sing "Rejoice, the Lord Is King." Pray for comfort and courage for all who suffer unjustly, and specifically for those mentioned during the class session.

Planning for Next Sunday

Ask the class to read Jonah 1–2 and reflect on times when they have faced unwanted tasks or tried to avoid difficulties or responsibility.

LESSON 2   JUNE 14

Running Away from God

Background Scripture: Jonah 1–2

The Main Question—William H. Willimon

What is your image of one who is a "prophet of God"? Well, a prophet is someone who is sent by God to speak God's word. A prophet is someone like Jeremiah who believed that God's hand was upon him from the time he was in his mother's womb (Jeremiah 1:5). Or a prophet is someone like Isaiah who heard God call him and said, "Hear am I, send me" (Isaiah 6).

Prophets are those who go willingly when God calls, who dare to speak God's word, even when it is an unpopular word. Prophets brave public disapproval, make enemies of people in high places, speak the truth even when it hurts. Prophets obey God's will and speak God's word above all else.

In other words, prophets are not like us! You know how we are. We answer the call of God on Sunday morning at 11:00 am., if the weather is not too bad. We are willing to speak and enact God's word, if God's word happens to be a reassuring, pleasant, complacent word which everyone else is also speaking. We are not prophets.

Is it possible that God should call someone who did *not* go willingly? Would God dare to call a person who did everything possible to run away from God's call, to ignore the will of God for his life, to go in every direction except the direction which God had intended for him?

Is it possible that God should call *someone like us*? Welcome to the next two lessons on the "prophet" Jonah.

Selected Scripture

King James Version	**Revised Standard Version**
Jonah 1:1-9, 15-17	*Jonah 1:1-9, 15-17*
1 Now the word of the Lord came unto Jonah the son of Amittai, saying,	1 Now the word of the Lord came to Jonah the son of Amittai, saying,
2 Arise, go to Nineveh, that great city, and cry against it; for their wickedness is come up before me.	2 "Arise, go to Nineveh, that great city, and cry against it; for their wickedness has come up before me."
3 But Jonah rose up to flee unto Tarshish from the presence of the Lord, and went down to Joppa; and he found a ship going to Tarshish: so he paid the fare thereof, and went down into it, to go with them unto Tarshish from the presence of the Lord.	3 But Jonah rose to flee to Tarshish from the presence of the Lord. He went down to Joppa and found a ship going to Tarshish; so he paid the fare, and went on board, to go with them to Tarshish, away from the presence of the Lord.
4 But the Lord sent out a great wind into the sea, and there was a	4 But the Lord hurled a great wind upon the sea, and there was a

JUNE 14 LESSON 2

mighty tempest in the sea, so that the ship was like to be broken.

5 Then the mariners were afraid, and cried every man unto his god, and cast forth the wares that *were* in the ship into the sea, to lighten *it* of them. But Jonah was gone down into the sides of the ship; and he lay, and was fast asleep.

6 So the shipmaster came to him, and said unto him, What meanest thou, O sleeper? arise, call upon thy God, if so be that God will think upon us, that we perish not.

7 And they said every one to his fellow, Come, and let us cast lots, that we may know for whose cause this evil *is* upon us. So they cast lots, and the lot fell upon Jonah.

8 Then said they unto him, Tell us, we pray thee, for whose cause this evil *is* upon us; What *is* thine occupation? and whence comest thou? what *is* thy country? and of what people *art* thou?

9 And he said unto them, I *am* an Hebrew; and I fear the Lord, the God of heaven, which hath made the sea and the dry *land*.

....

15 So they took up Jonah, and cast him forth into the sea: and the sea ceased from her raging.

16 Then the men feared the Lord exceedingly, and offered a sacrifice unto the Lord, and made vows.

17 Now the Lord had prepared a great fish to swallow up Jonah. And Jonah was in the belly of the fish three days and three nights.

Key Verse: **Jonah rose up to flee unto Tarshish from the presence of the Lord. (Jonah 1:3)**

mighty tempest on the sea, so that the ship threatened to break up. 5 Then the mariners were afraid, and each cried to his god; and they threw the wares that were in the ship into the sea, to lighten it for them. But Jonah had gone down into the inner part of the ship and had lain down, and was fast asleep. 6 So the captain came and said to him, "What do you mean, you sleeper? Arise, call upon your god! Perhaps the god will give a thought to us, that we do not perish."

7 And they said to one another, "Come, let us cast lots, that we may know on whose account this evil has come upon us." So they cast lots, and the lot fell upon Jonah. 8 Then they said to him, "Tell us, on whose account this evil has come upon us? What is your occupation? And whence do you come? What is your country? And of what people are you?" 9 And he said to them, "I am a Hebrew; and I fear the Lord, the God of heaven, who made the sea and the dry land."

....

15 So they took up Jonah and threw him into the sea; and the sea ceased from its raging. 16 Then the men feared the Lord exceedingly, and they offered a sacrifice to the Lord and made vows.

17 And the Lord appointed a great fish to swallow up Jonah; and Jonah was in the belly of the fish three days and three nights.

Key Verse: **Jonah rose to flee to Tarshish from the presence of the Lord. (Jonah 1:3)**

As You Read the Scripture—Charles T. Klinksick

The book of Jonah is a unique bit of religious literature. It pictures God's dealings with one man and his times, while revealing the Lord's intentions

FOURTH QUARTER

and methods. The language describing God's doings is overly simple, but figuratively it indicates his intent: "*hurled* a great wind" (1:4), "*appointed* a great fish" (1:17), "*spoke* to the fish" (2:10) and "*appointed* a plant" (4:6), a worm (4:7), and a sultry east wind (4:8).

Jonah himself is a historical person mentioned in 2 Kings 14:25, living about 750 B.C. or earlier. The book is written about him, but probably by someone else to whom Jonah had told the story. A reader feels close to Jonah because of what he has said and the rather close characterization of him. But our opinion of him is harsh because of his disobedience and his later disappointment with God's fairness. The book should, like the book of Job, be read as a beautiful literary composition full of basic religious truths and expectations. The fish and problems of explaining Jonah's survival are incidental to far more important points, such as God's concern for proclaiming repentance to distant outsiders, his mercy upon the repentant city, and his persistence in correcting Jonah's thinking.

Jonah 1:1. Jonah, a Hebrew name meaning "dove," was a prophet from Gath-hepher, identified as a city a few miles northeast of Nazareth. "Amittai" means truth, or truth-telling.

Verse 2. Nineveh was on the Tigris River, five hundred miles eastward. It was "that great city" of more than 120,000 people (4:11), capital of Assyria in Mesopotamia. It was enclosed by a rectangle of walls nearly eight miles around. Jonah was to "cry against it," meaning preach against its wickedness—a lonely voice in an evil city. He rebelled and refused to go.

Verse 3. Tarshish, westward from Joppa on the Mediterranean Sea, was possibly Tartessus in Spain, or some remote place where Jonah believed the Lord would not find him. The ship was a sizeable cargo sailing vessel with oars.

Verses 4-14. The storm was so violent that the crew cast cargo overboard to lighten it. The captain decided this was not just a weather problem; the storm was divine retribution or punishment for some great wrong. Who was the cause of it? Casting lots eliminated all but one, who was presumed to be the guilty one—Jonah. The crew quizzed him: What's behind all this? Your occupation? Where from? Your nationality? To his credit Jonah confessed he was a God-fearing Hebrew running from the Lord's presence.

He was willing to let himself be a sacrifice to save the ship and crew. The sailors were reluctant to throw him overboard; first they tried their best to row toward shore, without success. Then they prayed fervently for mercy.

Verses 15:16. The storm ended when Jonah was pitched overboard. It was frightening. The crew was humbly religious—they feared the Lord, they offered a sacrifice, and they made vows. Jesus' stilling of a storm caused a similar response in his disciples (Mark 4:41).

Verse 17. It was "a great fish" that swallowed Jonah whole. We are not told what kind or how large. This was a Mediterranean Sea fish, not an inland lake creature. The account is believable. He was confined the better part of three days. Jesus ratifies the entire account by his references to Jonah in Matthew 12:40-41; 16:4; and Luke 11:29-32.

Jonah had wanted to escape the Lord's presence but was miraculously trapped. The story could have ended here, but this is part one, and there is more to come. God was not finished with Jonah.

JUNE 14   LESSON 2

The Scripture and the Main Question—William H. Willimon

The Word of the Lord Came to Jonah

"I wish God would speak to me, I wish God would tell me what to do!" she said. She sat in my office, trying to figure out what God wanted her to do with her life. She was in her last year of college, and now she was beginning to panic over what she ought to do after she left the university.

"I would like to serve God, to do what God wants me to do with my life, but I can't figure out what that is. How does someone hear the voice of God?" she wanted to know.

She was raising a tough modern question. Many modern people complain that they no longer hear God speaking to them. The voice of God, which sometimes seems ever present to biblical people, never seems present to us. God's voice was always intruding into biblical people's lives, telling them what to do, demanding that they go this way or that. Why can't we hear God's voice today?

At the beginning of the book of Jonah, there is God's voice, speaking in ways that are clear, unambiguous, and definite. "Now the word of the Lord came to Jonah the son of Amittai, saying, 'Arise, go to Nineveh, that great city, and cry against it; for their wickedness has come up before me'" (1:1-2). If we could only get a word from God like that, we would . . .

We would probably respond just like Jonah, wouldn't we? That is, we would do everything in our power to ignore God! "But Jonah rose to flee to Tarshish from the presence of the Lord" (1:3).

God's voice can be a fearful, terrible intrusion into our lives; it certainly was for Jonah. There he was, minding his own business, going about his own typical, everyday, normal, well-adjusted life. Then everything was turned upside down by that intruding, disturbing voice of God.

Can that be the reason why we no longer seem to hear the voice of God today? It may not be the case that God no longer speaks to modern people. Rather, it may be the case that modern people like you and me are no longer listening, are no longer obeying or responding to the voice of God.

The young person who sat in my office that day, pondering her life, said that she wanted God to speak to her, to tell her what to do with her life.

"Have you ever considered being a teacher?" I asked her. "You are a good student, a good communicator. We desperately need good teachers in our public schools. Have you ever considered that?"

"No, not me! Teachers make too little money. I'm tired of having to scrape to make ends meet. My mother was a teacher, and she had a terrible time of it. No, I want a job that would be better paying and a bit less demanding."

"Well," I continued, "there are a number of church-related jobs that might be just the place for your talents . . ."

"No, that's not a good idea, either. I volunteered in various capacities in the church while I was growing up, and frankly, I really don't like church people all that much. I find many people in the church to be petty, mean, and difficult to work with."

Now, I ask you, could it really have been said, in this person's life, that God was not speaking to her? Of course, my voice is that of a pastor, not the voice of God. Perhaps it was not the will of God for this young person to become a teacher or a church leader. But if it were the will of God for her to go into one of these vocations, would she have done so? No. She had her own opinion of what was right for her, her own definition of the limits for her commitment.

In that way, I suppose that this young person is much like each of us. We say that we want God to use our lives, to tell us what to do. But then we have our own sense of what God ought to tell us, of how far God should ask us to go.

The problem may not be that God is not speaking. The problem may be that we are like Jonah, and if God should ever call our name, give us our marching orders, lay hold of our lives, we should, like Jonah, flee "from the presence of the Lord" (1:3). There is God, telling Jonah to go and speak to the residents of Nineveh, and here is Jonah, standing on the dock with tickets in his hand for Tarshish!

The great Christian writer C. S. Lewis once noted that whereas preachers often go on about "Man's search for God," they more accurately (and much more biblically) should be talking about "God's search for man." As Lewis said, "To act as if man is out looking for God is to be as silly as talking about the mouse's search for the cat!"

Jonah is on board a ship bound in the opposite direction from the way God has commanded him to go. After all, he is no fool. He knows something about those terrible Ninevites. They were bitter, terrible enemies of Israel. A person goes out to preach to Nineveh, he doesn't know where he might end up. Some prophet, this Jonah! Here is a person to whom God's word has come, and it has produced not Isaiah's "Here am I, send me!" but rather "Get me out of here!"

But here is a God who will not be so easily put off. God pursues Jonah, even out on the dark sea. A terrible storm arises. All are in danger of perishing. Someone must be responsible for this terrible storm that has come upon us, reason the sailors (1:6-10). They decide that the culprit must be Jonah.

Here is a depiction of a God who is resourceful, determined, even ruthless in getting what he wants. He wants Jonah and is willing to turn the whole sea loose, to make the waves roar and the wind howl, if need be. Like a great cat pursuing the escaping mouse, this God will go to any lengths to get at his reluctant prophet.

It's just a story. You and I may be somewhat put off by this primitive picture of a God who resorts to storms at sea and big fishes to work on people's lives. Yet the story of Jonah is a true story in that it is a true depiction of the nature of a God who uses every means possible to get at us, to get at those who are the objects of his love. For I remind you that God is not only after Jonah but also after the people of Nineveh, determined that they also should hear of his justice and mercy. God has now decided that Jonah, despite his faults, is the instrument of that divine mercy, and so God will not be easily thwarted from his plans.

You and I probably spend more of our lives like Jonah, fleeing the love and will of God rather than searching for God—sometimes with good reason. God's will can do as much to disrupt and make difficult our lives as to bless our lives. This great, loving, resourceful God does not deal in trivialities. This is the God of the raging sea, the howling storm, the big fish, and the relentless pursuit. Get mixed up with this true, real, living God, and your life will never be the same! Ask Jonah about it.

JUNE 14 — LESSON 2

The Sign of Jonah

Perhaps this helps to explain why, when one day his critics came to Jesus and demanded a sign from him (Matthew 12:38-42), Jesus rebuked them. Jesus rebuked them because they already had a sign from God, standing before them, in the flesh, God's own son. Here they were, cooling their heels, waiting for God to speak and to act, and here was God standing before their very eyes.

Then Jesus said that the only sign they would get would be the "sign of the prophet Jonah" (Matthew 12:39). What is this sign of Jonah?

Jonah stands as an ever-present reminder of the perils of ignoring the will of God. In Jonah's day, God was determined to be merciful even to those who were bitter enemies of God's Chosen People. Jonah resisted such boundless mercy and fled from the will of God.

In Jesus' day, God was also determined to be merciful. Yet those who were poring over the Scriptures, ceaselessly trying to figure out the will of God, were the very ones who missed the will of God when it stood before them as Jesus the Christ. Did not they howl at him when he ate with sinners? Did not they criticize him for the company he kept?

Yet Jesus came preaching no new and unknown religion. The God he revealed was the same God who was depicted in the "sign of Jonah," the God who reaches out beyond our narrow boundaries and loves even the people of Nineveh.

Is that one reason why, in the church of the first four centuries, one of the most popular Christian symbols depicted by the first Christian artists was Jonah. For them it symbolized the resurrected Christ; even as Jonah was in the belly of the big fish for three days, so Christ was in the tomb for three days. But I think it also was a strong symbol of the call of God upon each of our lives, and the perils involved in ignoring or resisting that divine summons.

Even today, especially today, the "sign of Jonah" ought to be posted over the door of every Christian church. This story ought to be told to every contemporary Christian, to remind each of us of God's great, boundless love for all people, even the people whom we refuse to love. And then to remind us of the perils of saying that we are listening for God to speak, only to disobey the voice of God when it is spoken over our little lives.

Helping Adults Become Involved—Douglas E. Wingeier

Preparing to Teach

Read the entire book of Jonah, plus Isaiah 6:1-8; 2 Kings 14:25; samplings in Ezra and Nehemiah, and Matthew 12:38-42. Also read on Jonah 1–2 from one or more of the commentaries listed in lesson 1.

In a spirit of prayer, examine your heart to discover times when you have been reluctant to hear and follow God's voice, through refusing unwanted tasks, avoiding frightening situations, dodging difficulties, or shunning responsibility. Also pray for your class members during the week, that they may become more open and responsive to God's leading through study of the Jonah story.

The purpose of this lesson is to help class members become more receptive to hearing and following God's will. Use this outline:

FOURTH QUARTER

    I. The word of the Lord came to Jonah.
    II. The word of the Lord comes to us.
    III. The sign of Jonah: then and now.

Introducing the Main Question

Begin with a dramatic reading of Jonah 1–2, asking for volunteers to take the parts of Jonah, God, the captain, the sailors, and the narrator. After the reading, emphasize the point that whether or not this was a historical event, it is a story true for all time because it describes human efforts to avoid God and God's relentless pursuit of us to carry out the divine purpose.

Ask the class; Are we called to be prophets? Have you been called by God? How have you responded? What does God want you to do with your life? How do we know it is God who is speaking to us? In the discussion emphasize that God calls all persons to lives of service and witness, that we can test a voice by how consistent it is with the loving Spirit of Christ, and that we like Jonah try to evade God's purpose for us because it seems difficult and demanding.

Developing the Lesson

I. The word of the Lord came to Jonah.

Locate Palestine, Tarshish (possibly southern Spain), and Nineveh (Assyria, present-day Iraq) on a map. Have someone read 2 Kings 14:25 to show that Jonah was a historical figure. Explain that because Nineveh was a large, foreign city, it is understandable that small-town Jonah was averse to going there.

Remind the class that the main concern of God in this story is for the salvation of the people of Nineveh, the capital of a pagan, non-Jewish, enemy nation. Most scholars believe this book was written after the return from exile (in the fifth or fourth century B.C.)—about the same time as Ezra and Nehemiah. Yet its spirit is in sharp contrast to the narrow nationalism of those writers. Have Ezra 9:10-12 read aloud as a sample of this exclusivism. God cares about all the people of the earth, not just those who read the Scriptures and say their prayers, the writer of Jonah is telling us.

Next consider the situation of the ship's captain and sailors. Fearful, superstitious, beset by danger, their first concern was saving their own skins. Neither prayer to their gods nor throwing some of the cargo overboard to lighten the load did any good. So suspecting the storm to have been caused by the sin of someone on board, they cast lots and found Jonah to be the culprit.

Not wanting anyone to perish, they at first rowed for land. But when this failed, asking forgiveness of both Jonah and God, they had no choice but to offer Jonah up as a peace offering to an angry god. When they threw him into the sea, the storm soon subsided.

Typical people of their day (and ours) these sailors had a pragmatic concern for survival, wanted to do the right thing, performed the religious rites they knew, but in the end put their own self-interest first. They were oblivious to the larger drama of salvation in which they were playing a bit part—the loving pursuit of Jonah and Nineveh by the God of the universe.

Ask the class to what extent this describes their situation in life, and how this self-protecting bystander role might be overcome.

JUNE 14 LESSON 2

Now read aloud Isaiah 6:1-8, and discuss the contrast between Isaiah's "Here am I, send me" response and Jonah's effort to evade God's call. What makes the difference?

If the question comes up as to whether one can live three days inside a fish, respond with either "with God all things are possible" or "we don't know, but the story's point is not the fish but God seeking Jonah and Jonah running from God."

II. The word of the Lord comes to us.

Ask the class for instances of God calling people today and our running away. Examples that could be cited: refusing to teach Sunday school or accept other church or community responsibilities; devoting all one's time and resources to private enjoyment rather than the well-being of society and the world; "spending our children's inheritance"; ignoring opportunities to witness for Christ; refusing to accept challenges in the form of new ideas, difficult tasks, or stretching experiences; and avoiding intimacy and conflict in personal relationships.

Tell Dr. Willimon's story of the student who wanted God to tell her what to do but had already made up her mind what she wanted to hear. Ask the group: What influences in the lives of people today prevent us from hearing God's voice? How can these barriers be penetrated? Has this ever happened in our lives? What did/will it take to get us to hear what God wants to say to us? How can the church help make people more receptive to God's call and leading?

Dr. Willimon says that God is "resourceful, determined, even ruthless in getting what he wants." Ask the class if this fits their concept of God, then discuss any differences that emerge. If they see God as patient and genteel in dealing with people, ask how they explain the relentless God in Jonah and the Good Shepherd who goes out to "seek and save the lost."

III. The sign of Jonah: then and now.

Have Matthew 12:38-42 read aloud. Follow Dr. Willimon in explaining what Jesus meant by the sign of Jonah. This story is a parable of our efforts to avoid the loving, seeking God. There is also a parallel between Jonah's three days inside the fish and Christ's time in the tomb. So the sign of Jonah—then and now—is God's call to repentance, to do God's will, and to accept the power of the resurrected Christ to transform us from avoiding to responding, from running to serving, from fearing to bold telling of the Story.

Helping Class Members Act

Conclude the lesson by asking the class with which characters in the story they most identify—the seamen (self-serving bystanders, oblivious to the drama of salvation going on around them), Jonah (insensitive to God's call and avoiding a hard assignment), or the willing servant who accepts the call, found in Isaiah 6. Most, if honest, will find parts of all three in themselves.

Challenge the group to avoid the mistake of Jonah by staying open to God's invitation and accepting opportunities for witness and service. Ask for reports from the committees set up last week to address individual and social injustices, and remind the class that these are opportunities for them to respond to God's call.

FOURTH QUARTER

After a period of silent prayer and self-examination, read Jonah 2:2-9 as the prayer of both Jonah and all who acknowledge our unfaithfulness and thank God for forgiveness. Close by singing "O, Zion Haste" or "Out of the Depths I Cry to You."

Planning for Next Sunday

Ask the class to read Jonah 3–4 and come ready to discuss the questions, How is God's grace disturbing? (lesson title). Why was Jonah angry? (4:1). Where is our Nineveh? (field for evangelistic outreach).

LESSON 3   JUNE 21

Disturbed by God's Grace

Background Scripture: Jonah 3–4

The Main Question—William H. Willimon

Disturbed by God's grace? Can that be the title for today's lesson from the prophet Jonah? How could God's grace possibly be disturbing? The word "grace" is the way we translate the biblical word for "gift." God loves us not because of what we have done but rather because of the sheer graciousness of God's love. God's love comes to us not as our achievement but rather as a gift, unearned and unmerited.

This graciousness sounds like the best deal a person ever had. God is grace. Thus Jesus told stories about the goodness of God's grace: He described the owner of the vineyard who paid every worker the same amount of money, even those who worked for only a few hours. Then there was the loving and gracious father who threw a party for his returning prodigal son. Remember Jesus' parable about the self-righteous Pharisee and the money-grabbing tax collector who stood before the temple and prayed? Remember which one returned to his home after prayer "justified"? It was the tax collector! God is grace!

What could be disturbing about a gracious God?

God's grace is potentially disturbing because whereas the father's grace felt great to the returning prodigal son, it felt like a real slap in the face to his older brother. Whereas the owner's reckless generosity was wonderful for the people who worked in the vineyard only one hour, it was terrible to those who had sweated among the vines all day. It was great for the humble tax collector to be surprised by the unmerited love of God at the temple that day, but lousy for that proud Pharisee.

How do *you* feel when you witness the sheer, unmerited graciousness of God toward sinful humanity? Theoretically we ought to feel good about God's grace. Actually, we don't. Why is God's grace sometimes so disturbing?

JUNE 21 — LESSON 3

Selected Scripture

| **King James Version** | **Revised Standard Version** |

Jonah 3:1-5, 10

1 And the word of the Lord came unto Jonah the second time, saying,

2 Arise, go unto Nineveh, that great city, and preach unto it the preaching that I bid thee.

3 So Jonah arose, and went unto Nineveh, according to the word of the Lord. Now Nineveh was an exceeding great city of three days' journey.

4 And Jonah began to enter into the city a day's journey, and he cried, and said, Yet forty days, and Nineveh shall be overthrown.

5 So the people of Nineveh believed God, and proclaimed a fast, and put on sackcloth, from the greatest of them even to the least of them.

10 And God saw their works, that they turned from their evil way; and God repented of the evil, that he had said that he would do unto them; and he did *it* not.

Jonah 4:1-4, 10-11

1 But it displeased Jonah exceedingly, and he was very angry.

2 And he prayed unto the Lord, and said, I pray thee, O Lord, *was* not this my saying, when I was yet in my country? Therefore I fled before unto Tarshish: for I knew that thou *art* a gracious God, and merciful, slow to anger, and of great kindness, and repentest thee of the evil.

3 Therefore now, O Lord, take, I beseech thee, my life from me; for *it is* better for me to die than to live.

4 Then said the Lord, Doest thou well to be angry?

Jonah 3:1-5, 10

1 Then the word of the Lord came to Jonah the second time, saying, 2 "Arise, go to Nineveh, that great city, and proclaim to it the message that I tell you." 3 So Jonah arose and went to Nineveh, according to the word of the Lord. Now Nineveh was an exceedingly great city, three days' journey in breadth. 4 Jonah began to go into the city, going a day's journey. And he cried, "Yet forty days, and Nineveh shall be overthrown!" 5 And the people of Nineveh believed God; they proclaimed a fast, and put on sackcloth, from the greatest of them to the least of them.

10 When God saw what they did, how they turned from their evil way, God repented of the evil which he had said he would do to them; and he did not do it.

Jonah 4:1-4, 10-11

1 But it displeased Jonah exceedingly, and he was angry. 2 And he prayed to the Lord and said, "I pray thee, Lord, is not this what I said when I was yet in my country? That is why I made haste to flee to Tarshish; for I knew that thou art a gracious God and merciful, slow to anger, and abounding in steadfast love, and repentest of evil. 3 Therefore now, O Lord, take my life from me, I beseech thee, for it is better for me to die than to live." 4 And the Lord said, "Do you do well to be angry?"

FOURTH QUARTER

10 Then said the Lord, Thou hast had pity on the gourd, for the which thou hast not laboured, neither madest it grow; which came up in a night, and perished in a night:

11 And should not I spare Nineveh, that great city, wherein are more than sixscore thousand persons that cannot discern between their right hand and their left hand; and *also* much cattle?

Key Verse: Should not I spare Nineveh, that great city, wherein are more than sixscore thousand persons that cannot discern between their right hand and their left hand; and also much cattle? (Jonah 4:11)

10 And the Lord said, "You pity the plant, for which you did not labor, nor did you make it grow, which came into being in a night, and perished in a night. 11 And should not I pity Nineveh, that great city, in which there are more than a hundred and twenty thousand persons who do not know their right hand from their left, and also much cattle?"

Key Verse: Should not I pity Nineveh, that great city, in which there are more than a hundred and twenty thousand persons who do not know their right hand from their left, and also much cattle? (Jonah 4:11)

As You Read the Scripture—Charles T. Klinksick

The story of Jonah at Nineveh in chapters 3 and 4 is complete without the account in chapters 1 and 2. But they belong together to report the outcome of Jonah's missionary assignment and to complete the record of God's dealings with Jonah and with the Ninevites.

Jonah 3:1-4. The second time Jonah obeyed the word of the Lord. Somehow after being cast up on the Mediterranean seacoast, he made the five-hundred-mile journey to Nineveh. He may not have been enthusiastic, but he did what the Lord told him. The city is described as requiring three days to cross, which equals sixty miles (at twenty miles per day); or it could have been densely populated and (from archaeological evidence) only eight miles across. Population estimates are from 600,000 up to 1 million persons. Jonah headed into the heart of the city. His message was "Destruction in less than six weeks." The implied message was "Repent from your wickedness and escape destruction!"

Verse 5. "The people . . . believed God." They took Jonah seriously as a prophet from God. They gave up their feasting and put on old clothes and plain sackcloth—everyone, in royalty or in poverty. The king removed himself from his throne and followed the Hebrew custom of sitting on ashes. He ordered a city-wide fast with prayers. Details are not given, but Jonah was effective.

Verse 10. They repented ("turned from their evil way"). God relented. He eased off from the threat of destruction. This was consistent with the covenant he had with Israel, which was, in short: Be faithful to me and I will be your God; fail me and I will not deliver you. Joshua had explained this clearly to the Israelites (Joshua 23:15-16). Jonah had threatened, the Ninevites had heeded, and God had displayed his grace and love.

Jonah 4:1-3. Jonah was very angry. He had expected the equivalent of fire and brimstone, a military defeat, or at least a shattering earthquake. But because the Ninevites were sorry, God did not overthrow the city, and Jonah was disappointed. He turned against the Lord and complained.

"When I was back home, isn't this what I said would happen? That's why I ran away. I knew you were too kind to want to hurt people." He felt the Lord had tricked him into prophesying doom that would never come. Now he wanted to die. He was wallowing in self-pity and blaming God for his misery.

Verse 4. The Lord did not debate or argue with him. He replied in the form of a simple question: "Do you do well to be angry?" Jonah said nothing.

Verses 10-11. After two nights or more outside the city, Jonah was still fuming. "I do well to be angry, angry enough to die" he sputtered to God (verse 9). His mental (and religious) health was not good. He had failed in his attempt to run away. He had failed to bring about the downfall of Nineveh because his preaching was heeded. He was bitter because a large castor oil plant that had shaded him had died, and he was hot and weak from a sultry east wind. He was a ripe candidate for suicide.

The whole story ends abruptly on a positive note of challenge by the Lord. He says, in effect, "If you can feel sorry about a plant dying, shouldn't I have mercy on this city of over 120,000 uneducated people?" There was no answer from Jonah. God had the last word.

The Scripture and the Main Question—William H. Willimon

Arise, Go to Nineveh

Again we are pondering the actions of Jonah, the prophet who wanted to be anything but a prophet. Last week we studied Jonah's reluctance to obey God's command to "Arise, go to Nineveh, that great city, and proclaim to it the message that I tell you" (3:2). We really couldn't blame Jonah for his reluctance. After all, Nineveh was the bitter enemy of Israel, source of countless troubles and terrors. Why would any normal, self-respecting Israelite want to go there on a preaching mission?

Jonah heads in the opposite direction from Nineveh. God, as the story goes, would not be so easily put off. A great fish is sent to swallow Jonah, and after giving him three days in its belly to think things over, spews Jonah back up on shore. Jonah relents and heads to Nineveh.

Fortunately, God gives Jonah the sort of message that an Israelite wouldn't mind preaching to such foreign heathen: "Yet forty days, and Nineveh shall be overthrown!" (3:4). The fulfillment of that message would be the prayer of every good, loyal, patriotic Israelite, who would just love to see Nineveh brought to its knees by the fierce judgments of God.

As things turn out, to the utter surprise of Jonah, Nineveh was brought to its knees by the great mercy of God. Lo and behold, the king of Nineveh and the entire city were so moved by Jonah's proclamation that they all went out, repented, and prayed to God for forgiveness, begging that God would spare them (3:6-9).

The writer of the book of Jonah gives us only a line or two of Jonah's preaching. But he must have been a most effective preacher for his preaching to yield such results among the Ninevites. What a response! From the palace to the poorest hovel, everything in Nineveh (even the livestock! verses 7-8) turned toward God.

FOURTH QUARTER

It Displeased Jonah Exceedingly

One would think that Jonah, while astounded, would be pleased. His great, risky preaching mission had ended in astounding success! I am a preacher myself, and I can testify that one of the great difficulties of preaching is that the preacher so often sees little result from his or her labors. Occasionally, but only occasionally, someone's life does appear to be changed through the hearing of a sermon. But concrete, visible, measurable change is a rare phenomenon in preaching. Which makes it all the more astounding to read the rather miraculous results of Jonah's sermon, particularly when one recalls how little Jonah wanted to preach in the first place!

One would think that Jonah would be pleased.

"But it displeased Jonah exceedingly, and he was angry" (4:1). Why would Jonah be so angry that God's word was heard by the Ninevites and responded to by them, and that they were then shown mercy by God? Is not God's grace a wonderful, beautiful thing?

Not necessarily, from our point of view. Jonah is furious because the Ninevites, those dreaded and hated enemies of God's people, turned toward the God of Israel. "I told you something terrible like this might happen when you sent me way over here!" says Jonah to God. Jonah is sickened by God's grace. He becomes depressed and wishes he were dead.

Does this seem like a strange response? I ask you, how did your church school class respond when it heard that convicted Watergate crook Jeb Magruder had been converted and was headed for Princeton Seminary to become a Presbyterian pastor? Was there great rejoicing that God's grace had won a new and superbly talented servant of the gospel?

Jesus says that heaven goes wild over the one sinner who repents and rejoices much more over this one who comes back to God than over the ninety and nine who have no need of repentance. Heaven celebrates such repentance, but do we?

All would have been well for Jonah if Nineveh had acted the way he had hoped that they would. They should have turned their backs upon the word of God, looked in the other direction, proceeded on in their heathen ways. Then Jonah could have said to God, "See, I told you so, these pagans were not worth your love."

But the worst thing happened. Nineveh actually repented and, in so doing, proved that God's love really has no bounds, that God is able to love and to bring back even those not within our narrow boundaries.

And when that happens, we, those who have convinced ourselves that we are in the boundaries, that we are the specially loved insiders, are sickened by the sight of it.

What good is it for us to be here this Sunday morning, praying, tithing, believing, studying our lesson from the Bible, if God is going to go out and be gracious even to those who have never set foot within our cozy church? If God is going to go out and be gracious to *them*, then we'll just get sick and wish that we were dead rather than to have to live with a God whose love is that big and surprising.

Thou Art a Gracious God

Once there was a church that decided to have a great evangelistic emphasis. They would pray, then develop a plan to go out and witness to people within their community, ask them to come to their church, and try to win them to the Lord.

Plans were made. Members in the church were enlisted to go door to door throughout the neighborhoods and witness for Christ. Visitors were formed into teams. Every Sunday afternoon for a month, the teams met at the church, had prayer, then went out into the neighborhood.

Unfortunately, despite their evangelistic efforts, the results were very disappointing. Few of those who were visited showed any interest in coming to their church or even in continuing conversation with the visitors. The members began to lose hope.

Then the chairperson for evangelism noted, "You know, we have gone to most of the homes in the neighborhood around here, but not all."

"Really?" they asked, astounded because there had not been one inch of territory not covered by the visitation teams.

"Yes," said the chairperson, "we have overlooked the mobile home park a few blocks away. We haven't gone there."

There was silence among the would-be evangelists. Then someone said, "But we didn't think *they* would be interested. Are they really our sort of people?"

"But I thought we were going out to win people for Christ. To find *his* 'sort of people,'" the chairperson responded.

Only one team volunteered to visit in the mobile home park. "It probably won't do any good," someone predicted, "they just are not church-type people."

The one team went door to door among the residents of the mobile home park. They were received warmly by most of the residents. They were told that they were the only church visitors who had ever been there.

I suppose that you know the rest of the story. It was straight out of the book of Jonah. The next Sunday, after the day of the mobile home park visitation, one new family plus three other individuals kept their word and visited the little church, more new people than had ever visited on any previous Sunday in memory.

At last the church's evangelistic efforts were a great success. At last the harvest had born fruit. At last the church had succeeded in finding an effective means of communicating the mercy and love of God!

At last they had succeeded in being disturbed by God's grace.

"I don't know that this evangelistic visitation idea was all that great," mumbled one member. "We ought to have planned things a little better."

"We should have been a bit more careful," said another. "We wouldn't want to do anything that might damage our warm fellowship here or change the basic nature of our congregation."

The only thing the chairperson of evangelism said in response was this: "Go home, each of you, and read the book of Jonah, all four chapters."

Helping Adults Become Involved—Douglas E. Wingeier

Preparing to Teach

Read Jonah 3–4 and the commentaries on it. Also read the three parables mentioned by Dr. Willimon as being similar to this Jonah story in emphasizing God's unmerited and disturbing grace (Matthew 20:1-16; Luke 15:11-32; and Luke 18:9-14).

FOURTH QUARTER

Ponder the three questions assigned at the end of the last session, and be prepared to share your thoughts about them.

Pray for class members, that through study of this lesson they may grow spiritually in their capacity to accept God's undeserved grace offered to themselves and others, and to reach out with evangelistic concern to persons different from themselves.

Collect newspaper clippings and stories from magazines like *Sojourners, The Other Side,* and *Guideposts,* that depict persons or groups who are either in need of or have unexpectedly received God's unmerited grace.

The aim of this lesson is to enable class members to recognize that God's grace is extended to the undeserving and to open their hearts and church to all kinds of persons. The following outline may be used:

    I. Arise, go to Nineveh.
   II. And Jonah was angry.
  III. A gracious God.

Introducing the Main Question

Divide the class into three groups, and assign each group to read and discuss one of the three parables of Jesus listed in "Preparing to Teach." (Or have three class members read them aloud, and then discuss them as a total group.) For each parable ask: What is the main point Jesus is making in this story? Help them discover that in each parable Jesus is teaching that God's grace is extended to the unworthy, unlovely, and undeserving, and that this really upsets the so-called fine, upstanding citizens in each case.

Then draw the connection to the Jonah story. Jonah was angry with God for not punishing the Ninevites, even though they repented in response to his preaching, because after all, weren't they pagans, sinners, and the enemies of Israel?

Ask Dr. Willimon's questions at the end of "The Main Question": How do *you* feel when you witness God's unmerited grace? Why is God's grace so disturbing?

Developing the Lesson

I. Arise, go to Nineveh.

Rehearse the story of Jonah—God's call to him to preach in Nineveh (the capital of mighty Assyria), Jonah's reluctance and running away, his eventual journey and preaching there, their unexpected repentance from the king on down, and God's response in rescinding his judgment. Include background information on Nineveh from "As You Read the Scripture" and the commentaries you consulted. Explain why Jonah was understandably resistant to preaching in Nineveh.

Ask the third of the advance preparation questions: Where is our Nineveh (field of evangelistic outreach)? Consider types of people in your area, sections of your city or country, refugees, the homeless, and persons of other ethnic groups, languages, nationalities, sexual orientations, political persuasions, or life-styles. What is the response of your class to reaching out to some or all of these persons in the name of Christ and the church?

II. And Jonah was angry.

Ask the second of the advance questions: Why was Jonah angry? After discussing the group's ideas, share Dr. Willimon's observations on this question. Jonah wanted the Ninevites to pay for their sins. God's free grace that took them off the hook when they repented was too much for him.

Compare Jonah's attitude to those of the elder brother, the all-day workers, and the proud Pharisee in the three parables. Ask class members to share similar feelings of self-righteousness and resentment when the undeserving are rewarded, the guilty pardoned, or the unlovely accepted. Cite the examples of Watergate conspirators Jeb Magruder, and Charles Colson and others from your news clippings and magazine stories.

If you have found none, this story, reported by Joyce Hollyday in the December 1989 issue of *Sojourners,* might be shared. A small group of Brazilian peasants, pushed off their land by government and business interests wanting it for development, tried to resist, move on, and start over. Each time the police came in with force, destroying houses and crops and wounding and killing people.

In despair, most were ready to give up and die of starvation, but some of the women got an idea, looked up where the members of Congress lived, and went with their children to sit on their elegant front lawns.

When the Congressmen's wives went out to offer them bread, the mothers said, "We want no bread or money from you. We are going to die. Since this is a nice place, we would like to die here." And they told of how their land was soon to be stolen, their children would starve, and Congress was voting to make it all legal.

The wives called their husbands to ask them not to pass the bill. The people were allowed to stay on their land, and their hope for life and the future was restored.

In discussing this story, ask: Who are the Ninevites here? Who is Jonah proclaiming God's mercy and love? Who might have felt displeased or angry and for what reasons? Where is grace operating? Do not expect 100 percent agreement in your group.

III. A gracious God.

Ask the question in the lesson title: How is God's grace disturbing? After the class has discussed it, explain that God revoked the promised punishment of Nineveh after they repented of their sin. Jonah was upset because he felt God should make them pay the penalty for all the harm they had done to Israel over the years.

Discuss ways in which God confounds our narrow, judgmental, protective attitudes today with the grandness and inclusiveness of his grace. Examples might include acceptance of a pregnant teenager who wants to keep her baby, a divorcee, ethnic neighbors, a Spanish-speaking congregation that is growing, or a church member about to come out of prison after serving a sentence for a crime. What is God's attitude toward such persons in the light of today's study of Scripture? What should our attitude be?

Helping Class Members Act

Now tell Dr. Willimon's story of the church that evangelized in the trailer park but were reluctant to accept those who came. Ask: How is this like Jonah? How is this like us?

FOURTH QUARTER

Go back to the groups identified earlier as being possible Ninevites. Discuss whether you might reach out to them in the name of Christ, how you would go about it, what church members' responses might be, and what guidance for this venture you might get from the Jonah story. If the group is ready, plan how to take this proposal to appropriate church committees for implementation.

Close by singing "Lord, Speak to Me" or "There's a Wideness in God's Mercy." Pray that God will forgive our narrow and vindictive attitudes, help us to be accepting of all God's children, and empower us to reach out and share God's love and mercy with the unlovely and undeserving.

Planning for Next Sunday

In addition to reading the book of Nahum, ask class members to watch the news during the week for instances of the struggle against injustice, and to bring at least one such news item to class next Sunday.

LESSON 4   JUNE 28

Good News for God's People

Background Scripture: Nahum

The Main Question—William H. Willimon

We are in the middle of a crime epidemic. At least that is what the newspapers and magazines are saying. Our nation is confronted with an unprecedented outbreak of violence and criminal activity. Just this morning I picked up our local newspaper and read that a prominent local politician had been indicted on charges of bribery and extortion, two people had been shot in a local bar during an argument, and a young person who was a member of a prominent local family died of a drug overdose. I am sure that you could pick up your local newspaper on nearly any morning and read much the same.

Of course, we are fortunate to live in a country of laws. Through the efforts of police, law enforcement officials, and the judiciary, many of those who are responsible for these crimes will be brought to justice. When justice is done, we are pleased. There is a sense that a proper balance has been restored to life. Those who have done wrong have been punished, the good have been vindicated.

The accomplishment of justice is the main theme of our "cops and robbers" novels and television shows. In the beginning, some crime is committed. Then, through the efforts of the courageous police officer, the brilliant detective, or the crusading attorney, criminals are brought to justice. By the end of the story, righteousness has again triumphed, and injustice has been punished.

Surely one reason for the perennial popularity of our murder mysteries, courtroom dramas, and detective stories is that we derive great satisfaction from seeing justice done. But our joy in seeing justice done is based on the

JUNE 28 · LESSON 4

truth that in real life, justice is not always done. In the murder mystery, the police catch the criminal more predictably than in real life. In the televised courtroom drama, the attorney is able to bring the law to good effect more often than in our actual law courts.

The cry for justice, the plea that righteousness should win and evil should be defeated, is an ancient hope, buried deep within the human spirit. Whose side is God on in the struggle against injustice?

Selected Scripture

King James Version

Nahum 1:2-3, 6-9, 12-13, 15

2 God *is* jealous, and the Lord revengeth; the Lord revengeth, and *is* furious; the Lord will take vengeance on his adversaries, and he reserveth *wrath* for his enemies.

3 The Lord *is* slow to anger, and great in power, and will not at all acquit *the wicked:* the Lord *hath* his way in the whirlwind and in the storm, and the clouds *are* the dust of his feet.

6 Who can stand before his indignation? and who can abide in the fierceness of his anger? his fury is poured out like fire, and the rocks are thrown down by him.

7 The Lord *is* good, a strong hold in the day of trouble; and he knoweth them that trust in him.

8 But with an overrunning flood he will make an utter end of the place thereof, and darkness shall pursue his enemies.

9 What do ye imagine against the Lord? he will make an utter end: affliction shall not rise up the second time.

Revised Standard Version

Nahum 1:2-3, 6-9, 12-13, 15

2 The Lord is a jealous God and avenging,
  the Lord is avenging and wrathful;
 the Lord takes vengeance on his adversaries
  and keeps wrath for his enemies.

3 The Lord is slow to anger and of great might,
  and the Lord will by no means clear the guilty.

6 Who can stand before his indignation?
  Who can endure the heat of his anger?
 His wrath is poured out like fire,
  and the rocks are broken asunder by him.

7 The Lord is good,
  a stronghold in the day of trouble;
 he knows those who take refuge in him.

8 But with an overflowing flood
  he will make a full end of his adversaries,
 and will pursue his enemies into darkness.

9 What do you plot against the Lord? He will make a full end;
  he will not take vengeance twice on his foes.

FOURTH QUARTER

12 Thus saith the Lord; Though *they be* quiet, and likewise many, yet thus shall they be cut down, when he shall pass through. Though I have afflicted thee, I will afflict thee no more.

13 For now will I break his yoke from off thee, and will burst thy bonds in sunder.

··

15 Behold upon the mountains the feet of him that bringeth good tidings, that publisheth peace! O Judah, keep thy solemn feasts, perform thy vows: for the wicked shall no more pass through thee; he is utterly cut off.

Key Verse: **The Lord is good, a strong hold in the day of trouble; and he knoweth them that trust in him. (Nahum 1:7)**

---

12 Thus says the Lord,
"Though they be strong and many,
they will be cut off and pass away.
Though I have afflicted you,
I will afflict you no more.

13 And now I will break his yoke from off you
and will burst your bonds asunder."

··

15 Behold, on the mountains the feet of him
who brings good tidings,
who proclaims peace!
Keep your feasts, O Judah,
fulfil your vows,
for never again shall the wicked come against you,
he is utterly cut off.

Key Verse: **The Lord is good, a stronghold in the day of trouble; he knows those who take refuge in him. (Nahum 1:7)**

As You Read the Scripture—Charles T. Klinksick

Nahum is a literary gem that properly comes after the lessons from Jonah. It was written for Judah as a double message about God and Nineveh. Chapters 2 and 3 are stunning poetic descriptions of the warfare, destruction, and desolation Jonah probably had in mind 150 years earlier when he prophesied God's judgment upon Nineveh. (Note the previous Jonah lessons.) The words of Nahum are first-hand realism—accurate, terse, and horridly beautiful. All three chapters contain theology, prophecy, and poetry. The permanent overthrow and plunder of Nineveh, the flood that mired the city, and the fiery death of its king took place about 612 or 623 B.C.

In Hebrew the first letter of each line after the superscription formed a literary acrostic using the first half of the Hebrew alphabet, the way we would begin the first line of a hymn with an *A* word, the second with a *B* word, the third with a *C* word, and so on. The content describes what the Lord God is like in his doings.

Nahum 1:1. An oracle is a divinely inspired pronouncement or utterance. The author is Nahum, who is otherwise unknown. His name means "comfort" or "compassion." The location of Elkosh is uncertain, though presumed to be in Judah.

Verses 2-3. Old Testament history indicates these strong characteristics of God, but few statements describing him are this plain-spoken about vengefulness. These verses can best be understood in reverse order, from the last phrase to the first. They point out that the Lord will hold the guilty accountable; that he is patient and powerful; and that he will punish his adversaries. A more positive statement of how the Lord works can be noted in Psalm 103:6-8.

The sentence form is typical of Hebrew poetry: a positive statement followed by the same truth stated in a new way, negatively, with opposites, reversed, or simply in different words. For example "jealous," then "wrathful," are linked by "avenging"; and "adversaries" equals enemies linked by a common idea-verb, "takes"/"keeps."

The majesty of clouds being merely dust from the Lord's feet striding across the sky is an ultimate in descriptive poetry.

Verses 6-9. The seventh verse is a very reassuring statement set between two dire declarations and rhetorical questions. The Lord is remarkably good, as explained so fully in Psalm 107, with its invitation to give thanks. See also Psalm 46:1. "Vengeance twice" in verse 9 means there will be no second time. Once will end the matter. The Lord is both a threat and a hope.

Verses 12-13. We understand this to be addressed to the Israelites, who have been oppressed by the Assyrians. When the capital of the Assyrians, Nineveh, is overthrown, Judah will have freedom. The Lord God will accomplish this.

Verse 15. This is simply prophecy of good news. The wording is the same in the fifty-second chapter of Isaiah, who adds "how beautiful" (Isaiah 52:7). Imagine a runner coming from over the mountains with the welcome news that peace has been agreed upon. No more fighting! Before addressing Nineveh in the rest of his prophecy, Nahum tells Judah to remain faithful, for the wicked shall not prevail. The Lord is the God of salvation as well as of judgment and vengeance. Under him wickedness will stop.

The Scripture and the Main Question—William H. Willimon

A Jealous and Avenging God

We begin today's scripture from the prophet Nahum with some rather strong words (verses 1-2):

> The Lord is a jealous God and avenging,
> the Lord is avenging and wrathful,
> the Lord takes vengeance on his adversaries
> and keeps wrath for his enemies.

I don't know about you, but I have not heard too many sermons lately which speak of God as wrathful and full of vengeance. Most of the sermons I hear, when they ascribe human attributes to God, speak of God as a loving Father, a caring parent, a good friend. Would a kind and loving God also have enemies? Is it possible for someone to be so opposed to God that God has declared that person an enemy?

A typical response is to say, "Well, of course, those words describing the wrath and the vengeance of God were written by an Old Testament prophet. Nahum, being a man who was limited by his Old Testament concepts, tended to think of God as a God of wrath and anger. We now know better. Jesus came preaching about a God of love and mercy."

Unfortunately, that explanation for today's scripture, though widely used, will simply not work. As you have probably found out in this series of lessons on the Old Testament prophets, there is certainly as much mercy and love in the Old Testament as in the New. The loving Father Jesus describes is the same God whom Israel worshiped.

Perhaps the same could be said of God looking back from the New Testament to the Old. The God who is angry at injustice and vengeful toward the enemies of righteousness whom Nahum describes is also the God of Jesus. When Jesus encountered evil and injustice, he did not simply smile and say, "God loves you." He rebuked evil. On many occasions he reacted with anger and indignation toward injustice and wrong-doing. We have not told the whole story of Jesus if we present him as "gentle Jesus, meek and mild."

Of course, there really is no way for someone to be on the side of justice without being utterly opposed to injustice. There is no way for someone to be an advocate for good without being an enemy of evil. While Nahum says that "the Lord is slow to anger" (1:3), the same merciful Lord "Will by no means clear the guilty."

The wrath of God is the inevitably dark side of the love and mercy of God. A God who merely sympathized with suffering humanity, ringing his hands over injustice but unwilling or unable to do anything about the injustice, would not be much help to us in our times of trial. The prophet Nahum describes a God who is considerably more engaged in the alleviation of human suffering than in merely passive, detached sympathy. Here is a God who actively takes up our cause during our times of trial. Here is a God who not only cares about us but who acts in our behalf when we are victims of injustice.

A number of years ago, a major Protestant denomination revised its worship book. While the book was being revised, someone recommended that the traditional "Prayer for Enemies" that had appeared in the older prayerbook be dropped because "we Christians have advanced to the stage where we no longer have any enemies."

That may be a rather sad commentary on today's church. While Jesus clearly commanded us to pray for our enemies and to bless those who persecute us, he also warned us that the truth of the gospel has a way of making its own enemies. In fact, it could be argued that a church without enemies is not really being a church!

Today's scripture from the prophet Nahum reminds us that God has enemies. God has enemies not because God is in the business of punishing others. Rather, we human beings seem to be in the business of living by what is false rather than by what is true. We prefer our wills to God's will. Thus there are always people who put themselves in opposition to the way of God. The first word of today's scripture from the prophet is that God takes an active role against those who oppose the ways of God.

The Lord Is Good

> The Lord is good,
> a stronghold in the day of trouble;
> he knows those who take refuge in him.
>
> (1:7)

There are two sides to today's scripture from the prophet Nahum. We begin with an assertion of the anger and the wrath of God. God gets angry at the presence of human injustice and takes action against those who do wrong. But God is also good. The anger of God is an extension of the love and mercy of God. The prophets speak of a God who is active. Here is a God who does not just sit up in the heavens, disinterested, detached from human need. Rather, "He knows those who take refuge in him" (1:7). Even those who were made to feel terribly insignificant by human injustice are intimately known by God. The poor black woman living in Soweto, the starving mother and her children in the African desert, the desperate family living in the Mexican barrio, are all known intimately to God. At least, that is the claim of the prophet.

One might ask if we, in our contented, relatively affluent situation, can truly hear these words of the prophet? Nahum's words may sound harsh to us. After all, we are contented. God is in his heaven, and all is right in the world, as far as we are concerned. We don't really need a God who acts. Nor do we need a God who takes sides in the interest of justice and punishes injustice. Because of our comfortable situation, can we really hear these comforting words of Scripture?

It is obvious that these words are addressed to people who are in pain, people who are on the receiving end of injustice. The actual historical context may be the persecution of God's people by the Assyrians. But they apply today to any group that is suffering oppression by others. When one is suffering oppression, one wonders whether wrongdoers will ever get what they deserve. In this life, things seems so unequal. Injustice seems to triumph more often than justice. Here is a powerful word to those who suffer:

> Behold, on the mountains the feet of him
>   who brings good tidings,
>   who proclaims peace!
> (1:15)

God's bad news to the oppressor is good news to the oppressed. God's mercy toward those who suffer wrong is balanced with God's punishment of those who do wrong. Here is a word to be asserted in the face of great difficulty. Things are not always equal in this life. Not everything works out for the best today. However, this powerful word of the prophet asserts that eventually, ultimately, God's justice *does triumph*. God will have his way, and his way is always one of justice and righteousness.

Helping Adults Become Involved—Douglas E. Wingeier

Preparing to Teach

Read the book ot Nahum and the commentaries on the verses identified for this week's study. Watch one or two television crime or courtroom dramas to have freshly in mind the typical plot of the triumph of Justice over evil, as outlined by Willimon. Collect clippings or notes of several news stories of the struggle against injustice to take to your class.

FOURTH QUARTER

Read Luke 1:47-55 (the Magnificat) and Luke 4:18-19 (Jesus' announcement of his mission), and compare their message to that of Nahum.

Pray for class members individually, both with regard to immediate needs they may be facing and also that their sensitivity to injustice and commitment to oppose oppression may be deepened through this study.

Your aim this week is to help class members grow in their understanding of a God whose love of the poor and oppressed also involves wrath and judgment against the oppressor, and to join with God in the struggle against injustice. Use the following outline:

I. A jealous and avenging God.
II. The Lord is good.

Introducing the Main Question

Invite class members to share instances of injustice reported in the news during the past week. Have your own items ready to contribute. Stories regarding housing evictions and homelessness; prison conditions; hunger and poverty; oppression in South Africa, Central America, or Asia; health care costs and inequities; consumer rights; bailouts of large corporations; promotion of infant formula in Third World countries; evasion of prosecution for white-collar crime; invasions of small countries by big countries; and the like may be mentioned.

As I write these words, I have just returned from leading a work team in helping to build a school in a poor barrio in Nicaragua. At our farewell celebration, two war veterans in wheelchairs, victims of contra land mines, praised us as North Americans for helping them build up their nation, in contrast to the policies of our government—the contra war and the trade embargo—that were destroying them. Working alongside us were mothers who had lost sons and children who had lost fathers in that United States-sponsored war.

We were in the midst of a people of hope, in spite of the injustice they were facing. Over and again, they asked us to use our influence to stop contra aid and the trade embargo, in order to bring peace to their land, so they could develop their country and determine their own destiny. Our hearts ached with compassion for their suffering and filled with anger at the misguided policies that were causing it.

Hopefully, by the time you read this, peace with justice will have come to Nicaragua, and their people will be free of United States intervention and able to invest their all-too-meager resources in providing education, health care, housing, and other human services to their own people, as has been their deep desire all along. But at this time of writing, the people of Nicaragua are still suffering intolerable injustice and awaiting the fulfillment of the promise of Nahum, "I will break his yoke from off you and will burst your bonds asunder" (1:13).

Have the group discuss the contrast between the seemingly interminable uphill struggle against this kind of injustice and the "quick fix" of television detective and courtroom dramas. Why are these stories so popular? Why is justice so hard to achieve in the real world? How is God involved in this struggle?

JUNE 28   LESSON 4

Developing the Lesson

I. A jealous and avenging God.

Give the historical background of Nahum from "As You Read the Scripture" and the commentaries. The overthrow of the tyrannical Assyrian empire, hoped for by Jonah (see previous lesson), is now promised by Nahum. Israel's suffering under the yoke of oppression will be relieved by their jealous and avenging God.

Ask: When you get angry and punish your children, is that inconsistent with your love for them? Why do you punish them? Is judgment a contradiction or an expression of love? How does this relate to God's nature and attitudes toward us?

Ask: Is the God of the Old Testament a God of wrath, while the New Testament God is one of love? Ask the class for examples of God's love in the Old Testament and God's judgment in the New. The lessons on Jonah in this series, Isaiah 43, 53, and 55, Jeremiah 31, and Hosea 11 are evidence of the former. And Jesus' cleansing of the temple (Matthew 21:12-13), warnings of hell (Mark 9:42-49), woes against the Pharisees (Luke 11:37-52), and prediction of the last judgment (Mark 13) demonstrate the wrath of God against the enemies of justice.

Clearly, it is the same God in both Testaments, a God who rebukes evil and expresses love through judgment when that is what is needed.

Discuss the following statements of Dr. Willimon's: "There is no way for someone to be an advocate of good without being an enemy of evil"; "Is it possible to be so opposed to God that God has declared that person an enemy?"; "The truth of the gospel has a way of making its own enemies"; "God takes an active role against those who oppose the ways of God."

Go back to the contemporary situations of injustice mentioned earlier, and discuss how God's love and justice could best be expressed in each circumstance. How can we as Christians cooperate with God to see that God's love and justice are done in those situations?

II. The Lord is good.

While Nahum forecasts doom for the evil empire, there is good news for the faithful. Quote 1:7 and 15.

God cares about the plight of the poor and the oppressed. Ask two persons to look up and read aloud Luke 1:50-53 and Luke 4:18-19. Ask: What is the main point of each of these passages? How do they compare with the message of Nahum? How are God's love and justice to be expressed to the poor and oppressed, in the view of all three passages? How will God's wrath and punishment on the oppressor be carried out?

Do Nahum's words sound harsh to you, as Dr. Willimon suggests? Does our comfortable situation prevent us from hearing these words of comfort? How might the recipients of injustice hear them differently than we?

Discuss Dr. Willimon's assertion that "God's bad news to the oppressor is good news to the oppressed." Are we among the oppressed or the oppressors?

Helping Class Members Act

Return again to the situations of injustice mentioned early in the session. Choose one that is close to the class and on which they would like to make an

FOURTH QUARTER

impact, cooperating with God in the struggle for justice. Analyze the blocking and enabling forces to greater justice in two columns on the board. Determine which blocking forces the group might work to reduce or remove, so that the forces for justice might more readily prevail. Make assignments for work on these issues, with members to report back at a later session.

In closing sing "O Young and Fearless Prophet" or "The Voice of God Is Calling," and pray for peace and justice in the world and courage and strength for your group to carry out their chosen project effectively.

Planning for Next Sunday

Ask the class to read the book of Habakkuk in preparation for next week. Also have them recall times of national and personal crisis and ask themselves how they felt about God's faithfulness in those situations.

LESSON 5   JULY 5

Faithfulness in Crisis

Background Scripture: Habakkuk

The Main Question—William H. Willimon

Yesterday, we in the United States celebrated our day of national independence. The Fourth of July is not only a time for fireworks, picnics, and vacations. It is also a time to remember. Anytime we look back on the history of our country, we remember many of the crises our country has survived. The quality of the nation is measured by its ability to live through times of great difficulty.

The quality of an individual is likewise measured by that person's ability to withstand crises. As you look back on your own life, you probably measure your life through significant moments in which your life was interlocked with the life of our nation. Where were you when Pearl Harbor was attacked? Do you remember what you were doing the day that President John F. Kennedy was shot? I suspect that you know exactly where you were and what you were doing when the space shuttle *Challenger* exploded. These national crises were also crises in your life.

In times of national or personal crises, we come to a turning in the road. One path ends, and we stand on the threshold of a new beginning. New beginnings are frightening because we cannot predict what the future holds. Times of crises are therefore times of testing of faith. Will our faith sustain us through this time of difficulty? We sing about the faithfulness of God and church, we read Scripture that proclaims that God is with us during times of difficulty. But is this true? Will this be true for us during our time of crisis and dislocation?

JULY 5   LESSON 5

Many years ago, the prophet Habakkuk faced a crisis in his land. He cried out to God. Would God stand beside him during this time of testing?

Is God faithful during time of crisis? This is the question that lies behind today's lesson.

Selected Scripture

King James Version

Habakkuk 1:1-7

1 The burden which Habakkuk the prophet did see.

2 O Lord, how long shall I cry, and thou wilt not hear! *even* cry out unto thee *of* violence, and thou wilt not save!

3 Why dost thou shew me iniquity, and cause *me* to behold grievance? for spoiling and violence *are* before me: and there are *that* raise up strife and contention.

4 Therefore the law is slacked, and judgment doth never go forth: for the wicked doth compass about the righteous; therefore wrong judgment proceedeth.

5 Behold ye among the heathen, and regard, and wonder marvellously: for *I* will work a work in your days, *which* ye will not believe, though it be told *you*.

6 For, lo, I raise up the Chaldeans, *that* bitter and hasty nation, which shall march through the breadth of the land, to possess the dwellingplaces *that are* not their's.

7 They *are* terrible and dreadful: their judgment and their dignity shall proceed of themselves.

Habakkuk 2:1-4

1 I will stand upon my watch, and set me upon the tower, and will watch to see what he will say unto me, and what I shall answer when I am reproved.

Revised Standard Version

Habakkuk 1:1-7

1 The oracle of God which Habakkuk the prophet saw.

2 O Lord, how long shall I cry for help,
and thou wilt not hear?
Or cry to thee "Violence!"
and thou wilt not save?

3 Why dost thou make me see wrongs
and look upon trouble?
Destruction and violence are before me;
strife and contention arise.

4 So the law is slacked
and justice never goes forth.
For the wicked surround the righteous,
so justice goes forth perverted.

5 Look among the nations, and see;
wonder and be astounded.
For I am doing a work in you days
that you would not believe if told.

6 For lo, I am rousing the Chaldeans,
that bitter and hasty nation,
who march through the breadth of the earth,
to seize habitations not their own.

7 Dread and terrible are they;
their justice and dignity proceed from themselves.

Habakkuk 2:1-4

1 I will take my stand to watch,
and station myself on the tower,
and look forth to see what he will say to me,
and what I will answer concerning my complaint.

FOURTH QUARTER

2 And the Lord answered me, and said, Write the vision, and make *it* plain upon tables, that he may run that readeth it.

3 For the vision *is* yet for an appointed time, but at the end it shall speak, and not lie: though it tarry, wait for it; because it will surely come, it will not tarry.

4 Behold, his soul *which* is lifted up is not upright in him: but the just shall live by his faith.

Key Verse: **Behold, his soul which is lifted up is not upright in him: but the just shall live by his faith. (Habakkuk 2:4)**

2 And the Lord answered me:
"Write the vision;
    make it plain upon tablets,
    so he may run who reads it.
3 For still the vision awaits its time;
    it hastens to the end—it will not lie.
If it seem slow, wait for it;
    it will surely come, it will not delay.
4 Behold, he whose soul is not upright in him shall fail,
    but the righteous shall live by his faith.

Key Verse: **Behold, he whose soul is not upright in him shall fail, but the righteous shall live by his faith. (Habakkuk 2:4)**

As You Read the Scripture—Charles T. Klinksick

Habakkuk (pronounced Ha-*back*-cook) is another short literary composition full of historical and theological truth. The Chaldeans (Babylonians) had recently conquered Nineveh (see lesson on Nahum), and now they are exceeding the Assyrians in rampant violence. They would inevitably attack Judah, and Jerusalem would fall.

Chapters 1 and 2 are dialogues between the complaining writer and the Lord. Chapter 3 is a majestic prayer hymn or psalm, which the Dead Sea Scroll of Habakkuk does not have. Habakkuk's problem is that all the wrong things are happening, and the Lord is not intervening. The problem is a common one, but the degree of violence, destruction, and injustice is extreme.

Habakkuk 1:1-4. Habakkuk is "the prophet" mentioned in verse 1; nothing is known of his background. The time of his prophecy is approximately 598 B.C. His cry is a personal one, but he speaks for all who are seeking deliverance.

"O Lord, how long?" is an appropriate outcry at many points in personal life or national history, but it was urgent at this time for these people. Note the words and their cumulative implications: wrongs, trouble, destruction, violence, strife, and contention. The law is not respected, the wicked corner good people, and justice is perverted. There is no end in sight.

Verse 5. This is the Lord's reply to the prophet. In effect he is saying, "Look beyond yourselves and be surprized. You wouldn't believe what I am doing if I told you."

Verses 6-7. Here is a providential paradox. God is using a terrorist nation to answer Judah's cry for help. There probably was much more in the background: How righteous was the complainant? Exactly what unbelievable work was God planning? How could the Holy One justify using guilty men to accomplish his good? The Caldeans are described in verse 7. They decide for themselves what justice is. Pictures are added through verse 11.

Habakkuk continues his dialogue with complaints and questions, to the end of the chapter.

Habakkuk 2:1. How the prophet backs off to meditate by himself until the Lord gives him a clear answer. The tower reference may be literal or poetic. Either way, he is taking a watch-and-wait attitude. His expectancy becomes God's opportunity.

Verse 2. The answer came, with instructions for communicating it. He was to write it in large letters on "tablets." These probably were wax-covered boards on which a message could be incised with a stylus. The words were to be large enough for a runner to read while passing it. No fine print!

Verse 3. This is a comment on how a revelation works: It is timely, progressive, and truthful. It is unhurried and undelayed. The point is, wait for it; don't be impatient.

Verse 4. "Behold," meaning look, take note: The evil soul within causes failure, and righteous living requires faith. The second half of the verse is quoted by Paul in Romans 1:17 and Galatians 3:11 and contains a key concept of the Protestant Reformation. The doctrine of justification by faith undergirds the whole concept of forgiveness and grace in the New Testament. For Habakkuk and Judah, it meant the complaints of righteous people are to be met by faith in God. Conversely, unrighteous and unbelieving people will always falter and fail.

The Scripture and the Main Question—William H. Willimon

Strife and Contention Arise

A number of years ago, at the University Chapel where I preach, the throng emerged from the chapel choir's annual performance of Handel's *Messiah*. It was a cloudy, early December afternoon. The crowd, which had just heard the choir sing of glory to God and the coming of the Prince of Peace, emerged to find hundreds of students gathered around automobile radios in the chapel quadrangle. What was going on?

They were listening to the radio reports, which had just come in, of the bombing of Pearl Harbor.

Not a single life would be unchanged after that fateful Sunday afternoon. Every person went home, pondering the irony between the beautiful biblical poetry put to music by Handel in his *Messiah*, contrasted with the reports of the carnage at Pearl Harbor.

"That was the saddest, most frightening Christmas I have ever had," recalled one man who was in the congregation that day.

How far the biblical promise of peace on earth seemed then from the realities of modern war.

The ancient prophet Habakkuk lived through a time of chaos as frightening and devastating as our modern experiences of war. The book of Habakkuk opens with the prophet's cry of anguish:

> O Lord, how long shall I cry for help,
>   and thou wilt not hear?
> Or cry to thee "Violence!"
>   and thou wilt not save?
> Why dost thou make me see wrongs
>   and look upon trouble?
> Destruction and violence are before me
>   strife and contention arise. (1:2-3)

FOURTH QUARTER

You have to hand it to the Bible. Although for us, on Sunday morning, dressed in our Sunday best, religion is a time to hide from life's difficulties, a time for sweet words and nice thoughts, that is not the Bible's way. When biblical people hurt, they cry out. When they are confused, they tell God about their confusion. When they are angry, they pour out their anger before the throne of God.

Habakkuk's anguished cry is a typically honest biblical outburst. So the first lesson to be learned from today's Scripture is that it is fully permissible to be fully honest with God about anguish, confusion, fear, and dread. God is not offended by our anguish. Prayer need not be a time for sweet platitudes, pious clichés and vague, meaningless speech. Prayer can be a time for an honest, straightforward, up-front outburst.

Habakkuk is talking to God. The prophet is telling God how it is with his soul. Everything is laid bare. There is no pretension or deceit here. The prophet is at the end of his rope. The fierce armies of the Chaldeans are at the door of Israel. What will become of God's Chosen People? With destruction threatening and oblivion imminent, Habakkuk does not know which way to turn next. So he turns to God in an honest, heartfelt outburst: "For the wicked surround the righteous, so justice goes forth perverted" (1:4). The bad seems to triumph over the good. There is corruption and injustice throughout the land. Is not this the core of our anguish during times of crisis?

And the Lord Answered Me

Habakkuk stationed himself on his tower to scan the horizon to see what, if anything, God would say in response to his plea. He received an answer, a vision from God.

The vision Habakkuk received may not have been the one he wanted. "The vision waits its time," he was told; "if it seem slow, wait for it; it will surely come, it will not delay" (2:3).

Habakkuk's vision reminds me of a person in my congregation who said one night as we were having a discussion about prayer, "God always answers prayer. But sometimes God's answer to us is no."

God's answers to our anguished cries are not always the answers we ask for. When he prayed for deliverance in the Garden of Gethsemane, asking that the cup of death pass from him, Jesus received no for an answer.

Habakkuk did not receive no for an answer from God. However, he was told that God's response to the plight of his homeland might not be as fast as he would like. These things take time. God's time is not the same as our time. We grow impatient. We want what we want, and we want it now. Our impatience is understandable, particularly when we are going through tough times. But God's visitation to us is a gift of God, not something we can have on demand, not something that we control. Therefore patience is an essential virtue for people of faith.

"The righteous shall live by faith," says the vision (2:4). Martin Luther read that verse and his insight led to the Protestant Reformation. Luther took the verse to be a prooftext on his doctrine of justification by faith rather than good works. In the context of Habakkuk, it is probably an exhortation for faithful patience on the part of those who wait for God to act in their lives.

We must live by faith. That means we must allow God to respond to our crises in God's own good time.

JULY 5 LESSON 5

The Vision Awaits Its Time

I have just finished rereading the exciting historical account of the last days of the Nazi occupation of Paris, *Is Paris Burning*? In the last days of Paris, as the Germans were gradually losing their grip upon the beautiful city after the Allies' Normandy invasion, the French Resistance was divided on what to do next. One group, the Communists, wanted to begin an armed rebellion against the Nazi occupiers so that they could ensure Communist control of a liberated city after the Allied troops arrived.

The other group, the Gaullist Party led by General DeGaul, wanted to wait until the allied forces approved the beginning of a popular uprising. That way, fewer Frenchmen would lose their lives and the city might be spared from destruction by the departing Nazis.

The impatient Communists got their way. Despite pleas from the Allies to wait a few more days for deliverance, they began fighting the Nazis in the streets of Paris. The superior German forces ruthlessly crushed the rebellion, destroying many beautiful buildings in the process.

As you know, Paris was eventually liberated, but not because of the impetuous acts of the Parisian Communists. The Gaullists waited on the arrival of their allies, and they succeeded in recapturing and holding the now-free Paris.

Sometimes we so want justice, deliverance. At times, God seems so slow. Patience is an essential virtue of people who are praying, not that our will but God's will be done.

Helping Adults Become Involved—Douglas E. Wingeier

Preparing to Teach

This lesson on Habakkuk deals with one of the most profound and difficult questions human beings face: How can a good God remain "silent when the wicked swallows up the person more righteous than he" (1:13)? Why do the innocent suffer while evil and injustice prosper?

This issue was also touched on in lesson 1 on Obadiah. Review that material, and also the ideas in the books by Leslie Weatherhead and Harold Kushner cited in lesson 1 of this quarter.

Read the book of Habakkuk and one or more commentaries on it. Chapter 14, "The Transition to the Babylonian Era," in Gerhard von Rad's *The Message of the Prophets*, also provides helpful background.

Read Mark 14:32-42, the story of Jesus in Gethsemane, and Romans 1:17, Galatians 3:11, and Hebrews 10:38 on justification by faith.

Note that the book contains three distinct literary forms: a dialogue between the prophet and God in 1:2–2:5, five woes against a wicked nation in 2:6-20, and the long psalm in chapter 3, written for use in temple worship.

Also be aware that scholars differ on the historical period to which the book belongs. The traditional view is that the Chaldeans mentioned in 1:6 are the Babylonians who conquered Judah in 587 B.C., which would place the book around 600. But a commentary on Habakkuk discovered with the Dead Sea Scrolls in 1947 supports the view that the reference is to the Greeks (Greek: *Kittim*) not the Chaldeans (Greek: *Kasdim*), which would

FOURTH QUARTER

date it much later, at the time of the conquest by Alexander the Great, begun in 334 B.C.

Whichever it was, the central theme is the same. A searching prophet dares to question God's apparent way of working in the world, and finds an answer in trustful faith.

Pray for wisdom to deal helpfully with this question and to relate this scripture meaningfully to the life concerns of your class members.

Your purpose is to help the class reflect prayerfully on life crises and to deepen their trust in the God who stands with us in those times. You may organize the lesson as follows:

        I. Strife and contention arise.
       II. The vision awaits its time.
     III. The righteous live by faith.

Introducing the Main Question

Begin by asking class members to share stories of crisis times in their lives, the life of your church, or the history of the nation. Because of the proximity of July 4, the three recent events in American history mentioned by Dr. Willimon—Pearl Harbor, the Kennedy assassination, and the Challenger explosion—might be a good place to start. Church emergencies, such as a fire, loss of a beloved pastor or lay leader, or a divisive conflict, might also be mentioned.

In terms of personal crises, those that have hit me the hardest have been the illness of my mother, the death of my father, a threat to my marriage, and a temporary estrangement from one of my children.

Cultivate a caring, supportive climate in the class for the sharing of these experiences. If the group is large, divide into smaller groups of three or four so that more can share and more intimate support can develop.

Once the stories are out, gently guide the group into a discussion of the following questions: How did you *feel* while going through these experiences? Could you sense God's presence with you? What made God seem present or absent? Could you trust God to bring a loving outcome, even in the midst of the sense of pain and unfairness? What helped or hindered your ability to trust?

Developing the Lesson

I. Strife and contention arise.

Have someone read these verses aloud. Give the historical background from "As You Read the Scripture" and your commentary study. If you prefer the Greek to the Chaldean dating, read *Harper's*, or another Bible dictionary for information on Alexander the Great.

Draw parallels to the crisis experiences just shared, in terms of the wrongs done, the feeling of loss and despair, the suffering endured, the sudden twist of fortunes, the cry for help, and the sense of God's absence or deafness to our need.

II. The vision awaits its time.

Have these verses read aloud. Ask: In your crisis times, were you impatient to have the wrongs righted, the despair transformed into hope, the suffering be over, your bad fortunes reversed, the cry for help answered *now*, God's absence overcome by a mighty spiritual uplift?

Emphasize Dr. Willimon's point that it is permissible to be honest with God about our negative feelings and our cries for relief. Also emphasize that our prayers are often not answered in the way we wish. Share an experience of your own in this regard, or ask the group for examples.

In my own life, I had been praying for peace in Central America, the Middle East, and South Africa for a number of years, without visible results. Suddenly my son went off to Nicaragua as a United Methodist mission intern, and then I felt a call to go there myself to help build a school. Could this, have been God's way of nudging me to be a partial answer to my own prayer?

Have Mark 14:32-42 read aloud, and emphasize that even Jesus in Gethsemane did not receive the answer he wanted to his prayer that the cup pass from him. Sometimes God's answer to our prayers leads us into even greater risk and crisis than what we are seeking to escape.

The word Habakkuk receives from God is "Patience." The answer to his prayer is neither yes nor no, but "Wait." The vision of peace and justice to come is plain, but it will be slow in coming. The people of faith must be patient.

Relate this word of counsel to the crisis situations shared by class members. Ask: Are you able to wait for God to act in your situation? Can you trust God to deliver or transform or empower or sustain or make new, as you are praying and hoping, or to do something different—and better—than you can imagine?

III. The righteous live by faith.

Have three class members read these same words in Romans 1:17, Galatians 3:11, and Hebrews 10:38. Explain that while for Habakkuk this meant faithful patience to wait for God to deliver Judah from the scourge of the Chaldeans or Greeks, Paul and later Martin Luther have made justification through faith in Christ the cornerstone of the Christian message.

Habakkuk's (and our) response to the problem of innocent suffering is (1) to really believe that God will transform situations of suffering and injustice into the shalom vision of the Old Testament and Jesus' promise of the coming kingdom or new age, and then (2) to work with God to help bring this to pass, "on earth as it is in heaven."

Helping Class Members Act

Review the crisis experiences shared earlier, and ask members to consider what they might do to help God's redemptive purpose be accomplished in those situations.

Call for reports from the members or task groups working on the justice issue identified in the last session. Plan your next steps and make new assignments as appropriate.

Sing either "Prayer Is the Soul's Sincere Desire" or "Work, for the Night Is Coming," then close by praying the Lord's Prayer together.

Planning for Next Sunday

In addition to reading Zephaniah 1-2, ask class members to think about the causes of hopelessness in our world and the sources of hope in their own lives and to come prepared to share these thoughts.

UNIT II: A REMNANT IS SAVED
Horace R. Weaver

TWO LESSONS **JULY 12-19**

Unit II consists of two sessions from the prophet Zephaniah. The first lesson, "Seek the Lord," July 12, warns of God's intention to judge all people who refuse to worship God. The second lesson, "Renewal of Life," July 19, discusses God's promises that a faithful remnant will be saved.

LESSON 6 **JULY 12**

Seek the Lord

Background Scripture: Zephaniah 1-2

The Main Question—William H. Willimon

A recent survey of American college students revealed that well over half believe that we will have a nuclear confrontation within their lifetime. What does it do to a people to believe that their world could be utterly destroyed in the twinkling of an eye?

Recent events remind us all that we live on a fragile planet. There is a disaster at a nuclear power plant. An oil tanker has a collision at sea, and hundreds of miles of coastline are threatened. We surround ourselves with nuclear weapons, so many nuclear weapons that we could destroy the world sixty times over, according to some estimates.

Today's scripture reminds us that the majority of humanity has always lived on a fragile planet. Zephaniah's world was smaller than our own. When he heard God say, "I will utterly sweep away everything from the face of the earth" (1:2), he probably thought God spoke of the coming destruction of Jerusalem. We live in a time when not only Jerusalem, but every living thing could be utterly swept away from the earth. So there is a sense in which the ancient words of the prophet Zephaniah have particularly relevant meaning for our generation. Zephaniah saw storm clouds gathering over his beloved land. It seemed to him as if the world as he knew it was coming to an end. It is at this point that we modern people begin to make contact with the ancient prophet. Storm clouds are also gathering on our horizon. A majority of our people know that we face a threatening and uncertain future.

Where is our hope when it seems as if there will be no more tomorrow? That is the ultimate question behind today's lesson.

JULY 12　　　　　　　　　　　　　　　　　　　　LESSON 6

Selected Scripture

King James Version

Zephaniah 1:1-3, 7, 12

1 The word of the Lord which came unto Zephaniah the son of Cushi, the son of Gedaliah, the son of Amariah, the son of Hizkiah, in the days of Josiah the son of Amon, king of Judah.

2 I will utterly consume all *things* from off the land, saith the Lord.

3 I will consume man and beast; I will consume the fowls of the heaven, and the fishes of the sea, and the stumblingblocks with the wicked; and I will cut off man from off the land, saith the Lord.

....

7 Hold thy peace at the presence of the Lord God: for the day of the Lord *is* at hand: for the Lord hath prepared a sacrifice, he hath bid his guests.

....

12 And it shall come to pass at that time, *that* I will search Jerusalem with candles, and punish the men that are settled on their lees: that say in their heart, The Lord will not do good, neither will he do evil.

Zephaniah 2:1-3

1 Gather yourselves together, yea, gather together, O nation not desired;

2 Before the decree bring forth, *before* the day pass as the chaff, before the fierce anger of the Lord come upon you, before the day of the Lord's anger come upon you.

Revised Standard Version

Zephaniah 1:1-3, 7, 12

1 The word of the Lord which came to Zephaniah the son of Cushi, son of Gedaliah, son of Amariah, son of Hezekiah, in the days of Josiah the son of Amon, king of Judah.

2 "I will utterly sweep away everything
　from the face of the earth," says the Lord.

3 "I will sweep away man and beast;
　I will sweep away the birds of the air
　and the fish of the sea.
I will overthrow the wicked;
I will cut off mankind
　from the face of the earth," says the Lord.

....

7 Be silent before the Lord God!
For the day of the Lord is at hand;
　the Lord has prepared a sacrifice
　and consecrated his guests.

....

12 At that time I will search Jerusalem with lamps,
　and I will punish the men
who are thickening upon their lees,
　those who say in their hearts,
'The Lord will not do good,
　nor will he do ill.'"

Zephaniah 2:1-3

1 Come together and hold assembly,
　O shameless nation,
2 before you are driven away
　like the drifting chaff,
before there comes upon you
　the fierce anger of the Lord,
before there comes upon you

FOURTH QUARTER

3 Seek ye the Lord, all ye meek of the earth, which have wrought his judgment; seek righteousness, seek meekness: it may be ye shall be hid in the day of the Lord's anger.

the day of the wrath of the Lord.
3 Seek the Lord, all you humble of the land,
who do his commands;
seek righteousness, seek humility;
perhaps you may be hidden
on the day of the wrath of the Lord.

Key Verse: **Seek ye the Lord, all ye meek of the earth, which have wrought his judgment; seek righteousness, seek meekness. (Zephaniah 2:3)**

Key Verse: **Seek the Lord, all you humble of the land, who do his commands, seek righteousness, seek humility. (Zephaniah 2:3)**

As You Read the Scripture—Charles T. Klinksick

Zephaniah, Habakkuk, and Jeremiah were contemporaries. Josiah was king of Judah from 640 to 609 B.C. The times were violent all around. Scythian barbarians were pouring down through Palestine from Asia Minor to the borders of Egypt. The Assyrians had ruled viciously, until overcome by the Chaldeans. Judah was smug and sin-ridden, and Jerusalem was ripe for capture. Zephaniah's theme was "The day of the Lord is at hand" (1:7), "the day of the wrath of the Lord" (2:2-3). Note verses 14, 15, and 16 of chapter 1. The book sweeps from emphasis on total overthrow of everyone, everywhere, in chapter 1, to hope for survival for Judah in the end of chapter 3.

Zephaniah 1:1. Though not mentioned as a prophet, Zephaniah is traced back to his great-great-grandfather, Hezekiah, king of Judah from 715 to 697 B.C. Josiah as king had tried to purge his nation of its evils. It was a turbulent period of idol worship and nationalistic power clashes. Zephaniah speaks out for God with authority.

Verses 2 and 3. The words imply an end to mankind. Note the ending of 1:18, which reminds us of God's resolve in the days of Noah to "blot out man . . . from the face of the ground" (Genesis 6:7). It seems that either Zephaniah was overstating the Lord's intentions, or the text is a clue to how righteously wrathful the Lord had become. Righteous indignation is one of the attributes of God. Note how Jesus indignantly cleansed the temple of money dealings (Luke 19:45-46).

The Lord had been displaced from the center of worship by alien idols and superstitious magical practices. The time had come for reckoning "the day of the Lord." "I will," says the Lord, five times in verses 2 and 3.

Verses 4-13. Specifically, Jerusalem will be set upon. The Lord will search out the men who think God will neither bother nor bless them. "Lees" are the dregs of wine that settle to the bottom of empty wine bottles, jugs, or cups. "Thickening" means becoming crusty, hardened, or callous. The Lord's wrath will land on them as well as others. Their indifference will not excuse them.

Zephaniah 2:1-2. Zephaniah softens his broad, sweeping threats. He writes kindly to his nation and offers hope. He invites them to assemble *before* the Lord's fierce anger comes. There is still time.

Verse 3. This is addressed to the portion of the population that is *humble*. Proud people won't pay attention, but those who try to do what the Lord commands and expects, as the Ten Commandments require (Exodus 20:1-17), have a chance. The message says to seek three things: the Lord, righteousness, and humility. Similarly, Jesus would later tell his followers to seek his kingdom and his righteousness (Matthew 6:33). Zephaniah's offer of hope begins here with the idea of being hidden from the Lord's wrath, "perhaps." The offer of safety and security is amplified greatly by the close of chapter 3, as the book ends.

A prophet has an exceptional role. He is more than a day-to-day plodder. He senses where he is in history. He reads his times morally and interprets them from the viewpoint of the Lord, to whom he is sensibly alert. He awesomely is aware of where all this is leading. He is under a compulsion to speak out. He is factual, poetic, historical, and far-seeing. He is a remarkable person of faith in the eternal nature of God as a personal being and in the ability of human beings to respond to him for their own good. His purpose is to serve primarily as a Rescuer, not to aggrandize himself. Zephaniah was one of these.

The Scripture and the Main Question—William H. Willimon

I Will Utterly Sweep Away Everything

"I will utterly sweep away everything from the face of the earth," Zephaniah hears God declare (1:2). These are harsh, threatening words. You and I are unaccustomed to thinking of God as an avenger, a harsh destroyer. For us, God is the loving creator, the maker of worlds rather than the destroyer of life.

What shall we do with this rather terrifying image of God as the devastator of Israel rather than its patron and protector?

One possible explanation: When Zephaniah had this vision, he was showing that he was a man of his times. These are the thoughts of an Old Testament man, a man who probably lived more than seven hundred years before Christ. Old Testament people like Zephaniah had an inadequate view of God. For them, God was a harsh, wrathful deity. Now, after Jesus, we know better. God is love. God is complete grace and mercy.

Unfortunately, this explanation doesn't really help us out of our dilemma with these tough words from Zephaniah. Such an explanation implies that the Old Testament is not really a vessel of God's Word, that its revelation is flawed and so inadequate as to be irrelevant. We ought to remind ourselves that the Old Testament was the only Scripture Jesus and his disciples knew. When Jesus used Scripture to speak of God, he quoted from the Old Testament. While for us Jesus is the fulfillment of the Old Testament, the correction for any inadequacies of interpretation of the Hebrew Scriptures, he claims to be the *fulfillment* of those Scriptures. As Christians we are not free to dismiss Old Testament revelation as somehow superseded or negated by the New Testament.

Second, the claim that the Old Testament as an inadequate, primitive depiction of a wrathful, merciless God is a grave injustice to the Old Testament. There is plenty of grace and love within the Old Testament. Admittedly, the book of Zephaniah has plenty of harsh, uncompromisingly judgmental language, but there is also plenty of grace, even in Zephaniah.

FOURTH QUARTER

This prophetic book ends not in wrathful condemnation of wayward Israel but in a merciful, gracious promise of deliverance for suffering Israel:

> Sing aloud, O daughter of Zion;
>   shout, O Israel!
> Rejoice and exult with all your heart,
>   O daughter of Jerusalem!
> The Lord has taken away the judgments against you,
>   he has cast out your enemies.
> (3:14-15)

On the other hand, there is plenty of wrath and judgment in the New Testament:

> I came to cast fire upon the earth; and would that it were already kindled! . . . Do you think that I have come to give peace on earth? No, I tell you, but rather division; for henceforth in one house there will be five divided, three against two and two against three; they will be divided, father against son and son against father, mother against daughter and daughter against her mother, mother-in-law against her daughter-in-law and daughter-in-law against her mother-in-law. (Luke 12:49-54)

Here are words of Jesus that would be worthy of inclusion in the harshest prophecies of Zephaniah!

So we might well ask ourselves, Why is a God of love and mercy, and God's son, Jesus, speaking in such harsh, terrible terms?

The Fierce Anger of the Lord

Anthropomorphism—can you say the word? It is a big and fancy word that means simply that we human beings tend to describe God in ways that are human. We speak of God as a loving father. We talk about God being moved to pity. When asked about the nature of God, Jesus told a story of a father and his two sons. God waits for us to return to him just like that father waited for the return of his prodigal son. Or God is like a woman who loses a valuable coin and turns her house upside down, sweeping until she finds the lost coin. God seeks us just like that sweeping woman, says Jesus. This is anthropomorphism, ascribing certain human attributes to the indescribable God.

But we cannot take our anthropomorphism in only one way. If God feels love for us, why can't God feel anger toward us? If God cares for us, why can't God also punish us?

Let's indulge in a little anthropomorphism of our own: If you are a parent, you understand quite easily how it is possible to love a child very dearly and yet at the same time be terribly, fiercely angry with that child. You know what it means to punish a wayward child not out of hate but out of your great love for that child.

I believe this bit of anthropomorphism lies behind today's scripture from Zephaniah. God loves Israel. In fact, God created Israel, first through covenant with Abraham and Sarah and their heirs, then through God's merciful deliverance of Israel from Egyptian slavery. Yet God's beloved people have gone astray, have bowed down to other gods and have forsaken

God's commandments. Why cannot God also be terribly angry with Israel while at the same time loving Israel?

Actions have consequences. If Israel chooses to live like any other nation, doing injustice, persecuting the poor, living with one another not as brothers and sisters but as strangers, then God will treat them as any other nation, as a nation that has no God.

We may debate whether the punishment Israel suffers in its time of trial was brought on by the direct, punitive intervention of God or simply developed as a consequence of Israel's actions. Nevertheless, the prophet sees the nation's current situation as deserved because of the nation's infidelity. God is grieved. God is angry. There is judgment.

We live in a nation that invented the most awesome, terrible weapon ever known to humankind. We chose to use that terrible weapon against the civilian population of two Japanese cities, the only time in history that any nation has ever used nuclear weapons against anyone else. Since that day, we have spent decades developing more nuclear weapons, stockpiling weapons on top of weapons.

Now we find ourselves in a terribly vulnerable situation. It is ironic that the very force, nuclear power, that was to bring us security and stability, freedom from war and destruction, has become a major possibility for our nation's total destruction, indeed, the utter destruction of the whole planet. The bomb that was to be our servant in our desire for power over our own destinies has become our master. Vast amounts of our national resources go into the care and feeding of our bombs. We face the possibility of complete annihilation with the push of a button.

Could it not be said by someone, perhaps someone who studied today's prophecies from Zephaniah, that we are being "punished" for our sin?

Helping Adults Become Involved—Douglas E. Wingeier

Preparing to Teach

The lessons for this week and next, based on the prophet Zephaniah, juxtapose the doom and hope themes of much Old Testament prophecy. As a descendant of the good king Hezekiah (715–687 B.C., 1:1), Zephaniah was a relative of the current king, Josiah (640–609 B.C.). But he preached before the young king had become strong enough to institute the reforms of 622 B.C. (2 Kings 22–23), so he confronted the corrupt practices of his day. We can thus understand why he is so vehement in denouncing the sins of his society and predicting its wholesale destruction.

His prophecy is less concerned with justice for the poor than with criticism of the top levels of national life—court officials (1:8), judges, cult prophets, priests (3:3-4), idolatrous practices (1:4-6), adoption of foreign customs and dress (1:8), religious indifference (1:12-13), and proud boasting (3:11).

His description of the coming destruction of Jerusalem (1:10-13) is probably based on the invasion of the Fertile Crescent by the Scythian hordes, which took place around 625 B.C. The prophet sees in these marauders a sign of the even more ominous Day of Yahweh, when God will bring just and terrible retribution upon Judah and her neighbors, while rescuing a righteous remnant—an increasingly common theme in the later prophets, especially Daniel.

FOURTH QUARTER

The book of Zephaniah has four sections: God's judgment on Judah (1:2–2:4), God's judgment on the nations (2:5-15), woe to Jerusalem (3:1-8), and God's blessing on Judah (3:9-20). The first two are dealt with in this lesson, the last two in the next.

Read the entire book, commentaries about it, and the article on the Day of the Lord in *The Interpreter's Dictionary of the Bible.*

Collect from magazines and newspapers items that forecast doom for our nation and planet—environmental crises, nuclear testing, wars and rumors of wars, urban decay, declining standards of health and education, family disintegration, and the like. Search through issues of *Sojourners* and *The Other Side* for articles on current issues of this sort, which you may quote in class.

Pray for wisdom and guidance that your preparation and teaching of this lesson may make class members more concerned about global issues of peace, justice, and the integrity of creation, which is the aim of this lesson. Use the following outline:

    I. Signs of doom in Zephaniah's time
   II. Signs of doom in our time
  III. Hope in the face of hopelessness

Introducing the Main Question

Ask members to share the causes of hopelessness in the world, which they were asked to think about during the week. To "prime the pump," offer some of your news items at this point. As this is being written, an oil spill, a hurricane, an earthquake, a nuclear accident, an invasion, a civil war, and an assassination have all taken place in recent months. What is happening in 1992?

Ask class members how they *feel* about these events. Are they discouraged about the future of the world? Depressed? Optimistic? Spurred to try to change the course of history? Or do they try to ignore these happenings by becoming preoccupied with daily responsibilities in family, work, and church?

Now ask how they see God being active in these world-shaking events. Is God angry at human sin and using these happenings to express displeasure and judgment? Is God grieving over humanity's greedy, self-centered exploitation of the earth and inhuman treatment of "the least of these"? Is God suffering and struggling with abused creation to restore the order and harmony of the shalom vision? Or is God so grand and majestic that what seem to us to be dire and cataclysmic disasters hardly cause a ripple in the cosmic scheme of things?

Developing the Lesson

I. Signs of doom in Zephaniah's time

As someone reads aloud 1:4-13, have the class pick out the offenses specified by the prophet. Write these on the board.

Ask: Why would these abuses make God so angry? Is it God that is angry, or just Zephaniah? Does God get angry? Share Dr. Willimon's discussion of the mistaken contrast between the Old Testament God of wrath and Jesus' God of love. Refer back to the examples of love in the Old Testament and judgment in the New mentioned in lesson 4, and also to Jesus' statement, "I came to cast fire upon the earth," quoted by Dr. Willimon from Luke 12:49-54.

Open up Dr. Willimon's treatment of anthropomorphism. Discuss whether it is appropriate to draw parallels to parental attitudes and ascribe human attributes when thinking about God?

Emphasize that at least from Zephaniah's perspective, Judah's leaders had violated God's commandments, which had made God extremely angry. Whether through the Scythians or from some other source, Yahweh would bring punishment and devastation upon his disobedient people.

II. Signs of doom in our time

Referring to the natural and human disasters discussed earlier, ask: Does God have just cause for anger at a disobedient people in our time? What are the likely consequences of our ravaging the environment, our stockpiling nuclear weapons, our craze for acquiring ever more consumer goods, our exploitation of Third World countries, our blatant support of military dictatorships and death squads in Central America and Asia, our denial of housing and human services to the poor of our own land?

It may be difficult for class members to accept that the judgment of God may be aimed at our own nation, just as it was at ancient Judah. Have 1:2-3 and 2:1-4 read aloud. Ask the class to imagine what it might have been like for the people of Judah to hear these words of Zephaniah. How would they have reacted? How can we keep ourselves open to hear the criticism of prophetic voices in our time? Cite paragraphs from *Sojourners* or *The Other Side* giving specific content to such criticism. What message does God want to give to the United States in our time? Does this message give us a sense of hopelessness or hope?

III. Hope in the face of hopelessness

Ask class members to share the sources of hope in their lives from their pre-class reflections. Such things as strong national leaders, the younger generation, progress in technology, changes in Eastern Europe, and current signs of peace and prosperity may be mentioned.

Read 2:3 once again. This holds out a glimmer of hope that *perhaps* those who seek the Lord, righteousness, and humility will be spared on the Day of the Lord. Drawing on your research on the Day of the Lord, explain that the Old Testament prophets use this phrase to refer to a coming time of judgment and catastrophe, in which evil will be destroyed and the righteous saved.

The source of hope in the face of this grim calamity is not political leadership or scientific progress, not military might or material affluence, not even family love and church attendance. Rather, the only source of hope is humble repentance and trust in the saving power of God.

Helping Class Members Act

Review progress on class justice projects begun at earlier sessions. Plan next steps and new assignments. Sing "O God of Every Nation" or "This Is My Song." Close with a litany in which mention one-by-one of the various present-day signs of doom discussed in class is followed by a group response, such as "Good Lord, deliver us" or "Forgive us, O God."

FOURTH QUARTER

Planning for Next Sunday

Study of Zephaniah will continue next week. Have the class read chapter 3 and continue thinking about the sources of hope in their lives, in light of the brief discussion of that near the end of this lesson.

LESSON 7   JULY 19

Renewal of Life

Background Scripture: Zephaniah 3

The Main Question—William H. Willimon

Here, in the middle of the lazy, beautiful, restful summer, things are at peace. The summer is a wonderful time of rest and relaxation, a respite from the usual cares and worries that occupy our lives through so much of the year.

In such a peaceful context, today's scripture from the third chapter of Zephaniah may be difficult to teach to your adult class. After two chapters of scathing rebuke and dire prediction of terrible disaster, the prophet at last hears from God words of comfort and hope. Life shall be renewed. God will again turn back toward his people, lay aside his anger, and bless them.

Here are words not addressed to people who were content, on vacation, safe and secure. They are words addressed to a people who are at the end of their rope, people who know what it means to hit bottom, to be lost and bereft of any resources.

Yet we ought to remind ourselves that these words from the prophet can still be our words. While people in your class may not be, at this moment, in a time of crisis, everyone in your class either has been or will be living in such a time. It happens to us all.

Also, even though we may not be in desperate circumstances at this moment, we are linked, in Christian compassion, to those who are. What is our word of hope to them?

So even though it is the middle of summer, July vacation and all that, it is possible for the questions raised by life at its most desperate moments to be answered by today's word from Scripture.

Selected Scripture

King James Version	Revised Standard Version
Zephaniah 3:12, 14-20	*Zephaniah 3:12, 14-20*
12 I will also leave in the midst of thee an afflicted and poor people,	12 For I will leave in the midst of you

JULY 19   LESSON 7

and they shall trust in the name of the Lord.

a people humble and lowly.
They shall seek refuge in the name of the Lord,

....

14 Sing, O daughter of Zion; shout, O Israel; be glad and rejoice with all the heart, O daughter of Jerusalem.

15 The Lord hath taken away thy judgments, he hath cast out thine enemy: the king of Israel, *even* the Lord, *is* in the midst of thee: thou shalt not see evil any more.

16 In that day it shall be said to Jerusalem, Fear thou not: *and to* Zion, Let not thine hands be slack.

17 The Lord thy God in the midst of thee *is* mighty; he will save, he will rejoice over thee with joy; he will rest in his love, he will joy over thee with singing.

18 I will gather *them that are* sorrowful for the solemn assembly, *who* are of thee, *to whom* the reproach of it *was* a burden.

19 Behold, at that time I will undo all that afflict thee: and I will save her that halteth, and gather her that was driven out; and I will get them praise and fame in every land where they have been put to shame.

20 At that time will I bring you *again*, even in the time that I gather you: for I will make you a name and a praise among all people of the earth, when I turn back your captivity before your eyes, saith the Lord.

14 Sing aloud, O daughter of Zion; shout, O Israel!
Rejoice and exult with all your heart,
O daughter of Jerusalem!

15 The Lord has taken away the judgments against you,
he has cast out your enemies.
The King of Israel, the Lord, is in your midst;
you shall fear evil no more.

16 On that day it shall be said to Jerusalem:
"Do not fear, O Zion;
let not your hands grow weak.

17 The Lord, your God, is in your midst,
a warrior who gives victory;
he will rejoice over you with gladness,
he will renew you in his love;
he will exult over you with loud singing

18   as on a day of festival.
"I will remove disaster from you,
so that you will not bear reproach for it.

19 Behold, at that time I will deal with all your oppressors.
And I will save the lame
and gather the outcast,
and I will change their shame into praise
and renown in all the earth.

20 At that time I will bring you home,
at the time when I gather you together;
yea, I will make you renowned and praised
among all the peoples of the earth,
when I restore your fortunes before your eyes," says the Lord.

FOURTH QUARTER

Key Verse: The Lord thy God in the midst of thee is mighty; he will save, he will rejoice over thee with joy; he will rest in his love. (Zephaniah 3:17)

Key Verse: The Lord, your God, is in your midst, a warrior who gives victory; he will rejoice over you with gladness, he will renew you in his love. (Zephaniah 3:17)

As You Read the Scripture—Charles T. Klinksick

Chapter 3 of Zephaniah's book contains a quick shift from emphasis on rebelliousness to a remarkable proclamation of joy because the Lord will forgive and save a humble remnant in Israel. After blunt threats, warnings, and prophecies in chapters 1 and 2, aimed in all geographical directions, the writer concludes with majestic poetry extolling "the King of Israel, the Lord, in your midst" (3:15). Without this conclusion the book of Zephaniah would be a fearsome tale of disasters, but with it the last seven verses promise salvation and invite loud praises.

Zephaniah 3:12. The last words of verse 10 indicate it is the Lord speaking in the statement beginning with verse 11: God will leave humble people in Israel. They will not be the proud and wicked judges, prophets, or priests mentioned in verses 3 and 4. They are to be the lowly survivors, not the worshipers of pagan idols, but persons who know the name of the Lord, the God of Israel. He is their refuge and strength. (See Jeremiah 16:19 for a confessional description.)

Verse 14. This is Zephaniah's call for action: sing, shout, rejoice, and exult. It is addressed to all Israel.

Verses 15-16. Two things will be gone: (1) all guilt, the judgments against Israel, and all the causes of judgment, and (2) your enemies, governmental and religious exploiters, and military troops. The reference to the Lord as king of Israel is understood as prophecy. The God-with-us (Emmanuel) king is spiritually present, the prince of peace.

"On that day" (not the day of wrath of 1:8-10, 15-16) you need not be afraid. Zion is Mount Zion, the temple site in Jerusalem; it means all Zion's people. The advice about weak hands is amplified in the New Testament letter to the Hebrews (12:12-14), which refers to "drooping hands" to be lifted up after experiencing God's discipline.

Verses 17-18. The victory is more than in physical matters. (See 1 Corinthians 15:57 and 1 Chronicles 29:11.) God in your midst makes you victorious. He will rejoice over you like a warrior-husband returning to love his bride gladly, overjoyed to the point of singing. The disasters of chapter 1 are gone. You are the object of his affections.

Verses 19-20. This is the grand climax of the book. Warfare always ends with one party's embarrassment. Defeated oppressors deserve punishment or mercy; I will deal with that, says the Lord. War leaves the wounded, the lame, the discards, and the suffering poor; I will change all that, he says. Warfare displaces families and nations, as in the Babylonian captivity, but I will bring you home and gather you, he adds. More than that, the Lord promises fame, praise, and new fortunes. The recognition will be as widespread as the threatened desolation first spoken of. Zephaniah's book is a brief, but pungent prophecy about vengefulness of God upon rebellious people and his merciful concern for humble people in Judah. It is a call for a change of heart, hope, greatness of faith, courage, love of the Lord God and loyalty to him, and belief in the joy that God will give. For God's people it means a bad beginning, a good ending!

Ultimate questions about a book like this are, When shall all this take place? Is this an Israel-Jerusalem prophecy, or does its pattern include any similar nations? Has it been fulfilled then or since, once or more than once? Does this apply to modern Israel and its ever-hurting Jerusalem? It is of most importance to remember that Zephaniah's prophecy is not primarily about cities and their people, like Jerusalem and the Israelites, but is about God, the Lord of all. Zephaniah reported on how the Lord, in a time of wrath, conducts his affairs. It is a narrative about the "I Am" (Exodus 3:14) of desolation and salvation, the God of Zion and of history everywhere, forever. Thirty times in the three chapters the Lord says "I." Through Zephaniah he is describing his dealings. This book is a motion picture of God in action.

The Scripture and the Main Question—William H. Willimon

Seek Refuge in the Name of the Lord

It has sometimes been said of soldiers in time of war, "There are no atheists in foxholes." In other words, when the bullets are whirring around us and things seem terribly desperate, everyone, even people who normally don't have much to do with God, turns to God.

I have never much cared for this statement about there being no atheists in foxholes. I don't like this image of people who never turn to God until they have exhausted every other possible remedy and then, in final desperation, having tried everything else to deliver themselves, at last turn and "try" God.

However, it does at least raise the question of where one does turn when one is utterly desperate. I'm not talking about all the little worrisome and annoying setbacks that everyone faces in life from time to time. Most of us have resources for living through such temporary difficulties. We know how to think about more pleasant matters, or how to be patient, telling ourselves, "This too shall pass."

I'm talking about times of utter, complete desperation when all seems lost, words of comfort are cheap and pointless, there is nothing to be said, nothing to be done. Thank God, such times don't come often in most lives, but they do come. What do we do then?

We don't like to think that life will ever be this way for us. We Americans enjoy thinking of ourselves as conscientious, competent, able people. For every problem, there is a solution, usually some solution of humanly derived means. When faced with problems, all we have to do is to think hard, get ourselves together, marshal our resources, and overcome that problem through sheer human ingenuity and effort.

This self-confident attitude carries us through most of life's problems, and it has enabled our society to make great contributions to the betterment of humanity. But it is not enough for the bleakest, most desperate, terrible situations of life. Then, face-to-face with tragedy, our backs against the wall, no way out, our self-confidence crumbles, and we are forced to reach out to some power greater than our own.

Today's scripture arises out of just such a period in Judah's history. Because of Judah's terrible wickedness, not only Judah and Israel but the whole world shall suffer terribly (1:14-18). Zephaniah goes through all classes of society, merchants and traders (1:10-13), court officials and the royal family (1:7-9), as well as all the nations of the world (2:4-15), telling them that God will show wrath to them all because of the evil they have done. There will be terrible, universal suffering

> a day of distress and anguish,
> a day of ruin and devastation,
> a day of darkness and gloom,
> a day of clouds and thick darkness.
> (1:15)

Yet God's wrath shall not last forever. A righteous remnant shall remain, "For I will leave in the midst of you a people humble and lowly" (3:12).

Although none of us would wish trouble upon ourselves and although we would be hard pressed to say that our troubles are sent from God, is it not possible to say that our times of trouble are often times when we find ourselves growing closer to God? In Zephaniah's day, the proud, arrogant, godless ones were purged through the terrible times of crisis in the nation. Now, after the crisis, all that will be left will be those who have been humbled in the crisis, those who have again learned to "seek refuge in the name of the Lord" (3:12).

The Lord Is in Your Midst

To these now humbled, still, obedient believers, the Lord of Israel returns and takes up their cause in their distress. The same God who had, in effect, declared war upon the unrighteous ones in Judah and Israel now says to the sufferers that he shall stand on their side, shall fight for them, shall become "a warrior who gives victory" (3:17).

Here is a God who just doesn't sit back in detached empathy, wringing his hands in sorrow at our sorrows but basically doing nothing. This God actively takes up our cause, fighting on our side against all that would cause us to lose faith.

Frankly, I don't hear much talk about this kind of God. Is it because we modern people find it difficult to believe in a God who acts, who responds actively in behalf of the needs of people? We prefer a God who is little more than some vague, ill-conceived cosmic force, impersonal, inactive, aloof. Or perhaps we have trouble conceiving of Zephaniah's warrior of a God because we are so content, so self-sufficient and confident, that we have no need for such a God. Thank you God, but we would rather do it ourselves.

Let us be reminded, on this pleasant July Sunday, that very few of the world's people have the luxury of thinking that they are in total control of their destinies. The mass of the world's people find themselves this day in much the same state as the people of Israel and Judah in Zephaniah's day. They are vulnerable to the assaults of evil politicians, violent wars, famine, political oppression, natural disasters, disease, and terrible poverty. What hope is there for them?

If there is hope, it will be based upon the assertion of the existence of a God who not only cares but who acts, a God who is strong enough to set things right, a God who is able to take up their cause as his own. If there is to be renewal of life out of death, then that renewal must come through the efforts of a God who is on the side of life rather than death. This great God may not fight and make war the way that earthly rulers do, but nevertheless this God must fight against wrong in order to be a God of righteousness. This God must be able to struggle against evil, or this God is not good.

Because there is such a God, waiting, standing beside those who are poor and oppressed, there can be real cause for hope, even in the most desperate situations of life. No situation, however bleak, is beyond the reach of this great God. Therefore, there can be cause for rejoicing. For the prophet says that this God not only is ready to fight in behalf of those who have no one to take up their side, but this God is also ready to rejoice with them when they are victorious (3:17). At the great day of victory and jubilation, God will be there, "with loud singing as on a day of festival" (3:17).

I Will Bring You Home

On most Sundays, in most sermons, in most churches of my acquaintance, the sermons, the hymns, the religious talk is mostly about us. That is, church is mostly a time for us to get together and decide what we ought to do to live better lives, or to have more happiness, or to achieve more success. Sunday is a time for us to gather and to become motivated to go out and do what we know we ought to be doing.

Of course, much of the Christian faith is concerned with our becoming motivated to do what we know God wants us to do. But a steady diet of this sort of religion has a way of becoming insufferably moralistic, boringly human centered. There isn't much room left for God if all that needs doing in the world is of our own human devising.

Today's lesson from Zephaniah is an invitation to rise above such human-centered pettiness. The God depicted in these prophetic utterances is a big God, whose hands are busy with big matters. This God does not exist merely to run our petty errands, soothe our little aches and pains. This God is about nothing less than the creation of a new heaven and a new earth.

> Behold, at that time I will deal with all your oppressors.
> And I will save the lame
>   and gather the outcast,
> and I will change their shame into praise. (3:19)

Today is a pleasant summer Sunday. Many of us are here in church not out of desperation but merely out of habit. Yet can we stretch our imaginations to the point of conceiving the existence of people whose situation is so desperate, so utterly without hope of merely human solution, that it is up to God to help them or they are without help? Can we conceive of a God so active, so big and so loving, that he will not rest until justice and mercy flow like a river upon all the world's dispossessed and oppressed?

That's a big assignment for a pleasant July Sunday. But then, the world's needs are great, and so is the love of God.

Helping Adults Become Involved—Douglas E. Wingeier

Preparing to Teach

The Scythian invasion spares Jerusalem. Surrounding nations are devastated, but somehow Judah is not attacked. The dire warnings of

FOURTH QUARTER

Zephaniah, however, may have served to awaken his people to repentance and a renewed trust in Yahweh. The reform of Josiah is about to begin.

The woes of 3:1-8 are followed by a mood shift in verses 9-20, in which God's blessings on Judah are extolled. Verses 14-18 are a joyful hymn of celebration, which Zephaniah may well have used to lead temple worshipers in thanking God for deliverance from the Scythian scourge.

The threat of disaster has humbled God's people (verse 12). They will be renewed in God's love (verse 17). God has promised to bring them home and restore their fortunes (verse 20).

Read what one or more commentaries have to say about Zephaniah 3. Make a list of the sources of hope in your own life, especially in times of discouragement. Think of things like the support and encouragement of friends, the love of family members, belief in a mentor or coach, a parent's faithful care when you are sick, the confidence that things will get better, the pull of a goal you greatly desire, the satisfaction of a job well done, or the example of one who went before you.

Ask God to instill in you a genuine sense of hope, so that you may communicate this to your class through the way you teach, as well as the words you speak.

Your aim is to help class members examine their sources of hope and learn to distinguish between relying on earthly circumstances and trusting in the love and power of God. Use this outline:

      I. Examining our sources of hope.
     II. God in our midst.
    III. I will bring you home.

Introducing the Main Question

Begin by asking the class to name times when they have been in need of comfort and hope. This may better be done in small groups of three or four, where persons are encouraged to share at a deeper level. Assure them that all that is shared will be kept confidential, and that the purpose is to enable class members to be supportive and helpful to one another. Take the risk first by sharing one of your own experiences. Examples might include a lingering, debilitating illness, the loss of a job, failure in a task or examination, a broken relationship, or a financial setback.

After each person has shared, ask: In what had you placed your hope? How did you feel when it let you down? What was God saying to you in that circumstance? From whence did comfort come? How did/will hope grow in the aftermath?

After several have shared, ask: How can we be helpful to one another and persons outside the church in such times of discouragement? What word of hope do we have to offer?

Developing the Lesson

I. Examining our sources of hope.

Invite members to report the sources of hope on which they tend to rely, and list these on the board. Some can come from their through-the-week reflections, others from the experiences just shared. Then go over the list and evaluate the dependability of each item. Was it reliable in the actual situation? Under what circumstances might it fail? To what could we turn in its absence? How might God use it to sustain and encourage me? Might this become a substitute for God, and lull me into a false complacency?

Read back through Zephaniah and identify Judah's intended sources of hope—priests and rites (1:4-5), officials and princes (1:8), trade (1:11), houses and vineyards (1:13), fortified cities and battlements (1:16), silver and gold (1:18), judges and prophets (3:3-4), and haughty pride (3:11). How does this list compare with ours? Why are we humans so prone to place our hope in things earthly and material?

II. God in our midst.

Divide the class into two groups (men and women or north and south) to read responsively the hymn of joy in 3:14-18. Ask: What is the source of hope here? Note that the God celebrated here is not one of outer space or the distant future or the heroes of faith, but the God in *our midst.*

Introduce Dr. Willimon's contrast between our tendency to trust in American ingenuity and the desperation of life's bleakest circumstances, when such self-confidence crumbles. Relate this to Judah's situation in Zephaniah's time and to the experiences shared earlier in the session.

The people of Nicaragua face awesome difficulties. A massive earthquake in 1972 destroyed their capital city. Forty years of the brutal Somoza dictatorship left them with few schools, hospitals, or trained leaders, plus divided loyalties and a big debt. The United States-sponsored Contra war and trade embargo have cost fifty thousand Nicaraguan lives and set their economy back forty years. Hurricane Joan devastated vast coastal and mountain areas. Peasants in the mountains have lost homes, crops, lands, sons, and limbs to vicious Contra attacks.

But the one thing they have not lost is hope. Why? Because Nicaraguans are a deeply Christian people—over 90% of them (70% Catholic, 20% Protestant)—and many are highly committed to their faith. Never have I been so profoundly affected by the intense faith, hope, and joy of an entire people!

Mothers who lost husbands and sons band together to make clothes, run shops, and build homes for refugees. Wounded war veterans on artificial limbs run a cooperative farm. Farmers who have lost their crops for lack of a repaired irrigation pump due to the embargo turn their energies to building homes with Habitat for Humanity. The children whose school we were building worked as hard as we did painting, digging, and hauling dirt. Worship, Bible study, prayer, and Christian discipleship are at the heart of their struggle to resist the oppressor, determine their destiny, and build their nation. I was several times moved to tears by the genuine faith, dedication to struggle, and joyful hope of these suffering people!

They could sing with Zephaniah, "The Lord is in your midst; you shall fear evil no more. . . . Let not your hands grow weak. . . . Your God . . . will renew you in his love" (3:15-17).

III. I will bring you home.

The promise to the faithful goes on—to remove disaster, deal with oppressors, save the lame and outcast, change shame into praise, and bring the home (3:18-20). The God in our midst renews us in love and joins us in the struggle to transform pain into praise and a hostile world into a home of comfort and healing.

FOURTH QUARTER

God is at work in Nicaragua, doing just that. I was there, and I testify that it is so.

Point to instances in the experiences shared earlier in which members found hope and a home through seeing God at work around them.

Helping Class Members Act

Ask: How can we work with God to offer hope and a home to persons around us in trying circumstances? Perhaps the justice project they are involved in is doing that. Ask them, in addition, to think of persons to whom they can offer a word of hope during the coming week.

Close by singing "Hope of the World" or "Great Is Thy Faithfulness." Offer a prayer for all in need of hope, a home, and renewal in love, and for class members to dedicate themselves to be God's instruments to help this happen.

Planning for Next Sunday

Next week begins a new unit on 1 and 2 Timothy and Titus. Have class members read through all three letters, then study 1 Timothy 1. Also ask them to list the standards by which they distinguish the true from the false.

COURSE 2: Guidelines for Ministry

UNIT I: GUIDELINES FOR LEADING

THREE LESSONS   **JULY 26–AUGUST 9**

This course of study consists of two units that focus on instructions to Timothy and Titus about how to carry out their ministry. The lessons in this course provides guidelines for the ministry of all Christians. Certain familiar passages have been purposely omitted so that students might concentrate on often-neglected passages. Reputable scholars disagree over the authorship of Timothy. You will discover this is the case with the writers of these units. They simply do not agree. Regardless of how your class resolves the issue of authorship, remember that the important element is the message being conveyed, not the authenticity of the writer.

Unit I, "Guidelines for Leading," includes three lessons from Timothy. The first lesson in the unit urges leaders to understand what they teach. The second lesson encourages leaders to discipline themselves for service by living godly lives. The third lesson advises leaders to choose their priorities carefully in order to live virtuous lives.

"Hold to Sound Doctrine," July 26, searches for belief systems based on sound teaching. "Train Yourself in Godliness," August 2, clarifies how adult Christians seek positive role models. "Set Your Priorities," August 9, advises us to reorder our lives so that the most significant events in life have first place in our daily choices.

LESSON 8 JULY 26

Hold to Sound Doctrine

Background Scripture: 1 Timothy 1

The Main Question—William H. Willimon

"The thing that I like about being a member of this church," said the man on the third row from the front, "is that you can believe pretty much whatever seems right to you personally."

"Well, look," she said, "I'm a Baptist, you're a Methodist, but the main thing is not so much what you believe as long as you are sincere, right?"

These opinions about Christian doctrine, although held by lots of people, just happen to be wrong. Believing whatever seems right to you personally has little to do with believing as a Christian, and a belief is not right simply because somebody sincerely believes it. Adolf Hitler was as sincere as Francis of Assisi, except that one man lived and died by what was true, whereas the other lived and died by a lie. While clear thinking isn't the answer to every problem in life, it is possible for people to be in misery not because their hearts are not right or because they are bad people but because they are confused. If people become confused at a cloverleaf intersection, think how much more confused they are apt to be about God.

As contemporary Christians, we all need to think as clearly and as faithfully as we can about God. Thinking about God is called *theology*, and all of us do it even if we don't know that's what we are doing, because everybody tries to make sense out of life, wonders what we are doing here, would like to know where we will be tomorrow. So there are no non-theologians, there is just good theology and bad theology.

How can we think faithfully as modern believers? This is the question that guides us in today's lesson.

Selected Scripture

King James Version

1 Timothy 1:3-11, 18-20

3 As I besought thee to abide still at Ephesus, when I went into Macedonia, that thou mightest charge some that they teach no other doctrine,

4 Neither give heed to fables and endless genealogies, which minister questions, rather than godly edifying which is in faith: *so do.*

5 Now the end of the commandment is charity out of a pure heart, and *of* a good conscience, and *of* faith unfeigned:

6 From which some having

Revised Standard Version

1 Timothy 1:3-11, 18-20

3 As I urged you when I was going to Macedonia, remain at Ephesus that you may charge certain persons not to teach any different doctrine, 4 nor to occupy themselves with myths and endless genealogies which promote speculations rather than the divine training that is in faith; 5 whereas the aim of our charge is love that issues from a pure heart and a good conscience and sincere faith. 6 Certain persons by swerving from these have wandered away into vain discussion,

FOURTH QUARTER

swerved have turned aside unto vain jangling;

7 Desiring to be teachers of the law; understanding neither what they say, nor whereof they affirm.

8 But we know that the law *is* good, if a man use it lawfully;

9 Knowing this, that the law is not made for a righteous man, but for the lawless and disobedient, for the ungodly and for sinners, for unholy and profane, for murderers of fathers and murderers of mothers, for manslayers,

10 For whoremongers, for them that defile themselves with mankind, for menstealers, for liars, for perjured persons, and if there be any other thing that is contrary to sound doctrine;

11 According to the glorious gospel of the blessed God, which was committed to my trust.

....

18 This charge I commit unto thee, son Timothy, according to the prophecies which went before on thee, that thou by them mightest war a good warfare;

19 Holding faith, and a good conscience; which some having put away concerning faith have made shipwreck:

20 Of whom is Hymenaeus and Alexander; whom I have delivered unto Satan, that they may learn not to blaspheme.

Key Verse: **Now the end of the commandment is charity out of a pure heart, and of a good conscience, and of faith unfeigned. (1 Timothy 1:5)**

7 desiring to be teachers of the law, without understanding either what they are saying or the things about which they make assertions.

8 Now we know that the law is good, if any one uses it lawfully, 9 understanding this, that the law is not laid down for the just but for the lawless and disobedient, for the ungodly and sinners, for the unholy and profane, for murderers of fathers and murderers of mothers, for manslayers, 10 immoral persons, sodomites, kidnapers, liars, perjurers, and whatever else is contrary to sound doctrine, 11 in accordance with the glorious gospel of the blessed God with which I have been entrusted.

....

18 This charge I commit to you, Timothy, my son, in accordance with the prophetic utterances which pointed to you, that inspired by them you may wage the good warfare, 19 holding faith and a good conscience. By rejecting conscience, certain persons have made shipwreck of their faith, 20 among them Hymenaeus and Alexander, whom I have delivered to Satan that they may learn not to blaspheme.

Key Verse: **The aim of our charge is love that issues from a pure heart and a good conscience and sincere faith. (1 Timothy 1:5)**

As You Read the Scripture—Charles T. Klinksick

Timothy was the son of a Greek man and a Jewish woman named Eunice. Paul had met him at Lystra, where he was well spoken of (Acts 16:1-3). His faith and that of his mother and grandmother Lois was sincere and notable

JULY 26   LESSON 8

(2 Timothy 1:5). He was chosen and prepared by Paul to be a fellow minister in his missionary travels.

Ephesus was a port city on the eastern shore of the Aegean Sea. Its population was three hundred thousand or more. Its theater could seat twenty-four thousand persons. A large harbor and river, public baths, libraries, business places, and marble-paved streets made it the most important Roman city in western Asia Minor. The temple of Diana overlooking the lower city and harbor was larger than a modern football field.

Paul labored two years in establishing Christianity in Ephesus and sent Timothy as his replacement. See Acts 19:23-41 for details about life in Ephesus.

1 Timothy 1:3-4. Christianity in Ephesus was threatened by "certain persons" (verses 3 and 6) emphasizing mythology and speculative religion. Except for two names mentioned in verse 20, we do not know to whom Paul was referring or how they were operating. He is instructing Timothy to confront them with sound doctrine.

Verse 5. In one sentence Paul states the philosophy of Christianity: Our aim is *love, a pure heart, a good conscience,* and *sincere faith.* For Timothy this meant not fighting or bickering but counseling and convincing others by honest conversing from the heart. Seldom has the motif of missionary methodology been put so simply and clearly.

Verses 6-7. Here is the problem: legalism. These persons, trying to be teachers, were imposing conduct requirements. This is the inevitable temptation in every religious system: "You must do what our rules say, or you won't be religiously right!" Paul knew this contradicted his emphasis on divine grace, forgiveness, and faith as pure doctrine. God and love are more than law and obedience alone. He expounds on the function of the Law in his letter to the Romans (chapters 4 and 5) and in the third chapter of his letter to the Galatians. Legalists, he says, do not know what they are getting into when they make the Law by itself primary. "Vain discussion" is useless talk, unconvincing debate.

Verses 8-11. In itself the Law has a good and rightful use; it defines wrong for those who know no rules. Using some of the Ten Commandments, Paul names specifically the kinds of persons who need Law teaching. Sodomites are homosexuals. Kidnappers included persons who stole children to bring up as slaves. Perjurers are people who lie when they have taken an oath to tell the truth. "Whatever else" summarizes other unnamed types of wrongs against God and good government.

Verses 18-20. This is Paul's pastoral and fatherly advice to his spiritual son and brother minister. "Good warfare" is highly honorable and convincing talk, not nasty, hateful, or unfair tactics. Hang on to your faith and good conscience, he is saying.

Rejecting conscience is to wreck one's faith, like a ship breaking apart on rocks. Losing everything, it ends faith's journey. Alexander was probably the coppersmith mentioned later by Paul in his second letter to Timothy (2 Timothy 4:14). Hymenaeus is unknown except for Paul's reference to him with Philetus (2 Timothy 2:17). The statement "delivered to Satan" can mean put out of the church, excommunicated. Paul despaired of them but hoped they would learn a lesson from this. He is warning Timothy about people like these.

FOURTH QUARTER

The Scripture and the Main Question—William H. Willimon

The Gospel with Which I Have Been Entrusted

We wonder what false teaching the writer of 1 Timothy is concerned with. "Myths and endless genealogies which promote speculations rather than divine training" (1:4) doesn't really tell us much. Whatever the nature of this false teaching, it has, in the writer's mind, the character of idle, insignificant, distracting speculation that only causes trouble in the minds of believers.

When it comes down to it, as religions go, Christianity is a very simple, straightforward religion. Every word that Jesus is recorded as having said to his disciples would scarcely fill an average newspaper. Jesus frequently rebuked those who wanted to add to his teaching or to embellish what he said with speculation about the nature of the future, the date of the end of the world, and other esoteric matters.

Ever since the Christian religion began, there has been a tendency among certain persons to embellish the teaching of Jesus, to speculate on more arcane ideas. These opening verses of 1 Timothy are evidence that, right at the very first, the early church had to deal with matters of false doctrine, the problem of those who were not content to leave matters as they were with the straightforward teaching of Jesus.

This tendency continues today. From time to time the church is confronted with individuals or groups within the church who claim to have discovered some new or else some neglected teaching. Sometimes they tend to "major in the minors," seizing upon some heretofore obscure passage and elevating this snippet of doctrine to the level of major importance.

I have met Christians who sincerely believe in reincarnation, astrology, communication with the dead, and similar practices that are definitely not a major concern of Scripture. I feel that the writer of 1 Timothy would assign such beliefs to the level of "vain discussion" (1:6).

Why is it wrong for us to explore these new, unusual ideas? On the basis of today's text, I can think of at least two objections to such speculation: First, belief is no easy matter. We have our hands full, as Christians, just following the Master who asked us to call all people our brothers and sisters, to turn the other cheek when attacked, and to give him our whole devotion, without adding anything else to make belief even tougher. Struggling believers, trying to have faith in Christ, may become confused and distracted because the church becomes preoccupied with pointless discussion of purely speculative fringe issues. Could that be what today's scripture means by referring to "certain persons" who "have made shipwreck of their faith" (1:19)?

Second, the writer of 1 Timothy says that the aim of our teaching in the church is "love" (1:5). Too often, esoteric, strange teaching becomes a means of division in the congregation. Some claim to have received some special revelation, some secret teaching that has been made available to some but not to all. This divides the church into the haves and the have-nots, so far as belief is concerned. "I am a graduate school Christian; you are only a kindergarten Christian," these believers often imply.

Perhaps because of these dangers of false doctrine, every church, even churches that claim to be relatively free of dogmatism and complex doctrinal statements, specifies what sound doctrine is. Sound Christian doctrine must be, first, *biblically based*. Our doctrines are derived from and answerable to the Bible. The Bible is the source and the test of all Christian belief. If a belief conflicts with the teachings of the Bible, then something is wrong with that belief. Of course, there are cases in which the Bible cannot tell us exactly which belief is true and which is false. However, the Bible does point us in the right direction, and if a belief is not a major concern of the Bible, it should probably not be a major concern of ours.

Second, sound Christian doctrine should be *available to all*. The teaching of Jesus was direct, straightforward, and accessible to all, even to those who had little or no formal education, even to those who were not very intelligent. He was criticized by the intellectuals of his day for being naive and simplistic in his teaching. Therefore, the church has historically been quite suspicious of any doctrine that was so complex, so intricate and abstract, that it could only be grasped by some believers and not all.

Third, sound doctrine should be *faithful to tradition*. We are not the first generation of Christians. Our beliefs come as our inheritance from the suffering, believing, witnessing church of the past. Any new revelation, any claim of new doctrine, must therefore fight for itself with the church's past doctrine. The writer of 1 Timothy appeals to the gospel "with which I have been entrusted" (1:11). Our tradition is a wonderful trust from the saints of the past and a contemporary measurement for belief.

This Charge I Commit to You

Why should the early Christian writer of 1 Timothy make such a fuss over doctrine? Do these fine points of belief really make that much difference? The writer claims that wrong thinking leads to wrong action. Confusion in doctrine leads to confusion in morals (1:8-11).

Today, we tend to psychologize people's problems. Every problem is reduced to some difficulty within a person's personality. The important question is not, What do you think? but rather, How do you feel? Such a view is an inadequate concept of how human beings behave. Sometimes people are in misery not simply because they are psychologically confused but because they are intellectually confused. Their minds are filled with wrong ideas, unfounded claims, untrue notions.

Any church that neglects its responsibility to help its members think clearly about their faith is not being true to biblical faith. In the Bible, in books like 1 Timothy, we see early Christian teachers struggling to help their new Christians think about God, to use their minds in godly ways, and to bring some intellectual order out of the conflicting claims they heard. This is important, loving, pastoral work.

I feel that many of our people have been vulnerable to the appeals of religious cult groups and their strange, confused, and potentially damaging ideas because we have not done a good job of helping people to mature in their faith, to be able to discern true from false doctrine and to think from a biblical point of view. Cast adrift in a sea of their own limited notions, unsure of what orthodox Christian belief really is, they are easy targets for cults and other religious groups that prey upon the hearts and minds of the misinformed.

Of course, one reason why you and your class have gathered together on this July morning is to do theology, to think clearly as Christians and to discern the true from the false.

FOURTH QUARTER

The work you do in your class as you do theology is holy, ancient activity, as old as 1 Timothy, yet every bit as needed today as it was then.

Helping Adults Become Involved—Douglas E. Wingeier

Preparing to Teach

The letters to Timothy and Titus, which we study in these six lessons, are known as the Pastoral Epistles. Most scholars think they were not written by Paul but by one of his disciples near the end of the first century A.D. The movements of Paul as described in these letters do not fit the chronology of Acts and could only be accounted for if he had been released from prison in Rome and gone on another missionary journey.

Also, the doctrinal issues discussed in these letters did not arise until late in the century, decades after the traditional date of Paul's death, 64 A.D. Paul's characteristic teaching about the Law, faith, cross, and flesh and spirit, as found in other epistles, are all ignored or treated differently in these letters.

Instead, the focus is on church organization, discipline, and loyalty to church tradition. The sentence structure is different from that typically employed by Paul, and his characteristic phrases are absent. The main purpose of these letters is to defend orthodox doctrine and sound morality against heretical teaching. They do so through contradiction, denunciation, ridicule, and appeal to "the truth" and "the good teaching"—a different spirit from that found in Paul's other letters.

The key themes in 1 Timothy are faithfulness to the truth and the maintenance of a good conscience (1:5, 19; 3:9), moral and spiritual guidelines for church leaders (3:1-13), the example of the Christian teacher (1:16; 4:12-16), and the goodness of creation and our right to enjoy it (4:3-5).

Read the entire unit and all three epistles to get an overview. Helpful commentaries will be *Harper's*, *The Interpreter's Bible*, *The Interpreter's One-Volume Commentary*, *Peake's*, and Barclay's *Daily Study Bible*. Edward Blair's *Abingdon Bible Handbook* gives concise background information.

Study the verses in this lesson and the commentaries about them. Reflect on your own criteria for discerning truth from falsehood. Read the "Our Theological Task" section of the 1988 United Methodist *Book of Discipline*, especially pages 80-86. Pray for skill and guidance to help your class develop confidence to think theologically and to discriminate wisely among truth claims, which is the aim of this lesson. Use the following outline:

　　　　I. Competing claims to truth
　　　　II. Loving God with our minds
　　　　III. Guidelines for thought and behavior

Introducing the Main Question

Invite two members to read aloud the first two paragraphs in "The Main Question." Ask: Do you agree? Why or why not? Emphasize that there *is* a difference between right and wrong, truth and error.

Then ask: Are you theologians? Emphasize that all Christians are called to think about God and to relate belief to life experience, which is the task of theology. Quote Dr. Willimon: "There are no non-theologians, only good and bad theology."

Developing the Lesson

I. Competing claims to truth

Ask the class to name ideas and beliefs about which they have heard differing opinions. Political issues (the arms race, involvement in Central America, gun control), ethical issues (abortion, homosexuality, ecology), and religious issues (infant baptism, life after death, salvation outside Christianity) might be mentioned. Ask: How do you react to these conflicting viewpoints? Are you swayed one way and then the other, confirmed in your own beliefs, or simply confused?

Note that this was the situation in the time of 1 Timothy. Paul's teachings had been contradicted by "certain persons" who were teaching "different doctrine" and "occupying themselves with myths and . . . speculations" (1:3-4). Give the background of the Pastoral Epistles from "As You Read the Scripture," "Preparing to Teach," and the commentaries. Each Christians needed guidance in how to assess these issues wisely and in keeping with the Pauline tradition. Is this what we need as well?

II. Loving God with our minds

This is my definition of doing theology. Theology is not limited to scholars, pastors, and experts. If we love God, our minds are included, which means thinking about our faith and relating it to our daily lives. We cannot be content with avoiding the issues or just accepting what others tell us. Our Christian discipleship demands that we face the issues, wrestle with the pros and cons, acknowledge our differences, seek guidance from Scripture, tradition, reason, and experience, then make up our minds and act on our convictions.

Above all, we must accept and respect one another when we disagree, even while seeking to convince one another. For, said Jesus, "By this shall all people know that you are my disciples, *if you have love for one another*" (John 13:35). This is what is meant by "the aim . . . is love that issues from a pure heart and a good conscience and sincere faith" (1:5).

III. Guidelines for thought and behavior

Ask the class for their standards for separating the true from the false, about which they have been thinking this week. Write them on the board.

Note that the writer points to "the glorious gospel of the blessed God" as the criterion for "sound doctrine" (1:11), but nowhere defines what he means by this, or the Law, good conscience, or sincere faith—phrases he uses to denote the truth to which he asks us to hold fast.

Now, as then, we are left to discern this for ourselves. John Wesley, in his famous quadrilateral, has given us the guidelines of Scripture, tradition, reason, and experience to help us determine faithful, relevant positions on the issues we face. Explain these from the material you have read in the United Methodist *Book of Discipline*. *Scripture* provides reliable guidance when related to the literary context, Biblical life-world, faith themes, and our life concerns. *Tradition* is helpful when seen as a dynamic, ongoing process that shapes identity and life-style, and not as static, constricting forms inherited from the past. *Experience*, the raw material from which our

FOURTH QUARTER

beliefs come, is composed of our needs, feelings, intentions, and behavior, in interaction with outer limits and possibilities. *Reason* is the process of interpreting experience as a basis for decision and action, in light of our previously acquired understandings of the world, right and wrong, and our own self-image. (*Working Out Your Own Beliefs,* Abingdon Press, 1980, describes how to use these guidelines in doing theology.)

Helping Class Members Act

Discuss one of the controversial issues mentioned earlier, taking care to draw on the resources of Scripture, tradition, reason, and experience and to show love and respect for one another's point of view. When the time runs out, close off the discussion and remind the class that what they have been doing is loving God with their minds, an expression of the "love that issues from a pure heart and a good conscience and sincere faith" (1:5). Ask how they feel about this process.

Conclude with the hymn "Immortal, Invisible" (based on 1 Timothy 1:17) or "We Believe in One True God." Then offer a prayer asking God for wisdom to discern the truth, love to accept those who differ, and courage to live our beliefs.

Planning for Next Sunday

Ask members to read 1 Timothy 4 and to ask one person outside the class two questions: What does it mean to be a Christian disciple? What training is needed to be an effective disciple?

LESSON 9   AUGUST 2

Train Yourself in Godliness

Background Scripture: 1 Timothy 4

The Main Question—William H. Willimon

Toward the end of Matthew's gospel, Jesus gives his disciples their marching orders. He tells them to "go and make disciples of all nations, baptizing . . . teaching . . ." (Matthew 28:19-20).

Just in case anybody thinks that following Jesus is something that comes naturally, an inborn inclination, a matter of nice people gradually becoming a bit nicer, Jesus settles all that in this Great Commission. Disciples are not born. You have to *make* disciples.

The way Jesus invites us to walk is a narrow way, so against the stream, so uncommon, that anything less than intentional, careful, Christian formation will not do. If being a Christian were merely a matter of breathing the air and drinking the water, absorbing a little godliness by osmosis, then we wouldn't need the church, wouldn't need help from our

AUGUST 2   LESSON 9

friends. We could be Christians the same way that people become Rotarians or members of the Women's Garden Club. We could hand them a membership card and a lapel pin rather than half drowning them by baptism.

From all that we know of Jesus and his demands upon us, being a disciple of his is a good deal more demanding, requiring more than the completion of a pledge card and the right hand of fellowship. Discipleship requires a lifetime of training, trial and error, struggle, correction, prayer, and a host of virtues that cannot be had simply by wanting them.

An athlete, preparing for some difficult athletic competition, enters into rigorous training. Why shouldn't we Christians expect the same need for rigorous training in order to be effective disciples?

That is the question behind today's scripture from 1 Timothy.

Selected Scripture

King James Version

1 Timothy 4

1 Now the Spirit speaketh expressly, that in the latter times some shall depart from the faith, giving heed to seducing spirits, and doctrines of devils;

2 Speaking lies in hypocrisy; having their conscience seared with a hot iron;

3 Forbidding to marry, *and commanding* to abstain from meats, which God hath created to be received with thanksgiving of them which believe and know the truth.

4 For every creature of God *is* good, and nothing to be refused, if it be received with thanksgiving:

5 For it is sanctified by the word of God and prayer.

6 If thou put the brethren in remembrance of these things, thou shalt be a good minister of Jesus Christ, nourished up in the words of faith and of good doctrine, whereunto thou hast attained.

7 But refuse profane and old wives' fables, and exercise thyself *rather* unto godliness.

8 For bodily exercise profiteth little: but godliness is profitable unto all things, having promise of the life that now is, and of that which is to come.

9 This *is* a faithful saying and worthy of all acceptation.

Revised Standard Version

1 Timothy 4

1 Now the Spirit expressly says that in later times some will depart from the faith by giving heed to deceitful spirits and doctrines of demons, 2 through the pretensions of liars whose consciences are seared, 3 who forbid marriage and enjoin abstinence from foods which God created to be received with thanksgiving by those who believe and know the truth. 4 For everything created by God is good, and nothing is to be rejected if it is received with thanksgiving; 5 for then it is consecrated by the word of God and prayer.

6 If you put these instructions before the brethren, you will be a good minister of Christ Jesus, nourished on the words of the faith and of the good doctrine which you have followed. 7 Have nothing to do with godless and silly myths. Train yourself in godliness; 8 for while bodily training is of some value, godliness is of value in every way, as it holds promise for the present life and also for the life to come. 9 The saying is sure and worthy of full acceptance.

FOURTH QUARTER

10 For therefore we both labour and suffer reproach, because we trust in the living God, who is the Saviour of all men, specially of those that believe.
11 These things command and teach.
12 Let no man despise thy youth; but be thou an example of the believers, in word, in conversation, in charity, in spirit, in faith, in purity.
13 Till I come, give attendance to reading, to exhortation, to doctrine.
14 Neglect not the gift that is in thee, which was given thee by prophecy, with the laying on of the hands of the presbytery.
15 Meditate upon these things; give thyself wholly to them; that thy profiting may appear to all.
16 Take heed unto thyself, and unto the doctrine; continue in them: for in doing this thou shalt both save thyself, and them that hear thee.

Key Verse: **Exercise thyself rather unto godliness. . . . For Godliness is profitable unto all things, having promise of the life that now is, and of that which is to come. (1 Timothy 4:7-8)**

10 For to this end we toil and strive, because we have our hope set on the living God, who is the Savior of all men, especially of those who believe.
11 Command and teach these things. 12 Let no one despise your youth, but set the believers an example in speech and conduct, in love, in faith, in purity. 13 Till I come, attend to the public reading of scripture, to preaching, to teaching. 14 Do not neglect the gift you have, which was given you by prophetic utterance when the elders laid their hands upon you. 15 Practice these duties, devote yourself to them, so that all may see your progress. 16 Take heed to yourself and to your teaching; hold to that, for by so doing you will save both yourself and your hearers.

Key Verse: **Train yourself in godliness; for . . . godliness is of value in every way, as it holds promise for the present life and also for the life to come. (1 Timothy 4:7-8)**

As You Read the Scripture—Charles T. Klinksick

The purpose of this letter and especially of its fourth chapter can be found in Paul's personal word of explanation to Timothy in verses 14 and 15 of chapter 3. He said, "I am writing these instructions so that, if I am delayed, you may know how one ought to behave in the household of God, the church." Paul was the experienced pastor, Timothy the young, still-learning minister assigned to the Ephesus congregation as Paul's representative. This is pastor-to-pastor advice about personal conduct and congregational life.

Paul's concern is not just the problem of tangential teachings mentioned earlier (Chapter 1) but hypocrisy, spiritual deceit, and demonic doctrine. He knows what is being promoted, and he doesn't want Timothy or the Ephesus believers to be caught in such errors.

1 Timothy 4:1. We do not know when or how the Spirit expressly spoke of defection from faith, but the problem was clearly referred to by Jesus. In his parable of the sower he said the word would be snatched away from believing hearts by the devil (Luke 8:12; Mark 4:15).

Verse 2. "Liars whose consciences are seared" is best understood as those deceivers whose consciences showed permanent evidence of evil, as if a branding iron had marked them. They not only lie, but their teachings go against good sense.

Verses 3-5. Marriage and eating have always been regarded as normal human privileges. To deny the right to marry or to eat is not in keeping with God's purposes. Paul says if you can be thankful for having food, God created it to be eaten. He implies that meals should be graced by a statement from God's word and a thankful prayer.

Verse 6. This is not only a matter of knowing these things for yourself but also of passing this information on to others. Ministry is teaching others that good which has sustained you. Timothy was not a minister of Paul, but of the Messiah (Christ) Jesus.

Verses 7-9. The seventh verse is a disclaimer. Christian ministry is concerned with truth, the gospel. Excluded are godlessness, superstitions, fables, folktales, and myths. Good teaching, good preaching, and good ministering are nothing but good news. Godliness requires training by critical thinking, awareness of God, and self-discipline. It has double value: a good life now and a life good for eternity. The ninth verse is an editorial affirmation by Paul (See 1 Timothy 1:15).

Verse 10. This is a statement of the purpose of missionary ministry based on the Christ-statement in John 3:16.

Verses 11-16. Paul now tries to reinforce Timothy. He wants him to be in charge unhesitatingly, as an educator, a youthful example, and a leader in public services. Timothy was possibly thirty to thirty-four years old, much younger than Paul. His personal conduct was to be above question. His reading and explanations of the holy Scriptures and his preaching were to be expressions of the spiritual gift assured him when he was ordained. This was to be a growth ministry, not a time of coasting along but a time of progress. If you take heed to yourself, you will benefit ("save," in all senses of the word) yourself and your audiences. Ephesus needed a minister like that.

The Scripture and the Main Question—William H. Willimon

Practice These Duties

Let us begin today's lesson by noting that the word "disciple" is related to the much more troubling and decidedly old-fashioned word, "discipline," a word that evokes bad memories of your third-grade piano teacher, Coach Smith with the whistle around his neck, and boot camp days at Fort Bragg. We're not much into discipline these days, are we?

But the writer of the fourth chapter of 1 Timothy would find it unimaginable that one could be a disciple, could follow a master whose name is Jesus, without discipline—the conscious, intentional submission of feelings, time, talents, and projects to the will of God as revealed in Christ. Disciples are made, not born.

Unfortunately, discipline isn't plentiful these days. What abounds is freedom, or at least what we call freedom. What we call freedom is the maximum amount of space to do whatever it is that we jolly well want to do. We have "freedom of choice," which means that we are set loose to choose a maximum number of options for our lives. But on what basis shall I choose, and to what end? Ah, there's the rub in our freedom.

My society—the affluent, upwardly mobile, American one, that is—enables me to be free, to decide, to choose, to roam at will. But it gives me absolutely no help in deciding what is worth having, on what basis my freedom of choice becomes interesting, truly freeing, and the free exercise of the best of my humanity. My society tells me that I'm free, but it cannot tell me what to do with my freedom. So left to my own devices, I merely lunge toward whatever craving I have at the moment. When asked what I'm up to, I'll tell you that I'm "meeting my needs." However, since I have no coherent view of myself beyond the bounds of my own momentary desires, no goal in mind for my life beyond what I feel like I might want right now, what I call "need" is mostly an amorphous bundle of desire, a self-indulgent, ever-changing blob of ego.

Little wonder that increasing numbers of our fellow Americans report that even in this supposedly most free of all nations, they feel anything but free. They feel trapped, their lives hemmed in by a growing chemical addiction, irresponsible parents, selfish children, and an endless treadmill of buying, consuming, and craving. Didn't George Bernard Shaw define hell as that place where you *must* do what you *want* to do? Having now unlimited freedom to express our sexual, economic, intellectual, and political desires without the constraints of any notion of a higher value, God, or anything beyond the simple fact that we want to, we live in something that feels very much like, well, hell. An oversexed society is just another manifestation, like an overconsuming economy or an overly bureaucratized state, of our dilemma of being all decked out with our rights and our freedom and have absolutely nowhere to go.

Which is to suggest that we may be the first generation in a long time to be able to say again a good word for that old-fashioned word, discipline. To be a disciplined person is to be someone who has some means of being able to say yes and no (no small achievement in a self-indulgent age). Without some goal, some vision of the good beyond the confines of the moment or our own egos, we tend to say yes to everything out of fear that we might say no to the very thing that would make our lives worth living. In this sense, some of our promiscuity, overindulgence, and consumptiveness is more "moral" than it first appears. We buy expensive cars or drift from person to person not because we are simply immoral but rather because somewhere within us we are desperate for meaning.

The Christian claim is that Jesus Christ, and only Jesus Christ, is the means whereby we are enabled to make sense of ourselves. By becoming attached to Christ, in having our lives caught up in his work in the world, our lives are given significance. We become fellow workers with him. Our lives take on new meaning since we are now about work that is more important than my desires for the moment. I am freed from the deadly necessity of having to please everyone, having to create some self-derived significance for my little life, because my life has been subsumed in his light.

A disciple is a person of discipline because the disciple has as a life project nothing less than imitation of the master. As Augustine said, "We imitate whom we adore." Any practical, daily disciplines we Christians employ—prayer, Bible reading, small group study, devotional reading, working at the soup kitchen, going to church meetings—are our means of being more adoring of and therefore more faithful to the one who reached out to us and said, "Follow me."

I meet lots of people today who are hungry for discipline. They have discovered that freedom *from* is not nearly as interesting as freedom *for*. Realizing that life (despite all our mechanisms for avoidance), whether it is lived well or poorly, eventually costs everything we've got, it is better to expend one's life for something that's worthy rather than worthless. Sick of wandering about without chart or compass, without guide or goal, they hunger for form, structure, direction in life. I want to say to them, if they happen to show up at our church, "Congratulations, you've come to the right place."

Nourished on the Words of the Faith

I think that many times we evangelical Christians have put too much emphasis on feelings and faith. We have often presented the Christian faith as something that one feels, an experience in one's heart. Now, feelings are fine, as far as feelings go. But feelings are notoriously fickle. So what you need, if you are going to stay Christian, is some means of keeping faithful even when you don't feel like it, even when it doesn't please you to live righteously, even when it doesn't feel good to do justice to others.

How many people have found that their initial religious fervor grew cool with the passing of time and the fading of the emotional experience from their memory? They were enthusiastic with the first steps of faith but neglected the next steps. They were born again, as Christians but never grew to Christian maturity. Jesus deserves mature, well-equipped disciples.

So we must gather on a regular basis at church and name the name and tell the story. We must remind one another of the Christian values that are often so easily subverted by the world's values. We must correct and encourage one another. As the writer of 1 Timothy says it, "Train yourself in godliness; for while bodily training is of some value, godliness is of value in every way" (4:7-8).

When we reduce the Christian faith to a mere one-time emotional experience, a momentary "high" one feels at some ecstatic moment, we endanger our ability to withstand the forces that subvert discipleship. So we must train. How? "Attend to the public reading of scripture, to preaching, to teaching. . . . Practice these duties, devote yourself to them, so that all may see your progress" (4:13,15).

If you want to learn to throw a baseball very well, you must practice throwing a baseball. It helps greatly if you very much enjoy throwing a baseball. But even if you have much natural talent for throwing a baseball, there will come a time when you must simply do it as a matter of training and practice rather than simple enjoyment. You will never learn to do it well, as if by second nature, if you do not train for it, practice throwing the ball well, do it as a matter of discipline.

Discipleship, following Jesus, is much like learning to throw a baseball well. There are some people who really seem to be Christian by natural inclination. That helps. However, even for those who seem naturally disposed to it, training is necessary. The world being what it is, the demands of Jesus being what they are, one must be well equipped if one is going to survive as a vibrant, effective disciple today.

FOURTH QUARTER

Helping Adults Become Involved—Douglas E. Wingeier

Preparing to Teach

Pray for class members by name, keeping in mind their current life situations and asking God to guide you in helping them become more aware of and committed to the goal of becoming faithful disciples.

Remember that the disciple who writes these letters is interpreting Paul's mind and purpose for a later day, with the aim of strengthening the church's ministry in the congregations founded by Paul and then developed by leaders like Timothy and Titus. It was a common practice for a disciple to write in the name of his master and to ascribe insights to him in keeping with his teachings.

Interview at least one person, asking the questions on discipleship given at the end of the last lesson. Think through your own answers to these questions as well.

Read 1 Timothy 4 and commentaries on it. Also study Matthew 28:19-20 and Mark 8:34-38. Your aim is to help members recognize the claims of Christian discipleship and the need for sound, effective discipleship training. Use this outline:

I. Discerning the truth
II. Training in godliness
III. Setting an example

Introducing the Main Question

Begin by asking: What is the difference between being a Christian and being a member of Rotary or the Garden Club? List answers on the board. Point up the difference, in terms of the demands of following Jesus.

Ask for answers to the first interview question, What does it mean to be a Christian disciple? List these elsewhere on the board. The following may be mentioned: A disciple is dedicated, serves willingly, gives of self, puts Christ first, bears witness, seeks to win others, makes sacrifices, works for justice.

Compare the two lists. Discuss: Have we made the church more like a club than a movement? How can we better emphasize the claims of discipleship? How should our training be shaped to better equip persons for discipleship as well as membership?

Ask persons to read aloud Matthew 28:19-20 (the Great Commission) and Mark 8:34-38 (the cost of discipleship). Comment that we need rigorous training and a high level of commitment to fulfill these claims.

Ask for answers to the second interview question on discipleship training, and write them up. Elements like leadership skills, Bible study, theological understanding, support groups, prayer, and worship may be lifted up. Point out that training must also include the three elements emphasized in this lesson: guidance in discerning truth, equipping for godly leadership, and accountability for setting an example.

Developing the Lesson

I. Discerning the truth

Have verses 1-5 read aloud. Explain that the false teaching here is gnosticism, which emphasized that the spiritual is good while the physical is evil. Ask: What are ideas and life-styles in our time that lead people away from faithful discipleship? Cite Dr. Willimon's discussion of the self-centered pursuit of need-satisfaction through promiscuity, overindulgence, and consumerism as one prominent contemporary heresy.

Ask: How do you discern the truth that undergirds faithful discipleship? Offer the following biblically based guidelines:

1. God does loving things. God wants us to do the loving thing. What is the most loving way to address the issue at hand?

2. God's will is justice and peace. God wants us to foster justice and peace locally and in the world. How can justice and peace best be served in relation to this issue?

3. God suffers when persons get hurt. God wants us to make choices that involve us redemptively in other people's pain. How can our involvement in this issue be redemptive?

4. It is more blessed to give than to receive. God wants us to give ourselves rather than protecting ourselves. How can we give of ourselves in relation to this issue?

5. God created persons to live in covenant community. God wants us to be accountable to one another within this covenant of grace. How will we manifest our care for each other on this issue?

6. God forgives us when we choose wrongly and repent. God wants us to forgive rather than be judgmental. How will we manifest an attitude of forgiveness on this issue?

7. God has created a world of ambiguity; certainty is the opposite of faith. God wants us to risk choosing in faith, trusting the Spirit's guidance and grace when we miss the mark. Are we willing to act on our convictions, accepting the possibility that we could be wrong but knowing that God and our faith community will love us anyway?

II. Training in godliness

A second dimension of discipleship training is equipping Christians for godly living and leadership. After reading verses 6-10, point out the five kinds of advice being given to Timothy and all church leaders.

1. Do not give orders; take the gentler, humbler approach of advising and suggesting. Don't command, but rather "put instructions before" your brothers and sisters in a way that leaves them free to respond (6*a*).

2. Base the training on "the words of the faith and of the good doctrine." Christian disciples must be nurtured in the study of Scripture, the teachings of Jesus, and the truths of Christian tradition (6*b*).

3. Avoid the frivolous and superficial. Base the training on the essentials of Christian identity and witness. Don't let "godless and silly myths" deter you from the central task of taking up the cross, following him, and sharing the good news by word and deed (7*a*).

4. Focus on training in godly living. Other kinds of leadership skills, represented by the phrase "bodily training," are important and worthwhile but should not substitute for the pure, honest, faithful living of the Christian life. Discipleship training should hold us accountable to these standards (7*b*-8).

5. The goal is a relationship with the living God. Make prayer, worship, and the nurture of the spiritual life primary in the training process (10).

These are the *disciplines* that make *disciples*, as Dr. Willimon puts it.

FOURTH QUARTER

III. Setting an example

As verses 11-13 are read, ask members to listen for aspects of discipleship and leadership in which Timothy is to set an example. Divide into two listening groups, one to identify personal qualities and the other public or corporate functions.

The first group might come up with characteristics like love, loyalty, and purity, of which we are to be an example. The second group could mention leadership roles like Scripture reading, exhortation, and teaching. Point out that the latter, plus prayer, are the basic elements in Christian worship, and that regular worship nurtures the strong Christian character expressed in the first set of qualities. Worship is basic to the discipleship training that forms exemplary character.

Helping Class Members Act

Have the class evaluate your church's current leadership/discipleship training in terms of the above guidelines. Formulate a revision in light of what you have learned. Who will carry this proposal to your pastor and see that it is considered?

Sing in closing either "Go, Make of All Disciples" or "Take Up Thy Cross." Then read 1 Timothy 4:14-16 as a charge to the group. Call for sentence prayers of new levels of commitment to faithful discipleship.

Planning for Next Sunday

Ask members to read 1 Timothy 6:2*c*-21, watch "Life-styles of the Rich and Famous" or a similar television program, ponder their life goals and priorities, and come next Sunday ready to share these with the class.

LESSON 10   AUGUST 9

Set Your Priorities

Background Scripture: 1 Timothy 6:2*c*-21

The Main Question—William H. Willimon

I remember the great preacher, Carlyle Marney, noting in a sermon that, "You had better be careful what you ask for in life, because most of us will be given what we want."

The statement seemed patently untrue to me. Get what we want? How can that be?

Marney continued, "If you want security above all else, you can get it. However, you may also get boredom. If you want freedom, more than anything else in the whole world, it is possible for you to attain complete freedom. But be careful. You may also obtain complete loneliness, an

AUGUST 9 LESSON 10

unfortunate byproduct of complete freedom. Be careful. You will probably get what you want."

I began to see the preacher's point. While not always the case, life often does give us what we want. Sometimes, the greatest problem facing us lies not in not getting what we want but in wanting what is wrong.

We had therefore best be careful while setting our goals, determining our priorities, for we may very well attain our goals. In writing to his beloved Timothy, Paul urged the young man to "aim at righteousness, godliness, faith, love, steadfastness, gentleness" (6:11). Set your priorities well for they become the goal, the orientation points for the living of your life.

How can we set worthy goals for our lives?

Selected Scripture

King James Version

1 Timothy 6:6-14, 17-21

6 But godliness with contentment is great gain.

7 For we brought nothing into *this* world, *and it is* certain we can carry nothing out.

8 And having food and raiment let us be therewith content.

9 But they that will be rich fall into temptation and a snare, and *into* many foolish and hurtful lusts, which drown men in destruction and perdition.

10 For the love of money is the root of all evil: which while some coveted after, they have erred from the faith, and pierced themselves through with many sorrows.

11 But thou, O man of God, flee these things; and follow after righteousness, godliness, faith, love, patience, meekness.

12 Fight the good fight of faith, lay hold on eternal life, whereunto thou art also called, and hast professed a good profession before many witnesses.

13 I give thee charge in the sight of God, who quickeneth all things, and *before* Christ Jesus, who before Pontius Pilate witnessed a good confession;

14 That thou keep *this* commandment without spot, unrebukeable, until the appearing of our Lord Jesus Christ:

Revised Standard Version

1 Timothy 6:6-14, 17-21

6 There is great gain in godliness with contentment; 7 for we brought nothing into the world, and we cannot take anything out of the world; 8 but if we have food and clothing, with these we shall be content. 9 But those who desire to be rich fall into temptation, into a snare, into many senseless and hurtful desires that plunge men into ruin and destruction. 10 For the love of money is the root of all evils; it is through this craving that some have wandered away from the faith and pierced their hearts with many pangs.

11 But as for you, man of God, shun all this; aim at righteousness, godliness, faith, love, steadfastness, gentleness. 12 Fight the good fight of the faith; take hold of the eternal life to which you were called when you made the good confession in the presence of many witnesses. 13 In the presence of God who gives life to all things, and of Christ Jesus who in his testimony before Pontius Pilate made the good confession, 14 I charge you to keep the commandment unstained and free from reproach until the appearing of our Lord Jesus Christ;

FOURTH QUARTER

17 Charge them that are rich in this world, that they be not highminded, nor trust in uncertain riches, but in the living God, who giveth us richly all things to enjoy;
18 That they do good, that they be rich in good works, ready to distribute, willing to communicate;
19 Laying up in store for themselves a good foundation against the time to come, that they may lay hold on eternal life.
20 O Timothy, keep that which is committed to thy trust, avoiding profane *and* vain babblings, and oppositions of science falsely so called:
21 Which some professing have erred concerning the faith. Grace *be* with thee. Amen.

Key Verse: **Follow after righteousness, godliness, faith, hope, patience, meekness. (1 Timothy 6:11)**

17 As for the rich in this world, charge them not to be haughty, nor to set their hopes on uncertain riches but on God who richly furnishes us with everything to enjoy. 18 They are to do good, to be rich in good deeds, liberal and generous, 19 thus laying up for themselves a good foundation for the future, so that they may take hold of the life which is life indeed.

20 O Timothy, guard what has been entrusted to you. Avoid the godless chatter and contradictions of what is falsely called knowledge, 21 for by professing it some have missed the mark as regards the faith.
Grace be with you.

Key Verse: **Aim at righteousness, godliness, faith, love, steadfastness, gentleness. (1 Timothy 6:11)**

As You Read the Scripture—Charles T. Klinksick

Chapters five and six of his first letter to Timothy reveal Paul's remarkable ability to "read" types of people and to comment on their problems. He does not preach to Timothy with elegant textual theology but counsels about wise and cautious religious dealings among age groups (1 Timothy 5:1), widows (5:3-16), church elders or persistent sinners (5:17-22), slaves (6:1-2), conceited wranglers (6:3-5), and the money-lovers (6:9-10). He concludes with advice about the godly man Timothy is expected to be. Because there is so much to be said, we are studying only fourteen verses of the sixth chapter. They have many present-day implications.

1 Timothy 6:6-8. Contentment does not mean having a lazy attitude, nor does it mean trying to own everything. Having a godly sense of satisfaction because of enough food, clothing, and shelter is a plus in itself "great gain," verse 6). "There are no pockets in shrouds" is the proverbial way of saying you can't take it with you (verse 7).

Verses 9-10. Money itself is not the problem. Roman and Greek coins, huge credits, subsidies, and briberies were a money network enmeshing Ephesian citizens. The craving, the love of this commodity called money, is the root of all the evils that tempt the poor and snare the rich. It erodes faith and causes heart disease.

Verse 11. This is addressed to Timothy, but it applies to anyone trying to be God's man or woman. "Shun" means stay away from, avoid by all means. "Aim" means to point oneself toward a goal or target. The fruit of the Spirit, Paul says (Galatians 5:22), is "love, joy, peace, patience, kindness, goodness, faithfulness, gentleness, self-control." Taken together, they constitute righteousness and godliness, goals for every Christian person.

Verse 12. "The good fight" is a tacit battle in which the weapons are not hatred but love, kindly deeds, courage that believes without fear, patience and a sense of time, a smile or a bit of humor, and help from almighty God. Paul has been fighting this kind of warfare, he will tell Timothy in his next letter (2 Timothy 4:7). It includes eternal living that began with a confession of faith, possibly Timothy's ordination as a minister.

Verses 13-14. "With God as my witness, I, Paul, charge you, Timothy . . ." is the effect of this statement. The commandment is the order given in verse 12. The imminent return of the Lord was expected by the New Testament apostles. The main point is that Paul's minister is to be above reproach or question, pure in conduct.

Verses 17-19. Those who are admittedly rich are not to be criticized or told to unload their riches but to be taught humility, spirituality, and liberality. Riches are their building blocks for the good life ahead.

Verses 20-21. This is a very personal letter. "O Timothy" is a plea, clinching all that has preceded. There is danger in Ephesus. This group of believers could lose its Christianity. Paul therefore is advising him to avoid the pitfalls of false knowledge and the godless talk it stirs up. It has already caused some persons to misbelieve.

"Grace"—Paul ends each of his letters with some form of a wish that the grace of God may be with his reader(s), a beautiful ending. His name was not added here, because the "To" and "From" with names were usually written on the top outer edge of the scroll (note the form of verse 1 of chapter 1).

The Scripture and the Main Question—William H. Willimon

The Love of Money

Earlier this week, I watched a silly television show called "Life-styles of the Rich and Famous." On this particular segment, viewers were taken to an exclusive resort on the French Riviera where we were enabled to look in on the rich at play. One person complained that she was spending two thousand dollars a day on her hotel room. Another person described how he and his girlfriend had just spent fifteen hundred dollars on one meal.

All of this in a world where many starve from lack of bread.

Today's scripture from 1 Timothy begins with concern about making money our priority. It is not necessarily concerned that through our conspicuous consumption we may be depriving others of their necessities. Rather, it is concerned that what making money our goal does to us.

As a young pastor I heard Pastor Richard Neuhaus, a distinguished Lutheran writer and scholar, comment that "early on in a person's ministry, he or she ought to decide how much money it will take for him or her to live on. If one is not clear about that, one can never be too committed to the Christian ministry."

It has never occurred to me to make a decision about how much money it would take for me and my wife to be happy. I suppose that if asked how much money I needed, my answer would simply be, "More!"

Yet making more money our major goal in life leads to spiritual destruction, according to 1 Timothy 6:6-10. When money is our priority, we

FOURTH QUARTER

"fall into temptation," "into many senseless and hurtful desires." Our lives become cluttered, preoccupied with things. What should be a mere desire is transformed into necessity. This is not a suitable condition for those who have been called to discipleship.

Do you agree with the author that "the love of money is the root of all evils"? (6:10). When one looks at our consumptive, overly materialistic society, it is difficult not to agree. The other day I was talking about contemporary health problems with a physician at our university. I asked him which modern disease concerned him the most. Heart disease? Lung cancer? AIDS?

His reply surprised me. "I believe that the greatest contemporary health problem is materialism," he said. Materialism? "Our hospitals are full of people who have a variety of problems which affect their hearts, their circulatory systems, which encourage them to overeat, to smoke, to drink. When you probe deeper into the causes of their addiction, their poor health habits, why they are unable to sleep at night, nine out of ten times the problem is money. We are literally working ourselves, worrying ourselves, to death."

So 1 Timothy claims not only that because of the priority of money "some have wandered away from the faith" but also many have "pierced their hearts with many pangs" (6:10).

When asked what foe he feared the most, what factor could be most detrimental to his then-fledgling Methodist movement in England, John Wesley replied, "the love of riches." Wesley knew that many a person's initial ardor and commitment to the Christian faith is dampened through materialism.

A pastor waters down his sermons and fails to preach boldly because he fears that he might lose his job, or that major financial contributors to his church might protest.

Jane gives up her vocation as a church school teacher because she now has a house at the lake and, rather than teach her class, now wants her weekends free to enjoy her new recreation cottage.

Tom leaves home nearly every day at 7:00 A.M. and does not return until well after 9:00 P.M. When asked why he is working so hard, Tom always replies, "I'm doing it for my family." Yet everyone knows that Tom's marriage is in trouble and that his two children have grown up as if they had no father at all.

As I said, it is difficult to argue with today's scripture when it asserts, "The love of money is the root of all evils."

Aim at Righteousness

Someone once said, "Show me your checkbook stubs and I will tell you whom you worship." Or, as Jesus once said, "Where your treasure is, there is your heart also." In our society, we tend to act out our deepest needs, try to fill our deepest insecurities, demonstrate our most cherished values, through our money.

Therefore, it becomes particularly important for each of us to examine our priorities, to ask ourselves what goals we are aiming for. The Bible has made money a spiritual issue, a matter of idolatry, worship of false gods in place of the true God. Whom do we worship?

I work at the university. One of the great privileges of being here is that

AUGUST 9   LESSON 10

I come into contact with many idealistic, earnest young people. Many of them show a desire to do something worthwhile with their lives, to expend their lives in service to others, to give of themselves in some sacrificial work in behalf of the less fortunate. Some of them become teachers in remote areas of our country. Others give their talents in God's work in some mission field.

Yet I have been here long enough to see many of these idealistic young adults lose their youthful altruism. Sadly, for most of them, their idealistic outlook on life does not last. In a few years, they are back for their first college reunion, and they seem to have changed. They gave up their desire to do something for others. Now they are busy looking after themselves, fitting into the usual treadmill of getting and acquiring.

The love of money is a powerful tempter in life.

Therefore, I think that I agree with today's scripture. Early on in life, it is important for each of us to set priorities, to decide what goal we shall aim for. Many lives never hit a worthy target because they are never aimed. Life being what it is, it is so easy to become distracted, to allow the nonessentials to crowd out the essentials, to lose touch, to go astray.

Of particular concern to me are young married couples. When a couple comes to me as their pastor, planning their marriage, and I counsel them concerning the challenges of marriage, I often ask them, "Do you know the major cause of marital distress in our country?"

Sometimes they respond with "incompatibility" or "sexual problems." No. The major cause of marital distress is *money*.

More marriages will fall on hard times in disputes between husbands and wives over money than for any other reason. Therefore, one of the most important things a young couple can do is to attain clarity over how they will handle the finances of their marriage.

I see too many young couples who say that they are waiting to get married until they have paid for their two cars, have a nice home in which to live, good appliances, and so forth. Now, it is a good thing that they realize that marriage involves financial responsibility. But it bothers me that, so early in their marriage, they are letting these material things determine the shape of their relationship. Probably their parents began marriage with far fewer material possessions, and I do not think that their parents were a bit worse off for it. When people make their marital happiness conditional upon how many things they have acquired, I believe that they have fundamentally misunderstood what marriage is all about.

If that applies to marriage, it also applies to life itself. Money cannot make a life. It can be an enrichment for life, but never can it be a worthy goal in life. Never.

A Good Foundation for the Future

Not long ago, the lively youth evangelist Dr. Anthony Campolo preached in our campus chapel. Dr. Campolo is internationally renowned for his vibrant appeal to youth. Toward the end of his sermon, Dr. Campolo said, "I loved the old version of the TV show, 'Star Trek.' The best thing about the show was the way it began. Do you remember the words? 'Go where no man has ever been.'"

I wondered to myself what on earth this "Star Trek" diversion had to do with Dr. Campolo's sermon!

FOURTH QUARTER

"'Go where no one has ever been!'" he shouted. "Now here you are at the university. Most of you are preparing to be stockbrokers, bankers, lawyers, business executives. Now, that's OK. The only trouble is, THAT'S BORING! Anybody can do that! Why don't you go out of here and do something exciting? Why don't you go where no one else is going? Why don't you go follow Jesus Christ!"

Helping Adults Become Involved—Douglas E. Wingeier

Preparing to Teach

Think of each class member—their relationships, opportunities, problems, and dreams. Pray that this lesson will help them examine their priorities and revise their goals in light of the guidelines in this chapter of 2 Timothy.

Keep in mind that the Pastoral Epistles are more like church manuals than personal letters, written with church members as well as leaders in mind. They contain instructions and admonitions to help pastors and laity keep the faith, avoid false teaching, and maintain high moral standards.

Read 1 Timothy 6:2c-21 and commentaries about it. Also read the story of the rich young ruler and its subsequent verses (Mark 10:17-25). Make your own list of goals and priorities and evaluate them in relation to the critique of materialism in today's scripture and the aims mentioned in verses 11 and 18.

Reflect on how your goals and priorities have changed as you have grown older. What has caused the changes? Are they for the better or the worse, as judged by today's passage?

Watch "Life-styles of the Rich and Famous" or a similar television program, and critique it in terms of the values emphasized in this lesson.

Your aim is to help members assess their life goals and priorities in light of the standards presented in 1 Timothy 6, and to support one another in carrying out any new priorities the class may collectively set. Use this outline:

      I. The love of money.
     II. Aim at righteousness.
    III. A good foundation.

Introducing the Main Question

Open with the story of the rich young ruler (Mark 10:17-22). Ask: What were this man's strong points? What were his priorities? What kept him from following Jesus? Why did he choose as he did? How can/do material things get in the way of faithful discipleship?

Read the Marney quote from "The Main Question": "Be careful what you ask for in life, because you will be given what you want." Ask the class what they think this means, then share Dr. Willimon's explanation. Does this square with their experience of life?

Now divide the class into groups of three or four to share the goals and priorities they were asked to bring. Have each small group discuss and report on the goals they have in common, the discrepancies in their priorities, and changes they would like to make to become more faithful Christians. Write these on the board.

Developing the Lesson

I. The love of money.

Look at the list of goals and priorities and put a dollar sign beside any of them that cost money to achieve. Discuss: How important is money to our life goals? How do we distinguish luxuries from necessities? Is an affluent life-style a means to an end or an end in itself? What distinguishes us from the persons portrayed in "Life-styles of the Rich and Famous"? Is it just a difference of degree, or of basic values?

Have someone read verses 6-10. Ask: Why are we not content with just godliness? Why, knowing that we brought nothing into the world and can take nothing with us, do we still strive to acquire more and more? What are the temptations and snares we can fall into when we desire more things? Is the love of money really the root of all evils? What makes it so seductive?

Ask for examples from current events or the members' own lives of how the quest for things leads persons astray, into, for instance, gambling, graft, exploitation of workers, waste of natural resources, damage to the environment, stock market manipulations, substance abuse, and putting acquisition above family relationships. Discuss Dr. Willimon's illustrations of the pastor, Jane, Tom, and young couples. Do these examples fit with class members' experience?

II. Aim at righteousness.

As verses 11-16 are read, ask members to note the aims to which the writer is calling Christians to devote themselves. These include righteousness, godliness, faith, love, steadfastness, gentleness, the good fight of faith, eternal life, and keeping the commandment. Ask the group to come up with everyday examples of each of these qualities.

Compare these with the group's goals, and note which of the scriptural goals are represented in the group's list.

Have the group reflect on how their priorities may have changed through the years. Were they ever like Dr. Willimon's idealistic young adults at one time, and if so, to what extent have they lost their youthful altruism and become "busy . . . fitting into the usual treadmill of getting and acquiring?" What has caused this shift? How can we better incorporate into our lives the goals advocated by the writer of 1 Timothy?

Help the group identify specific behaviors that will do this, such as tithing, faithful church attendance, contributions to mission causes, participation in mission trips and work projects, sponsorship of a refugee family, consultation with other Christians on major purchases, responsible leadership in church and community, and a regular discipline of prayer and Bible study. List these on the board.

III. A good foundation.

Invite two members to go out of the room to plan a role play of a conversation between a parent and a teenager leaving for college. The parent is to advise the young person on the elements of a sound foundation on which to base his or her future life. While these two are out, have the rest of the class brainstorm items they would include in such a foundation. Write

FOURTH QUARTER

these on the board, but cover them up before the two come in. After the role play, uncover the list and compare it with what was advocated in the role play.

Now read verses 17-21, and note the aspects of "a good foundation for the future, so that they may take hold of the life which is life indeed" that are emphasized—"to do good, to be rich in good deeds, liberal and generous." Ask: Why does the writer consider this a better foundation than haughtiness about "uncertain riches"? How does this foundation compare with the ones implied in our lists of priorities and made explicit in our role play? What changes would we want to consider in our goals for the next stage of our lives, in order to be sure of having "a good foundation"?

Helping Class Members Act

Allow five minutes of silence for members to write new goals and priorities for their lives, reflecting today's discussion.

Join hands in a closing circle. Sing "Take My Life, and Let It Be" or "How Firm a Foundation." Invite members to voice their newly made commitments in brief prayers of dedication. After each prayer, have the group respond with "Take hold of the life which is life indeed!"

Planning for Next Sunday

Have members read 2 Timothy 2:1-19, memorize verse 15, and come ready to share how regularly they read the Bible, which parts of it are most meaningful to them, and what are the obstacles to making the Bible a more vital resource to their spiritual life and growth.

UNIT II: GUIDELINES FOR SERVING

THREE LESSONS   **AUGUST 16–30**

"Guidelines for Serving" includes three lessons, two from 2 Timothy and one from Titus. "Respect God's Word," August 16, encourages leaders to teach God's message correctly. "Serve Faithfully," August 23, underscores the need for leaders to be faithful in their ministry for God. "Demonstrate Christian Living," August 30, encourages leaders to set good examples for believers.

LESSON 11   AUGUST 16

Respect God's Word

Background Scripture: 2 Timothy 2:1-19

The Main Question—William H. Willimon

The great, faithful German martyr, Dietrich Bonhoeffer, asserted in his famous book, *The Cost of Discipleship,* that every

> revival of Church life always brings in its train a richer understanding of the Scriptures. Behind all the slogans and catchwords . . . there arises a quest . . . for Jesus Christ himself. What did Jesus mean to say to us? What is his will for us today? How can he help us to be good Christians in the modern world? . . . Let us get back to Scriptures, to the word and call of Jesus Christ himself.

Bonhoeffer testifies to the centrality of God's Word, as contained in the Bible, for the vitality of the church. Without this word, the church is cast adrift, left to its own limited, human devices. As Bonhoeffer says, every revival, every reformation and resurgence of the church, is linked to a renewed grappling with God's Word.

Which is to assert that the study you will do this Sunday in your class is essential, life-giving work for the church. In getting "back to the Scriptures," you are really going forward into the future, because study of the Bible gives us the resources we need to be faithful modern disciples. None of us knows what demands the future holds for each of us, what tests of faith life may send our way. Therefore, we must study the Scriptures and arm ourselves for faithful discipleship.

A few years after Bonhoeffer wrote these words about the connection between the Bible and Christian discipleship, he was to pay the ultimate price of biblically based discipleship. He was hung by the Nazis because of his Christian-motivated resistance to Hitler.

How can you and I become equipped to handle the challenges that life may put to us as disciples of Jesus Christ?

Selected Scripture

King James Version	Revised Standard Version
2 Timothy 2:1-15	*2 Timothy 2:1-15*
1 Thou therefore, my son, be strong in the grace that is in Christ Jesus.	1 You then, my son, be strong in the grace that is in Christ Jesus, 2 and what you have head from me before many witnesses entrust to faithful men who will be able to teach others also. 3 Take your share of suffering as a good soldier of Christ Jesus. 4 No soldier on service gets entangled in civilian pursuits,
2 And the things that thou hast heard of me among many witnesses, the same commit thou to faithful men, who shall be able to teach others also.	
3 Thou therefore endure hard-	

ness, as a good soldier of Jesus Christ.

4 No man that warreth entangleth himself with the affairs of *this* life; that he may please him who hath chosen him to be a soldier.

5 And if a man also strive for masteries, *yet* is he not crowned, except he strive lawfully.

6 The husbandman that laboureth must be first partaker of the fruits.

7 Consider what I say; and the Lord give thee understanding in all things.

8 Remember that Jesus Christ of the seed of David was raised from the dead according to my gospel:

9 Wherein I suffer trouble, as an evil doer, *even* unto bonds; but the word of God is not bound.

10 Therefore I endure all things for the elect's sakes, that they may also obtain the salvation which is in Christ Jesus with eternal glory.

11 *It is* a faithful saying: For if we be dead with *him*, we shall also live with *him*:

12 If we suffer, we shall also reign with *him*: if we deny *him*, he also will deny us:

13 If we believe not, *yet* he abideth faithful: he cannot deny himself.

14 Of these things put *them* in remembrance, charging *them* before the Lord that they strive not about words to no profit, *but* to the subverting of the hearers.

15 Study to shew thyself approved unto God, a workman that needeth not to be ashamed, rightly dividing the word of truth.

***Key Verse:* Study to shew thyself approved unto God, a workman that needeth not to be ashamed, rightly dividing the word of truth. (2 Timothy 15)**

since his aim is to satisfy the one who enlisted him. 5 An athlete is not crowned unless he competes according to the rules. 5 It is the hard-working farmer who ought to have the first share of the crops. 7 Think over what I say, for the Lord will grant you understanding in everything.

8 Remember Jesus Christ, risen from the dead, descended from David, as preached in my gospel, 9 the gospel for which I am suffering and wearing fetters, like a criminal. But the word of God is not fettered. 10 Therefore I endure everything for the sake of the elect, that they also may obtain the salvation which in Christ Jesus goes with eternal glory. 11 The saying is sure:

If we have died with him, we
  shall also live with him;
12 if we endure, we shall also reign
  with him;
  if we deny him, he also will deny
  us;
13 if we are faithless, he remains
  faithful—
for he cannot deny himself.

14 Remind them of this, and charge them before the Lord to avoid disputing about words, which does no good, but only ruins the hearers. 15 Do your best to present yourself to God as one approved, a workman who has no need to be ashamed, rightly handling the word of truth.

***Key Verse:* Do your best to present yourself to God as one approved, a workman who has no need to be ashamed, rightly handing the word of truth. (2 Timothy 15)**

AUGUST 16 LESSON 11

As You Read the Scripture—Charles T. Klinksick

Second Timothy was written from Rome. Paul was imprisoned for the second and final time. Nero was emperor; Rome had burned for four days in 64 A.D., with the Christians being blamed for it; and death was coming soon for Paul. The letter does not say where Timothy was, but we can assume he was still in Ephesus. Its message is solemn, straightforward, and uncomplaining. It is full of practical advice based upon Christ-theology. Paul was in his sixties at this time. His main point of reference throughout the letter is Christ Jesus (see 1:1-2, 9-10, 13; 2:1, 3, 8, 10; 3:12, 15; 4:1). This is the gospel (1:11), the reason for good conduct and for suffering, Paul says.

2 Timothy 2:1-2. What you have heard me preach, teach to others, he says. To be "strong in grace" means to be thankfully close to Jesus Christ in all possible ways.

Verses 3-7. Suffering is to be expected. Some people do not want the gospel of grace and goodness; 3:2-4 describes such persons. Three vocations illustrate the price and discipline of being a professional. A *soldier's* responsibility is toward his outfit, the military, and his commanding officer; a pastor's highest loyalty is to the Chief Shepherd, Jesus Christ. An *athlete* wins only if he complies with all the rules of the game; a minister cannot win by cheating. The *farmer* has to work hard for what he expects to harvest; a missionary must put in long days before he deserves to see results. There are no shortcuts that avoid suffering to achieve value.

Verses 8-10. Paul is saying, "Remember, I am suffering, like a criminal, in bonds, because of the gospel. My purpose is to have those whom God calls ["the elect"] obtain eternal glory through Christ Jesus, the risen descendant of David. I am enduring everything for their sake. Nothing holds back God's good news" ("the word of God").

Verses 11-13. These couplets are like a short hymn, although commentators suggest no poetry with which to identify them. They can stand on their own merit. Paul's reference to "the saying" would seem to imply this is a quote from a known source.

The idea of verse 11 is stated by Paul in chapter 6 of Romans: "If we have died with Christ, we believe that we shall also live with him" (verse 8).

Verse 12 can be found in the words of Jesus: "He who endures to the end will be saved" (Matthew 24:13); "Come . . . inherit the kingdom prepared for you" (Matthew 25:34); "Whoever denies me before men, I also will deny before my Father who is in heaven" (Matthew 10:33).

God's faithfulness (verse 13) was cited by Moses (Deuteronomy 31:6), "It is the Lord your God who goes with you; he will not fail you or forsake you." The same thought is quoted in Hebrews 13:5.

Verse 14. "Them" refers to the men Timothy was to train as teachers (2:2) and to possibly all believers who will listen. This reminder is similar to Paul's warnings in his earlier letter (1 Timothy 4:7 and 6:20). He amplifies his warnings further in verses 16 and 17. Orators in these Roman Empire days excelled in playing games with words and logic. They delighted in twisting thoughts and words enough to corner an opponent with rhetoric. Paul was advising: Speak wisely and carefully so what you say cannot be manipulated against you.

Verse 15. Religion's currency is truth. This verse is good for memorizing by every minister, church school teacher, seminarian, and parent. It would be useful posted on a plaque in every church office, pastor's study, sacristy, and faculty lounge. No Timothy is to be faulted if he does his best before God.

The Scripture and the Main Question—William H. Willimon

Be Strong in Jesus Christ

In writing to a young disciple named Timothy, Paul urges him to "be strong in the grace that is in Christ Jesus" (2:1). How does one grow stronger in faith? To describe the path to resilient, firm faith, Paul reaches for three vivid metaphors from everyday life. A soldier on duty conforms his entire life to satisfy the demands of "the one who enlisted him" (2:4); single-minded devotion to duty to the commanding officer is offered as an analogy for Christian discipleship. For an athlete to win the prize, he must discipline his efforts to win by the rules of the game (2:5). Only the farmer who works hard in the fields is destined to reap a good harvest (2:6).

The point is obvious. Christian discipleship requires rigorous, disciplined devotion. Do you believe that this is a point missed by many contemporary disciples? In a culture accustomed to having everything in an instant, with push-button speed, the notion that faithful discipleship takes time may seem strange. In a hedonistic society in which pleasure is always chosen over pain, in which millions try to go through life with a minimum of effort and pain, Paul's exhortation to "share in suffering as a good soldier of Christ Jesus" (2:3) seems odd. Yet here it is, in the Bible—we will never be strong disciples without hard work, discipline, even suffering.

Too often American evangelical Christianity presents the Christian faith as the best deal a person ever had, the solution to all of our aches and pains, a good way to make happy people even happier. How does that vision of faithfulness square with the assertions of today's scripture from 2 Timothy, or even with your own experiences of being a Christian?

We are saved by grace. In Christ, God accepts us just as we are. But we must not let our first steps in faith be the end of the story. Here is a narrow way that requires a lifetime of effort. Staying a Christian involves confrontation with that four-letter word modern people abhor, "*work*."

Perhaps you thought that being a Christian was a simple matter of feeling certain warm fuzzies within your heart, thinking a few lofty thoughts on a once-a-week basis, getting together occasionally with a few other nice people. No, here it is in the Bible, in 2 Timothy. Following Jesus requires work.

Present Yourselves to God

"Present yourself to God as one approved, a workman who has no need to be ashamed, rightly handling the word of truth" (2:15).

Paul moves from his images of soldier, athlete, and farmer to the image of a workman, a master craftsman who takes justifiable pride in his handiwork because it is excellently done. Your life, he seems to say, ought to be crafted carefully, so that on the day when you present your handiwork before God, you will not be ashamed.

When I think of a craftsman, I think of the curator of organs at our chapel. Here is a man who is a craftsman of the old school. Maintenance of

AUGUST 16 — LESSON 11

organs requires the ear of a musician, the hands of a master woodworker and metalworker, the eye of an artist, and great patience. I have watched our curator work for hours carefully fashioning just one small organ pipe until the air flowed through it to make the perfect sound.

You ought to treat your life like that, says today's scripture. Through our study of God's Word, by laying our lives alongside of the Bible, using the Bible as a yardstick to measure ourselves, our lives can become works of art of which we need not be ashamed.

I like to think that the letters to Timothy were written by Paul, an older Christian, to Timothy, a young person just starting out on the way of discipleship. It therefore seems appropriate that much of the advice given has to do with the necessity for Christian discipline, the need for young Timothy to dare to discipline his life in obedience not to his own appetites or preferences but rather to the demands of Scripture. Now we're talking about discipline. Disciples are those who have disciplined their lives on the basis of the demands of biblical faith.

As I have mentioned above, I spend a good deal of time talking to young adults who are planning to marry. When a couple comes to me to talk marriage, I sometimes ask them, just to get things rolling, if they are already living together. Many of them are honest enough to admit that they are.

"So why in the world would you want to get married?" I ask. "You're already having sex, doing the dishes together, sharing groceries, toothpaste. What on earth could I or the church give you that you don't already have?"

In their response, they invariably say things like "I just need to hear him say the words" or "We're looking for more long-term commitment."

To which I say, "Congratulations! You've come to the right place. We're in the long-term commitment business. At last you're ready for a promise. That's marriage."

Frustrated by their inability to sustain a relationship with God by purely spontaneous feelings, embarrassed by the superficiality of their lives, many people today are reaching out for the structures of commitment. That's called *discipline*.

They've come to the right place when they walk into your church. Rather than reducing your life together as a congregation to the lowest common denominator, a matter on which nine of ten Americans can agree, a life-style indistinguishable from that followed by everybody else, even those who aren't following Jesus, I believe that we ought to ask more of our people rather than less, ought to build congregations that test the limits of our faithfulness, that expose us to ever-deepening dimensions of commitment. The future belongs to churches who create the communal structures and the forms of congregating that are able to sustain discipleship in an unbelieving world. I believe that the effectiveness of your adult church school class will be measured by how well you, in your Sunday study of the Bible, enable your members to conduct themselves in their Monday through Saturday world. Are you giving your people the skills, the insights, and the discipline they need to survive as Christian disciples today? Does the same kind of equipment for discipleship, which we witness in 2 Timothy, occur in your adult class?

A while back I met a man on our campus who announced to me that he was a Mormon. "Just been a Mormon for a few years," he said. "We Mormons really believe a lot of strange things."

FOURTH QUARTER

"I might have said that," I replied, "but it surprises me to hear *you* say that about your church. What made you a Mormon?"

Without hesitation he replied, "I love my family." He then explained to me how he was "just an average person" who feared that he lacked the personal and moral resources to fulfill his marital responsibilities without help. Now, since his family affiliated with the Latter Day Saints, he is in church most nights of the week, has had his social life rearranged by the church, and is totally engaged in church work in his spare time. His family is thriving and together, unlike the majority of the families in his neighborhood.

There was a day when that same conversation could have been had by substituting the name of any mainline denomination for "Mormon." A stanza in one of my favorite Charles Wesley hymns emphasizes this need for disciplined, long-term, biblical discipleship:

> A charge to keep I have,
> A God to glorify,
> A never-dying soul to save,
> And fit it for the sky.
> To serve the present age,
> My calling to fulfill;
> O may it all my powers engage
> To do my Master's will.

Paul, an older Christian giving good advice to a younger one, urged young Timothy to respect God's Word by fashioning his life in accord with the dictates of Scripture, to handle the "word of truth" as a master craftsman, to discipline all aspects of his living so that when it came time for him to render account of himself to God, he would have "no need to be ashamed."

Helping Adults Become Involved—Douglas E. Wingeier

Preparing to Teach

Reflect honestly on the place the Bible holds in your own religious life. Reading James Smart's *The Strange Silence of the Bible in the Church* will help you understand the reasons why many church people do not read the Bible faithfully. Robert McAfee Brown's *The Bible Speaks to You* will make the biblical message vital and relevant to the life issues faced by you and your class members. And Richard J. Foster's *Celebration of Discipline* will provide a rich resource for dealing with the disciplines of the Christian life.

Note that contrary to the scholarly opinion cited earlier, both Dr. Willimon and Dr. Klinksick assert that Paul wrote 2 Timothy. Use your judgment as to how much class time to spend on the authorship issue. Get the perspectives of several commentaries. Blair's *Abingdon Bible Handbook* offers a compromise position.

A church leader near the end of the first century is concerned about the increase of heretical teaching and the decline of zeal and enthusiasm. He addresses the situation by writing a letter from Paul to Timothy, in which Paul predicts the problems the writer already is facing. Thus this letter, purporting to be addressed to Timothy, is really an appeal from an apostolic leader to all the churches and their pastors to set things straight, uphold the true and oppose the false, and defend the faith regardless of the consequences.

It urges Timothy to be steadfast in faith, rekindle God's gift (1:6), witness unashamedly (1:8), suffer bravely (2:1-13), contend with false teachers by handling the word rightly (2:15), be a pure vessel (2:20-26), and follow the example of Paul (3:10-17), who is facing death and awaiting the crown of righteousness (4:6-8).

Read the entire letter, study 2:1-15 and commentaries on it, and memorize verse 15. Your aim is to help the class consider honestly their present attitude toward and use of the Bible, develop greater appreciation for its centrality to the Christian life, and find ways of practicing regular daily Bible study. Follow this outline:

> I. The Bible: present practice
> II. God's word: source of strength
> III. Rightly handling the Word

Introducing the Main Question

Ask: Where do we turn for guidance on being good Christians in today's world? Answers may include the Bible, the church, and respected leaders. Read the quote from Bonhoeffer, and tell how he paid with his life for following God's leading through Scripture to join an unsuccessful plot on Hitler's life.

Emphasize along with Dr. Willimon that because "study of the Bible gives us the resources we need to be faithful modern disciples," we must "get back to the Scriptures, to the word and call of Jesus Christ himself."

Developing the Lesson

I. The Bible: present practice

Divide the class into small groups to discuss the questions they were asked to think about in advance: their present Bible-reading practices, the most meaningful parts of it, and the obstacles to making it a vital resource. To avoid embarrassment, share your own responses first, acknowledging honestly your own questions and struggles. Ask group reporters to write their reports on the board.

Note the present practices and favorite passages briefly, but focus on the obstacles. These may include archaic and abstract language, lack of time, lack of background knowledge, dependence on the pastor's specialized training, irrelevance to the complex contemporary world, lack of skill in interpretation, proof-texting by literalists, lack of self-discipline, busy schedule. Agree that all are understandable reasons for our failure to pay sufficient attention to the Bible.

Then ask: How can we overcome these obstacles so as to make better use of the Bible as a vital resource?

II. God's word: source of strength

Read 2:1-7. Mention the three examples of "being strong in the grace" (verse 1)—the soldier, the athlete, and the farmer—and the characteristics of each as explained by Drs. Willimon and Klinksick. These represent the ideal toward which Timothy and we are urged to strive.

FOURTH QUARTER

They also offer strategies for overcoming the obstacles to faithful Bible study. Like the soldier, we must set priorities that satisfy Jesus, the one who enlisted us, and that thereby keep us from getting entangled in nonessential pursuits. Like the athlete, we must follow the disciplines of Christian discipleship—participation in worship and sacrament, prayer and support groups, personal devotions, witness and service projects, stewardship, and fasting—if we are to find the time and will to study the Scriptures faithfully. And like the farmer, we have to work hard at the task. Share Dr. Willimon's concern about evangelical Christianity's presenting the faith as a way to happiness and warm fuzzies without much disciplined effort.

Ask: Will these strategies make us strong in the faith? What help do we need to better employ them? Can we covenant together to practice the disciplines of Christian discipleship, including regular Bible study?

III. Rightly handling the Word

Have the class recite 2:15 from memory; discuss its meaning. Share Dr. Willimon's image of the organ curator as an example of a master craftsperson, a worker who need not be ashamed. Ask the class to name others who fit this description. Do they want to be able to read the Bible with this kind of devotion and expertise? How can they acquire this skill?

Here are eight guidelines for "rightly handling the word" that will help them move in that direction:

1. Try to understand the biblical life-world out of which the passage comes.
2. Relate parts to the whole; see the passage in relation to the overall biblical story and message.
3. Look for unifying themes; test the message of a passage against the central threads of love, redemption, faith, and the just sovereignty of God.
4. Identify the intentionality of the passage; briefly state its central point.
5. Relate the biblical message to the contemporary life-world, present-day life concerns, and your own life situation; make it relevant.
6. Test your interpretation with the teaching of the church; don't trust a privatized point of view.
7. Expect God to speak and act. Bible study is not passive acquisition of knowledge; it changes lives!
8. Be ready to respond; God calls you to act in response to your study.

Helping Class Members Act

Invite the class to covenant together to engage in a daily Bible study and prayer discipline. Ask them to spend at least fifteen minutes a day in studying the Bible, praying for each other and the needs of the world, and in receptive silence, waiting for God's guidance and strength.

Share Dr. Willimon's closing words about commitment, discipline, and the communal structures of discipleship. Tell his story about the man who became a Mormon to help him fulfill his responsibilities. Ask: could this be said of our church as well?

Close by singing "A Charge to Keep I Have," "Take Time to Be Holy," or "Break Thou the Bread of Life." Invite sentence prayers of commitment to

AUGUST 23　　　　　　　　　　　　　　　　LESSON 12

the group's new covenant of spiritual disciplines, followed by the Lord's Prayer in unison.

Planning for Next Sunday

For daily Scripture readings in their new covenant of discipline, members may go back and read 1 and 2 Timothy, paying special attention to 2 Timothy 3:10–4:58 for next week. Also have them think of an experience in which they received ministry, identify what made it ministry, and come prepared to discuss the question, Who and what is a minister?

LESSON 12　　　　　　　　　　　　　　　　AUGUST 23

Serve Faithfully

Background Scripture: 2 Timothy 3:10–4:8

The Main Question—William H. Willimon

I have a pet peeve about the way we refer to people who perform Christian ministry. Sometimes we call our ordained clergy, our pastors, by the name "minister." "The Reverend Mr. So-and-So is our minister," we say. Of course, this person is a minister, an ordained, official servant of the church. But this person is not the *only* minister. Through baptism, all Christians are "ordained" to share in Christ's service to the world (see 1 Peter 2:5-6). Every one of us is a "minister" who has as a vocation to serve the world as Christ has served us. From among these "ministers," some have been set apart to be pastors and teachers, servants of the servants, ministers to the ministers. These persons are our ordained clergy. But their ministry in no way supersedes or makes them superior to the ministry of all Christians.

Therefore, when we are speaking of ordained clergy, I think we ought to call these people priests, or pastors, or clergy, rather than simply ministers, because that implies that the clergy are the real, the only, ministers, and that the laity have no ministry. Which is just plain wrong.

A clerical friend of mine has on his calling card, "St. John's Church. Pastor, The Rev. James Smith. Ministers, Every Member of the Congregation."

Each adult in your class this Sunday has a ministry, a vocation to serve faithfully. How might each of us, in our own unique way, be a better minister? That is today's question.

FOURTH QUARTER
Selected Scripture

| King James Version | Revised Standard Version |

2 Timothy 3:10-17

10 But thou hast fully known my doctrine, manner of life, purpose, faith, longsuffering, charity, patience,

11 Presecutions, afflictions, which came unto me at Antioch, at Iconium, at Lystra; what persecutions I endured: but out of *them* all the Lord delivered me.

12 Yea, and all that will live godly in Christ Jesus shall suffer persecution.

13 But evil men and seducers shall wax worse and worse, deceiving, and being deceived.

14 But continue thou in the things which thou hast learned and hast been assured of, knowing of whom thou hast learned *them;*

15 And that from a child thou hast known the holy scriptures, which are able to make thee wise unto salvation through faith which is in Christ Jesus.

16 All scripture *is* given by inspiration of God, and *is* profitable for doctrine, for reproof, for correction, for instruction in righteousness:

17 That the man of God may be perfect, throughly furnished unto all good works.

2 Timothy 4:1-5

1 I charge *thee* therefore before God, and the Lord Jesus Christ, who shall judge the quick and the dead at his appearing and his kingdom;

2 Preach the word; be instant in season, out of season; reprove, rebuke, exhort with all longsuffering and doctrine.

3 For the time will come when they will not endure sound doctrine; but after their own lusts shall they heap to themselves teachers, having itching ears;

2 Timothy 3:10-17

10 Now you have observed my teaching, my conduct, my aim in life, my faith, my patience, my love, my steadfastness, 11 my persecutions, my sufferings, what befell me at Antioch, at Iconium, and at Lystra, what persecutions I endured; yet from them all the Lord rescued me. 12 Indeed all who desire to live a godly life in Christ Jesus will be persecuted, 13 while evil men and impostors will go on from bad to worse, deceivers and deceived. 14 But as for you, continue in what you have learned and have firmly believed, knowing from whom you learned it 15 and how from childhood you have been acquainted with the sacred writings which are able to instruct you for salvation through faith in Christ Jesus. 16 All scripture is inspired by God and profitable for teaching, for reproof, for correction, and for training in righteousness, 17 that the man of God may be complete, equipped for every good work.

2 Timothy 4:1-5

1 I charge you in the presence of God and of Christ Jesus who is to judge the living and the dead, and by his appearing and his kingdom: 2 preach the word, be urgent in season and out of season, convince, rebuke, and exhort, be unfailing in patience and in teaching. 3 For the time is coming when people will not endure sound teaching, but having itching ears they will accumulate for themselves teachers to suit their own likings, 4 and will turn away

AUGUST 23   LESSON 12

4 And they shall turn away *their* ears from the truth, and shall be turned unto fables.
5 But watch thou in all things, endure afflictions, do the work of an evangelist, make full proof of thy ministry.

from listening to the truth and wander into myths. 5 As for you, always be steady, endure suffering, do the work of an evangelist, fulfil your ministry.

Key Verse: Preach the word; be instant in season, out of season; reprove, rebuke, exhort with all longsuffering and doctrine. (2 Timothy 4:2)

Key Verse: Preach the word, be urgent in season and out of season, convince, rebuke, and exhort, be unfailing in patience and in teaching. (2 Timothy 4:2)

As You Read the Scripture—Charles T. Klinksick

Paul knew his life and ministry would end soon. He was very anxious for Timothy to carry on unhesitatingly. The last half of chapter 3 and first half of chapter 4 of his second letter to Timothy are like a last will and testament. They state Paul's final wishes clearly and specifically instruct on what should be done. The words leap the centuries and apply to every confirmed Christian who takes commitment and ministry seriously. Paul's death is reported to have come by beheading on the Ostian roadway outside of Rome in 67 A.D. This was after he had spent his last two years under house arrest in that city (Acts 28:30-31) during the murderous close of the rulership of Emperor Nero.

The text can be summarized with these five statements: (1) Remember me as an example; (2) suffering is inevitable; (3) the Holy Scriptures are your mainstay; (4) continue as a steady evangelist, preaching urgently at all times and teaching persuasively and patiently; (5) my end and reward are near.

2 Timothy 3:10-11. Paul's style and deeds had been exceptional. He was not a hater of anyone but a patient teacher of faith and the love of God. At Antioch and Iconium the Jews and Gentiles had driven him from their cities, and at Lystra the hotheads had stoned him. But he returned later to preach again (Acts 14:21-22).

Verses 12-13. The price of Christ-living is persecution, according to Paul. Jesus had said the persecuted would be among the blessed (Matthew 5:10-11). With calmness Paul had experienced godly peace within himself. Deceivers will always cause suffering.

Verses 14-17. These are statements to be cherished. They indicate Timothy had good training in the holy writings at home and possibly in a synagogue. Note the emphasis on learning, faith, salvation in Christ Jesus, and inspiration of the Scripture. Here are all the ingredients for equipping a grown man or woman of God for doing what is right and helpful. The Holy Scriptures are beneficial for training in doctrine, for refuting what is erroneous, for changing wrong conduct, and for showing how to put righteousness into practice. The intended result is completely good conduct and every kind of good service. Timothy and his learners were not to be half-Christians.

2 Timothy 4:1-2. As he did in his first letter (1 Timothy 6:14), Paul again *charges* Timothy. This is a strong statement, with God as witness. The

439

mandate is to preach the word of God, the biblical truth of good news. "In season and out" means any time, favorable or not. Timothy is not to run short of patience. A loving teacher is durable.

Verses 3-4. This would be a delightful figure of speech if it were not so bluntly true. It was a time for neo-orthodoxy, new interpretations, or philosophical "discoveries" that appealed especially to young listeners. Fiction is more attractive than truth. To accumulate ear-pleasing teachers implies numbers and rounding up a faculty in a new school of thought. Timothy would be facing a trend toward new myths authoritatively taught.

Verse 5. What to do? Don't fold! Carry on despite the hurt. Be a faithful minister of the good news truth. Verses 6-8 are a kind of personal footnote. Paul is saying, "My time is up; I am looking forward to glory with the Lord."

The Scripture and the Main Question—William H. Willimon

Convince, Rebuke, and Exhort

In the late 1890s, a small, soft-voiced woman had just finished a scathing attack upon the evils of the alcohol industry. Out of the large audience stepped a very large, visibly angry man, shaking his finger at her and shouting, "You mind your own business!"

The woman faced him unafraid. "I *am* minding my own business," she replied calmly but firmly. "Men, women, children are *my* business because they are *God's* business."

The woman was Frances E. Willard, president of the Women's Christian Temperance Union, who eventually became a member of the Hall of Fame in the nation's capitol. Her work captured the attention of the nation, and her organization was the first, and by far the largest, most influential women's organization in the world.

In 1884 Mary Reed volunteered for mission work in India. When she returned to Cincinnati six year later, one day she happened to notice strange sores on her face and hands. She had contracted the dreaded disease of leprosy. Rather than resign herself to her condition as a curse, she regarded it as a divine call to witness. Mary returned to India, where she spent her life ministering to lepers there as director of the Chandag Heights Leper House.

William and Catherine Booth, aflame with concern for the poor and the downtrodden in mid-nineteenth-century England, walked out of a church meeting, criticizing their church for its sorry "passion for respectability." They went on to found the Salvation Army, which even today spans the whole globe with its work in behalf of those whom society has forgotten.

Born in Mayesville, South Carolina, in 1875, Mary McLeod Bethune was the child of former slaves. At age nine she could pick 250 pounds of cotton per day, but she could neither read nor write. When the Northern Presbyterian Church opened a school for blacks five miles from her house, Mary enrolled there and studied for ten years. When she later graduated from college, she wanted to be a missionary to Africa. Eventually, though, she said, "God made me a missionary to all people of all races in the United States."

She founded Bethune-Cookman College in Florida, and in 1974, an eighteen-foot bronze statue was erected in her honor in Washington, D.C., the first statue on public ground to honor the memory of either a black person or a woman.

A common factor unites all these diverse people. They were all convinced that each of them had a vocation to be a minister, to share the gospel in word and deed. None of them thought that Christian ministry was mainly something that a bunch of lay Christians paid other "professional" Christians to do in their behalf. Ministry in the name of Christ was for them the duty, the joy, of each and every believer.

Earlier, in the First Letter to Timothy, Paul told Timothy not to feel ashamed or inadequate because he was only a young person. None of us should feel ashamed because of inadequacies in our education or background. Once God has called someone to some area of Christian ministry, God has a way of giving us the equipment we need to fulfill that ministry. God calls whom God wants, and God equips whom God calls.

Be Strong in Christ Jesus

As Paul tells young Timothy in today's scripture, if you are going to be a faithful minister, you need to be strong. Jesus can't use too many hothouse Christians who wilt easily when exposed to the fierce glare of difficulty. "As for you, always be steady, endure suffering, do the work of an evangelist, fulfil your ministry" (4:5).

Paul wants young Timothy to be the sort of disciple who values obedience to the demands of God's word above all else—popularity, public approval, comfort, success. Nothing can take precedence over subservience to the demands of Scripture (4:1-4).

As you enter the university chapel where I preach, you must first pass through a wonderfully carved limestone arch over the front door. There, staring down in dignity, are assorted heroes, saints of the faith. They serve as reminders of the cost of discipleship. There is Martin Luther; the Florentine friar, Savonarola; and Bible translator Wycliff; all are presided over by John Wesley and the first bishops of American Methodism, Thomas Coke and Francis Asbury. (My Lutheran friends express befuddlement over why Wesley, Asbury, and Coke stand higher than Martin Luther. I tell them that the reason is simple and nontheological: Methodists paid for the chapel.) Although gathered from diverse times and places in the church's life, one factor unites these now-silent, still, staring witnesses: *All of them were troublemakers, disturbers of the peaceful status quo.*

More than one was burned at the stake. (In the Bible, the word we translate as "witness" is also the root for the word "martyr.") All of them suffered public disapproval but dared to swim against the stream. I can think of no better way to welcome people into the church than with these visible reminders of the potential cost of discipleship. They stand there as silent but eloquent rebuke whenever church people, in Bishop Francis Asbury's words, try to be "like other people" and contemporary disciples degenerate into merely "honorable" people. Every time we enter the church, we take our place within that glorious procession of misfits, troublemakers, protesters, and saints, who obeyed God's word more faithfully than the opinions of people.

So when visiting local Methodist Societies, founder John Wesley often asked a question that, if answered wrong, could send their preacher

FOURTH QUARTER

packing off to another place: Who has your preacher made angry this past year?

Of this possibility, Wesley had warned his preachers. He said that the life of a circuit rider was not "the way to ease, honour, pleasure or profit. It is a life of much labour and reproach." We are "liable to be beaten, stoned, and abused in various manners. Consider this, before you engage in so uncomfortable a way of life."

Equipped for Every Good Work

I am convinced that all ministry worthy of the name Christian, whether that ministry is lay or clerical, begins in a person's being confronted by the demanding, transforming, liberating word of God as contained in the Bible. We receive our vocation, our marching orders, by listening to Scripture. Our lives are judged, corrected, and trained for righteousness (3:16) by careful, lifelong attentiveness to the words of the Bible. Perhaps that is why Paul seems to put the proclamation, study, and enactment of Scripture at the very heart of his exhortation to young Timothy.

Grappling with Scripture is still at the heart of all ministry.

George works sixty-hour weeks in the heart of one of our nation's great cities. By day he is a staff member at a church and community-sponsored clinic for victims of AIDS. By night George walks the streets looking for intravenous drug users, talking to them, giving them literature about how to prevent AIDS. On weekends he is usually speaking on the AIDS epidemic in a church. So I asked him, "George, what led you to give your life so totally to this work?"

He looked a bit sheepish, as if his answer to my question was going to sound dumb. "Why? Well, I was in church on Sunday. The preacher read the story about how Jesus called little Zacchaeus down out of the tree, how Jesus went to dinner with him. Of course I knew the story since childhood, doesn't everyone? Well, the preacher noted how Zacchaeus, though he had lots of money, was an outcast, someone who was despised by the community. Yet Jesus reached out to him, linked himself with him, ate with him. The preacher remarked, just as a kind of side comment, 'If you want to be with Jesus, you'll usually find him with the outcasts.' And I thought about AIDS, about the suffering of these people. I thought to myself, 'Where would Jesus be if he were walking the streets of our city?'"

Hearing George's story reminded me that, even today, even in a church that is often quite timid and tame, God's word is still taken seriously. A person like George listens to a simple little Bible story, and one never knows what might happen! One witnesses an ordinary life like George's transformed into a living, courageous, compassionate ministry, and one is confronted with modern proof that Paul was right: "All scripture is inspired by God and profitable for teaching, for reproof, for correction, and for training in righteousness, that the man of God may be complete, equipped for every good work" (3:16-17).

Helping Adults Become Involved—Douglas E. Wingeier

Preparing to Teach

Read 2 Timothy 3:10–4:8 and the commentaries on it. Also read the chapter on "The Ministry of All Christians" in the United Methodist *Book of*

AUGUST 23 LESSON 12

Discipline (especially paragraphs 101–111), or a comparable reading from your denominational book of order. An additional resource on lay ministry useful for this lesson is William Diehl's *Christianity and Real Life*.

Think of the unique ministry of each class member, and pray for their effective witness and service to Christ in their respective workplaces.

The purpose of this lesson is to help class members think of themselves as ministers, claim their ministries, and draw strength and resources for their ministry from this study of Scripture. Use the following outline:

> I. Follow a worthy example.
> II. Equipped for the work.
> III. Fulfill the ministry.
> IV. I have kept the faith.

Introducing the Main Question

Begin by dividing into groups of three to share experiences of receiving ministry from others. Instances of invitation, care, service, inspiration, confrontation, support, and the like may be described. Ask a reporter from each group to list on the board the qualities that caused persons to think of these acts as ministry.

William Diehl, in *Christianity and Real Life*, names four types of lay ministry: aid that helps persons at their point of need, words that point persons to Christ, strategies to change systems to make them more just and humane, and ethical decisions and acts that are honest and upright. Try to place each of the acts of ministry shared by the group in one of these categories.

Now ask: What is a minister? The obvious answer is any person who exhibits these qualities and performs these acts. Next ask: Who is a minister? Whether the group equates this term with pastors and clergy or sees all Christians as ministers, emphasize the ministry of the laity, citing ideas from "The Main Question" and the *Book of Discipline* in support.

Point out that the message in today's passage, while addressed to Timothy, is meant for *all* ministers, lay and clergy alike—this includes us! The writer gives us ministers four kinds of advice, which form the points in the outline used below.

Developing the Lesson

I. Follow a worthy example.

Paul is held up as a model of discipleship worthy of emulation. His teaching, behavior, life goal, faith, patience, love, courage, and endurance of persecution all are exemplary.

We ministers need a model and mentor, someone whom we admire, whose advice and example we can follow. Jesus, of course, is a prime example, and Paul a close second. Ask the class to name persons of faith whose example they have sought to follow.

Use Dr. Willimon's illustrations—Frances Willard, Mary Reed, the Booths, and Mary McLeod Bethune. Others who might be mentioned are Martin Luther King, Jr., Archbishop Oscar Romero, Dorothy Day, Mother Teresa, or a favorite grandmother, teacher, or pastor. Identify the

FOURTH QUARTER

outstanding qualities of ministry in each of the persons named, and add these to the list of ministry characteristics begun earlier.

As ministers, most of us need someone to go before us and show us the way. Paul did this for Timothy. Others have done it for us. Will we do it for those who come after us?

II. Equipped for the work.

Ministers need not only an example but equipment. The primary tool mentioned here is Scripture—the sacred writings that are to be learned and firmly believed, that provide instruction for salvation, that are inspired by God, and are useful in teaching, reproof, and training in righteousness.

Ask the class how they did this week in their new discipline of daily Bible study. What struggles did they face? What further help do they need? Do they feel better equipped for ministry in the workplace through having read the Bible? Refer back to the guidelines for Bible study discussed last week. Allow time for the group to counsel and support each other in finding guidance for getting this piece of equipment for their ministry firmly in place.

III. Fulfill the ministry.

As these verses are read aloud, ask the group to listen for the qualities of faithful ministry that are mentioned. Add these to the list of ministry qualities already on the board as they call them out—witnessing, consistency, persuasiveness, willingness to confront, patience, persistence, courage to endure suffering, evangelism. Now ask the group to look over the list, and add any other characteristics they find necessary but still missing.

By now the list of expectations for faithful ministry is probably getting pretty long and intimidating. Ask: How do you feel about trying to live up to these high standards? What resources do we have to help us? What happens when we fail? Accept their feelings of inadequacy, but remind them that Christ stands with them, we have each other for support, and the grace of God supports and forgives us when we don't quite measure up.

IV. I have kept the faith.

One who did measure up, at least in the eyes of an adoring disciple writing forty years after his death, was the Apostle Paul. Have someone read verses 7-8. The faithful minister will be rewarded! The crown of righteousness is awaiting not only Paul but all who love and serve Christ. Discuss: What should be the primary motivation for faithful ministry—obedience to Christ, the gratitude of those we serve, an inner "good feeling" from helping others, or this promise of a heavenly reward? Think back to the experiences of received ministry shared earlier and ask: What motivated those persons to minister as they did? Ask the same question about the persons cited as ministry models.

Finally, ask: What is our motivation? What should it be?

Helping Class Members Act

Ask members to identify a situation in their life or workplace where their ministry is needed. Have them share the strategy they intend to follow during the next week to address that situation, keeping in mind the four

AUGUST 30 — LESSON 13

possible types of ministry mentioned earlier—aid, word, change, and ethics. Have each member agree to pray specifically for one other member's ministry each day during the week.

In closing sing "Forth in Thy Name, O Lord" or "Jesu, Jesu." Pray for wisdom, strength, and courage for class members as they seek to be faithful in their covenant of discipline and their individual ministries during the coming week.

Planning for Next Sunday

As part of their study discipline, ask the class to read the book of Titus, with special focus on 2:7-8, 11-14 and 3:1-8. Since next week is the final one in this unit, ask them also to review the previous five lessons, reflect prayerfully on their observance of their covenant of discipline and this week's ministry strategy, and come prepared to share in a group evaluation of their study and action during these weeks.

LESSON 13 — AUGUST 30

Demonstrate Christian Living

Background Scripture: Titus

The Main Question—William H. Willimon

Medieval theologians once debated the difference between the visible and the invisible church. There was the visible church, that is, your church, my church, the church on the corner of Elm and Main Street, the church we can see and hear and touch. Then there was something called the invisible church, that is, the church as God meant it to be in purity, fidelity, and authenticity.

The problem they were struggling with, of course, was the sad state of the visible church. Was ever a group of people called to such a noble and challenging task? Called forth to be the body of Christ in our world, we Christians have a high vocation.

Did ever a group of people fail more miserably? Beset from the beginning by internal squabbles, bickering, backsliding, and infidelity, the church has rarely been pure and undefiled. Where is the church, the real, pure, spotless church that is promised in Scripture?

The answer, said some of the theologians, lies in the difference between the church you can see and the church you can't see. Don't be bothered, they said, by the flaws and shortcomings of the churches you can see. There is an invisible church, known only to God, made up of the real, committed, solid Christians. This is the true church.

Unfortunately, most of us know better than to buy into this kind of rationalization for the shortcomings of the church. There is only one church, the church we can see, the church in the here and now. If that

FOURTH QUARTER

church isn't the church, then the body of Christ is in sad shape. There is no way of weaseling out of the plain truth that Christ is known by the sort of lives he produces, that we must embody the faith of which we speak, and that we are called to be models to others of what Christ can do with ordinary people.

Are we contemporary Christians really called to be, in the words of Paul to Titus, "a model of good deeds"? That is the rather frightening question behind this Sunday's scripture.

Selected Scripture

King James Version

Titus 2:7-8, 11-14

7 In all things shewing thyself a pattern of good works: in doctrine *shewing* uncorruptness, gravity, sincerity.

8 Sound speech, that cannot be condemned; that he that is of the contrary part may be ashamed, having no evil thing to say of you.

....

11 For the grace of God that bringeth salvation hath appeared to all men.

12 Teaching us that, denying ungodliness and worldly lusts, we should live soberly, righteously, and godly, in this present world;

13 Looking for that blessed hope, and the glorious appearing of the great God and our Saviour Jesus Christ;

14 Who gave himself for us, that he might redeem us from all iniquity, and purify unto himself a peculiar people, zealous of good deeds.

Titus 3:1-8

1 Put them in mind to be subject to principalities and powers, to obey magistrates, to be ready to every good work,

2 To speak evil of no man, to be no brawlers, *but* gentle, shewing all meekness unto all men.

3 For we ourselves also were

Revised Standard Version

Titus 2:7-8, 11-14

7 Show yourself in all respects a model of good deeds, and in your teaching show integrity, gravity, 8 and sound speech that cannot be censured, so that an opponent may be put to shame, having nothing evil to say of us.

....

11 For the grace of God has appeared for the salvation of all men, 12 training us to renounce irreligion and worldly passions, and to live sober, upright, and godly lives in this world, 13 awaiting our blessed hope, the appearing of the glory of our great God and Savior Jesus Christ, 14 who gave himself for us to redeem us from all iniquity and to purify for himself a people of his own who are zealous for good deeds.

Titus 3:1-8

1 Remind them to be submissive to rulers and authorities, to be obedient, to be ready for any honest work, 2 to speak evil of no one, to avoid quarreling, to be gentle, and to show perfect courtesy toward all men. 3 For we ourselves were once foolish, disobedient, led astray,

AUGUST 30 · LESSON 13

sometimes foolish, disobedient, deceived, serving divers lusts and pleasures, living in malice and envy, hateful, *and* hating one another.

4 But after that the kindness and love of God our Saviour toward man appeared,

5 Not by works of righteousness which we have done, but according to his mercy he saved us, by the washing of regeneration, and renewing of the Holy Ghost;

6 Which he shed on us abundantly through Jesus Christ our Saviour;

7 That being justified by his grace, we should be made heirs according to the hope of eternal life.

8 *This is* a faithful saying, and these things I will that thou affirm constantly, that they which have believed in God might be careful to maintain good works. These things are good and profitable unto men.

slaves to various passions and pleasures, passing our days in malice and envy, hated by men and hating one another; 4 but when the goodness and loving kindness of God our Savior appeared, 5 he saved us, not because of deeds done by us in righteousness, but in virtue of his own mercy, by the washing of regeneration and renewal in the Holy Spirit, 6 which he poured out upon us richly through Jesus Christ our Savior, 7 so that we might be justified by his grace and become heirs in hope of eternal life. 8 The saying is sure.

I desire you to insist on these things, so that those who have believed in God may be careful to apply themselves to good deeds; these are excellent and profitable to men.

Key Verse: In all things shewing thyself a pattern of good works. (Titus 2:7)

Key Verse: **Show yourself in all respects a model of good deeds.** (Titus 2:7)

As You Read the Scripture—Charles T. Klinksick

Titus was Greek (Galatians 2:3). Paul calls him "my true child in a common faith" (Titus 1:4), "my partner and fellow worker in your service" (2 Corinthians 8:23). His background is unknown, but he was with Paul in Jerusalem, Corinth, Macedonia, and Crete. He is mentioned appreciatively many times in Paul's second letter to the Corinthians. He seems more aggressive than young Timothy and apparently was a capable organizer.

Paul had left Titus at Crete (Titus 1:5), the large island at the east end of the Mediterranean Sea. There were one hundred cities or towns in Crete. The Cretans had a reputation for being "always liars, evil beasts, lazy gluttons" (1:12), as well as being violent, greedy, and quarrelsome. His assignment was to straighten things out and appoint church leaders in every town (1:5-9).

Christianity in Crete, as in Ephesus and Corinth, was a flower of hope in a wild-growing field. We read of unruly men, empty talk, deception, corrupt thinking, religious hypocrites, alcoholism, disobedience, stealing, and conceit. The important points of this letter are positive statements about the goodness Titus was to show and teach to those who believe in God.

Titus 2:7-8. Titus personally as preacher and teacher was to be an example, "a model of good deeds," with whom no one could find fault. He was not to be unethical, flippant, or mouthy. Good teaching would require integrity, seriousness, and logical soundness.

FOURTH QUARTER

Verses 11-14. Here is a brief summary of divine doctrine and human response: God's grace has appeared for mankind's salvation, by the gift of Jesus Christ to redeem us, who are to respond with purified lives. These verses tell what God has done and what we should do. Verse 13 anticipates the future return of Christ as Judge and glorious Savior. The paragraph is a statement about the past, the present, and the future.

Titus 3:1-2. The text from verses 1 through 8 is a mini-sermon to one person, Titus. Part A is practical advice about good citizenship: respect for authorities, obedience, honesty in work, no slander or quarreling, gentleness, and courtesy. Praying for civil authorities was also advised in Paul's first letter to Timothy (2:1-2).

Verses 3-4. Part B is a confession of "our" previous foolish sinfulness. Paul says "we ourselves" as a general statement about all Christians who, like himself, before the goodness of God became known to them lived shamefully. It is a needfully honest admission between the preacher and the learner.

Verses 5-6. Part C is doctrine, the gospel of good news of God's own doing. We have not earned our salvation; we are saved by his mercy. The washing and renewal are understood to refer to baptism. It is through Jesus Christ our Savior that we have the Holy Spirit and newness of life. This is a key passage in support of the sacrament of baptism, which assures forgiveness and the gift of the Holy Spirit.

Verses 7-8. Part D is consequences or benefits: justification by the grace of God and assurance of eternal life. "The saying is sure" equals an Amen. Paul's insistence indicates his concern for purity in the church as the bride of Christ, "holy and without blemish" (Ephesians 5:27).

The Scripture and the Main Question—William H. Willimon

Sober, Upright, and Godly Lives

In my introduction to this week's lesson, I suggested that a "rather frightening question" lay behind our passage from Paul's Letter to Titus. Are we really expected to be visible models of Christian life? The question is frightening because if we have even a shred of honesty, most of us must admit that, even as Christians, we share all of the natural, normal human weaknesses. Christians feel all of the temptations, urges, passions, and emotions that are inherent in the human heart. So who among us can be expected to be "a model of good deeds?"

Besides, what about the grace of God? Isn't the message of Jesus that we are forgiven, accepted and loved just as we are? Jesus came into the world to save sinners—isn't that so? God's grace accepts us even when we are unacceptable because of our bad thoughts and bad deeds. There is always grace.

Paul also speaks to Titus of divine grace. "For the grace of God has appeared for the salvation of all," he says (2:11). Grace means gift. God's love comes to us as a gift, undeserved, unmerited, unearned. God loves us for nothing.

Yet after this mention of grace and the gift of God's love comes a long string of ethical exhortations. God's grace is busy, "training us to renounce irreligion and worldly passions, and to live sober, upright, and godly lives in this world" (2:12). Whatever the gift of God's grace means, it does not mean that we are thereby freed from responsibility for our lives. In fact, by the grace of God, we are enabled to accept responsibility for our actions, to form our lives in accordance with God's will for us. Because Christ "gave himself for us to redeem us from all iniquity and to purify for himself a people of his own who are zealous for good deeds" (2:14), we are able to give ourselves more fully to Christ. We give ourselves to Christ not by simply giving him our hearts or our disembodied souls but by giving him our daily lives "in this world" (2:12).

As the German language helps us to say it, every *gabe* ("gift") entails an *aufgabe* ("assignment"). The grace of God evokes responsibility. Because God has claimed us, saved us, redeemed us, we are freed to lay claim to our lives, to make our little lives count for something, to reveal, in our daily living, the power of the grace of God to transform ordinary people like us into models of Christian living.

One of my theological heroes is John Wesley. This eighteenth-century church reformer and father of Methodism put much emphasis on Christian formation, that is, on the necessity for daily, real-life embodiment of our Christian beliefs in our lives. One of the most distinctive features of Wesley was his linkage, within his own life, of aspects of the "holy living" tradition with an evangelical emphasis on conversion. Holy living meant offering up one's whole life to God as a living sacrifice, loving God and one's neighbor as completely as possible, and attempting to imitate Christ in our daily lives.

One of John Wesley's favorite books was *The Imitation of Christ* by Thomas à Kempis. There he read that "high curious reasons make not a man holy nor righteous, but a good life maketh him beloved with God" (Book I). Or, as Wesley himself never tired of saying, Christianity is considerably more that "true opinions." It is a way of life—"holiness of heart and life," said Wesley.

Jesus urged his disciples to "take up your cross *daily*." Every moment of our lives, even the apparently insignificant moments, are moments to be walked with God. Every aspect of our lives can be held accountable to God because, as Paul told Titus, the world is quite right in judging the power of God's grace by looking at our lives as examples of that grace at work in our world.

Faith Demonstrated by Example

In one of my former churches, we were discussing the formation of our yearly confirmation class for teenagers. Confirmation had traditionally been a time to collect the teenagers and put them through a series of afternoon classes on church history, biblical interpretation, beliefs, and so on. As the Christian Education Committee discussed confirmation for that year, someone asked an appropriate and fundamental question: What is the purpose, the goal, of confirmation? How many of us became or stayed Christian because we read a book and went to a class?

Then someone said, "What we really want out of confirmation is about a dozen youth who, in their adult lives, come to resemble John Black." She had named one of the "saints" of our congregation, an ordinary person who lived his life in an extraordinarily Christian way.

"That's it!" we said. "All we want is a dozen youth who, in their beliefs and lives, come to look like our best Christians. Is it too much to ask of our confirmation?"

FOURTH QUARTER

"Now how on earth do we go about doing that?" asked another.

So we put our heads together and went to work creating a method of confirmation that would be appropriate to our goal. We agreed that confirmation has as its goal *discipleship*, the production of people who more closely resemble, in their life-styles, beliefs, and values, disciples of Jesus. Confirmation is nothing less than giving people the equipment they need now to be disciples.

The manner in which most of us became Christian was by looking over someone else's shoulders, emulating some admired older Christian, taking up a way of life that was made real and accessible through the witness of someone else. So while books, films, lectures might play a part in confirmation, they will all be subservient to the main task of putting young Christians in close proximity with exemplary older Christians, "mentors," we shall call them, who invite these younger Christians to look over their shoulders as they both attempt to be Christian.

We drew up a new approach to confirmation, based upon our assumptions. We asked groups in our congregation, "Who comes to your mind as an adult in this church who would be especially good in helping our youth deepen their faith?" We then took these (confidential) lists of names and selected twelve adults, ranging in age from twenty-three to sixty-eight. We contacted each of them, telling them what we were asking them to do. We then assigned each of our ten youth to a mentor, or Guide, as we eventually called the adult leader.

A setup meeting was called. The youth met their Guides, and the Journey (as we called it) began. To each pair we gave a one-sheet list of learning activities that had been devised by the committee. We told them to proceed at their own pace, and to follow their own interests.

Among the fifteen or so activities were the following:

- Read the Gospel of Luke together. As each of you read at home, keep a notepad with you, and note those passages you find interesting, confusing, or inspiring. Every two weeks, make some time to discuss what you have read.
- Attend Sunday services together for the next three months. After each service, discuss your reactions, questions, and impressions of the service.
- Get a copy of our church's budget. Find out where the money goes. Discuss together how each of you decides to make a financial commitment to the church.

When the Sunday of Confirmation finally arrived, each adult Guide stood before the church with his or her confirmand and told the church what this young disciple was bringing to the church—some aspect of personality or personal talent. Then each confirmand thanked the congregation for one gift—a church school teacher, a helpful sermon—that had proved helpful to his or her growth as a disciple.

I describe all of this because I feel that the church needs to see that one of its greatest resources is its ability to bring generations of disciples together. A renewed sense of the unique way the church makes Christians through example and model is an essential part of any response to our young.

An essential need of a congregation is to appreciate and appropriate those extraordinary people who are in their congregations and are able to provide significant models to the rest of us of what it means to be the church.

Helping Adults Become Involved—Douglas E. Wingeier

Preparing to Teach

Pray for each member by name, asking God to strengthen and guide them as they practice their covenant of discipline and carry out their ministry strategy during the week.

Since this is the last lesson in this unit, review the previous lessons and be prepared to lead the class in reconstructing the major themes of the unit, which has dealt with various dimensions of Christian discipleship. These may be summarized as follows:

- Lesson 8, "Hold to Sound Doctrine." Think theologically about experience, and discriminate wisely among truth claims.
- Lesson 9, "Train Yourself in Godliness." Accept the claims of discipleship and seek training for the task.
- Lesson 10, "Set Your Priorities." Assess and revise your life goals in terms of biblical standards.
- Lesson 11, "Respect God's Word." Keep regular Bible study central to your life of discipleship.
- Lesson 12, "Serve Faithfully." Claim and fulfill your ministries.
- Lesson 13, "Demonstrate Christian Living." Be a model of good deeds, based in salvation by grace.

Today's lesson focuses on the book of Titus, which like 1 and 2 Timothy is a Pastoral Epistle purportedly written by Paul to one of his younger disciples. Its central themes are church organization, the importance of sound teaching in contrast to false doctrine, and instruction about moral behavior.

It deals with three main subjects. Chapter 1 describes the requirements for elders or bishops (these terms were used interchangeably in the early church) in dealing with false teachers and local problems. Chapter 2 outlines approaches to different groups in the church—older men and women, younger men, and slaves—and then summarizes the expectations of believers in response to God's grace. Chapter 3 develops ethical guidelines for Christians, including obedience and honesty; the avoidance of quarreling, passions, and hatred; and the practice of lovingkindness, courtesy, and gentleness growing out of God's mercy in Christ and the Holy Spirit.

Read the entire book and commentaries on it, focusing on 2:7-8, 11-14 and 3:1-8. Your aim is to help class members accept responsibility for being an example of upright Christian living in response to God's grace in Christ. Use this outline:

      I. A model of good deeds
     II. The grace of God
    III. Holiness by God's mercy

FOURTH QUARTER

Introducing the Main Question

Begin by giving the background of the letter to Titus, based on information in "As You Read the Scripture," "Preparing to Teach," and your commentary study. Then ask: Should Christians be expected to set a high moral example for others in the community? How do you feel about this expectation being laid on you? What is the result when Christians don't live up to this expectation?

Introduce Dr. Willimon's treatment of the visible and invisible church. Ask: Do you agree that this is just a rationalization for the church's shortcomings, that the only church there is, is the one we see, and that Christ is known by the lives he produces? What impression do people have of Christ through our lives?

Developing the Lesson

I. A model of good deeds

After reading these verses aloud, ask members to name Christians who fit this description. Well-known persons such as Albert Schweitzer, Mother Teresa, Dag Hammarskjold, Dietrich Bonhoeffer, Dorothy Day, Georgia Harkness, Cesar Chavez, Frances Willard, Dom Helder Camara, Martin Luther King, Jr., and John and Susanna Wesley could be mentioned, as well as family members, pastors, and local people whose Christian faith and life have been exemplary.

List these persons on the board. Beside each write the quality of life the class thinks makes them a "model of good deeds." Ask members to share anecdotes out of these person's lives that illustrate the qualities and bring them to life. Ask: What enabled these persons to develop these qualities in their lives?

II. The grace of God

The answer to this question is the grace of God. No one can live an exemplary life in his or her own strength. Only by relying on God's grace in Christ Jesus can we live the way God wants us to, and even then, when we slip, as we tend to do, we need God's forgiveness and strength to carry on.

Have 2:11-14 read aloud, then share Dr. Willimon's thoughts about grace as a gift evoking responsibility and Wesley's emphasis on holy living.

III. Holiness by God's mercy

As these verses are read aloud, ask members to identify the traits of holy living that are mentioned. Emphasize that these are not "deeds done by us in righteousness, but by God's own mercy, by the washing of regeneration and renewal in the Holy Spirit" (3:5). It is only possible to live a holy life through salvation in Christ.

Give Dr. Willimon's example of the adult mentors or guides in his confirmation class, and ask whether class members would be interested in serving that way in your church. (Give the names of those who are to your pastor and Education Committee.)

Helping Class Members Act

Ask members to report individually on how they have done with the covenant of discipline and their ministry strategy during the past week. In

AUGUST 30   LESSON 13

keeping with the theme of this lesson, remind them both that as Christians we are expected to set an example in these areas, and also that there is grace and forgiveness through Christ when we do not measure up.

Briefly review all the lessons in this unit, along the lines mentioned in "Preparing to Teach." Ask members to recall ideas, illustrations, and experiences from sessions that were especially meaningful. Discuss: What have been the highs and lows of this study? What stands out that you will remember? How has your faith been challenged and your commitment to discipleship deepened? What decisions have you made? How have your lives been changed, or how will they be? What have you learned about Christian discipleship, and how are you putting it into practice?

Sing the first two verses of "Are Ye Able." Then join in this litany of dedication:

Leader: To seek to discern the truth and live by it,
Group: We commit ourselves, O God.
Leader: To accept the claims of Christian discipleship and undergo training for this task,
Group: We commit ourselves, O Christ.
Leader: To assess our life's priorities and goals and to bring them into line with the standards of your Word,
Group: We commit ourselves, O God.
Leader: To engage in regular study of the Bible as the foundation of our life of faith,
Group: We commit ourselves, O Christ.
Leader: To accept your call to ministry and seek to carry it out faithfully in our places of work,
Group: We commit ourselves, O God.
Leader: To strive to be a model of good deeds, by your mercy and grace,
Group: We commit ourselves, O Christ.
UNISON: GRACE, MERCY AND PEACE, FROM GOD THE FATHER AND CHRIST JESUS OUR LORD. AMEN. (1 Timothy 1:2*b*)

Close by singing the last two verses of "Are Ye Able."

Planning for Next Sunday

Ask members to read next week's background scripture and to pray for God's guidance and strength in living out the themes and challenges of this study with faithfulness and joy.